The Book on Bush

ALSO BY ERIC ALTERMAN

When Presidents Lie: Deception and Its Consequences (forthcoming)
What Liberal Media? The Truth About Bias and the News
It Ain't No Sin to Be Glad You're Alive: The Promise of Bruce Springsteen
Who Speaks for America? Why Democracy Matters in Foreign Policy
Sound & Fury: The Making of the Punditocracy

ALSO BY MARK GREEN

What We Stand For: A Platform for a Changing America (ed., forthcoming)
Selling Out: How Big Corporate Money Buys Elections, Rams Through Legislation,
and Betrays Our Democracy
Mark Green's Guide to Coping in New York City
The Consumer Bible
Changing America: Blueprints for the New Administration (ed.)
America's Transition: Blueprints for the 1990s (ed.)
The Challenge of Hidden Profits: Reducing Corporate Bureaucracy and Waste
(with John Berry)
Reagan's Reign of Error: The Instant Nostalgia Edition (with Gail MacColl)
Who Runs Congress? (with Michael Waldman)
The Big Business Reader (ed.)
Winning Back America
Taming the Giant Corporation (with Ralph Nader and Joel Seligman)
Verdicts on Lawyers (ed. with Ralph Nader)
The Other Government: The Unseen Power of Washington Lawyers
Corporate Power in America (ed. with Ralph Nader)
The Monopoly Makers (ed.)
The Closed Enterprise System
With Justice for Some (ed. with Bruce Wasserstein)

The Book on Bush

How George W. (Mis)leads America

ERIC ALTERMAN
AND
MARK GREEN

VIKING

VIKING
Published by the Penguin Group
Penguin Group (USA) Inc., 375 Hudson Street,
New York, New York 10014, U.S.A.
Penguin Books Ltd, 80 Strand,
London WC2R 0RL, England
Penguin Books Australia Ltd, 250 Camberwell Road, Camberwell,
Victoria 3124, Australia
Penguin Books Canada Ltd, 10 Alcorn Avenue,
Toronto, Ontario, Canada M4V 3B2
Penguin Books India (P) Ltd, 11 Community Centre, Panchsheel Park,
New Delhi – 110 017, India
Penguin Books (N.Z.) Ltd, Cnr Rosedale and Airborne Roads, Albany,
Auckland, New Zealand
Penguin Books (South Africa) (Pty) Ltd, 24 Sturdee Avenue,
Rosebank, Johannesburg 2196, South Africa

Penguin Books Ltd, Registered Offices:
80 Strand, London WC2R 0RL, England

First published in 2004 by Viking Penguin,
a member of Penguin Group (USA) Inc.

1   3   5   7   9   10   8   6   4   2

LIBRARY OF CONGRESS CATALOGING IN PUBLICATION DATA
Alterman, Eric.
The book on Bush : how George W. (mis)leads America / Eric Alterman and Mark Green.
p.   cm.
Includes bibliographical references and index.
ISBN 0-670-03273-5
1. Bush, George W. (George Walker), 1946–   2. United States—Politics and government—
2001–   3. Bush, George W. (George Walker), 1946—Ethics. I. Green, Mark J. II. Title.
E902.A45 2004
973.931'092—dc22   2003065775

This book is printed on acid-free paper. ∞

Printed in the United States of America
Set in Stemple Garamond
Designed by Jaye Zimet

Contents

★

The Book on Bush

1. Introduction

The Power of Audacity

✭

"All public policy should revolve around the principle that individuals are responsible for what they say and do."
—George W. Bush, 1994

When George W. Bush ran for president in 2000 he was presented to the nation by his campaign handlers and a sympathetic media as a nice-enough fellow who didn't take himself or much of anything else—save perhaps his family and religion—too seriously. Though polls consistently showed that a majority of voters held views closer to those of Democratic candidate Al Gore—and, indeed, a 52 percent majority did end up voting for Al Gore or Ralph Nader—even most of Bush's opponents did not see his presidency as much of a threat to their beliefs.

While Bush had the reputation of being a conservative from a conservative state, he did not strike voters as particularly ideologically motivated. The media served his purposes here by focusing not on his record in Texas, or on the scale of the tax cut he proposed, but on his personal story of youthful dissolution before finding faith, along with his apparently charming habit of handing out nicknames to everyone he met. George W. Bush, the self-described "compassionate conservative," was said to be different from the Republican hard-liners in Congress, who, in President Bill Clinton's terms, held up the nation's business with a politically inspired shutdown of the government and impeachment of the president. True, few people found themselves awed by Bush's intellect, but the argument went that a man who knew himself, as Bush appeared to, was preferable to one who knew many things but needed to rely on pollsters to tell him what to say.

Nothing about Bush's genial campaign—or Al Gore's, for that matter—

motivated Democrats to commit themselves strongly to his defeat. The *New York Times* reported just before Election Day that "the gap in intensity between Democrats and Republicans has been apparent all year," with Republicans fighting tooth and nail for their man, and Democrats taking a more diffident attitude to theirs. Polls showed that Gore voters by two-to-one were more willing to accept a Bush victory after the Florida fiasco than vice versa. The retiring Democratic senator and liberal icon Daniel Patrick Moynihan told the *Times,* "There is no great ideological chasm dividing the candidates. . . . Each one has his prescription-drugs plan, each one has his tax-cut program, and the country obviously thinks one would do about as well as the other."

Bush's victory in the highly disputed fight in Florida and his failure to get more votes than Gore nationally further contributed to the belief that America's forty-third president would govern from the happy middle of the partisan divide. "Given the circumstances," wrote the commentator Joe Klein in the liberal *New Yorker* magazine, "there is only one possible governing strategy: a quiet, patient, and persistent bipartisanship."

Few predictions in recent political history have proved quite so mistaken. Once sworn into office, a potential bait-and-switch occurred as George W. Bush proceeded to embark on the most radical presidency in modern times. In fact, his hard-right agenda strikes out in so many directions simultaneously that it's nearly impossible for the average citizen to keep up. In his first term as president, Bush has sought to explode precedents in almost every area of governance, whether the policy in question be foreign or domestic, popular or unpopular, old or new, effective or not. He has done so in contempt of the opinions of not only his opponents but also many of the corps of professional experts who are charged with nonpartisan evaluation of government programs purely from a standpoint of efficacy. To find an apt parallel in American history one would have to go all the way back to FDR's New Deal and wartime mobilizations. But Roosevelt was contending with the Great Depression and the near-collapse of world capitalism, and later with the declaration of war against the United States by two highly industrialized great powers bent on world domination, Nazi Germany and Imperial Japan. Bush, in contrast, is driven almost exclusively by a near-religious belief in the rectitude of his ideological convictions on domestic matters and by the shock of a single albeit devastating terrorist attack by a group of stateless, pre-modern Arab fundamentalists. There is literally no comparison.

To be fair to the pontificating pundits, it was not easy—at least at first—to discern just how differently from his campaign rhetoric Bush intended to govern. There were few precedents for Bush's transformation, either in America's political past or in Bush's own personal history. "I remember describing Bush as an incrementalist when he was down here, and he was," said Bruce Buchanan, a professor of government at the University of Texas.

"He was not throwing the long pass. He was not a policy ideologue by any stretch of the imagination."

Early profiles of Bush paid tribute to his quiet sense of religious commitment and his easygoing "aw-shucks" manner. *Time*'s Jay Carney discerned in Bush "an immutable core" and called the president a man of "preternatural equanimity." Frank Bruni of the *New York Times* wrote, "Mr. Bush's is the impish grin, a deliberate signal of confidence and good cheer. He revels in unpretentiousness, and he seems wholly undaunted by his new responsibilities." When Bush came to Washington, *USA Today* announced in a bold front-page headline, "Bush charm offensive gains ground." Here was a classic case of the media as an enabler, encouraging the elevation of style over substance.

While it is important not to "misunderestimate" George W. Bush—personally, we think him dumb like a fox—it is no less important to address the consequences of his self-defined limits of intellectual inquiry. "I was never a great intellectual," he said in 1986. "We're [the Bush family] not serious, studious readers. We are readers for fun." In 1999 Bush explained to conservative commentator Tucker Carlson that he didn't like to read long books, especially books about policy. His advisors have admitted that the staff usually limits him to three or four thirty- to forty-five-minute "policy time" sessions per week, about what Bill Clinton engaged in per day. Then, more often than not, the president sloughs off responsibility with the admonishment, "You guys decide it." It was therefore hardly surprising when our forty-third president told Fox News in the fall of 2003 that he rarely read beyond the headlines of the day's newspapers. Even Bush friends and boosters cannot vouch for the extent of his knowledge. Neoconservative strategist Richard Perle damned with faint praise when he told *Vanity Fair*, "The first time I met Bush 43, I knew he was different. . . . One, he didn't know very much. The other was that he had the confidence to ask questions that revealed he didn't know very much."

It was dismaying though obviously not disqualifying that president-elect George W. Bush entered office with less understanding of American history and the world than probably any twentieth-century predecessor. But lacking Eisenhower's or his own father's worldliness or JFK's or Clinton's intellect, Bush is prone to grab onto a useful intellectual framework like a life preserver and then not let go—whether it's Myron Magnet's sour interpretation of the sixties in *The Dream and the Nightmare*, Marvin Olasky's irrationally exuberant view of the value of government faith-based programs in *The Tragedy of American Compassion*, or Paul Wolfowitz's Pollyannaish analysis of the likely consequences of an American invasion of Iraq.

Bush's lack of the most rudimentary knowledge of the areas in which he sought to pursue radical change did not strike him or his advisors as in any way limiting. The president is rarely allowed by his handlers to speak directly to the media on matters of policy, and he has reduced the number of regular presidential press conferences held on average by his four predecessors in office by nearly three-quarters. (By the fall of his third year, the father Bush had held sixty-one press conferences; his son by the same time, nine.) They happen often enough to indicate that Bush does not take presidential preparation much more seriously than he took his course-work as an affirmative-action–legacy student at Yale. Asked for instance, in July 2003, whether he might revisit the case of Israeli spy Jonathan Pollard, Bush replied, "Well, I said very clearly at the press conference with Prime Minister [Mahmoud] Abbas, I don't expect anybody to release somebody from prison who'll go kill somebody." Clearly Bush had never even heard of Pollard, who is only the most famous foreign spy to be captured and tried in the United States in the past thirty years and whose jail sentence remains a significant bone of contention in U.S.-Israeli relations. One could literally fill books with examples of cases where Bush demonstrated less knowledge about a given topic than would a decently educated graduate student.

Bush's combination of a low base of knowledge coupled with his admitted lack of intellectual curiosity might be less worrisome in a less ambitious politician. No president can know everything and, as Bush defenders argued during the election, many presidents have been book smart and real-world stupid—and vice versa. But the advent of the second Bush administration witnessed a fully united Republican Party driven by the engines of the religious right, big business and the neoconservative worldview—and piloted by a famously stubborn Texan.

For example, Bush's unwillingness to depart from an original premise—get Saddam; tax cuts are always good—reflects a focus and willpower that are much commented-on traits. "We don't second-guess out of the White House. We don't adjust the plan based on editorials," he said with an edge of disdain during the run-up to the invasion of Iraq. A supporter told the *Washington Post* that Bush "learned that anguishing doesn't pay. He doesn't let his own inner core be supplanted by the hand-wringing of policy wonks." *Post* reporter David von Drehle concluded, "Bush tends to make a decision only once. He doesn't anguish afterward. He doesn't really anguish much to begin with."

But if the facts are merely a political convenience to prop up his first instincts, then where do Bush's first instincts come from? If W's thinking is more catechismic than empiric—that conclusions produce "facts" rather than facts producing conclusions—how does he arrive at his predetermined conclusions?

The answer, we believe, is that he begins any policy consideration with three fundamental questions: What does the religious right want? What does big business want? What do the neocons want? Convinced by political advisor Karl Rove that the way to a second term is to "activate the base"—that is, not alienate it, as his father did when he raised taxes after promising, "Read my lips, no new taxes"—Bush first and foremost wants to satisfy his core conservative constituencies. And if facts clash with the established orthodoxy, he'll stick with his base, not the facts.

First, Bush's own religiosity is well known. He's both a "born again Christian" who kicked alcohol and found God at forty with the help of family friend Billy Graham, and a politician who keenly understands, in G. K. Chesterton's view, that America is a "nation with the soul of a church." Of course, it's traditional for presidents to be observant, to regularly invoke God and attend church. Difficulties can arise, however, if either a public official appears indebted to religious zealots or bases policy significantly on his particular religious beliefs. Most prominently, John F. Kennedy—who understood how the Founding Fathers' aversion to European religious intolerance led to the First Amendment's separation of church and state—told the Greater Houston Ministerial Association in September 1960 that the pope and the Catholic Church didn't control him. "I believe in a president," he said, "whose religious views are his own private affair." Unlike Kennedy, however, Bush appears to weigh religion—and religious voters—far more heavily on his scale of policy. "The president feels that one of the contributory factors to his father's loss is that he didn't get as many evangelical votes as Reagan did," said Dr. Richard D. Land, president of the Ethics and Religious Liberty Commission of the Southern Baptist Convention and an intimate of Karl Rove's. Michele Cottle of *The New Republic* put it more bluntly: "Karl Rove would likely rather risk an international holy war than a drop in Bush's support among Christian conservatives."

Second, if Bush has ever broken with the big-business community, it doesn't come to mind. But the marriage of big business and politics isn't just the world that Bush grew up in; from oil to the Texas Rangers to fund-raising, it's all he's ever known (see chapter 4). Ralph Nader teased in 2000 that "George Bush is a corporation running for president disguised as a person." *The Economist,* at the other end of the spectrum, concluded that a trust-busting Teddy Roosevelt "may be George Bush's favorite president, but Mr. Bush is a business school graduate who has stuffed his administration with multimillionaire chief executives. There can be no doubt where his sympathies lie." And when he seeks to raise $200 million for his 2004 presidential campaign, he doesn't go to union workers for $25 direct-mail gifts but gets several hundred business "pioneers" to raise at least $200,000 each. No one tells these business bundlers to give back a little of their tax windfall to the man whose policies made it possible. No one has to.

Third, and perhaps most costly, following September 11, 2001, President Bush fell under the sway of a group of neoconservative ideologues placed in his administration by Dick Cheney and focused primarily in the Pentagon and vice president's office. These ideologues viewed the attacks less as a national tragedy than a strategic opportunity to implement a program of unilateral global empire for the United States, beginning with a "preventive" war against Iraq. Because Bush and his advisors were willing to deceive Congress and the nation about both the level of threat Iraq presented, as well as its (all-but-nonexistent) connections to the true perpetrators of the terrorist attack on New York and Washington, they succeeded in perpetrating a war against the wishes of the population of virtually every nation on earth. Meanwhile, candidate Bush's promise of a foreign policy that would be "humble in how we treat nations that are figuring out how to chart their own course" was consigned to the dustbin of history.

By the time the two authors of this work set down to examine Bush policies in major areas of domestic and foreign policy, it was everywhere evident that they were not simply ad hoc reactions to problems as they arose. Rather, they were conscious attempts to reorder the priorities of the U.S. government both at home and abroad and permanently alter Americans' relationship with their government, with one another, and with the rest of the world. Few of these policies were even hinted at during the 2000 election, and since then none of them has been honestly presented in language that would alert Americans to the extreme path their government has undertaken. That, in a nutshell, is why we are writing this book: to ensure that Americans do not go to the polls in 2004 without being fully armed with the facts regarding the radical transformation of our political life that began on that fateful day that the United States Supreme Court intervened to prevent a full and fair count of the votes in Florida. Some books and articles have argued that President Bush cannot be trusted to tell the truth, a contention with which we agree. Others have noted that his foreign policies have caused the United States to be reviled across the world as never before, without in any way appreciably increasing our security. We agree as well. Still others focus on Bush's favoring of the wealthy over the poor, and the contempt, rhetoric notwithstanding, with which his administration treats average Americans. Again, we concur.

What is lacking from these accounts is a detailed map of the entire political and policy landscape. Yes, President Bush frequently dissembles. Yes, he can be fanatical. Yes, he is also often ill prepared and uninterested in acquiring the knowledge necessary to make informed decisions about complicated policy questions. But what will the consequences be for the country and the world of the ascension to the highest office in the land by a man who is willing to deceive the nation on behalf of policies that stem from the most extremist element of his already quite conservative party?

Rather than taking on the thankless role of Cassandra, *The Book on Bush* seeks to walk readers through this administration's specific policies with an eye toward revealing what Bush and his conservative warriors would prefer to conceal. We aim to demonstrate, based on the evidence presented by expert analyses, the likely consequences of an environmental policy run for the benefit of the energy industry; an economic policy that beggars the poor, comforts the rich, and destroys the basis of fiscal solvency for the nation; an education policy that "leaves behind" those most in need; a science policy that flatters the prejudices of theological fundamentalists; and a foreign policy that creates hatred and terror where none existed before, undermining our alliances and threatening our security.

In each of these cases, the Bush modus operandi has been to say one thing and do another, whether promising tax saving for everyone but giving the lion's share to the wealthy few or vowing to protect America from threats while inflating nonexistent ones and ignoring those against which we can be defended. How does he do it? There are a variety of methods that add up to what playwright Arthur Miller terms Bush's "power of audacity."

Sometimes the president seems to think that vagueness, non sequiturs, and tautology are enough to explain away his political problems. How long will there be an American presence in Iraq?—"As long as necessary but not a day longer." Did you get where you are because of your famous father?—"I love my Dad." Drugs as a youth?—"When I was young and reckless, I was young and reckless." Is war with Iraq really a last resort? "When I say I'm a patient man, I mean I'm a patient man." It is sad to say about our democracy, but this nonsense often works.

Another frequent maneuver is to talk left/govern right to the point that Bush seems to think he can get away with anything if he declares its opposite. One is reminded of great magicians who (mis)direct audiences to focus on the visible left hand while the hidden right one behind the back pulls off the trick. For example, in his admiring memoir *The Right Man*, loyal Bush speechwriter David Frum paid tribute to the president's stem cell "compromise" in the summer of 2001: "Because Bush summarized all points of view so sympathetically, he was able to win the support of his viewers for his own not at all middle-of-the-road position." Few Americans probably realized that this sympathetic-sounding man was, in fact, throwing up ideology-inspired roadblocks in the search for potential cures for Parkinson's, Alzheimer's, and cancer.

Then there is what Joshua Micah Marshall has called "the confidently expressed, but currently undisprovable assertion." Bush took the country to war with Iraq on the basis of arguments that turned out to be patently false—and understood by most experts at the time to be so—but could not be disproven without an invasion. Especially with the president arguing the contrary daily, how could anyone say for certain that Saddam Hussein had no nuclear weapons or even no significant ties to al Qaeda? The intelligence experts quietly made their case against such claims, but Bush and Cheney just brushed them aside with their confidently asserted, largely fictional pronouncements. "There is no doubt in my mind that Saddam Hussein was a threat to world peace," said Bush after the invasion of Iraq. "And there's no doubt in my mind that the United States, along with allies and friends, did the right thing in removing him from power. And there's no doubt in my mind, when it's all said and done, the facts will show the world the truth." He can say he has no doubt three times or three hundred times, but the issue isn't about "doubt in his mind"; it's about whether a unilateral invasion and occupation of an Arab country was worth the cost.

Much the same is true of Bush's program of tax cuts for the wealthiest few. Almost no one with even a college degree in economics really expects them to offer a cure for the myriad problems that ail the economy, and in many respects they are the problem itself. But all of this is hard to prove in the face of Bush's repeated assertions about his "jobs and growth" package. Bush, meanwhile, speaks as if the future will fall into line with his beliefs once it recognizes his personal resolve. "The President and his advisors," concluded a *New York Times* editorial, "obviously believe that the constant repetition of several simplistic points will hypnotize the American people into forgetting the original question."

Another Bush rhetorical strategy, identified by journalist Renana Brooks, is his masterful use of emotional language to dominate debate while ignoring the substance of the question at hand. She notes, for example, "Rather than explaining the relationship between malpractice insurance and sky-rocketing health-care costs, Bush summed up: 'No one has ever been healed by a frivolous lawsuit.'" The multiple fiscal and monetary policy tools that can be used to stimulate an economy were downsized to: "The best and fairest way to make sure Americans have that money is not to tax it away in the first place." The controversial plan to wage another war on Iraq was simplified to: "We will answer every danger and every enemy that threatens the American people." These are all empty phrases but they serve their purpose in making all further discussion unnecessary. There are good guys, who want to prevent frivolous lawsuits, to make sure Americans have money, and to prevent threats to the American people, then there is everybody else. Which side are you on?

And, of course, there is that time-honored tactic of so many presidents: outright dishonesty. Few Americans were aware—at least until we learned the truth about Iraq—how George Bush "had such a high regard for the truth," as Lincoln said of a rival, "that he used it sparingly." The problem wasn't just "16 words" about Iraq supposedly purchasing enriched uranium but some 160,000 words—that is, much of what the administration says day in and day out on policy after policy. When *Washington Post* reporter Dana Milbank collected a number of these in a front-page story in late October 2002, he couched them in linguistic circumlocutions, such as that Bush's statements represented an "embroidering of key assertions." Presidential statements were clearly "dubious, if not wrong." The president's "rhetoric has taken some flights of fancy . . . taken some liberties . . . omitted qualifiers," and "simply outpace[d] the facts." The words *President Bush lied* do not appear in Milbank's story and have yet to appear in any newspaper account in any major national newspaper, insofar as we are aware.

Part of the reason is deference to the office and the belief that the American public will simply not accept a mere reporter's calling the president a liar. Part of the reason is the nature of the political culture of Washington, where it is somehow worse to call a person a liar in public than to be one. Another motivation is the inherent caution of the journalism profession on this most sensitive of topics. Former *Washington Post* editor in chief Ben Bradlee notes that "even the very best newspapers have never learned how to handle public figures who lie with a straight face. No editor would dare print this version of Nixon's first comments on Watergate for instance: 'The Watergate break-in involved matters of national security, President Nixon told a national TV audience last night, and for that reason he would be unable to comment on the bizarre burglary. That is a lie.'"*

We know that President George W. Bush is not the first president to mislead, misstate, fudge, or falsify in a pinch, citing national security needs to be sure. What distinguishes his efforts here is the frequency and scale of the dishonesty, as well as the resolve with which he commits himself to it. ABC News's scrupulously nonpartisan Web publication "The Note" observed early in the Bush presidency that the president and his advisors were unusual in modern times for the degree to which they were willing to insist that "up is down" and "black is white. While the public doesn't necessarily see or pay attention to all of this," the authors added, "there has been a corrosive effect on the filter through which media and political elites view administration statements and actions."

Michael Kinsley succinctly describes the Bush administration technique: "What's going on here is something like lying-by-reflex. If the opposition accuses you of saying the world is round, you lunge for the microphone to declare your passionate belief that it is flat." The ferocity is often accompanied by insouciance. What is odd about the Bush technique is that frequently no one in the administration appears to concern himself with whether such deceptions are necessary or even credible. Kinsley adds, "Bush II administration lies are often so laughably obvious that you wonder why they bother. Until you realize: They haven't bothered. If telling the truth was less bother, they'd try that, too. The characteristic Bush II form of dishonesty is to construct an alternative reality on some topic and to regard anyone who objects to it as a sniveling dweeb obsessed with 'nuance,' which the presi-

---

*While many officials in his administration frequently lie, we are agnostic about the specific proposition that "Bush is a liar" because that is both unknowable and even irrelevant. What is important and provable is that he can't be taken at his word since he constantly distorts and misleads, either because he's willfully lying or because he's misleading himself and then us. A leader whose religious certitude is unleavened by deep knowledge—and who believes that changing one's mind is a sign of weakness—can easily lapse into serial dissembling to justify policies based more on faith than on facts.

dent of this class, I mean of the United States, has more important things to do than worry about."

Yet while Bush unabashedly continues to make such misstatements and sleights-of-rhetoric, many Democrats and the media lack the coherence to call him on them. "Like orthodox Marxists who pick apart mainstream economics and anthropology as the creations of 'bourgeois ideology' or Frenchified academic postmodernists who 'deconstruct' knowledge in a similar fashion," Joshua Micah Marshall notes, Bush and his ideological supporters reject " 'the facts' as nothing more than the spin of experts blinded by their own unacknowledged biases. The result, as we are seeing in the land of Iraq and in the sea of red ink currently engulfing the federal budget, is that by the time Bush has been disproven, we are stuck with the results of his ideologically driven policies."

The result of these tactics—together with many others described in subsequent chapters—is that the massive political, social, economic, and environmental revolutions currently underway in America are taking place just beneath the radar screen of public debate. The very nature of our society, our government, and our nation's relationship with the rest of the world are being transformed in ways that may endure for decades, and yet most Americans are only dimly aware that George W. Bush is a different sort of leader than, say, his father, or even his political role model, Ronald Reagan.

Another way of putting this, as author William Greider does, is that President Bush is actively seeking "to roll back the twentieth century." The draining of the public treasury to benefit the very rich is just the start of an effort designed to reduce government to a size where, as close Bush ally and conservative political organizer Grover Norquist has so memorably said, you can finally "drown it in the bathtub." Some of the evident aspects of this historic redirection as Greider identifies it include the elimination of federal taxation of private capital "as the essential predicate for dismantling the progressive income tax"; the gradual "phase out [of] the pension-fund retirement system as we know it, starting with Social Security privatization but moving eventually to breaking up the other large pools of retirement savings . . . and converting them into individualized accounts"; the withdrawal of "the federal government from a direct role in housing, health care, assistance to the poor and many other long-established social priorities, first by dispersing program management to local and state governments or private operators, then by steadily paring down the federal government's financial commitment"; the restoration of the "churches, families and private education to a more influential role in the nation's cultural life by giving them a significant new base of income—public money"; the strengthening of the hand of business enterprise against "burdensome regulatory obligations, especially environmental protection, by introducing voluntary goals and 'market-driven' solutions"; and the defenestration of labor unions and all forms of organized labor. Abroad, there is an attempt to abandon virtually all international obligations and constraints that in any way impinge on America's unilateral ability to define and act upon its own self-interest in a fashion of its own choosing—the "good opinion of mankind" as Thomas Jefferson defined it, be damned.

Some of the above might sound implausible to the point of being unimaginable. We can only wish that this were so. But all that is required for radical conservatives to remake America in their own image through the power of the presidency, the Congress, and the courts is for the rest of us to avert our eyes and pretend that it is just not taking place. That would be the triumph of the power of audacity. In the pages that follow we intend to document both the failures of a far-Right House and other dangerous changes President Bush and his allies have in store for the nation. This is one case, to borrow W.'s penchant for theologically inspired language, wherein "the devil" may really be in the details. Here they are. Don't say you weren't warned.

2. Drill and Cough

W.'s Environmental and Energy Policies

✭

"Every environmental issue confronts us with a duty to be good stewards. As we use nature's gifts, we must do so wisely. Prosperity will mean little if we leave future generations a world of polluted air, toxic lakes and rivers and vanished forests."

—George W. Bush,
during the 2000 presidential campaign

In a nation nearly equally divided along political lines, the environment is a rare issue on which a strong consensus has emerged. A comprehensive 2000 survey found that 62 percent of Americans think we're spending too little on the environment, compared to only 7 percent who believe we're spending too much. By a more than 2 to 1 margin, Americans believe that environmental laws and protections don't go far enough.

Through presidential leadership and citizen efforts, America in the past three decades has managed an impressive record of environmental accomplishments: creating a vast network of protected parks, forests, and wetlands; improving air and water quality; and safeguarding against the extinction of vital animal and plant species—all while continuing to grow its economy by leaps and bounds along the way.

George W. Bush seemed to grasp the importance of environmental values during his presidential bid, and his stump speeches contained numerous references to preserving our national treasures. He boasted a Texas record of bringing together environmentalists, businesses, and politicians to mold pragmatic solutions. He even promised to control greenhouse gas emissions, with a campaign pledge to place a cap on carbon dioxide (CO_2) that went even further than Vice President Gore's.

Bush's "green" rhetoric led some conservatives, such as columnist Thomas J. Bray, to wring their hands in public: Would George W., like his father before him, go too far toward appeasing moderate suburbanites and then find himself "unable to fend off the continued assault on the industrial economy?" In fact, a close look at Bush's record in Texas, his oilman's background, and his list of campaign contributors (all on display in chapter 4) would have eased Bray's mind considerably. Today his environmental campaign promises seem as distant as Bob Jones University and Broward County.

Under the guises of "eliminating bureaucratic red tape" and "self-auditing," Bush and his appointees—many of them former industry lobbyists or lawyers—have taken aim at the most fundamental environmental laws in our country. The results so far include the weakening of our clean air and clean water laws; the opening up of our national parks and forests to mining, drilling, and logging interests; an energy plan giving multi-billion-dollar subsidies to the oil, gas, and nuclear industries; and the replacement of tough environmental and public health standards with voluntary industry controls.

If these policies sound like the fulfillment of a wish list handed to Bush and Cheney by the energy and timber industries, that's because they are. Having made record contributions to the Bush campaign, these industries have since gotten a substantial return on their investment. Yet President Bush continues to proclaim himself a moderate on environmental issues, announcing grand plans on Monday, then cutting the legs out from under them on Tuesday through Friday. Again, the power of audacity has opened up a credibility chasm. George W. Bush's environmental strategy appears to be talk globally, harm locally . . . and hope the voters don't notice.

Global Warming Heads-Up

The air and ground assault began even before the inaugural glow had worn off. Fewer than sixty days into his presidency Bush declared that he was dropping his campaign pledge to cap carbon dioxide emissions, the leading contributor to global warming. Yet just two weeks earlier, his EPA administrator, Christine Todd Whitman, had announced after congressional testimony: "This president is very sensitive to the issue of global warming. . . . There's no question but that global warming is a real phenomenon. . . ." Likewise, President Bush's then treasury secretary Paul O'Neill described the threat of global warming as being equal to that of a nuclear holocaust. In 2001 a report from the nonpartisan National Academy of Sciences concluded that carbon dioxide and other gases spewed from such man-made sources as factories, power plants, and motor vehicle exhaust pipes were indeed being trapped in the atmosphere and beginning to cause global warming. This study warned that global temperatures could rise anywhere from three to ten degrees Fahrenheit over the coming century, risking catastrophic damage around the globe.

What then, one asks, had spurred the president to change his mind? A White House spokesman explained that "CO_2 should not have been included as a pollutant during the campaign. It was a mistake." Bush himself argued that "important information" had been brought to his attention and that he was "responding to reality."

That "important information" apparently came directly from the oil and coal industries. Among the documents ultimately pried out of Vice President Cheney's National Energy Policy Task Force was the resignation letter of Jane Hughes Turnbull, a member of the National Coal Council (a governmental advisory group), which warned that Bush's reversal was "profoundly shortsighted [and] an obvious and expedient response to industry interests." The numerous e-mails and letters of gratitude from coal, oil, and gas industry groups also found among the task force documents hint at the hammerlock in which these businesses held Bush during those early months. It was surely no coincidence that the fossil fuel industry had lavished Governor Bush with almost $3 million in campaign contributions during the 2000 presidential campaign.

In place of mandatory caps on greenhouse gases, Bush announced a plan to seek an 18 percent decrease by 2012 in the "emissions intensity" of carbon dioxide pollution from power plants and utilities. But notice the sleight of hand: "emissions intensity" is a measure of emissions as a percentage of economic output. Because the administration forecasts significant growth over the next decade, by Bush's own calculations, carbon dioxide emissions will actually *increase* 14 percent in the next ten years.

More significantly, the reductions in his plan are voluntary, and therefore similar to past unsuccessful ventures. "There's no evidence that would convince the administration [voluntary reductions] will work," says Howard "Bud" Ris of the Union of Concerned Scientists. "We've had a voluntary approach since 1990 and thirteen to fifteen percent more carbon emissions since then. . . . I don't even think the Bush administration believes it. It's a smoke-screen." Here's why: If companies fall on hard times, there's nothing to stop them from simply canceling their voluntary reductions. Or if they want to report on compliance for only a portion of their business, they can.

The ineffectiveness of such voluntary reductions—will voluntary speed limits on the highway be next?—became clear at the announcement ceremony for the program in January 2003. Disappointed at the commitments received from industry, the administration moved the event from the White House to the cafeteria at the Department of Energy, where, despite the best efforts of media handlers, confusion lingered in the air. Edison Electric and six other power sector groups stated their pledge to reduce "emissions intensity" by 3 to 5 percent before 2012. However, as the *Los Angeles Times* reported, the Energy Information Agency's 2003 Annual Energy Outlook had projected that the electric industry, under business-as-usual policies, would already be reducing its emissions intensity by 7 percent over that time. The Bush administration apparently believed that the industries' pledges were on top of the 7 percent baseline reduction. But, when pressed, Edison president Thomas Kuhn confessed that his commitment was for an *absolute* 3 to 5 percent reduction. "That would not be our understanding," publicly retorted an exasperated Energy Undersecretary Bob Cart. "The electric power sector needs to do more than 3 percent to 5 percent absolute over this time period."

President Bush further deflated efforts to reduce carbon dioxide emissions by removing the United States from the Kyoto Protocol, the internationally negotiated program to limit CO_2. Bush had said all along that he would not submit the treaty to the Senate, so his decision itself was no surprise. It was his complete disengagement from the international environmental process—first refusing to cap greenhouse gases domestically, then pulling the United States out of Kyoto—that generated such worldwide anger. While Bush promised the media that the United States would continue working multilaterally, in the corridors of international diplomacy people regarded the world's only superpower and biggest polluter as pulling up stakes on a problem that demands international cooperation. Consider, for example, that the radiation from Chernobyl fell on Bridgeport, Connecticut—a perfect example of what UN secretary general Kofi Annan calls "problems without passports." The later hostility of European countries to Bush's Iraq policies was sown by his handling of Kyoto—in the antiwar editorials of 2003, they often linked his unilateralist foreign policy with his unilateralist environmental policy. In the international press, Bush's CO_2 announcement was referred to as "suicidal," "tragic," "irresponsible," "outrageous," "a low point in world environmental history"—and that was just from our allies. The (Scottish) *Sunday Herald* wrote of the president's speech: "It was the callousness of his words, the naked self-interest of his sentiment and the disregard he showed for the health and safety of the rest of the world, that really shook people."

The United States has continued in these policies despite the emergence of a genuine scientific consensus that global warming has already begun. John Harries, the scientist who led a study published in *Nature* in 2001, wrote of the threat of carbon dioxide: "We're absolutely sure, there is no ambiguity. . . . [The] greenhouse effect is operating and what we're seeing can only be due to the increase in the gases."

The 1990s was, according to NASA's Goddard Institute, the warmest decade in a thousand years, and 2001 and 2002 were two of the three warmest years since the 1800s. British scientists attributed Europe's record-breaking summer temperatures in 2003 to global warming. Temperatures in the Arctic region have already risen seven to nine degrees Fahrenheit, and the once massive glaciers of the Andes region have shrunk by as much as 60 percent in some areas—all the result of man-made pollution, scientists believe. And unlike most "airborne" pollutants, which dissipate or fall to Earth in a few years, greenhouse gases will stay in the atmosphere for as long as a century, making the need to reverse emissions increases particularly urgent.

To justify his turnabout on global warming, President Bush has had to reject two decades' worth of climate research—research on which the United States has spent $18 billion between 1990 and 2000, more than Japan and the entire EU combined. Since taking office, Bush has repeatedly asked panels of scientists and industry leaders for input, only to disregard it when the results don't please him. According to Bud Ris of the Union of Concerned Scientists, "The administration has fallen into a trap: They commission a panel, get a response that [global warming] is serious, and then they don't know what to do."

In 2001 additional reports from the National Academy of Sciences and the Intergovernmental Panel on Climate Change unequivocally stated that global warming is occurring and that man-made pollution is responsible. Even the Global Climate Coalition, an industry lobbying group that for years published anti-climate-change reports, disbanded that year as its members found themselves on the wrong side of scientific and public opinion. Philip Watts, the chairman of Royal Dutch Shell (once a member of the coalition), summed up the revised position of many businesses: "Amid all this uncertainty, we have seen and heard enough in Shell to say we stand with those who believe there is a problem and that it is related to the burning of fossil fuels."

Bush, however, remained unimpressed, citing the "incomplete state of scientific knowledge of the causes of, and solutions to, global climate change." In reality, the only things incomplete are the Bush administration's own assessments of our country's environmental health. As we will discuss in chapter 9, the Bush White House has made a habit of altering data or simply removing references to global warming from otherwise comprehensive environmental reports. The EPA deleted the entire global warming section from its landmark Report on the Environment after the White House Office of Management and Budget insisted that the EPA inject industry-sponsored scientific reports into the chapter. An internal EPA memo leaked to the National Wildlife Federation captured the agency's frustration: "Conclusions of the [National Research Council] are discarded. . . . Uncertainty is inserted where there is essentially none. . . . Most important, the [Report] no longer accurately represents scientific consensus on climate change."

Despite all the global warming evidence on the table, Bush's proposal is to spend yet another decade studying the problem, thereby ignoring the problem.

On this subject Republicans embrace not science but spin. A 2002 memorandum sent to Republican strategists by Frank Luntz, the pollster who helped craft the 1994 "Contract with America," advises Republicans to call themselves "conservationists," not "environmentalists"; to talk of "climate change" instead of the more alarming "global warming"; and to foster skepticism about the science of environmental problems. "Should the public come to believe that scientific issues are settled," he warns, "their views about global warming will change accordingly."

Energy, Inc.

The first six months of the Bush administration were a giddy time for the fossil fuels and nuclear industries. After eight years of treading lightly around Bill Clinton's centrist energy policies, the "Old Fuels Club" was warmly welcomed back into the White House. Not only were their opinions sought, but these companies were even asked to help write the largest review of energy policy since Jimmy Carter preached conservation in a cardigan.

By the time the Bush-Cheney energy policy was announced, in June 2001, the oil, gas, coal, and nuclear industries were slated to be awarded $28 billion in tax breaks and the keys to some of our country's most precious natural assets. Indeed, the debate over energy—how it's supplied, how it's financed, and how it's consumed—has been one of the defining issues of George W. Bush's presidency.

The Bush energy plan was developed in closed-door sessions by Vice President Cheney and his National Energy Policy Task Force (which is described in greater detail in chapter 5, "Secrecy and Civil Liberties"). During that process, scientists and environmentalists were kept on the sidelines while energy companies threw a nonstop party. Of the 400 organizations that sought meetings with the vice president or the task force in that period, 194 were granted access—158 energy companies, 22 labor unions, 13 environmental groups, and a lone consumer organization. Energy Secretary Spencer Abraham, one of the key officials responsible for drafting the final document, turned down a request for a meeting with environmental groups in February 2001, citing his "busy schedule." In a sense that statement was true: during that period, documents released later under judicial order show, he met with 109 industry representatives.

Much of what is known about the Energy Task Force meetings either leaked out slowly or was pried out with the help of the court system, only to be censored. Examples include:

★ In a March 18–22, 2001, e-mail exchange between Joseph Kelliher, the energy secretary's top assistant, and Dana Contratto, a natural gas lobbyist interested in building a pipeline in the Caspian Sea, Kelliher solicitously asked, "If you were King, or Il Duce, what would you include in a national energy policy, especially with respect to natural gas issues?" The Energy Task Force ultimately recommended developing a Caspian pipeline.

* A March 22, 2001, e-mail from Bob Slaughter of the National Petrochemical Refiners Association tells Department of Energy officials that "the EPA's enforcement campaign against U.S. refineries should be halted and reexamined." Slaughter was referring to the agency's practice of filing suit under the Clean Air Act when refineries increase production at their dirtiest plants but don't improve pollution controls. Cheney's Energy Task Force recommended overturning that enforcement policy and the Bush EPA soon followed suit.

From the e-mail trail, it isn't hard to discern the identity of the "industry representatives" who had access to Secretary Abraham and Vice President Cheney during the formation of the Energy Plan. Indeed, their calendars during the spring of 2001 read like a list of the largest contributors to the Republican Party. During the 2000 election cycle, energy companies gave George W. Bush nine dollars for every one dollar they gave to Al Gore. Among oil and gas companies, the figures were even more skewed: fourteen dollars to Bush for every dollar to Gore. When the Energy Task Force made its list of people it would see, it apparently remembered well who had given (and how much) and who had not. Among the repeat visitors-cum-campaign-contributors were

* Nuclear Energy Institute (19 visits, $437,404)

* Edison Electric Institute (14 visits, $598,169)

* National Mining Association (9 visits, $575,496)

* American Gas Association (8 visits, $480,478)

* Southern Company (7 visits, $1,626,507)

* Exelon Corporation (6 visits, $910,886)

One energy company stands above the rest in terms of its political influence. That company met with task force members six times and with Vice President Cheney at least three times. Its name: Enron, a donator of $1.1 million to the GOP in 2000 and another $300,000 for the Bush inauguration. According to Secret Service logs, Cheney had two additional meetings with Enron chairman Ken Lay in the spring of 2001. What resulted from all these get-togethers? An independent evaluation of the Bush energy bill by American Family Voices, an advocacy group for middle- and low-income families, showed that seventeen different policy initiatives included in the plan directly benefited the rogue corporation.

Inside the Bush White House, "diversity" means having a president and a vice president who come from *two entirely different energy companies.* Frederick D. Palmer, the chief lobbyist for Peabody Energy, the world's largest coal-mining company, acknowledged that the pro-energy attitude goes far deeper than merely what meetings and money could foster. "We're all on the supply side—the electric utilities, the coal companies—and the energy plan is basically a supply side plan, but that's not the result of back-room deals or lobbying the vice president. People running the United States government now are from the energy industry."

The Energy Plan that ultimately emerged was a nineteenth-century proposal with twenty-first-century window dressing. While the White House repeatedly pointed out that the plan had forty-two recommendations on conservation and only thirty-five that dealt with energy supply, the supply-side recommendations were specific, whereas the conservation ones were vague and exhortatory. The message was clarified by Vice President Cheney when he famously mocked energy conservation as a "personal virtue" in a major speech just before the plan's release. Carl Pope, the chairman of the Sierra Club, attributed this outlook to a sort of West Texas machismo: "Real men don't build windmills. Real men build oil wells."

Just how dirty was the final bill? On CBS's *Face the Nation,* Vice President Cheney asserted, "Virtually all of the recommendations for financial incentives and assistance tax credits and so forth are for conservation and increased efficiency and renewables. There are no new financial subsidies of any kind for the oil and gas industry."

Of course that statement was false. According to a detailed report published by Taxpayers for Common Sense, the U.S. Public Interest Research Group, and Friends of the Earth, Bush's energy bill would lavish $28 billion in subsidies and tax breaks on the oil, gas, coal, and nuclear industries. (The giveaways included a $3 billion investment credit for the development of "clean coal" technology and $500 million in relief for certain oil and gas companies from paying royalties they owe to the government.) The $28 billion provided for by the Bush Energy Plan, when added to the $33 billion in subsidies those industries were already scheduled to receive, amounted to a grand total of $61 billion—or a cost of $220 for every American.

Cheney also absurdly claimed that his proposal was consistent with eleven of the twelve planks in the Sierra Club's energy proposal, an ambitious plan that included forty-mile-per-gallon fuel efficiency standards, the goal of 20 percent of America's energy coming from renewables by 2020, and a steep reduction in carbon dioxide emissions (all obviously missing from the Bush plan). Ironically, it was the Sierra Club's response—"If Bush really believes these plans are similar," said Carl Pope, "then Arthur Andersen must be checking his math"—that finally procured them a meeting with Cheney. As Pope later described the meeting: "We sat there and said, 'We don't think that your plan does anything that our plan does. You have the same subject areas. You have a section called Renewables, but there's nothing in it.' And they said, 'Well, this isn't really our plan, this is a work in progress. We're going to change it.' Which they never did of course."

Ironically, Bush's insistence on passing a comprehensive energy plan, complete with all the oil and gas subsidies and the Alaskan drilling projects, has prevented improvement of America's energy grid. In the days after the devastating East Coast blackout of August 2003, President Bush and his advisors blamed it on failure to pass his Energy Plan. In fact, when Congressional Democrats proposed spending $350 million to modernize the grid in 2001, the proposal was summarily rejected by the White House and Republican leaders, who would only improve the electrical grid when combined with tax giveaways and new drilling.

The Bush administration has been equally negligent in dealing with the development of renewable energy sources. During the 2000 campaign Bush had declared, "To enhance America's long-term energy security, we must continue developing renewable energy." Yet in the first budget he submitted to Congress, he slashed funding for renewable energy by 50 percent. Even after the stirring tribute to the hydrogen car in Bush's January 2003 State of the Union address, the budget he soon submitted left funding for other renewable energy programs completely flat. Senator Byron Dorgan of North Dakota had to fight simply to maintain the $55 million—that's only 19 cents per taxpayer—wind production tax credit, which has enabled wind power to operate more cheaply and effectively in the past decade.

The misrepresentations go on and on. Yet few Americans will ever read the Bush Energy Plan, and both George W. and Karl Rove know that. The goal is to muddle the debate and, by doing so, confuse the public so that they'll either stop blaming the administration or just stop paying attention. Again, the Bush administration has followed the advice of Republican strategist Frank Luntz, who told them in a memo: "A compelling story, even if factually inaccurate, can be more emotionally compelling than a dry recitation of the truth."

Energy Security Blankets

On November 8, 2001, less than two months after the September 11 attacks, Energy Secretary Spencer Abraham wrote in the *Wall Street Journal*, "The House knows—and the Senate would agree if allowed to vote on it— that [the Alaskan National Wildlife Refuge] would reinforce energy security by increasing domestic oil production." "Energy security," a term that reflects the relationship between our country's oil dependence and its implications for national security, has returned to common parlance in the last three years. More often than not, it's used as a justification for drilling in Alaska.

The Bush administration seems to believe that there are few problems in the country that drilling in the Alaskan National Wildlife Refuge (ANWR) wouldn't alleviate. When California experienced blackouts, Bush advocated drilling. In the weeks after September 11, Senator James Inhofe (R-OK)—on behalf of the Bush administration—attempted to push through legislation to open the ANWR. And as the country was bracing for war with Iraq, again the drumbeats were heard in Alaska.

But in January 2002, 63 percent of voters surveyed rejected Bush's argument that drilling in ANWR would enhance national security, oil independence, and jobs, with 47 percent "strongly opposing" it. A year later, the results were roughly the same: While a higher number (45 percent) accepted the proposition that ANWR drilling would reduce our Middle Eastern oil dependence, 62 percent still opposed the project.

While drilling in the ANWR wouldn't be the apocalypse some environmental groups claim, the available evidence indicates that it would have a significant harmful effect on local animal species and on the physical condition of one of America's most magnificent locales. In 2002 a group of Republican lawmakers who support ANWR drilling commissioned a National Research Council panel (composed of experts from oil companies, scientific institutions, native Alaskan groups, and an environmental organization) to study the ecological impact on the nearby North Slope of Alaska, where drilling has been permitted for the past thirty years.

The results were not what the senators had hoped. The panel reported a drop in the reproductive rates of some bird species and the local caribou herd. Their findings also detailed a disturbed habitat, littered with abandoned infrastructure, permanent scars that have eroded "the spiritual and aesthetic values of the barren yet majestic region." Of particular relevance to the ANWR debate, they warned that current warming trends in the Arctic could make future projects even more destructive.

ANWR does not offer short-term energy relief, either. If development started today, oil wouldn't start flowing from the region for at least ten years, and production wouldn't reach full capacity until 2020 or later.

Nonetheless both President Bush and Secretary Abraham have repeatedly attempted to justify the project, offering assurances that ANWR's oil reserves could help pry us from the grip of OPEC. Abraham wrote that the ANWR contained "the equivalent of ten years of oil from the Persian Gulf." Bush later claimed the reserve could produce 16 billion barrels of oil. In fact, the U.S. Geological Survey, in its most current and extensive assessment, says, "Technically recoverable oil within the ANWR 1002 [the section Bush has proposed opening to drilling] is estimated to be between 4.3 and 11.8 billion barrels, with a mean value of 7.7 billion barrels." According to the same report, at a market price of $24 per barrel, the "economically re-coverable" value would be only 5.2 billion barrels. Based on Energy Information Administration data, these estimates reveal that drilling in ANWR would supplant OPEC oil not for ten years, as Secretary Abraham claimed, but only eighteen to thirty-six months.

In the grand scheme, all these numbers are but drops in the global gas tank. Richard Fineberg, former oil and gas advisor to the governor of Alaska, notes, "People ignore the basic fact that roughly ninety-seven percent of the world's oil is outside the U.S., and no amount of drilling will alter this picture significantly." According to the Rocky Mountain Institute, an environmental think tank, a 0.4 mile-per-gallon improvement in the fuel efficiency of our country's auto fleet (equivalent to the improvement made on average every month from 1979–85), would save more oil per day than the Alaskan reserve would produce.

Ultimately, ANWR is less about oil than about oil money, the $1.9 million poured into George W. Bush's presidential campaign by his supporters in the oil industry, supporters who will make more money and more donations if the ANWR is opened for business.

If domestic drilling simply cannot bring America energy security—and with such environmental risks on the line, why should we even undertake the effort?—an investment in vehicle fuel efficiency, by comparison, would yield far better economic and environmental returns. In 2003, according to the EPA, the fuel economy of American cars fell to 20.4 miles per gallon, its lowest point in twenty-two years, a period during which engine, brake, and safety technologies all improved dramatically. Perhaps hoping to demonstrate that the problem wasn't as bad as environmentalists claimed, the newly elected Bush administration commissioned a report from the National Research Council on automotive fuel efficiency. The report disclosed that, in fact, automakers already have the technology to increase the fuel efficiency of SUVs to 25 to 30 miles per gallon and of standard cars to 40 miles per gallon. The Bush administration, in response, committed to raising SUV fuel efficiency standards by a mere 7 percent to 22.2 miles per gallon over the next few years—while adamantly opposing a bipartisan 2002 bill proposed by Senators John McCain (R-AZ) and John Kerry (D-MA) that would have raised the overall fuel efficiency standards to 36 miles per gallon by 2015.

This is a major lost opportunity. "If the vehicles on the road today averaged 40 miles per gallon, we would save more than 3 million barrels of oil a day, more than we currently import from the Persian Gulf," notes Daniel Becker, the director of the Sierra Club's Global Warming and Energy Program. "The degree of duplicity this administration has shown—in wanting to pillage the Alaskan wildlife for six months of oil but turning its back on programs that would save ten times as much oil by requiring our vehicles to go further on a gallon of gas—is unparalleled."

President Bush's embrace of hydrogen car technology in his 2003 State of the Union address was commendable—hydrogen fuel cells may one day have the potential to replace the internal combustion engine. But in another gap between rhetoric and result, the five-year, $1.2 billion FreedomCAR program Bush announced then looks like little more than a "green" coat of paint. It includes no timetable or even a requirement for an actual prototype, and the price tag is less than 20 percent of what DaimlerChrysler spends on research and development every year. "If it was a really serious effort, on the scale of the Manhattan Project, we'd be talking about a $24-to-27-billion project," explains Bud Ris of the Union of Concerned Scientists. "Hydrogen is the holy grail of the environmental movement, but it'll take twenty to thirty years. It's not worth doing it if we're robbing the money from things that are already working." And in focusing on cars that won't be on the market for some twenty years, President Bush deflects attention from the highly efficient hybrid gas-electric engines that are in showrooms today.

Given its ardor for tax cuts, the Bush administration should be providing tax breaks to Americans who buy more efficient cars and SUVs. Instead, the president is maintaining perverse incentives that do just the opposite. Bush's newest round of tax cuts would allow small business owners and the self-employed to take a special deduction for the purchase of extra-large sport utility vehicles. This "Hummerdinger of a tax loophole," in the phrase of Al Kamen of the *Washington Post,* would allow a doctor or an accountant to deduct $87,000 of the value of the purchase of a $102,000 Hummer H1.*

Policies that fail to make cars more fuel efficient and keep us dependent on Middle East oil are not merely oversights. The automakers work hard to influence political jurors, with contributions of $2.7 million into Republican and Democratic campaign coffers in the 2000 election cycle and another $2 million in 2002. They will continue to fight fuel efficiency standards as they always have, just as they fought seat belts in the 1960s and 1970s and air bags in the 1980s.

Political courage involves more than talking tough to tyrants. It also means standing up to domestic political forces that, through their anticonservation, proindustry practices, keep us perpetually embroiled in that region. After September 11, President Bush had an opportunity to rally public opinion and resources toward the goal of independence through improved fuel efficiency. Such an initiative would have strengthened our domestic economy and our national security and would have attracted

---

*A sales representative for Hummer of Alaska, Chris Thorpe, wrote in a promotions letter: "Allow me to introduce you to a fabulous opportunity. A tax 'loophole' so big you could drive a Hummer H2 through it. Imagine being able to purchase the #1 large luxury SUV in America today . . . and receive a deduction for the entire purchase amount from your taxes this year! How is this possible? Thanks to the Bush administration's recent economic stimulus package, small businesses and the self-employed are eligible to deduct the entire purchase cost of new equipment up to $100,000 the year of the purchase."

overwhelming public support. But due to a deadly mix of industry money, political ideology, and eloquent deceptions, he squandered the opportunity.

Dirty Skies

In the thirty years since the Clean Air Act was passed "air quality" has evolved from an oxymoron into something most Americans regard as a right. Los Angeles is no longer the smog capital of the world, factory towns in the Rust Belt are livable again, and many of our country's worst polluters have been fined and forced into compliance. Overall, since the passage of the Clean Air Act, air pollution has declined by 25 percent. Nonetheless, many Americans are still plagued by pollution. Numerous studies have directly linked power-plant emissions to childhood asthma, respiratory disease, and other internal health problems—a 2000 review of the scientific literature by Abt Associates, a consultancy that does work for the EPA, estimated that 30,100 Americans die every year from power-plant-related disease.

On the subject of the environment and clean air, President Bush often sounds like one of his Republican heroes, Teddy Roosevelt, as when he declared in 2001, "We must seek the best ways to achieve the common goal of leaving to posterity a nation of fresh air, clean water, and natural beauty. These policies arise from the conviction that a healthy environment is a national concern and requires an active national government."

To back up his proclamations, the president announced the following year his "Clear Skies Initiative." Clear Skies would set new pollution levels for three pollutants: sulfur dioxide, nitrogen oxides, and mercury. The program would build on the cap-and-trade system first utilized for sulfur dioxide under Father Bush's Clean Air Act of 1990. President Bush 43 promoted the supposed benefits of his plan in unambiguous terms: "Clear Skies will reduce air pollution from power plants by seventy percent, the most significant step America has ever taken to address this problem—while using a market-based system to keep electricity prices affordable for hardworking Americans."

But here's the twist: a year before Clear Skies was officially rolled out, Bush's EPA had a meeting with the Edison Electric Institute in which the agency outlined the pollution targets it was planning to implement under the Clean Air Amendments signed by Bush's father. Side by side, the numbers speak for themselves: George W.'s plan would in the short term allow 125 percent more sulfur dioxide, 68 percent more nitrogen oxide, and 420 percent more mercury than the laws already in the books.

The numbers shell-game is only part of the problem. Jumping into market-based pollution programs for nitrogen oxide and mercury will also pose particular health risks for which the Clear Skies Initiative has failed to account. Unlike sulfur dioxide, which is usually spewed high into the air and dispersed over hundreds of miles, the effects of mercury are mostly local, so if a few plants in an urban area purchase a large number of mercury credits, we could see dramatic mercury increases in that area even while national levels decline. Mercury poses the greatest threat to infants and pregnant women: A 2003 EPA reported showed that 8 percent of American women of childbearing age have mercury levels in their blood above the "reference dose" (i.e., at levels that risk neurological damage and other adverse effects in utero and in nursing infants). In light of that finding, Bush's proposal to allow 420 percent more mercury than the EPA wanted and his refusal to place a cap on localized mercury emissions hardly seem "compassionately conservative."

This notion of a "right to clean air" is embodied by the Clean Air Act, a bill signed by President Nixon and strengthened by President George H. W. Bush. The act was founded on a series of fundamental compromises between government, business, and the environmental groups. That spirit of compromise is embedded in the EPA's New Source Review guidelines: The government wouldn't impose pollution controls on older plants, but new plants had to be built with the best available technology, and older plants couldn't expand or increase their emissions unless they simultaneously upgraded their pollution technology. The tradeoff, at the time, seemed fair— EPA assumed most of the older plants would be closed down by the end of the twentieth century, anyway.

It hasn't worked out that way. By the late 1990s, a surprisingly large number of those dirty, older plants were still in business and responsible for the greater proportion of the overall emissions of nitrogen oxide and other pollutants. The Clinton administration reacted by strengthening enforcement at the EPA, to force cleanups when maintenance or improvements increased emissions at a plant. In 1999 and 2000, the EPA filed lawsuits against nine major power companies and dozens of individual power plants, whose combined emissions represent a third of all factory pollution in the United States and are responsible for more than 5,000 premature deaths each year. In court-approved settlement agreements, the first companies had started to comply. "EPA was finally calling their bluff. We had them over the barrel," explained Eric Shaeffer, at the time EPA's head of the Office of Regulatory Enforcement.

Then a new Bush moved into the White House, an industry wasted no time in seeking to modify or repeal New Source Review. A group of utilities hired Haley Barbour, a former Republican National Committee chairman, to be their chief lobbyist in Washington. Around the same time, the Southern Company, one of the businesses being sued by EPA and a one-million-dollar-plus contributor to the Republican Party in 2000, sent Cheney's Energy Policy Task Force a strongly worded memo arguing that relaxed New Source Review standards would help guarantee energy security (and, no doubt, their own corporate profits). The Task Force included Southern's recommendation in its final proposal, and the Bush administration officially announced the lowered standards in 2003.

The "*New* New Source Review" standards would basically allow the 17,000 oldest, dirtiest power plants in America to keep on belching away. Whereas today the grandfathered plants can't make modifications that would increase their emissions, the Bush rule would allow each facility to spend annually up to 20 percent of the value of the plant's total equipment—in some cases, tens or even hundreds of millions of dollars—on replacements and improvements, even if those "improvements" increase total plant emissions. In other words, over five years, an energy company could rebuild its entire facility (20 percent in each year), increase its total pollution, and evade environmental standards. That means more smog and acid rain in midwestern and northeastern states, more kids contracting asthma, and no relief for families living under the shadow of refineries and chemical plants.

It was particularly ironic that Bush made the New Source Review announcement while visiting a Michigan power plant that emits 102,000 tons of sulfur dioxide every year and—thanks to the eased regulations—won't have to reduce that pollution for another seventeen years. Although Bush asserted that his approach would not contribute to air pollution, two scientific studies—by the GAO and by the Council of the State Governments—concluded that the rule change would add 1.4 million tons of air pollution in twelve states. The New York *Daily News,* a paper that endorsed George W. Bush in 2000, complained, "The rule change is a direct assault on the environment. Bush is putting Big Business ahead of clean air. Let's at least be honest about it, Mr. President. Admit that EPA now stands for Environmental Pollution Agency."

Of course, even strict environmental standards work only if there's someone enforcing them. Bush's 2003 EPA budget would continue a three-year effort to slash the number of enforcement jobs. With fewer people available to enforce the laws, the result is not surprising. Since Bush took office, civil environmental penalties are down almost 50 percent, the number of pounds of pollution to be cleaned up is down 20 percent, and EPA is conducting three thousand fewer inspections each year.

The Bush administration, therefore, is reducing not pollution but enforcement. Not only has Bush's EPA not brought any new Clean Air Act cases since it's been in office, but, in one of the greatest regulatory capitulations of this or any administration, the agency in November 2003 dropped dozens of previously filed lawsuits against companies for pollution because of the circular reasoning that the companies might no longer be in violation of Bush's more relaxed interpretation of the Clean Air Act—an idea that, not surprisingly, came from Vice President Cheney's Energy Task Force.

Former press secretary Ari Fleischer blamed the enforcement drop-off on the rigidity of the New Source Review guidelines, asserting, "What often happens in these federal regulations, while they may have a sound that seems to be very well-intended, the actual impact on the country is just the opposite. And that's what's happened here, with the way these rules are enforced. And the President believes that as a result of the actions announced today [relaxing the standard], it will lead—just as his Clear Skies Initiative does—to less pollution in the air."

The president's belief is so far the only evidence the White House has been able to marshal in support of weakening New Source Review. "The data to defend that assertion has been repeatedly requested but has never been produced," explains Greg Wetstone of the Natural Resources Defense Council. "It's a thinly disguised effort to revisit and undermine the basic compromise that made the Clean Air Act work in the first place." In July 2002 congressional testimony, Assistant Attorney General Thomas Sansonetti acknowledged the shortage of data, deferring and deflecting senators' requests for numbers that would justify changing the New Source Review standards.

According to the Bush administration, the higher emissions allowed will nonetheless be offset by factories and energy companies voluntarily reducing their pollution. Take away the regulations, they argue, and companies will undertake environmental improvements that they're afraid of starting today. But these are the same companies who have fought every air quality improvement effort over the last forty years and whose irresponsible practices provoked the Clean Air Act in the first place. In the end, what we're left with is another "faith-based initiative": ease controls on our country's biggest polluters, then pray that they clean things up on their own.

In this courtroom, Bush arrives as a repeat offender. Facing a state ranking number one in total air pollution and pollution-related cancer risk, then governor Bush tried the same approach to address power plants that had been grandfathered by Texas's earliest clean air laws. His 1997 proposal, literally written by members of the oil and gas industry, asked power plants to voluntarily clean up their pollution.* During the 2000 presidential campaign, Bush often referred to this bill as his "biggest environmental achievement" and a model for the market-based solutions he would bring to Washington. The problem is that three years later, according to the *Corpus Christi Caller-Times*, fewer than 10 percent of the seven hundred plants

---

*According to an internal DuPont Corporation memorandum, "The draft concept paper (attached) was developed by a very small (2–3) group of companies from upstream oil & gas. . . . The belief was clearly communicated at the meeting that this industry group was going to be in the leadership role in transforming the concepts into a program that would be approved by the Governor's Office. . . . I told the group that I believe that TNRCC will be in the lead on this very soon. Clearly, the 'insiders' from oil & gas believe that the Governor's Office will 'persuade' the TNRCC to accept whatever program is developed between the industry group and the Governor's Office. I don't believe that will be the case. . . . The concept put forward was that the industry group and the Governor's Office would develop the program, then take it to some broad-based group, including public representatives, who would then tweak it a little bit and approve it. . . . The concept paper has no 'meat' with respect to actual emissions reductions. One of the [industry] leaders actually stated that emissions reductions was not a primary driver for the program."

covered by the law had in fact volunteered to reduce emissions, and pollution at the grandfathered plants had been reduced by less than 3 percent. Fewer than six months after Bush had left Texas for the White House, the Texas legislature declared Bush's voluntary program a failure and replaced it with a mandatory pollution control scheme.

Failure, of course, is a relative concept. From a political perspective, the voluntary program proved a significant success. Not only did grandfathered companies contribute significantly to Bush's gubernatorial and presidential campaigns, but the superficial effort also gave Governor Bush something to trumpet during the presidential campaign and allowing him to talk tough on polluters. During the October 11, 2000, presidential debate, he declared: "We need to make sure that if we decontrol our plants that there's mandatory—that the plants must conform to clean air standards, the grandfathered plants. That's what we did in Texas. No excuses. I mean, you must conform." But the truth is that the Texas plan was neither mandatory nor successful. If the president is going to invoke Teddy Roosevelt as his environmental role model, he should pay attention to something else TR said: "Compliance with the law is demanded as a right, not asked as a favor."

Public Health versus Private Interests

Most presidents make careless errors in early weeks, and one of Bush's occurred when his EPA attempted to overturn a Clinton administration regulation that would've tightened the limits on arsenic in public drinking water. Environmentalists and editorialists reacted with outrage, the Bush administration did a "mea culpa," and the proposal was dropped.

This gaffe would be excusable were it not representative of a pattern of environmental hostility during the first three years of the Bush administration. Its approach on public health laws has typically been to first ask industry which regulations they hate most, then eliminate or weaken those laws, and if the public notices and reacts, declare their action an administrative mistake and move on to something new.

Take the case of testing poor children for lead poisoning. In the spring of 2002 the Department of Health and Human Services (HHS) was considering abandoning its mandatory lead testing for tens of thousands of children on Medicaid. Lead, which can contribute to anemia, kidney damage, and even brain damage, is particularly dangerous to the very young; and because lead paint has not been removed from many public housing units, the poorest children have the greatest exposure to it (according to 2002 data, at least 535,000 Medicaid children have lead poisoning). The Bush administration's approach would have allowed states the flexibility to determine how much lead testing they should perform, despite government figures showing that only 10 percent of poor children were screened by states in 1999 and 2000. When physicians and public health advocates loudly protested and threatened a hearing, HHS disavowed the plan, blaming a "career civil servant" and saying it was all a big misunderstanding.

The weakening of the Clean Air Act was clearly no "misunderstanding." That landmark 1972 legislation arose when citizens, having seen children sickened by drinking water, sludge in Lake Erie, and the Cuyahoga River ablaze, finally decided enough was enough. While the act has had mixed success since its enactment, President Bush himself declared its legacy was that "our lakes and rivers are much cleaner than they were thirty years ago." But in the last three years, his administration has repeatedly threatened this legacy, usually loosening standards when corporate interests beckon.

Consider mountaintop-removal mining, perhaps the most environmentally and aesthetically destructive extraction process in the history of an industry notorious for ecological carelessness. In this process, rather than building a mineshaft into a mountain, mining companies use explosives to shear off the mountain's top, exposing the coal within. It is a cheap way to get to coal, but disposing of the resulting rubble is not so easy. For twenty-five years, the Clean Water Act has forbidden mining companies from dumping such waste into the valleys and streams below.

In May 2002 the Bush administration redefined "fill material" in order to allow mining companies to legally dump their waste in these areas, despite that mountaintop mining practices have already destroyed thousands of miles of streams in the Appalachians, killing fish and wildlife. During flood season this silt and rubble is also carried far downstream into drinking water sources.

The Bush White House has argued that failure to change the regulation would have forced the West Virginia coal companies out of business; of course, these same coal companies made it their business to spend $3.6 million supporting Republicans in the 2000 and 2002 election cycles (88 percent of their total political spending) and had unfettered access to Vice President Cheney's Energy Policy Task Force.

West Virginia is not the only place where destructive mining practices are threatening drinking water. After a decade of study, the EPA reported that "mining in the western United States has contaminated stream reaches in the headwaters of more than forty percent of the watersheds in the West." Rather than intervening to monitor mining more closely, the Bush Interior Department instead overturned a Clinton administration rule restricting mining projects when they will cause "substantial irreparable harm" to a given area's environment.

While Christie Whitman's EPA deserves considerable credit for forcing General Electric to clean up its PCB contamination in the Hudson River, on most other environmental health controversies the record of Bush's environmental officials has been consistently poor:

✳ The Bush Administration deliberately misled New Yorkers about health risks after the World Trade Center disaster. In press releases issued on September 16 and September 18, 2001, the EPA announced that the air in lower Manhattan was clear and that people should feel safe returning to work in that area. A stunning 2003 report by the EPA's own inspector general revealed not only that EPA lacked the knowledge to make such "blanket statements" but that the White House intervened to delete more cautionary language. For example, EPA draft language stating that asbestos levels were three times higher than national standards in certain areas was changed to read "slightly above the 1 percent trigger for defining asbestos material." According to the report, at the request of the White House Council on Environmental Quality, language warning of particular danger to asthmatics and the elderly was stricken, as was an advisory notice that residents and businesspeople should have their buildings professionally cleaned. The EPA's whitewashed notice (deceptively) calmed people down, encouraged citizens to return to their homes, induced some businesses to reopen quickly—but at what cost? A study at the University of California–Davis found that the debris pile "gave off gases of toxic metals, acids and organics for at least six weeks . . . like a chemical factory," threatening the pulmonary health of both workers at the site and people who lived and worked nearby. A May 2003 poll of lower Manhattan residents found that 31 percent reported pulmonary problems that dated to the September 11 attacks.

✳ The administration passed taxpayers the bill for cleaning up toxic waste. From 1980 to 1995, cleanups at large toxic waste sites in the Superfund program were supported in part by a trust fund, established by levying a tax on polluting industries. Both the Reagan and Bush 41 White Houses backed this "polluter pays" principle because it was fair and it worked. Since the Republican Congress took over in 1995 and refused to reauthorize the tax, the fund has shriveled from $3.8 billion to flat-broke as of October 2003. In addition, the Bush budget allocated barely half of the $450 million that the EPA's regional offices sought for these cleanups. Without the trust fund in place, Superfund cleanups are down 41 percent from the average of the Clinton years, and the future of the Superfund program is in jeopardy. Taxpayers now end up footing the bill by themselves, and local communities may now be forever stuck with highly toxic sites in their neighborhoods.

The premise behind so much of this attempted regulatory rollback is that regulation is a costly interruption for the business community. Yet a crucial study in late 2003 documented that, overall, environmental regulation was well worth its costs—costing business $23 billion to $26 billion a year but generating $120 billion to $193 billion in such benefits as reduced hospitalization, fewer lost workdays, and fewer premature deaths. The source: an Office of Management and Budget study.

Open Season on National Treasures

Before television cameras and on the campaign trail, President Bush and his top lieutenants refer to themselves not as "environmentalists" but as "conservationists," aligning themselves with the Republican Party's early-twentieth-century history of setting aside land and forests as permanently protected areas. Interior Secretary Gale Norton, in her Senate confirmation hearing, declared, "If confirmed, I intend to make the conservation of America's natural treasures my top priority." Quite the opposite, however, is true: Secretary Norton has actually rescinded an order protecting 2.6 million acres of wilderness in Utah and declared that the Bush Interior Department had zero interest in setting aside wilderness lands in the future.

President Bush's forest policies similarly reflect that conservation is far from the top priority. In early January 2001, after two years of public input, the Clinton administration finalized a rule—the so-called Roadless Rule—that would protect sixty million acres of national forest from additional road-building and development. The Bush administration first sought to discredit the Roadless Rule as an environmental land grab. Bush's statement during the October 11, 2000, presidential debate is emblematic: "[They] took 40 million acres of land out of circulation without consulting local officials. . . . I just cited an example of the administration just unilaterally acting without any input." His statement was completely false. In fact, the Forest Service conducted six hundred public hearings on the proposal and received more than a million letters from Americans urging the service to strengthen it.

In 2001, when the Roadless Rule was challenged by industry groups, Bush's Department of Justice refused even to defend it in court, reasoning that the policy was insensitive to timber companies and local interests. Environmental groups intervened on the government's behalf, and, in late 2002, the Ninth Circuit Court of Appeals strongly confirmed the legitimacy of both the original Roadless Rule and the process used to create it.

With its public relations and legal remedies exhausted, the administration tried a new tack. *Appearing* to capitulate, the administration announced in June 2003 that it would retain the Roadless Rule after all—with a couple of footnotes. First, Bush's version of the Roadless Rule would exempt the millions of acres of undeveloped forest in Alaska's Tongass National Forest, opening up for timber sales an area that "contains nearly 30 percent of the world's unlogged coastal temperate rain forest." Incidentally, it announced, no environmental impact statement would be necessary because there would be "no significant environmental impact" in exempting this magnificent rain forest from the logging ban. Second, the Bush administration would consider requests from state governors to further relax the restrictions on road-building and logging in those states' national forest land. Western governors will no doubt soon be lining up around the corner to hand in their "requests."

As it turns out, the Roadless Rule was just a warmup. President Bush's true intentions for our nation's forests became clearer by the summer of 2002, when in the aftermath of tragic forest fires he announced major overhauls to the way America's national forests are managed under the misnamed "Healthy Forests Initiative." Bush described it with a high-minded flourish few could dispute: "This isn't a chance for one political party to get an upper hand on another political party, this is just common sense for what's best for not only the forests, and the preservation and conservation of forests, but what's best for the people who live around the forests. That's what this is."

The centerpiece of the plan is a fire-prevention proposal that would allow logging companies to cut large-diameter trees from the middle of our forests in exchange for their obligation to thin trees and brush near residential areas. The plan purportedly has the worthy goal of protecting houses from fire danger, but it will in fact allow logging companies to focus much of their attention far from at-risk communities. "It's a license to steal," concluded Marty Hayden, legislative director for the legal group Earthjustice. "To pay for it, you need big trees, in areas that are not close to communities. [But] these are older trees, deep in the forest, that are exactly what we do not need to be thinning." That's because large-diameter trees, though highly valuable as pulp and paper, are especially fire-resistant. Without them, the forest loses its strongest natural barriers against the spread of fire.

Likewise, there is no scientific consensus on industry-led stewardship projects like the ones Bush's plan recommends. Even the study cited by proponents of Healthy Forests concludes that, because only five of the eighty-four pilot projects had been completed, Congress should "exercise serious caution" before making them permanent. So while the White House requests yet another decade of study for global warming, this not nearly completed pilot program represents enough evidence to open our national forests to wholesale logging.

Worse, Healthy Forests wouldn't actually mandate that the timber companies remove the forest underbrush that contributes so greatly to forest fires: doing the fire-prevention work would be an afterthought, dependent on the loggers making enough profit from harvesting large trees to fund the brush removal. If the timber companies decided not to clear the brush, the proposal has no mechanism to force their hands. As a result, the logging industry gets a sweetheart deal and fire-threatened communities get the shaft.

Why is the Bush administration more focused on timber sales than on the true sources of forest fires? Perhaps it's because the administration's point man on forests, Agriculture Undersecretary Mark Rey, was a top official at the American Forest and Paper Association, a logging industry interest group, prior to his government position. In a telling gesture, key Bush administration officials, including Rey, spoke at a February 2003 meeting in Portland, Oregon, during which timber industry leaders discussed contributing up to $275,000 each for a PR campaign supporting the Healthy Forests Initiative. "The Bush administration has told people in our industry, 'We need your help,'" according to Ray Wilkeson of the Oregon Forest Industries Council. In return for industry's help, Bush's proposal would allow the Forest Service to waive the environmental impact statements, public hearings, and fish and wildlife protections usually required before giving the green light to forestry projects.

The White House justified these dramatic moves by blaming "analysis paralysis" and obstructionist environmentalists. As President Bush declared when announcing the Healthy Forest Initiative, "We have a problem with the regulatory body there in Washington. I mean, there's so many regulations, and so much red tape, that it takes a little bit of effort to ball up the efforts to make the forests healthy. And plus, there's just too many lawsuits, just endless litigation."

As the old saying goes, "Interesting if true." But *is* forest litigation out of control? A 2003 General Accounting Office (GAO) report concluded that of the 762 fire-prevention projects proposed by the Forest Service in the past two years, fewer than 25 were litigated, and 95 percent of them proceeded in fewer than 90 days. While environmental impact statements undoubtedly require time and energy, they have been successfully utilized for thirty years, and they play a vital role in ensuring that a company or industry doesn't run roughshod over environmental values.

National forests are not the only resources that have come under Bush's relentless attack. Over the last three years, the White House has pushed numerous mining and drilling projects on public lands or near protected areas. Behind these measures is a crew of Bush-appointed regulators who only three years ago were lobbying on behalf of the industries they're now supposed to be regulating. Conflicts of interest are commonplace:

✦ Deputy Interior Secretary J. Steven Griles, a former lobbyist for the coal-bed methane industry, consulted for several companies vying to drill in Wyoming's Powder River Basin in the late 1990s. Apparently, he forgot to check his lobbyist card at the door. Despite signing two recusal memos in which he promised not to participate in decisions that affected formal clients, Griles tried to block an EPA report that criticized the environmental effects of coal-bed methane development in the Powder River Basin.

* Interior Department solicitor William Geary Myers previously lobbied to preserve federal grazing subsidies. Now he represents Interior in grazing cases—and on his watch, the Interior Department backed off its plan to double the fees for grazing on public lands it charges ranchers (currently ranchers pay only 10 percent of market value).

* Assistant Secretary of Energy for Fossil Energy Carl Michael Smith, himself a veteran of the oil industry, famously informed a group of oil and gas representatives that his job was to determine "how best to utilize taxpayer dollars to the benefit of industry."

To Dan Becker of the Sierra Club, the problem is not merely the presence of energy, mining, and timber industry people in government—all administrations include some representation from corporate America—but the power they command. "The key lobbyists for all the key industries now hold key positions in this administration. The level of animus that they bring to their activities is unparalleled. The Reagan administration had [Interior Secretary] Jim Watt but this administration has twenty-five Jim Watts, and in fact Gale Norton was one of Jim Watt's top deputies."

What are the results when industry is invited to regulate itself? On the watch of these "regulators," the Bush administration has pushed for: drilling on the border of Utah's Arches National Park, a project ultimately halted by a federal judge; drilling off the shore of South Padre Island, Texas; logging 10 million board feet of timber from the Sequoia National Monument; and yet more drilling near the coast of Santa Barbara, California, even though virtually every Republican politician in California opposes it. President Bush was kinder to the coastal waters of Florida after his brother, Governor Jeb Bush, subjected the Interior Department to a yearlong full-court press and convinced them in 2002 to abandon plans for offshore drilling there (an election-year gift for the brother who delivered Florida in 2000).

In that same spirit the Bush administration has backed off from thirty years of protection for our nation's wetlands. In the early 1990s, President George H. W. Bush established the well-intentioned "no net loss" policy for America's wetlands: If you fill in a wetland, you have to replace it locally with a wetland of the same size. The EPA of Bush 43 quietly abandoned "no net loss"; but rather than protecting existing wetlands, the administration continues to push for wetlands replacement projects, even though two separate reports by the National Academy of Sciences and the General Accounting Office showed that 80 percent of these wetlands replacements are failures.

Wetlands may only be the tip of the Clean Water iceberg. In early 2003 the Bush EPA announced that it would reopen the long-settled question of what bodies of water are covered by the Clean Water Act. Before the

Clean Water Act of 1972, 70 percent of America's waters were too polluted for swimming or unable to support fish and wildlife. Three decades later, standing under the shade of redwoods in California's Sequoia National Forest, President Bush 43 said, "Our lakes and rivers are much cleaner than they were thirty years ago. Firm limits on toxic emissions have greatly improved the quality of the air we breathe. And I'm proud that it was my dad's signature on the Clean Air Act amendments of 1990 that helped reduce acid rain and urban pollution." But defying his father's legacy, President Bush 43 himself has pulled far back on the actual enforcement of these laws, ignored global warming, and preferred drilling in Alaska to auto fuel efficiencies, a record that has provoked harsh conclusions from environmental lawyer Robert F. Kennedy Jr.:

> If you polled experts they'd say that this Bush is the worst environmental president in our history. But unlike Newt Gingrich's open assault a decade ago, he's doing it quietly through his agencies via rules changes to eviscerate thirty years of environmental law. If he even partly succeeds, we'll no longer have effective environmental laws anymore. We'll be like Mexico, having nice-sounding laws with no mechanism to enforce them.

3. Déjà Vu-doo Economics
The Real Faith-Based Policy

"My economic security plan can be summed up in one word: jobs."
—President George W. Bush, 2002

"For the sake of fiscal sanity, the United States Senate must . . . get us to head towards a balanced budget."
—President George W. Bush, 2002

Presidents running for reelection are largely judged on two big subjects—peace and prosperity, not necessarily in that order of importance. "I know from bitter experience," wrote Richard Nixon, "how in both 1954 and 1958 economic slumps contributed to substantial Republican losses."* Of course, because George W. Bush witnessed his father harpooned by the 1991–92 recession and the slogan, "It's the economy, stupid," he smartly focused most of his domestic political capital on the economy. His economic goal is also his de facto political goal: a more than 3 percent GDP growth rate in the first and second quarters of 2004, which is the historic threshold for incumbent presidents separating sure losers from favorites.

All new presidents are dealt a particular card from a previous administration they must figure out how to play: for Eisenhower it was Korea; for Kennedy, the Soviet threat; for Nixon, Vietnam; and for Clinton, the weak economy. Bush's early hand contained two big economic cards—one widely discussed, one not—that were especially challenging: (a) how to overcome

---

*In 1984, of the 48 percent of Americans saying the economy had gotten better, 80 percent voted for President Reagan; in 1992, of the 72 percent saying the economy was worse, 68 percent voted for challenger Bill Clinton.

sluggishness and continue record growth and (b) how to shrink a quietly widening wealth-income gap that was eroding the middle class. Eventually he'll be assessed on how he managed these two topics. Did his policies lead to strong growth and boost the middle class, or not?

The Economy—January 2001

For all the controversy over Reaganomics, its most significant legacy was the quadrupling of the federal debt at a cost to American taxpayers of tens of billions annually in interest payments. Over the twelve years of Reagan-Bush, wages stagnated, workers' productivity stalled, investment languished, poverty rose by 6.5 million people, and income inequality steeply climbed. Average GDP growth for these years was a modest 2 percent. "There was no supply-side revolution at all," wrote Will Hutton in *A Declaration of Interdependence*, "just a scale of enrichment at the top that beggared belief."

Naturally, Democratic presidential nominee Bill Clinton focused on economic issues in 1992, promising tax increases on top earners and tax cuts for the middle class to stimulate growth. But once in office, he was persuaded by economic advisor Robert Rubin to pay heed to the bond market, and so dropped the middle-class tax cuts, hiked tax rates from 31 percent to 39.6 percent for those earning over $250,000 annually, and slowed spending, with the result that the deficit began to shrink.

As deficit reduction (and crises abroad) gave investors confidence in the United States, interest rates declined and growth took off. Eight years later, the Clinton economy had created a record 22 million jobs, real income for median families rose twice as fast in his eight years as the prior twelve, 7.7 million escaped poverty, and deficits had turned into surpluses for the first time in twenty-four years.

Liberals had learned a surprising lesson: in a globalized economy, when money could drain away from a country with fiscally unsound policies, fiscal discipline—even balanced budgets—could be stimulative. By 1999 the budget that was plunged into the red by Reagan's tax cuts was finally balanced, and by 2001 it was running a surplus. Al Gore and other Democrats made plans to use that surplus as the basis for securing Social Security and Medicare, the two big entitlement programs that will face a cash crisis when baby boomers retire. Rarely has an administration of one party bequeathed to a president of another such fundamentally promising prospects.

But the business cycle remained in force and, as George W. Bush appeared on the Capitol steps to take the presidential oath, clouds had already begun appearing on the economic horizon. The geometrically expanding Internet-tech bubble burst in 2000, erasing hundreds of billions in paper wealth and leaving behind excess inventories. Foreign investors and American consumers—the latter with $300 billion more to spend after home refinancings—were propping up an economy that was saving and spending too little. Manufacturing jobs were continuing their flight to low-wage countries abroad. And unlike the recession of 1991, when the Federal Reserve raised interest rates to cool off inflation, this time the problem was not too much demand for too little supply, but the reverse—the economy needed some public-sector stimulus to get back on its feet.

That's Rich—January 2001

While a tribune of the economic elite such as George W. Bush certainly hoped no one would notice, the data are indeed damning: one of the greatest social shifts in America in the past half-century is the growing gap between the rich and the rest of us—in terms of income and wealth.

What's most striking is the reason for the division. In the 1990s it was not that the poor were getting poorer—they weren't. Rather, the inequality was entirely the result of an astonishing increase in wealth among the very top individuals and families, in a concentration of capital not seen since the Gilded Age.

Based on IRS data, the earnings of the top 1 percent of all Americans grew from 14 percent of all income in 1990 to nearly 21 percent in 2000—or double that of the bottom 40 percent. From 1973 to 1995 workers saw their real incomes actually decline (though it rose at the end of Clinton's second term); the pay of the average CEO rose from about ninety times that of the average worker in 1988 to more than four hundred times in 1999. Even these stunning ratios understate the differences between managers and line workers because they omit the perks of high office: executives, for example, often receive freebies for which their employees have to pay. Although the last payout for GE's Jack Welch was $120 million, still his retirement package includes a Manhattan apartment with fully paid-for flowers, wine, laundry services, postage, and housekeeping services—as well as tickets to sporting events. Federal Revenue chairman Alan Greenspan called the phenomenon "infectious greed," as executives from Enron's Ken Lay to Global Crossing's Gary Winnick took nine-figure payouts.

The story on wealth is even more dramatic. While 1 percent *earns* almost 21 percent of income, the top 1 percent have come to *own* nearly 50 percent of all financial wealth; 5 percent owns 70 percent. (Housing and Social Security wealth is more progressively distributed.) The overall numbers are more dismal for the black and Latino families: black households had fifty-four cents of income and twelve cents of wealth for every dollar in a white household; for Latinos it was sixty-two cents and four cents.

Actually, when viewed over the time frame of a century, things haven't changed very much. While FDR's assault on "concentrated power" did diminish the concentration of income and wealth, the percentages of income and wealth controlled by the richest 1 percent rose in 2000 back to where they were in 1900. These inequalities have been tolerated by an American public that mistakenly believes that either it's already in a top bracket (19 percent believe they're in the top 1 percent, a statistic Garrison Keillor would understand) or it may be. But while there are obviously exceptions, the myth of mobility is losing its force: in 1970, it was four times more likely that a student would go to college if he or she were in the richest one-fourth as compared to the poorest one-fourth; but by 2000, this disparity had grown to ten times more likely.

Nothing succeeds like excess, joked Oscar Wilde, but even much of the business press had begun to regard the disparities as offensive. To illustrate an article about executive pay, *Fortune* put a pin-striped pig on its cover, and *The Economist* similarly chided "those pigs and their love of the trough." In his *Wealth and Democracy,* Kevin Phillips spoke of a "plutoc-racy [due to] the ability of wealth to reach beyond its own realm of money [to] control politics and government as well." Phillips gloomily concluded, "In just a little over two centuries the United States went from being a so-ciety born of revolution and touched by egalitarianism to being the country with the industrial world's biggest fortunes and its largest rich-poor gap." While this gap has slightly shrunk recently due to the decline of hot IPOs (Initial Public Offerings) and the stock market, the 2003 economic recovery and current federal policies mean it won't remain there for long.

Bushomics: Less Taxing, More Filling?

In the 140-year history of federal income taxation there has been a con-tinuing struggle between two schools of political economy. One believes that higher progressive taxation paying for social services is, in Justice Holmes's formulation, "the price we pay for civilized society." The revenue from the first federal income tax, signed into law by President Lincoln to pay for the Civil War, "was essential to saving the Union and freeing the slaves," in the conclusion of author Stephen R. Weisman in *The Great Tax Wars.* During the 1930s President Roosevelt finally rejected Hoover eco-nomics and, in a burst of what came to be called Keynesianism, increased federal taxation and spending in order to revive the economy, establish an economic safety net, and save capitalism from itself.

George W. Bush, in contrast, is a star student in the second school, which regards income taxes as a four-letter word—not a necessary evil, just evil. From John D. Rockefeller ("When a man has accumulated a sum of money within the law, the people no longer have any right to share in the earnings resulting from the accumulation") to conservative economic gurus Frederic Hayek and Milton Friedman, this school believes that high taxes (a) dis-courage investment and growth and (b) encourage social spending, which reduces self-esteem and incentives to work.

As a candidate and officeholder, Bush has been remarkably consistent and persistent on the subject of taxation. Although his original 1997 proposal as Texas governor to cut property taxes by $1 billion failed (because he would also have had to increase sales taxes at the same time), he took credit for a constitutional amendment that subsequently increased the homestead tax exemption, a step that enabled him to run for president three years later as having enacted "the largest tax cut in Texas history." (Few saw any real cuts because, in a development to be reprised just six years later as president, most local school districts were forced to significantly raise their tax rates to make up for shortfalls created by Austin.) When announcing for president in Cedar Rapids, Iowa, on June 12, 1999, the very first policy issue he mentioned was taxes. "We'll be prosperous if we reduce taxes," he said, a theme returned to often as a candidate: "Everybody who pays taxes ought to get relief"; "tax cuts will be financed exclusively out of the non–Social Security surplus"; "for years politicians in both parties have dipped into the [Social Security] trust fund to pay for more funding. And I will stop it"; "it's *your* money"; and, in the first Bush-Gore debate, "after my [tax] plan, the wealthiest of Americans will pay more [in] taxes of the percentage of the whole than they do today."

To Bush and Company, tax cuts were *the* economic elixir—the right remedy if there was a surplus, the right remedy if there was a deficit, the right remedy if we were at war, the right remedy *period.* The president's focus and repetition brought to mind the axiom that "if you only have a hammer, everything looks like a nail." Grover Norquist, among the most important conservative strategists now in Washington, colorfully concluded that, "What Mae West said of sex is true of taxes—even bad tax cuts are good." During the invasion of Iraq, House majority leader Tom DeLay asserted that "there is nothing more important in the face of war than cutting taxes," something America had never done in any of its wars, until Iraq.

In three tax reductions over the course of three years, President Bush has radically changed America's fiscal policies. Individual income tax rates are down, especially for the highest earners; the tax on corporate dividends has been cut by about half (varying by bracket); the tax on capital gains has fallen from 20 percent to 15 percent; the estate tax is on track to be phased out in 2010; high-income families can save up to thirty thousand dollars tax free; the child tax credit rose from five hundred dollars to one thousand dollars, for most children; and the "marriage penalty" is being eliminated for some families.

It's difficult to estimate the entire cost of Bush's tax program because, as Allan Sloan wrote in *Newsweek,* "the legislation has so many tax sunrises and sunsets—Washington's terms for cuts' beginnings and ends—that it should be called the Fiddler on the Roof Act." The president added to the confusion by confidently dismissing the Democratic $350 billion alternative in May 2003 as "little bitty"—yet signing the following month a $350 billion package that he confidently called "a bold package of relief." The best estimate is that his three legislated reductions combined total nearly $2 trillion for the coming decade (and far more if all are extended), making them the largest cumulative tax cuts in American history.

Supporting this massive program have been six rationales, six refrains sung again and again by the Bush chorus. Let's examine each.

> ✳ **Tax cuts stimulate growth and jobs.** "The president does believe that cutting taxes is the best way to spur growth and therefore to have a return to bigger surpluses" (Office of Management and Budget director Mitch Daniels, 2001).

While Bush may try to emulate much about the Reagan administration, he has also shrewdly avoided their mistakes. David Stockman, Reagan's budget director and popularizer of "supply-side economics," has since regretted this "terribly unfortunate" term not because it was wrong but all too accurate, something like Trent Lott's toast to Strom Thurmond and segregation. Bush has embraced the theory, if not the rhetoric.

Recessions often occur when higher interest rates, established to cool off inflation, also have the intended effect of reducing investment and spending, thereby slowing the economy. Then, a combination of more spending, lower taxes, and/or lower interest rates spur demand and stimulate investment—as happened in 1972 and 1991. One problem of the 2001–02 recession and weak recovery, however, was not too little supply but too much. Businesses were utilizing only 75 percent of their industrial capacity, the lowest in twenty years, because of what Alan Greenspan famously called "irrational exuberance"—they had overestimated the tech boom and overinvested in capacity for which there was no market.

But if a modest stimulus was modestly desirable, "tax expenditures" of more than $2 trillion over the course of a decade, flowing largely to the wealthiest Americans to provide an estimated $100 billion stimulus when needed in 2003, seemed a classic case of "burning down the house to roast the pig." If the policy goal was to stimulate the economy, (a) why not cut payroll taxes—most taxpayers pay more in FICA than in income taxes—since average-income families are more likely to spend their tax breaks while wealthier families are more likely to save theirs; or (b) why not just send the money to strapped states as revenue sharing? (Eventually, Bush accepted a relatively small revenue-sharing component as the price of enactment of his 2003 package.) Since the states' eighty-billion-dollar cumulative deficit in 2003 was the highest in five decades—forcing many to reduce health care for the poor, close parks, increase class size, boost tuition at state schools, lay off police, and, in Missouri, unscrew every third light bulb—states would surely spend the money quickly. "In times like this, states usually get a little extra help from Washington," teased former President Bill Clinton, "but instead they're going to give the money to me. I get the money."

Economy.com, a leading independent research group, studied how different tax approaches would boost the economy compared to its cost: a dollar spent extending unemployment benefits would increase GDP by $1.73; a dollar tax cut for low-income individuals would produce $1.34 but for high-income individuals only 59 cents; and phasing out dividend taxes would generate a paltry 9 cents for every dollar in revenue loss.

But these data collide with supply-side theory, which in essence assumes that you motivate the rich with more money and motivate the poor with fewer services. (Pennsylvania Republican Rick Santorum, a top Senate ally of the Bush White House, said that "making people struggle a little bit is not necessarily the worst thing.") But with little evidence that such an approach creates incentives to be more entrepreneurial or work harder, Bush's tax package was far more of a straight transfer of wealth than an economic stimulus. Indeed, when the administration's tax program was put through several public and private computer models—including one by the Congressional Budget Office—they all predicted only tiny revenue losses or gains but no sustained revenue increases. Even the Council of Economic Advisors, in its *Economic Report of the President,* concluded that the tax cuts would *not* pay for themselves, directly contradicting the reassuring comments of both the president and vice president.* Recall how the real-world result of the comparable Reagan cuts of 1981 was huge revenue losses and annual deficits that took fifteen years to eliminate.

So it came as no surprise to mainstream economists that, nearly three years after taking office and with his economic program enacted largely intact, the Bush jobs engine revved up in reverse. For the first time since President Hoover in 1929, a new president experienced a net job loss of more than 2 million, compared to an average 3 million job *gain* for each of the eight years of the Clinton administration. In just three years America has endured a 50 percent increase in the unemployment rate, the loss of one in six manufacturing jobs, and repeated extensions of unemployment compensation because people are out of work longer. Goldman Sachs economists called this not just a "jobless recovery" but a "job-loss recovery"; as economist Jared Bernstein of the Economic Policy Institute said, jobless recovery is "indistinguishable from a recession for many working families."

So how did Bush deal with this proven failure? Like the character in *Chicago* who said, "You going to believe what you see or what I tell you?," Bush in 2003 brazenly attacked the problem head-on. "That six percent [jobless] number should say loud and clear to members of both political parties in the U.S. Congress, we need robust tax relief so our fellow citizens can find jobs"—even though four-fifths of the job losses *followed* his 2001

---

*Bush: the growth package will "lay the groundwork for future growth [and] the added benefit of higher revenues for the government"; Cheney: "the president's package will . . . increase tax revenue to the federal government ultimately."

tax relief. So when press secretary Ari Fleischer said in mid-2003 that "tax cuts have helped create jobs and to promote growth in the economy," he must have had the economy of the Cayman Islands in mind.

* **All will benefit, not just the rich.** "The Bush tax cuts benefit all Americans but reserve the greatest percentage for the lowest income families" (GWB, 1999).

This comment from candidate Bush was reiterated by Fleischer, insisting that people in the lowest tax bracket would "benefit the most" from the tax package, and was reinforced by the Republican National Committee Web site, controlled by the White House: "Who benefits under the President's plan?" asked the site the month that the 2003 package passed. "Everyone who pays taxes—especially middle-income Americans—as tax rate reductions passed by Congress are made effective immediately."

The President also kept heralding the statistic that the "average" family would get back $1,083 from his proposed 2003 cuts. This combination of populist rhetoric and actual data would be more appealing, however, if it were true. But based on data from the Tax Policy Center, 80 percent of Americans will get three-fourths *less* than W.'s claim of an "average" tax cut of $1,083. Filers in the middle quintile of the income spectrum—the "median" household—would receive only $227, and that before increased local and state taxes due to federal cutbacks are subtracted. And the 42 percent of taxpayers who are neither married nor have children would get a "little bitty" $50 on average, according to Citizens for Tax Justice. By including in his "average" the $20,762 each of the top 1 percent of all tax filers would receive and the $89,509 returned to those 0.2 percent earning a million or more annually, Bush's figure perfectly fit Mark Twain's definition of a "stretcher"—literally true but misleading. In a congressional hearing, OMB director Mitch Daniels himself admitted under questioning that "averages can be misleading," which did not stop his on-message boss from repeating and repeating the $,1083 figure.

Overall, 50 million households—36 percent of all households—get *no* benefit from this 2003 plan, either because they pay no federal taxes or they are among some 8 million low-income singles without children or income from dividends or capital gains. Ironically, this happens to be exactly the number of taxpayers that Bush, in their second debate, said *Gore's* plan would ignore: "He [Gore] says he's going to give you tax cuts; 50 million of you won't receive it. He wants to make sure the right people get tax relief. *That's not the role of a president to decide right and wrong*" (italics ours).

What kind of "fuzzy math" could defend the fact that more than a third of households would get zero benefit from a plan declared to help "all"? In an editorial that gave chutzpah a bad name, the *Wall Street Journal* congratulated these taxpayers for being "lucky duckies" because they paid no income taxes at all. This ideological arithmetic, however, conveniently neglected the reality that 90 percent of all workers with income under $100,000 pay more in Social Security payroll taxes than income taxes. So it's circular for Bush defenders to say that, since the president chose to reduce income taxes but not payroll taxes, those not enjoying that chosen benefit can't complain, notwithstanding the president's assertion that "all" would benefit.

Nor did all children enjoy the childcare tax credit increase to $1,000. After enactment, it was discovered that nearly 8 million children in poor families had been omitted entirely. House Republicans (again) argued that it was wrong to extend such credits to families that didn't pay federal income taxes; the White House blamed congressional Democrats for demanding a $350 billion ceiling over the decade for tax expenditures—even though helping these children had never been included in either the White House or House of Representatives versions and even though the $350 billion was a largely fictitious figure that will likely grow to $1 trillion, according to Speaker Dennis Hastert and Ways and Means chair Bill Thomas. A *Washington Post* editorial reflected the popular indignation: "If it makes sense to help families with children, why shouldn't the aid go to those who need it most? . . . if one goal of the tax bill is to pump money into the economy quickly, why not give it to those most apt to spend it?"

After a media firestorm hit, the White House said it "preferred" to include these children. But all President Bush and congressional Republicans had to do to fund this increased child-care credit for all children was reduce the tax rate on the top tier down to 35.3 percent instead of to 35 percent—the slight difference being enough to finance the credit for 8 million children. "Ain't gonna happen," said the ever-reliable majority leader Tom DeLay. Apparently, only a $20,762 average tax cut per top earner, not say a $20,000 one, would provide the desired incentive to invest and work.

Despite the political disclaimers, Bush's program grossly favored the already wealthiest Americans. While bigger earners obviously received bigger absolute cuts—42 percent of the benefits went to the top one percent—the Bush cuts were also larger in *percentage* terms for the highest-income brackets than middle and low-income quintiles: after the cuts, the richest 1 percent of Americans earning more than $337,000 annually will enjoy a 15 percent reduction in their taxes (2003–10) while the remaining 99 percent receive only a 7 percent reduction. And contrary to Bush's claim in the debate that the wealthiest Americans would end up paying a bigger slice of the tax pie, Citizens for Tax Justice found that the share paid by top earners fell.

To obscure those unequal effects, the Bush Treasury Department suddenly altered the standard table on a tax package to present data in a different way—cuts appeared as a percentage of federal *income* taxes rather than *all* taxes paid, as it had been in the past, in order to make the percentage reductions appear more even. The Democratic staff of the House Government Reform Committee published a chart demonstrating how leading government officials pushing this "growth" program saw their own respective portfolios grow: annual tax savings for Vice President Dick Cheney were $116,002; Defense Secretary Donald Rumsfeld up to $604,059, and Treasury Secretary John Snow up to $842,377. But the median household savings, again, were a measly $227.

Sleights of hand also attempted to hide savings to business beneficiaries. "We estimate that 23 million small business owners across America," went another favorite Bush claim, "will receive an average income tax cut of $2,042" from his tax proposal. But he got that factoid by including five hundred thousand well-off people who are "chapter S corporations" or have passive investments in partnerships in the same group as those who ran a corner deli. According to the Tax Policy Center, 80 percent would get less than $2,042 and half tax cuts of $500 or less.

It was left to Senator John McCain (R-AZ) to cut through the fog of false data and point out that the bulk of the tax cuts "goes to wealthier Americans. I would like to see some of that redistributed more heavily to middle-income and low-income Americans."

  ★ **Deficits either won't exist, will be small, will be manageable—or won't matter.** "We can proceed with tax relief without fear of budget deficits, even if our economy softens" (GWB, 2001). "Our budget will run a deficit that will be small and short-term" (GWB, 2002).

It's not surprising that a presidential candidate or newly minted president would have an easier time predicting good results than obtaining them. But for a projection to be off by $9 trillion in three years is unusual.

Of course, *temporary* deficits are fine, even desirable, so long as they spur growth during recessions or slowdowns, or take the form of investments for future growth (student loans, roads and bridges). While Bush frequently argued for his tax cuts as a stimulus, his proposed 2003 tax reductions were actually 5 percent short-term stimulus and 95 percent post-recession–end-of-decade cuts that baked structural deficits into the economic pie. The Council of Economic Advisors itself projected *permanent* annual deficits of several hundred billion dollars for decades to come, and those estimates did not even include the costs of the war and the ensuing reconstruction.

The first Bush budget of April 2001 predicted a surplus of $334 billion for 2003. Speaking about the administration's ten-year forecasts projecting huge surpluses, OMB director Mitch Daniels confidently promised Congress, "Well, we really can't miss." A year later, however, the OMB predicted a deficit of only $80 billion in 2003 and a balanced budget by 2004. By early 2003 it announced that there'd be a deficit of $300 billion in FY 2004, but only four months later reestimated that year's deficit to be $455 billion (again, not including the costs of Iraq)—a figure that was second only, in constant dollars, to that of Bush's hero, Ronald Reagan, in 1983. Although Bush pledged in 1999 that "tax cuts will be financed exclusively out of the non–Social Security surplus," his administration took $159 billion from Social Security, which meant that the real deficit was $614 billion. Even worse, the projected $5.6 trillion surplus (2002–11) had by now disappeared, to be replaced by a likely deficit of over $4 trillion instead.

From "can't miss" to record shortfalls, what went so wrong? "A recession we inherited and a war we did not choose have led to the return of deficits," explained the president in early 2003. But his statement is false in every respect. First, the initial projected deficits *preceded* the first estimate of a $75 billion cost for the war of April 2003. Second, whether a good or bad idea, Iraq was unquestionably an elective war—the first "preventive" war in our nation's history. And third, according to the National Bureau of Economic Research, the recognized arbiter of the start and end of recessions, the recession formally began in March 2001—a fact the president himself originally acknowledged in a radio address in November 2001. ("This week, the official announcement came that our economy has been in recession since March. And, unfortunately, to a lot of Americans, that news comes as no surprise."). Only nine months later he changed his version of events. ("I want you all to remember that when Dick Cheney and I got sworn in, the country was in a recession.")

Bush's no-fault defense struggled to avoid the elephant in the living room—his tax cuts. Director Daniels went to Capitol Hill in February 2003 and, in a pure display of denial, told a stunned Senate Budget Committee that it was "bunk" to attribute any significant part of the deficit to cuts. Meanwhile his own OMB was then estimating reduced revenues from tax cuts of $1.5 trillion over ten years. Of the more than $9 trillion plunge in federal accounts, the Congressional Budget Office estimates that more than a third is due to the tax cuts. Finally, in his July 2003 press conference, Bush himself admitted under questioning that they accounted for 25 percent of the deficit. Independent estimates, however, which properly assume the 2003 tax cuts are extended and other likely costs will occur, are much worse. The Concord Coalition, Goldman Sachs, and the Center on Budget and Policy Priorities estimate ten-year deficits of between $4 trillion and $5 trillion; even when growth recovers, the center concludes, annual deficits won't fall below $420 billion in any year.

After projecting a $455 billion deficit, Mitch Daniels's successor at OMB, Joshua Bolton, said it was "manageable" because it was less, as a percentage of gross domestic product, than Reagan's record. According to Treasury Secretary John Snow, "If you look at this budget as a percentage of GDP, they decline and they get down to well under one percent [by the end of the decade]. That's a modest deficit." But Snow didn't include either the costs of Iraq* and Afghanistan or the costs of extending current tax cuts or the several hundred billion filched from the Social Security Trust Fund. Nor did his total include the myopia factor—that is, the Bush administration's track record has been wrong close to 100 percent of the time on such predictions. Deficits are more critical now than they were in the 1990s. Back then it was plausible, if not necessarily wise, for an administration to try to "prime the pump" with tax cuts or spending with little ultimate consequence. Now governments are held to a more rigorous standard by hyperactive capital markets, which renders the administration's blithe assurances more spin than substance.

A number of significant problems likewise undermine the administration's Pollyannaish forecasts. First, a cresting "age wave" of tens of millions of baby boomers will begin retiring and receiving Social Security and Medicare in 2011—which makes Bush's deficits now far worse than Reagan's in 1981–83. By the 2020s these costs will likely reach 12 to 15 percent of the GDP, compared to 6.8 percent in 2004. Second, given the popularity of prescription drugs as a Medicare benefit, there will likely be a $400 billion to $800 billion added price tag this coming decade, not to mention additional rising health care costs. And third, because the Alternative Minimum Tax is scheduled to hit a politically untenable 40 million people by 2010, common sense dictates that Washington will buy some of it back, costing at least another $400 billion.

The response of mainstream economists has been harsh. Rudy Penner, former Republican head of the Congressional Budget Office, said "There are a lot of pretty radical ideas here. I would have preferred a few less bold initiatives to avoid the bold increases in the deficit." Nobel Economic Laureate Robert Solow was even harsher: "There has been a dissipation of the huge budget surplus, and all we have to show for that is the city of Baghdad."

Nonetheless, President George W. Bush pushed his 2003 tax package through the Republican Congress. Failing to argue persuasively that the deficits would be nonexistent, or modest, or temporary, or manageable, Bush and Company retreated to their final defense, which in effect was— *whatever.* Deficits didn't really matter, anyway. This about-face was not without some embarrassment.

In 1996 Representative Sue Myrick (R-NC) won the "deficit hawk" award of the Concord Coalition; Representative Tom DeLay (R-TX) said, "By the year 2002, we can have a federal government with a balanced budget or we can continue down the present path toward fiscal catastrophe"; Senator Orrin Hatch (R-UT) wrote that a balanced budget amend-

---

* As of this writing, the administration claims that, because it can't precisely estimate the cost of maintaining 140,000 troops in Iraq, it would for budget purposes assume they're zero.

ment was "our first priority [because] continued deficits would devastate future generations." Just five years ago Republicans wanted to add a constitutional amendment requiring a balanced budget, even as critics complained that it would sully the Constitution to enshrine one particular economic theory in its text. When the amendment came to a vote, while Clinton was still president, every Senate Republican and 223 out of 226 House Republicans voted for a balanced budget amendment. Fifty of 51 Senate Republicans and 218 of 229 House Republicans voted for the 2003 tax cuts, however, assuring instead an ocean of red ink.

Administration officials proved even more "flexible." Glenn Hubbard, chair of Bush's Council on Economic Advisors, disparaged the supposed link between deficits and interest rates as "Rubinomics," referring to the most successful Treasury secretary of the modern era, "and we think it is completely wrong." But that view is hard to reconcile with one expressed in Hubbard's own textbook—*Money, the Financial System and the Economy*—which had earlier concluded, "By the late 1990s, an emerging federal budget surplus put downward pressure on interest rates. . . . It's all right to run a deficit during a recession, as long as the deficit is clearly temporary. But both the numbers and the [Bush] administration's search for excuses tell us that there's nothing temporary about the red ink." N. Gregory Mankiw, replacing the fired Lawrence Lindsay as CEA head, had previously ridiculed the supply-side economics of President Reagan as "fad economics" conceived by "charlatans and cranks. It threatens the very foundation of our culture." National Economic Council director Stephen Friedman was once a member of the bipartisan Concord Coalition pleading for balanced budgets.

The relationship between deficits and interest rates is, in fact, a complicated one, and can be debated reasonably. Two points, however, are undeniable. First, all these people went from deficit hawks to borrow-and-spend Republicans without any serious explanation of their turnabout. Second, a consensus among economists agrees that there *is* a relationship: when the deficit rises, "it does affect long-term interest rates, it does have a negative impact on the economy," said Federal Reserve Board chairman Alan Greenspan in February 2003 testimony. If one believes in the "law" of supply and demand— and if the government soaks up a lot of available credit due to its large borrowing—the price (interest rate) of the dwindling credit remaining will predictably rise. A Goldman Sachs analysis concluded that interest rates would have been 2 percentage points higher in 1999 if the annual deficit hadn't been eliminated. Indeed, the deficit–interest rate relationship is built into the economic models used by the Federal Reserve, CBO, OMB, and both Democratic and Republican White Houses. Brookings economists William Gale and Peter Orszag found that nearly all "studies that (properly) incorporate deficit expectations in addition to current deficits . . . tend to find economically and statistically significant connections between anticipated deficits and current long-term interest rates."

★ **Spending must be constrained to reduce the deficit or the size of government, or both.** "Unrestrained government spending is a dangerous road to deficits" (GWB, 2001).

President Bush adopts the popular conservative parlance against federal spending, appropriate for an ex-governor of a state that was fiftieth in per capita spending on public services during his term. When it comes to Bush's domestic spending as president, *New York Times* columnist Thomas L. Friedman wisely suggests translating his words "tax cuts" to mean "service cuts" and offers up the slogan: "Read my lips—no new services."

The Bush administration has occasionally tried to get tough with spending, especially since several trillion dollars over a decade in "tax expenditures" (the accepted phrase for foregone revenue) doesn't leave a lot of room for it. While proposed and enacted budgets are constantly changing, the Bush White House in early 2003 insisted on at least a ten-billion-dollar reduction from spending levels approved *unanimously* only a half-year earlier by the Senate Appropriations Committee—in a year it was also seeking a fifty-nine-billion-dollar tax cut. The Center on Budget and Policy Priorities tracked significant proposed reductions in the Low Income Home Energy Assistance Program, unemployment training, maintenance and repairs to public housing, child care and education for disadvantaged children, veterans programs, school lunches, college loans, and Medicaid. Over the decade, the proposed cuts (most of which were abandoned due to political pressure) totaled $475 billion—or about the same as the tax reduction for all those earning over $337,000 annually.

Unlike Reagan, however, Bush doesn't dramatically attack the programs he seeks to shrink—indeed, quite the opposite.

★ In April 2002, the president went to Albuquerque to praise Lucy Salazar, a grandmother who tutors pre-K kids and collects books for a reading program called Project Even Start. But Bush's FY 2003 budget effectively cut Even Start funding by 20 percent, with New Mexico's share falling from $1.7 million to $1.4 million.

★ Bush visited a Boys and Girls Club in Wilmington, Delaware, in April 2001, calling it a "faith-based program . . . based on the universal concept of loving a neighbor just like you would like to be loved yourself." Six days later his FY 2002 budget called for cutting Boys and Girls Clubs funding by $60 million.

★ The prior month, Bush traveled to the Egleston Children's Hospital in Atlanta and praised it as "a place of love." The *Atlanta Journal and Constitution* described how Bush "got misty-eyed as [Vicki] Riedel, a forty-five-year-old mother from DeKalb County, recounted her daughter's battle with cancer," even though congressional Republicans wouldn't restore $35 million in the Bush budget to the Children's Hospital Graduate Medical Education program that trains pediatric physicians at such hospitals.

The Bush administration's anti-spending zeal could be seen most clearly in its effort to shrink "entitlement programs" by urging states to switch their Medicaid programs to a block grant: states switching would get increased funding, while those refusing would not receive any of a projected $13 billion boost. But no states have yet accepted such block grants because they quickly figured out that it really meant "block that grant!"—that is, the bait of increases would last only seven years, after which federal payments would fall significantly.

The credibility and consistency of Bush's anti-spending ethic was undermined when he pushed for and signed the $180 billion Farm Security and Rural Investment Act of 2002 to win political points in crucial farm states—even though, for example, it boosted agricultural subsidies 80 percent to twenty-five thousand cotton farmers with an average net worth of eight hundred thousand dollars. The president's tough talk on spending is belied by the fact that he hasn't vetoed one spending bill in three years. Also, Republican spending was apparently better than its Democratic cousin. An Associated Press report that same year described how Republican control of Congress led not so much to cuts but to shifts in spending from Democratic to Republican districts, "from poor rural and urban areas to more affluent suburbs and GOP-leaning farm country."

> For instance, spending on child-care food programs was slashed 80 percent; public and Indian housing grants were virtually eliminated; rental housing loans for rural areas and special benefits for disabled coal miners were cut by two-thirds; and the food stamp program was cut by a third.
>
> But Congress under GOP rule also directed more money to programs that disproportionately benefit GOP districts. Direct payments to farmers increased sevenfold during the six years of GOP rule; business and industrial loans quadrupled; home mortgage insurance went up 150 percent; and crop insurance assistance jumped by two-thirds.

W.'s spending program reflected his basic values to simultaneously send refunds to those who don't need them and cut programs for those who do. The administration's supporters have acknowledged the reality: tax cuts and spending cuts, wrote the patron saint of conservative economics in 2003, Milton Friedman, "will be an effective restraint on the spending propensities of the executive branch and the legislature." At a 2003 conference on the Bush presidency, economist Allen Schick concluded that one lesson of Bush's economic policies "is that it is better to have a smaller government with a bigger deficit than a bigger government with a smaller deficit." There is a certain perverse logic in building up huge deficits so future Congresses can say "stop me before I spend again," like a compulsive gambler putting everything down on a long shot to cure his habit.

Senator Daniel Patrick Moynihan (D-NY) first spotted this syndrome when he derided President Reagan's program of "strategic deficits" as an effort to starve and therefore shrink the public sector. Bush 43 is moving rapidly toward Reagan's goal. The Center on Budget and Policy Priorities reports that after enactment of the FY 2004 budget, federal revenues will fall to about 16.5 percent of the gross domestic product, "the lowest level, as a share of the economy, since 1959," which was before we assumed the huge costs of such programs as Medicare, Medicaid, and environmental protections.

"It's nuts, stone-cold nuts," said Senator Kent Conrad (D-SD). "And they're not nuts and they're not stupid. They're smart people and they know what we know, that the deficit will explode when federal expenditures peak. And that's when I had this revelation: the only rationale for what they're doing is that they plan to fundamentally gut Social Security and Medicare. To sustain benefits and keep the social contract as is would require an unprecedented tax increase to 30 percent of GDP [from 20 percent]. Or we'll have to eliminate the rest of government as we know it. This is radical, radical stuff."

So when George W. Bush is safely back at his Crawford, Texas, ranch clearing brush and writing his memoirs, here will be the options for a successor president confronting far higher costs and far lower revenues: "Balancing the budget by the end of the coming decade (i.e., in 2013)," concluded an unusual, joint report of the business-oriented Council for Economic Development, the liberal Center for Budget and Policy Priorities, and the Concord Coalition, "would entail such radical steps as: raising individual and corporate income taxes by 27 percent; or eliminating Medicare entirely; or cutting Social Security benefits by 60 percent; or shutting down three-fourths of the Defense Department; or cutting all expenditures other than Social Security, Medicare, defense, homeland security, and interest payments on the debt—including expenditures for education, transportation, housing, the environment, law enforcement, national parks, research on diseases, and the rest—by 40 percent."

Kent Conrad is an elected Democrat and, despite his reputation for sincerity and smarts, could be discounted as partisan. Not so the bipartisan Concord Coalition, which gave the Bush administration an F for a fiscal policy of "deficits, deception and denial." And not *Washington Post* columnist David Broder, the voice of the Washington political establishment. "I asked one of my favorite Republican economics guides what he thought of the new Bush tax plan," he wrote. "This man—a veteran of the Nixon and Ford administrations and a friend and advisor to many officials in the Reagan and two Bush administrations said, 'it may be the least defensible policy ever.'" Professor George Akerlof, the 2001 winner of the Nobel Prize for Economics, agreed. Complaining that the debate over Bush's economic policy "has so far been much too polite," Akerlof concluded that "the proper reference point is that the Bush fiscal policy is the worst in 200 years. . . . What we have here is a form of looting."

★ **Taxation of dividends is unfair and hurts seniors.** "Double taxation of dividends is bad for our economy. Double taxation is wrong." (GWB, 2003).

President Bush is technically correct when he says that taxing dividends is taxing money twice, since the corporation pays taxes on its gain and then the shareholder does. There's also some validity to the argument made by Stephen Friedman, director of the National Economic Council (NEC), that "double taxation of dividends creates a bias toward corporate borrowing because the interest on debt is tax deductible whereas dividends are at present neither deductible nor exempt from tax at the recipient level."

But why does the president worry only about double taxation of corporate profits? Workers pay income taxes *and,* on the same income, sales taxes, excise taxes, cigarette and alcohol taxes, state and local taxes, and taxes on interest earned on their bank certificates of deposit. Property taxes, too, are levied on already taxed income. And, of course, average workers pay the Social Security and Medicare payroll tax of 7.65 percent. Authors Donald Bartlett and James Steele describe a family with $60,000 in wage income: "Of that, $3,720 is deducted from its paychecks for Social Security taxes, and an additional $870 is taken out for the Medicare tax. That's $4,590 that the family never sees. Nevertheless, that money is taxed as personal income, as if the family received it. What it amounts to is a tax upon a tax."

By choosing to focus on the multiple taxation of corporate dividends rather than, say, on food and clothing, Bush seeks to help the nearly 8 million Americans with incomes over $100,000 and receiving dividends. The Urban-Brookings Tax Policy Center estimates that two-thirds of the $364 billion in dividend tax savings over a decade will go to the top 5 percent of taxpayers, precisely the people already benefiting from the other Bush tax cuts. These "lucky duckies" are not the blue-collar workers paying "double taxation" in payroll taxes. To camouflage this choice, President Bush plucks at our heartstrings by adding that "a lot of seniors count on dividend income in order to survive." In fact, they don't. Here Bush exploits the imagery of the word "seniors" as he earlier used the connotation of "average" to mislead listeners. For 40 percent of his dividends tax cut going to the elderly would accrue to only the 2.5 percent of the elderly earning over two hundred thousand dollars, while the two-thirds of all seniors earning under fifty thousand dollars receive only 11 percent—not to mention that many seniors already have their retirement money in tax-deferred 401(k) accounts.

Nor are corporate taxes so historically high that it's now urgent to reduce taxes on owners rather than labor. While corporations paid a third of all federal tax receipts in 1945 and 25 percent in the 1950s, this percentage fell to only 7 percent by 2001, putting the U.S. twenty-eighth out of twenty-nine OECD countries (Organization for Economic Cooperation and Development); only Iceland is lower. At the same time, the ability of corporations to threaten to flee to low-tax states or countries has significantly reduced their local tax bill. And according to IRS estimates, American companies and wealthy individuals dodge seventy-five billion dollars annually in owed taxes by establishing phony offices or mail drops in offshore tax havens. After Bush's dividend reductions, this is money not even taxed *once.* Yet in late 2003, the Republican House—notwithstanding the ballooning deficit and declining share of corporate taxes—was pushing hard for $142 billion more in reductions in, of course, corporate taxes.

* **The "death tax" should end.** "It's not fair to tax the same earnings twice—once when you earn them, and again when you die—so we must repeal the death tax" (GWB, 2002).

In the mid-1990s Speaker Newt Gingrich's office set up a fund that staff had to contribute to if any used the words "estate tax" rather than "death tax." This humorous tactic reflected the political reality that those who frame the canvas get to paint the picture. Slowly, steadily, successfully, President Bush and fellow Republicans rechristened a tax on estates *at* death as a tax *on* death, which nicely conflates and confuses Benjamin Franklin's famous aphorism that "nothing in this world is certain but death and taxes."

Because guns and uniforms in wars have to be paid for, the idea of an inheritance tax was initially considered by Congress during the War of 1812 and first enacted by the North during the Civil War. Rates were set at 1 to 6 percent, depending on the size of the property inherited and the relationship of the deceased to the beneficiary. When the war ended, so did the tax, only to be revived in the War Revenue Act of 1898 on estates over ten thousand dollars. Republican Teddy Roosevelt pushed to make permanent what he called "a progressive tax on all fortunes." At the time, twenty-seven states already had their own versions of an inheritance tax. The tax finally became permanent in 1916 on the eve of World War I, despite the opposition of business interests who denounced it as "plain outright robbery."

But if *someone* had to pay for desired public services, why not those who were both very wealthy and unable to take it with them? Especially after great fortunes arose during the Gilded Age, many Americans feared an aristocracy of wealth being locked in generation after generation if great inheritances could be passed on and grow decade after decade (due to the magic of compound interest). Moreover, an estate tax encourages the wealthy to put some of their assets into tax-exempt charitable enterprises—foundations, universities, hospitals, museums—so they can both memorialize themselves and advance the public good. Last, based on the conservative (later to be called supply-side) premise that low taxes encouraged wealth accumulation and the work ethic, taxing the estates of the deceased super-rich couldn't discourage them; at the same time, giving it all to those born to the right parents certainly didn't encourage the work ethic among heirs. Quite the opposite, hence the derisive terms "idle rich" and "heir-heads." As the great industrialist Andrew Carnegie once observed, "The parent who leaves his son [*sic*] enormous wealth generally deadens the talents and energies of the son, and leads him to a less useful and less worthy life."

Into this history stepped George W. Bush. He was determined to spare a very small number of very wealthy taxpayers from paying such taxes—in 1999, a mere 467 estates worth over $20 million each paid a quarter of all estate taxes—even though the federal government would lose $680 billion in revenue in the decade after elimination (2011–20).

The president offered two arguments in support of abolition. First, again, it's "double taxation." Second, in his own words, "Every family, every farmer and small-business person should be free to pass on their life's work to those they love, so we will abolish the death tax." He could have added "every grandmother, every paralyzed veteran, and every hungry child," and it would have been as effective, and inaccurate. For this tax was largely imposed on the one group he chose not to mention—the 1.4 percent of the wealthiest households inheriting taxable estates over one million dollars. Indeed, although Bush kept using the example of a family farm taxed into extinction with the frequency of Ronald Reagan's welfare queen, it, too, proved apocryphal. Even the pro-repeal American Farm Bureau couldn't find a single example of such a farm. When Democrats offered to raise the exemption from estate taxes to a very ample $3.5 million, the all-or-nothing-repeal lobby and Bush White House refused, understanding that they would forfeit their populist appeal if only six thousand estates of multimillionaires were annually left to be taxed.

Bush did get the estate tax reduced and then eliminated by 2010, but because of congressional maneuvering it is currently scheduled to be restored in 2011. An unusual lobby has come into existence to oppose its permanent repeal. Reflecting Andrew Carnegie's reasoning, United for a Fair Economy and Responsible Wealth is led by Bill Gates Sr. and includes his son, Bill Gates, the richest man in the world, and Warren Buffett, the runner-up.

Declaring the Class War

A president who believes in "preventive" military wars certainly understands the value of preventive rhetoric in political wars. At the start of the 2003 battle over his "jobs and growth plan," while talking to reporters at his Crawford, Texas, ranch on January 2, Bush said, "I understand the politics of economic stimulus—that some would like to turn this into class warfare. That's not how I think."

What should it be called, then, when a father and his son attacked rival Michael Dukakis for representing the "Harvard boutique"? Or when Bush 43 told AP reporter Scott Lindlaw—during a monthlong vacation at his ranch—"Most Americans don't sit in Martha's Vineyard swilling white wine." Or when W., telling how a teacher and a fireman had difficulty finding a doctor during a pregnancy, blasted high medical malpractice rates, concluding with "What we want is quality healthcare, not rich trial lawyers"? Writing in the *Washington Post,* E. J. Dionne observed that "if setting up a teacher and a firefighter against 'rich trial lawyers' is not class warfare, then Karl Marx is the current editor of the *Wall Street Journal*'s editorial page."

In George W. Bush we have a president who's a fourth-generation business heir, a man who never really pounded the pavement but accumulated his wealth through family contacts and favors. As president, he moves aggressively and successfully to enact a fiscal program that (a) reduces taxes on the "investor class" more in percentage terms than on the middle class, (b) abolishes the "dead billionaires' tax" (estate tax), (c) shifts the burden of taxes to "earned" income and away from "unearned income" (dividends and capital gains), and, for good measure, (d) changes IRS practice so fewer multimillionaires are audited and more poor people are. (The number of civil fraud penalties against corporations plunged two-thirds, from 555 in 1993 to 159 in 2002.) Given that tax cuts for the top 1 percent equal all the cuts to the bottom 90 percent—and given the trillions of dollars quietly shifting from the accounts of labor and future generations to today's investor class—George W. Bush is redistributing wealth far more than George McGovern or Huey Long ever dreamed possible. These large movements of money reflect the law of intended consequences and are neither incidental nor accidental. For Bush to attack others for engaging in class warfare is the speeder blaming the radar gun.

In an op-ed entitled "Billionaires Don't Need Another Tax Break," Warren Buffett analyzed the effect of the proposed tax break on dividends:

> The taxes I pay to the federal government are roughly the same proportion of my income—about 30 percent—as that paid by the receptionist in our office. My case is not atypical—my capital gains and ordinary income—nor is it affected by tax shelters (I've never used any). As it works out, I pay a somewhat higher rate for my combination of salary, investment and capital gain income than our receptionist does. But she pays a far higher portion of her income in payroll taxes than I do.
>
> Now the Senate says that dividends should be tax-free to recipients. Supposed this measure goes through and the directors of Berkshire Hathaway (which does not now pay a dividend) therefore

decide to pay $1 billion in dividends next year. Owning 31 percent of Berkshire, I would receive $310 million in additional income, owe not another dime in federal tax and see my tax rate plunge to 3 percent.

And our receptionist? She'd still be paying about 30 percent, which means she would be contributing about ten times the proportion of her income that I would to such government pursuits as fighting terrorism, waging wars and supporting the elderly. Let me repeat the point: Her overall federal tax rate would be ten times what my rate would be.

Yet Karl Rove insists that when President Bush has "a choice between Wall Street and Main Street," he comes on down on the side of "the little guy." This is elitism masquerading as populism, as even conservative economists and commentators acknowledge. Economist Kevin Hassett of the American Enterprise Institute agrees that it "makes perfect sense" that Bush's tax plans had a pro-rich, anti-middle-class redistributional impact. "The middle class is predominately labor income," and Bush's cuts help those enjoying "unearned income" like capital gains. Christopher Caldwell, senior editor at the conservative *Weekly Standard,* argues that

> The middle class benefits in this plan are wholly illusory. . . . In a modern economy, relative wealth matters. The middle class, in certain circumstances, must compete against the rich as if in a luxury market—not just for luxury goods but for the staples of life. What do middle-class parents want for their children? A house in a neighborhood with a good public school system, orthodontia, a college education, maybe even (heaven forbid) a kidney transplant. The prices for all these commodities will be bid up when top earners start getting their annual five-figure windfalls.

Putting numbers to these conclusions was the Citizens for Tax Justice. Interest owed on the debt for the typical middle class family will be $1,200 annually, or more than double their average $578 tax savings, by 2006; yet the top 1 percent's tax savings would significantly exceed any interest paid on their debt. Ultimately, rhetoric about a "jobs and growth" program for the middle class is, to borrow David Stockman's famous phrase to describe Reaganomics, a "trojan horse" to hide a policy that's more about transferring wealth than creating it.

Seeking and accumulating wealth is a good thing, and there will always be class distinctions in America. But do we really want our president to widen them on purpose? Speaking on ABC, George Will remarked that attacks on Bush's fiscal plan were due to pure "envy, which was not a sin most

Americans felt." Actually, the sentiment involved is not envy, but fairness, which requires no apologies.

"Dispassionate Honesty"?

Unlike such subjective exercises as movie reviews or beauty contests, the economy is more like bowling—you can keep score. How have the Bush economy and economic plan actually performed three years after their inception? How did he play the economic cards he was dealt? "The Bush family," wrote *Los Angeles Times* reporter Ron Brownstein of the eerily similar economic performances of Bush 41 and Bush 43, "is on an intergenerational losing streak."

All of Bush 43's economic predictions and promises quoted previously in this chapter were either false when he said them or later became untrue. *All.* Here's a quick review: the recession did not start under Clinton; the debt was not paid down; deficits appeared pre-Iraqi war and weren't small or short-term; Bush did siphon off much of the Social Security surplus; he did not cut tax rates more for lower-paid workers—exactly the opposite; and "everybody" who pays taxes did not get a tax cut. Bush was, however, prescient in the first Bush-Gore debate when early on he predicted that "you're going to be hearing a lot of phony numbers about what I think." What he didn't say was that he would be their source.

There should be no surprise that phony numbers reflect failed policies. "Facts are stubborn things," President Reagan once said, and here are the facts. First, middle-class working families have been under sustained assault for three years. Not since Herbert Hoover has a president presided over such a steep net job loss. Over Clinton's eight years, the American economy *grew* by an average of 239,000 jobs per month; in Bush's first thirty months, the number of jobs per month *declined* by an average of 69,000. Eighteen percent of all American workers reported being laid off between mid-2000 and mid-2003. "In short," wrote Jon E. Hilsenrath on page one of the *Wall Street Journal* in May 2003, "the U.S. is experiencing the most protracted job market downturn since the Great Depression."

Two-thirds of workers who were laid off received less than two weeks' notice, no severance, and no health benefits. "A lot of people say there's a safety net," explained Carol E. Van Horn of Rutgers University's Center for Workforce Development. "It's more like getting shoved off a cliff without a net." In the "temping" of America, many new jobs are temporary slots without benefits or prospects. Thirty million Americans—or one in four—earn no more than $18,100 a year, the current poverty benchmark for a family of four. Median pay, the best barometer of a family's economic health, rose 14.5 percent under Clinton, to a high of $43,848 in 2000, then fell 3 percent, to $42,409, over Bush's first two years. In response to the economic crisis of no or low-pay work, the Bush administration seeks to reduce overtime pay to millions of households (see "Labor Pains" in chapter 8), cut by half proposed increases to federal workers, refuse to allow the unionization of Homeland Security Agency workers—and reduce tax rates far more for high-income owners than low-paid workers.

Second, deficits are on a record pace and at double the percentage that would warrant censure if engaged in by a member of the European Union. Third, not only are states, as mentioned, suffering their worst shortfalls in a half century, but they are the last ones out from what is a fiscal shell game at best, a federal Ponzi scheme at worst. The president sends out scores of billions in tax-rebate checks to popular applause while governors and mayors—who by law have to balance their budgets annually—are left to pay for Bush's purchased popularity.

An early sign of this federal-state tension—and of future conflicts in post-Bush Washington—were the spectacles in Alabama and Arkansas. Alabama Republican governor Bob Riley—who in six years in Congress bragged that he never voted for a tax increase—felt compelled in 2003 to seek a state tax hike of $1.2 billion, or eight times the largest previous increase, to close a $675 million deficit and improve failing schools. The born-again Baptist governor explained that he had no choice if his state was to be fiscally responsible. His referendum—opposed by the Alabama Republican Party but supported by the Alabama Democratic Party—ultimately failed in a two-to-one vote. Similarly in Arkansas, Republican governor Mike Huckabee said that his and other states faced a "galloping" crisis that was sabotaging their ability to fund essential services like hospitals and schools. "It comes down to deciding how many inmates you will release from prison," he said, and "which colleges and nursing homes you will close."

True, in the short term, President Bush's stimulative policies—massive increases in military spending, $400 child-care tax credit checks—should produce the illusion of adequate growth for his 2004 election. Indeed, when the child-care credit checks hit in July and August 2003, consumer spending on durable goods spurted—and so did third-quarter growth—only to subside when consumer spending fell in September. For in the long term Bush planted several economic time bombs for his successor to defuse. Budget deficits and trade deficits will be exploding at the very time that (a) monetary policy may be unavailable after the Federal Reserve has already cut interest rates thirteen times in 2002–03, (b) fiscal policy can hardly tolerate more red ink, and (c) foreign investors won't forever pay for our excess consumption.

Economist Paul Krugman, writing in *The Great Unraveling*, was not sanguine:

> One of these years, and probably sooner than you think, the financial markets will look at the situation, and realize that the U.S. gov-

ernment has made inconsistent promises—promises of benefits to future retirees, repayment to those who buy its debt, and tax rates far below what is necessary to pay for all of it. Something will have to give, and it won't be pretty. In fact, I think the United States is setting itself up for a Latin American–style financial crisis, in which fears that the government will try to resolve its dilemma by inflating away its debt causing interest rates to soar.

The combination of these dismal numbers and political exigencies presumes that if your head's in the oven but your feet are in the freezer, then "on average" you're a fine 98.6 degrees. When Bill Gates walks into a restaurant, everyone's "average" tax cut there skyrockets but the guys washing the dishes in the back are not leaving in Porsches.

But no amount of data manipulation can answer the big question—how could President Bush have missed by so much? Again, he doesn't analyze facts to arrive at conclusions. Instead, he arrives at conclusions—a misnomer surely in this context—and then works backward to find supportive "facts." So when the truth proves embarrassing, the dissembling begins. Should we freeze the generous tax cuts to the top 1 percent to pay for Iraqi reconstruction, Vice President Cheney was asked on *Meet the Press.* Oh, no. "An awful lot of the returns in that top bracket are small businesses, and they provide an awful lot of job growth in this economy." Actually, of course, an awful lot of data show that the top bracket is populated with the richest Americans.

How do policies so antithetical to the majority of workers get proposed and enacted? When first revealed, Bush's fiscal plans received the Bronx cheer. A *Washington Post*–ABC News poll found the public favored spending on social priorities over tax cuts by 67 percent to 29 percent; by 53 percent to 41 percent, Americans preferred to reduce the federal deficit than their taxes. The way Republican members could ignore the sentiments of their constituencies required "partyology," a neologism of ex-representative Tim Penny (D-MN). Even though it must not be fun for the GOP to have to explain to working families why they pay a higher tax rate on their bank interest than their wealthy neighbors do on their dividend income, elected Republicans robotically do it to advance a party structure that perpetuates their money, incumbency, and majority. "They've got a president who has a dumb idea," says Penny, "and because he's their president, they're going through mental gymnastics to explain why they're getting rid of a history of fiscal responsibility."

Ultimately, Bushomics—like President Reagan's "voodoo economics," so named by Bush's own father—is part payoff and part politics. It rewards donors and incumbents in an elaborate back-scratch. Because money shouts in American politics, the top 1 percent who pocket the bulk of tax cuts also coincidentally give more in contributions than the bottom 99 percent combined. According to Democratic pollster Stan Greenberg, regressive taxation "is all about deepening support with your loyalists and taking a very enthusiastic loyalist base into the [2004] election." That seems politically plausible: of some 40 million Americans making under thirty-five thousand dollars, about a third voted; of 33.4 million making over seventy-five thousand dollars, three-fourths voted. But this is a very expensive strategy for the rest of America.

"The question is," asked then OMB director Mitch Daniels in 2002, "what would you not do? Would you not try to spur economic growth? Would you not continue the strengthening of our defenses and the prosecution of the war on terror?" But Daniels knew that President Bush didn't want to debate options but was on a mission to put supply-side economics into practice. When the White House did organize forums of economists on January 21 and April 2, 2002, "they only called people who agreed with them," said Stephen S. Roach, the chief economist of Morgan Stanley. "These meetings are not forums for debate," Ethan S. Harris, chief economist of Lehman Brothers, concurred. "Basically 90 percent of the people are kind of preaching to the choir, and maybe they have one or two middle-of-the-road people. They really don't seem to want to hear opposing views."*

George W. Bush wouldn't—indeed probably couldn't—think outside the skybox. And just when America needed, in the phrase of the *Financial Times,* "dispassionate honesty" to steer through our economic straits, we are having to endure the exact opposite—a passionate dishonesty using myths, misstatements, half-truths, statistical tricks, and rhetorical rouge to cover up a failed economic policy.

---

*Contrast this scenario with the one in September 1974, when President Gerald R. Ford asked twenty-eight economists, including some prominent liberals, to share their economic proposals at a White House conference on economics.

4. When Laissez Isn't Fair

How a Business President
Handles Business Fraud

⋆

"I got to know Ken Lay when he was the head of the—what they call the Governor's Business Council in Texas. He was a supporter of Ann Richards in my run in 1994. And she had named him the head of the Governor's Business Council. And I decided to leave him in place, just for the sake of continuity. And that's when I first got to know Ken and worked with Ken."
—President George W. Bush, January 10, 2002

Business fraud is as old as business itself. Merchants in 600 BC tried to corner the Grecian olive market. The Bible mentions sellers who short-weighted their customers. In the seventeenth century the rise of the first modern corporation—the British East India Company—was helped along when it obtained duty-free treatment for its exports by thoughtfully providing Far Eastern Mogai rulers with paintings and carvings. Jonathan Swift saw the problem clearly when he wrote, "The Lilliputians look upon fraud as a greater crime than theft . . . for they allege that care and vigilance may preserve a man's goods from theft, but honesty has no defense against superior cunning."

Jonathan Swift, meet Enron. Even before that spectacular rise and collapse, the irony of the most successful corporate citizens occasionally being the most corrupt was not lost on politicians as astute as George W. Bush and Karl Rove. Early on they knew to be careful about looking like, in the self-mocking phrase of *Forbes,* a "capitalist tool."

George W. Bush has gone to great lengths to promote an aw-shucks image as a self-made entrepreneur from Midland, Texas. While it's true he grew up in Texas (though he was largely schooled in the East), that element of geography has little to do with the privileged petri dish from which he comes. His father was not only the forty-first president of the United States but also the scion of senators, Wall Street bankers, captains of industry, and wealthy New Englanders descended from seventeenth-century settlers and fourteenth cousins to Queen Elizabeth. Barbara Bush, born Barbara Pierce, also comes from a wealthy, politically connected family, one that is related to the fourteenth president of the United States, Franklin Pierce. High family status is surely no disqualification for success in high office, as FDR showed. But television images of a brush-clearing ranch hand notwithstanding, the forty-third president is the beneficiary of a business elite whose implement of choice was not a plow but a Rolodex.

After a lackluster career at Andover and Yale, where he was remembered more for bonhomie than books, and after an MBA from Harvard Business School, George W. made his way back to Texas to follow in his father's footsteps: spinning family loans and contacts into black gold by digging for oil. (For the best detailed summary of his personal history, see Bill Minutaglio's *First Son: George W. Bush and the Bush Family Dynasty* [1999].) Unfortunately, the golden age of oil drilling in Texas had ended, and Bush's business collapsed. But because he could always fall back on the family name, his failed Arbusto Energy was bought by Spectrum 7, which also failed, only to be bought by Harken Energy in a deal that brought Bush onto Harken's board of directors, paid him a nice annual consulting fee, spotted him a bunch of free stock, and gave him low-interest loans to buy more. Not bad for a business leader who by the age of forty had only steep losses to show for his efforts.

In 1991 he managed to sell his 212,000 shares of Harken stock for $850,000 to a private buyer, which kept Harken afloat and propped up its stock price with a $30 million investment in an off-the-books partnership formed in 1990. These maneuvers occurred weeks before the stock tumbled on word of both the company's bad financial news and impending war in the Middle East. But Bush then rolled his new wealth into a stake in the Texas Rangers baseball team. That venture was a big deal for Bush, for though he freely admits to being essentially a glad-handing front man with a golden name, his success with the Rangers enabled him to claim a business prowess that had previously escaped him. "It solved my biggest political problem in Texas," he has said. "There's no question about it and I knew it all along. My problem was 'What's the boy ever done?'" When the team was later sold, his coinvestors rewarded him with a $15 million profit in gratitude for his famous name and investment of $600,000. And suddenly, Bush was a wealthy man, perhaps not by Texas standards but by all others.

This personal biography obviously both appeals to the corporate community and affects Bush's own view of the world: Our first oil company/MBA president naturally views the world through the eyes of a CEO. The result is a record that both his admirers and detractors regard as probusiness and anticonsumer, and other chapters discuss his well-known enthusiasm for corporate tax cuts, business subsidies, and "tort reform." Indeed, if George W. Bush has ever taken an initial position contrary to the interests of the business community, it does not come readily to mind. Here are several representative examples, small and large, of how corporate interests invariably trump consumer and environmental interests in Bush's Washington:

* **The California Energy Crisis.** In the spring and summer of 2001 California suffered from a shortage of electricity, soaring energy costs, and rolling blackouts affecting millions of people. Governor Gray Davis pleaded with the Federal Energy Regulatory Commission (FERC) to step in and set price caps to ease the crisis. On April 17, 2001, during the height of the controversy, Vice President Cheney met with Enron CEO Ken Lay, the largest beneficiary and cause of the crisis according to later investigative reports. The very next day, in a rare interview with the *Los Angeles Times,* Cheney dismissed price caps as "short-term political relief for the politicians," bluntly declaring, "I don't see [price caps] as a possibility." Enron's Ken Lay has been the largest individual donor to Bush's political career, contributing to his two gubernatorial campaigns and the 2000 presidential election. (For more on this episode, see chapter 2, "Drill and Cough.")

* **Bankruptcy Laws.** President Bush has strongly supported a federal bankruptcy bill that protects credit card companies from individuals declaring bankruptcy, despite a stagnant economy with growing unemployment and growing bankruptcies. The bill also exempts the multi-million-dollar homes of those corporate executives who have watched their businesses crumble amidst scandal. MBNA America, the largest credit card company in the United States, was Bush's largest corporate donor during the 2000 election cycle.

* **Homeland Security.** The last place one would suspect a corporate giveaway would be in the Homeland Security bill, but that's exactly where you'd find an unrelated provision to shield drug manufacturer Eli Lilly from litigation related to thimerosol, an additive in a variety of children's vaccines that contains mercury and may cause autism. Bush's first budget director, Mitch Daniels, is a former Eli Lilly executive. Bush appointed the company's president, CEO, and chairman, Sidney Taurel, to the Homeland Security Advisory Council.

* **Manure Runoff.** Factory farms regularly spread onto nearby land liquid animal waste that flows into waterways, killing fish and polluting drinking water. Throwing out the recommendations of the Clinton administration, the Bush EPA decided to allow factory farms to write their own permit conditions and to shield them from liability for the environmental damage they cause. The Bush-Cheney campaign received $2,636,625 from agribusiness interests, including more money from the livestock industry than any federal candidate in a decade.

* **The FCC.** On June 2, 2003, the Republican-majority Federal Communications Commission—run by President Bush's choice for chairman, Michael K. Powell—approved sweeping changes to media ownership rules that would allow for greater consolidation of mass media across the nation. Among six major changes, the FCC made it easier for national networks to buy local affiliates and threw out the ban that prevented a company from owning a newspaper and a television or radio station in the same media market.

  New York Times columnist William Safire declared that "no other decision made in Washington will more directly affect how you will be informed, persuaded and entertained." One of the two dissenting votes on the panel, Michael J. Copps, complained that the decision "empowers America's new media elite with unacceptable levels of influence over the ideas and information upon which our society and our democracy so heavily depend." But how did such a tidal wave of changes occur when critics from across the spectrum—from Bernie Sanders (I-VT) to Trent Lott (R-MS)—were vocal opponents of media consolidation? And when more than 750,000 citizens contacted the FCC to complain about further media consolidation and urge the commissioners to vote against the changes?

  It certainly didn't hurt that lobbying the commission were nearly all big media companies, including Clear Channel, now the dominant owner of radio stations in America with 1,225, about 970 more than its nearest competitor; its vice chairman is the individual who in 1998 purchased the Texas Rangers and made the soon-to-be president a multimillionaire. (The company also no doubt pleased President Bush when it organized several prowar demonstrations during the buildup to the Iraq conflict, under the banner of "Rally for America.")

  But then, in a surprising development, a normally disciplined Republican Congress balked. The House voted 400 to 21 to block the rules, and the Senate 55 to 40 to pass a "resolution of disapproval." In response the Office of Management and Budget released a statement concluding that "the Administration believes that the new

FCC media ownership rules more accurately reflect the changing media landscape." And President Bush himself told Fox News: "I support what Michael Powell did. He took a long, deliberative process."

But before the Congress could formally vote down these pro-oligopoly rules and before Bush could veto, on September 3, 2003—one day before the rules were scheduled to take effect—the Third Circuit Court of Appeals blocked, at least temporarily, implementation of the changes. The court argued that "given the magnitude of this matter and the public's interest in reaching the proper resolution, a stay is warranted pending thorough and efficient judicial review."

* **Postwar Contracts.** Although there are hundreds of companies, both U.S. based and otherwise, that will be involved in the $100-billion-plus reconstruction of Iraq, three in particular—Halliburton, Bechtel, and MCI/WorldCom—have emerged as the leading examples of the quid-pro-quo relationship between donors, friends, and officials of the Bush White House, or what has been derided as "crony capitalism."

   Six companies were secretly invited by the Pentagon to bid for up to $900 million in initial postwar contracts. These six—Bechtel, Halliburton (via its subsidiary, Kellogg, Brown & Root [KBR]), Fluor Corp., Louis Berger Group, Parsons Corp., and Washington Group International—contributed a total of more than $3.5 million to candidates over the past two election cycles, with two-thirds going to Republicans.

   The Dallas-based Halliburton had previously been run by Dick Cheney as CEO. When Cheney left in 2000 to join the Bush ticket, he was given a retirement package of company stock worth more than $33 million. To this day Cheney still receives more than $160,000 a year from Halliburton as part of a deferred compensation package, even though he said in September 2003 that he has "no financial interest in Halliburton of any kind and haven't had now for over three years." The *New York Times* said the statement "is true only if you don't count the stock options Mr. Cheney continues to hold and $367,690 in deferred compensation he has reported receiving so far while vice president—on top of the $20 million severance package awarded in 2000."

   While the parent company has engaged in problematic accounting procedures and offering $2.4 million in bribes to a Nigerian official, its KBR subsidiary is raising other red flags, for example, by overcharging taxpayers in similar situations (i.e., the Balkans in the late 1990s). Despite its history of problems, in March 2003 KBR won a closed process (without a single competing bid) for an Iraq-related contract which, depending on the complexity and breadth of the project, could be worth up to $7 billion over the following two years.

Bechtel has been similarly favored. It's as politically connected as Halliburton, with current board members that include former secretary of state George Shultz. Bechtel, which gave $1.3 million to campaigns between 1999 and 2002, 59 percent of which went to Republicans, was awarded an initial contract of $34.6 million, with possible funding of up to $680 million over the following eighteen months.

MCI/WorldCom presents an especially striking example of blind government patronage. After pulling off the single largest corporate securities fraud in U.S. history (involving up to $9 billion in overstated profits, leading to $175 billion in lost shareholder value), it was awarded by the Bush administration a no-bid $30 million contract to build a wireless network in Iraq. The administration bestowed this contract despite the company's recent history and the fact that it is not a wireless carrier, nor does it have any experience in building such a network. While the country remains desperate for phone service of any sort, only the inexperienced MCI is allowed to provide it. MCI/WorldCom donated more than $2.6 million to federal campaigns in the past two election cycles, with 60 percent going to Republicans.

But there was one example when the Bush administration, devoted as it was to the theory of laissez-faire (literally "leave alone"), had to abandon ship. When Admiral John Poindexter's office at the Pentagon came up with the idea of an online futures trading market where speculators could in effect invest on the probabilities of a particular terrorist attack, as a way to stay ahead of such eventualities, the public outcry led Defense Secretary Rumsfeld to drop the idea, and Poindexter, too.

The Genius of Capitalism

It's more than a little ironic that the first two years of the Bush administration coincided with the biggest corporate scandals and bankruptcies since Teapot Dome in the 1920s. The man that Big Business put in the White House through record campaign contributions and counted on to deliver a friendlier regulatory environment was faced with managing a falling economy riddled with corporate malfeasance. And the first company on the corporate rap sheet happened to be the largest contributor to Bush's political career.

Enron was not merely the first but also about the biggest domino in a sequence of fallen companies, in part because of the intimate relationship between Enron and the White House. Author Kevin Phillips describes the link: "[N]ot in memory has a single major company grown so big in tandem with a presidential dynasty and a corrupted political system. Indeed, the Bush family has been a prominent and well-rewarded rung in Enron's climb to national political influence. In retrospect, it's unclear whether the Bush dynasty built Enron or vice-versa. . . . The question now is whether what went up together will come down together."

The administration is staffed by numerous former employees and consultants to the energy-industry player. Former economic advisor Lawrence Lindsay, for one example, simultaneously worked for the Bush campaign and was paid $50,000 per year as a consultant to Enron. The *Washington Post* wrote that "[d]uring the campaign, Lindsay described Lay's contribution as key. The cozy relationship—in which Bush campaign advisor, being paid by Enron, placed an Enron idea on the candidate's agenda—served as one more reminder of the political influence and reach of the once-giant energy company. Its ties extend deep into President Bush's staff, appointments, cabinet members, friends, family—and his own past." In fact, the Bush-Cheney Recount Fund paid Enron more than $13,000 for the use of its corporate jets during the Florida recount. (Cheney's former company Halliburton received $2,400 for the same purpose.) But beyond such circumstantial ties are the ways in which those connections colored the White House response to the Enron scandal, and how Enron's troubles mirror the indiscretions that Bush and Cheney have been accused of in their own days at Harken and Halliburton, respectively.

Enron's sins are numerous and complex. Some of its behavior was patently illegal, like the manipulation of California's energy markets. Some of it was very smart business for Enron and very bad politics for the Bush administration. Enron, for example, successfully pushed its agenda to Cheney's Energy Task Force, meeting with the group on six occasions, with Lay meeting three times individually with Cheney. Indeed, the Bush-Cheney energy bill that came out of these private meetings contained seventeen different policy initiatives that directly benefited Enron.

Ken Lay likewise pushed for more friendly faces on the Federal Energy Regulatory Commission (FERC). According to Curtis Hebert Jr., then the chairman of the FERC, Lay offered him Enron's continued support if "[Hebert] changed his views on electricity deregulation." Hebert refused the offer, told the press of the incident, then resigned his post by the end of the summer. Lay also gave face-to-face and written input to White House personnel officer Clay Johnson on two other nominees to the commission, the only business executive to do so. Hebert was replaced by Pat Wood, one of the candidates that Lay recommended, and former head of the Texas Public Utility Commission, to which he had been appointed by then governor Bush—also on a recommendation by Lay.

While some of Enron's activities may even have been legal within the broadest interpretations of the tax code—which their lawyers and their accountants at Arthur Andersen were only too happy to argue—they were all symptoms of the same illness, a companywide obsession with cutting corners on the journey to profits. The Enron business plan involved eliminating government rules wherever their political muscle allowed, and failing that, bending or breaking them when necessary.

Enron's worst problems stemmed from shady accounting that spun gossamer profits. The indiscretions of former army secretary Thomas White (2001–03), the vice president of Enron Energy Services before his appointment by President Bush, include actions he took after joining the administration—such as conducting eighty-four meetings and phone calls with Enron *while* in office, many taking place before he divested himself of Enron stock and in the weeks after September 11, when one would have thought him busy with other matters. His unit at Enron, which specialized in privatizing energy utilities, is at the center of the California price-fixing scandal. According to the *Washington Monthly,* Enron booked profits upfront from multiyear deals made during White's tenure as vice president over Enron's Energy Services, which allowed executives like White, "whose bonuses were tied to performance, to collect millions of dollars before the company had realized any profit."

Jeff Skilling, succeeding to the CEO position after Ken Lay, was most proud of convincing the SEC to allow Enron to count projected earnings from long-term energy contracts as current earnings, despite the possibility that the money wouldn't be collected for as long as twenty years, if ever. This enabled Enron to meet analysts' estimates at will by claiming future revenue as current revenue whenever the company needed it. While technically legal, these methods are obviously misleading. Illegal, however, was Enron's habit of shifting both real profits like the $1.5 billion in trading profit reaped during the California energy crisis, and paper profits, like those from the recognition of long-term contracts, into reserve accounts, the purposes of which were to manage earnings growth. The profits in reserve were released during periods when real earnings would slow or fall to make it appear that earnings were continuing to grow.

Another dubious accounting device was the use of subsidiaries called "special-purpose entities" that were owned by Enron through shell corporations. These entities effectively hid risky ventures so that losses and debt were kept off Enron's book, even though the risks were in reality still carried by Enron, and when those risks didn't pan out, the company still had to pay. Enron's CEO, auditors, board of directors, and lawyers all failed in their oversight duties by authorizing or ignoring these transactions.

As it neared collapse Enron worked hard to bulk up its cash flow, and it leaned heavily on its many contacts in the Bush administration for help right up until the scandal leaped to the front pages. Pressures on the White

House and the FERC to avoid imposing price controls in California's energy market during the rolling blackouts of spring 2001 successfully allowed Enron to pull in billions more in revenue than it did the previous spring. Vice President Cheney personally pressed the Indian government to pay Enron $64 million for power generated from an Enron power plant south of Bombay. The president was also prepared to raise the subject with the Indian prime minister, but, according to documents obtained by the (New York) *Daily News,* "a November 8 E-mail, whose sender and recipient are blacked out, warned, 'President Bush cannot talk about Dabhol.'" It is a safe assumption that this change of plans occurred after someone realized that having the president intercede for his biggest campaign contributor on behalf of a bill from a foreign government might not look kosher on the nation's front pages.

In February 2001 one of the first acts of the new administration was to withdraw support for an effort by the international Organization for Economic Cooperation and Development (OECD) to crack down on the type of offshore tax havens that Enron used with great success to avoid taxes— as, too, did Bush's Harken and, especially, Cheney's Halliburton, which on Cheney's watch increased its number of offshore subsidiaries in tax-friendly countries from nine to forty-four, improving Halliburton's tax position from a $302 million payment in 1998 to a rebate of $85 million in 1999. The following summer, however, Bush condemned such tax havens, saying, "I think we ought to look at people who are trying to avoid U.S. taxes as a problem. I think American companies ought to pay taxes here."

Administration officials had done nearly all they could to help Enron, but when in late October 2001—after the public disclosure of Enron's severe financial problems—Lay made phone calls to Secretary of Commerce Don Evans and Secretary of the Treasury Paul O'Neill, they drew the line. In defending his late inaction as Enron faltered and fell, O'Neill fliply commented, "Companies come and go. . . . It's part of the genius of capitalism." President Bush claimed that none of his close advisors warned him of the impending disaster.

But then, Bush claims a lot of things about his relationship with Enron that are very hard to believe. He denies that Enron or Ken Lay had undue influence over the creation of White House energy policy, even though Cheney has resisted releasing information on the formulation of that policy.

Bush also denies that he and Ken Lay are close friends, despite a history of connections between the two that date back to business deals in 1986 between Bush-led Spectrum 7 and Lay-led Enron, Lay's prominent support of Bush's father in the 1988 presidential election, and W.'s 1988 contact with the Argentine government lobbying on behalf of Enron's interest in a pipeline proposal. He even went so far as to say that Ken Lay "was a supporter of Ann Richards in my run in 1994." Ken Lay remembers the situation quite differently. In an interview with PBS's *Frontline* on March 27,

2001, he admitted, "I'd worked very closely with Ann Richards also, the four years she was governor. But I was very close to George W. and had a lot of respect for him, had watched him over the years, particularly with reference to dealing with his father when his father was in the White House and some of the things he did to work for his father, and so did support him." In that 1994 campaign, Lay contributed $37,500 to the Bush campaign, three times what he gave to Ann Richards. And Enron as a whole— including Enron's PAC and other corporate executives—contributed almost eight times more to Bush than to Richards.

Harken Energy

Bush has been dodging this heat-seeking missile since he first ran for governor of Texas in 1994 and again during the 2000 campaign for president. The issue was resurrected in 2001, due to the similarities between the behavior of the companies caught in the corporate scandals and his own behavior on Harken's board of directors.

Is it fair to go back into Bush's and Cheney's history to examine their business dealings? If Republicans thought it was worth $70 million in taxpayers' money to have a special counsel investigate a failed land deal of the Clintons from the 1970s called Whitewater—which turned up no wrongdoing by the first family—it seems both fair and relevant to go back to the early 1990s to look at not just one investment but business careers that both shaped two leaders' current policies and helped them attain their current offices.

Harken Energy is a Texas energy company that in 1988 purchased a failing Spectrum 7, run by George W. Bush. As part of the deal, Bush was put on the corporate board and also paid as a consultant. He was as well given loans by Harken at cheap rates so that he could buy company stock, which, as noted, he later used to secure more loans from a bank at which he was a director to invest in the Texas Rangers. (After the corporate meltdown of 2002, he called for a ban on these same kinds of sweetheart loans to insiders.)

He eventually sold his stock in Harken on June 22, 1990, sixty-three days *after* receiving a memo from Harken's president about the company's "liquidity crisis," thirty-five days *after* receiving another memo from Harken's executive vice president on the "negative repercussions" of a failure to extend corporate loans, fifteen days *after* receiving a memorandum from Harken's president describing the company as "in jeopardy," eleven days *after* an audit committee meeting discussing the devaluation of two Harken subsidiaries, and seven days *after* receiving a letter from Harken's attorneys warning about selling stock based on insider information . . . but a few weeks *before* the company publicly released bad financial news, causing the stock price to plummet. He then conveniently failed to file notice of these sales with the SEC for eight months. Bush has claimed on different occasions that the SEC lost the forms or that his lawyers forgot to send the forms, finally throwing up his hands in a July 8, 2002, press conference, saying, "As to why the Form 4 was late, I still haven't figured it out completely." The SEC briefly investigated George W. Bush over a decade ago. True to form, Bush produced few documents, and those he did submit to the SEC, according to the SEC report on the Bush investigation, "provide little insight as to what Harken nonpublic information he knew and when he knew it." Nevertheless, although investigators never interviewed him, the SEC halted the investigation without absolving him but without bringing any formal charges.

The day after it closed the investigation in August 1991, the SEC received documents from Bush that detailed the warning that Harken's lawyers had given to the board on June 15, 1990, a week before Bush's June 22 stock sale, about selling stock after hearing bad news. This letter suggests that Bush had reason to worry about the impropriety of selling his stock at that time and that the SEC presumably could have used this evidence before ending its investigation. The document, appropriately titled "Liability for Insider Trading and Short-Term Swing Profits," addressed the solution to the above-mentioned "liquidity crisis." On May 17, 1990, Bush attended a board meeting in which he was told that Harken was three days away from running out of cash. A few days later, Harken spun off two troubled divisions in a deal financed by the Harvard Management Fund, an institutional investor that manages Harvard University's huge endowment. The deal was publicly announced on May 22, 1990, but the rights offering was not priced until October 1990.

Following the May 22 announcement, Bush asked Harken for advice on selling his stock. Harken's law firm, Haynes and Boone, responded with the missing document, which warned: "The act of trading, particularly if close in time to the receipt of the inside information, is strong evidence that the insider's investment decision was based on the inside information. . . . Unless the favorable facts clearly are more important than the unfavorable, the insider should be advised not to sell." However, according to the *Boston Globe,* Bush told the SEC during its investigation of his stock sale that "Haynes and Boone informed [Bush] that they had met internally to consider the issue and, based upon the information they had, they saw no reason why Bush could not sell his shares."*

---

*Harken's losses, and Bush's profits, could very well have been monumentally worse without this divine intervention from Harvard. While the group denies its investments were motivated by the presence of Bush on the Harken board, its first investment took place within a month of Bush joining Harken and escalated to $50 million in June 2000, as the company faced dire financial trouble and Bush sought to sell his own shares. At that time, Harken, a small troubled company absent from the ranks of the Fortune 1000, represented Harvard's seventh-largest stakehold. According to William Black, a top federal bank regulator during the Reagan and first Bush administrations, "[T]his is beyond nuts from an institutional investor's standpoint. You don't see the Harvards of the world doing things like this." Black told the *Boston Globe* that "he did not investigate the Harken partnership for political reasons."

In a press conference eleven years later, on the day before the president's Wall Street speech on corporate accountability, the following exchange took place:

> Q: Mr. President, you've said that you didn't know, when you sold your Harken stock, that the company was going to restate its earnings. As a member of its audit committee, how could you not know that its earnings had not been properly accounted for?
>
> THE PRESIDENT: Because that fact, that fact came up after I sold the stock. And the SEC fully looked into this. All these questions that you're asking were looked into by the SEC. And again, I repeat to you, the summary—which I think you've seen—I hope you've seen it; if not, we'll be glad to get it to you—said that there was no case there.

While Bush said the lawyers' letter flashed a green-for-go signal, in fact the letter—arriving after the SEC investigation—flashed a red-for-stop signal. But Bush didn't. Also, an October 1993 memo from the SEC states that halting the investigation "must in no way be construed as indicating that the party has been exonerated or that no action may ultimately result." And does it need to be said that Bush's father was the president at the time and had appointed four of the five SEC commissioners, including the chairman, or that the general counsel at the SEC was the James Doty who represented Bush in his purchase of the Texas Rangers a few years before?

During his tenure on the Harken audit committee, Bush voted in 1989 to approve a deal in which Harken sold an unprofitable subsidiary called Aloha Petroleum to an "independent" subsidiary, turning real losses into fake profits and propping up the stock price at the same time. Sound familiar? For both Harken and Enron, hiding these kinds of losses required a rapidly growing cash flow that was difficult to maintain. The Aloha deal allowed Harken to record a profit on the deal of $7.9 million dollars, which in turn enabled it to claim losses for the year of only $3.3 million. Alfred King, former managing director of the Institute of Management Accountants, commented on the Aloha transaction that "the people at Enron could have gone to school on this thing." An SEC investigation of the sale forced Harken to restate its earnings—that is, admit that it had been lying all along, bringing Harken's losses for 1989 up to $12.6 million. Before news of the restatement hit the press and before the stock price dove, Bush cashed out.

Although Bush sold his stock in the nick of time, he absurdly maintains that, despite his seat on the audit committee, he didn't know about the coming bad news. He also claims to have voted *against* the offshore tax shelters in the Caymans, despite the records of the board meetings that are available, which show that he actually voted *for* the offshore shelters. When he is pressed further on the subject, Bush says he doesn't remember, yet he refuses to ask the SEC to release records of its investigation, referring the press to Harken for records of its directors' meetings. Harvey Pitt, President Bush's chosen head of the SEC during 2002, said publicly that he would release the SEC records if Bush asked, but Harken has said it won't release the records at all. When pressed on the subject at his July 8 press conference, the man who is proud of his moral clarity when it comes to evil abroad could only ambiguously answer that "sometimes things aren't exactly black and white when it comes to accounting procedures."

Halliburton

Before joining Bush on the Republican ticket, Dick Cheney served for five years (1995–2000) as CEO and Chairman of Halliburton, a Texas-based energy-services company, an experience he often referred to during the 2000 campaign as "a great success story." It was certainly a great success for Cheney, but the jury is still out on whether Halliburton and its shareholders will laud or rue his tenure.

Like Bush, Cheney sold stock before bad financial news regarding his company was made public. In August 2000, Cheney made an $18.5 million profit on stock sales that he was not required to make until his swearing-in as vice president the following January. Two months later, in October 2000, Halliburton released news that its engineering and construction business would not meet revenue expectations and that the company was under investigation for overbilling the government. While Cheney sold his shares at Halliburton's all-time peak of $52 per share, by the end of the year the price had fallen to $35 and by January 2002, down to $10. There has been no investigation of Cheney's sales, and there likely won't be one in the future. "The developments at Halliburton since Cheney's departure leave two possibilities," the Washington Post concluded. "Either the vice president did not know of the magnitude of problems at the oilfield services company he ran for five years, or he sold his shares in August 2000 knowing the company was likely headed for a fall." That is, Cheney acted either incompetently or unlawfully.

The questionable stock sale is only one of several Halliburton controversies. In 1998 the company began counting projections of cost overruns on its construction contracts as revenue before the work was completed, a decision that padded the company's bottom line by $89 million that year— roughly one quarter of the firm's annual revenue—and that the SEC is now investigating. Not surprisingly, Arthur Andersen was Halliburton's accountant at the time, and Cheney was so pleased with its work that he filmed a promotional video commending his experience with the now-dismantled accounting firm: "I get good advice, if you will, from their people based upon how we're doing business and how we're operating—over and above just the sort of normal by the books auditing arrangement." According to Halliburton's current CEO, David Lessar, Cheney was aware of the accounting changes. While the SEC hasn't interviewed the vice president yet, the nonpartisan and conservative watchdog group Judicial Watch has filed a shareholder suit against Cheney and Halliburton claiming that because Halliburton overstated its earnings by $445 million from 1999 through 2001, shareholders lost their shirts when the fraud was revealed and the stock tanked in response.

Despite Halliburton's troubles since Cheney left there for public office, he has stonewalled the press on every related subject—whether his stock sales, or asbestos liability assumed after Halliburton acquired Dresser Industries, or the SEC accounting investigation—and refers all questions to Halliburton, which conveniently declines to comment. Like Bush, Cheney calls for business leaders to step up and assume responsibility, claiming that "where corporate greed and malfeasance causes honest people to lose their jobs, life savings, and pensions, the people's confidence in the system is undermined—and the wrongdoers must be held to account." That's easy for Cheney to say, given the $32 million early-retirement package Halliburton awarded him when he stepped down to run for vice president, despite being too young to collect it. Unfortunately, Halliburton was not quite as generous with the hundreds of employees acquired with Dresser. While they continued in the same jobs they held before the acquisition, technically they resigned from Dresser and were rehired by Halliburton, thereby collectively relinquishing $25 million worth of their pension.

There's more to the Halliburton story than just the company's accounting maneuvers. Halliburton has shown just how profitable it can be to hire a former secretary of defense as your company's CEO and then return him to public service to become vice president. In the vice-presidential debate of October 5, 2000, Cheney remarked on his successful business career that "the government had absolutely nothing to do with it." In fact, the government had everything to do with it. With Cheney at the helm of Halliburton, the company doubled its earnings from government contracts, from $1.2 billion in the five years prior to $2.3 billion during Cheney's five-year tenure. In the last two years alone, Halliburton won $1.5 billion in federal loans and insurance subsidies compared with the $100 million the company received in the five years before Cheney joined them. A Halliburton subsidiary even tried to do business with Saddam Hussein, but was denied permission by the Clinton administration (see chapter 11).

Broadway on Wall Street

In the aftermath of the Enron scandal, President Bush had an opportunity to quiet critics who maintained that he couldn't independently and vigorously clean up Corporate America. Instead, Bush continued to cling to the idea that Enron—though quickly followed by WorldCom, Adelphia, Tyco, et al.—was the single rotten apple in an otherwise responsible business barrel. As late as June 28, 2002, Bush reassured Americans that "it's important for our fellow citizens to understand that, by far, the vast majority of our leaders in the business community are honest and upright people." The *Daily News* responded to such assurances with disbelief: "Bush is dreaming—or he's misinformed." The newspaper went on to cite a 1998 *Business Week* poll that asked CFOs if other executives had requested that they misrepresent results; 55 percent said they were asked to cheat, and 12 percent admitted to having done so.

Bush's assertion likewise did not prevent such critics as fellow Republican senator John McCain from calling for SEC chairman Harvey Pitt's resignation. When weeks of public and congressional fervor for reform refused to die down, Bush released his "Ten-Point Plan on Corporate Responsibility." Then WorldCom imploded. Pressure exponentially increased for the Senate and House to move quickly on the Sarbanes and Oxley bills, respectively, aimed at reforming the complex accounting and corporate governance structures at public companies.

On July 9, 2002, President Bush went to Wall Street to give a much anticipated condemnation of and prescription for the avalanche of corporate scandal that had crashed down on the business landscape. An understandable crisis of confidence had hit investors who had lost billions on companies they believed to be robust.

His Wall Street speech was long on exhortatory generalities but short on substance and specifics. Delivered at the Regent Wall Street Hotel to a crowd of about a thousand corporate CEOs and Wall Street leaders against a backdrop on which the words "Corporate Responsibility" were printed over and over in bold letters, Bush's wooden speech satisfied few except, perhaps, the CEOs against whom he allegedly railed. According to (New York) *Newsday*, executives emerged from the Regent Hotel "grinning like they'd just been handed fat new stock-option deals. . . . The executives Bush came to pillory, they swore they loved the speech. And why not? Savvy Wall Streeters realized what any half-intelligent person would. This was for the cameras." Once again, instead of exposing a broken system that needed fixing, he blamed a degradation of moral fiber among a few corporate executives.

He warned the crowd of Wall Street executives gathered to hear him that "we will use the full weight of the law to expose and root out corruption. My administration will do everything in our power to end the days of cooking the books, shading the truth, and breaking our laws." The rest of the president's remarks that day were lacking in specifics, contrary to his own history of business practices, or just plain contradicted by his actions as president. He demanded "truly independent directors," though he wouldn't have qualified while on the board of Harken. Bush even went so far as to blame business schools and urge them to "be principled teachers of right and wrong, and not surrender to moral confusion and relativism." One Wall Street executive in attendance commented that "[h]e mentioned a lot of things that the Securities and Exchange Commission already does." Rather than calling for increased oversight, stricter rules, or any number of reforms, he spent the majority of his time suggesting "a new ethic of personal responsibility in the business community." Who needs far stronger laws when morality alone can save us from greed?

The president did propose "tough new criminal penalties for corporate fraud," adding that such "legislation would double the maximum prison terms for those convicted of financial fraud from five to ten years. Defrauding investors is a serious offense, and the punishment must be as serious as the crime." Unfortunately, all prosecutors will tell you how hard it is to actually convict individual executives of criminal fraud, hidden as they are behind the collective corporate form, without the extraordinary devotion of government resources.

Cheney had privately advised the president to go easy on Wall Street that day, but the Bronx cheer the president received for his Wall Street speech led him to change his rhetorical course. Bush and Karl Rove are nothing if not politically astute about popular sentiment, and the president's next few speeches began to sound as if Ralph Nader had won the White House in 2000. At the signing of the Sarbanes-Oxley bill on July 30, the president boasted that "corporate misdeeds will be found and will be punished. . . . [T]he maximum prison term for common types of fraud has quadrupled from five to twenty years." In a speech on August 7, he continued to talk tough, warning, "For corporate leaders found guilty of fraud and theft, there will be no more easy money, just hard time."

The creation of the new Corporate Fraud Task Force within the Justice Department was announced by the president in his Wall Street speech as "a corporate crimes SWAT team." But as CorpWatch, a progressive watchdog group devoted to corporate responsibility, reports, "There's no additional funding or staff, just a directive that a bunch of government agencies talk to each other more often about the things you'd expect they'd be talking to each other about a lot these days—securities fraud, mail and wire fraud, money laundering, and tax fraud. In fact, . . . Bush actually reduced the number of FBI agents on the corporate crime beat by fifty-nine, redeploying them for the anti-terrorism effort. So it looks like the Fraud Task Force is itself a fraud."

We certainly haven't been able to rely on the Ashcroft Justice Department. According to records compiled by the Transaction Records Access Clearinghouse, a nonpartisan research center at Syracuse University, during the first six months of the 2002 fiscal year, the number of white-collar crimes referred to prosecutors was the lowest since the late 1980s. And the percentage of the referred white-collar crimes accepted by assistant U.S. attorneys was less than 50 percent (compared to 80 percent for drug crimes).

The president also told his audience, "I urge board members to check the quality of their company's financial statements; to ask tough questions about accounting methods; to demand that audit firms are not beholden to the CEO; and to make sure the compensation for senior executives squares with reality and common sense." A leader truly interested in cracking down on corporate corruption could have proposed legislation to require board members to be completely independent of management; to prevent CEOs from actively choosing the audit firm; to prohibit a single firm from providing auditing, consulting, and accounting services; and to require auditing firms for a company to rotate every few years, or even return the auditing role to a fully funded federal agency. Again, when it comes to the profit motive, suggesting voluntary virtue is a throwback to the era before Upton Sinclair disclosed the sickening conditions in food processing plants in his 1906 classic, *The Jungle.*

Finally, the president audaciously said, "I challenge compensation committees to put an end to all company loans to corporate officers." But again, the business president only "challenges" board members to behave responsibly, rather than "challenging" Congress to pass laws that will actually protect shareholders. Of course, one could sympathize with the president's tough bind on this point, considering that he received exactly this type of loan while he was on the board of Harken.

The speech was roundly panned by a broad range of commentators. Missing from the president's proposals were basic provisions like real funding increases for the SEC, protections for whistleblowers, limitation of offshore tax havens, restrictions on misbehaving companies doing business with the federal government, rules on expensing of stock options, and very many specifics. *Newsday* wished there was more on "the far-too-interlocking relationship between companies and the auditors who are supposed to give clear and unbiased evaluations of their finances." The *Financial Times* noted that the reform bill in the House that Bush preferred "is backed by the accounting firms (and would leave regulation in the industry's hands), instead of the Senate bill, which would increase government oversight." *The New Republic* pointed out that "Bush's plan wouldn't create a new felony for securities fraud, as an amendment by Senator Pat Leahy would do, and it simply increases the sentences for the narrow criminal categories of wire and mail fraud."

The day after his speech the Dow dropped 282 points, the largest one-day fall since the September 11, 2001, terrorist attacks.

On July 30, 2002, the political fervor for corporate reform culminated in the signing of the Sarbanes-Oxley Act. Among its other initiatives, the act created the Public Company Accounting Oversight Board (PCAOB).

Prior to the passage of the bill, the accounting profession was regulated by the Financial Accounting Standards Board (FASB), an "independent" regulatory body whose entire budget was paid by the accounting industry itself. Under the Sarbanes-Oxley Act, the FASB will continue to set accounting rules, while the new PCAOB will oversee the accounting firms and their clients. The presence of the new oversight board in the Senate version of the bill and its absence from the House version was one of the main reasons the White House preferred the House bill. This didn't prevent Bush from accepting credit for its inception: "My administration pressed for greater corporate integrity," said the president in the East Room at the bill signing. "A united Congress has written it into law. And today I sign the most far-reaching reforms of American business practices since the time of Franklin Delano Roosevelt." All presidents from Johnson to Reagan enjoy FDR comparisons, but while Roosevelt was responsible for creating the SEC and many of the modern regulatory agencies, President Bush fought against the creation of the PCAOB, and only signed the bill under considerable political pressure.

The Securities and Exchange Omission

Professor Joel Seligman, dean of Washington University Law School and author of the definitive history of the SEC, wrote in an article after the Enron debacle: "A widespread belief appears to have evolved in the United States financial community that time-honored rules such as those that discourage conflicts of interest are quaint and easily circumvented. Too frequently, in recent years, sharp practitioners in business, investment banking, accounting or law appear to have challenged the fundamental tenets of 'full disclosure of material information' or 'fair presentation of accounting results.'"

President Bush, not eager to contest these entrenched beliefs of the banking industry, set the tone for the SEC early in his administration through his appointment of Harvey Pitt as its chairman. A longtime lawyer for the accounting industry, Pitt spearheaded their fights against the proposed reforms of his predecessor, Arthur Levitt. To his later regret, Levitt backed down after taking a beating in Congress from the Pitt-led accounting lobby and from members of Congress from both parties. In 2000, as Levitt proposed a rule prohibiting accounting firms from offering both auditing and consulting services to their clients, forty-six senators and representatives wrote letters of opposition to Levitt. In the ten years prior, these forty-six received $39 million in contributions from the industry.

Levitt, in his recent book, *Take On the Street,* describes Pitt's position on auditor independence: "[E]ach firm would customize its specific standards, and each auditor would determine whether he was in compliance." Levitt and others thought "self-regulation by the accounting profession is a bad joke." Former SEC chairman Roderick Hills believed "the system itself needs a major overhaul." But Pitt's position had not changed a bit between the time he represented the accounting industry and his tenure at the SEC. Even after Arthur Andersen demonstrated that allowing one firm to provide accounting and consulting services was a bad idea, Pitt continued to hedge on whether the practice should be outlawed. In an interview with Tim Russert on *Meet the Press,* he responded to a question about this issue by saying, "I want to see an absolute prohibition that is in the hands of the audit committee or independent directors to decide upon." In English, this means that Pitt wanted to allow boards of directors—like those at Enron—to decide if their accounting firms—like Arthur Andersen—should be allowed to audit the results of their own consulting. How this would prevent the kinds of conflicts of interest that prevented Arthur Andersen from doing its job was anyone's guess.

None of this history meant that Pitt would necessarily run the SEC as a tool of the accounting industry. When President Franklin Roosevelt appointed former Wall Street insider Joseph Kennedy to be the first chair of the SEC, Kennedy confounded critics by turning his insider knowledge to good use in regulating the industry from which he came. But Pitt instead called to mind the less auspicious presidency of former president George Bush by promising a "kinder, gentler place for accountants." Following this promise, delivered in a speech to the American Institute of Certified Public Accountants, Pitt was accused of pandering to the accounting industry by suggesting that he would be much more willing to quietly settle problems with the industry in a way that his predecessor Levitt was not.

Even after the demise of Enron, much of the media remained unimpressed with the way Pitt had stayed so close to his old clients. According to *Newsweek,* "The problem is not that Pitt represented the accounting industry and corporate defendants as a lawyer (and thus has recently had to recuse himself twenty-nine times from pending SEC cases). . . . The problem, as New York attorney general Eliot Spitzer notes, is that Pitt has 'internalized the values of his clients.' He came in talking about a 'kinder, gentler' SEC, and held cozy meetings with the folks he should be regulating aggressively."

Spitzer, who led the charge against investment banks for trading positive stock ratings in exchange for lucrative banking deals, defended his entry onto traditional SEC turf by charging that "[i]f the SEC had been pursuing this [analyst issue] aggressively, then for me to have jumped in would have been wasteful and perhaps inappropriate. But there was a vacuum, [which] had to be filled in order to protect the small investor." Only after Spitzer released explosive internal e-mails showing analysts privately disparaging what they were publicly promoting did Pitt get on board.

But Pitt's zeal in investigating Wall Street wavered when it came time to appoint a head to the new accounting oversight board. He at first chose John Biggs, a pension fund CEO who had demonstrated an ardor for real reform, but under pressure from the accounting lobby, he reversed course. *Fortune* reports that "his SEC colleagues were embarrassed and appalled. A fellow commissioner puts it this way: 'This was the single most important decision the chairman had to make, and he's made a total mess of it.'" Instead of Biggs, Bush's SEC chair turned to William H. Webster, a former FBI and CIA director with little accounting experience, and, more important, the head of the audit committee of U.S. Technologies, an Internet company that was itself under investigation for securities and wire fraud. After Pitt's selection of Webster but before Pitt submitted his selection to the other SEC commissioners, Webster notified the chairman how at U.S. Technologies he had dismissed outside auditors when they complained of serious financial problems. Apparently, Pitt didn't think that Webster's failure of judgment in fulfilling his oversight duties as a corporate director was relevant to his appointment as head of a body that would oversee the accounting industry. So he failed to tell the other SEC commissioners before they approved Webster.

When this information came to light in November 2002, it was the second shoe falling. A tidal wave of public criticism and unattributed quotes from White House aides provided no wiggle room: Pitt resigned as SEC chair, and Webster stepped down as head of the new oversight board shortly thereafter.*

Aside from the Pitt appointment, Bush's true views on keeping corporate America honest are best reflected in his budget requests for the SEC. Prior to the Enron scandal, the president's first budget proposal in April 2001 for the 2002 fiscal year raised the SEC's budget by a scant 3.5 percent from $423 million to $439 million, forcing the commission to cut its staff by fifty-seven employees—this despite its expectations that the volume of complaints in 2002 would increase by 60 percent, from 81,500 to 136,500. The SEC bravely accepted the budget but warned that "[u]nfortunately, and perhaps ironically, we only have the ability to operate at this funding level because of the severe staffing problems we currently face."

After Enron blew up in late 2001 and early 2002, Bush either underestimated the magnitude of the financial disasters on the horizon or he had no interest in preparing for them: his response was to ask Congress for a mere 3.5 percent boost to the 2002 SEC budget, or basically just keeping up with inflation. Pitt admirably defied his president by requesting $91 million more, or a 20 percent boost, but even that amount would later seem insuf-

---

*Bush's replacements for Pitt and Webster have shown that the administration has finally understood the public's and the Senate's desire for credible regulators. William Donaldson, a respected Wall Street banker and former head of the New York Stock Exchange, was easily confirmed as chairman of the SEC. One of his early decisions was to nominate William McDonough, president of the New York Federal Reserve, to take Webster's place at the head of PCAOB. McDonough was hailed in Washington as an excellent choice, and his nomination was approved unanimously by the SEC commissioners. He has so far taken a tough but fair tone with the accounting profession, promising that he will hold them to both the letter and the spirit of the Sarbanes-Oxley Act.

ficient. After the WorldCom scandal broke, Bush, in his Wall Street speech, upped his request to $100 million more for the SEC, while the House, more sensitive to the public outrage, approved an increase of $300 million. The 2002 budget ended up at $513 million, while 2003's came to $776 million. Inexplicably, Bush promised to use only $568 million of the $776 million that Congress appropriated. The message was clear: We want the SEC to do its job, but not too well.

To put all of these budget numbers in perspective, the figure that Senate Republicans are pushing for 2004, $650 million, represents only a 3 percent annual rise in the SEC's budget since 1992, while average daily trading at the New York Stock Exchange has risen 21 percent over the same period, and the amount of discovered corporate fraud, obviously, has so grown that companies like Enron, WorldCom, Adelphia, and Tyco have become household names.

5. Secrecy and Civil Liberties
"Watch What [You] Say"

"America will always stand firm for the non-negotiable demands of human dignity: the rule of law; limits on the power of the state; respect for women; private property; free speech; equal justice; and religious tolerance."

—President George W. Bush,
January 2002 State of the Union address

Throughout our history the government has at times felt it necessary to suspend democratic principles during emergencies, on the Lincolnian argument that occasionally you have to amputate the foot to save the body. It happened with the passage of the Alien and Sedition Acts of 1798 to silence critics of the Federalist Party, and again during the Civil War when President Lincoln suspended the right of habeas corpus. It happened in 1919 and 1920 when Attorney General A. Mitchell Palmer conducted his notorious and largely warrantless raids against suspected Bolsheviks and "hyphenated-Americans"; during World War II when 120,000 Japanese Americans were interned on suspicion of espionage simply because of their ethnic heritage; and again during Senator Joseph McCarthy's anti-Communist witch hunts in the 1950s. Each time, these abrogations of individual rights and expansions of government power were regarded as essential responses to national security emergencies and each time later regretted as unnecessary, even counterproductive.

Secrecy

Secrecy is a favorite tactic of government officials who want either to hide their mistakes or to pretend that policy tailored for special interests was fitted for the general public. Rather than deceiving or misleading, it's easier to just say nothing at all—at least that way you can't be accused of incompetence or lying. The problem is that secrecy is inherently misleading in a system like a democracy, which depends on an open government, an informed citizenry, and a public debate to arrive at good decisions.

Since Vietnam and Watergate caused public trust in the government to plummet to historic lows, Americans have been steadily engaged in the process of increasing access to government and accountability by government. A number of laws passed in the post-Watergate era—the Presidential Records Act, the Federal Advisory Committee Act, and the Freedom of Information Act, strengthened by a 1974 amendment—all reach for these lofty goals. Reducing secrecy is not only about maintaining the balance of power between the government and the public, however, for it is also fundamental to making good policy. Justice Louis Brandeis's axiom that "sunshine is the best disinfectant" is as relevant to special-interest government as it is to corporate abuses. From the FBI's secret lists of supposed Communist sympathizers to the Pentagon Papers, secrecy allows government either to quietly intrude upon Americans' privacy and individual liberties or to adopt policies that bypass the "consent of the governed"—or both. As the late senator Daniel Patrick Moynihan put it, "Secrecy is for losers."

Speak Little (and Carry a Very Big Stick)

Since taking office, President Bush has made it clear that he's comfortable with his the-less-disclosure-the-better CEO management style. Independent of the war on terrorism, his administration has consistently reduced the flow of information about domestic economic policy. The Bush White House decided to replace the Office of Management and Budget's traditional ten-year budget forecasts with five-year ones as the long-term forecasts began to look increasingly dim as a result of the president's huge, back-loaded tax cuts. And effective January 2003, the White House discontinued a monthly mass layoff report released by the Labor Department—the same report that was also dropped by Bush's father and then reintroduced by Clinton in 1995. When the department was contacted by the press for a reason for stopping the reports, its response was at least consistent: no comment. (The monthly mass layoff report was restored after much criticism later in 2003.)

It's not just the economy. As we've mentioned, the General Accounting Office was forced to pursue Vice President Cheney for more than a year for details of his closed-doors meetings with an unnamed "Energy Task Force" that helped draft the administration's energy policy. At first, the White House justified its secrecy on this project by claiming that the meetings were just among internal staff and sent Interior Secretary Gale Norton onto the Sunday morning talk shows to proclaim, "What we're talking about . . . is essentially cabinet officers meeting together. And I'm not aware that any administration has ever had public comments before cabinet officers can sit down together."

Over time, however, a very different story emerged. As chapter 2 described, energy firms were present at the meetings while environmental representatives cooled their heels outside. The GAO ultimately sued the Executive branch for the first time in its eighty-one-year history for records of the meetings, arguing that a failure to release the documents would be "fatal to its ability to perform functions that it has in the past for Congress and the public." The Bush administration essentially escaped disclosure due to a technicality—the lower court ruled not that Cheney had a right to keep the documents secret but that the GAO comptroller lacked the standing to bring the lawsuit. Cheney, however, was compelled by other lawsuits—especially one by the Natural Resources Defense Counsel—to turn over eleven thousand pages of documents from the process. The materials showed that the task force had made 714 direct contacts with industry representatives and only 29 with identified nonindustry groups.

What was so crucial to hide in this case? Cheney, Fleischer, and the other public faces reiterated that it was an issue of principle, that our leaders must have the freedom to meet in secret with whomever they choose. But John Dean, former White House counsel, saw a more sinister rationale: "[Cheney] told the *Today* show that he wants to 'protect the ability of the president and the vice president to get unvarnished advice from any source [they] want.' That sounds all too familiar to me. I worked for Richard Nixon."

The squabble over the Energy Task Force is only the "tip of the iceberg," adds Dean, of the Bush administration's ongoing effort to keep secrets from Congress as well. This is a disturbing thought when you consider that congressional oversight over executive branch functions, especially such hidden activities as intelligence and national security, is one of the cornerstones of our governmental system of checks and balances. President Bush's attitude appears to be that Congress can write the checks, but the executive will dictate the balance.

The 107th and 108th Congresses have been battling the White House for access practically since inauguration day. For eighteen months the Department of Justice was unwilling to share with Congress an account of how it was implementing the powers it was granted under the USA Patriot Act, which prompted outgoing Republican congressman Bob Barr to conclude, "Their attitude seems to be that even Congress isn't entitled to know how they're using the authority that Congress gave them."

The Bush administration even stonewalled prewar congressional requests for an estimated cost of the war in Iraq, forcing Congress to debate the budget without any idea of what turned out to be one of the government's largest expenditures in the upcoming year. That lack of transparency has extended into the postwar period as well, as lucrative reconstruction contracts were handed off in a secret bidding process like choice party favors to the Bush administration's favorite corporate insiders. These contracts were being awarded to U.S. firms by secret invitation only, instead of the usual public notice process, as chapter 4 discussed in more detail.

Senator Ron Wyden (D-OR) has bipartisan support for a bill calling for the administration to explain its decision to sidestep standard bidding procedure. "You look at this process, which is secret, limited, or closed bidding, and you have to ask yourself: 'Why are these companies being picked? How's this process taking place, and is this best use of scarce taxpayer money?" asked Wyden. "The administration has been keeping the taxpayers in the dark with respect to how this money is being used, and that information ought to be shared."

The Bush administration's invariable response when accused of being unusually secretive? There is no increased secrecy, silly. The president's press secretary calmly assures us that they "are more accessible and open than many previous administrations. . . . [T]he bottom line remains the president is dedicated to an open government, a responsive government, while he fully exercises the authority of the executive branch." Why be open when you can impose secrecy while *saying* you're open?

From Keeping Records to Keeping Secrets

Signs of secrecy emanated from the Bush White House well before September 11. The first was the controversy over 68,000 pages of Ronald Reagan's presidential correspondence, documents that were due to be released on the very day of Bush's inauguration under the terms of the 1978 Presidential Records Act (PRA). Passed in the aftermath of public outcry over the kind of executive high-handedness that had precipitated Watergate, the PRA was intended to facilitate public access to presidential records. Except for specified exempt materials, it mandated the release of presidential documents after a period of no more than twelve years after a chief executive leaves office. But when the national archivist informed the Bush administration that the Reagan papers, the first set of such documents to come up for release under the act, were dressed and ready to go, White House counsel Alberto Gonzales quashed their release. After sitting on the records for nearly ten months, Bush signed Executive Order 13233, which he and members of his administration touted as nothing more than a procedural measure that would ensure the documents' orderly (though not timely) release.

Even the most casual reading of the two legal documents, however, reveals the disingenuousness of this portrayal. The PRA is premised on the presumption of openness, stating that the national archivist has "an affirmative duty make such records available to the public as rapidly and completely as possible." The executive order, in contrast, is based on secrecy, setting up a cumbersome procedure where both the incumbent and former presidents have the right to a virtually indefinite review of any documents up for release. The EO also shifts the burden from the executive branch to justify the refusal to release a particular document to a party seeking a document to have "a demonstrated, specific need" for the records.

Questioned about these discrepancies, the administration's nimble equivocations began. Gonzales, who drafted the order, maintained the changes were necessary because an incumbent president is "in a better position to decide whether or not the release of documents of a former president do, in fact, jeopardize, say, the national security of this country." The Bush administration has certainly learned this lesson of September 11 well: drop the words "national security" into a press briefing—and confuse secrecy with security—and you are accorded immediate deference.

In this case, documents from a former administration that may have relevance to current national security concerns are already exempt from release, under the terms of the 1978 law. Executive Order 13233, however, clearly has nothing to do with national security, although it may have something to do with job security—namely, shielding Bush staffers who served under Reagan from potential embarrassment for ill-advised decisions such as Iran-Contra. Then press secretary Ari Fleischer, however, held firmly to the party line, calling the national security need a "classic case in point" while, with typical "sleight of mouth," lauding the EO as an "orderly process" that would help people get more information about their government. President Bush himself characterized the order as laying out a process that will "enable historians to do their job."

Why then were so many historians up in arms about it? American University historian Anna K. Nelson condemned how "this order sets up a minefield in front of what was a straightforward piece of legislation." Other scholars protested that the order steps beyond the law by effectively allowing the vice president the right to invoke executive privilege as well, a right that has no basis in the law or the Constitution.

The majority of the Reagan documents were eventually released by the spring of 2002, but Executive Order 13233 still stands, ready to protect any documents from the first Bush administration when they "go up for parole" in 2005.

Freedom from Information

While President Bush was undermining one pillar of the laws designed to keep the government open, his attorney general was happily assailing another. On October 12, 2001, Attorney General John Ashcroft issued a memorandum to all federal agencies announcing a new policy for handling Freedom of Information Act (FOIA) requests. The memo was distributed quietly in the midst of the fear and confusion over the anthrax attacks; no public announcement was made, no press conference was scheduled, and no justification was given for the directive, which effectively undermines the FOIA, our nation's most treasured sunshine law.

Enacted in 1966, the act gives members of the public a legal right to access information from federal agencies, subject to certain exemptions. The FOIA is relied on extensively by journalists, historians, community action groups, and others seeking to preserve government access and maintain government accountability. According to Gary Bass, executive director of the independent government watchdog group OMB Watch, "Editors at the *Orlando Sentinel* wanted to see just how central FOIA really was, so they asked reporters to put a little sunshine icon by every story they wrote that required the use of FOIA or other government openness procedures. Turns out that more than 70 percent of the stories had a sunshine! People don't realize the extent to which we rely on these laws for ensuring some understanding of what's happening in our communities."

Ashcroft's memo essentially reverses the Clinton administration's policy of presumed disclosure to one of presumed closure. While Attorney General Janet Reno's 1993 FOIA directive urged the disclosure of documents unless "foreseeable harm" would accrue from their release, the Ashcroft memo encourages agencies to withhold records unless they lack a "sound legal basis" to do so. The text of the memorandum proclaims that the Justice department is "committed to full compliance with the FOIA," as "it is only through a well-informed citizenry that the leaders of our nation remain accountable to the governed and the American people can be assured that neither fraud nor government waste is concealed." Good words, but emblematic of the Bush White House understanding that a president can do almost anything so long as he repeatedly and forcefully insists he's doing the opposite. Lucy Dalglish, executive director of the Reporters Committee for Freedom of the Press, notes that the Ashcroft memo "sends a message throughout the entire federal government to stonewall or deny requests whenever possible."

Because Ashcroft's directive was in the works before September 11, national security provided a convenient cover but was not its driving motivation. Tellingly, it directs agencies to make "full and deliberate consideration of the institutional, commercial, and personal privacy interests" that would be implicated by any disclosure. That expresses as much a concern for corporate security as it does for national security, a concern bolstered by the FOIA exemptions contained in the Homeland Security Act of 2002.

Those exemptions include "critical infrastructure information" shared voluntarily with the Department of Homeland Security. At first glance this may seem like a reasonable provision; after all, we don't want detailed plans of nuclear power plants and other potentially vulnerable infrastructure floating around in the public domain so that terrorists can easily compile a laundry list of targets. However, the language of the act is unnecessarily broad, creating what Representative Janice Schakowsky (D-IL) has called "a loophole big enough to drive any corporation and its secrets through."

When pressed on the reason for such vague language, the Bush administration responded with characteristic doublespeak. Although Richard Clarke, first Clinton's and then Bush's top cybersecurity advisor (now retired), admitted that current law already allowed for the protection of critical infrastructure information, he added, "that doesn't persuade companies to give us the information. Their lawyers believe they need additional protection; therefore we need to get additional protection." When a panel of administration representatives, including Secretary of State Colin Powell, Attorney General John Ashcroft, and Secretary of Defense Donald Rumsfeld were specifically asked about the need for further FOIA exemptions in testimony before the House Select Committee on Homeland Security in July 2002, they deflected the question. Powell kindly suggested the Congress take up their concerns with the Director of Homeland Security.

When Governor Ridge eventually did make an appearance before the Senate Judiciary Committee to talk about the Homeland Security bill, Senator Patrick Leahy (D-VT) admonished him:

> This is a proposal born in secrecy and rushed to the stage before the legislative plans were ready and on the same day this committee was hearing powerful testimony from a whistleblower about intelligence failures. Exempting the new department from laws that ensure accountability to the Congress and to the American people makes for soggy ground and a tenuous start—not the sure footing we all want for the success and endurance of this endeavor.

The problem with the proposal is that the Homeland Security Act exempts not only information about potential vulnerabilities but also any information that a corporation may deem "critical"—a determination left to the corporation's own discretion. And once shared with the Department of Homeland Security (DHS), that information is not only off-limits to the public but its use by the government is also severely restricted. In most cases, DHS cannot release the information to other agencies or use it to correct the vulnerability without written consent from the company that shared it; the act does not even require the company itself to take any steps to fix the problem. In addition, once information is shared with DHS, it cannot be used in a civil suit. In the past, this is precisely the sort of information that environmentalists and community action groups, among others, have used to monitor chemical plants, energy facilities, and corporate abuses. Hamstringing the public's right to know even further, the act criminalizes whistleblowers who lift the lid on company malfeasance.

While no one wants to give potential terrorists a helping hand, no one should want corporations to use September 11 as an excuse to shroud their activities in the kind of secrecy for which they have been lobbying for years, except perhaps an administration that favors corporations almost as much as it favors operating in secret.

Misinformation and the Media

In the immediate aftermath of September 11, Congress and the public were willing to let the president do nearly anything he thought necessary to protect national security. Heightened secrecy was presented as part and parcel of the government's efforts to combat future terrorist threats. The administration spent that blank check, sweeping up hundreds for alleged terrorist ties or INS violations and then ordering their detention and deportation hearings to be completely closed, battling Congress over information about the enforcement of the Patriot Act, and, in a moment of supreme irony, appointing (originally) Henry Kissinger to head an "independent" commission to investigate September 11.

Over time fewer and fewer Americans seemed willing to buy the link the Bush administration was trying to draw between "more secret" and "more safe," and criticism of unwarranted expansions of government secrecy began to mount. While an earlier appeals court ruling had supported secret deportation hearings, the Sixth Circuit struck them down as unconstitutional, with Circuit Judge Damon J. Keith eloquently admonishing the Bush administration in August 2002 that "democracies die behind closed doors."

Through the now-defunct Office of Strategic Influence (OSI), the Pentagon planned a worldwide propaganda campaign, including possibly the use of falsified stories planted in the foreign press, to bolster international sympathy for the American cause. When news of the office's Orwellian mandate broke in the press in early 2002, Bush administration staffers were quick to stonewall. Undersecretary of Defense Douglas Feith declined to comment while Secretary Donald Rumsfeld maintained that "the Pentagon does not lie to the American people. It does not lie to foreign audiences."

Yet lying seems to be precisely what the OSI was designed to do. A senior Pentagon official admitted that its propaganda campaign was designed to run the gamut from "the blackest of black programs to the whitest of whites." The news sources that broke the story concurred that the Pentagon plans included planting a mix of true and false stories in the foreign press and sending pro-American e-mails from disguised addresses, while using such covert operations as cyber attacks to disrupt anti-American coverage abroad.

Any war waged against terrorism must include an information component. Government officials are understandably eager to counter the propaganda bin Laden and his minions have been distributing through mosques, Islamic schools, and over the airwaves of Al-Jazeera. And it's no secret that the American government, through the CIA and the U.S. Army Psychological Operations Command (PSYOPS), has been distributing pro-American propaganda for years. However, the targets in the past have primarily been hostile nations. Purposefully distributing misinformation to media outlets in friendly nations is not only distasteful, it also can backfire badly, straining allied relations and creating cynicism when we want truthful stories to be believed. And if any of the misinformation makes its way back to American news outlets, which is likely in this age of the instantaneous Internet media, the administration could find itself in violation of a law that forbids governmental propaganda campaigns in the United States. Eventually, sustained public criticism forced the Pentagon to shut down the OSI in February 2002.

Privacy and Liberty

The Bush administration has gone to great lengths to assure the American people that the war on terror is a war for freedom—to protect our freedoms at home and liberate those suffering under oppressive regimes that breed or harbor terrorists abroad. From Operation Enduring Freedom to Operation Liberty Shield to Operation Iraqi Freedom, the White House has portrayed President Bush as a committed freedom fighter—and those who dare to criticize his policies as freedom's enemies. Yet President Bush has chosen to defend our freedoms in a manner that often reduces them. This is a government that exploits secrecy to reduce privacy—and liberty.

The disconnect between President Bush's pro-personal-liberty rhetoric and pro-government-authority policies began long before September 11. During his presidential campaign, one of his catchphrases was "government if necessary, but not necessarily government." As governor of Texas, he took an anti-big-government stance typical of southern conservative Republican businessmen when in April 1996 he insisted, "We must reduce the role and scope of the federal government, returning it to the limited role our forefathers envisioned when they wrote the Tenth Amendment to the Constitution, giving the states all power not specifically granted to the federal government."

Yet despite paying lip service to the conservative philosophy of small government, Bush as governor demonstrated a fondness for assertions of executive power that restricted constitutionally guaranteed freedoms. Members of environmental and community groups peacefully protesting against a proindustry clean-air bill backed by then-governor Bush were arrested for demonstrating on a sidewalk outside the governor's mansion, although protesters had often assembled there in the past. Bush defended the arrests as carried out pursuant to a change in the rules governing protest activity, but those new rules were never made public. According to Jay Jacobsen, an executive director of the ACLU observing the protest, "The motive is clearly to stop their speech." Governor Bush was also criticized by civil liberties groups for vetoing a bill intended to improve the process by which Texas courts appointed attorneys for indigent defendants, increasing their chances of a fair and speedy trial. But it would only be as president, responding to the new scourge of terrorism, that his views on government and liberty would truly be tested.

The USA Patriot Act

On October 26, 2001, after a greatly truncated congressional debate held in the midst of the traumatic and bewildering anthrax attacks that occurred hard on the heels of September 11, President Bush launched his counter-terrorism strategy when he signed the "Uniting and Strengthening America by Providing Appropriate Tools to Intercept and Obstruct Terrorism" Act of 2001, known by its acronym as the "USA Patriot" Act. Given the devastation of the attacks and the pressure to come up with some response, it was very difficult for Congress to present a reasoned critique of the administration's demands. After what was more a stampede than a debate, the Patriot Act passed the Senate with only one dissenting vote. (The honor belongs to Senator Russ Feingold [D-WI], who cautioned: "I believe we must, we must, redouble our vigilance. We must redouble our vigilance to ensure our security and to prevent further acts of terror. But we must also redouble our vigilance to preserve our values and the basic rights that make us who we are.")

"The bill before me takes account of the new realities and dangers posed by modern terrorists," the president said at the bill signing. "It will help law enforcement to identify, to dismantle, to disrupt, and to punish terrorists before they strike." Attorney General John Ashcroft made clear his motivation for pushing the changes incorporated in the Patriot Act, telling a conference of U.S. attorneys that they were directed toward "an enemy that lives among us, turning our freedoms into the means of freedom's destruction." As for the possibility of eroding freedom in its name, Ashcroft assured his audience that the bill's solutions were "firmly rooted in the Constitution, secure in historical and judicial precedent, and consistent with the laws passed by the Congress."

There were clearly flaws in the structure of U.S. law enforcement and intelligence efforts pre–September 11 that failed to anticipate the attacks. In this context, the Patriot Act does take several useful steps toward bolstering national security, including provisions to encourage consolidation between law enforcement and intelligence agencies, to beef up border control and airport security, to stiffen visa review procedures and to tighten controls over biological and chemical toxins. Other sections of the act are more troubling, as they give the Executive unprecedented powers of indefinite preventive detention over immigrants, authorize secret searches and surveillance at standards much lower than the Fourth Amendment's mandate of "probable cause," and broaden the definition of domestic terrorism to the extent that it could be applied to the activities of legitimate political protestors.

A few small, eloquent voices have begun to express their concerns, such as small-town librarians who were destroying records daily to protect their borrowers from the FBI's expanded powers to review all book and computer records at libraries. Assistant Attorney General Daniel J. Bryant defended this FBI power in a letter to Senator Patrick Leahy (D-VT), saying, "Any [such] right of privacy is necessarily and inherently limited since . . . the patron is reposing that information in the library or bookstore and assumes the risk that the entity may disclose it to another." Librarians, however, thought otherwise. "We felt strongly that [the destruction of records] had to be done," said Linda Wilson, a librarian in Monterey Park, California. "The government has never had this kind of power before. It feels like Big Brother." As part of his fall 2003 stumping tour to defend the Patriot Act, Ashcroft belittled the "hysteria" of those asserting that "local libraries are under siege by the FBI," claiming that federal investigators have never used their expanded Patriot Act authority to check library records. But don't bother to ask librarians whether or not this is true—they can't tell you. The section of the act that grants the expanded powers also forbids librarians to divulge whether or not they've been contacted by the FBI. "No library can counter" Ashcroft's assertion, said University of North Carolina–Chapel Hill law library associate director Anne Klinefelter, "because they're prevented by law from saying they've been visited by the FBI."

As a sop to critics, Justice Department spokespeople have repeatedly asserted that Section 215 does not target Americans and that searches executed under it remain constrained by a standard of probable cause. This is simply not true; Section 215 merely specifies that searches targeting "a United States person" cannot be conducted "solely upon the basis of activities protected by the First Amendment to the Constitution." And, far from needing to show probable cause of criminal activity, the government must only show that the records are relevant to an ongoing counterterrorism or counterintelligence investigation, a standard that Attorney General Ashcroft himself admitted is "lower than probable cause."

After the law's enactment, Ashcroft assured the Judiciary Committee that "each action taken by the Department of Justice . . . is carefully drawn to target a narrow class of individuals—terrorists. Our legal powers are targeted at terrorists. Our investigation is focused on terrorists. Our prevention strategy targets the terrorist threat." The *New York Times,* however, reported that federal law enforcement officials are increasingly using Patriot Act powers to investigate crimes that have little or nothing to do with terrorism. Despite the attorney general's public statements reiterating the act's narrow focus, the Justice Department has internally emphasized a much broader mandate. A guide to a 2002 Justice Department employee seminar on financial crimes, for instance, said, "We all know that the USA Patriot Act provided weapons for the war on terrorism. But do you know how it affects the war on crime as well?" In a report submitted to Congress in September 2003, the Justice Department admitted that hundreds of cases not related to terrorism have been pursued under the law. The problem is that several of the powers granted law enforcement in the act extend to criminal investigations unrelated to terrorism. Section 218, for example, amending the Foreign Intelligence Surveillance Act (FISA), allows the secret Foreign Intelligence Surveillance Court* to grant warrants for official surveillance as long as gathering foreign intelligence constitutes a "significant purpose" of the surveillance. The use of FISA warrants is particularly open to abuse because they are issued on the basis of secret evidence and are not subject to the Fourth Amendment standard of "probable cause" for search and seizure. The FBI need have no suspicion of criminal activity to obtain a FISA warrant, only a belief that the target of the warrant is an "agent of a foreign power."

Because the FISA standard is so much lower than the Fourth Amendment standard of probable cause, it was never intended for use in domestic criminal investigations. The wording of Section 218, however, allows the FBI recourse to a FISA warrant in criminal investigations, as long as some claim of a foreign intelligence component—related or not to terrorism—can be made. Far from being "firmly rooted in the Constitution," this power raises serious constitutional questions; federal courts have ruled that FISA "is not to be used as an end run around the Fourth Amendment's prohibition of warrantless searches." A Foreign Intelligence Surveillance Court of Review ruling in November 2002 raised this prospect by upholding new surveillance guidelines proposed by Attorney General Ashcroft that would make it easier for Justice Department lawyers to apply for FISA warrants and to share information with criminal prosecutors.

Under the Patriot Act, the amendments to FISA's powers expire on December 31, 2005, but many of the act's other expansions of federal law enforcement power are not subject to similar "sunset" clauses. Section 213 authorizes sneak-and-peek searches, allowing federal agents to conduct secret searches and seize property without first notifying the individual being searched as long as the court issuing the warrant finds "reasonable cause to believe that providing immediate notification of the execution of the warrant may have an adverse result." This may be a useful tool for agents wor-

---

*FBI requests for intelligence warrants must be approved by the Foreign Intelligence Surveillance Court (FISC), a secret court composed of seven rotating judges. Unlike all other courts, records of FISC proceedings are sealed and not available to defendants or their lawyers. The Foreign Surveillance Court of Review is an appellate panel that handles appeals of the cases that come before FISC.

ried about alerting suspects to an imminent search, but to characterize it as anchored in the Constitution and judicial precedent is misleading.

During the congressional debate over the Patriot Act, card-carrying ACLU liberals and anti-big-government conservatives joined forces to protest its particularly broad expansions of executive power. Indeed, the act's most vocal opponents in Congress were conservatives such as Dick Armey (R-TX) and Bob Barr (R-GA), who succeeded in forcing congressional oversight of the FBI's Carnivore e-mail surveillance program. "The Justice Department in the U.S. today, more than any federal agency," Barr warned, "seems to be running amok and out of control."

Ashcroft himself, as a senator, had opposed the FBI's Carnivore e-mail surveillance program over concerns that it would lead to unwarranted invasions of individual privacy. Yet as attorney general he has gone so far as to blame critics for wanting to do away with "virtually all of the new tools Congress has passed and the administration has authorized" in order to return the nation to the "culture of inhibition" that existed before September 11.

This is simply not true. In fact, in 1995 it was the Democrats who sought to expand federal authority to conduct roving wiretaps and broaden the definition of domestic terrorism. Several Republicans, however (including then senator Ashcroft), voted to table that amendment to the Antiterrorism and Effective Death Penalty Act of 1996, with Senator Orrin Hatch (R-UT) then observing, "I do not think we should expand wiretap laws any further. . . . We must ensure that in our response to recent terrorist acts, we do not destroy the freedoms that we cherish."

The Antiterrorism and Effective Death Penalty Act signed into law by President Clinton in reaction to the World Trade Center and Oklahoma City bombings expanded many federal counterterrorism powers. The act criminalized the donation of material or monetary support to terrorist organizations, allowed the government to deny entry to the United States to aliens associated with terrorist organizations, and gave the Department of Justice authority to deport aliens for supporting terrorism based upon secret evidence.

In fact, the key government official who ignored terrorism threats pre–September 11 may be Ashcroft himself. In his budget proposal for fiscal year 2003 sent to the Office of Management and Budget on September 10, 2001, none of the sixty-eight programs for which Ashcroft requested spending increases related directly to counterterrorism efforts. And a memorandum circulated to department heads earlier in that year listed Ashcroft's top seven priorities for the Department of Justice—none of which involved countering terrorism, despite the advice of outgoing National Security Advisor Sandy Berger that the new administration's greatest foreign policy problem would be terrorism. (See chapter 10 for more discussion.)

Notwithstanding concerns about Patriot I, the Bush administration was quietly preparing a sequel for months without seeking input from, or indeed even informing, Congress. Hardly anyone on Capitol Hill knew that the Domestic Security Enhancement Act of 2003 (DSEA), a bill intended to expand upon the Patriot Act, was in the works until a Department of Justice staffer leaked a draft to the Center for Public Integrity in early 2003. The executive branch is admittedly not obligated to share draft proposals with Congress, but at the very least it shouldn't lie about them; in response to direct inquiries, legislators were repeatedly told that no such legislation was in the pipeline, and even Ashcroft himself denied its existence a week before the leak. Senator Patrick Leahy accused Justice Department officials of telling his staff outright lies, adding that the department's secrecy was worrisome, as it suggested that when a formal proposal was presented, "we're supposed to roll over and play dead and just pass it."

As disturbing as the secrecy in which it was concocted is the substance of the proposal itself. In response to the barrage of criticism the draft met once it was leaked to the press, Justice Department spokeswoman Barbara Comstock insisted that "the department's deliberations are always undertaken with the strongest commitment to our Constitution and civil liberties."

Section 501 of the draft act would allow the executive branch to strip American citizens of their citizenship by inference of their association with any group the attorney general alone has designated as terrorist. Section 501 leaves the Justice Department free to exercise its discretion to detain and deport citizens without all the pesky inconvenience of a public trial.

Mindful of the growing public outcry against the Patriot Act and any proposed sequels (more than 150 municipalities and three states have enacted legislation condemning the act as antithetical to the principles of liberty in the Bill of Rights) the Bush administration stepped up its PR machine to defend its expanded powers—and had the temerity to ask for more. Ashcroft hit the road on a sixteen-state, eighteen-city "Patriot Act tour" to drum up support for the act, while President Bush used the two-year anniversary of the September 11 attacks to call for greater federal search and surveillance powers. And as many congressmen were still stewing over the leaked DSEA draft, Senator Orrin Hatch was quietly drafting a revised version focused on expanding federal powers to fight drug-related terrorist activity. The bill, known as the Victory Act, includes some expansions similar to proposals axed by Congress in the debate over the original Patriot Act. Other provisions, such as a broad grant of authority to use administrative subpoenas (which do not require judge approval) to seize records sought in connection with terrorism investigations, if anything, take the disdain for fundamental civil liberties in the most objectionable parts of the Patriot Act to an even higher level.

But then, many of the expanded powers of the Patriot Act and the additional wish list in the draft DSEA are not all specific responses to the extraordinary security concerns raised after September 11. Many are powers that federal law enforcement agencies have long been itching to be granted, despite the FBI's documented history of harassment of legitimate dissent in its 1956–71 COINTELPRO campaign. During the negotiations over the Patriot Act, Representative Armey recalls being told by a Justice Department official, "This isn't new; we've been asking for this for a long time." To which Armey responded, "We've been saying no for a long time." This Republican appreciated a truth about government uttered decades earlier by a congressman during the debate over the 1917 Espionage Act: "Yet we are going ahead with this as a war measure, although when enacted it will be permanent in its operation; and I very much fear that with the best of intention we may place upon the statute books something that will rise to plague us."

Privacy Is Not Partisan

Reversals on privacy began well before September 11. In 2000 William Safire asked candidate George W. Bush the key, pending question about consumer privacy: did he favor (a) an opt-out provision, forcing consumers to affirmatively state they didn't want a seller to distribute his/her name, credit report, medical record, or (b) an opt-in provision, putting the burden on sellers to obtain a consumer's consent? Governor Bush replied "opt in," the proconsumer position. But two years later his Department of Health and Human Services took the opposite stance when it reversed Clinton administration rules requiring that hospitals get a patient's written consent before disclosing sensitive medical information to drug companies, insurers, or other outsiders.

"The protections of the Fourth Amendment are clear. The right to protection from unlawful searches is an indivisible American value. Two hundred years of court decisions have stood in defense of this fundamental right. The state's interest in crime-fighting should never vitiate the citizen's Bill of Rights." These are the words not of the ACLU but of Senator John Ashcroft, who now as attorney general is leading the Bush administration's attempt to expand the federal government's surveillance capabilities to monitor reams of information about ordinary Americans even absent suspicion of criminal activity.

Consider the Bush administration's earlier efforts to peep over the walls of privacy that have traditionally protected Americans from constant government scrutiny. The Pentagon's "Total Information Awareness" initiative was problematic not only because of its blatantly *1984*-ish name and mission statement, which declared the initiative would "imagine, develop, apply, integrate, demonstrate, and transition information technologies, components, and prototype closed-loop information systems that will counter asymmetric threats by achieving total information awareness that is useful for preemption, national security warning, and national security decision making." It was also revealing because of whom the White House had chosen to lead it—Admiral John Poindexter, whose involvement in the Iran-Contra scandal earned him convictions on five felony counts that were overturned later on appeal because of a technicality. Press Secretary Fleischer assured us that "Admiral Poindexter is somebody who this administration thinks is an outstanding American, an outstanding citizen, who has done a very good job in what he has done for our country, serving in the military."

Privacy issues are not a topic that concerns just the paranoid antigovernment fringe. A broad-based coalition of groups from the Eagle Forum and the Free Congress Foundation on the right, to the ACLU and People for the American Way on the left, has coalesced to demand greater oversight and accountability for any executive programs that threaten individual privacy.

These concerns arose over two other big-brother-like programs—the Terror Information and Prevention System (TIPS) and the Computer-Assisted Passenger Pre-Screening System (CAPPS II). Operation TIPS was announced by President Bush in January 2002 to encourage ordinary Americans to get involved in the fight against terrorism. According to the Justice Department, TIPS was to provide "a national system for reporting suspicious and potentially terrorist-related activity," involving "millions of American workers" such as truck drivers, utility repairmen, and postal employees, "who, in the daily course of their work, are in a unique position to see potentially unusual or suspicious activity."

Beyond the likelihood of its unleashing a deluge of irrelevant information on law enforcement officials already struggling with limited resources, civil liberties and privacy advocates decried the initiative as creating a corps of "government-sanctioned Peeping Toms," paving the way for a culture of neighbor-spying-upon-neighbor reminiscent of the excesses of Communist governments. Because such a measure certainly didn't sound as if it came from a small-government, Tenth Amendment Republican like George W. Bush, when Ari Fleischer was asked about TIPS and TIA, all he could offer was that "the President supports . . . efforts to prevent terrorists from engaging in any attacks against the United States, while making certain that the constitutional rights and liberties of the American people are protected. That's what the president is going to make certain what [sic] is done." Evidently Congress did not think that the president was doing enough: led again by libertarians such as Representative Armey, it suspended funding for the TIA project and quashed the TIPS initiative in amendments to the Homeland Security Act.

The proposed CAPPS-II is an airline surveillance system that profiles passengers and assigns them a risk-assessment score that determines whether they are allowed to fly. Privacy-rights advocates such as the Electronic Privacy Information Center have criticized the program not only because of its questionable efficacy but also because of its lack of transparency—that is, although the Transportation Security Administration (TSA) announced the creation of the database in January 2003, they published no information on procedures for appeal or redress if an individual believes that he or she has been inaccurately or unfairly scored.

That is not just a hypothetical problem—there's much anecdotal evidence of bewildered citizens refused permission to fly because their name appeared on an FBI no-fly list. In August 2002, Jan Adams and Rebecca Gordon, two white middle-aged women from San Francisco with a history of peaceful antiwar activism, were barred from boarding a flight from San Francisco to Boston after their names showed up on an FBI blacklist. Arshad Chowdhury, a first-generation South Asian American MBA student at Carnegie Mellon University, was also stopped from boarding his cross-country flight. Even after FBI agents at the airports cleared him, Northwest Airlines refused to allow him to fly. Jayashri Srikantiah, an ACLU attorney, observed, "The problem with this list is that there is no accountability. People don't know why their names were put on this list, and they don't know how to get them off." Adams and Gordon were eventually allowed to fly, but only after their boarding passes were branded with a large crimson "S," signaling that they were to be targeted for special searches at every stop.

Guilt by Ethnicity

On September 25, 2001, Attorney General Ashcroft told the Senate Judiciary Committee, "Just as American rights and freedoms have been preserved throughout previous law enforcement campaigns, they must be preserved throughout this war on terrorism. This Justice Department will never waver in our defense of the Constitution nor relent in our defense of civil rights." Considering the manner in which Ashcroft's Justice Department has approached the investigation of suspected terrorists, one wonders to which previous law enforcement campaigns the attorney general was referring.

Few would argue with Justice Arthur Goldberg's famous observation that the Constitution "is not a suicide pact." However, as Justice Stephen G. Breyer noted in April 2003, "We know that terrorism is a problem. We also know we live in a country that wants to protect basic civil liberties." The challenge is to find an appropriate balance between the two, a challenge which Ashcroft has not met.

The immigration sweeps Ashcroft ordered after September 11 involved more than twelve hundred noncitizens from mainly Muslim countries, arrested for technical violations such as expired student visas—which seems to conflict with his earlier declaration that Justice would go after only suspected terrorists. One, Mohammed Rafiq Butt, a Pakistani who had done nothing wrong except overstay his visa, died of a heart attack in jail after being detained without charge for thirty-three days. Immigration and Naturalization Service (INS) regulations normally mandate that aliens can be held for only forty-eight hours before charges must be filed, but Ashcroft modified the guidelines to allow individuals to be held for a "reasonable time," which for many translated into months, without charges being brought or a suspicion of criminal activity. Even the last INS commissioner, James Zigler, voiced his disapproval of this policy, stating he believes that it is inconsistent with the Immigration and Naturalization Act. The immigration sweeps were carried out under a cloak of extreme secrecy: Two years after September 11, the Justice Department was still refusing to release the names of those detained on immigration charges and material-witness warrants.

The department's excuses for the secrecy appear as disingenuous as they are malleable. One Justice attorney argued before a federal appeals court that releasing the names would provide al Qaeda with clues as to how the United States conducts counterterrorism investigations, while at the same time Ashcroft, in an analysis George Orwell would have admired, maintained that the secrecy was necessary to protect the detainees' privacy. (Keeping them in jail was another way to assure their privacy.) Yet none of the men picked up on immigration violations was charged in connection with the September 11 attacks, and some, contrary to immigration law, were held for months on end. Nevertheless, Ashcroft has continued to maintain that the Justice Department's "efforts have been carefully crafted to avoid infringing on constitutional rights while saving American lives. We have engaged in a deliberate campaign of arrest and detention of law breakers. All persons being detained have the right to contact their lawyers and their families."

The actual experiences of the detainees, however, suggest otherwise. *60 Minutes* interviewed Mr. Hady Omar, an immigrant from Egypt with a wife and child who are U.S. citizens, who was arrested on September 12. Law enforcement officials told Omar he had been apprehended because he purchased an airline ticket from a computer terminal in the same Kinko's where Mohamed Atta, a September 11 hijacker, had earlier purchased a ticket. Omar was kept in solitary confinement in a maximum-security prison for two months, with the lights on twenty-four hours a day. When he asked to call a lawyer, he was told that he could not use the phone. Omar was charged with overstaying a tourist visa (although he was married to an American citizen, had a work permit, and had applied for permanent residency), but he was ultimately released after two and a half months in custody.

Others fared worse. Ali Yaghi, an immigrant from Jordan, also with an American citizen wife and child, had lived in upstate New York for fifteen years and was expecting his green card in the mail. What he got instead was ten months in solitary confinement. Claiming its evidence was secret, the FBI refused to talk to Yaghi's lawyer and finally deported Yaghi to Jordan—without telling his family. "I was not notified of it. Nobody was notified," said his wife Shokriea, adding that her children ask every day when they will see their father again. The Justice Department office charged with investigating the immigration sweeps has been inundated with allegations of comparable civil rights abuses. Not surprisingly, they don't want to discuss them. According to *60 Minutes* correspondent Bob Simon, "We wanted to talk with Attorney General Ashcroft or, in fact, anyone from the Justice department, about what happened to Hady Omar and the other detainees. They declined."

Ashcroft himself guessed that probably "about 97 percent" of the people detained on immigration charges have no relationship to any sort of terrorist activity. The actual number is *100 percent*—for in the summer of 2003, the department finally acknowledged that no one in its initial sweeps had been linked to al Qaeda or charged with any terrorist activities.

Is the harassment and detention of hundreds of members of an immigrant minority warranted in order to find the one or handful who may be linked to terrorists? It's an interesting moral question. On a purely utilitarian calculus, if some detentions and questioning could plausibly stop an attack of the magnitude of September 11, such actions could be justified. But what if there was only a one in one thousand chance—or one in a million—that mass detentions could deter some terrorist event? What if the planned attack was of a much smaller scale? And what weight should be accorded to fundamental principles of justice, rather than pure utility? Such questions point out the flaws of a policy that targets people according to their ethnic or religious background rather than according to a suspicion of criminal activity. Racial profiling of course *could* stop criminal activity but is no more justified when applied to Muslim men by the INS than when applied to black men by local police.

Before September 11, President Bush himself expressed his disapproval of such policies. "Earlier today, I asked John Ashcroft, the attorney general, to develop specific recommendations to end racial profiling," he said in February 2001. "It's wrong, and we will end it in America." In fact, during a 2000 campaign debate against Al Gore, Bush specifically protested the profiling of Arab-American men, saying, "Arab-Americans are racially profiled in what's called secret evidence. People are stopped, and we got to do something about that."

In his 192-page report in June 2003, Department of Justice inspector general Glenn A. Fine found a massive program of preventive detention where those incarcerated were presumed guilty until the FBI found them innocent, a bureaucratic process often taking months. While the law narrowly allows for such imprisonment if there's a specific showing that a suspect may flee the jurisdiction, in this case the 762 detainees languished in jail for months in order to send a message about future immigration policy.

Fine's report documents that many of their families were either not told they were being held or where they were held, and many were either denied counsel or given the names of lawyers with incorrect phone numbers, or lawyers who had already said they wouldn't represent these immigrants. Yet when department lawyers raised objections about the legality of some of these tactics, they were ignored by senior officials.

When the media sought comment from Ashcroft about these devastating findings by his own inspector general, who could not be attacked as unpatriotically undermining the war on terrorism, Justice Department spokeswoman Barbara Comstock expressed vindication.

> The Inspector General report is fully consistent with what courts have ruled over and over—that our actions are fully within the law and necessary to protect the American people. . . . We make no apologies for finding every legal way possible to protect the American public from further terrorist attacks.

A few days later, Attorney General Ashcroft finally responded, saying with a shrug, "We make no apologies." Nor did he alter or apologize for an unprecedented immigration policy, announced just two months earlier, that the AG on his own could detain refugees without any specific findings if he determines their release might endanger the national security, a policy first directed at arriving Haitians in late 2002.

Under this new policy and the policy incarcerating 762 detainees, there are also some 680 accused "enemy combatants" being held without access to lawyers or charges at Guantánamo Bay and in conditions that have led to several suicide attempts. Further, there are some four thousand other Arab or Muslim foreign nationals detained after trying to register under INS rules. In short, more than five thousand Arab nationals have been held in preventive detention in the United States, causing enormous distress and anger in the targeted communities without any real law enforcement results to show for it.

The September 11 sweeps were just the beginning of the Bush administration's consistent undermining of the standards of our criminal justice system when it comes to terrorist suspects, establishing what the *Washington Post* has called an "alternative legal system." By an executive order issued on November 13, 2001, President Bush decreed that individuals suspected of terrorist activity could be detained and tried under military authority.

Since the Justice Department hasn't even released the names of the hundreds of "suspects" detained after September 11, it's not impossible to envision a scenario under the Cheney rationale where someone is arrested, thrown into military confinement and held there indefinitely, brought to trial before a kangaroo court on secret evidence, and incarcerated indefinitely or even executed—all out of the public's sight and away from judicial supervision.

Robert Rubin, the legal director of the Lawyers Committee for Human Rights, notes, "If we want to challenge secret trials of dissidents in Peru or China, we obviously have lost that moral footing when we treat our own people the same way." Cheney's assertion that suspected terrorists do not deserve the same safeguards as other "criminals" skillfully but rhetorically conflates "suspects" with "criminals" and therefore leads even conservatives like William Safire to castigate Bush for "suspending, with a stroke of his pen, habeas corpus for twenty million people."

Calling upon military tribunals to try suspected terrorists caught during conflict overseas may be necessary, but doing so on American soil is inimical to liberty and of doubtful constitutionality. It was misleading for Ashcroft to defend the president's use of military tribunals as secure in judicial and historical precedent when he said, "For centuries, Congress has recognized this authority and the Supreme Court has never held that any Congress may limit it." Although a military commission did try the conspirators behind Lincoln's assassination, the Supreme Court issued a stern ruling in 1866 declaring the use of military tribunals to try those suspected of antigovernment activity unconstitutional even in wartime, as long as the civilian courts were still operational. Terrorists as infamous as Sheik Omar Abdel Rahman, the suspected architect of the 1993 World Trade Center bombing, have been successfully tried in regular criminal courts without damaging national security interests.

So far, the Bush administration has turned to methods other than a military tribunal for suspected terrorists (although the president designated six suspects as eligible for trial-by-tribunal in the summer of 2003). During his 2003 State of the Union address, President Bush informed the nation that more than three thousand suspects have been arrested in other countries, and that "many others have met a different fate. Let's put it this way, they are no longer a problem to the United States and our friends and allies." The president's jaunty comment was met with a rousing cheer, but the thinly veiled implication that the leader of the world's only hyperpower is publicly sanctioning assassinations should be repugnant to a country that goes to war to uphold the rule of law.

Such a might-makes-right approach was also evident in the Bush administration's circumvention of the Geneva Conventions by simply declaring captured suspected terrorists to be "unlawful combatants." But once we implicitly and impatiently dismissed the Geneva Conventions as annoying technicalities, it certainly didn't help our case in the court of world opinion when we accused Iraq of mistreating American prisoners under the same conventions.

Speak No Evil

President Bush and his Attorney General John Ashcroft as a team make a sort of reverse Wizard of Oz—here the innocuous, charming wizard is presented to the public to hide the fact that behind the curtain lies a fire-exhaling monster reducing fundamental freedoms to ashes with a single smoldering breath.

At first glance, Attorney General John Ashcroft appears an unlikely figure to be leading a crusade to expand executive powers. His past record places him, as indicated, with religious and libertarian conservatives traditionally distrustful of a powerful federal government. Since September 11, however, Ashcroft has presided over the greatest expansion of federal law enforcement powers in memory, seeking a fundamental shift in the legal system from the investigation and punishment of past crimes to the prevention of future ones, something like a real-life version of Tom Cruise running his Office of Pre-Crime in *Minority Report*.

As Ashcroft was overseeing the restriction of civil liberties of Americans in the name of security, he was also questioning the patriotism of any who challenged these policies, saying to the Senate Judiciary Committee in December 2001: "To those who pit Americans against immigrants, and citizens against non-citizens; to those who scare peace-loving people with phantoms of lost liberty; my message is this: Your tactics only aid terrorists—for they erode our national unity and diminish our resolve. They give ammunition to America's enemies, and pause to America's friends. They encourage people of good will to remain silent in the face of evil." Some of this "with us/against us" rhetoric coming out of Washington has fostered a new intolerance in a number of communities, as a kind of informal patriotism-police discourages bona fide criticism of Bush or his policies.

In July 2002, a San Francisco man got into an argument with several acquaintances at his gym over President Bush's conduct of the War on Terror. Agreeing that "Osama bin Laden is an asshole," he added, "Bush is a bigger asshole than bin Laden will ever be because he bombs people all over the world for profits." Several days later, the man was treated to an unannounced house call by the FBI. Two young agents dropped by his apartment to conduct an impromptu interview, informing him, "We've heard that you've been discussing President Bush, oil, Osama bin Laden..." before reassuring him that "you do, of course, have freedom of speech." The San Francisco man is not an immigrant. He is not a Muslim, or even an Arab. He is an American citizen named Barry Reingold, whose family fled Germany and Russia.

Stories like Reingold's may be the exception, but they are becoming more frequent. From the Chinese American college student who was visited by the FBI for saying the word *bomb* over the phone when talking about a video game, to the Jewish-American woman threatened with an FBI subpoena because of her involvement with the peaceful protest group Women in Black, to the upstate New Yorker arrested at a large private mall for wearing a T-shirt saying "Peace Is Good," more Americans, it seems, are being harassed for participating in legitimate First Amendment activity.

The Bush administration's response to September 11 has thus far not sunk anywhere near the depths of the Palmer or McCarthy eras. But as noted New York University law professor Stephen Schulhofer has said, "To measure performance by these standards is to set the bar terribly low; these were sorry historical embarrassments." It was President Teddy Roosevelt who set the bar of speech during a crisis at the proper level, with a sentiment that Ashcroft would do well to remember. During the First World War he said, "To announce that there must be no criticism of the president, or that we are to stand by the president, right or wrong, is not only unpatriotic and servile, but is morally treasonable to the American people."

Georgetown law professor David Cole has closely studied the Bush administration's legal response to September 11 and terrorism. The threat we face is real, concluded Cole, yet the response is one TR would not have approved:

> With the exception of the right to bear arms, one would be hard pressed to name a single constitutional liberty that the Bush administration has not overridden in the name of protecting our freedom. Privacy has given way to Internet tracking and plans to recruit a corps of 11 million private snoopers. . . . Physical liberty and habeas corpus survive only until the President decides someone is a "bad guy." Property is seized without notice, without a hearing, and on the basis of secret evidence. Equal protection has fallen prey to ethnic profiling. Conversations with a lawyer may be monitored without a warrant or denied altogether. . . . And the right to a public hearing upon arrest exists only at the Attorney General's sufferance.

But if Ashcroft has been contemptuous of First Amendment rights, he's been passionate in his support of the death penalty and the Second Amendment "right" to bear arms. Ashcroft believes that expanding the death penalty will deter terrorists, logic that probably would have surprised September 11 hijackers and other suicide-homicide bombers. And despite Supreme Court decisions affirming the "right" to bear arms for "well regulated militia" but not individual citizens, he at least refused to let the FBI check its audit logs of gun purchases to determine if any of those "suspected terrorists" had recently purchased a firearm. This is a strange decision from someone who has voiced his intention to mobilize all the resources of the Justice Department "toward one single, overarching, and overriding objective: to save innocent lives from further acts of terrorism." Apparently, the attorney general loves gun owners even more than he loathes terrorists.

6. Mismanaged Health Care

Privatization versus Patients

★

"We will make prescription drugs available and affordable for every senior who needs them."

—George W. Bush, in a televised advertisement
from the 2000 presidential campaign

A national poll conducted in 2002 found that only 17 percent of those questioned believed that the nation's health care system "works reasonably well" whereas 80 percent believed either that "we need to completely rebuild the system" or that the health system needs "fundamental changes." Americans' dissatisfaction isn't surprising. People who have private health insurance are seeing their benefits erode and out-of-pocket payments rise. Growing numbers of full-time workers are finding themselves among the nation's more than 43 million uninsured, and nearly 75 million Americans lack health insurance over a two-year period—one out of every three non-elderly Americans. Deteriorating finances are forcing hospitals to reduce staffing levels, Medicare premiums are rising at double-digit rates, and woe to anyone who has to pay for his prescription medications entirely out of pocket—every year since 1998, prescription-drug spending has increased by at least 15 percent.

President Bush's ℞ for these ills is less government and greater reliance on the private sector. The government's function "is not to centralize, nor is government's role to control the delivery of medicine," he told a medical college audience in February 2002. In his 2003 State of the Union address, he said that the problem of high medical costs and the uninsured "will not be solved with a nationalized health care system that dictates coverage and rations care."

Of course, many Americans already have their health coverage dictated and their care strictly rationed—not by government but by the same for-profit managed care insurers Bush says should play an even greater role in the nation's health care system. But among the consequences of the polemical piñata of "less government" are weak protections for personal health information privacy and few federal patients' rights laws on the books.

President Bush's simple "blame government first" approach and reliance on the private sector to fix the health care crisis shouldn't surprise anyone. He has never in his career focused on issues involving health care, while health service companies, health insurers, and the drug industry have been big sources of funding for Bush's campaigns and for those of his Republican colleagues. In instance after instance on health issues, when presented with policy options, George W. Bush has favored companies over patients.

Medicare

President Bush has proposed to "expand" Medicare coverage, "improve its services," "strengthen its financing" and "give seniors more control over the health care they receive." These were welcome words to the millions of older Americans struggling with rising treatment copays, escalating deductibles, and out-of-pocket drug expenses. But of course they were just that: words.

Prescription-drug coverage is the Medicare expansion many seniors would like to see most. Four out of ten seniors, including one-third of Medicare beneficiaries, still receive no help with their drug bills. Older Americans with drug coverage are experiencing declining annual benefit maximums and rapidly rising copayments. According to a 2003 study by the Project Hope Center for Health Affairs, only the Japanese pay more than Americans for brand-name prescription drugs.

Because Bush and his strategists understand the political importance of this issue, he was quick to take a position on it during the first presidential debate: "Let me make sure seniors hear me loud and clear. . . . All seniors will be covered. All poor seniors will have their prescription drugs paid for." When Vice President Gore interjected—"Let me—let me call your attention to the key word there. He said all 'poor' seniors"—Bush reassured viewers, "Wait a minute, all seniors are covered under prescription drugs in my plan."

During the third presidential debate, Bush asserted that, "step one [is] to make sure prescription drugs is [sic] more affordable for seniors" is "to have prescription drugs as an integral part of Medicare once and for all." Resonating with "compassionate conservatism," he said, in his 2003 State of the Union address, "Medicare is the binding commitment of a caring society. We must renew that commitment by giving seniors access to preventive medicine and new drugs that are transforming health care in America." More specifically he added: "Seniors happy with the current Medicare system should be able to keep their coverage just the way it is. And just like you—

the members of Congress, and your staffs, and other federal employees—all seniors should have the choice of a health care plan that provides prescription drugs."

Fine words, but the fine print did not support them. According to Bush's actual plan, to get any meaningful drug coverage, seniors would have had to leave traditional Medicare and join a private managed care plan. So if you loved your own physician, you faced a choice of the right doctor or affordable drugs, but not both, a choice the president did not explain, or even imply. Democrats also blasted the plan for failing to cover all Medicare beneficiaries. Influential Republicans like Senator Olympia Snowe (ME), Senator Charles Grassley (IA), and Representative Billy Tauzin (LA) publicly voiced similar concerns.

In response to the criticism, the administration released a slightly modified plan a few months later. Seniors who chose to remain in traditional Medicare would now be offered a prescription-drug discount card and protection from "high out-of-pocket prescription drug expenses"—"high" being defined as more than $7,000 a year. Seniors spend on average $2,400 a year on prescription drugs—the cost of arthritis, high cholesterol, and high-blood pressure drugs typically run $1,200 to $1,500 each—but since most seniors do not spend enough to hit the $7,000 threshold, Bush's plan offered them nothing. So Bush's debate comeback to Gore promising coverage to "all seniors" was proved false. And low-income beneficiaries would get a mere $600 annual prescription-drug subsidy.

Medicare beneficiaries who wanted greater drug coverage than this would have to switch either to "Enhanced Medicare," which would provide a standardized drug benefit but require paying an additional premium and signing up for a private managed care plan, or to "Medicare Advantage," which though not requiring an additional premium would be based on the current private Medicare+Choice plans, with no guarantee of drug coverage.

Medicare+Choice has been a bust. Though many of its plans cover drugs, 89 percent of Medicare beneficiaries have chosen to stay with traditional Medicare rather than switch. Marilyn Moon, an economist and Medicare expert with the Urban Institute, reports that organizations contracting with Medicare to provide counseling and to inform Medicare beneficiaries "find a disturbing pattern of denials of care" with Medicare+Choice plans: "Patients are often denied access to care from specialists outside the network who have particular expertise in a given procedure."

The private plans offered through "Enhanced Medicare" would similarly have restricted members to limited rosters of participating physicians, labs, and hospitals; imposed referral requirements for specialists; and charged substantial copays. The list of covered drugs would be much more limited than in traditional Medicare. In response, the administration argued that competition among private plans and with traditional Medicare would help ensure quality and efficiency. But with no standardization of coverage and benefits in either "Enhanced Medicare" or "Medicare Advantage," beneficiaries would find comparison shopping among plans next to impossible. And without comparison shopping, there can be no competition.

As in so many other areas, the Bush administration was satisfied with good rhetoric rather than good results—that is, the language of "choice" and "affordable prescription drugs for seniors" *is* the intended result, not necessarily an effective plan actually taking a real bite out of seniors' drug bills. In Bush's 2003 State of the Union speech, the president said he was committing $400 billion more to Medicare over the next decade, mostly to fund the drug coverage. Health and Human Services secretary Tommy Thompson told reporters shortly after, "Four hundred billion dollars, you have to admit, is a lot more than what seniors have right now. Because right now they have nothing in Medicare to pay for drugs."

True, something was better than nothing. But (a) Marilyn Moon estimates that between 2002 and 2012, Medicare beneficiaries will spend more than four times this amount on prescription drugs, and that giving Medicare beneficiaries drug coverage comparable to what federal employees receive—as the president implied in his 2003 State of the Union address—would actually cost $900 billion over the next decade, and (b) Bush's promised $400 billion would be largely offset by hundreds of billions of dollars of *cuts* in nondrug Medicare spending, to be achieved in large part by persuading seniors to switch to private plans. Secretary Thompson underlined the importance of the administration's privatization plans when he told journalists that the drug plan "is dessert, this is what everyone is talking about," but if Congress passes only a prescription-drug plan, the momentum for longer-term Medicare (market-based) reform would be jeopardized.

Bush's Medicare plan, however, was not dessert but the equivalent of several entrées for pharmaceutical manufacturers. If drugs were simply added to the list of traditional Medicare benefits, the government could negotiate substantial drug-price discounts. Since Medicare beneficiaries account for 43 percent of the nation's drug costs, the feds could have driven a hard bargain on behalf of patients. But providing drug coverage through a large group of private health plans shifts the negotiating advantage to drug makers, giving them billions of dollars in extra sales annually without fear of heavy discounting.

Robert Hayes, president of the Medicare Rights Center, a national Medicare advocacy organization, concluded that the administration's Medicare drug plan "appears to have been written by the pharmaceutical industry." The industry's substantial campaign contributions to Bush and the Republicans certainly gave them access. The Bush presidential campaign received at least a half-million dollars from pharmaceutical firms, more than four times the amount Al Gore received. Rather than take any chances, the pharmaceutical industry then bankrolled $625,000 of the estimated $17 million cost of the inaugural celebrations. Meanwhile, during the 1999–2000 election cycle, 76 percent of the pharmaceutical industry's $20 million in direct campaign contributions to candidates and party committees went to the GOP. Health services companies and HMOs also gave $8.2 million during the 1999–2000 election cycle, with 60 percent of that sum going to Republicans.

Ultimately, though, the Bush administration's Medicare plans were driven by its uncompromising free-market ideology, one that seeks to privatize as many government programs as possible. Representative Sherrod Brown (D-OH), who tracks the drug and health care industries as closely as any member of Congress, says the administration is "carrying out a twenty-year intellectual jihad against Medicare with false claims that it is financially unsustainable and going bankrupt. The administration has been steadily weakening the program from within—and is frankly trying to make Medicare less attractive by cutting out outreach services and basically demolishing what was generally a good customer service apparatus."

By mid-2003 the Bush administration was painted into a corner. Strong public support for giving traditional Medicare beneficiaries a real drug plan forced Bush to back down and support a Senate proposal that provided the same drug benefits for *all* Medicare beneficiaries, whether they switched to a private plan or not. Still, as the pharmaceutical industry insisted, instead of simply adding drug benefits to the existing Medicare program, prescription medication benefits would be provided through new "drug-only" plans run by private insurers. Such an arrangement assures drug makers that no single government drug plan covering all beneficiaries could apply its enormous market clout to dictate lower prices. To curb Medicare costs and lure traditional Medicare beneficiaries, the compromise Senate plan also offered private "Medicare Advantage" plans—an array of health maintenance organizations, preferred provider organizations, and other insurance plans—that include some additional coverage such as preventive services. But even with sweeteners, the Congressional Budget Office estimated that the private plans would attract only 2 percent of the nation's 40 million Medicare beneficiaries. Not surprisingly, most older Americans remain very reluctant to trust their health to managed care organizations and private insurance.

While this Bush alternative did represent progress, it split leading Democrats into those who thought its half loaf worthwhile (Senator Edward M. Kennedy) and those who didn't (Senator Hillary Clinton). Objectors pointed out that it would still leave millions of seniors each with thousands of dollars in prescription-drug bills. Drug coverage would entail a $35-a-month premium and a $275 annual deductible, and would pay only half of a senior's drug costs up to $4,500. Between $4,500 and $5,800, coverage would cease, leaving a "doughnut hole" just at the point where many seniors need help the most, and would resume picking up a portion of "catastrophic" outlays above $5,800.

The Drug Industry

Bush's Medicare proposal demonstrated the enormous power the pharmaceutical industry wields in Washington, especially among Republicans. The industry's trade group, the Pharmaceutical Research and Manufacturers Association (PhRMA), runs one of the capital's most effective lobbying operations. In 2003, PhRMA budgeted $121 million for trying to win friends and influence legislative and regulatory enemies; in 2004 it was expected to spend 23 percent more. Cozy relations between the industry and the administration have been cemented by hires like Mitch Daniels, previously Eli Lilly's vice president for strategy and policy, and, until May 2003, Bush's director of the Office of Management and Budget. In July 2001 President Bush nominated Michael J. Astrue, a pharmaceutical industry lawyer, to head the Food and Drug Administration. But Astrue's appointment was blocked by Senator Edward M. Kennedy (D-MA), who chaired the Senate committee that would consider the nomination, because he was too close to the industry. In a letter to the president, Kennedy and six fellow Democrats wrote, "It would be unprecedented for the commissioner to be appointed from an industry regulated by the FDA." But having sent Harvey Pitt to the Securities and Exchange Commission, and the Ken Lay–recommended Patrick Wood III to the Federal Energy Regulatory Commission, such a choice was hardly unusual for George W. Bush.

GENERIC DRUGS

Once a brand-name drug's patent expires, generic drug makers are free to manufacture and sell the same formulation. Because the resulting competition causes prices to tumble and brand-name profits to decline, drug makers of brand names naturally guard their patents fiercely.

Generic drug makers need FDA permission before they can sell a generic version of a brand-name drug. So manufacturers can—and frequently do—sue to prevent their doing so. Filing such a lawsuit automatically delays the generic rollout for thirty months, giving the brand-name drug company time to file a new patent that only slightly alters the drug, typically in a meaningless way.

In an October 2002 Rose Garden presentation President Bush announced that a new regulation his administration was proposing would keep the brand-name drug makers at bay and give the generic makers a fair shot. The enacted regulation now prevents manufacturers from piling patent on top of patent and thirty-month stay on top of thirty-month stay. "Our message to brand-name manufacturers is clear," Bush said. "You deserve the fair rewards of your research and development. You do not have the right to keep generic drugs off the market for frivolous reasons." He continued, "By this action we will reduce the cost of prescription drugs in America by billions of dollars and ease a financial burden for many citizens, especially our seniors."

Again, check the fine print. The regulation would not permit generic drug companies to seek prompt court decisions on frivolous new patents filed by brand-name companies, which the organization Families USA called, "an effective tool to prevent the industry's abusive, anti-competitive practices." The regulation also failed to address the widespread practice by brand-name manufacturers of paying generic makers to keep the generic version off the market.

The administration's proposed regulation, moreover, proved to be considerably weaker than a bill to stop brand-name drug makers' antigenerics practices that had passed the Senate only a few months earlier, a bill that would have prohibited the payoffs and not permitted even a single thirty-month stay. The Congressional Budget Office estimated that the Senate bill would save consumers twice as much as the administration's regulation.

THE "PRICE CONTROLS" STRAW MAN

A report released by the Department of Health and Human Services (HHS) in 2002 illustrated the parallelism of White House and industry concerns about the remote possibility that someone in government may somehow try to rein in the galloping increases in prescription-drug prices. The report discussed the threat of "the potentially serious consequences to medical innovation and overall health posed by attempts to contain drug expenditures by implementing government controls." In fact, the department raised a nonissue because there is no federal legislation pending to impose such controls.

The HHS report merely repeated the PhRMA line, laid out by its president, Alan Holmer, on National Public Radio, "Believe me, if we impose price controls . . . and if you reduce the R&D . . . it's going to harm my kids and it's going to harm those millions of Americans who have life-threatening conditions." In fact, for the average drug introduction, manufacturers spend at least as much on marketing and advertising as on research, according to the Center for Medical Consumers. A report by Families USA, using information provided by the SEC, found that eight of the nine largest publicly traded pharmaceutical companies spent two to three times more on advertising, marketing, and administration than they did on research and development.

There are more examples of the Bush administration acceding to drug industry concerns, including a 70 percent decline in enforcement by the FDA against false and misleading pharmaceuticals advertising; a proposed FDA rule that would allow drug companies to make claims about effectiveness for purposes for which it was not approved; and the administration's plan to roll back a rule requiring manufacturers to conduct pediatric studies on new drugs and to help avoid underdosing and overdosing by requiring manufacturers to place information gained from the studies in the drug's label. (In April 2002 the FDA reversed its position on the pediatric-drug rule but stated that the rule still needed to be "updated.")

Patients' Rights and HMOs

During the third presidential debate, Governor Bush said, "You know, I support a national patients' bill of rights, Mr. Vice President. And I want all people covered. I don't want the law to supersede good law like we've got in Texas." Yet the following year, as president, Bush supported a House bill that threatened to do exactly that. Frank M. Fitzgerald, Michigan's Republican insurance commissioner, warned, "The House bill appears to preempt all state internal and external review laws. If that becomes law, I would have a real concern about the ability of people to get an appropriate and adequate review of adverse decisions by HMOs."

George W. Bush's record of opposing effective patients' rights laws stretches back to his first term as governor, when he vetoed the Texas Patient Protection Act. Passed with only a few no votes, the act contained many commonsense measures that were being adopted in other states, such as a fair and prompt process to appeal coverage denials and a requirement to apply a "prudent person" standard for determining if an HMO has to cover an emergency room visit. Although Bush argued the act would have increased health care costs too severely, it was enacted over his veto.

As president, Bush nonetheless repeated his assertion that he supports a patients' bill of rights for dealings with HMOs. In July 2001 he went so far as to list "patient rights" as one of three priorities for his administration when Congress went back into session that year. And he's taken occasional public swipes against HMOs, as when he said in his 2003 State of the Union address, "Instead of bureaucrats and trial lawyers and HMOs, we must put doctors and nurses and patients back in charge of American medicine."

But again, the legislation he actually backs would substantially limit, not expand, patients' rights. For instance, during the 2000 campaign Bush said that when he was governor he had supported a new Texas law—the first in the nation—allowing state court lawsuits against HMOs for harm done when they deny medically necessary care. During the third presidential debate on October 17, he bragged, "We're one of the first states that said you can sue an HMO for denying you proper coverage. . . . If I'm the president . . . people will be able to take their HMO insurance company to court. That's what I've done in Texas and that's the kind of leadership style I'll bring to Washington."

Leadership for patients' rights? Actually, when faced with a veto-proof 28-to-3 vote in the Texas Senate in favor of the bill and a 121-to-20 Texas House vote against his weaker alternatives, Governor Bush acceded to the right-to-sue measure's becoming law without his signature after trying to kill it. After being sworn in as president, Bush stated in no uncertain terms that lawsuits against HMOs should be heard only in federal courts, where damage payouts are much more limited than in state courts: "I will not support a federal law that subjects employers to new multiple lawsuits in fifty different states." In February 2001, speaking against the Kennedy-McCain patients' bill of rights legislation that allows state court lawsuits, he declared, "We can't have a patients' bill of rights that encourages and invites all kinds of lawsuits, because the ultimate effect will be to run up the cost of business, particularly for small businesses."

Bush was so opposed to state court lawsuits that on June 21, 2001, he vowed to veto the Kennedy-McCain bill if it ever came to his desk. The White House claimed the measure would lead to an "explosive growth" in lawsuits and that it "could cause at least 4 to 6 million Americans to lose health coverage." Of course, the actual record of state court lawsuits against HMOs in the ten states that now permit them reveals that Bush's claim is nonsense. Texas, for instance, saw just fifteen such lawsuits between 1997, when the law was enacted, and 2001. Other states have had similar experiences.

The president also complained that the Kennedy-McCain bill "circumvents the independent medical review process in favor of litigation." Again, this is false. The bill requires a patient to complete the review process before suing unless he has suffered "irreparable harm." In addition, Bush clearly exaggerated when he claimed that Kennedy-McCain would subject employers to "frequent litigation in state and federal court." In fact, employers are required to pay damages if and only if they directly participate in decisions that cause injury or death.

The Bush administration preferred a very different sort of patients' rights bill. An eleventh-hour compromise in August 2001 arranged by the White House and Representative Charlie Norwood (R-GA) allowed state court lawsuits but required much more restrictive federal rules to be applied instead in malpractice cases. The compromise measure also created a special, greater burden of proof, called a "rebuttable presumption," that plaintiffs would have to meet. The House bill, moreover, threatened to supersede states that allow state court lawsuits against HMOs using state court rules. The Bush-Norwood bill also threatened to supersede laws in forty states that require HMOs to arrange for an independent medical review of their decisions to deny coverage for a requested treatment or procedure.

As of fall 2003 the House and Senate still hadn't agreed on a compromise patients' rights bill, although a federal appeals court ruling in February 2003 did allow plaintiffs to sue HMOs in state courts.

Medical Malpractice Insurance

Bush's close relations with tort-reform forces date back to his gubernatorial campaigns. Capping court awards was one of the four issues he focused on during his 1994 campaign and was included at the insistence of advisor Karl Rove. In *Bush's Brain*, their book on Rove, authors James Moore and Wayne Slater note that "tort reform didn't have the same public appeal as education or crime, but it was an issue most important to Rove's business clients and potential contributors." "I sort of talked him into that one," Rove indiscreetly once admitted of a policy that nicely dovetailed with another Rove goal of unlinking Democrats from their donor base (trial lawyers) in order to defund them.

An analysis of Bush's gubernatorial campaign fund-raising by Texans for Public Justice established that Rove was right about the issue's campaign contribution potential. The group reported that "tort-dodging individuals and PACs, which seek to limit the liability of businesses that injure consumers, workers or communities" contributed $4.1 million (15 percent) of Bush's war chest during his two campaigns for governor.

Convinced of the issue's power in 1994, he pushed it again during his re-election campaign, and, as president, Bush continues to repeat the refrain that "excessive" medical malpractice lawsuit payouts are dramatically increasing the cost of health care. In Scranton, Pennsylvania, in early 2003, he said, "Excessive jury awards will continue to drive up insurance costs, will put good doctors out of business or run them out of your community and will hurt communities like Scranton. . . . There are too many lawsuits in America, and there are too many lawsuits filed against doctors and hospitals without merit." The year before, Bush told a cheering audience of 2,300 crowded into Madison Central High School's gym in Madison, Mississippi, "In this state, the lawsuit industry is devastating the practice of medicine. Too many frivolous lawsuits in this state have been filed against doctors. That's a fact. And too many jury awards are out of control."

Actually, it's not a fact. While there are no doubt publicized cases of very high punitive awards—and people legitimately can differ on his proposal to cap awards for pain and suffering at $250,000 and limit the period of time patients have to sue—his "facts" are largely fictions:

> ✳ "Out-of-control" juries are not contributing to higher malpractice insurance rates. According to the federal National Practitioner Data Bank, from 1991 to 2001 malpractice lawsuit payouts grew an average of 6.2 percent annually. *Business Week* noted that this was "almost exactly the rate of medical inflation" during this period, and they dismissed as "a myth" the claim that "[R]unaway jury awards are forcing insurers to raise rates." An analysis of Pennsylvania medical malpractice awards after Bush's Scranton speech found that, from 2000 to 2002, the number of jury awards of $1 million or more in Pennsylvania actually *dropped* by 50 percent (from 44 to 22) while the overall amount of these awards *decreased* by more than 75 percent (from $415 million to $93 million). According to the National Practitioner Data Bank, the total number of malpractice claims paid in Pennsylvania from 1995 through 2001 rose only from 957 to 1,049.
>
> *Business Week* in 2003 also contradicted the view that "courts

are clogged with an exploding number of claims," pointing out that "claims against the industry have actually been flat since 1996."

* Rising malpractice insurance *costs* are rarely "putting good doctors out of business," as Bush claims. Malpractice insurance costs amount to only 3.2 percent of the average physician's revenues. From 1987 to 2002, the amount spent on medical malpractice insurance increased 52 percent, less than half the 113 percent increase in medical services inflation over this period. A few days after President Bush made his dramatic statement about the "devastating" impact of lawsuits on medical practice in Mississippi, the *Biloxi Sun Herald* reported that medical practice in the state was in fact expanding: "Medical groups have claimed that doctors are fleeing Mississippi, relocating to states with more stable legal climates. In fact, the state has gained 564 doctors over the past five years. . . . Only four states have grown faster in physician population." More recently, Congress's General Accounting Office carefully investigated the widely publicized claims that doctors are leaving or retiring in states that do not cap court awards for pain and suffering. Its report, released in August 2003, concluded, "The problems we confirmed were limited to scattered, often rural, locations and in most cases providers identified long-standing factors in addition to malpractice pressures that affected the availability of services."

* Judges already can and do dismiss "frivolous" lawsuits brought "without merit." That's how the legal system works, as when in 2002 a New York City judge dismissed a highly publicized lawsuit against McDonald's brought by a teenager who blamed her obesity on eating too many Big Macs. Arthur Levin, president of the Center for Medical Consumers, observes that what those who complain of "frivolous" lawsuits seem to be saying is that any lawsuit in which there exists doubt about whether the defendant was wrong is "frivolous."

Not only do tort-reform assertions evaporate under the heat of scrutiny, but Bush's proposals would, if enacted, affirmatively hurt tens of thousands of people who experience grievous losses because a doctor or hospital has made a preventable mistake. "Think of it this way. You are a woman twenty years old and you expect to live to the average life expectancy for females of seventy-seven. Let's say you are going in for surgery and they make a terrible mistake with anesthesia, leaving you brain damaged and permanently in a wheelchair. A two hundred fifty thousand dollar cap is equivalent to only twelve dollars a day for the rest of your life," says Frank Clemente, head of Public Citizen's Congress Watch in Washington, D.C. When court awards are effectively limited to "economic damages"—consisting of monetary losses such as lost lifetime earnings and support—"pain and suffering" compensation may be nearly all that's left for survivors of people without marketable value, such as retired people, homemakers, and infants.

And with the cost of investigating and bringing a medical malpractice case often exceeding one hundred thousand dollars, many victims would find it difficult to retain a lawyer to try a case when the "pain and suffering" award is capped at only two hundred fifty thousand dollars, which of course is exactly what the medical interests that gave $4.1 million to George W. Bush in the 1990s want.

So what *does* cause the high medical malpractice insurance premiums that have become so controversial? Along with so many other investors, insurance companies have taken a beating on their investments in recent years, while the low interest rates insurers earn on investments have also hurt. These investments compose much of the reserve funds insurers are required to maintain. When investment returns were soaring a decade ago, insurers engaged in ardent price competition. But now they are shoring up these funds by raising premiums.

There are also undeniably high rates of medical malpractice and errors. A study by the National Academy of Sciences released in 2000 concluded that up to 98,000 people unnecessarily die in hospitals every year because of deficiencies in quality of care and safety. The Harvard Medical Practice Study, issued in the early 1990s, found that at least 95,000 people die and hundreds of thousands are injured in hospitals each year in some part as the result of preventable medical errors. Nonetheless, in 2002 President Bush proposed a 16 percent reduction in the budget of the Agency for Healthcare Research and Quality, the agency that focuses on reducing medical errors.

The cap on lawsuit pain and suffering awards, which in 2003 passed the House of Representatives with Bush's support, covers cases brought not only against doctors and hospitals but also against insurance companies and makers of pharmaceuticals and medical devices. When Bush focuses all his public remarks on how "out-of-control verdicts" are putting "good doctors out of business," listeners can imagine TV doctors like Marcus Welby and the *ER* staff being forced to hang up their stethoscopes. He neglects to mention how his campaign contributors in the drug and insurance and medical-device industries—think Dalkon Shield and silicone breast implants—would also benefit.

The Uninsured

According to President Bush in his 2002 State of the Union address, "Americans know economic security can vanish in an instant without health security." In the following year's address, he observed, "Yet for many people, medical care costs too much—and many have no coverage at all."

These observations are consistent with his prior comments in presidential debates, "There is an issue with the—the uninsured. There sure is. . . . We need a program for the uninsured. They've been talking about it in Washington, D.C. The numbers of uninsured have now gone up for the past seven years."

But the number of uninsured adults at any time continued to rise during the Bush presidency, from 41 million in 2001 to more than 44 million in 2003. The administration's plan for helping them would do nothing to arrest this trend and in fact could exacerbate it. The plan has three major elements: medical savings accounts, tax credits, and association health plans.

MEDICAL SAVINGS ACCOUNTS (MSAs)

In the second presidential campaign debate on October 11, when asked what he would do for the uninsured, Bush said, "Well, I've got a plan to do something about that. It's to make health care affordable and available this way: First, there are some who should be buying health care who choose not to. . . . Some of the healthy folks. You know, the young kids say, 'I'll never get sick; therefore I'm not going to have—don't need health care right now.' And for those, what I think we need to do is to develop an investment-type vehicle that would be an incentive for, for them to invest. Like medical savings accounts with rollover capacity. In other words, you say to a youngster, 'It'll be in your financial interest to start saving for future illness.'"

Bush offered a somewhat more comprehensive explanation of MSAs during a speech at the Medical College of Wisconsin in February 2002: "Instead of paying a large premium every month for services you may not use, I believe we ought to have an account that allows a person to pay a much smaller premium for major medical coverage, and then put the savings into a health account, tax free. . . . The money is your money . . . not the government's money. If you don't use it, it's yours to keep. And for the more affordable premium, you also get catastrophic care, protection in case of serious illness."

Under the administration's MSA proposal (building on a 1996 demonstration program), Americans could buy a stripped-down high-deductible health insurance plan that covers only catastrophic care and invest the rest of what they would have spent in a comprehensive plan in a special tax-free MSA. They could then save this money for future medical needs. There are several obvious flaws, however, in this concept:

* MSAs provide yet another tax shelter for the wealthy. According to the Center on Budget and Policy Priorities, there are no limits on how much money can be saved in MSAs. After retirement, the money can be withdrawn and used for nonmedical purposes without penalty.

* The center also concluded that MSAs could double the cost of premiums because the accounts "would be most attractive to healthier people" who are "not deterred by the high-deductible policy they would purchase." The less-healthy people remaining would concentrate in traditional health plans, whose premiums would consequently soar, jeopardizing the health insurance of a significant number of Americans.

* MSAs start with a misassumption that uninsured Americans have enough extra income both to buy a stripped-down policy and then invest in a tax-free account. How realistic, for example, is it to expect middle- and low-income young people just getting started in life to follow Bush's advice and open one of these accounts? And how likely is it that there will be enough money in the account to pay for medical expenses that are not covered by the bare-bones policy?

* MSAs put individuals in the unenviable position of competing with big corporations and employee groups to buy health insurance. The big players will get all the discounts.

In an unguarded moment, Bush acknowledged the severe limitations of MSAs. At a February 2000 campaign appearance in Florida, a woman told candidate Bush that her son had a chronic, life-threatening illness and that the health insurance did not cover everything he required. She wanted to know what he would to about it. As *New York Times* reporter Frank Bruni wrote, "The candidate, who has yet to articulate a comprehensive health plan, seemed stumped. He sang the praises of medical savings accounts, then acknowledged that it was too late for the woman to start one and that he really had no specific remedy for her. 'I'm sorry," Bush ended with. 'I wish I could wave a wand.'"

Tax Credits

Bush proposes an annual refundable tax credit of one thousand dollars a year to help individuals and three thousand dollars to help families buy health insurance. Since health insurance premiums generally cost two or three times this much, people who need assistance the most—say, a parent earning thirty thousand dollars a year at a small business that has no health plan—would still find health insurance unaffordable. "His proposal is like throwing a ten-foot rope to a person in a forty-foot hole. It simply provides no relief," comments Ron Pollack, executive director of Families USA. And without any controls over premiums, the extra federal money would likely just cause premiums to escalate even faster than currently projected.

Bush's current tax credit plan is even stingier than the one he proposed during the second presidential debate, which involved a credit of two thousand dollars per individual. It is also less generous and less targeted to those who really need help than the tax credit his father once proposed. In his State of the Union address in 1992, President George H. W. Bush said, "We make basic health insurance affordable for all low-income people not now covered. We do it by providing a health insurance tax credit of up to $3,750 for each low-income family."

ASSOCIATION HEALTH PLANS (AHPs)

At the Medical College of Wisconsin in February 2002, Bush touted association health plans as a way for small businesses to reduce the cost of buying health coverage for their employees: "A stand-alone-small business doesn't have purchasing power in the marketplace. We ought to allow employers to pool together . . . so that they can get the best deal for their workers, just as large corporations are allowed to do." Association health plans were included in the Bush-backed patients' rights bill that passed the House in August 2001.

The Congressional Budget Office estimated that AHPs could reduce premiums for small business by 13 percent. While there's no doubt that AHPs might encourage some businesses to begin to offer health insurance to their employees, the catch is that AHPs would be largely exempt from state regulations such as those requiring plans to provide mammography, bone marrow transplants, and mental health coverage. Chances for consumer fraud would increase because the plans would operate outside of the ambit of state consumer protection laws.

The National Governors Association, the National Conference of State Legislatures, the National Association of Insurance Commissioners, and National Small Business United oppose AHPs for another reason: insurers would be able to "cherry-pick"—to sign up companies with younger, healthier workers and avoid those with older, sicker ones, who would end up paying more for insurance than before. Speaking in favor of AHPs in March 2002, Bush said, "It makes no sense, no sense in America, to isolate small businesses as little health care islands unto themselves." Instead, he'd isolate small businesses with older and costlier workers because insurers would avoid them.

Medicaid

The Medicaid program gives millions of Americans access to doctors, hospitals, nursing homes, and home health care. Speaking about improving Medicaid in one of his weekly broadcasts in August 2001, President Bush said, "The goals of Medicaid are too important to get bogged down in a bureaucracy. My administration cares about results, about getting Americans broader and better medical coverage." But in February 2003 the administration unveiled a dramatic Medicaid restructuring plan that would not "broaden" but instead shrink coverage for millions. In presenting the proposal, HHS secretary Tommy Thompson said, "The time to modernize Medicaid is here. . . . The old Medicaid rules are a straitjacket, restraining creative new approaches that could preserve coverage and expand it to more Americans in need."

Rather than providing financially hard-pressed states with more federal dollars to help cover their share of soaring Medicaid program expenses (states generally pick up half the cost), Bush's "creative new approach" was to tell the states that they would be free to slash benefits for the one-third of Medicaid recipients who are considered "optional beneficiaries"— largely those who are not on welfare and are not poor children. This one-third of the Medicaid population accounts for two-thirds of Medicaid's costs. States could save billions by cutting back benefits for optional beneficiaries like the elderly and the disabled or by charging them higher copays and raising eligibility levels.

The plan would also give states moderately increased federal funding for Medicaid and child health insurance programs, but only if they agree to switch from a reimbursement-for-services to a block grant payment system, and to accept *lower* federal Medicaid payments starting in 2011. Under a block grant system, states that exceed their grants have to cover the excess costs themselves. With pharmaceutical costs soaring and an aging population, states that accept this bargain will risk running short of federal money even before 2011. The block-grant program would ultimately result in a substantial reduction in federal funding for state Medicaid programs. The flat amount provided by the block grant program—irrespective of the current economic situation—would also be a hugh hindrance to the success of state Medicaid programs, preventing them from picking up necessary slack when the economy is bad and unemployment high. Governors from both major parties, including President Bush's brother, Florida governor Jeb Bush, understandably enough expressed severe reservations. A ten-governor National Governors Association task force, including Governor Bush, proposed an alternative plan that would protect states from Medicaid funding shortfalls. Rhonda Medows, head of Florida's Agency for Health Care Administration, assured the *New York Times* that Governor Bush was "right there with the other governors. . . . He's a responsible man. He doesn't want to take money up front and dump problems on his successor." Representative Sherrod Brown (D-OH) predicted that if the president's plan stands, "ultimately in Lansing, Sacramento, Columbus, and Springfield there will be a gargantuan fight between the nursing home industry and children's advocates over a diminishing pie—a fight no one should ever want to see played out in our state capital."

President Bush can certainly try to simultaneously cut taxes for the wealthiest and medical services for the poor, but it is Orwellian for him to proclaim his desire to increase "health security" while pursuing policies that would in reality increase the number of uninsured Americans.

Medical Privacy

During the 2000 campaign, Governor Bush called privacy "a fundamental right," and stated, "I believe . . . every American should have absolute control over his or her personal information. I believe that it is especially important to protect highly sensitive medical, genetic, and financial information. As president, I will prohibit genetic discrimination, criminalize identity theft, and guarantee the privacy of medical and sensitive financial records." He also then assured a *Business Week* interviewer, "I'm a privacy-rights person," insisting that people should "opt in" to sharing their personal information and, before information is shared, "the company has got to ask permission."

After taking office, it appeared that Bush would live up to his campaign statements and ensure that Americans would control their own medical information. In April 2001, medical-privacy advocates were surprised and elated when pro–privacy regulations that had been proposed by the Clinton administration were allowed to go into effect. These rules said that patients must consent before their medical records could change hands.

But only a year later, the self-styled "privacy person" abruptly changed course. In April 2002, the Bush administration proposed modifying the privacy regulation to remove the requirement for patient consent before medical records may be used or disclosed for the purposes of treatment, payment, and health care operations. There would be no more opportunity to "opt in," just an ex post facto notification of the patient.

The Bush administration claimed that they revised the new regulation to carry out a provision in the Health Insurance Portability and Accountability Act (HIPAA) of 1996 to foster the development of a national health information network that would make provider bills and insurance claims easier to process. But the administration cleverly slipped in a redefinition of the term *marketing* so that it allows for protected health information (PHI) to be disclosed to drug manufacturers and other health care services. These companies can then send direct mail advertisements or make unsolicited telemarketing calls—targeted to patients based on their diagnosis—that encourage the recipients to purchase a certain product or to switch to an alternative treatment. The direct marketer need not disclose that they paid for the PHI.

For example, a company that makes a new cholesterol-reducing drug could pay a pharmacy chain to send a letter to people with high cholesterol informing them of their new product. Or, even more troublesome, what if, as Representative Henry Waxman (D-CA) suggests, "you are diagnosed with a stigmatizing condition? You could receive unsolicited telemarketing phone calls about treatments." The congressman, ranking minority member of the House Health Subcommittee, also warns that the new rule could lead to more health complications because "there may be harmful potential side effects and interactions with some drugs" that consumer marketing might not adequately explain. Worse, when direct marketing is based on sensitive PHI purchased from health care providers, "the entire atmosphere of trust required for quality medical care" could be undermined.

In July 2002 Waxman and six of his House colleagues sent a letter to Secretary Thompson objecting to this new "broad loophole." Thompson never responded. The regulation began to be applied in April 2003.

Smoking and Tobacco

The Bush administration appears to be of two minds when it comes to smoking. President Bush has publicly announced, "Tobacco use is the single most preventable cause of death and disease in the United States, causing more than four hundred and forty thousand premature deaths annually during 1995 to 99." In 2003 his administration declared that it did not intend to drop a major lawsuit filed by the Clinton administration against tobacco companies for fraudulent marketing of cigarettes. Although Attorney General Ashcroft had previously given mixed signals, saying the lawsuit didn't appear very strong, the Justice Department had amassed new evidence that it says proves the industry manipulated nicotine content, intentionally marketed cigarettes to minors, and tried to hide the dangers of smoking. In addition to seeking $289 billion in "ill-gotten gains," the Justice Department is asking for severe restrictions on advertising, a prohibition on labeling cigarettes "low tar" and "mild," and a requirement to disclose all ingredients. But Attorney General Ashcroft has already floated the idea of settling the lawsuit. On this one pro-health, anti-tobacco initiative, will the Bush administration "stay the course"?

In February 2003, however, the White House rejected a proposal by its own expert advisory committee—the Interagency Committee on Smoking and Health—to increase the federal cigarette tax by two dollars a pack in order to fund a comprehensive smoking cessation initiative. The committee estimated that the initiative would have over time prevented 3 million premature deaths.

The administration also has vigorously fought international efforts to discourage smoking. On March 1, 2003, the 171 nations composing the World Health Organization (WHO) approved a historic Framework Convention on Tobacco Control. The convention asks nations to enact a comprehesive ban on tobacco advertising, promotion, and sponsorship and to require strongly worded warning labels on cigarette packages. The United States held out for months as the lone (if powerful) dissenter, until it finally capitulated.

Thomas Novotny, a Clinton administration appointee to the negotiation over a global draft Framework Convention on Tobacco Control, had been doing his best to thread the needle between pro-tobacco forces in Congress who would have to ratify the treaty and measures called for by the overwhelming evidence of dangers caused by smoking. The convention would have supported mandatory cigarette taxes, a ban on smoking in most closed public spaces, and a ban on some forms of tobacco advertising, particularly those that were designed to appeal to children. As *Mother Jones* magazine reported, just as the deal was about to be concluded, however, Novotny received a midnight phone call from William Steiger, a godson of President Bush 41 whom President Bush 43 had appointed to be director of the U.S. Office of Global Health Affairs. The result, once again, was the forced repudiation of all the positions the United States had previously worked so hard to convince other nations to embrace. Six weeks before Novotny received his midnight missive, lobbyists for the Philip Morris corporation forwarded to Bush officials a thirty-two-page letter detailing the company's stance on the treaty. The company presented eleven separate revisions it wanted, designed to weaken its enforcement provisions, as well as a number of issues it wanted taken off the table entirely, following up the letter with a soft-money contribution of $57,764 to the Republicans. Shortly thereafter, the United States officially adopted ten of the eleven positions requested by the Philip Morris lobbyists. As a result, "We had to back down on any sort of agreement for restricting cigarette advertising, any sort of pro-tax stand, and any policies on secondhand smoke restrictions," Novotny told reporter Barry Yeoman. The United States also reversed itself and came to oppose efforts to ban descriptive terms like "low-tar," "light," and "mild," which, according to our own National Cancer Institute, deceive smokers into thinking that products are less likely to cause cancer than others.

With the treaty now replete with watered-down provisions to suit the administration's liking, the Bush team decided to ask all 191 countries to reopen negotiations. The American contingent now announced that they could not accept the agreement as long as it included a "no-reservations" clause, which would prevent countries from disregarding any provisions they found unacceptable. Finally, "much to the surprise of many around the world," in the words of Bush's own secretary of health and human services, Tommy Thompson, the administration reversed itself in spring 2003 and agreed to add its name to the now-watered-down treaty. Nearly 5 million people die each year from tobacco use, according to the World Health Organization. This number is expected to double in twenty years, with nearly all the increase to come from the developing world.

Given the enormous campaign contributions Bush and fellow Republicans received from the tobacco industry, these stances should not surprise anyone. Common Cause and the National Center for Tobacco-Free Kids Action Fund report that tobacco companies have given more than $24.8 million in political donations to federal candidates, national parties, and nonparty political action committees since 1997. Republican candidates and committees received $20.2 million, or 81 percent of the tobacco industry's contributions.

Any fair weighing of President Bush's health policies would conclude that he appears far more concerned with the health of his donors' wallets than the health of Americans. His administration's consistent obeisance to the wishes of the drug and insurance industries and its insistence on private sector approaches to all public policy problems, if unchecked, will continue to compromise the health and finances of all but the most well-off.

7. Race

In the Picture, Not the Program

★

"[Some think that we candidates] will say anything to get elected. But there's a record, and that's what I hope people look at."
—George W. Bush,
third presidential debate, October 17, 2000

Remember the podium at the Republicans' 2000 National Convention? It was choreographed to reflect the diversity of America itself. Children from almost every racial and ethnic group performed on stage; the percentage of nonwhite speakers exceeded by fivefold the percentage of nonwhite delegates. General Colin Powell spoke about "reaching out to minority communities and particularly the African American community." Governor Bush derided "division," preached "tolerance," and rightly declared that "bigotry disfigures the heart." And in the subsequent fall campaign, it seemed that hardly a day went by without the appearance of an appealing picture of the Republican nominee with beaming, beautiful black schoolchildren.

Yet George W. Bush still received only 8 percent of the African American vote in the 2000 general election, even less than Ronald Reagan in 1980. Why?

The Southern Strategy

The Republican "southern strategy," as Richard Nixon originally framed it, permits Republican candidates to appeal to "angry white males" while providing plausible deniability to the fair-minded of both sexes. Trent Lott praised openly the neo-Confederate Council of Conservative Citizens (CCC) at meetings of their members in 1992 and 1995 and then later claimed he thought the CCC was just a "benign conservative" group. Ronald Reagan preached his support for "states' rights" at his 1980 presidential announcement right outside of Philadelphia, Mississippi, which just happened to be where three black civil rights activists had been murdered in the summer of 1964. And, of course, George H. W. Bush's 1988 presidential campaign benefited from the broadcast of the notorious Willie Horton ad, a political commercial featuring a black parolee who committee a brutal murder after his release.* Julian Bond, chairman of the NAACP, explained the process. "It's clear . . . [that George W. Bush] and his party have long depended on attracting support from this virulently racist minority element in their party and they come back to it time and time and time again. And when they're uncovered they profess ignorance."

While George W. Bush didn't invent the southern strategy, he has certainly mastered it. With his campaign in jeopardy after the hard-charging John McCain won the New Hampshire primary by eighteen points, Bush sought out a religious-right audience at Bob Jones University just prior to the pivotal 2000 South Carolina primary to "defend our conservative philosophy." At the time Bush visited the Bob Jones campus, it had a ban on interracial dating, and its founder had proclaimed on the school's Web site that Roman Catholicism and Mormonism were "cults which call themselves Christian." In his red-meat speech, Bush failed to take a stand against the school's bigoted and intolerant policies. Not until several days later, when he faced a potential backlash among Catholics in the Michigan primary, did Bush write in a letter to the archbishop of New York, Cardinal John O'Connor. "On reflection, I should have been more clear in disassociating myself from anti-Catholic sentiments and racial prejudice. It was a missed opportunity, causing needless offense." The letter was written *after* he had won the primary in South Carolina.†

Another missed opportunity in that state occurred when Bush ducked the contentious issue of the Confederate flag with a veiled reference to states' rights that really wasn't so hard to decipher for the neo-Confederates to whom it was aimed. "I believe the people of South Carolina can figure out what to do with this flag issue. It's the people of South Carolina's decision."

---

*The Bush camp denied paternity, blaming an independent group, one that nevertheless had obvious affiliations with the vice president's effort.

† Questioned about his visit to Bob Jones during the South Carolina primary, Bush refused to apologize, stating that he would bring his message to all that would listen regardless of viewpoint. But when Larry King called him on his refusal to meet with the Log Cabin Republicans, a gay and lesbian grassroots group, Bush falsely said on CNN, "Well, they made a commitment to John McCain." The Arizona senator immediately corrected the record, as did Kevin Ivers, spokesperson for the Log Cabin Republicans, since the group hadn't made any endorsement.

Affirmative Inaction

In a letter to *USA Today*, published on Election Day, November 7, 2000, George W. Bush wrote, "I am a uniter, not a divider and, as the governor of Texas, that is how I have led. It is how I will lead in the White House." After six years as governor and now as president, one would think that Bush "the uniter" could point to some accomplishment in the civil rights arena—some issue on which he has brought people together across racial lines. But when asked on July 8, 2002, by the media about his civil rights record and his decision not to meet with the NAACP, this was his entire answer: "Let's see. There I was sitting around the leader with—the table with foreign leaders, looking at Colin Powell and Condi Rice." Lacking any substantive policy in this area, Bush is left with no choice but this defensive comment; however, it opens the door of inquiry into how these two talented advisors attained the positions they hold today. The answer is that they benefited from the very types of affirmative action programs that Bush wants to eliminate.

Whether Bush even understands the concept of affirmative action is impossible to determine. During the third presidential debate on October 17, 2000, he responded to a question about his stance on this issue by saying, "If affirmative action means quotas, I'm against it." Then, on Dr. Martin Luther King Jr.'s birthday in 2003, Bush unveiled his Justice Department's brief in opposition to the University of Michigan affirmative action program. Four times he claimed that the Michigan policies amounted to a "quota system," which was false. Unlike the sixteen "special admissions" positions at the UC Davis Medical School, which the Supreme Court invalidated in the 1978 *Bakke* decision as an unconstitutional quota, the Michigan Law School had no such set-asides. When plaintiff Barbara Grutter applied in 1997, sixteen white students were admitted with lower grades and test scores than she. The percentage of minority students varied each year with the applicant pool. "Let's set the record straight," University of Michigan president Mary Sue Coleman said. "We do not have—nor have we ever had—quotas or numerical targets in either the undergraduate or the law school admissions system. By far the overwhelming consideration is academic achievement." Even former independent counsel Ken Starr said in an interview, "I'm not sure I would say it is a quota system," conceding that, despite giving added weight to minority applicants, the term *quota* is not the "most full articulation of [the] principle."

In midsummer 2003 the Supreme Court issued its holding in the University of Michigan cases—*Grutter v. Bollinger* and *Gratz v. Bollinger.* While critical of the plan used for *undergraduate* admissions, which awarded specific point values for different qualities—ranging from athletic ability to legacy status to race of the applicant—as too "mechanical," Justice O'Connor approvingly wrote for a 6 to 3 majority that the *law school* had engaged in a "highly individualized, holistic review of each applicant's file" in which race counts as *a* factor but not *the* factor. The Constitution, she concluded for the majority, "does not prohibit the Law School's narrowly tailored use of race in admissions decisions to further a compelling interest in obtaining the educational benefits that flow from a diverse student body."

President Bush argued that awarding points for being a minority is not equivalent to awarding points for "any academic achievement or life experience." If Bush is as opposed to preferences as his words suggest, why doesn't he speak out against all preference systems, including the one he benefited from that is still in full force today—legacy admissions. (At Princeton, for example, 35 percent of legacy candidates are accepted, whereas only 11 percent of nonlegacy applicants are accepted.) According to Wade Henderson, the executive director of the Leadership Council on Civil Rights, "For this President to turn around and criticize the University of Michigan's program when he himself clearly benefited from a form of affirmative action guaranteeing admission to the sons and daughters of prominent alumni—that seems to me as especially hypocritical." As for those who dismiss affirmative action as "reverse discrimination," columnist Michael Kinsley nicely punctures their argument: "Would you rather have a gift of 20 points out of 150 to use at the college of your choice? Or would you rather have the more amorphous advantages President Bush has enjoyed at every stage of his life?"*

Given the sensitivities about a problem older than America, the Bush Justice Department's brief in the Michigan case walked a fine line, singing the praises of diversity while speaking harshly of the only programs proven to have achieved that goal. In announcing the brief's filing, Bush said, "I strongly support diversity of all kinds, including racial diversity in higher education. But the method used by the University of Michigan to achieve this important goal is fundamentally flawed."

"The modus operandi is to speak centrally and act from the Right," said Bruce Buchanan, a professor of government at the University of Texas. "The conservative constituencies won [the brief's condition], because they got exactly what they want. And the minority constituency, who is exactly what the Republican Party is courting, get the soft words." In an earlier era, Dr. Martin Luther King Jr. warned in his "Letter from a Birmingham Jail" that it is not the Ku Klux Klan or White Citizens Council that will be the "Negro's great stumbling block." To the contrary, he declared, "the white moderate . . . who constantly says: 'I agree with you in the goal you seek, but I cannot agree with your methods'" is the greatest threat to opportunity for all Americans.

---

*George W. Bush was a mediocre student. With a 1206 (out of 1600) SAT and a C average at Andover, he was admitted to Yale. With grades like a 73 in Introduction to the American Political System, a 71 in Introduction to International Relations, and a C average for his undergraduate career, Bush was nonetheless accepted to Harvard Business School, graduating in 1975. Interestingly, when Bush was rejected from the University of Texas Law School in 1973, his father never knew that he had applied.

When confronted with this issue as governor of Texas, Bush pulled a similar fake left and drive to the right. He was cool to a bill that guaranteed the top 10 percent of students in each high school admission to one of the schools in the Texas State University system. But when it was passed by the Democrats in the Texas legislature, he signed it "with considerable fanfare" and has continued to advocate this admissions scheme as a candidate and president. In the third presidential debate with Al Gore on October 17, Bush said, "In our state of Texas I worked with the legislature, both Republicans and Democrats, to pass a law that said if you come in the top 10 percent of your high school class, you're automatically admitted to one of our higher institutions of learning, college. And as a result, our universities are now more diverse. It was a smart thing to do. What I called it, I labeled it affirmative access."

The brief filed by the Bush Justice Department in the Michigan case states: "[T]he Texas program has enhanced opportunity and promoted educational diversity by any measure." While it is true that minority enrollment is up at both the University of Texas at Austin and Texas A&M, this is owing to increased enrollment overall. But proportionally, according to a 2003 study done at the University of Texas at Dallas, minorities represent a *smaller* share of enrollment than prior to the ban on affirmative action. Further, as a percentage of all high school graduates, the number of minorities is increasing in Texas, so even keeping the minority share of enrollment constant in the Texas University system would, in effect, be lessening opportunity for minority graduates.

"Affirmative access" programs simply don't make the grade in pursuit of diversity either analytically or empirically. "Access" programs can only be applied to state undergraduate colleges, not the highly selective private institutions that often determine the composition of our ruling elites. Nor do they apply to graduate and professional schools, in Texas or elsewhere. Further, such programs rely on the continued existence of racially segregated secondary schools, since the only way to ensure diversity at the undergraduate level is if there are all-black schools producing a top tenth who are by definition all black. In fact, under affirmative access in Texas, black students make up 12 percent of graduating students but only 6 percent of students graduating in the top 10 percent of their high school class. And finally, the president's support of a voucher system to encourage students to leave failing schools would have the opposite effect of encouraging students to *stay* in failing schools so that they can graduate in the top 10 percent of their "minority" class and be accepted to college in Texas.

The Michigan case might have been one of the few times that Bush found himself on the opposite side of the aisle from business and military interests. Some sixty-five large corporations and more than twenty distinguished former military leaders filed friend of the court briefs favoring the University of Michigan's affirmative action policy. Colleges and universities are talent pools for corporate and military recruiters, who recognize that on-campus diversity helps students develop an understanding of different cultures. According to one of these briefs, this understanding better enables future employees to "appeal to a variety of consumers" and work with colleagues and clientele from various backgrounds; diversity "facilitate[s] a unique and creative approach to problem-solving."

And the president found himself at odds as well with his own secretary of state. Speaking to a group of students at the Supreme Court on the evening of April 30, 2003, with Justice O'Connor sitting in the front row of the audience, Powell was asked by a student for his opinion on affirmative action. The secretary seized the opportunity and delivered a ten-minute soliloquy about his support for affirmative action, declaring that he was in fact a "beneficiary," and that, while his enthusiasm for such programs ran contrary to the president's policies, he nonetheless lauded affirmative action as a means of achieving diversity. Powell, who had been introduced by O'Connor, could not have been unaware that his remarks were being listened to carefully by a person who everyone believed would be the swing vote in the then-upcoming Michigan decision.

In a version of John Mitchell's—"Watch what we do, not what we say"— the president again was trying to have it both ways, taking a stand against quotas, while lauding "diversity." But Justice O'Connor, speaking for a court with seven of nine justices appointed by Republican presidents, wouldn't let him do so. She wrote that the brief failed to explain "how such plans could work for graduate and professional schools." Further, she continued, schemes like the president's 10-percent plan "may preclude the university from conducting the individualized assessments necessary to assemble a student body that is not just racially diverse, but diverse [in a way that reflected] all the qualities valued by the university."

Of course, new ways of achieving diversity should be explored and considered, but as of now, cutting through all the posturing and rhetoric, the effective choice remains between imperfect affirmative action and de facto segregation. An expert testified in the Michigan case that if affirmative action were ended at the University of Michigan Law School, minority enrollment would drop from 14.5 percent to 4 percent. As former University of Michigan and current Columbia University president, Lee Bollinger, put it on the *Charlie Rose* show, "Banning affirmative action would lead to the resegregation of American education." On the issue of a racially segregated or integrated America, President George W. Bush has found himself on the wrong side of history.

Nevertheless, performing a pirouette more adroitly than a ballerina, President Bush "applauded" the Court "for recognizing the value of diversity on our nation's campuses." A naive reader of this statement could scarcely know that its speaker was in fact congratulating the justices for adopting a position he had asked them to reject.

Not a Lott of Lincolns

Another barometer of Bush on race can be found in l'affaire Lott. In late 2002, Senate majority leader Trent Lott made his now infamous statement on the occasion of Strom Thurmond's birthday that "[i]f the rest of the country had followed [Mississippi's] lead" in voting for then-segregationist presidential candidate Thurmond in 1948, "we wouldn't have had all these problems over all these years." Even ardent conservatives quickly condemned him. The *Weekly Standard*'s William Kristol urged Lott's resignation as the leader of the Senate Republicans, calling his praise of segregationist Thurmond "ludicrous."

When Bush himself finally did comment five days after Thurmond's birthday party, it was only through press secretary Ari Fleischer. "The president has confidence in [Lott] as Republican leader, unquestionably," Flesicher declared and went on to tell reporters that Bush viewed Lott's apologies as the "final word" on the matter. But it wasn't. When the controversy continued, President Bush told an audience of black clergy in Philadelphia two days later, "Recent comments by Senator Lott do not reflect the spirit of our country. He has apologized and rightly so." Then Fleischer, speaking to a *New York Times* reporter on December 15, said that "emphatically and on the record, the president doesn't think Trent Lott needs to resign [his leadership post]." While Bush never publicly called for Lott's resignation as leader, behind the scenes the White House was coaxing the Mississippi senator to step aside for a Bush favorite, doctor and senator Bill Frist. "They've got a skilled surgeon coming in to run the Senate, and they used a surgeon's skill to remove Lott without leaving any fingerprints," said admiring former Democratic National Committee Chairman and Bush friend, Robert S. Strauss.

The Republicans repeatedly claim to be the "party of Lincoln," but if they really were adhering to the ideals of Abraham Lincoln, they would probably have a more contemporary figure to idolize instead of having to reach back a century and a half for faux inspiration. In fact, Lott's sin was not that he told a lie, but that he told the truth.*

Ironically, during the Lott contretemps, a similar racial problem uncomfortably arose for the Republicans when Bill Back announced his candidacy for chairmanship of the Republican Party of California. Back had sent out an e-mail newsletter that included the statement: "History might have taken a better turn" had the South won the Civil War. It also said that "the real damage to race relations came not from slavery, but from Reconstruction, which would not have occurred if the South had won." When the

---

*Nor was this the first time. As chairman of the Republican Party's platform committee in 1984, Lott stated, "The spirit of Jefferson Davis lives in the document of principles and positions guiding the GOP." In a 1992 speech in Greenwood, Mississippi, Lott told a group from the openly racist Council of Conservative Citizens: "The people in this room stand for the right principles and the right philosophy. Let's take it in the right direction, and our children will be the beneficiaries."

national leader of the Republican Party, President George W. Bush, was asked about Back's candidacy and comments—in this case without the kind of public pressure that forced his hand with Lott—he literally had nothing to say.

A Confederacy of Dunces

President Bush's cautious approach to issues of race and intolerance were evident as early as his governorship of Texas, when he refused to attend the funeral of James Byrd Jr., a young black man dragged to his death tied to a pickup truck driven by racists. Nor did Bush show any public compassion over this worldwide publicized tragedy. When Byrd's sister later pleaded with the governor to sign the Hate Crimes bill that would bear her brother's name, Bush simply responded no, and that was it.

The Texas House did pass the James Byrd Jr. Memorial Hate Crime Bill, and Governor Bush, under pressure, said he would consider the bill if it was passed by the Senate. But Senate Republicans, after meeting with a member of his staff, voted to kill the measure. According to Bush biographer Molly Ivins, "This was the 'Let's Not Embarrass the Governor' session, and Bush's political problem was simple: He was about to run for the nomination of a party in which Christian-right voters make up one-third of the Republican primary vote. He could not afford to be associated with a bill that could be interpreted as giving special rights to gays."

James Byrd's sister, Louvon Harris, summed up her feelings about Governor Bush after the legislation failed. "If he had his way, he would be standoffish to black America. But since he's running for president, he has to do his campaigning as if he loves all people. But I have my doubts about that. I think it's all a ploy. I'm not in a position to judge anybody's heart, but actions speak louder than words."

Based on his words, you'll never catch Bush himself talking like a Dixiecrat, but the appropriate message seems to get conveyed on his behalf whenever necessary. After Bush's Bob Jones University speech, for example, a whispering campaign, begun through telephone "push polls," spread the word through the state of South Carolina that Senator John McCain had a black child; in fact, McCain had adopted a child from Bangladesh.

Another implicit wink to the Old South is Bush's relationship with neo-Confederate groups, which dates back to his time as governor. He is listed as a donor in the annual report of the Museum of the Confederacy in Richmond, Virginia, at least through 1999, having raised money for the organization's annual ball. The affair is held in an old slave hall, Tredgar Iron Works, where slaves were forced to build war material for the Confederate army; the theme of the 1996 ball was "Bonnie Blue Ball," a celebration of the blue flag of the secessionist confederacy. Also as governor, Bush in 1996 wrote a letter honoring the Sons of Confederate Veterans, a group that has, according to *Southern Exposure,* "repeatedly offered a platform for avowedly white supremacist organizations like the Council of Conservative Citizens."

Then there's Richard T. Hines, whom historian Sean Wilentz terms one of the "most outspoken and influential neo-Confederates in the country." A former editor of the virulently racist *Southern Partisan* and a close friend of Bush advisor Karl Rove, Hines wrote in the *Washington Times,* after the Lott affair, "This brouhaha has caused many people to look afresh at the issues in the War of 1861–65, to the decided benefit of the memory of the Confederate Cause." Hines has criticized Governor James Gilmore of Virginia for issuing a resolution acknowledging the "horrors of slavery" during Confederate Heritage Month and in 1996 protested the placement of an Arthur Ashe statue in Richmond, Virginia, claiming that "the intent of the placement of the statue was to debunk our heritage." Hines's own Web site, meanwhile, touts his connection to the president, claiming that "his history of political activism was, most recently, extended to aid the campaign of President Bush in the South Carolina primary of the 2000 presidential election" and that he "has an active voice in the current Bush administration." Hines helped finance a 250,000-piece pro-Bush mailer extolling Bush's support for the Confederate flag, for example, prior to the South Carolina primary and, according to the *Wall Street Journal* and *Newsweek,* was crucial to Bush's victory there, which in turn was crucial to his nomination.

Beyond such characters in the neo-Confederate world, however, are the president's own presidential appointees. In nominating John Ashcroft as his attorney general, Bush said, "There's no question in my mind that this is a person who believes in civil rights for all citizens." Yet Ashcroft, in a 1998 interview in the racist *Southern Partisan,* stated, "Your magazine helps set the record straight. You've got a heritage of doing that, of defending Southern Patriots like Lee, Jackson, and Davis. Traditionalists must do more. I've got to do more. We've all got to stand up and speak in this respect, or else we'll be taught that these people were giving their lives, subscribing their sacred fortunes and their honor to some perverted agenda."

In announcing Gale Norton's nomination as secretary of the interior, the president described her as "a former attorney general of Colorado with a reputation for building consensus on divisive issues." Yet Norton had told a conservative group in Denver in 1996 that "we lost too much" in the Civil War, referring to the states' rights agenda.

When it comes to judicial appointments, Bush has likewise proven his consistency on civil rights. He has said that he hopes to pick justices in the mold of Antonin Scalia and Clarence Thomas, neither of whom are known for their pioneering decisions advancing racial justice. After Trent Lott accidentally reopened the question of the Republican Party's relationship to segregation, the president had an opportunity to live up to the rhetoric of his inaugural address, when he proclaimed, "Our unity, our union, is the serious work of leaders and citizens in every generation. And this is my solemn pledge: I will work to build a single nation of justice and opportunity." Recall how President Richard Nixon stood up to his anti-Communist base by visiting Red China; how President Bill Clinton demanded and won a balanced budget from fellow Democrats; and how Everett Dirksen, the Republican Senate minority leader, supplied the key votes to pass the civil rights bills in the 1950s and 1960s. But when George W. Bush's moment came after the Lott affair, he instead shrank to the occasion and winked at his confederate base by reappointing Judge Charles Pickering to the Fifth Circuit (see chapter 8) and opposing the affirmative action policy of the University of Michigan.

Suppressing Minority Voters

While the Republican southern strategy is unstated but obvious, it also runs the risk of being self-defeating, given rising populations of minority voters. A corollary Republican strategy to the racial wink-and-nod, therefore, has been the periodic suppression of minority voters.

There is, of course, a long history of preventing minorities from voting—from the three-fifths clause of the U.S. Constitution to literacy tests in the South to Senator Theodore Bilbo's (D-MI) observation in 1946 that "the way to keep the nigger from the polls is to see him the night before." In recent years such practices have become less blatant but remain an art form for some Republicans nonetheless. They paint broad enough strokes to achieve their desired effect, but do so in subtle enough shades that they can deny they're even painting. Consider just four of many examples from the 2002 elections:

★ This sign was posted throughout the predominantly minority areas of Baltimore prior to the 2002 election:

> **URGENT NOTICE**
>
> COME OUT TO VOTE ON NOVEMBER 6TH
>
> BEFORE YOU COME OUT TO VOTE
> MAKE SURE YOU PAY YOUR:
>
> —PARKING TICKETS
> —MOTOR VEHICLE TICKETS
> —OVERDUE RENT
>
> AND MOST IMPORTANT, ANY WARRANTS!

★ In Arkansas, Republican poll monitors demanded to see black voters' identification cards and took photographs of them. Arkansas law requires no such identification. According to Michael Cook, executive director of the Arkansas Democratic Party, Republicans were saying, "If you don't have your ID, you can't vote, you gotta go home." There were no reports of this sort of behavior in the white neighborhoods.

* In Michigan Republican leaders publicized that they would have a large number of "spotters" in the heavily Democratic (and heavily minority) precincts around Detroit. In Florida, a telephone marketer (client "unknown") called Democratic voters and told them to cast their absentee ballots after Election Day, at which point their votes would no longer count.

* The night before the Louisiana senatorial runoff election, a flyer appeared in New Orleans housing projects advising voters that if they were unable to vote on Election Day, they could simply show up at the polling place three days *later* to cast their ballots. In that same race, the Republican party paid for posters, and black men to hold those posters, that read, "Mary [Landrieu], if you don't respect us, don't expect us."

The Democratic Party noted similar problems in Florida, Missouri, South Carolina, and New Jersey, among numerous other states in 2002— yes, 2002, not 1962 or 1862. "I do think that the existence of these programs over a long period of time," said Wade Henderson, "without discouragement from the party for their use, in effect gives a tacit sanction for this program to continue."

But instead of speaking out, the leader of "the party of Lincoln," George W. Bush, has stood idly by while the Civil War amendments resulting from Lincoln's leadership are being eroded.* Congress, however, did respond.

As a result of the Florida 2000 election debacle and other voter-suppression

---

* An additional form of minority voter suppression is "felony disenfranchisement" laws. "The Florida election imbroglio was not just about dimples and chads, butterfly ballots and VotoMatics," wrote Josh Rosenkranz of the Brennan Center for Justice. "Most importantly, it was about a scandal that received no attention: state laws stripping millions of citizens with past felony convictions of the right to vote, adding up to the most significant formal disenfranchisement of our time." In fact, the state of Florida had at least 200,000 ex-felons, people who had already paid their debt to society, yet who were not permitted to vote in the 2000 presidential elections. State felon and ex-felon disenfranchisement laws have disenfranchised an estimated 3.9 million Americans nationwide, 1.4 million of whom are black men. In seven states that deny the vote to ex-offenders, one in four black men has been permanently stripped of the right to vote.

"It is no surprise that many of the states that permanently bar ex-felons from voting are southern," observes Representative James Clyburn (D-SC). "These arcane laws stem from the era where Jim Crow laws were in effect to deny voting rights to blacks. Just as states imposed literacy tests and poll taxes in order to exercise voting rights, some used criminal convictions as yet another way to reduce black power at the polls."

Florida governor Jeb Bush has been on the front lines of this formal disenfranchisement, purging voter lists of any ex-felons or those with names similar to ex-felons. His brother should be quietly grateful, for he has felon and ex-felon disenfranchisement laws to thank, in part, for his current title—since the bulk of the some 200,000 disenfranchised ex-felons in Florida are black and would likely have voted overwhelmingly Democratic, a number that would have easily surpassed W.'s 537 vote margin in winning the state and presidency. To the best of our knowledge, George W. Bush has never spoken about felon disenfranchisement laws.

efforts, Congress passed the Help America Vote Act (HAVA), which the president signed into law on October 29, 2002, stating: "Every registered voter deserves to have confidence that the system is fair and elections are honest, that every vote is recorded, and that the rules are consistently applied."

The act provides that the federal government will help the states replace their outdated voting systems with more reliable technology, even setting a minimum standard of reliability for voting machines. Much of the good that will be done through these provisions, however, will be undermined by so-called ballot-integrity measures jammed into the law by insistent Republican members of Congress, led by Senator Mitch McConnell (R-KY).

Under the HAVA, for example, anyone who registered by mail and has not previously voted must show photo ID, a utility bill, bank statement, or some government document with his name and address on it. A Justice Department study in 1994 reported that blacks in the state of Louisiana were one-fifth as likely as whites to have a driver's license or other picture ID. Getting these can be a major expense and can therefore function as a de facto poll tax on the poor, who remain disproportionately minority and vote disproportionately for Democratic candidates. Such a demand "doesn't make it harder to commit fraud; it just makes it harder to vote," wrote Laughlin McDonald in *The American Prospect.* While Republican senators claim they fear fraud, what they apparently fear is more voters.

Walking the Talk

A Republican president wanting to ensure that the electoral "system is fair and elections are honest" would have fully funded the election reform measures aimed at fixing the antiquated system that failed us in 2000. Not only is the ostensibly pro-voting-rights HAVA being enforced in ways that may actually discourage voting, it is further weakened by President Bush's proposed 2004 budget, in which he allots HAVA a meager $500 million, a fraction of the $3.9 billion that the act authorizes. A Republican president truly interested in racially moderating his party would speak not only occasionally *to* minority audiences, but also *with* minority leaders, even if he might be asked a tough question or two. Yet President Bush has refused to meet with the Congressional Black Caucus for three years, citing scheduling difficulties, and has ducked every interview request made by Black Entertainment Television and Tom Joyner's radio show, a program appealing to a mostly black audience. Kweisi Mfume, the president of the NAACP, complained, "You can't be president when you only want to deal with some of the people."

And with not one black Republican in the Congress, a Republican president serious about diversity could have recruited even a single black conservative to run in a safe Republican congressional district. Bush hasn't. Last, a Republican president seriously interested in promoting racial tolerance could have pledged to reject any support in his next campaign from known racists like Richard Hines or repudiated any connection he has with groups that preach hate under the guise of "heritage."

So, in response to the question that opened the chapter: Why did George W. Bush get only 8 percent of the black vote in the 2000 presidential election? Because black voters care more about results than speeches. Professions of a commitment to equality ring hollow when accompanied by veiled appeals to neo-Confederates, the appointment of far-right and anti-civil-rights judges, a frontal attack on affirmative action, and a lack of interest in protecting the right to vote for those who fought so hard to gain it.

8. Reality Bites
Watch What We Say . . .

★

EDUCATION
No Politician Left Behind

"And that's exactly the kind of budget I submitted to the United States Congress. . . . It's a budget that says we could spend more money on the public's education system around America. It's a budget that prioritizes education."
—President George W. Bush, April 5, 2001

When George W. Bush ran for president his most significant governing credential was his education record in Texas. He made more than a hundred campaign stops at schools in 1999–2000 and touted his heavy involvement in Texan education reform, where as governor in 1998 he averaged a speech a week on education. Once elected, President Bush labeled his first week in the White House "education week."

But when independent observers looked more closely at the "Texas Miracle"—the catchphrase used to describe the state's dramatic turnaround on education—it turned out to be more of a mirage.

First, many of the state's most significant changes were implemented well before Bush entered office and were spearheaded by the state's 1983 Select Committee on Public Education—led, ironically, by the man who helped defeat his father in 1992, Ross Perot. Perot and his cohorts conducted a ten-month tour and study of the state's education system, proposing a sweeping set of reforms embodied in the state's 1984 legislation, H.B. 72, which was signed into law by then governor Mark White in 1985.

Second, a thorough investigation by the RAND corporation of the state's progress in education noted that the dramatic improvements on its own Texas Assessment of Academic Skills (TAAS) tests did not correspond to the mediocre improvements on the National Assessment of Educational Progress (NAEP) tests. Even more disappointingly, the gap in scores between whites and students of color was widening, not shrinking. "According to NAEP, the gap is large and increasing slightly. According to TAAS, the gap is much smaller and decreasing greatly," the RAND report concluded. These discrepancies raised "very serious questions" about the validity of the TAAS gains that were the sole basis of Bush's "Texas Miracle."

In the first presidential debate of the 2000 election, Governor Bush claimed that "Testing is the cornerstone of reform. You know how I know? Because it's the cornerstone of reform in the state of Texas." But while there were improvements in Texas's (and other states') scores on NAEP, RAND judged progress on the basis of five key factors: smaller class sizes, more resources for teachers, more kids in pre-K programs, lower teacher turnover, and more money spent per student. High-stakes testing was not a critical factor of student academic success.

High-stakes tests did finally make it into the news in Texas between September 1998 and May 1999, but not in the way Bush intended. The pressure and emphasis on test scores led to accusations in Austin, Dallas, and Houston of teachers helping students cheat on their tests and of administrators changing the identification numbers of low-performing students to exclude their damaging data from the final TAAS ratings.

The things that *did* work in Texas were notable, important achievements—they just didn't have much to do with Governor Bush's reign in Austin and they bore no resemblance to the education policies he pursued as president. When Bush proposed the sweeping set of education reforms included in the massive No Child Left Behind Act of 2001, it was obvious that he had not been a good student of his own record in Texas.

No Child Left Behind: A Primer

In his foreword to the No Child Left Behind Act (NCLB)—the reauthorization and restructuring of the Elementary and Secondary Education Act, first passed in 1965—President Bush began with the promise that "bipartisan education reform will be the cornerstone of my administration." And while the events of September 11 shifted his focus away from domestic policy, at the one-year anniversary of the bill's signing in 2003, Bush still spoke of his "deep passion to make sure every child gets educated in America" and called the bill "the most meaningful education reform probably ever."

While it's possible to debate whether the bill produced "meaningful" education reform, it does certainly, at the least, represent a massive change in approach to the subject. No Child Left Behind brings the federal government into local public school policy-making to an unprecedented extent and does so via Bush's repeated demand to schools that "if you receive federal money, we expect you to show results." Bush usually refers to "results" interchangeably with "accountability," the buzzword of No Child Left Behind, which is measured primarily through the favorite mechanism of conservative school reform—high-stakes testing.

Bush's plan requires states to test students in reading and math annually in grades three through eight and at least once in high school. Districts must compile scores for each school and for certain subgroups (racial and ethnic minorities, low-income students, students with disabilities, and students with limited English proficiency). Schools then release "report cards" on student performance and must demonstrate "adequate yearly progress" in each subgroup each year. Schools that fail to make progress in each category for two consecutive years must use their Title I federal funds (money distributed specifically to high-poverty schools) to provide supplementary education to any student who desires it. (This "supplementary education" can take the form of tutoring, extra classes, and other help. For-profit and religious organizations are eligible to provide such services—and receive the government funding that pays for such services—as long as they are approved by the state.) The low-performing school must also offer students the option to transfer to better-performing schools, which cannot deny transfer requests based on capacity alone.

President Bush's No Child Left Behind has many other components—including a requirement for states to hire only "highly qualified" teachers in core subjects by the end of the 2005–6 school year and a focus on phonics-based reading instruction—but the high-stakes testing requirement has dominated the discussion of the act. Can high-stakes testing at a low cost significantly improve our nation's schools?

Debates on public education usually boil down to a question of money. Serious education reform is incredibly expensive, and enforcing this law is no exception. Apparently, however, no one told President Bush's Office of Management and Budget.

Fuzzy Funding

In the world of federal legislation, there's a huge difference between *authorization* and *appropriation*. Authorizations stipulate how much money Congress is allowed to spend on a given program, while appropriations indicate how much they actually spend. So it's not uncommon to have an authorization level much higher than an appropriation level—that way the bill's sponsors can brag about the massive amount of money slated to be spent on their project while knowing that the program will never be fully funded.

No Child Left Behind, however, was supposed to be different—that is, the rare bill that received the maximum amount of money allowed in the bill's authorization level.* At its signing, for example, President Bush promised; "The new role of the federal government is to set high standards, provide resources, hold people accountable, and liberate school districts to meet the standards.... We're going to spend more on our schools, and we're going to spend it more wisely." It was such statements that enabled the bill to be written and passed with a bipartisan slate of cosponsors in Congress—Representatives John Boehner (R-OH) and George Miller (D-CA) in the House and Senators Judd Gregg (R-NH) and Edward Kennedy (D-MA) in the Senate. All four were influential in the bill's passage and publicity, making pit stops at public schools around the country with the president immediately after the law's signing. One year later, however, Miller and Kennedy were noticeably absent from the president's celebration of its one-year anniversary, and Miller held his own press conference on the steps of the Department of Education.

As it happened, No Child Left Behind programs were appropriated only $22 billion—some $4 billion short of the law's authorized level. The numbers the following two years were even worse, when Bush actually proposed *cuts* to those programs each of those years.

"Part of the issue [is that] we passed the bill for tougher standards with higher funding down the road," explains Alex Knox, a member of the democratic staff of the House Committee on Education and the Workforce. But the budgets proposed for the entire Department of Education in fiscal years 2003 and 2004 (about $50 billion and $53 billion, respectively) show it's been the road not taken. "I mean, clearly it's not a priority for the administration," Knox adds.

Recall that this is the "education president" whose wife travels throughout the country reading to small children because education is the "cornerstone" of her husband's domestic agenda. But facts are facts. Bush's much publicized $1 billion increase in Title I funding, for example, still falls $6 billion short of the FY 2004 authorization level called for in the No Child Left Behind Act. And even the meager 5.3 percent increase Bush proposed in 2004 was accomplished only by eliminating forty-five other programs ranging from rural education to dropout prevention. The 2004 budget proposal also reduces funding for research-proven methods of increasing student successes—like teacher recruitment and training—while earmarking $75 million

---

* It's possible to see a wide spectrum of different numbers referring to the same budget proposals because of the way federal budget numbers are calculated. Most people, however, prefer to use only the "Discretionary Funding" total in the Department of Education's budget when referring to the department's total budget. Mandatory funding is susceptible to things like interest rates and previously passed statutes and is immune to budget battles in Congress, making its contribution to the number somewhat meaningless when it comes to establishing funding priorities. The discretionary totals are, therefore, the numbers that are used in this chapter.

for "choice" programs that could be used to move children in public schools to private ones and proposes tax credits for parents who send their kids to private schools.

These retreats on Bush's commitment to NCLB come at an especially inopportune moment for state lawmakers, who are faced with huge budget deficits and a new education mandate that does not provide the funding needed to accomplish its goals. According to the National Conference of State Legislatures, seventeen states cut K-12 funding in 2002, twenty states were forced to cut their K-12 education budgets in 2003, and twenty-one states were considering cuts to their K-12 programs in FY 2004. The irony, of course, is that states that choose not to comply with the NCLB regulations or schools that simply cannot meet the adequate yearly progress goals risk losing the one thing they most need to implement comprehensive school reform: money.

While the federal government provides, on average, only 7 percent of the funding for our nation's public schools, Title I money in particular is still crucial to the budgets of local school districts. Already, states are being told by Washington to set aside 20 percent of their Title I funds in anticipation of money that will then be transferred from the failing schools that need it the most and sent to private tutors or schools.

The Center on Education Policy in Washington has committed itself to a six-year study of the implementation of NCLB and found that, after its first year in operation, funding problems were among the most important issues to emerge with state lawmakers: "If education receives only the modest 2.8 percent increase [for FY 2003] proposed in the president's budget, this amount is likely to fall far short of what will be needed for states and school districts to effectively implement the new law."

How can Bush claim to be a champion of public school education while flatlining or effectively downsizing the Department of Education's budget? Again utilizing the presidential bully pulpit to repeat a mantra until people focus on the phrase and not the policy, Bush makes the simple claim that "better schools require more than just funding." He's even gone so far as to compare the $158 billion targeted to the education of low-income children through Title I as a process similar to "pumping gas into a flooded engine." But to this day Title I, which serves only about one-third of the children eligible for its help, is closer to E than F on its gas gauge.

But Bush has been able to downplay the importance of funding in education reform and instead to focus on a simplistic formula of testing and test scores. Ironically, by confusing "accountability" with "testing," he puts all the onus on schools, not politicians. Think of a coach yelling at runners to sprint faster without providing sneakers. Or imagine daily testing of a racecar or an infantry battalion without spending adequately for tires and training. Thus can a coach—or president—himself escape accountability by the conservative tactic of focusing on results without resources.

"Cheap" Rhetoric

High-stakes tests—tests whose results are tied to material consequences like funding, graduation, and teachers' pay raises—encapsulate what Bush and Company believe to be the real problem with public education: laziness. This is what Bush means when he declares: "Low standards will yield low results. We've got to raise the bar and expect the best of every classroom in America," an attitude summed up by one of his favorite catchphrases, "the soft bigotry of low expectations." Because he believes that the only thing holding test scores down is lazy schools and lazy students, attaching a dollar sign or diploma to the tests will be sufficient incentive for children and teachers to perform up to par. In other words, transfer the private sector's motivator of money into public education.

"What's important about results is it begins to change the whole attitude in the schools," President Bush has said. "Schools used to say—and still do in some places—they ask the question, gosh, how old are you? Well, if you're eight, you're supposed to be here. . . . And by having accountability as the cornerstone of reform, we begin to ask the question, what do you know. What do you know? It's a fundamental change in questions, isn't it? What do you know, instead of how old you are."

There are two problems with Bush's hyperreliance on high-stakes tests to solve our nation's education crisis. First, it is as logical to rely upon diagnostic tests as cures for our nation's ailing schools as it is, said one commentator, to "rely upon thermometers to reduce fevers." Of course it's essential to know which kids are doing well in school and which are not. Teachers regularly use tests in their classrooms to make informed decisions about what individual students need to improve their learning. At the same time, standardized tests allow schools and school districts to compare themselves with peer schools and evaluate necessary changes to curricula or programs. Looking at annual data of this kind is the only way schools can measure who's succeeding and, in Bush parlance, who's being left behind. So tests must be given to students—and schools, districts, teachers, and parents should look carefully at the results to figure out strategies to address emerging problems. The frequency of the testing regimen in No Child Left Behind, however, is of concern to educators who are asked to spend more time on test preparation and administration and less time working through their lesson plans. But the second question is whether material consequences should be tied to these diagnostic tools. Recent research responds with a resounding no.

Audrey Amrein of Arizona State University conducted the first nationwide study on the impact of high-stakes tests on schools. Twenty-eight states already depend upon high-stakes tests in their elementary schools, and eighteen give graduation exit exams, where students who fail them are not allowed to graduate. In 2002 Amrein and her colleagues compared scores from the statewide exams to scores on independent exams (the NAEP for elementary school students and the SAT/ACT for high school students) and charted the changes in both over time. Amrein, a former supporter of high-stakes testing, was surprised by what she found. While scores on the statewide exams—the tests that had real consequences attached to them—uniformly went up across the board, scores on the independent assessments actually decreased. On top of the already bad news, she also found that graduation rates fell and, not surprisingly, dropout rates rose. And in data that point to the philosophical alignment behind high-stakes tests, Amrein also discovered falling scores were concentrated in the South and Southwest, in areas with higher poverty rates, higher percentages of blacks and Hispanics, and with lower per-pupil funding.

Teachers, parents, and students already know that testing and learning are not one and the same; Amrein's research simply put solid science behind the anecdotal evidence. So the question now is how to embrace the concept of *genuine* accountability—not only the belief that every child in America is able to learn but also how to provide the tools for that success. Can it be done? Sure, says Amrein, by turning to research-based methods of improving student performance, like improved teacher quality and pay and smaller class sizes. But these are not likely to happen anytime soon, she says, because "that's the expensive route."

Headaches at Head Start

Shortly after taking office in 2001, Governor Bush suggested that "Head Start ought to be moved [from the Department of Health and Human Services] to the Department of Education, to highlight the need to make sure that our youngsters get a head start on reading and math"; in another speech, he argued that Head Start should become "first and foremost, a reading program."

But what are the consequences of this administrative shuffle?

Sarah Greene, president of the National Head Start Association, explains that moving the program to the Department of Education "dilutes and takes away the mission and goal of Head Start . . . which is to provide comprehensive services to children at risk through a holistic approach so that there's a permanent change in that child's life and that child's family life."

It is precisely this comprehensive approach that has made Head Start the success it is. At the program's reauthorization hearing in 2003, Dr. Edward Zigler, director of the Bush Center in Child Development and Social Policy at Yale University, told members of Congress, "My reading of the by-now voluminous evidence is that Head Start is clearly successful in achieving its primary mission, which is to prepare young children who live in poverty for school. The findings indicate that Head Start graduates are not only ready for the lessons they will receive when they begin school, but that they continue to achieve more. . . . It will continue to improve without sending it anywhere."

Despite widespread opposition from Head Start employees and child development researchers, a tidal wave of changes is potentially on the way for the nation's most comprehensive poverty program for young children. The Republican Senate in 2003 proposed the first budget cut to Head Start since 1968, and the Republican House approved Bush's plan for the smallest increase since 1996. Meanwhile, the Bush administration has mandated new literacy tests for all participants (kids aged three to five) in the program, to be administered up to three times a year—tests that Head Start advocates worry will turn into the high-stakes tests that have come to define No Child Left Behind.

Despite the president's comforting rhetoric, Greene worries that "during the first two years of this administration, Head Start has seen a tremendous drop in funding, and progress in expanding services and improving quality has also dropped. I don't know how you can say you're supporting a program," she adds, "and then not provide the funding."

It's All About Vouchers

In three years, President Bush has explicitly spoken of private school vouchers for public school students exactly twice. The V-word is rarely used around the White House, because it's not a popular concept with most Americans.

A 2001 poll conducted by the National School Boards Association/Zogby International found not only that vouchers lack majority support, but also that what support does exist is often based on a lack of information. While voters oppose vouchers 49 percent to 47 percent, the more information they're given about them (like how vouchers would drain public school funds), the more their support declines. Even more important, when given the option of introducing vouchers or other forms of school reform, voters prefer reforms like smaller class sizes by a margin of more than 2 to 1.

Vouchers are one of the nation's most controversial education topics. Research on voucher programs implemented here and in Europe has demonstrated negative side effects ranging from the "brain drain" that results when higher-achieving students flee the inner city for a private school to the money drain that results when public systems begin subsidizing the nation's private schools.

Because the public is familiar with studies pointing to such research about vouchers, "school choice" has been the rhetoric of preference for President Bush, appearing nine times in the president's speeches on the subject. There are other coded references to vouchers in comments like Bush's call for the federal government to "facilitate the capacity of parents to make different choices for their students" or in his declaration that "parents must be empowered to make different choices."

But Bush's education plan isn't really freeing anyone to make "choices" for their own schools or districts. Between the tightly circumscribed testing regimen and the withdrawal (and constant threat of withdrawal) of federal funds from low-performing public schools, it seems as if the only person making any school choices is Bush himself.

After Congress rejected Bush's initial voucher proposal in 2001, the president kept a relatively low profile on the issue. But in July 2003, Bush began pushing a new plan to provide $15 million in federal funds to vouchers for students in the District of Columbia. Using the word "scholarship" instead of "vouchers," he vowed the vouchers would help people "see the educational entrepreneurial spirit alive and well in D.C."

On September 9, 2003, the House of Representatives voted 209 to 208 to implement the nation's first federally funded vouchers program in the District of Columbia. The House Republican leadership scheduled the vote to coincide with a debate of the Democratic presidential candidates and ignored requests from the Black Caucus and Minority Leader Nancy Pelosi to reschedule the debate when their members could attend.

But assuming Bush is actually interested in education reform—and, based on his frequent, earnest statements, most people believe he is—what's the explanation for the seemingly self-defeating plans to heap requirements on already underfunded public schools and then to strip funding from schools that need it the most? Nancy Keenan—former state superintendent of Montana, the 2001 president of the National Council of State School Officers, and currently education policy director at People for the American Way—sees a huge credibility gap between the Bush administration's talk about education and its actual commitment to the issue. "When this administration underfunds public schools and sets unreasonable bureaucratic requirements that can't be met, they're setting schools up for failure because the real goal is to privatize public education. And who's left behind? Children of color and poor children. Instead of getting at the crux of the problem and really funding our schools, the Bush administration offers vouchers. Blaming the schools is like blaming a cemetery for dead people."

Going further, Noreen Connell of the Educational Priorities Panel argues that No Child Left Behind "was always meant as a vehicle for vouchers. . . . [I]t's structured that way all the way through." Connell believes that "there are a lot, a lot of technical implementation issues which I think were intentional." These issues—ranging from the difficulties in test development and approval by the Department of Education, to the (still) chronic underfunding of public schools, to the impending threat of monetary punishment—all work to create a public education disaster that ends with vouchers. Bush's plan gives schools three years to perform up to the administration's standards, but if in those three years additional resources and support aren't provided, failure seems predestined.

Yet Bush has been blaming away, blaming teachers and students as he drains the already meager budgets of local school districts while saddling them with more and more federal requirements. The education rhetoric sounds impressive, however, and photo-ops with kids learning to read makes for good PR. It's too bad someone hasn't educated the president on the real ABCs of public education—additional resources for teachers, pre-K programs, and smaller class sizes.

★

SCIENCE
The New Scopes Trials

"[W]e do not know how much effect natural fluctuations in climate may have had on warming. We do not know how much our climate could, or will change in the future. We do not know how fast change will occur, or even how some of our actions could impact it. . . . [N]o one can say with any certainty what constitutes a dangerous level of warming, and therefore what level must be avoided."
—President George W. Bush, June 11, 2001

What if the research agenda of the University of Texas science department were drafted not by the professors and scientists who actually conduct the studies but by, say, the alumni who funded the department? We might end up with research on the stickiness of Mr. Big's brand of adhesive glue instead of the development of an AIDS vaccine. Luckily, most research universities don't work that way.

The federal government, however, occasionally does, but instead of alumni, President Bush allows the interests of favored constituents to dictate his administration's science policies. When the religious right or big business weighs in on a matter of science, politics usually wins. So while the president may lack the powerful eloquence of William Jennings Bryan, in this world of science he's the smoother, modern equivalent of the Great Orator defeating the infidels of evolution in the Scopes Trial of 1925.

Within his first hundred days in office, Bush amassed a large portfolio of antiscience policies, including the United States's withdrawal from the Kyoto Protocol, a proposal to eliminate salmonella testing in school lunch meat (later withdrawn after the embarrassing headlines appeared), and a rejection of the decision to lower the legal amount of arsenic in drinking water. Perhaps his biggest misstep occurred when he dismissed concerns about global warming being largely a result of human activity.

What Global Warming?

Oil and gas companies, as documented by the Center for Responsive Politics, contributed more than $34 million to federal candidates during the 2000 election cycle, 78 percent of which went to Republicans. In 2002, thanks to the Bush administration, the energy industry had a banner year on climate policy. That February Exxon contacted the Bush White House to ask if Robert Watson, who at the time had been head of the UN Intergovernmental Panel on Climate Change (an organization of more than two thousand scientists from around the world) for six years, could "be replaced now at the request of the U.S.?" Watson had been vocal about the link between fossil fuels and rising global temperatures and a well-respected leader of this international committee. Two months later, the administration announced that it would not renominate Watson, who was out by May.

In June President Bush referred dismissively to a study by the Environmental Protection Agency as "the report put out by the bureaucracy," refusing to support its finding that humans are largely to blame for the earth's global warming. In September, the annual federal report on air pollution trends did not include its usual section on global warming after it was deleted by top officials at the EPA with White House approval. That December the administration "ignored a decade of peer-reviewed science" and called for five more years of study before taking any action on this worldwide problem. In light of the research that's already been conducted on the issue, Union of Concerned Scientists president Howard Ris said that this decision reflected not a pragmatic wariness of incomplete data, but a "real disregard for the science that has been learned so far."

The White House continued to tamper with the science of climate change in June 2003, when it once again deleted the section on global warming from an EPA report, a change one scientific expert compared to "the White House directing the secretary of labor to alter unemployment data to paint a rosy economic picture." The administration's head-in-the-sand approach to global warming was discussed in greater detail in chapter 2, but its policy position taken on behalf of friends of the White House is typical of its positions on many other science issues, chief among them, embryonic stem cell research.

Stem Those Cells

Stem cell research uses the inner cell material of a week-old embryo (often a discarded embryo created during in vitro fertilization processes) to produce large amounts of cells that can reproduce and—if directed correctly—become any type of cell in the human body. The mass of stem cells is created when the nucleus of an adult cell is transferred into an egg, which begins to divide after an electric current is run through it. At two weeks, the process is halted because the embryonic cluster already contains numerous stem cells. Stem cells are of vital interest because they have the unique ability to infinitely morph into other kinds of cells (a trait scientists refer to as pluripotency), making them appropriate for a wide range of scientific study.

Scientists have placed great emphasis on stem cell research because they believe it could play a key role in the development of cures for illnesses ranging from Parkinson's and Alzheimer's to diabetes. It's still too early to know what conditions stem cells may be able to help or even cure, but that, after all, is the whole point of continuing to expand and support research in the field.

President Bush, however, took a different view and on August 9, 2002, announced his "compromise" decision on the matter: "As a result of private research, more than sixty genetically diverse stem cell lines already exist," he said during his nationally televised address. "I have concluded that we should allow federal funds to be used for research on these existing stem cell lines, where the life-and-death decision has already been made." (The key word here was "existing"—as opposed to "new." The decision means that only stem cell lines currently in progress are now usable. Even extra embryos sitting frozen in fertility clinics would have to be tossed.) During this announcement, President Bush talked at great length of the seriousness with which he made his decision and claimed to have spent the preceding eight months consulting "scientists, scholars, bioethicists, religious leaders, doctors, researchers, members of Congress, my cabinet, and my friends."

But this decision involved little actual compromise, and in fact represented a huge victory for the far right. Bush's position was so extreme that, while he might have heard scientific opinion on the subject, he certainly didn't listen to it.

Most religious conservatives were pleasantly surprised by the announcement that federal funding of stem cell research would be so limited and restricted. While this research enjoys widespread support from the general public,* it passionately concerns many far-right conservatives. Ben Mitchell, a biomedical consultant for the Southern Baptist Ethics and Religious Liberty Commission, was quoted in *Southern Baptist Press News* comparing stem cell research to Nazi murders in the concentration camps. James Dobson, founder and chairman of the board of Focus on the Family, lauded the decision because President Bush's address "implied that life begins at

---

*An ABC News/*Washington Post* poll conducted on July 30, 2001—one week before President Bush's decision—found that 63 percent of Americans supported the research with only 33 percent claiming to be opposed. Public support for federal funding of stem cell research was similarly high: 60 percent of respondents supported it whereas 36 percent opposed it.

conception." Such comments led former White House speechwriter David Frum to deem President Bush's policy on stem cells "the biggest political victory the pro-life movement has had in years."

Bush's prejudices on the subject were also evident in the individuals he later appointed to the supposedly nonpartisan President's Council on Bioethics—a panel whose creation he announced during the stem cell speech. The *Southern Baptist Press News* applauded the appointees as "generally favorable" for "advocates of a sanctity-of-life ethic," while Richard Land, president of the Southern Baptist Ethics and Religious Liberty Commission, stated that "pro-lifers should be delighted" with the appointees. The council is ostensibly the organization charged with leading our diverse nation through the murky waters of cloning and other forms of genetic research. But instead of appointing a calm voice to lead the discussions, President Bush has appointed a reactionary ideologue cloaked in academic clothing, Leon Kass. Kass is a bioethicist at the University of Chicago who "has opposed or at least fretted about virtually every new reproductive technology." He opposed in vitro fertilization in the 1970s on the basis of *Brave New World*–esque fears of reproduction run amok and likes to refer to abortion as "feticide." In a recent issue of *The Public Interest,* Kass lamented the fact that today's young women live "the entire decade of their twenties—their most fertile years—neither in the homes of their fathers nor in the homes of their husbands; unprotected, lonely . . ." He goes on to blame everything from "woman on the pill" to sex education to the women's rights movement for the decline of old-fashioned courtship and claims that children of divorce are "maimed for love and intimacy."

Bush's announcement of his "compromise" was misleading in several critical respects. For example, the number of stem cell lines whose existence he asserted was inaccurate. An informal survey by *Science* magazine, the nation's leading science journal, claimed Bush's number sixty was "more than twice the number most scientists would cite." When the National Institutes of Health released its list of lines three weeks after the presidential address, the explanation for the leap upward became evident: the White House had a very loose definition of what counted as an "embryonic stem cell line." According to many observers cited in *Science,* the list of sixty-four was generated only because "NIH has established a low threshold of acceptability." In May 2003, under pressure from the scientific community, NIH director Dr. Elias Zerhouni reduced the number of widely available lines to the more accurate, but far less promising, *eleven.* The difference between sixty and eleven led science writer Stephen Hall to call the president's decision a "restrictive and disingenuous policy sold to the public on the basis of exaggerated information."

Also misleading was Bush's assurance that the lines he spoke of "have the ability to regenerate themselves indefinitely, creating ongoing opportunities for research . . . [l]eading scientists tell me research on these sixty lines has great promise that could lead to breakthrough therapies and cures." Roger Pedersen, an international expert in the world of stem cell research working out of the University of California at San Francisco, recently moved himself (and his research) to England, where government support makes this field a more promising pursuit. Pedersen explained that all lines approved by the Bush administration were cultivated on mouse "feeder" cells, meaning they do not have the potential for transplant into humans. Although there are a number of lines that have been off the mouse feeder cells for quite some time, there are still no human embryonic stem cell lines that have never been exposed to the mouse feeder cells. The federal restrictions on funding for the development of new stem cell lines also has served to greatly hamper progress in the field. Fourteen months after the president's decision, pediatric oncologist Dr. Curt I. Civin told a Senate subcommittee studying the issue that "[e]mbryonic stem cell research is crawling like a caterpillar . . . I am still waiting to receive my first stem cell line."

Many scientists like Dr. Pedersen prefer working within the English system, which encourages embryonic stem cell research while closely monitoring each project. For example, all research projects involving embryonic stem cells can only be conducted in order to address infertility and serious diseases and must be approved by the government's Human Fertilization and Embryology Authority.

As Michael Kinsley argued in his nationally syndicated column, it might be time for the president to make a change on this crucial policy.

> Bush cannot possibly believe that embryos are full human beings, or he would surely oppose modern fertility procedures that create and destroy many embryos for each baby they bring into the world. Bush does not oppose modern fertility treatments. He even praised them in his anti-stem-cell speech. It's not a complicated point. . . . If he's got both his facts and his logic wrong—and he has—Bush's alleged moral anguish on this subject is unimpressive. In fact, it is insulting to the people (including me) whose lives could be saved or redeemed by the medical breakthroughs Bush's stem-cell policy is preventing.

Sex and Scare Tactics

Bush's success with his far-right patrons on stem cell research was a feat matched only by his related success at chipping quietly away at reproductive rights. While the president himself may be pro-life, most of the country is solidly supportive of a woman's right to choose. (A CBS News/*New York Times* poll conducted on January 22, 2003—the thirtieth anniversary of *Roe v. Wade*—found that 77 percent of Americans were in favor either of allowing abortion to be generally available or available but with stricter limits than now.) Bush himself comes from a pro-choice family (though that position publicly changed when Bush 41 signed onto Reagan's ticket), and *Time*'s political columnist Joe Klein notes that where abortion is concerned, "You may have noticed that Bush doesn't talk about it very much. One suspects his wife, his mother, and quite possibly Karl Rove would kill him if he did." Former press secretary Ari Fleischer avoided directly addressing the question of whether President Bush supported overturning *Roe v. Wade,* never answering one way or the other. Bush's relationship with the "right-to-life" lobby is similarly equivocal. During the annual anti-abortion rally held January 22, 2001, just two days after his inauguration, President Bush announced that his first reversal of a Clinton administration policy would be to block federal funds from international family planning clinics that offer abortions or even present them as an option. While the policy itself is decidedly anti-choice, the way in which it was presented to the rally—via the cell phone of a Republican senator—is indicative of Bush's below-the-radar approach to the politics of reproductive freedom.

However delicately he handles the issue politically, Bush's own reproductive policies are decidedly anti-choice. In December 2002 he appointed Dr. David Hager to the FDA panel on reproductive health drugs, which determines whether a substance like RU-486—an anti-progesterone drug that induces spontaneous abortions when used early in a pregnancy—is safe enough for public use. (This panel also has the ability to hold up approval processes indefinitely if it chooses to do so.) Hager's appointment struck many observers as more than a bit odd, since he'd spent an awful lot of time lobbying alongside the Christian Medical Association in an attempt to halt the distribution of RU-486, which was finally approved by the FDA in 2000 for sale in the United States. Dr. Hager has written several books that urge women to turn to spiritual help for ailments ranging from premenstrual syndrome to headaches; *Stress and the Woman's Body,* for example, suggested that women imagine Jesus kissing them to help them end their extramarital affairs.

In June 2002 the National Cancer Institute—under pressure from congressional Republicans and HHS secretary Tommy Thompson—removed an online fact sheet explaining there is no link between abortion and breast cancer, even though mainstream groups like the American Cancer Society concluded that "the scientific evidence does not support a causal association between induced abortion and breast cancer." Rather than heed data, however, the supposedly nonpartisan National Cancer Institute replaced the original fact sheet with one insinuating that the science jury was still out on the issue (though that hazy formulation is also untrue). Under pressure, NCI later recanted and reposted a scientifically accurate fact sheet.

If Bush and other pro-lifers honestly want to decrease the number of abortions (which has been steadily dropping since 1990), a variety of constructive steps are open to them. But the president has characteristically limited thinking about the issue, believing, for example, that abstinence programs are the only way to teach teenagers about sex. "You know, I've heard all the talk about the abstinence programs, and this that and the other. But let me just be perfectly plain. If you're worried about teenage pregnancy, or if you're worried about sexually transmitted disease, abstinence works every single time."

While of course abstinence "works" if there's no intercourse, President Bush is willfully ignoring the fact that 46 percent of high school students and 80 percent of college students have sex outside of marriage and that 93 percent of men and 79 percent of women report that they have already had sex by the time they marry.

In fact, abstinence-only sex education has yet to show any evidence of actually helping to prevent the spread of sexually transmitted diseases or teen pregnancy. When asked about its effectiveness, Adrienne Verrilli, the director of communications with the Sexuality Information and Education Council of the United States, cites recent research on the topic: the only abstinence program that has been peer-reviewed and evaluated demonstrated that while the participants did postpone sex for eighteen months on average, they were 30 percent less likely than the control group to use contraception when they did have sex, a result Verrilli characterizes as a "backfire."

The Bush administration has nevertheless gone out of its way to fund these scientifically unsound abstinence-only-until-marriage plans, especially those administered through the Special Projects of Regional and National Significance (SPRANS) program. These programs worry health advocates because the eight-point definition of an "abstinence" program—to which all SPRANS participants must adhere—is too strict to be of any benefit and might in fact hinder the sex education of teenagers.* For example, these programs are allowed to discuss contraceptives only in terms of their risks and failure rates. The strict SPRANS definition of "abstinence education" is in fact the definition preferred by religious conservatives, and since President Bush took office, its funding nearly tripled.

Refusing to discuss condoms or exaggerating their failures is not smart policy when it comes to HIV/AIDS and STD prevention. It's also questionable science policy to nominate someone like Jerry Thacker to sit on the Presidential Advisory Council on HIV and AIDS. Thacker withdrew his nomination after controversy erupted over the appointment of a man who has described homosexuality as a "deathstyle" (as opposed to "lifestyle") and

---

*"Abstinence education" as defined by the SPRANS program means the program must teach (not simply refuse to contradict) concepts including the idea that "sexual activity outside the context of marriage is likely to have harmful psychological and physical side effects" and that "a mutually faithful monogamous relationship in the context of marriage is the expected standard of sexual activity." Such teaching ignores the lifestyle choices of the large majority of adult Americans who have had sex before they marry, to say nothing for gay teens who aren't allowed the option of having sex within the "context of marriage."

AIDs a "gay plague." Patricia Ware, the council's executive director and the person who suggested Thacker, resigned from the panel in the wake of the controversy. The panel includes Tom Coburn, the former Congressman who has expressed doubts over the effectiveness of condoms and opposes their use as a means of preventing sexually transmitted diseases (preferring to rely upon abstinence). The administration took its condom phobia a step further at the UN Special Session on Children when—along with Iran and Iraq—it forced the group to eliminate any reference to "reproductive health services and education" from its official declaration, including the use of condoms for HIV prevention.

Funding for scientific research in these areas is similarly stymied by the Bush political agenda. A *New York Times* article reported that federal officials have "warned" scientists "to avoid so-called sensitive language" and "key words" like "sex workers," "men who sleep with men," and "anal sex" when writing their grant proposals. Alfred Sommer, the dean of the School of Public Health and Johns Hopkins University, worried that such political pressure would compromise the mission of an arena that typically is free of such political influence.

Other Appointments

The administration's ability to politicize science is probably most evident on its appointments to scientific panels and committees. There are hundreds of such groups that make decisions ranging from the approval of drugs to deciding what research gets federal funds (like the research cited above) and what does not. These panels—perhaps most notably the Centers for Disease Control and Prevention's Advisory Committee on Childhood Lead Poisoning Prevention—have been particularly susceptible to the influence of the president's big-business supporters.

Bush and Company intervened at the precise moment the Lead Poisoning Advisory Committee was set to consider once again lowering the acceptable level of lead in the blood in light of new scientific evidence on the matter. Two 2003 studies—which appeared in the April 17 issue of the *New England Journal of Medicine*—have found new evidence of decreased IQ and delayed onset of puberty, both from levels of lead currently deemed acceptable by federal guidelines. But the administration rejected nominee Bruce Lamphear and dumped panel member Michael Weitzman, both of whom previously advocated lowering the legal limit. Instead, Secretary of Health and Human Services Tommy Thompson appointed William Banner—who has testified on behalf of lead companies in poison-related litigation—and Joyce Tsuji, who had worked for a consulting firm whose clients include a lead smelter. (She later withdrew.) Banner and another appointee, Sergio Piomelli, were in fact first contacted about serving on the committee not by a member of the administration but by lead-industry representatives who appeared to be recruiting favorable committee members with the blessing of HHS officials.

A similar case of stacking involved the CDC's National Center for Environmental Health, which reviews research and makes policy suggestions on a large range of public health policy issues, from bioterrorism to environmental toxins. When many of the committee members came up for renewal, committee chair Thomas Burke learned that fifteen of the committee's eighteen members were going to be replaced. In the past, HHS had asked Dr. Burke for a list of recommendations; this time, it had its own list, and Dr. Burke was not on it.

The new panel included numerous industry representatives, including chemical company favorite Lois Swirsky Gold, who denies many of the links between pollutants and cancer, and Dennis Paustenbach, who actually testified for Pacific Gas & Electric in the real-life Erin Brockovich court case. In fact, this administration sees nothing wrong with conducting an ideological litmus test for each of its potential appointees. For example, William Miller, a nominee to the National Advisory Council on Drug Abuse, was contacted by someone in Secretary Thompson's office after he'd been asked to consider the appointment. The caller asked a range of questions, including "Are you sympathetic to faith-based initiatives?" He was also asked whether he was supportive of abortion rights and whether he'd voted for President Bush. When he confessed that he had not voted for President Bush, he was asked to explain himself, and did not receive a callback.

The scientific community balked at these decisions. The American Public Health Association, for example, released an official policy statement November 12, 2002, that expressed its concern with "recent steps by government officials at the federal level to restructure key federal scientific and public health advisory committees by retiring the committees before their work is completed, removing or failing to reappoint qualified members, and replacing them with less scientifically qualified candidates and candidates with a clear conflict of interest. Such steps suggest an effort to inappropriately influence these committees."

Science magazine released an editorial signed by ten prominent U.S. scientists entitled "Advice Without Dissent" that railed against Bush's appropriation of the nation's system of scientific advisory committees and panels for political purposes. One of those scientists, Dr. Lynn Goldman at the Johns Hopkins University School of Public Health, is distressed at what she sees an eroding relationship between federal science agencies and the scientific community and eventually—when the ideological science is proven to be bunk—between government research on important public health topics and the scientific professionals in the field who desperately need, but no longer trust, that information.

Unlike previous administrations, the Bush White House, Goldman believes, has a "to the victor goes the spoils" approach to scientific research.

"That is what they're thinking, and what they don't understand is that everybody hasn't done it that way. Science isn't 'the spoils.' Science isn't something to be politicized based on who's elected." Anxiety within the science community has made its way across the Atlantic, with editors of Great Britain's premier scientific journal *The Lancet* expressing their own fears regarding Bush's influence over science policy in the United States:

> Expert committees need to be filled, by definition, with experts. That means those with a research record in their field and in epidemiology and public health. Members of expert panels need to be impartial and credible, and free of partisan conflicts of interest, especially in industry links or in right-wing ideology. Any further right-wing incursions on expert panels' membership will cause a terminal decline in public trust in the advice of scientists.

★

THE RIGHT JUDGES . . .
or Far-Right Judges?

"The role of a judge is to interpret the law, not to legislate from the bench."

—President George W. Bush, 2001

Nowhere is the religious right's relationship to President Bush more significant than in the arena of judicial appointments, where it can guarantee that its social agenda is advanced not for years, but for decades. On this point, the right and the left concur. Clint Bolick, a former Reagan Justice Department official, explained that "everyone on the Right agreed in 2000 that judicial nominations were the single most important reason to be for Bush." Senator Chuck Schumer (D-NY) added, perhaps in envy, "They realized if they took over the one unelected part of the government, they could govern for a generation."

With the U.S. Supreme Court hearing fewer than one hundred cases each year, the thirteen federal appellate courts, which usually hear cases using three-judge panels, almost always have the final say on questions of constitutional interpretation and federal law. Currently, Republican-appointed judges have a seven-to-two majority on the U.S. Supreme Court and a majority on eight of the appellate courts; three appellate courts have a majority of Democratic appointees, and two are evenly split. If President Bush's nominees fill the current vacancies, Republican appointees will control eleven appellate courts, and, with more retirements in the coming year, that figure could rise to thirteen by the end of 2004.

All federal judges are nominated by the president and then must be confirmed by a majority of the Senate before taking a seat for life on the federal bench. Often the relationship between the president and the Senate is one of consultation and compromise. President Clinton, for example, routinely consulted with GOP leaders about potential nominees, and even nominated several judges favored by Republican senators such as Orrin Hatch and Trent Lott despite complaints from many in his own party. President Bush has all but rejected such an approach and, instead, has nominated a cadre of far-right-wing judicial activists with the knowledge that, even if a few are blocked because of their extremist views, he will still manage to remake the composition of the federal judiciary for decades to come.

On the day he sent his first judicial nominees to the Senate, May 9, 2001, President Bush promised that everyone he would nominate "understands the role of a judge is to interpret the law, not to legislate from the bench." Once again, watch what he does.

One of Bush's first nominees to a federal appellate court was Texas Supreme Court Justice Priscilla Owen, who won distinction not as an academic or practicing attorney but as a conservative judicial activist eager to recast the law in her likeness—from protecting her corporate campaign donors against suits brought by workers (judges are elected in Texas) to adding new barriers to reproductive freedom. For example, although states can require that pregnant minors receive parental permission in advance of an abortion, parental consent statutes must include an alternative procedure through which the pregnant minor may receive authorization. The ability to "bypass" parental permission is vital in cases of parental abuse, such as when a father has raped and impregnated his own daughter, or when a young girl fears harsh parental reprisal for her condition. Texas's law instructs a court to grant a minor a bypass if the minor is "sufficiently mature and well-informed" to make the decision alone. Justice Owen, however, reads these words to require that the minor "[be] aware of and has considered that there are philosophic, social, moral, and religious arguments that can be brought to bear when considering an abortion. Owen's reading goes far beyond both the text of the statute and the interpretation given to the phrase by the Texas Supreme Court. Whatever one's view of abortion, this is surely an example of judicial activism. In another bypass case, then justice Alberto Gonzales, currently President Bush's White House counsel, criticized her dissent as "an unconscionable act of judicial activism," which would "create hurdles that simply are not found in the words of the statute."

With this record and the extraordinary coincidence of a Bush White House counsel's having previously condemned a Bush judicial nominee, Owen had a hard time in the Senate. After a contentious hearing, the Senate Judiciary Committee rejected her nomination on September 5, 2002, an action that historically has always killed a nomination. After the vote, Attorney General John Ashcroft complained that the Democrats were exhibiting "unfairness against qualified women." Not only was Ashcroft well aware that Owen's rejection had nothing to do with her gender, but while in the Senate he had frequently used a Senate rule to unilaterally bar the consideration of legislative measures in order to hold up President Clinton's nominees whose ideology was at odds with his own.

In January 2003, not to be dissuaded by a U.S. Senate exercising its confirmation powers under the Constitution, President Bush took an unprecedented step and renominated her. That maneuver may have had something to do with the fact that Bush's chief political advisor used to be on Owen's payroll: Karl Rove worked on her first campaign for the Texas Supreme Court in 1994, for which he was paid two hundred fifty thousand dollars. She was nonetheless blocked again in May by a Democratic filibuster that fell eight votes short of the sixty required to stop debate.

Owen was just the beginning. Prior to Bush's nomination of him to a federal appellate court, Dennis Shedd was a federal district court judge in South Carolina. As a district court judge, Shedd faced few restrictions on his judicial activism in attacking protections enacted by Congress. In one case, he invalidated the Driver's Privacy Protection Act by claiming that the federal government did not have the power to require that states keep driver's license records private. Even the conservative activist Scalia-Thomas-Rehnquist court thought Shedd went too far and *unanimously* reversed his decision. At Shedd's confirmation hearing in June 2002, Senator John Edwards (D-NC) asked if Shedd could recall another time when a federal trial judge had struck down an act of Congress only to be reversed by a unanimous Supreme Court. He couldn't think of one.

In another case, Judge Shedd struck down a portion of the Family and Medical Leave Act, the federal law that requires employers to give workers time off to care for a newborn child or sick relative. In order to invalidate part of the act, he claimed that a state agency cannot be sued by one of its employees for violating the law, invoking a complex legal argument that had not yet been recognized by his appellate court of the U.S. Supreme Court. Shedd's eagerness to attack federal laws that don't mesh with his personal ideology made him exactly the type of judge Bush promised not to nominate because he would "legislate from the bench."

Prior to his nomination to a federal appellate court by President Bush, D. Brooks Smith had been a federal judge since 1988. In several instances he acted in ways that appeared to violate the Code of Conduct for federal judges. In 1982, for example, Judge Smith became a member of a club that prohibited women from becoming members. At his 1988 confirmation hearing, Smith acknowledged that, if confirmed to become a federal trial judge, the Code of Conduct required him to resign from the club. If the command to resign wasn't already clear enough, the Senate Judiciary Committee unanimously passed a resolution in 1990 stating that it is "inappropriate" for federal judges to hold memberships in discriminatory clubs. Nonetheless, Judge Smith failed to resign from the club until 1999—eleven years after he recognized, under oath, his duty to give up his membership.

Miguel Estrada, Bush's nominee to the prestigious federal appellate court in Washington, D.C., was not confirmed after a bruising 2003 Senate battle because he couldn't persuade enough senators that he was a nominee of the highest quality. President Bush asserted that "Estrada is highly qualified [and] extremely intelligent." Democrats objected that Estrada, a forty-one-year-old lawyer who could reshape federal law for decades, had no judicial experience, virtually no record, and was unwilling to discuss his views on significant legal topics. At his confirmation hearing on September 26, 2002, Estrada claimed to have not given enough thought to *Roe v. Wade* to explain his views on the landmark abortion ruling. In an attempt to get some idea of Estrada's views on the law, Senator Schumer asked Estrada to "please tell us what three cases from the last forty years of the Supreme Court jurisprudence you are most critical of." "I'm not even sure that I could think of three that I would be . . . that I would have a sort of adverse reaction to," he replied, straining credulity all around the room.

Paul Bender was principal deputy solicitor general of the United States and Estrada's direct supervisor from 1993 to 1996. Based on their close work together, Bender concluded that Estrada is so "ideologically driven that he couldn't be trusted to state the law in a fair, neutral way. . . . Miguel is smart and charming but he is a right-wing ideologue." Such testimony and Estrada's dodging of questions led Schumer to call him "a far-right stealth nominee, a sphinxlike candidate who will drive the nation's second most important court out of the mainstream."

In February and March 2003, Senate Democrats held up a vote by the full Senate until Estrada provided more information on his judicial philosophy. They asked the Justice Department to release memoranda Estrada wrote while an attorney in the solicitor general's office, citing that such materials were turned over during the confirmation hearings of William Rehnquist and Robert Bork. The Justice Department refused.

The debate over Estrada quickly took on a racial dimension as Republican party leaders understood that the nomination played politically well in Latino communities around the country. Senator George Allen (R-VA), chairman of the National Republican Senatorial Committee, candidly acknowledged that, "I surely think it will help us with Hispanic voters." Many Hispanic leaders, however, fired back. As Congressman Ciro Rodriguez (D-TX), chairman of the Congressional Hispanic Caucus and a former judge, explained, "there are other highly qualified Hispanics who are not ashamed to discuss their views." He added, "That is the Republican strategy when it comes to minorities. Form over substance."

Presidential counsel Alberto Gonzales, himself Hispanic, even went so far as to assert that the Democrats were holding Estrada "to a double standard" because of his race. Yet Bush himself withdrew the nomination of Enrique Moreno to the Fifth Circuit Court of Appeals, despite Moreno's "well-qualified" rating from the American Bar Association. Moreno had been nominated by President Clinton and was never even given a hearing by the GOP-controlled Senate. Indeed, the Republican majority delayed the consideration of many of President Clinton's other Hispanic nominees, who never even received a hearing or a committee vote.

In total, 6.3 percent of President Clinton's judicial nominations were Hispanic Americans—a higher figure than any president who preceded him, and more than President Bush proposed. Currently, out of 179 federal appellate judges, only 10 are Hispanic, and 8 of them were appointed by President Clinton. President Bush has made only two nominations of Hispanics to federal appellate courts and he has not nominated any Hispanics to the two federal circuits with the highest percentages of Hispanic citizens.

With such an embarrassing record on past Hispanic nominees and Bush's withdrawal of the nomination of the highly respected Enrique Moreno, his administration might think twice about playing the race card in response to Democratic opposition to Estrada. For the nomination of Miguel Estrada is not about naming "quality" judges to the federal courts, or even "quality" Hispanic judges. As E. J. Dionne of the *Washington Post* wrote, "The fight over Estrada's nomination is not simply about him. It is about a concerted effort to pack our courts with representatives of a single point of view." No one has persuasively argued that President Clinton pursued a strategy of packing the judiciary with far-left judges. But if President Bush insists on nominating people more for their ideology than their intellect, he shouldn't be surprised if Democrats reject them for the same reason—*especially* since he's in a position to nominate so many judges in part because of an ideological Supreme Court opinion that picked him as president.

The Bush White House should also be especially careful about arguing race in the Estrada saga in light of its repeated push for Charles Pickering. Bush nominated Pickering, a federal trial judge in Mississippi, to a seat on the Court of Appeals for the Fifth Circuit which encompasses Louisiana, Mississippi, and Texas, in May 2001. The Fifth Circuit has a minority population of 44 percent (the highest of any federal court of appeals), yet, according to the Alliance for Justice, it has "issued many of the most extreme civil rights rulings in the country." Nonetheless, and despite the fact that only one African American currently sits on the eleven-member court, all three of President Bush's nominees, including Pickering, have been white.

By the time of his hearing before the Senate Judiciary Committee in October 2001, senators had learned that Pickering had published only ninety-five decisions out of the more than eleven hundred he has rendered in eleven years as a trial judge. Committee Democrats, not wanting Bush to put yet another recordless judge on the federal appellate bench, decided to call Pickering back for a second hearing after they had an opportunity to read his unpublished decisions and review his record. Following his second hearing and a more thorough airing of the many troubling aspects of his record on civil rights, possible violations of judicial ethics, and an extraordinary number of reversals of his decisions, President Bush came to his defense. On March 13, 2002, the day before the Senate Judiciary Committee was to vote on Pickering's nomination, Bush held a press conference and asserted that "Pickering is a respected and well-qualified nominee . . . [with a] very strong record on civil rights."

In fact, as a federal trial judge, Pickering displayed an impressive insensitivity to issues of civil rights and race. In one case, a man was convicted of burning an eight-foot cross on the lawn of an interracial couple with a young child. The defendant faced a severe sentence because of the federal mandatory minimum but Judge Pickering took ethically questionable steps to get the man a reduced sentence, ordering federal prosecutors to speak directly with the U.S. attorney general about the case and directly contacting a high-ranking Justice Department official. Senator John Edwards (D-NC) expressed concern that Judge Pickering violated the Code of Conduct for federal judges, which forbids such communications between a judge and attorneys for only one side of a case. Five experts on judicial ethics even wrote the Judiciary Committee to explain why his conduct violated the Code.

Pickering's questionable racial history surfaced long before his arrival at the federal bench. The Mississippi Sovereignty Commission was a state-funded agency established for the purpose of opposing integration. At his 1990 confirmation hearing before becoming a federal trial judge, Pickering testified that he "never had any contact" with the Sovereignty Commission. In fact, as a Mississippi state senator, Pickering voted to provide public funding to the organization. Moreover, a 1972 memorandum stated that state senator Pickering was "very interested" in one of the commission's investigations and had "requested to be advised of developments." Here, as columnist Joe Conason wrote, Pickering came "perilously close to lying under oath."

After Senator Trent Lott (R-MS) stepped down as the Republican leader in December 2002 because of his sympathetic remarks about Strom Thurmond's 1948 prosegregationist presidential campaign, President Bush had an opportunity to repudiate Pickering's troubling legacy. Lott had been Pickering's chief patron, and Bush could easily have distanced himself from the Senator's racial problems by accepting the Judiciary Committee's rejection of Pickering's nomination due to his anti–civil rights record. Instead, Bush went against the advice of many in his administration and chose to take the extraordinary step of renominating Pickering. According to an angry Julian Bond, chairman of the NAACP, "The renomination of failed judicial candidate Charles Pickering is a clear signal that the party of Lott has no intention of becoming the party of Lincoln and that they'll continue to play the race card and practice the politics of racial division." (Pickering was again voted down in October 2003.)

Demonstrating that ideology, not quality, is the preeminent characteristic President Bush uses to select his judicial nominees, he chose James Leon Holmes, the former president of Arkansas Right to Life, to take a seat on the federal trial court in Little Rock. In a 1997 newspaper article Dr. Holmes and his wife wrote that "the wife is to subordinate herself to her husband" and "the woman is to place herself under the authority of the man" in the same way that "the church is to place herself under the protection of Christ." In 1980 Dr. Holmes wrote a letter to the editor of a newspaper stating that "[c]oncern for rape victims is a red herring because conceptions from rape occur with approximately the same frequency as snowfall in Miami." (It snowed once in Miami the prior hundred years; thirty-two thousand women became pregnant that year as the result of rape.)

Two others from the Owen-Shedd-Holmes school of judicial temperament were Claude Allen and Alabama attorney general Bill Pryor. Nominated to the Fourth Circuit Court of Appeals in Richmond, Virginia, Allen was a spokesman for the Jesse Helms reelection campaign in 1984 when he declared that their Democratic opponent was vulnerable because of his links with "the queers." Pryor has also been nominated by President Bush to the U.S. Court of Appeals for the Eleventh Circuit, even though he has defended student-led prayer in public schools, supported displaying the Ten Commandments in state courts, and has called *Roe v. Wade* "the worst abomination of constitutional law in our history." *Washington Post* editors complained that, because of nominees like Pryor, "Mr. Bush cannot at once ask for apolitical consideration of his nominees and put forth nominees who, in word and deed, turn federal courts into political battlegrounds." Perhaps even more troubling than his extremist record is Pryor's founding of, and participation with, the Republican Attorneys General Association (RAGA), a group established to promote the election of Republican attorneys general. RAGA frequently solicits campaign contributions from the same corporations the attorneys general are charged with regulating, leading several Republican attorneys general to decline to join because of possible serious conflicts of interest. Pryor's solicitation of corporate contributions led Nan Aron, president of Alliance for Justice, to state that "There is no question that Pryor's conduct violates Alabama's Rules of Professional Conduct regarding attorney conflicts of interest." Grant Woods, a Republican and a former attorney general in Arizona, declined to join the association and commented that Pryor is "probably the most doctrinaire and the most partisan of any attorney general [he had] dealt with in eight years, so people would be wise to question whether or not [Pryor is] the right person to be nonpartisan on the bench."

The presidential prerogative to appoint judges and justices under Article II of the U.S. Constitution has periodically led to political feuding throughout our history. President Washington's very first nomination to the highest court was rejected in part because of his opposition to the Jay Treaty. FDR's frustrations led to his ill-considered court-packing plan, and the Robert Bork and Clarence Thomas fights of 1987 and 1991 still rankle—and motivate—Senate Republicans. President Bush, however, has taken the politicization of courts to a new level, ignoring shortcomings in judicial quality to nominate judges whose views, concludes Professor Cass Sunstein of the University of Chicago Law School, "are closer to the Republican Party platform than those of the framers." A prolific scholar and highly regarded moderate, Sunstein told a group of Senate Democrats how historically unusual Bush's nominees were:

> They want to cut back on what government is allowed to do—whether it's campaign-finance legislation, or affirmative action, or the right to sue for environmental violations. This Supreme Court has struck down more federal legislation at a higher annual rate than any other in the last half century. The new people want to strike down more. It's a radical agenda.
>
> We looked at thousands of opinions and we saw that Republican nominees really are different from Democratic nominees. And when you get three Republican nominees sitting together they get really conservative. We had a large enough sample, so that we could see proof of this in affirmative action, campaign finance, the Americans with Disabilities Act, judicial review of environmental regulations, and sex discrimination.

President Bush's disingenuousness about his selections for federal judges is more than matched by his party's hypocrisy on judicial nominees. Despite GOP assertions that Democrats were slow to confirm Bush's nominees when they controlled the Senate, the Republican Senate during the Clinton administration set the standard for obstruction and delay. Even though President Clinton nominated a largely centrist bench, the Republican Senate approved only 61 percent of Clinton's federal appellate court nominees, while Democrats approved 94 percent of Bush 43's nominees who had completed files. During the administration of Bush 41, it took an average of 77 days for an appeals court judge to be confirmed by the Democratic Senate. Under the Republican-controlled Senate in 1997–98, the average was 231 days, and in 1999–2000 it was 247 days, for President Clinton's appellate court nominees. Senator Orrin Hatch's Judiciary Committee often delayed votes for years—more than four years for Richard Paez's nomination to the Ninth Circuit Court of Appeals and more than three years in the case of William Fletcher's nomination to the same court; they wouldn't even give a hearing to Clinton White House aide Elena Kagan, who had to withdraw her name and three years later became the Dean of Harvard Law School. As Senator Patrick Leahy (D-VT), former chairman of the Judiciary Committee, remarked at a hearing, "We have confirmed more judicial nominees in less than fifteen months than were confirmed in the last thirty months that a Republican majority controlled the Senate."

Although Democrats had largely given Republicans a taste of their own medicine, confirming 132 judges and filibustering only 3 (Owen, Estrada, and Pryor), Republicans struck back. President Bush declared it a "crisis" because judicial vacancies "are causing delays for citizens seeking justice." (This was double Bushspeak, since (a) the vacancy rate was at its lowest in a decade and (b) Bush's own agenda would cut back on class action and plaintiff's lawsuits for "citizens seeking justice.") Nonetheless, Republican Senate leader Bill Frist began an attempt to thwart the Democrats by changing the hoary filibuster rule so that only fifty-one votes would be needed to approve a nominee or bill. Robert Caro, the National Book Award winner for his magisterial *Master of the Senate: The Years of Lyndon Johnson,* led a body of opinion that such a move would radically transform the Senate into a smaller House of Representatives. The *New York Times* editorialized that, while the filibuster "is not a tool to be used lightly[,] . . . it would damage our constitutional system if Senate Republicans tried to rewrite longstanding rules for advice and consent for immediate partisan gain."

Bush and Frist, however, pushed ahead with their effort to make it easier to confirm individuals who opposed many of the social and legal reforms of the past fifty years—and rejected an alternative proposal advanced by Senator Patrick Leahy, ranking Democrat on the Judiciary Committee, and the "dean" of Washington columnists, David Broder: "meaningful bi-partisan consultation in advance of any Supreme Court nomination." President Clinton had done just this with then judiciary chair Hatch before naming such consensus favorites as Ruth Bader Ginsberg and Stephen Breyer, but President Bush opted for confrontation over consensus.

*

POVERTY
"Heart"felt Indifference

"[A]n issue that is dear to my heart is the understanding that we need to help people help themselves."
—President George W. Bush, September 2, 2002

George W. Bush has labeled himself a "compassionate conservative," and he has demonstrated convincingly that he is precisely that: he speaks compassionately and governs conservatively. There is, and always has been, a great gulf between Bush's compassionate rhetoric and his conservative record.

President Bush's favorite organ is, by far, his heart. "I read a quote from a little girl from New York the other day that touched my heart, and I hope it touches yours." "Six months ago I . . . promised to fight for the things close to my heart." "I think the thing that has captured my heart the most is not only universal care for the weak and the suffering but also the strong focus on making sure every child is educated." "I have in my heart a prayer." "When I act, you will know my reasons. And when I speak, you will know my heart." In speaking of his heart, Bush hopes to differentiate himself politically from those earlier Republicans whose hearts couldn't get through airport metal detectors. In fact, George W. Bush must have an especially heartfelt affinity for the poor because he keeps creating more of them.

Feeding the Hungry with Words

In the 2000 campaign Bush stressed his role as governor of a "big" state. But one of the biggest things about Texas was the number of people without sufficient food: the federal government's annual report on hunger in America that year listed Texas as the state with the worst hunger problem in the nation.

In accepting the Republican Party's nomination for president, Bush assured America that he would "support the heroic work of homeless shelters . . . [and] food pantries . . . [and] people reclaiming their communities block by block and heart by heart." More than two years later, as president, just a few days before Christmas, Bush visited the Capitol Area Food Bank in Washington, D.C. "Those who are poor, those who suffer, those who have lost hope are not strangers in our midst: they're our fellow citizens," he said, accompanied by his wife, Laura. "And in this time of joy, in the time of blessing, we've got to remember that. To make the season complete and the season whole, we must help those who are in need." Even Bush, however, seemed to realize his rhetorical excess in mid-speech, begging the audience, "One of the things you've got to—I hope you'll recognize about me is sometimes I get a little wordy; I admit that. But I hope you view me as a man of action as well."

Here, in fact, were his "actions" only days prior to his visit to the food bank: the president proposed to cut off some 36,000 seniors' meal assistance; eliminate 50,000 slots in after-school programs for children and child care benefits for some 33,000 youngsters; and terminate heating assistance for 532,000 families during the Christmas season.

According to the latest available census report, the number of people living in poverty rose by 1.7 million in 2002, to 34.6 million. Median household income fell by $900 to $42,200. Further, the proportion of the national household income going to the top 5 percent of the population reached an all-time peak, while the proportion going to the bottom three-fifths dropped to an all-time low.

Welfare to Worse

In remarks in the East Room of the White House on January 14, 2003, Bush shared that "[he] wants to help people. That's what we ought to do in America. We want to help people who, in this land of plenty, have overcome some incredibly tough times, because of the lack of things—sometimes the lack of love; sometimes the lack of help; sometimes the lack of education." Ten months earlier, Bush had proclaimed: "I am proposing that every state be required within five years to have seventy percent of welfare recipients working or being trained to work at least forty hours a week. These work requirements must be applied carefully and compassionately." Bush's "compassionate" plan would actually force young mothers currently holding jobs under the federal welfare reform program to work an additional ten hours per week beyond the thirty hours required in the 1996 Welfare Reform Act. The new requirements would compel these women to work a full six hours more per week than the national average for women with children, without providing additional subsidies for child care and transportation, among other things necessary for working mothers to hold a job. Instead the president has proposed to limit funding for such assistance to $17 billion, the 1996 level, despite 11 percent inflation since that time.

Moving welfare recipients into the workforce is sound policy, as reflected by the bipartisan approach that President Clinton and Senator Robert Dole urged in 1996. In the strong economy of that time welfare reform increased employment among low-income mothers from 44 percent to 59 percent. While not popular with many on the left, Clinton's reform required most recipients to get off the rolls within two years, capped handouts at five years, and denied mothers additional subsidies if they had a child while receiving benefits.

But where the Clinton reform was tough, the Bush plan is unreasonable. President Bush refuses to recognize that mothers can't go to work if their children are home alone. Because it demands more work at the same time that it cuts child-care subsidies, the Bush proposal can force mothers to choose between a paycheck and their children. Ruth Brandwein, a former Suffolk County, New York, social services commissioner, asks: "If more people, even those working, are poor, and fewer jobs are available, does it make sense to require women—often with few skills, lack of education, and other barriers—to leave their children for long hours of work?"

At the end of 2002, nineteen states had extensive waiting lists for child-care subsidies. Indeed in Texas, at the end of 2001, more than thirty-six thousand were waiting for basic federal assistance that would enable them to care for their children. Yet Bush has proposed to cut Child Care and Development block grants by $200 million, child abuse prevention and counseling programs by $15.7 million, child care and education for preschool children by $20 million, and to eliminate the $250 million program that had gone to train pediatricians at the nation's children's hospitals. Of course, government spending is not limitless and, as President Kennedy said, "to govern is to choose." But these reductions were proposed by a president who inherited a $236 billion annual surplus, who had enacted a $1.3 trillion tax cut over ten years, and who had run on the slogan of "Leave no child behind." According to Maine's attorney general, Steven Rowe, "This is so shortsighted. For . . . one-fifth the [ten-year] cost of the [2003] tax cut, we could fully fund all of these programs" for the next ten years.

Unemployment Unpleasantness

Faced with the loss of her unemployment benefits during the Christmas season in 2002, Jo-Anne Hurlston of Washington, D.C., a former high school dean, said, "I don't even want to truly think about it. I have a twelve-year-old [daughter] to support." At the end of 2002 White House and congressional inaction put fear into the hearts of many Jo-Anne Hurlstons, refusing to pass any extension to the Temporary Federal Unemployment Assistance Program that was to expire over the Christmas holidays. After much pleading with the congressional Republicans, Democrat leaders Tom Daschle and Richard Gephardt wrote to President Bush on the twenty-first of November: "If you simply indicated your determination to enact this modest extension of unemployment insurance before the House adjourns, House Republicans would certainly drop their opposition." But while the Bush administration expressed "disappointment" that the House and the Senate could not come up with a timely bill, it did nothing to advance legislation. Finally, after more Democratic public pressure, in January the president urged and obtained legislation extending benefits, saying the bill "should bring some comfort to those of our fellow citizens who need extra help during the time in which they try to find a job."

Yet the legislation ignored the more than 1 million workers who had depleted all of their federal benefits and still couldn't find a job due to the lagging economy. And as of mid-January 2003 there were 1,012,200 workers who no longer received unemployment assistance and were still unemployed.

The number of workers unemployed for more than fifteen weeks has reached the level that it has under the Bush administration only twice since World War II—a period beginning in May 1982, and a period beginning in February 1992. While these two periods coincided with Republican presidencies, both Ronald Reagan and George H. W. Bush, faced with similar crises, kicked in substantially more weeks of unemployment assistance than Bush 43 has made available, along with significantly increased funding for food, fuel, and health care assistance programs. But according to a report of the Democratic staff of the House Appropriations Committee, "Instead of those services, the long-term unemployed in this downturn may have the opportunity to avoid taxation on any dividends received."

Hot Air Doesn't Keep the House Warm

During the second presidential debate George W. Bush pledged to fund the Low Income Home Energy Assistance Program (LIHEAP): "First and foremost, we got to make sure we fully fund LIHEAP, which is a way to help low-income folks . . . pay for their high fuel bills." In remarks to reporters on March 19, 2001, President Bush again spoke from the heart: "I am concerned that if we don't act in a commonsense way that our people will not be able to heat and cool their homes."

Yet in his 2003 budget proposal, Bush sought to cut federal energy subsidies for home heating from $1.7 billion to $1.4 billion, a decrease of approximately 18 percent. That translates into 438,000 fewer families receiving energy assistance from the federal government. "It's a grim situation," Bob Vondrasek, executive director of the South Austin Coalition, said. "People are living in the cold, they're trying to get by with kerosene heaters and charcoal grills, electric heaters. There will be fires, hypothermia. Strictly from the perspective of low-income households, it's kind of a third-world situation." How was this consistent with Bush's election-year pledge to "fully fund" LIHEAP? Health and Human Services spokesman Michael Musante explained: "You could call it a cut if you like. We're saying it's a return to the normal level of funding."

The Religious Solution

Bush's "faith-based initiative," his primary response to the nation's needy, was born out of a conversation he had in 1993 with University of Texas professor Marvin Olasky, the author of a scathing critique of the liberal welfare state entitled *The Tragedy of American Compassion.* Olasky preached that religious-based charities were a better means of aiding the poor than large government entitlement programs, and he believed that infusing faith into the welfare state would make up for any deficiencies that might rise out of a lack of funding. Without needing much convincing, Bush swallowed Olasky whole and later added this thesis to his presidential campaign's repertoire.

And he continued to push it as president-elect. At a meeting of faith-based organization leaders in Austin, Texas, shortly before Christmas, 2000, Olasky rapturously described how "Bush talked about how to 'change lives by changing hearts' and then emphasized ways of promoting the general welfare: 'the role of the government is to help social entrepreneurs.' . . . [H]e vowed to 'change the bureaucracy' from infatuation with process to an emphasis on results." Bush described a grand vision that day, leading the compassionate group gathered in Austin with his heart and his soul. His vision was of a government that did not distinguish between secular organizations and those of faith when handing out grants to provide social services. His vision was of a society in which the religious community provided services to those in need, filling the shoe traditionally worn by government. In conclusion, Olasky declared proudly that the Austin "meeting sounded like a revival itself."

George W. Bush sounded more like a pastor than a president in his December 2002 speech in Philadelphia unveiling his faith-based initiative. As much as Bush was trying to move the faith-based community into providing services that the government has traditionally provided, he was also trying to move the government into the arena traditionally reserved for the religious community. "We want more and more faith-based charities to become partners in our efforts, our unyielding efforts to change America one heart, one conscience, one soul at a time," he said. A year later, he added, "I believe government should welcome faith-based groups as allies in the great work of renewing America." In fact, Bush's welcome wagon would include a license to discriminate in hiring. In June 2003 President Bush called on Congress to "make it easier for federally funded religious groups to base their hiring decisions on a job candidate's religion and sexual orientation."

The religious right loves Bush's faith-based initiative, which is only to be expected, since the government will be sending large checks to these well-meaning people who will now have the opportunity to help those in the community that they were unable to assist before. But many more indigent than under the admittedly imperfect system in place since the New Deal will go without the assistance they need. Under Bush's proposal, the faith-based community may well be able to provide some improved services, due to their idealism and experience, but they will unfortunately never be able to make up for the cuts to the social safety net that have been described in this chapter. And when the needs of the community are not met, Bush can deny any responsibility. In essence, his faith-based initiative is a buck-passing program. The needs of society are not the federal government's responsibility anymore: sorry—call your clergy.

It was John DiIulio's job to convert Olasky's language into real services. President Bush called this University of Pennsylvania professor "one of the most influential social entrepreneurs in America" on the day he appointed him to lead the White House Office of Faith-Based and Community Initiatives—and later referred to him congenially as "Big John." But DiIulio left the White House within the year and publicly criticized the very program that he had been asked to lead, telling *Esquire*'s Ron Siskind that the White House "winked at the most far-right House Republicans, who in turn drafted a so-called faith bill that (or so they thought) satisfied certain fundamentalist leaders and Beltway libertarians but bore few marks of compassionate conservatism. . . . Not only that, but it reflected neither the president's own previous rhetoric on the idea nor any of the actual empirical evidence." Even Professor Olasky, while congratulating Bush's many public appearances to beat the drum of compassion, gave Bush "an F in terms of legislation at this point" at the end of 2002.

Regardless of how capably the nation's religious groups are able to meet the responsibilities of the government, the funding of these institutions by taxpayers is a constitutionally shaky proposition at best. "The Teen Challenge," for example, an "inherently Christian" program aimed at helping people get off drugs, would qualify for federal funding under Bush's faith-based initiative. The program does not require participants to convert to Christianity, but the group's leader, the Reverend John D. Castellani, testified before a House subcommittee in May 2001 that some of its clients become "completed Jews," better known as "Jews for Jesus."

Whether President Bush acknowledges it or not, religious institutions are going to provide religiously based services. Even the current director of the White House Office of Faith-Based and Community Initiatives, Jim Towey, recognized the concern. "This program is funding treatment, not worship. But what you would term 'worship' is integral to a successful treatment program." People should be able to turn to their faith for help in their private lives, but government should not, and cannot, constitutionally spend public money to provide that religion-based service.

Bush has gone as far as proposing that religious organizations be allowed to apply for federal housing assistance to build and renovate their buildings. His only requirement: that *part* of the building be used for social services. Yet this requirement will never be enforced simply because it's nearly impossible to police. As Bill Terry of the National Congress for Community Economic Development said, this will be like "trying to take the sugar out of cupcakes. The line can't be blurred." Congressman Barney Frank asked, "Are we going to start sending in the inspector general to charge people with committing a bar mitzvah?"

For all his rhetorical consistency and apparent sincerity, "compassionate conservatism" is more packaging than policy, as any comparison of words and deeds in George W. Bush's presidential term would show. His originally proposed 2003 budget began with (another) $726 billion tax cut, aimed primarily at the top income bracket, which would have forced cuts of $265 billion in entitlement programs over the next ten years—$165 billion of those reductions coming from programs aimed to assist low-income people. Federal funding for Medicaid would be slashed by $92 billion, veterans' benefits by $14 billion, food stamps by $13 billion, and school lunch and other child nutrition programs by $6 billion.

John DiIulio expressed his disappointment: "There is a virtual absence as of yet of any policy accomplishments that might, to a fair-minded non-partisan, count as flesh on the bones of so-called compassionate conservatism." Harvard University's Robert Putnam, author of *Bowling Alone* and a regular consultant to the Bush team, agrees: "He has always been rhetorically on the right side of the issue. They have not yet done nearly enough in practical terms to match the rhetoric. The compassionates win a lot of rhetorical battles, but when you look where the budget is, it shows hardly a hint of the compassionate." President Clinton, too, chimed in during the presidential race with a mocking analysis, telling a laughing Democratic Leadership Conference: "This 'compassionate conservatism' has a great ring to it, and I've really worked hard to figure out what it means. And the nearest I can tell, here's what it means. 'I like you—I do. And I would like to be for closing the gun show loopholes. And I'd like not to squander the surplus—you know, save Social Security and Medicare for the next generation. I'd like to raise the minimum wage. I'd like to do these things, but I just can't and I feel terrible about it."

Empirically the curtain seemed to close on "compassionate conservatism" with President Bush's performance on volunteerism and AmeriCorps. In a major address, he called on Americans to devote two years over the course of a lifetime to the cause. "I hope and ask that you serve your community you live in and your nation by two years of service, four thousand hours of service over your lifetime." Later, in his 2002 State of the Union address, in front of a TV audience of 50 million people, he called for an increase in the AmeriCorps program—a volunteer initiative started by President Clinton to encourage young people to perform community service—from fifty thousand to seventy-five thousand. "Americans are doing the work of compassion every day—visiting prisoners, providing shelter for battered women, bringing companionship to lonely seniors," he eloquently said. "These good works deserve our praise; they deserve our personal support; and when appropriate, they deserve the assistance of the federal government." Yet the following year, his administration quietly proposed not an increase but an 80 percent cut—from fifty thousand slots to ten thousand—for this program. After all, someone's got to sacrifice to pay for the large upper-bracket tax cuts, and where better to start than reducing opportunities for the young and the poor?

As president-elect Bush admitted to supporter Rev. Jim Wallis, a leader of Call to Renewal, a group of churches fighting poverty, "I don't understand how poor people think. [I'm] a white Republican guy who doesn't get it, but I'd like to."

✫

CRIME AND PUNISHMENT
Guns and Death

"[Politicians] should not respond to special interests. . . . They ought to respond to this interest—protecting the American people."
—President George W. Bush, 2002

On the issue of guns, George W. Bush is no hypocrite. He has not, per usual, adopted the John Mitchell axiom of saying one thing to misdirect attention away from doing another. Bush has been principled and consistent. Adopting the iconography of a western sheriff, he's tough on crime, tough on criminals, tough on terrorism, but soft on guns.

Again and again, he urges jurisdictions to "enforce the [gun control] laws on the books" and to put "violent criminals who commit crimes with guns behind bars—and keep them there." Bush's stress on "an era of personal responsibility" implies that the primary duty is individual, not societal. After the Columbine shootings in 1999, for example, he said, "this is a society that . . . has got to do a better job of teaching children right from wrong."

But while consistently pro-gun over the years, are his policies an honest effort to deal with the reality of a country that leads the Western world in gun violence—with 208 gun deaths in the United States for every 1 in Japan, 48 for every 1 in England, 30 for every 1 in Germany? Can one be both pro-gun and anti-crime?

The NRA Connection

Drawing a distinction between the National Rifle Association's views and George W. Bush's gun policies is an ultimately pointless task. As NRA president Kayne B. Robinson boasted at a private function prior to the 2000 election, "[if Bush wins,] we'll have a president where we work out of their office—unbelievably friendly relations." Grateful for his advocacy as governor, the NRA bestowed him with an A rating, "a dream come true" for the NRA, according to Nina Butts, the founder of Texans Against Gun Violence.

The NRA felt that Bush's 2000 candidacy was so important that they initiated a media (and fund-raising) campaign effort two to three times bigger than any it had ever undertaken. Gun rights political action committees and individuals pumped more than $4 million into Republican coffers in 2000, more than double their 1996 spending level of $1,734,937. The NRA saw Bush's ascendancy as an opportunity to "turn back the clock" on a Clinton-Gore administration that had imposed a five-day waiting period on handgun purchases, required criminal background checks to keep guns away from criminals, and banned nineteen types of assault weapons. Moreover, they looked forward, again in the words of Kayne Robinson, to a Bush win that would ensure a "Supreme Court that will back us to the hilt." For example, it could reverse the 1939 Supreme Court ruling in *U.S. v. Miller*, which concluded that the Second Amendment gave authorized state *militias* the right to bear arms, not *individuals*.

The NRA and George W. Bush seemed to have a smart, coordinated strategy for the 2000 election. Bush distanced himself from the group, saying little about it and not visiting it, and vice versa. Ralph Talbot, president of the Texas State Rifle Association (the Texas division of the NRA), observed, "I don't want to paint Governor Bush as being in the NRA's pocket or TSRA's pocket—that's not true at all. He's not. I think he's a fair man. He's not an extremist." However, when pressed about differences between Bush and the NRA, Talbot replied, "I can't think of any in recent time. [But,] I don't want to paint Governor Bush into a corner that doesn't give him any way out."

Concealed Weapons and Immunization

Running for governor in 1994, Bush complained that incumbent Ann Richards had "refused to let Texans vote on whether citizens of our state should be allowed to carry concealed weapons." A "concealed carry" law would make Texas a safer place," he added, and made an election-year pledge for a public referendum to decide whether to end the state's 125-year-old concealed-weapons prohibition. Yet once in the governor's mansion, Bush flip-flopped and pushed hard *against* the referendum, privately telling legislators during a late-night strategy meeting that "we [already] had a referendum on November eighth."

But police officers and mayors weren't persuaded. Mark Clark, the spokesman for the Combined Law Enforcement Association of Texas (CLEAT), a Texas-wide organization of 13,000 police officers, expressed concern that "the level of violence on the streets right now is unacceptable. It makes no sense to me as a police officer . . . to say, 'Let's put more guns out there to try and solve the violence issue.'"

In 1999, Governor Bush quietly signed an NRA-backed bill that prevented city, county, and local governments from suing firearm and ammunition manufacturers to recoup public money spent dealing with the consequences of gun violence. Spokesperson Karen Hughes explained the bill would prevent "frivolous lawsuits." Essentially, Bush argued that criminals—who usually have no resources—should bear the responsibility of lawsuits rather than the gun industry, which ignores the fact that it is the gun makers who could manufacture safer firearms. The Consumer Product Safety Commission data show that between 1972 and 1999, "nearly fifty thousand people have been killed in unintentional shootings." Immunizing the gun industry saves them potentially billions of dollars in lawsuits and reduces the pressure to make outlays to make guns safer. That would cost more money, which could drive down sales.

As governor and now as president, George W. Bush has never seriously advocated mandatory trigger locks, hidden serial numbers, or smart-gun technology.* If any of these technologies were either required by the government (much as government "performance standards" for cars reduce injuries and fatalities) or subsidized directly to make sure that new guns were safer, gun deaths would decline and, therefore, so would so-called frivolous lawsuits.

Now, as president, Bush—and the NRA—are pushing for national immunity for the gun industry. This would prevent gun-violence victims from bringing lawsuits against irresponsible gun dealers and manufacturers and compel judges to throw victims with pending cases out of court. For example, both of the Washington, D.C–area snipers were legally banned from making gun purchases, yet a negligent gun dealer allowed them to obtain a

---

* **Hidden Serial Numbers.** Under this system, unique numbers assigned to each gun are not visible to the user. The numbers are printed in extremely small type so that criminals will not be able to remove the serial numbers from their crime guns, which could block a police trace. **Smart-Gun Technology.** The owner needs something unique such as a fingerprint or a PIN to activate the gun. Currently, they have not been brought to market yet, though prototypes exist. **Trigger Locks (Child Safety Locks).** Using a lock and key mechanism, these protect children and others from being able to fire a gun.

powerful assault weapon anyway.* If his proposal is enacted into law, the families of the victims of the shootings will be unable to sue that gun dealer, setting the poor precedent that the federal government doesn't care if gun dealers act irresponsibly. As the Million Mom March organization points out, "Good gun dealers don't need immunity. Bad gun dealers don't deserve it."

Assault Weapons and Gun Trafficking

During the 2000 campaign Bush sought to inoculate himself against gun control critics by letting the public know, through his surrogates, that he supported the 1994 assault weapons ban's reauthorization. However, since he has become president, he has never explicitly mentioned the ban. Scott McClellan, the president's press secretary, assured the public in 2003 that Bush "supports the reauthorization of the current law."

When pressed about why Bush wasn't traveling the country using the bully pulpit to promote the ban, as he did to boost his tax cut plan, former press secretary Ari Fleischer replied that the president had two "top priorities [and they are] national security and . . . America's economy." He admitted in a follow-up question that the ban was not a "priority." Karl Rove, however, was less evasive when confronted by NRA activists in New Hampshire. He made clear that "the president will never have to address the issue because there aren't enough votes in Congress to pass the extension." The (New York) *Daily News*, which endorsed Bush in 2000, called in an editorial for the president to be "true to his word" and demanded that he stop playing "good cop/bad cop" with Tom DeLay and the rest of the GOP House leaders.

President Bush and Attorney General Ashcroft have also compromised their war on terrorism because of their gun views. The two barred the FBI from using the background check database to see if any of the post–September 11 detainees had bought guns. Although Bush has said, "We have a responsibility to deny weapons to terrorists and to actively prevent private citizens from providing them," his administration then issued warnings to proactive states against using the database to ferret out criminals with illegal guns. While President Bush condones curtailing some civil rights to increase security, his Justice Department seems bent on a narrow interpretation of the Brady Law, restricting state and local law enforcement from preventing gun crimes of foreign and domestic origin. It appears that they care more about the Second Amendment than the First, Fourth, Fifth, and Fourteenth.

---

*More than fifty of this dealer's gun sales were used by criminals in murders, robberies, and kidnappings. All of the sales, if this legislation is signed by President Bush, would be immune to victim lawsuits.

"I have concluded judgments about the heart and soul of an individual on death row are best left to a higher authority."

President George W. Bush

As with guns, a Republican president from Texas can be expected to favor the death penalty, and again there has been no hypocrisy or misdirection on this issue. Every Democratic nominee since 1968 (except for Michael Dukakis)—and every Republican nominee—has supported the death penalty, which has enjoyed continuing 65 to 75 percent majorities in America. George W. Bush, in his words, has "always believed that the death penalty will deter death; it'll save some victim": in 1998 he said, "All I can tell you is that for the four years I've been governor I am confident we have not executed an innocent person, and I'm confident that the system has worked to make sure there is full access to the courts." Ultimately, Bush oversaw 152 executions, the most of any modern governor. Unfortunately, his "confidence" is not the issue, but rather if the death penalty does indeed deter capital offenses, and that no innocents are executed.

The Execution President

According to Texas law, a governor can commute a death sentence only if it is recommended by the Texas Board of Pardons and Paroles. Although Governor Bush downplayed his influence over the Board and the ill-defined nature of its procedures, he picked all its members and paid each an eighty-thousand-dollar-a-year salary. "Bush has maintained a relatively removed posture," said Jim Mattox, a former attorney general of Texas. "The paroles board stands between him and the process, but there's no doubt if the governor tells the paroles board what he wants done, they do it."

As president, Bush again has a buffer on death penalty issues—this time in the form of Attorney General John Ashcroft. While the two men see eye to eye on an eye for an eye, at the federal level Ashcroft is attempting to implement the death penalty in ways that violate basic Republican principles favoring states' rights. He has been more than willing to ignore the recommendations made by, and delicate deals negotiated by, local prosecutors. As described by Aitan Goelman, a former federal prosecutor of nine years who worked on death penalty cases with the Department of Justice (including the Timothy McVeigh case), when the attorney general overrides local prosecutors he is bypassing those with the most knowledge and understanding of a given situation. In a Brooklyn case, for example, a murder defendant "promised to testify against others tied to a Colombian drug ring in exchange for a life sentence." Ashcroft ignored the work of local prosecutors and decided to push forward with a capital case. "To many federal prosecutors," says Goelman, "it appears that the presumption now in the DOJ is to seek the death penalty, and that exceptional circumstances are required to avoid it, rather than vice versa." Furthermore, Ashcroft's pursuit of federal death penalty cases in non-death-penalty jurisdictions like Michigan (capital punishment banned since 1846) and Puerto Rico (whose constitution since 1929 states that "the death penalty shall not exist") has created a great deal of anger, even backlash. Arturo Luis Davila Toro, president of the Puerto Rican Bar Association, complained, "We don't believe in capital punishment, and they are trying to impose it on us."

At the international level the U.S. position on the death penalty may be hindering the cooperation needed in the current war on terrorism. In November 2001 Bush signed a military order providing for the establishment of secret military tribunals and gave them the right to impose the death penalty. But many non-death-penalty countries—such as Spain and France—will not permit extradition of their suspected terrorists to the United States, where they could face a penalty banned in their own countries.

Is the Death Penalty Dying?

Today, the United States stands fourth in the world in executions performed, behind only China, Iraq, and Saudi Arabia. While at least 108 nations (including Russia) have abolished the death penalty, the United States remains the only major Western democracy not to have followed suit. The United States has also carried out more documented executions of child offenders than any other country since 1990. That places the United States at the head of a list comprising the Democratic Republic of Congo, Iran, Nigeria, Pakistan, Saudi Arabia, and Yemen. The United States and Somalia are the only states not to have ratified the UN's Convention on the Rights of the Child, which stipulates that capital punishment will not be applied to those under eighteen years of age.

None of this appears to concern President Bush, who at times displays an odd flippancy for so serious a subject. When the issue of his opposition to a hate crimes bill in Texas arose in the context of the notorious dragging death of James Byrd, he said in the second Bush-Gore debate, "Guess what? The three men who murdered James Byrd, guess what's going to happen to them? They're going to be put to death." Columnist Bob Herbert noted an "upbeat" quality to Bush's tone and that his "face brightened in a way that was unsettling to much of the nation." In the case of Karla Faye Tucker, a death row convert to Christianity, the worlds of the death penalty and religion awkwardly intersected for the religious president. But

Bush seemed unconflicted, doing his own imitation of a desperate Karla Faye Tucker, as described by an interviewer: "Please, Bush whimpers, his lips pursed in mock desperation, don't kill me."

Although President Bush is unwavering if not cavalier in his longtime support for the death penalty, his position is currently under the most sustained assault in decades.

DETERRENCE

While Bush asserts that the death penalty has deterrence value, a *New York Times* survey of September 2000 concluded that the homicide rate in states with the death penalty was 48 percent to 101 percent higher than in states without the death penalty. At the same time, FBI data showed that ten of twelve states without capital punishment have rates of homicide under the national average. For example, to compare states of generally comparable cultures, the homicide rate for North Dakota (non-death-penalty state) was lower than the homicide rate in South Dakota (death penalty state).

PROCEDURAL ERRORS

According to Columbia professor James Liebman's study of death penalty cases over a twenty-three-year period, "the overall rate of prejudicial error in the American capital punishment system was 68 percent. The courts found serious, reversible error in nearly seven of every ten of the thousands of capital sentences that were fully reviewed during the period." And four-fifths of these defendants given retrials were either ultimately given lesser sentences or, in 7 percent of the cases, found not guilty of any homicide at all.

The problem of incompetent lawyers in the death penalty system is one in which Bush should be well versed. In Texas, inconsistent standards and underfunding have led to a massive amount of incompetent lawyering, an affliction usually borne by poorer defendants. In the murder trial of Calvin Jerold Burdine, for example, a court later ruled that his lawyer "dozed and actually fell asleep during portions of [Mr. Burdine's trial]." The conviction was ultimately dismissed by the Fifth Circuit Court of Appeals.

RACIAL IMPACT

In his 2002 State of the Union address, President Bush proclaimed that "America will always stand firm for the nonnegotiable demands of human dignity, including 'equal justice.'" According to Amnesty International, the number of African Americans condemned to death in the United States is far out of proportion to their percentage of the defendant population. The statistics also indicate that the race of the victim likely plays a role in determining who will be executed. According to Amnesty International, 80 percent of those executed since 1977 were convicted of murders involving white victims, compared to 13 percent of those who were convicted of killing blacks.

DNA

Revolutionary breakthroughs in DNA testing are one of the newest tools being used in the death penalty system. According to the Innocence Project at the Benjamin Cardozo School of Law in New York, 123 people have been exonerated through postconviction DNA testing, including twelve death row inmates. DNA testing, however, will not be a magical fix for those hundreds now on death rows. In most prior criminal cases, there is no biological evidence available that can be tested.

It's difficult if not impossible to understand Bush's utter "confidence" that no one out of the 152 executed in Texas while he was governor was innocent. Given the sheer amount of cases plagued by incompetent lawyering, police and prosecutorial misconduct, lack of DNA evidence, unreliable eyewitness testimony, and a host of other failures in the system, it is inevitable that a number of innocent individuals have been—and will be—executed. It's odd that a conservative so critical of bureaucratic competence generally would suddenly assume that the criminal justice bureaucracy is flawless. According to Barry Scheck, head of the Innocence Project, "there's no doubt that there are many innocent people languishing on death row today and no doubt that some of Bush's 152 were innocent for this reason: on average one of every eight people sent to death row see their convictions later dismissed because of new evidence, including DNA."

Because of all these trends, at the end of his term former Illinois governor George Ryan commuted the death sentences of 167 people to life in prison. Ryan, a former death penalty supporter and Republican, declared a moratorium in 2001 after learning about the wrongful conviction of thirteen death row inmates. "Our capital system is haunted by the demon of error," said Ryan, "error in determining guilt, and error in determining who among the guilty deserves to die." Although he maintains that he never intended to be an activist on the issue, Governor Ryan said, "I have always reserved my right to change my mind if I believed it to be in the best public interest, whether it be about taxes, abortion, or the death penalty." But it is at least paradoxical, as author Wendy Kaminer has pointed out, that "mistrust of government, especially on the right, has long co-existed with faith that the criminal justice bureaucracy applies the death penalty with relative infallibility."

LABOR PAINS

"The safety and health of our nation's workforce is a priority of my administration."
    —President George W. Bush, March 21, 2001

On the very same day that the president made the pro-labor comment above, he repealed a major federal regulation on standards for workplace safety. The regulation, promulgated under President Clinton, set standards to prevent workplace injuries caused by ergonomic (equipment and workplace design) hazards. These dangers can cause carpal tunnel syndrome, tendinitis, and lower-back injuries and are the most widespread occupational health hazards in the United States. The regulation was the culmination of a process that had begun in 1989 under President George H. W. Bush. Responding to a request from several unions, then secretary of labor Elizabeth Dole agreed to initiate a standard-setting procedure for ergonomics regulation. After more than a decade of research on the harms caused by such injuries and the best way to prevent them—and thousands of pages of evidence and hearings—the Occupational Safety and Health Administration (OSHA) issued the final regulation in November 2000.

Responding to the president's reversal, David LeGrande, health and safety director of the Communications Workers of America, said, "Bush's statement that workplace safety is a priority for his administration is not in the slightest bit credible. It's just rhetoric. Bush is responding to the demands from the business community." Since Bush's repeal of the regulation, nearly 3 million workers have suffered injuries the regulation was designed to prevent. "If these injuries affected CEOs, we would see change tomorrow," said Senator Edward Kennedy. "But these injuries harm average workers—computer operators, waitresses, truck drivers, office workers—the people who keep America going every day."

Not only would the regulations have improved worker safety, they would also have saved the U.S. economy billions of dollars a year on a cost-benefit analysis: more than $9 billion would be saved every year in workers' compensation claims at a cost of only $4.2 billion. According to Charles N. Jeffress, former assistant secretary of labor for occupational safety and health, "One dollar of every three dollars spent on workers' compensation stems from insufficient ergonomic protection." In its report on ergonomic hazards, the National Academy of Sciences (NAS) found that the workers' compensation costs of these injuries is between $13 billion and $20 billion annually, while the overall costs to the economy are between $45 billion and $50 billion. Companies that have implemented ergonomics standards, such as Xerox and Coca-Cola, have seen decreases in absenteeism and injuries, morale improvement, and increased productivity. In Maine two sneaker manufacturers reduced their annual workers' compensation costs from $1.2 million to $89,000 and cut their lost and restricted workdays from 11,000 to 549 during a three-year period.

Compounding the problem of the ergonomics repeal was Bush's appointment of Eugene Scalia as the top lawyer in the Department of Labor. Scalia (son of Justice Antonin Scalia) has long opposed such workplace regulations, claiming that the targeted injuries are "quackery" based on "junk science." His assertions are ill informed at best and disingenuous at worst. In a report requested by Republicans in Congress, the nonpartisan National Academy of Sciences and the Institute of Medicine found that (a) 1 million Americans suffer from serious ergonomic injuries every year and (b) there's strong scientific evidence that the hazards causing these injuries can be prevented. Importantly, the measures endorsed by the NAS to protect against ergonomic injuries are identical to the main elements of the regulation Bush tossed out. New York State AFL-CIO president Denis Hughes believes that Bush and Rove "see unions as an independent stronghold of political power whose message is salient. It's a question of raw power." "For Bush and his political guru, Karl Rove," writes Robert Borosage, codirector of the Campaign for New Priorities, "labor is domestic enemy No. 1." By erasing a legislative achievement labor had advocated for more than ten years, Bush dealt a severe blow to workers and the unions to which they belong.

The White House uses other Scalia-like appointees to diminish the rights of workers. For example, President Bush has openly politicized the Occupational Safety and Health Study Section, which reviews applications for research grants on workplace safety issues. In 2002 the administration rejected three nominees to the panel, all of whom had significant experience in ergonomics. One nominee, Pamela Kidd, the associate dean of the College of Nursing at Arizona State University, was "offended" by the politically charged questions she was asked in interviews with the Bush administration. Laura Punnett, another rejected nominee and professor at the University of Massachusetts, said she was subjected to an ideological litmus test. This effort to keep advocates of an ergonomics regulation off a scientific panel has drawn harsh criticism from the scientific community. Anthony Mazzaschi, an assistant vice president at the Association of American Medical Colleges, derided the appointments process: "To stack [these] panels based on political preferences rather than scientific competency is doing everyone a disservice."

The disconnect between Bush's statements and actions on worker safety extend well beyond ergonomics standards. In the first two years of his presidency there were two tragic mine accidents. On September 23, 2001—in the worst mining disaster in seventeen years—an explosion in a Brookwood, Alabama, coal mine claimed the lives of thirteen workers. The following summer, nine miners were trapped underground for three days in a flooded coal mine in Green Tree, Pennsylvania, attracting worldwide attention. After the heroic rescue of the trapped miners, President Bush went to Pennsylvania to publicly praise them, saying, "It was their determination to stick together and to comfort each other that really defines the kind of a new spirit that's prevalent in our country, that when one of us suffer, all of us suffers [sic]." While Bush might be right about the existence of that spirit, it certainly didn't arise as a result of his policies. Shortly before praising the miners he had proposed cutting funding for the Mine Safety and Health Administration (MSHA) by $7 million (6 percent). Meanwhile, coal-mining deaths increased by 41 percent from 1998 to 2001.

One would have thought that, in the wake of the tragic deaths in Brookwood and the rescue at Green Tree, the Bush administration would better appreciate the need for diligent inspections and enforcement of mine safety laws. Indeed, in January 2003, the administration announced it would add fifty-five mining inspectors and $2.4 million for a new mine safety office. But a close examination of the agency's budget demonstrates that the White House actually cut the budget for mine safety enforcement by $4.7 million and changed the budgeting formulas to make it harder to figure out where the cuts were being made.

Of course, it's impossible to say if one or ten or fifty-five more inspectors might have saved the thirteen miners who perished in the Brookwood explosion—or the twenty-nine other miners who were killed nationwide in 2001. But an inquiry into Brookwood revealed that MSHA inspectors had cited the mine operator for thirty-one violations, but the inspectors never followed up to ensure the violations were corrected. And as of mid-2003, the administration hasn't even hired all the mine inspectors for whom Congress has appropriated the funds—the agency is fifty-five inspectors short in the coal-mine inspection division alone.

Many lobbyists and their officials used the tragedy of September 11 to push for pet items, whether "tort reform" or nuclear power for "energy independence." Similarly, when President Bush wasn't ridding Afghanistan of the Taliban or Iraq of Hussein, he was citing national security to strip more than two hundred thousand federal workers of their collective bargaining rights in the new Department of Homeland Security and other federal agencies. "The fight against terrorism," proclaimed his undersecretary for transportation, "requires eliminating many worker rights, including collective bargaining."

Bush was so insistent on his vision of denying federal workers their contracted-for rights that he delayed the creation of the Department of Homeland Security for months. In the summer and fall of 2002, the debate on the Homeland Security bill was essentially between Senator Joseph Lieberman's (D-CT) proposal that retained workers' rights and Bush's version, which eliminated these protections. Bush threatened to veto Lieberman's measure, dragging the debate out in the fall elections. This political tactic provided the Republicans with a hot-button issue on which to campaign and allowed Bush to question the patriotism of Senate Democrats and union members, claiming, while campaigning for Republican Congressional candidates, that "The Senate is more interested in special interests in Washington, and not interested in the security of the American people."

Unfortunately, Bush's political posturing came at the cost of delaying the creation of the Department of Homeland Security, which he said (after initially opposing it for months) was so vital to American security. But it had the additional effect of sending a clear message to labor and his right-wing base that there was almost nothing he wasn't willing to sacrifice in order to weaken organized labor and worker protections.

However politically effective it was, the claim that basic worker protections are incompatible with national security was simply implausible. Unionized federal employees are on the front lines of the war against terrorism and work in the Department of Defense, Air National Guard, Border Patrol, Coast Guard, and Customs Service, as were the municipal employees of New York City's fire and police departments on September 11, 2001. According to Border Patrol agent and local union president Mark Hall, "I do not understand how my role as union leader is incompatible with my oath to protect and defend the Constitution."

House majority leader Tom DeLay is one of Bush's top generals in his war against organized labor. In early 2003, DeLay signed a mass-mail fundraising letter that called labor leaders' efforts to organize federal workers "sickening" and "a clear and present danger to the United States." The letter went on to deride "union bosses' drive to use the national emergencies to grab more power." If DeLay had replaced "union bosses" with "the president's," he would have been closer to the truth. He later apologized for this letter after being called on it by Teamsters president James Hoffa.

On the remote, hypothetical possibility that unions did pose a threat to national security, existing federal law already gives the president the authority to bar unions when union rights are incompatible with national security objectives. In fact, Bush's elimination of worker protections may even undermine national security. According to T. J. Bonner, president of the National Border Control Council, many employees may quit rather than lose valuable worker protections. "If the administration's goal was to create a more mobile and agile workforce, then it's succeeded, because they'll be streaming out the door faster than you can say, ''Bye,''" Bonner says. When Bush claims he has "great respect for the federal employees" others may fear that the president might start to have great respect for them, too.

Bush's contentious relationship with labor is becoming obvious as his actions speak more clearly than his speeches. During her address at the AFL-CIO's winter meeting, Secretary of Labor Elaine Chao went out of her way to describe several examples of union corruption that were being prosecuted by the Labor Department (even though the prosecutions were of previous leaders often exposed by current leaders). This affront was infuriating but not surprising. "I have never seen a secretary of labor who is so anti-labor," explained John Sweeney, president of the AFL-CIO. Denis Hughes, president of the New York State AFL-CIO, commented that "Chao obviously felt we were the enemy as opposed to leaders of real organizations. I was struck by how uncomfortable she was around labor leaders. It's really illustrative that Bush would pick someone like this."

Chao's labor department has taken its offensive against labor to wage earners who count on overtime as a supplement to their income. The administration proposed new overtime rules that would have eliminated overtime for up to 8 million Americans, according to a report by the Economic Policy Institute (EPI). The proposed regulations would allow businesses to avoid paying overtime by classifying such employees as holding "positions of responsibility" and exempt many middle-income workers by capping overtime eligibility to those earning less than sixty-five thousand dollars a year. The impact of these regulations would be significant and severe. Almost 80 percent of the nation's 120 million workers are entitled to overtime, many relying on the additional wages for a significant part of their income. Police, firefighters, health technicians, and nurses are among those workers who would lose overtime protection under the proposal. (It failed to pass the House in October 2003.)

Yet the Bush administration estimated that "only" 640,000 workers would lose their overtime pay. According to Jared Bernstein, an economist with the EPI and author of the report, this estimate is a "vastly misleading undercount" because the proposed rules will give businesses an incentive to reclassify millions of hourly workers to avoid paying overtime. While the economics of who's hurt by the measure are obvious, so are the politics of who's helped. In a revealing *New Yorker* profile, Karl Rove indicated that his goal was achieving an era of Republican dominance by undermining the base of the Democratic party, which includes organized labor. Presumably, Rove was aware that of the $90 million that labor unions gave to candidates in 2000, 94 percent went to Democrats—and that public-sector unions, those most hurt by Bush's policies, gave Democrats $11 million and Republicans only $1 million.

9. Rules for Hyperpowers

"Because We Say So"

★

"Look, I know what I believe, and what I believe is right."
—President George W. Bush
to assembled G-8 leaders, Genoa, 2001

A New President for a New Hyperpower

When George W. Bush took the oath of office on a brutally cold and rainy January day in 2001, tens of thousands of protesters lined the streets of the capital to give vent to their anger about the much-disputed election. They failed to make much of an impression on the media, however, as, oddly, did the inaugural speech delivered by the man in question. Reporters, almost without exception, followed press spokesperson Ari Fleischer's lead in limiting their stories to the rhetoric of "unity," "healing," "one nation," and "bringing people together." As presidential scholar Fred I. Greenstein has noted, "The media coverage of Bush's inauguration focused on the dignified pomp of the occasion," rather than on either the manner in which Bush had achieved office, or on his failure to reach out to those who believed the country had been cheated by the final result.

Rather than the conciliatory speech that so many imagined or expected that day, Bush instead signaled the opening of an era of dominance by the extremely conservative Republican base, represented by the choice of cabinet members like the fundamentalist Christian John Ashcroft to oversee the nation's legal system, and a defense establishment filled with deeply ideological neoconservatives. The turn toward what had been considered the far right was particularly evident with regard to foreign policy. Instead of reaching out to foreign nations in the hopes of extending mutual cooperation and conciliation, Bush appeared to want to draw lines in the sand. "We will build our defenses beyond challenge, lest weakness invite challenge. We will confront weapons of mass destruction, so that a new country is spared new horrors. The enemies of liberty and our country should make no mistake, America remains engaged in the world, by history and by choice, shaping a balance of power that favors freedom," Bush declared. "We will meet aggression and bad faith with resolve and strength. And to all nations, we will speak for the values that gave our nation birth."

In both tone and content Bush's remarks sent a strikingly different message to the world than the admittedly sparse comments about foreign policy that he had made during the 2000 campaign. Back then, Bush warned against the danger of "overcommitting our military around the world" and implied that his predecessor, Bill Clinton, had been guilty of exactly this offense. He called upon his country to be "humble in how we treat nations that are figuring out how to chart their own course," adding, "It's important to be friends with people when you don't need each other so that when you do there's a strong bond of friendship." "If we're an arrogant nation," he would add, "they'll resent us. If we're a humble nation, but strong, they'll welcome us."

After the inauguration, even the closest Bush watchers in the United States and abroad could not help but wonder which president they would be getting in the Oval Office. This was not merely an academic question. For at the moment that George W. Bush put his hand on the Bible to recite the presidential oath of office, he assumed the leadership of the most powerful empire the world had ever seen. Judged merely by the size, capabilities, and sophistication of its military forces, the United States had, following the fall of the Soviet Union, moved beyond the category of superpower into an entirely new and perhaps unprecedented realm. Because it spends more on its military than all of the rest of NATO combined, analyst Gregg Easterbrook has observed that "the extent of American military superiority has become almost impossible to overstate." To take just one illustration, the U.S. Navy boasts nine supercarrier battle groups ringed by cruisers and guarded by nuclear submarines, with a tenth under construction. The world's closest competitor has zero. What about America's air force? The United States currently has more advanced fighters and bombers than all of the other nations of the world combined. It deploys three separate types of stealth aircraft (the B-1 and B-2 bombers and the F-117 fighter), with two more (the F-22 and F-35 fighters) about to go into production. Again, the world total for all America's competitors? None. The list goes on. The United States manufactures the world's only AWACS plane, JSTARS plane, and Global Hawk drone. According to Chris Hellman of the Center for Defense Information in Washington, using President Bush's budget increase requests for fiscal 2004, the cost of the U.S. military will be $399.1 billion, which includes $19.3 billion for the nuclear operation in the Department of Energy. That is more than six times as much as Russia, at $65 billion, and equivalent to the size of the next twenty-one largest militaries in the world *combined.* As historian Paul Kennedy concludes:

> Nothing has ever existed like this disparity of power, nothing. I have returned to all of the comparative defense spending and military personnel statistics over the past five hundred years [and] no other nation comes close. The Pax Britannica was run on the cheap, Britain's army was much smaller than European armies, and even the Royal Navy was equal only to the next two navies—right now all the other navies in the world combined could not dent American maritime supremacy. Charlemagne's empire was merely western European in its reach. The Roman Empire stretched farther afield, but there was another great empire in Persia, and a larger one in China. There is, therefore, no comparison.

But to express U.S. power purely in military terms is both to understate its reach and to fail to fully appreciate its role in the world. For power and influence in contemporary geopolitics involve more than guns and bombs. Here again, however, when measured by indices of what the political scientist Joseph Nye has termed *soft power* the United States is also the undisputed world heavyweight champion in a competition that has no other heavyweights, no light heavyweights, and not even many middleweights or welterweights. We are so far ahead in the competition that it's difficult to imagine who our competitors might be. For instance, Kennedy also notes that

> a full 45 percent of all Internet traffic takes place in this one country. About 75 percent of the Nobel laureates in the sciences, economics and medicine in recent decades do their research and reside in America. A group of twelve to fifteen U.S. research universities have, through vast financing, moved into a new superleague of world universities that is leaving everyone else—the Sorbonne, Tokyo, Munich, Oxford, Cambridge—in the dust, especially in the experimental sciences. The top places among the rankings of the world's biggest banks and largest companies are now back, to a large degree, in U.S. hands. And if one could reliably create indicators of cultural power—the English language, films and television, advertisements, youth culture, international student flows—the same lopsided picture would emerge.

The Personal Touch

The man who would have responsibility for all this power remained, on Inauguration Day, a mystery. In his six years in the Texas statehouse, the governor had precious little experience in the conduct of foreign relations; as a presidential candidate, he did not even hold a valid passport. Despite having a father who had served not only as president but also vice president, ambassador to China, and director of the CIA, Bush had made only a handful of brief trips abroad during his entire life. As a student, a businessman, a congressional candidate, and governor, Bush had left no record of taking any interest whatsoever in affairs beyond the nation's borders—with the exception, perhaps, of the unavoidable concession to reality in Texas, namely, Mexico. Indeed, aside from some tutorial sessions set up during the campaign, there is little evidence that George W. Bush was even familiar with the most rudimentary concepts of international relations. As Bush himself put it on the campaign trail, "Nobody needs to tell me what to believe," while admitting "But I do need somebody to tell me where Kosovo is." In one particularly worrisome campaign interview, Bush's face went blank when asked about the Taliban. When the reporter tried to feed him a helpful clue, mentioning "repression of women in Afghanistan," Bush responded, "Oh, I thought you said some band. The Taliban in Afghanistan. Absolutely. Repressive."

Taking a page from George Orwell, Bush partisans attempted to portray his ignorance of foreign affairs as a strength. National Security Advisor Condoleezza Rice argued, "He has on-the-ground experience, which I would say is much more valuable than if he had been attending seminars at the Council of Foreign Relations for the last five years." Moreover, Rice added, Bush "comes at this as an American with very, very American values." Just what these were, or how they related to such complicated questions facing the United States as peacekeeping, globalization, environmental security—not to mention the many challenges facing the United States in 2000 that could be addressed only in the context of global cooperation—Rice neglected to spell out.

Bush's most conspicuous value in January 2001 was utter certainty of purpose. No matter how complex a given problem or how thin his level of expertise, Bush never allowed himself to appear indecisive. In stark contrast to President Clinton, for instance, Bush never second-guessed himself. He did not allow extended discussions in his presence before reaching a decision on the proper course. Aides were expected to outline alternatives and recommend solutions, period. Complications were expected to work themselves out without his involvement. He was the CEO, not the detail man. As he would later put it, "My job isn't to nuance." If reality interfered with one of Bush's deeply held convictions or what he termed his commitment to "moral clarity," well, then reality would just have to wait.

Stories abound of the president's combination of a profoundly casual attitude toward preparation with a religious certitude in the infallibility of his conclusions. As governor, the *Los Angeles Times* has reported, Bush was absolutely "sweeping in his acts of delegation." Its reporters note that when he was given a lengthy report on a tragedy in which several Texas A&M students were killed in a bonfire, he did not even bother to read its executive

summary but instead left it to aides to highlight a few paragraphs of its conclusions. Even on questions of capital punishment, Bush would spend no
more than fifteen minutes on each case. There was, the authors note, "a
laid-back quality to his management of this time as governor, including an
extended midday break during which he worked out and had lunch." None
of this changed once he became president. Even on so crucial and demanding an issue as the Middle East peace process, Bush appeared to prefer ignorance to illumination, as if on principle. "He does not have the knowledge
or the patience to learn this issue enough to have an end destination in
mind," according to one of his own officials. Bush's own aides believed that
the president had "shown little interest in the details of the complex disputes in the region" and demonstrated "a viscerally negative reaction when
officials try to delve deeply into issues."

The foundational basis for Bush's impressive self-confidence appears to
lie in his personal belief—following a bout of near alcoholism and a born-
again religious experience—that his decisions are divinely inspired. Commerce Secretary Don Evans, perhaps the president's closest friend, echoes a
remark frequently made by chief speechwriter Michael Gerson, that Bush
believes "he was called by God to lead the nation." David Gergen, who
served in four separate White Houses and was close to many in the Bush
White House, would also observe, two years into the Bush presidency, that
the occupant of the Oval Office believed he "somehow may be an instrument of Providence, that part of what he's on is a mission that has some sort
of theological roots." Many, if not most, of Bush's speeches have been pep-
pered with theological references and sometimes even justifications, their
rhetoric often more appropriate to a Pentecostal preacher than the leader of
the world's most powerful secular state. But the perspective is helpful in understanding why Bush does not allow such earthly matters as truth to interfere with his mission:

* "The liberty we prize is not America's gift to the world, it is God's
gift to humanity."

* "We do not claim to know all the ways of Providence, yet can trust
in them, placing our confidence in the loving God behind all of life
and all of history."

* "Events aren't moved by blind change and chance . . . [but] by the
hand of a just and faithful God."

The conviction that God is his copilot has saved Bush a great deal of time
and worry as to how to proceed in choosing between various foreign policy
options that have been placed before him. David Frum, author of an almost
worshipful memoir of his brief tenure as a White House speechwriter, could
not help but admit that his hero was nevertheless "dogmatic; often uncuri-

ous and as a result ill-informed." (Frum also notes that during his time in the White House, "attendance at Bible study was, if not compulsory, not quite uncompulsory.") In the view of Richard Brookhiser, another Bush-admiring conservative intellectual, "Bush's faith means that he does not tolerate, or even recognize, ambiguity: there is an all-knowing God who decrees certain behaviors, and leaders must obey." His decisions, therefore, are limited by what Brookhiser generously terms these "strictly defined mental horizons."

Offering a hint of its future priorities—as well as its insouciant attitude toward intellectual consistency—on its third day in office, the Bush administration ended U.S. participation in the UN's population and women's reproductive health programs over their refusal to enact a gag rule for nongovernmental organizations (NGOs) that provide information about legal abortion services, counseling, or referrals (even if they receive no U.S. funding and even though these same referrals are legal in the United States). This decision, no doubt, pleased the Republican base, and was consistent with Bush's belief that his private religious beliefs made for good policy, but its likely effect will be to increase the number of abortions by as many as eight hundred thousand annually as family planning and educational services around the globe are deprived of badly needed funds. (Secretary of State Powell admitted that he disagreed with the decision but had no choice but to carry it out.)

The final quality Bush manifested in foreign policy might be termed the "good man" syndrome. In Bushworld, foreign leaders—and for that matter, nearly everyone, women included—fell into the category of either "good man" or "evildoer," with little differentiation beyond that. "Good men" had "no hatred in their hearts" and could be trusted to be "with us." "Non-good men" could not, and hence were understood to be on the side of the "evildoers." In many cases, it didn't seem to matter whether a "good man" had any demonstrable positive qualities—whether a commitment to freedom, democracy, or human rights—so long as he professed a belief in a higher power and distanced himself, if only rhetorically, from other evildoers.

One of the most remarkable demonstrations of this doctrine came in summer 2001 upon Bush's first meeting with Vladimir Putin, the ex–KGB chief and elected strongman of Russia, who was, at the time, in the process of conducting a brutal war against separatists in Chechnya and attempting to wipe out his internal opposition and vestiges of a free press. Bush announced to the world that he fully trusted the former spymaster because "When I looked at him, I felt like he was shooting straight with me." Bush claimed to have gotten a sense of Putin's "soul" and found the former KGB boss a "remarkable leader" and an "honest, straightforward man . . . who loves his family" and professed a sincere belief in God. Bush apparently failed to take a look at his briefing papers on this occasion, as his own advisor for national security, Condoleezza Rice, had urged, "If we have learned anything in the last several years, it is that a romantic view of Russia—rather than a realistic one—did nothing to help the cause of stability in Russia." That nation, she advised, remained "a threat to the West and to our European allies in particular." As *National Review*'s Ramesh Ponnuru put it, while Bill Clinton decried "the politics of personal destruction," George W. Bush wished to promote "the politics of personal affection."

Of course personal-affection politics works both ways. When Bush wasn't feeling very affectionate, he would practice the politics of personal pique. In fall 2002, for instance, at a summit in Los Cabos, Mexico, Bush grew impatient with Mexican president Vicente Fox, who was withholding his support for Bush's plans to invade Iraq, in conjunction with the views of 80 percent of his nation. During the planned joint press conference, Bush "glowered during Fox's windup and looked annoyed at the unruliness of the camera crews," according to a *Washington Post* report. "The last straw was when a cell phone went off, which infuriates Bush. . . . In a breach of protocol, Bush cut off the translator before Fox's answers could be rendered into English" and walked away. Bush threw another of these fits at a joint press conference with French president Jacques Chirac, though this time it was directed at a journalist, NBC's David Gregory, who had the temerity to ask a foreign leader a question in his own language—just as most foreign reporters courteously did for Mr. Bush. In this instance the leader of the Free World whined, "Very good, the guy memorizes four words, and he plays like he's intercontinental. I'm impressed. Que bueno. Now I'm literate in two languages."

These were hardly isolated incidents, for Bush's feelings about other leaders seemed to be among the most important determinants of U.S. foreign policy. He refused to congratulate German chancellor Gerhard Schröder on his election victory because he did not like the way the campaign had been run, and would not speak to Schröder when he called to offer his congratulations following the 2002 Republican electoral victory. When Bush traveled to Evian, France, for a Western summit in spring 2003, his spokespeople let it be known that he had no intention of speaking to the leaders of Germany or France. The post-Iraq policy, as Ms. Rice allegedly defined it, was "Punish France, isolate Germany, forgive Russia." Alas, as the pundit Anne Applebaum noted at the time, the policy made no sense whatever, even on its own terms of childlike pique: "Not only did the Russians support the French during the prewar squabbles at the United Nations, but a pair of Russian generals may also have advised Saddam Hussein, and Russian tracking equipment may have been used in the defense of Baghdad." "As the president sees it, Putin was led astray by bad companions," a "top official" told a *Wall Street Journal* reporter.

For America's deity-obsessed president, foreign leaders' professed belief in God sometimes seemed to be a sine qua non of U.S. foreign relations. It was surely no accident that Tony Blair's religiosity aided the two men's—

and hence, the Anglo American—relationship. And as the *New York Times* reported, "Mr. Bush has talked of bonding with Vladimir Putin over the story of a crucifix Mr. Putin's mother gave him," while "Jacques Chirac of France and Gerhard Schröder of Germany are adamantly secular. Mr. Schröder was the first German chancellor to refuse to end his oath of office with the customary 'so help me God.'" Bush often seems to think the religious beliefs of others are so critical a factor in a relationship that they trump almost all genuine differences. He was no doubt surprised by Turkey's unwillingness to go along with his plans for Iraq, despite a 96 percent rate of opposition to the invasion in that nascent democratic nation, because he had shared another of these moments with Recep Tayyip Erdogan, the devout Muslim prime minister. As Bush declared, "You believe in the Almighty, and I believe in the Almighty. That's why we'll be great partners."

In another of these bizarre instances, Bush once found himself confronted by a series of photographs of wounded Palestinian children by Crown Prince Abdullah of Saudi Arabia. Bush reportedly cried out, "I want peace. I don't want to see any people killed on both sides. I think God loves me. I think God loves the Palestinians. I think God loves the Israelis. We cannot allow this to continue." He then grabbed the hands of his guests and asked them to join him in prayer, as both sides looked on in an apparent state of shock. But while God may have loved both the Israelis and the Palestinians as His children, Bush loved only the former. Or rather, only Israel was represented in Mr. Bush's eyes by a "good man"—Prime Minister Ariel Sharon, whom Bush deemed to be a "man of peace." As a result, Sharon, like Mr. Putin, was given a free hand to defy Bush's wishes and deal with his enemies however he saw fit, irrespective of God's purported affections. Virtually all the progress made toward peace under the Clinton administration dissipated as a result.

Bush's apparent belief in his own divinely inspired infallibility is enforced within the administration to meet any contingency, which means the president is never to blame for anything unfortunate that happens on his watch. If an "evildoer" cannot be found to blame, a scapegoat is always at hand—together with an official denial that anyone associated with Bush would ever even imagine employing scapegoating tactics. On the Middle East question, for instance, Bush's spokesperson, Ari Fleischer, went so far in February 2002 as to try to praise his own boss's inaction by blaming ex-president Clinton's energetic peacemaking efforts for the recent outbreak of murderous violence there. "You can make the case that in an attempt to shoot the moon and get nothing, more violence resulted," Fleischer explained to inquiring reporters. "That as a result of an attempt to push the parties beyond where they were willing to go, that it led to expectations that were raised to such a high level that it turned into violence." Fleischer was eventually forced to apologize for this statement, but his boss never did. In fact, the president apparently thought his press secretary had turned in a terrific performance, for the next morning Bush sent word that he wanted Fleischer to walk with him across the South Lawn to the helicopter, in full view of the cameras, so that everyone could observe them.

Policies? We Don't Need No Stinkin' Policies

Bush's ignorance of the details of the issues on which he was called to decide and incuriosity about learning anything about them naturally left him particularly susceptible to the arguments made by his better-informed advisors. Of course such influence has had a bearing on the policies of every president, for no one individual can be expected to be expert—or even necessarily competent—in every area in which the United States president is called upon to make decisions. Good political instincts, coupled with competent staff work, have provided the basis for more "brilliant" presidential decisions than is commonly recognized—or even reported. But supporting Bush is a political operation that, in the words of former top-level aide John DiIulio, has had "no precedent in any modern White House." As DiIulio described it, "What you've got is everything—and I mean everything—being run by the political arm. It's the reign of the Mayberry Machiavellis." While DiIulio was referring to domestic policy, his arguments were relevant—if not directly analogous—to foreign policy as well. Excluding the case of the increasingly impotent Colin Powell, the primary motivation in the making of U.S. foreign policy has not been politics, narrowly conceived, but ideology. More specifically, it has been the unilateral exercise of U.S. power in support of the interests of the Republican right wing, its theological beliefs and its political allies.

Because George W. Bush took office with so little experience in international affairs, his foreign policy even more than his domestic policy would prove to be a reflection of the priorities of the men and women he chose to carry it out. First among equals in this arena was Vice President Cheney. Almost certainly the most influential vice president in U.S. history, Cheney was encouraged to attend any meeting at the White House he pleased. From the very beginning of the administration he was placed in charge of its most sensitive projects, from its still controversial review of national energy to the President's Budget Review Board.

Regarding foreign policy, according to journalist Harold Myerson, "Cheney's most distinctive contribution to this administration is his penchant for near-absolute executive power." While a member of the House of Representatives during the Reagan administration, Cheney argued for the president's authority to conduct a war against the Sandinistas in Nicaragua with no congressional involvement at all, even though the U.S. Constitution clearly defines war making as a congressional—rather than presidential—prerogative. As George H. W. Bush's secretary of defense, Cheney insisted that the first Gulf War required no congressional approval, either.

His first move as vice president was to inaugurate a series of secret energy-policy meetings in which he invited key industry lobbyists and executives to suggest and approve administration decisions.

Dick Cheney was not committed to untrammeled executive power for its own sake. Rather, he had a hard-line view of America's role in the world, in which power flowed exclusively from the barrel of America's guns. Allies and agreements, no matter how sympathetic to U.S. values and interests, were considered merely aggravating irrelevances. By virtue of the deference showed him by his boss, Cheney was able to use his appointment to oversee the presidential transition, stacking the new administration with an extremely effective network of likeminded neoconservatives: these included the hard-line secretary of defense, Donald Rumsfeld, and the extremely savvy and effective network of Paul Wolfowitz, Douglas Feith, Stephen Cambone, and Dov Zakheim in the Department of Defense; John Bolton in the Department of State; Elliott Abrams in the National Security Council; Zalmay Khalilzad in the Office of the President; and I. Lewis Libby in the vice president's office, together with the man who sometimes seemed to be pulling the strings while serving on the Defense Policy Board, and making himself wealthy selling his services to private industry, former Reagan-era defense official Richard Perle.

While most observers were confident that the much-admired war hero, Secretary of State Colin Powell, would be able to direct U.S. foreign policy from the titular office that oversaw it, Cheney, Rumsfeld, and their neoconservative operatives had other plans. When Paul Wolfowitz was asked why he sought the office of deputy secretary of defense, he reportedly answered simply, "Powell." And while conservative enough to be an old-fashioned Republican, Powell nevertheless remained committed to a traditional internationalist order based on U.S. support for multilateral institutions and other instruments of global (and nonmilitary) cooperation, a policy that soon left him struggling to maintain something more than figurehead status on many key issues. The tone of Powell's tenure was set early in the administration when he announced that he planned "to pick up where the Clinton administration had left off" in trying to secure the peace between North and South Korea, while negotiating with the North to prevent its acquisition of nuclear weaponry. The president not only repudiated his secretary of state in public, announcing, "We're not certain as to whether or not they're keeping all terms of all agreements," he did so during a joint appearance with South Korean president (and Nobel laureate) Kim Dae Jung, thereby humiliating his honored guest as well. A day later, Powell backpedaled. "The president forcefully made the point that we are undertaking a full review of our relationship with North Korea," Powell said. "There was some suggestion that imminent negotiations are about to begin—that is not the case." He later admitted to a group of journalists, "I got a little far forward on my skis." It would not be the last time. (After the Iraq war, Henry Kissinger was heard to refer to Powell and his advisors as "a small country that occasionally does business with the United States.")

Another key member of the Bush foreign policy team was his key tutor during the campaign and a former aide to his father, Condoleezza Rice. Writing in *Foreign Affairs* magazine just before being named to the top national security job, Rice complained that too many U.S. policymakers were "uncomfortable with the notions of power politics, great powers, and power balances." Addressing herself to what she believed to be the multiple failures of Clinton administration policies, Rice worried that this alleged discomfort tended to produce "a reflexive appeal instead to notions of international law and norms, and the belief that the support of many states—or even better, of institutions like the United Nations—is essential to the legitimate exercise of power." The result of this process, she warned, was "the 'national interest' is replaced with 'humanitarian interests' or the interests of 'the international community.'"

In drawing a distinction between her tough-minded, no-nonsense brand of analysis and the misguided, ineffectual humanitarian impulses animating Clinton-era policies, Rice seemed to imply a fundamental incompatibility between humanitarian and national-interest justification, as well as between multilateral and unilateral intervention. Yet no one, for instance, pursued a multilateral alliance more effectively than Bush's own father, together with James A. Baker, in the creation of the worldwide coalition that fought the first Gulf War. And though the attack against Iraq was undertaken strictly for reasons of national interest and defended as such (Baker eloquently justified the need for the action before Congress as "jobs, jobs, jobs"), it also had humanitarian benefits for the people of Kuwait. Since Rice served in the National Security Council during this period, one wonders if she deliberately unlearned the lessons of Bush I diplomacy in order to serve at the behest of his more unilateralist-minded son.

What Rice had dismissively termed the "reflexive appeal . . . to notions of international law and norms" proved to be congruent with the administration's own demonstrated contempt for the rule of law domestically, as it applied to the conduct of foreign affairs. In appointing his new administration Bush apparently made a concerted effort to recruit a number of former officials who had been personally and professionally disgraced—some were even indicted and convicted of criminal conduct—during the Iran-Contra scandal of the Reagan-Bush years. These appointments included

⋆ UN Representative John Negroponte, who during his years as Ronald Reagan's ambassador to Honduras turned a blind eye to a pattern of political killings in order to facilitate America's illegal war against the Sandinistas.

★ Acting Assistant Secretary of State for Inter-American Affairs Otto Reich, who, as head of the State Department's pro-Contra propaganda office, placed ghostwritten articles over the signatures of Contra leaders in the nation's leading opinion magazines and op-ed pages, smeared those journalists who would not go along as being in the pay (financial and sexual) of the Marxists, and generally publicized negative stories about the Sandinistas, whether true or not.

★ National Security Council staffer Elliott Abrams, who was forced to resign in disgrace from the Reagan State Department, accepted a plea bargain for his criminal conduct, and was disbarred in the District of Columbia and prevented from practicing law for his role in deliberately misleading Congress about his and Oliver North's secret plan to fund the Contra war. (Abrams was pardoned by President George H. W. Bush after he lost the election to Bill Clinton.)

★ Pentagon appointee John Poindexter was, like Abrams, indicted and forced to resign in disgrace from the Reagan administration for his role in deceiving Congress and, according to Poindexter, the president himself, in helping to guide the illegal activities associated with the Iran-Contra scandal. (Poindexter, like Abrams, was pardoned by Bush senior.)

These appointments sent a dual signal. In the first place, this was an administration that, ethically speaking, would make its own rules. After all, even if you admired Abrams et al. for breaking the law in pursuit of illegal plans to arm the Contras—as many Bush supporters, and particularly neoconservatives, openly did—you had to acknowledge that Poindexter achieved distinction by falling on his sword and bragging that he had deliberately kept the president uninformed about actions taken on his watch and under his name. This desire to preserve the president's "deniability" is the flip side of operating as a rogue, unregulated element in the government. It's hard to imagine that so disciplined a ship as the Bush administration relished that prospect unless they dismissed the entire story or were in the market for some future deniability themselves.

Viewed in its proper historical context, the Iran-Contra scandal can be seen as the precursor to much of the ideologically driven foreign policy of the George W. Bush administration. Abrams, Poindexter, William Casey, Ollie North, and others were willing to ignore historical constitutional strictures and pursue their own (secret) foreign policy agenda because they believed that whatever actions America took in the world to protect its own interests were by definition right. They could lie to Congress and the nation and do business with drug dealers, arms merchants, terrorists, and murderous dictators all in the service of an end that they believed justified all imaginable means: the national security of the United States and its mission to preserve "freedom" where it already existed and foster it where it did not.

Near the close of the twelve-year reign of the Republican presidents in 1992, then defense secretary Cheney oversaw the production of a strategic blueprint, the "Defense Planning Guidance Draft," which envisioned the United States as a colossus astride the world, imposing its will and keeping world peace through military and economic power. "The United States should be postured to act independently when collective action cannot be orchestrated," it brazenly announced. When leaked in final draft form, however, the proposal drew so much criticism among traditional Republicans, including President Bush's own personal brain trust, that it had to be hastily withdrawn and repudiated. But the ideas that underlay it refused to die and during the Clinton administration grew in influence as the original authors refined and updated them, drawing on the increasingly obvious gap in military power developing between the United States and the rest of the world. Restated in even bolder form in 2000 by a group of neoconservative intellectuals led by *Weekly Standard* pundits William Kristol and Robert Kagan, under the rubric of the Project for a New American Century (PNAC), the authors called for nothing less than the creation of a worldwide imperial American empire, with forces based all around the globe. "A Reaganite policy of military strength and moral clarity may not be fashionable today," the authors proclaimed, "but it is necessary if the U.S. is to build on the success of this past century and ensure our security and greatness in the next." Or to put the matter more simply, as one of its principal authors, Yale historian Donald Kagan, did in an interview with reporter Jay Bookman, "You saw the movie *High Noon*? We're Gary Cooper."

Among the report's signatories were current Bush administration officials Rumsfeld, Wolfowitz, Bolton, Libby, Cambone, Zakheim, and Abrams. And while all of these men were, in their own respective fields, hardened and sophisticated bureaucratic operators, it is quite possible that they would never have been able to put their ambitious plans to work—particularly given the opposition of Secretary Powell, the apparent ambivalence of NSC advisor Rice, and the lack of sophistication of George W. Bush—had the world not been transformed by the shock of September 11. For without the "war on terrorism" to provide justification for so much of what these men had been planning for the better part of a decade, just about all they could hope to have accomplished was the increased isolation of an increasingly arrogant America from the family of nations, including our closest allies. As for Bush himself, he had few delineated priorities coming into office, most of which concerned economic, social, and education policy. Gary Schmitt, a former Reagan administration intelligence expert who now runs PNAC for Kristol, observes, "Without 9/11, Bush might have been off wandering in the desert, in terms of foreign policy."

The major focus in the early period of the Bush administration was domestic issues—tax cuts, education reform, and "compassionate conservatism"—so long as not too much foreign turmoil appeared on the horizon. Indeed, the first nine months of the Bush presidency turned out to be relatively quiet ones internationally. A few minor controversies occurred, but these were mostly self-created, arising out of the administration's deliberate acts of commission, such as its April 1 unilateral withdrawal from the Kyoto Protocol, or acts of omission, such as the flaring up of the Israeli-Palestinian conflict following a Bush decision to withdraw its support for previous peacekeeping efforts.

Just about the only genuine drama of the period came in the spring of that year, when, on April 1, a U.S. spy plane collided with a Chinese fighter, whose pilot died. After the plane made an emergency landing at a military base in China, Bush insisted that he would not apologize, and the Chinese refused to release the twenty-four U.S. servicemen it held hostage until he did. In the standoff that ensued the president's inexperience frequently betrayed itself. For no apparent reason, and perhaps without even knowing what he was doing, Bush appeared on ABC's *Good Morning America* to announce that the United States would do "whatever it took" to defend Taiwan if China attacked. This pledge, long desired by the Taiwanese, had been specifically avoided by every president since the beginning of the nation's "two-China" policy in 1979, owing to the concern that it might embolden Taiwan's rulers to start a war. Various administration spokespeople stepped forward to insist that U.S. policy remained unchanged, but nobody really knew for certain whether Bush was trying to refashion it or even if he understood it in the first place. But the Chinese surely noticed it. "This shows that the United States is drifting further down a dangerous road," averred foreign ministry spokeswoman Zhang Qiyue. "It will . . . harm peace and stability across the Taiwan Strait, and further damage US-China relations." When Bush finally did apologize, without acknowledging he was doing so, much of the national media decided to give him a pass—except the neoconservatives. Writing in the *Weekly Standard* Robert Kagan and William Kristol thundered about "the profound national humiliation that President Bush has brought upon the United States." With his hemming and hawing, they complained, "President Bush has revealed weakness. And he has revealed fear. . . . The American capitulation will also embolden others around the world who have watched this crisis carefully to see the new administration's mettle tested."

The China standoff was thrust upon Bush, but most of the problems he faced during the first nine months of his presidency were of his own making. It was almost as if the hard-liners in the Pentagon and elsewhere were seeking to promote confrontations to pick fights here, there, and everywhere, as if to let the natives know there was a new gang in town, and they aimed to run things as they saw fit. The moderately conservative editor of *Newsweek International,* Fareed Zakaria, noted that President Bush's favorite verb is "expect." "He announces peremptorily that he 'expects' the Palestinians to dump Yasir Arafat, 'expects' countries to be with him or against him, 'expects' Turkey to cooperate. It is all part of the administration's basic approach toward foreign policy. . . . The notion is that the United States needs to intimidate countries with its power and assertiveness, always threatening, always denouncing, never showing weakness." It was perhaps no coincidence that Donald Rumsfeld, the man who, together with Dick Cheney, bested Colin Powell for control for the heart and mind of George W. Bush, was fond of quoting Al Capone the way some military men deploy Sun Tzu or Karl von Clausewitz: "You will get more with a kind word and a gun than with a kind word alone."

While Colin Powell struggled to preserve diplomatic continuity, along with a measure of cooperation with other nations on those issues where mutually beneficial goals remained possible, his colleagues were pursuing an alternative track in which the term *diplomacy* would be a decided misnomer. Despite Powell's efforts, in its first year the Bush administration repudiated pretty much every diplomatic effort in which the Clinton administration had invested itself from the Korean peninsula to the Persian Gulf. In addition to its withdrawal from peace talks in the Middle East and Korean peninsula, the administration promptly withdrew from five international treaties, doing so in what Zakaria termed "a language and diplomatic style that seemed calculated to offend the world." As his hagiographer David Frum would observe, "Bush was extraordinarily responsive to international criticism—but his response was to tuck back his ears and repeat his offense."

The very idea of foreign intercourse seemed to many inside the administration to be something vaguely unclean and un-American. Zakaria notes that neither Bush nor Cheney undertook much foreign travel—Cheney left the country only once during his first two years as vice president, and this trip, to the Middle East to attempt to secure support for a U.S. invasion of Iraq, was deemed to be a complete failure. The early-to-bed, early-to-rise president hosted virtually no state dinners for other foreign leaders, and he cannot be said to have encouraged much dialogue with other nations, irrespective of whether he was planning massive changes in U.S. positions on issue of major global significance. Secretary Powell admitted as much when he explained the standard operating procedure of his team to a group of European journalists. President Bush, said Powell, "makes sure people know what he believes in. And then he tries to persuade others that is the correct position. When it does not work, then we will take the position we believe is correct."

The most significant indication of the new U.S. unilateralism was undoubtedly Bush's decision, announced in March 2001, to withdraw from the Kyoto Protocol on global warming and discontinue U.S. participation in its future negotiation, without so much as notifying any of the other participants in advance. (Condoleezza Rice informed European Union ambassadors that the deal was "dead" at a private lunch.) Bush had spoken out in favor of the multination agreement on the campaign trail. Approved in 1997, though as yet unratified (and unlikely to be) by the U.S. Congress, the painstakingly negotiated accord called for thirty-eight industrial countries to gradually reduce the amount of greenhouse gas emissions each produced. The accord, however, would be meaningless without U.S. participation, because Americans account for approximately 25 percent of the world's greenhouse-producing gasses. If the Europeans went ahead alone, it would be U.S. companies that would derive the benefit, as they would be competing without incurring the added costs of controlling greenhouse gasses. The U.S. pullout faced Europe with the choice of either rewarding Bush for his intransigence or starting again from scratch.

Bush defended his position with the breathtaking argument that if the Europeans doubted the administration's commitment to preserving the environment, "all they need to do is look at home and see that we're making good progress on the environment at home. We changed wetland regulations. We will reduce the amount of arsenic in our waters. . . . [W]e've got money for our national parks." In fact, his administration was then in the process of actively undermining the regulation of the amount of arsenic in Americans' drinking water, and it tried to do the same with regard to the conservation of U.S. national parks, as chapter 2 recounts in detail. Regarding wetlands policy, Bush went so far as to refuse his own brother's request to try to save Florida's coastlines, so ideologically devoted was he to the sugar industry's profitable despoiling of the nation's natural resources for private profit. In the end nothing in Bush's alleged explanation has anything to do with the administration's unilateral sabotage of the Kyoto Protocol—which, one might add, was entirely gratuitous from a diplomatic perspective, since Congress had no intention of passing it and there was no possibility it would go into effect in any case.

Returning home from Europe, Bush admitted that he really couldn't care less what the rest of the world, especially Europe, thought of American actions abroad. The idea "of placing caps on CO_2 does not make economic sense for America," he explained, leaving no room for debate. Afterward, Bush bragged of his immovability: "I went to dinner, as Karen [Hughes] would tell you, with fifteen leaders of the EU, and patiently sat there as all fifteen in one form or another told me how wrong I was. And at the end I said, 'I appreciate your point of view, but this is the American position because it's right for America.'"

The Kyoto decision provided even more fodder for the hard-liners—now apparently including NSC chief Condoleezza Rice—to humiliate

Powell, which leads one to wonder how or why the proud general remained in his position to endure them. When, seeking to make the best of a bad situation, Powell promised the Europeans in July 2001 that the Bush team would come up with its own plan to replace the Kyoto Protocol in the fall, Rice explained elsewhere that no plan would be forthcoming, and the alleged deadline for American action was a figment of the secretary's imagination. EPA director Christie Whitman and Treasury Secretary Paul O'Neill soon saw their recommendations for addressing the problem dismissed by the president as well.

The administration's justifications for the repudiation of its other treaty commitments were hardly less contemptuous of those whose interests they affected or any more concerned with the chaos they spawned in their respective wakes. The Bush team elected to walk away from an eight-year effort to create an international Chemical and Biological Weapons Convention because the new inspection-verification provisions—initially advocated by the United States to combat germ warfare weapons—now appeared to risk the exposure of American companies' industrial secrets. "For six years everybody talks of the importance of verification," wrote London's pro-U.S. daily, *The Independent*, in what would soon become a familiar foreign scenario. "And then, America discovers that its facilities, too, would have to be verified. The brazen nerve! America might be treated as though it were just another country!"

A similar dynamic seemed at work in the Bush decision to reject U.S. participation in the International Criminal Court. The first new international judicial body since the World Court was created in 1945, the ICC largely reflected U.S. legal norms and practices. Because U.S. participation was deemed crucial to its success by nearly everyone involved, other nations went out of their way to accommodate many Bush administration proposals during the initial negotiating period. Yet Bush and Company insisted that U.S. citizens be exempted from its jurisdiction, and they even threatened to withdraw all funds for UN peacekeeping, even though, given the way the treaty was finally written, Americans had little if any exposure at all to its system of prosecution. (ICC jurisdiction assumes a nonfunctioning judicial system, or one that is unwilling even to carry out an investigation of alleged crimes, for starters.) In adopting this attitude over an issue with little pragmatic value, the administration chose to forgo the opportunity to shape the court's future working through the power of argument and precedent. This strategy can only be called self-defeating, unless one's ideological commitment to unilateralism outweighs any consideration of pragmatism in such decisions.

Many more such actions never made the front pages or the cable-TV shout fests. For instance, Bush officials scuttled a UN draft accord on the international sale of small arms, warning that it might constrain the legitimate weapons trade and infringe on the right of American citizens to bear arms. The purpose of the nonbinding agreement was to discourage the sale of small arms from fueling civil conflicts around the world through the creation of a monitoring system for all sales. John R. Bolton, undersecretary of state for arms control and international security affairs, had informed the other participants that our government would not support the accord's key provisions, among which was a proposed ban on private ownership of military weapons, including assault rifles and grenade launchers. Although these weapons were banned under U.S. law, that ban had been enacted during the Clinton administration over the objections of then senator, now attorney general John Ashcroft, and was opposed at the time by George W. Bush. Given that the United States is by far the world's leading exporter of such weapons—accounting for approximately $1.2 billion of the $4 billion to $6 billion worldwide total in 1998—any agreement that did not include its participation was, like the Kyoto Protocol, moot by definition. And so the Small Arms Agreement died—along with the approximately half a million people each year, more than 80 percent of whom are children, estimated by the UN secretary general's office to be victims of guns and explosives it sought to control.

We find yet another example of the Bush administration protecting the interests of big business by standing in the way of a global consensus for commonsense measures in its willingness to disrupt the adoption of a UN convention to ban corruption. Taking a position that the *Wall Street Journal* described as "a striking turnaround from several years ago, when the Clinton administration pressed a reluctant Europe to crack down on bribes," the Bush team fought hard to dilute the pact, in effect protecting the practice of bribes, illicit payments, and nepotism. U.S. negotiators, who were also interested in protecting the right of companies to make large illegal donations to political parties without suffering any consequences, complained that "funding issues are too complex for the pact because political systems vary so widely." In August 2003, the *Wall Street Journal* announced that the administration had "reached preliminary agreement with Europe and developing nations to water down a proposed global treaty against corruption by largely exempting businesses and political parties from the requirements."

Perhaps an even more egregious abandonment of fundamental standards of decency was the Bush administration's willingness to stand, together with the U.S. pharmaceutical industry, in the way of a global agreement to provide low-cost medicine to the developing world. Although every one of the 143 member nations of the World Trade Organization agreed upon a new plan on the trade of medicines, the United States blocked the proposal. According to the reporting in the *Wall Street Journal*, the administration, "under heavy lobbying from a pharmaceutical industry seeking to limit the scope of the deal, endorsed a list of some twenty infectious diseases that it was willing to address." Among the illnesses for which the administration left off treatments were heart-related problems, diabetes, cancer, and chronic respiratory diseases—maladies that afflict far more people than the ones for which low-cost drugs were to be provided, according to World Health Organization figures. Talks broke down as a result of the United States's refusal to compromise, and as of this writing, an agreement remains stalled on low-cost drugs for the Third World—which suits the U.S. pharmaceutical industry. (The industry had spent more than $50 million to help Republicans gain control of Congress in the November 2002 election alone.)

A similarly disturbing phenomenon was evident in the U.S. position in the free trade talks the administration conducted with the Southern African Customs Union (SACU), which includes South Africa, Namibia, Botswana, Lesotho, and Swaziland. At the end of 2002, according to estimates from UNAIDS, an umbrella group for five UN agencies, the World Bank, and the World Health Organization, nearly 30 million people in sub-Saharan Africa were living with (or dying from) HIV, with 3.5 million new infections taking place in 2002 alone. "National adult HIV prevalence has risen higher than thought possible, exceeding 30 percent" in much of the region, notes UNAIDS. HIV prevalence rates are 38.8 percent in Botswana, 31 percent in Lesotho, and 33.4 percent in Swaziland. South Africa has the world's largest population of people with HIV/AIDS. The crisis is one of the worst humanitarian disasters humankind has ever faced.

While the pandemic has many causes and complications, perhaps the greatest barrier to the treatment of the continent's tens of millions of victims—almost half of whom are under twenty-four—is the price of drugs that U.S. pharmaceutical companies charge to sell them there. Recognizing this, in 2001 all of the WTO countries—the United States included—affirmed the Doha Declaration on the Trade-Related Aspects of Intellectual Property Rights (TRIPS) Agreement and Public Health. This declaration stipulates that the TRIPS agreement "can and should be interpreted and implemented in a manner supportive of WTO members' right to protect public health and, in particular, to promote access to medicines for all," adding, "we reaffirm the right of WTO members to use, to the full, the provisions in the TRIPS agreement, which provide flexibility for this purpose." Under President Clinton, and initially under President Bush, a presidential order ensured that America would not request that any African nation offer patent protections above or beyond those required by the TRIPS accord. And when Congress passed the Trade Act of 2002, giving George W. Bush fast-track negotiating authority, it specifically mandated that the United States respect the Doha Declaration.

NGOs operating in Africa, including Doctors Without Borders/ Médecins Sans Frontières, Oxfam, Africa Action, Health GAP, Consumer Project on Technology, Global AIDS Alliance, ACT-UP Paris, and Essential Action have called on the administration to exclude intellectual property from the U.S.-SACU negotiations. But Bush has remained deaf to their pleas. U.S. trade representative Robert Zoellick explains that one of the chief aims of the Bush team is to "establish standards that reflect a standard of [patent] protection similar to that found in U.S. law and that build on the foundations established in the WTO Agreement on Trade-Related Aspects of Intellectual Property."

Big business is not the only outside force calling shots on U.S. global policy. The influence of fundamentalist Christians within the Bush team was so strong that the United States repeatedly refused to take part with the rest of the world in a basic convention raised in meetings of the UN Commission on the Status of Women. An objectionable phrase—which had been included in previous statements for approximately a decade—called upon member nations to condemn violence against women and "refrain from invoking any custom, tradition, or religious consideration" to avoid the obligation to halt it. One member of the Bush-appointed U.S. commission—Janice Crouse, of the conservative group Concerned Women for America—explained, "For too long, the feminists have been pushing a radical, special-interest agenda under the erroneous mantra made rhetorical cliché by Hillary Clinton: 'Women's rights are human rights.'" Meanwhile, the delegation's chair, Ellen Sauerbrey, a sometime Republican candidate, brushed off criticism with the claim, "I don't think we're aligning ourselves with countries who have bad records on human rights." In fact, joining the United States in its antifeminist obstructionism were such progressive nations as Iran, Pakistan, Sudan, and Libya.

The Bush administration position on trade adhered to the now familiar foreign policy pattern of "denounce and deceive." One of the few clear foreign policy positions Bush articulated during the presidential campaign was an unambiguous commitment to free trade. He warned that giving in to the temptation "to build a proud tower of protectionism and isolation" would be a "shortcut to chaos . . . invite challenges to our power" and result in "a stagnant America and a savage world." On this issue, moreover, he was considered a surer bet than his opponent Al Gore, because a Democrat supporting "free trade"—meaning, more truthfully, "free investment"—required the expenditure of considerable political capital, owing to the numerical strength of the party's "fair trade" constituencies, especially the labor movement. Supporting free trade as a Republican, however, demanded few if any concessions within the party, as the position was a natural ideological fit for the party of big business and untrammeled free enterprise.

Bush kept up the usual free trade rhetoric, telling graduates of the University of South Carolina, "Across the globe, free markets and trade have helped defeat poverty and taught men and women the habits of liberty." But at just about the first chance he was given he turned his back on free trade, vastly increasing protective tariffs on domestic steel and agriculture products to a degree never even contemplated by his Democratic predecessor (in some cases by more than 80 percent), just six weeks after he advised the members of the Organization of American States to resist those who "hold out the false comfort of protectionism." Apparently this advice did not apply when it affected jobs in such key swing states as Pennsylvania and West Virginia, or important agricultural constituencies. The farm subsidies will provide a windfall for massive agricultural conglomerates (who are, not surprisingly, Republican campaign contributors) but will close American markets to the poorest of the poor, while costing U.S. taxpayers an estimated $180 billion over the next decade.

While Congress plays a major role in farm policy, the steel subsidies were all the president's responsibility, and there can be no doubt that Karl Rove understood this when Bush made the decision. The *New York Times* quoted a steelworker explaining, "I may be a staunch Democrat, but I'll sure remember Bush for helping us." Even the administration's most loyal partisans found the hypocrisy hard to stomach. Conservative pundit George Will complained, "Proving himself less principled than Bill Clinton regarding the free trade principles that are indispensable to world prosperity and comity, President Bush has done what Clinton refused to do. In the name of providing 'breathing space' for the U.S. steel industry, which has been on the respirator of protection for decades, Bush has cooked up an unpalatable confection of tariffs and import quotas that mock his free trade rhetoric." Bush's friend and America's ally, British prime minister Tony Blair, termed the decision "unwarranted, unacceptable and wrong." Another expert complained that tariffs were "nothing more than taxes that hurt low- and moderate-income people." His name: Robert Zoellick; his title: U.S. trade representative for President George W. Bush. In November 2003, the World Trade Organization completed the circle, ruling that Bush's tariffs were illegal under international law, and opened the door to the sanction of more than $2 billion in penalties on U.S. exports unless Bush retreated.

In fact, the decision turned out to be a political loser as well as a policy nightmare. According to a study funded by steel-using companies, higher prices resulting from the tariffs ended up costing the industry roughly two hundred thousand manufacturing jobs, many of which went to China. Small machine-tool and metal-stamping shops complain that their costs rose by as much as 30 percent. Steel producers countered with their own numbers, but the argument certainly got the Bush administration's attention. When the United Steelworkers of America announced in August 2003 that it would be endorsing Democratic representative Richard Gephardt for president, the game was clearly up. A month later, administration officials let it be known that the tariffs would be either vastly reduced or rolled back entirely. Of course never did the president admit he had made a mistake or betrayed his "free trade" principles.

In Venezuela, it was not "free trade" that revealed the say-one-thing-do-another modus operandi of the Bush White House, but freedom itself. Just one day after the president celebrated Pan-American Day by proclaiming "democracy as the birthright of every person in the Americas," he and his advisors appeared to condone an attempted coup in Venezuela against the democratically elected Venezuelan president Hugo Chavez. Chavez, who had run afoul of U.S. foreign policy with his praise for Fidel Castro, among other sins, lost his job "as a result of the message of the Venezuelan people," according to Ari Fleischer. The latter, however, refused to term the military overthrow of a democratically elected president a "coup," insisting instead, "We know that the action encouraged by the Chavez government provoked the crisis."

While no clear evidence ever emerged to tie Bush administration officials to the coup in advance of its occurrence, the administration was in no more of a mood to adhere to the "humble" words of candidate Bush with regard to its actions in Latin America than it had been regarding Europe or the rest of the world, whose treaties it no longer supported. At a meeting of the Organization of American States that took place during the seventy-two-hour reign of the generals, Roger Noriega, the U.S. ambassador to the OAS, took the floor to chastise member states for failing to proclaim their support for the new (and short-lived) regime. "You can go all over Latin America and you will find disappointment," said Jorge Montano, a political consultant in Mexico City who served as ambassador to Washington from 1993 to 1995. "The behavior of this administration has been extremely erratic, proving their ignorance about what is going on in the region." Amazingly, the administration managed to top its own previous record for chutzpah in the aftermath of Chavez's reinstatement, as Condoleezza Rice warned him to "respect constitutional processes." This advice seemed to be useful only in the short term, for in December 2002, "in a statement that State Department and Pentagon officials said emanated from the National Security Council with little advance consultation with anyone outside the White House," according to the *Washington Post*, President Bush's spokesman, Ari Fleischer, announced that the United States believed the only way out of the crisis was "the holding of early elections." Alas, since Venezuela had no "constitutional processes" that would have allowed for the holding of such elections—any more than the U.S. Constitution does—this statement, according to *Post* reporter Karen DeYoung in Washington, "left many here and in Venezuela scratching their heads." Ms. Rice was apparently unavailable to explain just which processes—or whose constitution—she was instructing the Venezuelans to follow.

We Are the World

Perhaps the most significant of all the Bush administration's pre–September 11 diplomatic demarches into what former State Department official James Rubin termed "gratuitous unilateralism" was the president's announcement that he planned to withdraw from the U.S.-Russian antiballistic missile treaty. Claiming that "no treaty that prevents us from addressing today's threats, that prohibits us from pursuing promising technology to defend ourselves, our friends and our allies is in our interests or in the interests of world peace," Bush signaled plans to begin construction of a missile defense system that almost all disinterested analysts judged to be dangerously and ultimately fatally flawed. The notion of "protecting" America via missile defense proved to be yet another unhappy marriage of the president's ignorance, overconfidence, dishonesty, and hypocrisy. A best-case scenario would have the program turning out to be merely a waste of hundreds of billions of dollars; a worst case would be a dangerous nuclear arms race and the possibility of a catastrophic nuclear exchange in Asia or the Middle East.

The question of missile defense has become a kind of article of religious faith for most Republicans, like belief in God and the free market. Beginning in 1983 when President Reagan sprung the idea on all but a handful of his closest advisors, the United States has spent more than $70 billion attempting to solve the most rudimentary technical problems associated with creating a missile defense system and come up completely empty-handed. In fact, the entire notion has survived these past decades on the willingness of many of those in charge to cover up its obvious technical flaws or to create testing conditions designed to produce deceptive results. Never in its twenty-year history has any proposed system ever been subjected to a test that even remotely attempted to simulate the most rudimentarily imaginable form of missile attack, all the while continuing to fail tests explicitly designed to demonstrate its putative success.

In June 2003 the nonpartisan General Accounting Office issued a report warning that the planned Bush system put the nation "in danger of getting off track early and introducing more risk into the missile defense effort over the long term." It contained components "that have not been demonstrated as mature and ready" for incorporation with other elements, with testing that "has provided only limited data for determining whether the system will work." No wonder that, even as the Bush administration was readying the system's deployment, Defense Secretary Donald Rumsfeld tried to convince Congress to exempt it from the law that requires all weapons systems to undergo operational tests before being deployed in the field. Meanwhile, the director of the missile defense program, General Ronald Kadish, admitted that he had no idea whether the system chosen would work or even if it would have to be replaced entirely after it was deployed. "The final architecture is not knowable today because we have a lot more research and development to do," he explained. A July 2003 study by a twelve-member group under the auspices of the American Physical Society, the largest U.S. association of physicists, concluded that the intended Bush administration approach to just one aspect of the many complicated elements of such a system—the "boost-phase" hit—would push the limits of what is technically possible. It also found that these weapons would prove entirely ineffective against solid-fueled missiles that nations like North Korea and Iran are expected to deploy within the coming decade and a half. A month later, the Pentagon's Missile Defense Agency admitted as much, and suspended the program because, it noted, the technology involved was "not mature enough" to fund.

It gets worse. Even if missile defense could have been made functional, the proponents of building such a system have still never addressed themselves to the precise nature of the threat its enormous investment was designed to meet. Excluding the United States, just ten nations possess ballistic missiles. Of these, only China's and Russia's have sufficient range to reach the United States, a situation that has remained true since 1959 when Russia first tested its ICBMs and 1981 when China acquired its. And yet even this threat has diminished by roughly 60 percent, from more than a thousand to just four hundred or so in only fifteen years, owing to arms control agreements. The Russian force will likely fall by another 60 percent shortly merely for reasons of expense, while China has only about twenty ICBMs today and is not expected to increase that number beyond forty.

Moreover, not only is the U.S. homeland considerably less menaced by these missiles than in the past, but these same arms control agreements have pretty much freed most of Europe from the threat entirely, ridding the continent of all intermediate-range missiles. China alone still has them, and its force numbers only twenty. Once the United States embarks on a missile defense system, however, these nations could easily overwhelm its deterrent capacities simply by building more missiles, as it is impossible to imagine a system that is completely leakproof. Russia, China, Pakistan, and India would almost certainly embark on a new ballistic missile race under these circumstances, leading to greater instability and the increasing likelihood of a truly devastating war that could kill millions.

Alternatively, a defense, whether it worked or not, could embolden U.S. officials in the future to employ nuclear weapons on what had previously been a conventional battlefield. Bush's assistant secretary of defense for forces policy, Keith Payne, is a man who made his reputation two decades ago with a now notorious article about nuclear war entitled "Victory Is Possible." The article, coauthored with Colin S. Gray, spoke of defensive strategies that would enable the United States to endure a full-scale nuclear attack, and "reduce U.S. casualties to approximately 20 million . . . a level compatible with national survival and recovery." More recently, he has written approvingly of "multiple nuclear strikes" in a conventional war "if the locations of dispersed mobile launchers cannot be determined with enough precision to permit pinpoint strikes." (It was this very paper that convinced Donald Rumsfeld to put Payne in his sensitive job.)

In fact by investing less over a period of ten years than was spent in just the first seven months of 2003 on the missile defense system, the United States was able to eliminate more than six thousand nuclear warheads from the Russian arsenal. Still it starved this enormously cost-effective security program, along with most other efforts involved in preventing the proliferation of nuclear weapons to nations and groups that cannot be trusted to hold them. Things got so bad that private billionaires like Ted Turner and Warren Buffett had to fund efforts to secure a Belgrade facility that contained sufficient amounts of enriched uranium to make two bombs. While the United States has historically struggled to keep the nuclear threshold as high as possible, the Bush administration appears ready to begin erasing it, with all of the horrific implications of such a war one can imagine.

What is so infuriating about this strategy is that the arguments that favor a missile defense system are now so obviously questionable, at best. As the extremely low-tech al Qaeda attacks of September 11 conclusively demonstrated, Americans are vulnerable in thousands of ways to deadly attacks that cannot be prevented by the enormously expensive and politically provocative construction of a missile delivery system. Think of how many small boats pass along the harbors of our major cities every day, any one of which could conceivably kill millions of people with a delivery system no more powerful than an offshore dinghy. For a little more than half of what the Bush administration planned to spend in the 2004 budget on its pie-in-the-sky plan, as Fred Kaplan calculated in *Slate,* it could have provided the entire fleet of five thousand U.S. commercial jets with electronic flares, the hot emissions that U.S. military aircraft employ to deflect the anti-aircraft fire available to thousands of potential terrorists (and already tried against the Israelis).

Bush's warnings about threats from the "world's least-responsible states" to the contrary, it's hard to imagine that any "rogue" nation would ever be in a position to threaten the United States with an ICBM attack. Long before its military planes could become operational, the United States, armed with satellite intelligence, would likely knock out its missile-delivery capabilities, if we did not decide to simply obliterate it entirely. Being the most powerful nation on the planet by a factor of fifteen has significant advantages when it comes to deterrence.

Despite intense lobbying, including the proffering of billions in potential defense contracts, not one of America's allies could be talked into supporting Bush's plan to abrogate the ABM treaty and proceed with the creation of a unilateral ABM system. These nations worried not only about alienating Russia from the West but also about inspiring another U.S.-Russian nuclear arms race, and even more dangerously, one among China, India, and Pakistan, who would need only to increase the number of their launchers to overwhelm whatever imperfect system the United States decided to produce. The Bush plan would quite possibly inspire their embarkation on a rapid construction program to address this problem, thereby causing a dangerous and destabilizing arms race in one of the world's most explosive regions. Given Pakistan's vulnerability to home-grown Islamic militant takeover, this scenario inspires even greater alarm, particularly as it relates to the ongoing low-intensity war with India over Kashmir. And yet proceeding down this counterproductive and costly path was somehow preferable to actually taking steps that might help protect the nation from genuine threats. When the Senate and House Armed Services Committees passed an amendment that would have allowed the president to take more than $800 million from his missile defense program and transfer it to the Department of Homeland Security, Bush rejected the deal.

Why, really, did he do it? Again the defense contractors that were heavily invested in missile defense and stood to profit most heavily from its adoption were, almost without exception, significant contributors to the Republican Party. The Christian and conservative ideologues who formed the party's base believed it America's divine right to be protected from missile attack and were extremely unlikely to be aware of the multiple technological barriers that remained standing between Bush's proposal and its realization. The public was equally unschooled on the complexities that will undermine the effectiveness of any potential system, and as Frances FitzGerald has demonstrated, has labored for decades under the misimpression that America is already protected from a missile attack. By adopting the program so forcefully, Bush was able to present an image to the public of "strong" leadership, regardless of the prospect for success. Indeed, the issue is an almost perfect one from the standpoint of its political consequences. How many people would blame the president in the event of a successful nuclear attack against the United States for trying to protect the nation? In the far more likely event of no attack, how could Bush be proved wrong?

But the plan had a further advantage, as well, an ideological one, and as we will see, consistent with the emerging neoconservative consensus in the administration that it needed to start fighting wars in some places in order to reorder the world in accordance with American wishes. Writing in *The New Republic,* Lawrence F. Kaplan supported a missile defense scheme because it would enable the United States to contemplate military interventions across the globe without worry about retaliation. China's ambassador to the UN Conference on Disarmament also predicted, though hardly with Kaplan's enthusiasm, that the system would give the United States "absolute freedom in using or threatening to use force in international relations." As a RAND Corporation study put it, "[B]allistic missile defense is not simply a shield but an enabler of U.S. action." In fact, it may be far more the latter than the former, which one suspects would suit the Bush administration just fine.

The Bad Opinion of Mankind

In May 2001 the rest of the world had the chance to assemble at the United Nations and signal to the Bush administration just what it thought of its new attitude toward diplomacy, cooperation, and compromise. That May the United States found itself without a seat on the UN Commission on Human Rights for the first time since it was established in 1947. It was a clear rebuke of George W. Bush and the men and women who represented him. Whereas the United States had received written pledges of support from forty-one countries, only twenty-nine honored them during the secret balloting process. France won in a landslide, and Jean-David Levitte, the French ambassador to the United Nations, attributed his nation's new-found popularity to its foreign policy "founded on dialogue and respect," in clear contradistinction to that of the United States. The Communist Chinese used nearly identical language, observing that America's defeat demonstrated that it had "undermined the atmosphere for dialogue."

Ironically, the Bush position was held by a decided minority of his fellow citizens. When Americans were surveyed about their own foreign policy values and preferences, large majorities supported not the bellicose positions of the Bush unilateralists but the policies of conciliation and cooperation professed by the Europeans. According to an extensive survey of attitudes on both sides of the Atlantic undertaken by the German Marshall Fund of the United States and the Chicago Council on Foreign Relations in late 2002, approximately half of both surveyed populations named global warming as a major threat to national security. (Seventy percent of Americans surveyed said the United States should sign the Kyoto Protocol even when a possible negative impact on the domestic economy was cited; 65 percent supported American participation in the International Criminal Court even when the possibility of trumped-up charges brought against U.S. soldiers was mentioned as a potential liability.) Support to strengthen the UN stood in the high seventies on both sides, and there was majority support for strengthening institutions like the WTO and NATO. But while Europeans ensured that their governments accurately represented their feelings on these issues, U.S. citizens behaved in a far more apathetic, or perhaps deferential, fashion. They allowed the Bush administration to take position after position that contradicted their professed values because they were either insufficiently motivated or insufficiently organized to demand a more democratic response. As Ivo H. Daalder and James M. Lindsay of the Brookings Institution point out, "Polls throughout the 1990s found that fewer than 10 percent of Americans—and often less than 5 percent—named any defense or national security issue as the most important problem facing the United States. Even when people were pressed to name a foreign policy problem, the most common response polls turned up was 'Don't Know.'" So while neither Bush nor his advisors appeared to believe in the standard notion of international cooperation, considerations of right and wrong, and what Jefferson called the "good opinion of mankind," Americans' inattention provided an opportunity for the ideologues within the Bush administration to do with the nation's foreign policy virtually whatever they pleased.

10. A Nation Transformed, a Tragedy Exploited

✶

"My job will be to usher in the responsibility era, a culture that will stand in stark contrast to the last few decades, which has clearly said to America: 'If it feels good, do it, and if you've got a problem blame somebody else.'"

—Presidential candidate George W. Bush, 2000

See No Evil

In studying the pre–September 11 record it's hard to avoid the conclusion that, rhetoric notwithstanding, George W. Bush demonstrated a remarkably relaxed attitude toward the problem of fighting terrorism for the first nine months of his presidency.

In February 2001, shortly after taking office, Bush committed his administration to placing "a high priority on detecting and responding to terrorism on our soil." In reality, this "high priority" received no further presidential mention except on those occasions when Bush sought to make his dubious case for missile defense. When confronted with Clinton administration initiatives to address the problem in an aggressive fashion, the president's staff took a pass. Even when Bush appeared to confront the problem, he did so primarily by bureaucratic sleight of hand. On May 8, for example, the president announced the creation of a new Office of National Preparedness for terrorism at the Federal Emergency Management Agency, only to later cut the agency's budget by $200 million. With the exception of missile defense, Bush's constant themes during this period were tax cuts, education reform, and his program for "compassionate conservatism."

Clearly the president had his priorities, and terrorism safeguards were not one of them.

As a candidate, Bush had complained that the Clinton administration had invited challenge by failing to respond to previous terrorist attacks. For instance, one day after the October 12, 2000, attack on the USS *Cole,* candidate Bush proclaimed, "There must be a consequence." Yet an FBI document dated January 26, 2001—six days after Bush took office—demonstrates that even though U.S. authorities discovered what they deemed to be clear evidence tying the *Cole* bombers to al Qaeda, Bush did nothing.

Five days later a commission headed by Gary Hart and Warren Rudman released a detailed report on the urgent steps necessary to begin the process of protecting the United States against a terrorist attack. "States, terrorists and other disaffected groups will acquire weapons of mass destruction, and some will use them," the report warned. "Americans will likely die on American soil, possibly in large numbers." Hart even presciently predicted that the country was vulnerable to "a weapon of mass destruction in a high-rise building." The authors called for the creation of a department of homeland security combining and superseding the functions of the Immigration and Naturalization Service, the Border Patrol, and the Customs Service, a recommendation converted into legislation by Senator Joseph Lieberman (D-CT). Instead of embracing the plan, or seizing the initiative himself, Bush deliberately buried it. He announced a government-wide review to be overseen by Vice President Cheney and promised, "I will periodically chair a meeting of the National Security Council to review these efforts."

In fact, apparently neither Cheney's review nor Bush's chairing of NSC meetings on the topic ever took place. When White House press secretary Ari Fleischer was asked to list the vice president's policy portfolio at a press briefing on June 29, 2001, no mention was made of the review. When a reporter asked a specific question about whether Cheney might be heading task forces "after energy," Fleischer responded in the negative. The *Washington Post* later reported that no review ever took place; the problem was simply laid aside.

In contrast to the increasingly panicked Clinton terrorism team, top Bush advisors held only two meetings devoted to terrorism during the entire nine-month period before September 11. Conservative Republican Newt Gingrich, who had helped create the Hart-Rudman panel with Bill Clinton when he was Speaker of the House, was heard to complain, "The administration actually slowed down response to Hart-Rudman when momentum was building in the spring." Meanwhile, U.S. military commanders asked for additional funds to meet the domestic terrorist threat, and the Senate Armed Services Committee attempted to reprogram $600 million from Bush's beloved missile defense. The response: a promised presidential veto. The date: September 9, 2001.

After the cataclysmic events of September 11, Bush administration officials adopted the public stance that an attack like those on the World Trade Center and the Pentagon had been all but unimaginable up until the moments they took place. Taking refuge in hyperspecificity, President Bush explained, "Never [in] anybody's thought processes . . . about how to protect America did we ever think that the evildoers would fly not one but four commercial aircraft into precious U.S. targets . . . never." Condoleezza Rice followed a similar line: "I don't think anybody could have predicted that . . . [al Qaeda] would try to use a hijacked airplane as a missile." As Senator John McCain (R-AZ) points out, however, "the September 11 attacks were incredibly depraved but not, as it turns out, unimaginable." The *Sunday Times* (London) quoted a British senior Foreign Office source saying, "The Americans knew of plans to use commercial aircraft in unconventional ways, possibly as flying bombs." And in June 2001 the German intelligence agency, BND, informed the Americans that Middle Eastern terrorists were planning to hijack commercial aircraft and use them as weapons to attack "American and Israeli symbols which stand out." A member of the National Intelligence Council, the U.S. Intelligence Community's (IC's) center for midterm and long-term strategic thinking, later told the Associated Press that the plane-as-weapon scenario had long been considered in U.S. intelligence circles: "If you ask anybody—could terrorists convert a plane into a missile?—nobody would have ruled that out." Tom Clancy even wrote a novel in which just such an attack takes place, *Debt of Honor.* It was published in 1994 and sold millions of copies.

In retrospect, many of the dots were simply waiting to be connected. Back in 1995 an accomplice of Ramzi Yousef's who had trained as a pilot at three separate U.S. flight schools revealed that the mastermind behind the 1993 World Trade Center attack planned to hide bombs on twelve U.S.-bound airliners and crash an explosive-laden airline into the CIA. Six years later the National Intelligence Council received a Library of Congress–prepared report warning that al Qaeda suicide bombers "could crash-land an aircraft packed with high explosives" into the Pentagon, the CIA building, or the White House. This followed on an August 1998 intelligence report suggesting that a group of unidentified Arabs planned to fly an explosive-laden plane from a foreign country into the World Trade Center. These documents were passed along to the FBI and FAA. At the same time, in May and June of that year, the intelligence community began to acquire intelligence information indicating that Osama bin Laden's al Qaeda network intended to strike inside the United States, with the likely targets deemed to be New York and Washington; that summer, the target was narrowed down to the World Trade Center. This plot, however, was deemed too outrageous to be taken seriously, despite the fact that in 1994, French commandos had stormed a hijacked airliner, foiling a kamikaze attack on the Eiffel Tower. Intelligence forces in the Philippines had discovered similar plans in 1995.

Earlier in 2001, moreover, Italian military and police forces took seriously a report that al Qaeda terrorists might try to crash a plane into the G-7 meeting place and kill all of the assembled Western leaders and therefore positioned anti-aircraft missiles all around the city. President Bush decided to spend his nights on a U.S. aircraft carrier offshore, while the other Western leaders present opted to stay on ships as well. When the joint panel of the House and Senate Intelligence Committees released the nonredacted portions of its inquiry into the September 11 attacks in late July 2003, we also learned that the agencies had uncovered a message between al Qaeda operatives in the United States, dated December 1998, that read, "Plans to hijack U.S. aircraft proceeding well. Two individuals have successfully evaded checkpoints in dry run at NY airport."

Finally, and perhaps most significantly, Bush himself personally received two major briefings during the summer of 2001, one in the White House Situation Room and another on his ranch in Crawford. Each warned that a major terrorist attack against the United States, possibly carried out by al Qaeda, and possibly including hijacked planes, was likely in the offing. The latter memo read to Bush was entitled "Bin Laden Determined to Strike in U.S."—not "Bin Laden Determined to Strike U.S.," as Ari Fleischer would later argue. Condoleezza Rice would likewise claim, by way of partial exoneration, "The overwhelming bulk of the evidence was that this was an attack that was likely to take place overseas." It was not.

The warnings to Bush appear to have been based on information passed along by British, German, Israeli, Moroccan, Russian, Jordanian, and Egyptian intelligence, as well as by the U.S. intelligence community's own considerable resources. According to the Senate Intelligence Committee, the memo's authors worried "that members of al Qaeda, including some U.S. citizens, had resided in or traveled to the U.S. for years and that the group apparently maintained a support structure here." It raised the possibility that bin Laden would hijack planes and noted patterns of activity consistent with such a plan, as well as information acquired in May 2001 indicating a group of bin Laden supporters was planning attacks in the United States with explosives. "Something really spectacular is going to happen here, and it's going to happen soon," the government's top counterterrorism official, Richard Clarke, stated.

What did George Bush do after receiving his second serious warning of imminent danger to the nation whose protection and defense he had sworn to uphold? According to the *New York Times*, Bush "broke off from work early and spent most of the day fishing." Even though Attorney General John Ashcroft had already taken the precaution of no longer traveling by commercial jetliner, the president apparently did not allow the threats presented to him to interfere in any way with his monthlong August vacation. Major airline carriers were not even given any special alerts to be vigilant for potential hijackers. If Bush took any action at all, there's no evidence for it. Any information concerning this matter was redacted from the subsequent congressional inquiry, on the novel argument that to declassify "any description of the president's knowledge" would be to compromise national security. This was also the case for what might have been contained in his briefing that day.

It was not as if the United States lacked the means to protect itself. Following the *Cole* bombing, Clinton counterterrorism forces started working on an aggressive plan to retaliate against al Qaeda. Their plan to strike back reached then national security advisor Sandy Berger and other top officials on December 20, 2000. But with less than a month remaining in office and the Bush team about to take over, they decided it would be wrong to take an action that would tie the incoming administration's hands. Instead they took their case to the new administration in the hopes that some version of the plan might be enacted before it was too late. CIA director George Tenet termed al Qaeda a "tremendous threat" as well as an "immediate" one, while Berger warned Rice, "You're going to spend more time during your four years on terrorism generally and al Qaeda specifically than any other issue."

Clarke, who headed the counterterrorism office, then offered up a complete Power Point presentation to Rice, promising, "We would make a major error if we underestimated the challenge al Qaeda poses." Featuring a complete set of proposals to "roll back" al Qaeda, Clarke's plan envisaged the "breakup" of al Qaeda cells and their arrest and imprisonment. He also called for an attack on the financial network that supported the terrorists, freezing its assets, exposing its phony charities, and arresting its personnel. The United States would offer help to such disparate nations as Uzbekistan, the Philippines, and Yemen to combat the al Qaeda forces in their respective midsts. And finally, Clarke's proposal suggested a significant increase in U.S. covert action in Afghanistan with the goal of "eliminat[ing] the sanctuary" where the Taliban and bin Laden were operating in tandem. The plan recommended a considerable increase in American support for the Northern Alliance in their fight to overthrow the Taliban's repressive regime, thereby keeping the terrorists preoccupied with protecting their gains, rather than seeking new victories elsewhere. Simultaneously American military forces would begin planning for special operations inside Afghanistan and bombing strikes against terrorist-training camps.

It was an enormous undertaking, and *Newsweek* quoted one official as costing out the plan at "several hundreds of millions." Instead of acting on it, however, the Bush administration decided—as it did with the Hart-Rudman recommendations—to lay it aside and conduct its own review. Rice did not even bother to set up a high-level meeting to discuss the issue, but instead effectively demoted Clarke through a reorganization of the NSC structure.

As power in any strong hierarchy flows downward, the rest of the Bush team was hardly more concerned about meeting a potential terrorist threat.

All through the governmental system, the issue was moved, in the words of the chairman of the Joint Chiefs of Staff, General Hugh Shelton, "farther to the back burner." To take one example, terrorism requires large amounts of illegal cash, and much of the money used to finance the September 11 attacks was transmitted via an underground system of brokers called *hawala*. For instance, back in the spring of 1999, a Saudi government audit indicated that five of Saudi Arabia's billionaires had been giving tens of millions of dollars to al Qaeda, transferring money from the National Commercial Bank to accounts of Islamic charities in London and banks in New York that served as fronts for bin Laden. Such money-laundering operations are just as critical to the success of a terrorist operation as weapons or flight training. But U.S. Treasury Secretary Paul O'Neill, acting on the Bush administration's philosophy of laissez-faire for the wealthy, came into office seeking to weaken even the types of financial regulations designed to prevent money laundering by terror groups.

Before the Bush team came to power, previous administrations had worked with international organizations to suppress the kind of rogue banking activities that made money laundering by terror organizations and global drug smugglers possible. Most of these were conducted under the rubric of the Financial Action Task Force (FATF) of the Organization for Economic Cooperation and Development (OECD), located in Paris. Its most notable effort as of January 2001 was a "name and shame" campaign designed to humiliate nations with lax banking laws or enforcement practices into cooperating with the international community's effort to clean up the industry. The Bush administration suspended its cooperation with the FATF in May 2001, when Secretary O'Neill complained that it contradicted the administration's tax and economic priorities." Further U.S. cooperation, he announced, would henceforth be "under review"—yet another Bush administration "review" that ended abruptly on September 11.

At the Pentagon, Secretary of Defense Donald Rumsfeld felt that many of the Clinton-era antiterrorist efforts could be filed under "review" indefinitely. One tactic the Clinton team had been considering just before the transition began was the possibility of sending the CIA's Predator surveillance plane over bin Laden's camps in Afghanistan, armed with Hellfire missiles that were tested in February 2001, should any promising targets arise. The Predator had crashed in October 2000 and had required repairs, but the Clinton team had expected it to be flying again by March 2001. But through the spring and summer of 2001, when considerable intelligence might have been available, Rumsfeld did not approve the launch of even an unarmed Predator. Sources quoted in news reports at the time blame CIA poaching on traditional Department of Defense turf. The plane would begin flying again in October. At a meeting on September 4, 2001, which included the secretary of state, the secretary of defense, the director of the CIA, the chairman of the Joint Chiefs of Staff, the attorney general, the national security advisor, and Deputy Defense Secretary Paul Wolfowitz, the issue apparently came to a head. Richard Clarke told the *New Yorker*'s Jane Mayer, "Tenet said he opposed using the armed Predator, because it wasn't the CIA's job to fly airplanes that shot missiles. The Air Force said it wasn't their job to fly planes to collect intelligence. No one around the table seemed to have a can-do attitude. Everyone seemed to have an excuse."

But the CIA's level of engagement was also part of the problem. DCI George Tenet would argue, in retrospect, that beginning in 1998 he warned his subordinates of the al Qaeda threat: "We are at war. I want no resources or people spared in this effort, either inside the CIA or the community." In spring 1999 Tenet came up with what he called "the Plan" to deal with these terrorists, yet it was a plan without soldiers, weapons, or much of anything else. Tenet did not order up a National Intelligence Estimate on the threat, asked for no resources required to execute it, and did not even contact the FBI about how it might be implemented. As Fred Kaplan observed in *Slate*, Tenet "asked Congress for only the slightest increases in spending on counterterrorism—and, even so, the CIA ended Fiscal Year 2001 with millions of dollars in counterterrorism money left *unspent.*"

As for Justice, Attorney General Ashcroft's May 2001 Senate testimony averred that "our No. 1 goal is the prevention of terrorist acts." Meanwhile, at the time of the attack, Ashcroft was expending much of his time and energy focusing the bureau's efforts on such pressing problems as cancer patients' use of medical marijuana in California, and the operation of New Orleans whorehouses. When he first met with FBI chief Louis Freeh as attorney general, Ashcroft explained that his priorities would be two: "violent crime and drugs." According to a participant in the meeting, when Freeh tried to direct the conversation toward terror and counterterrorism, "Ashcroft didn't want to hear about it. More significantly Ashcroft also refused to devote significant resources to the antiterrorist cause. Only a few months later—on September 10, to be exact—the attorney general turned down an FBI request to add 149 field agents, 200 analysts, and 54 translators to its counterterrorism effort. He did so despite the fact that the FBI International Terrorism Section had more than a hundred fewer special agents working on international terrorism on September 11 than it did in August 1998. The Counter-Terrorism Center had only three analysts working full time on al Qaeda during 1998–2000, and only five on September 11.

The Justice Department's lack of concern for terrorist threats—like that of the White House itself—had consequences down the chain of command. One month after Ashcroft's testimony, in June 2001, veteran FBI agent Robert Wright authored an angry memo charging:

> Knowing what I know, I can confidently say that until the investigative responsibilities for terrorism are transferred from the FBI, I will not feel safe. . . . The FBI has proven for the past decade it

cannot identify and prevent acts of terrorism against the United States and its citizens at home and abroad. Even worse, there is virtually no effort on the part of the FBI's International Terrorism Unit to neutralize known and suspected international terrorists living in the United States.

Wright would also claim that the "FBI was merely gathering intelligence so they would know who to arrest when a terrorist attack occurred" rather than actually trying to prevent the attacks themselves. (It should be noted that Wright asked to speak entirely freely about what he knew to be taking place, but was denied permission by his superiors. He did not go the whistle-blower route, however, and so only a portion of what he said has so far been revealed.) Later in the month, CIA director Tenet, like Clarke a Clinton holdover, authored an intelligence summary for Condoleezza Rice in which he warned, "It is highly likely that a significant al Qaeda attack is in the near future, within several weeks." That message, like so many others, went unheeded.

Meanwhile, in Phoenix, Kenneth Williams, an FBI counterterrorism agent, had discovered large numbers of terrorist suspects signing up for aviation courses and asking about airport security. He immediately informed his supervisor, Bill Kurtz, a man known to be obsessed with al Qaeda. Together, on July 10, 2001, the two agents sent off a high-priority memo to headquarters raising the explicit possibility that Osama bin Laden might be trying to infiltrate America's civil aviation system, and proposed that the FBI monitor "civil aviation colleges/universities around the country." But the memo never made it anywhere in the FBI or Justice Department bureaucracy where it might have made a difference. Nor did it travel across the Potomac to the CIA."

Much the same dynamic could be found at work across the country in Minneapolis, where FBI agents had learned in August 2001 that suspected "twentieth hijacker Zacarias Moussaoui" was then enrolled in flying lessons. A known terrorist threat, Moussaoui was arrested and held, but the bureau did not even follow up a French wiretap connecting Moussaoui to bin Laden. The Minneapolis agents asked headquarters for a warrant to examine Moussaoui's computer and personal effects and to wiretap his phone. Not only did the FBI have the Phoenix memo at the time, it also had another from its chief pilot in Oklahoma warning that "large numbers of Middle Eastern males" were receiving flight training "all over the state." And yet according to a now-famous memo by FBI whistleblower Colleen Rowley, "FBIHQ personnel whose job it was to assist and coordinate with field division agents on terrorism . . . continued to, almost inexplicably, throw up roadblocks and undermine Minneapolis' by-now desperate efforts" to obtain a search warrant. With considerable bravery and dedication—particularly in light of the way bureaucracies are known to punish those who refuse to follow orders—the agents in question refused to give up. Defying protocol they slipped the information to their competitor, the CIA's counterterrorist unit. This earned them a major reprimand from their superiors, who continued to refuse them a warrant, right up until September 11.

Such incidents were, unfortunately, no anomaly. Upon learning of an al Qaeda gathering in Malaysia, the Special Branch, that nation's security service, was prevailed upon to monitor the meeting and take photos of its participants. Shortly after the Kuala Lumpur meeting, the CIA tracked two of the terrorists, Nawaf Alhazmi and Khalid Almihdhar, as they flew to Los Angeles, but didn't mention it to the INS or to the FBI. Both of these known terrorists were allowed to remain in the country and felt so secure in their status that neither one even bothered with precautions such as creating false names, passports, driver's licenses, and the like. Instead they lived, worked, and plotted under their own names and even listed themselves in the San Diego telephone directory.

Those numbers became inoperative, however, when the two men decided to use their easily obtainable flight training to crash a jumbo jet into the Pentagon on September 11, 2001. This particular story, while dramatic, is perhaps not so unusual. Apparently the hijackers had been in contact with at least fourteen individuals who had been the subjects of previous FBI counterterrorism investigations—of which a minimum of four were under active FBI investigation. Even with this level of activity Richard Clarke could later testify that when he visited several FBI field offices and asked agents what they were doing about al Qaeda, "I got sort of blank looks of 'What is al Qaeda?'"

Despite all of these now undeniable signals, FBI director Mueller contended, six days after the attack, "There were no warning signs that I'm aware of that would indicate this type of operation in the country." Not for nothing did this comment receive the designation "Whopper of the Week" from *Slate*. (As of this writing, in November 2003, George Tenet has still not provided the names of the agents responsible for this lapse. In fact, not a single U.S. official anywhere in the government has been disciplined for laxity on the job related to the catastrophic breakdown of security that allowed these incredible attacks to take place. Indeed, in a nearly inexplicable lack of accountability at the top, many key officials assigned to the CIA's bin Laden watch on that day have since been promoted.)

The preceding information raises the obvious, but painful, question: Could the suicide attacks of September 11 have been prevented? Was the Bush administration's lackadaisical approach to fighting terrorism ultimately at fault for the nation's naked vulnerability to nineteen men armed with box cutters and penknives? George W. Bush would later claim to have "seen no evidence today that said this country could have prevented the attacks." Vice President Cheney termed all suggestions to the contrary to be "incendiary," and "thoroughly irresponsible and totally unworthy of national leaders in a time of war." Even the usually apolitical Laura Bush got into the act by calling the questions about what the administration might have done as an attempt to "prey upon the emotions of people." But Senator (and Democratic presidential candidate) Bob Graham, former chairman of the Senate intelligence panel and cochairman of the congressional investigation, had a different answer. "The attacks of September 11 could have been prevented if the right combination of skill, cooperation, creativity and some good luck had been brought to task." As with so much about September 11, we will never know the full truth.

But certainly we can all agree that if the Bush administration had truly taken terrorism as seriously as Bush, Cheney, and nearly all its top officials claimed, and undertaken serious efforts in all of the areas described above, then Osama bin Laden and his murderous underlings would certainly have had more difficulty in carrying out their plans. Some of their sources of funds would have dried up; their agents would have been denied entry into the United States, wiretapped here and abroad, arrested or possibly even killed; their training centers would have been shut down; and the flight schools they used to learn their deadly craft would have been denied them. This is not the voice of 20/20 hindsight speaking; this is the information that was readily available to Bush and Company well before September 11. Vice President Cheney acknowledges, "There is no question but that there were failures." Unfortunately, despite the president's announcement that "we must uncover every detail and learn every lesson of September the eleventh," the administration has thwarted almost every official attempt to get to the bottom of what took place on that fateful day, and how it might have been avoided.

Ask Me No More Questions

According to General Wesley Clark, who headed U.S.-NATO operations in the war in Kosovo, it is "a basic principle of military operations [to] conduct an after-action review. When the action's over you bring people together. The commander, the subordinates, the staff members. You ask yourself what happened, why, and how do we fix it the next time?" And yet, Clark notes, "this has never been done about the essential failure at 9/11." President Franklin D. Roosevelt signed an executive order creating a commission to "ascertain and report the facts relating to the attack made by Japanese armed forces upon the Territory of Hawaii on December 7, 1941 . . . and to provide bases for sound decisions whether any derelictions of duty or errors of judgment on the part of United States Army or Navy personnel contributed to such successes as were achieved by the enemy on the occasion mentioned." This turned out to be just the first of *eight* government-led investigations into Pearl Harbor.

Setting aside the precedent of Pearl Harbor, among many others, where immediate and quite thorough investigations of intelligence failures were conducted during wartime, administration officials and their allies tried to argue that asking such questions about September 11 was too dangerous. "We don't need to hand the terrorists an after-action report," insisted Tom DeLay, the Republican House majority leader. Senate majority leader Tom Daschle reported that the vice president "requested on several occasions that we not have an investigation into this issue." The reason given by Cheney: the United States should not be diverted from the war against terrorism by a look backward. Cheney's rationale was given public voice by White House spokesman Ari Fleischer when he said in May 2003, "One hundred percent attention needed to be on fighting the war" at the time.

President Bush took the same position, insisting, "I have great confidence in our FBI and CIA," and saw no need for any investigation of their failures. Bush was forced to reverse himself, but not before Cheney intervened to prevent a painstaking compromise hammered out in Congress. Finally, the White House gave in to public outcry, particularly from the families of the dead, only to come up with the gruesomely comical notion of appointing one of the least credible figures in modern American history—Henry Kissinger—to oversee the investigation and with the guarantee that it could appoint six of the commission's ten members. As Maureen Dowd quipped in the *New York Times,* "Who better to investigate an unwarranted attack on America than the man who used to instigate America's unwarranted attacks? Who better to ferret out government duplicity and manipulation than the man who engineered secret wars, secret bombings, secret wiretaps and secret coups?"

Kissinger eventually decided to resign from the National Commission on Terrorist Attacks Upon the United States rather than reveal the names of his consulting clients, but the White House's next gambit proved no less inhibiting, when it budgeted precisely $3 million for the commission's investigation. (By comparison, a 1996 federal commission to study legalized gambling was given two years and $5 million, and the 2003 inquiry into the shuttle disaster's loss of seven lives is estimated to cost some $40 million. The inquiry into the Whitewater controversy, where no lives were lost, and only $30,000 was invested by the wife of a governor, ended up costing more than $70 million and resulted in not a single significant indictment.) When the September 11 commission requested a raise to $11 million, the Bush administration refused the funds. At that point, a Republican commission member complained that the White House was making it "look like they have something to hide." Stephen Push, a leader of the September 11 victims' families, thought it suggested "that they see this as a convenient way for allowing the commission to fail. They've never wanted the commission, and I feel the White House has always been looking for a way to kill it without having their finger on the murder weapon."

Eventually, the budget was raised to a still-inadequate $9 million, but little else changed. "We've been fighting for nearly twenty-one months—fighting the administration, the White House," Monica Gabrielle, whose husband, Richard, died on the 103rd floor of the World Trade Center's Tower 2, told Eric Boehlert of *Salon.* "As soon as we started looking for answers we were blocked, put off and ignored at every stop of the way. We were shocked. The White House is just blocking everything." Another September 11 family advocate—a former Bush supporter who requested anonymity—told Boehlert: "Bush has done everything in his power to squelch this [9/11] commission and prevent it from happening."

The choice to replace Kissinger, former New Jersey governor Thomas Kean, though widely lauded in the media, also turned out to be problematic as well. Kean immediately announced that he planned to remain president of Drew University and devote only one day a week to his work on the commission. And even that day would be compromised by Kean's associations. While chairing the commission, Kean continued to serve on the board of directors and executive committee at Amerada Hess, an oil company with extensive investments in Central Asia. As *Fortune* magazine observed, "Kean appears to have a bizarre link to the very terror network he's investigating—al Qaeda." In 1998, Amerada Hess formed an alliance with the Saudi oil company Delta Oil, calling it Delta Hess, which is invested in a number of oil-field and pipeline projects in Central Asia. Delta Oil has been one of the main financial partners in a controversial oil pipeline designed to go through Afghanistan. The company has been financially controlled by Khalid bin Mahfouz, and is connected to Mohammed Hussein al Amoudi. Both are said to be on a secret United Nations list of al Qaeda financers, and bin Mahfouz is Osama bin Laden's brother-in-law. In what *Fortune* terms to be an "interesting coincidence," three weeks before Kean's appointment onto the September 11 commission, Amerada Hess quietly severed its relationship with Delta Oil. George Mitchell resigned from the commission a few days earlier in part because of ties to al Amoudi. However, Kean's links to the company, along with its connections to al Amoudi and bin Mahfouz, were barely mentioned anywhere, outside of *Fortune* and a single Associated Press article.

In addition, Kean named University of Virginia historian Philip Zelikow as the committee's executive director. Formerly a member of George H. W. Bush's National Security Council staff, as well as a member of President George W. Bush's Foreign Intelligence Advisory Board, Zelikow was also coauthor with Condoleezza Rice of an admiring study of their ex-boss's (and the president's father's) handling of the end of the cold war. Without casting any personal aspersions on Professor Zelikow, who is also a first-rate scholar of the Cuban missile crisis, it is hard to imagine that anyone could conduct a thoroughly honest and potentially damning investigation of his friends and former colleagues. In October 2003, a group of families of September 11 victims wrote to the commission cochairs asking that Zelikow recuse himself "from any aspect of national security and executive branch negotiations and investigations" because of his past connections to the National Security Council and to key Bush administration officials. Other apparent conflicts of interest abounded as well. For instance, a Democratic nominee, Jamie Gorelick, was a member of the law firm Wilmer, Cutler & Pickering, which had been retained by Saudi prince Mohammed al Faisal in conjunction with lawsuits against the Saudi royal family by the families of September 11 victims.

Once the commission finally got under way the White House stonewalled its requests for information. Tim Roemer, a former Democratic congressman from Indiana, was initially denied access to the classified congressional report on which, by law, commissioners were to build their investigation, and in October Chairman Kean himself, a mild-mannered moderate Republican, became so frustrated by White House noncooperation that he threatened to subpoena the withheld documents.

Meanwhile Bush and Cheney waged a separate battle to prevent the publication of the congressional investigation of the September 11 breakdown, leaving House Intelligence Committee chairman Goss, a staunch Republican, to complain that the administration was going so far as to refuse to declassify even material about which intelligence officers had already testified. "Senior intelligence officials said things in public hearings that they don't want us to put in the report," said Goss. "That's not something I can rationally accept without further public explanation." One particular concern of the administration was the fact that the report allegedly named those "senior officials" who had received the alarming al Qaeda briefings and ignored them.

Blame Bill

One of the least attractive impulses of the Bush team, given the enormous number of mistakes they were later demonstrated to have made, was its attempt to blame the nation's vulnerability to attack on its predecessors. Vice President Cheney would later cite what he termed to be an insufficient response to events like the bombings of the World Trade Center, Khobar Towers, the U.S. embassies in Kenya and Tanzania, and the USS *Cole*, and observed that the Clinton administration's failure to deal with them aggressively had only invited further challenge. "Weakness, vacillation, and unwillingness of the United States to stand with our friends—that is provocative. It's encouraged people like Osama bin Laden . . . to launch repeated strikes against the United States, our people overseas and here at home, with the view that he could, in fact, do so with impunity."

Initially, the "Blame Clinton" assignment was delegated to Cheney's chief of staff, I. Lewis "Scooter" Libby. With a particular lack of grace, given his own administration's lack of response to the threat, he asserted: "Let's stack it up," and then proceeded to list the United States's retreat from Somalia, the bombing of the World Trade Center, the al Qaeda plot in the Philippines, the attempted Iraqi assassination of former president George H. W. Bush, the 1995 Riyadh bombing, the Khobar Towers bombing, the bombing of U.S. embassies in Africa, the bombing of the USS *Cole*, and the foiled millennium attack. "Did we respond in a way which discouraged people from supporting terrorist activities?" Libby asked. No, he charged, the Clinton administration's alleged weakness had encouraged "someone like Osama bin Laden to rise up and say credibly, 'The Americans don't have the stomach to defend themselves. . . . They are morally weak.'"

This tactic is doubly, perhaps triply, ironic because as Lawrence Korb, former assistant secretary of defense under Ronald Reagan, remarks, it was the Clinton administration that built up the military that the Bush team would later deploy so promiscuously. "Most of the credit for the successful military operation [in Iraq] should go to the Clinton administration," Korb noted. "The first Bush defense budget went into effect on October 1, 2002, and none of the funds in that budget have yet had an impact on the quality of the men and women in the armed services, their readiness for combat, or the weapons they used to obliterate the Iraqi forces."

9/11: Where Was George?

"On the eve of the fateful events of September 11," Fred Greenstein notes, "there was a widespread view in the political community that Bush was out of his depth in the presidency." Not once before the attack had America's president addressed the nation from the Oval Office, nor had Bush convened a single full-fledged, prime-time press conference. The president did not seem comfortable addressing either the media or the nation even on those occasions that seemed to demand it. (For instance, he did not even join in the welcoming ceremony for the crew of the spy plane when it returned from China, perhaps out of fear of being associated with the unacknowledged apology that preceded it.) Washington's preeminent establishment spokesperson, *Washington Post* pundit David Broder, complained that Bush had left the American people without a "clear definition" of their new leader. In a Gallup survey fielded the week before September 11, Bush's approval level reached the lowest of his presidency, just 51 percent, a full seventeen percentage points lower than Bill Clinton's on the day he was impeached. Things were getting so bad that many were already scrambling to jump off what they deemed to be a sinking ship. In his memoir, *The Right Man*, former Bush speechwriter David Frum admitted that he was planning to leave the White House prior to September 11, before the Bush presidency "unraveled."

September 11 changed all that, of course, and it is often described as the defining moment in the Bush presidency. It is surprising, therefore, that

Bush's behavior that day—along with that of his administration—has almost never been examined in any detail. This is all the more curious when one considers the fact that September 11 is among the most exhaustively chronicled days in human history and Bush, among the most heavily covered individuals. And yet many mysteries remain about how and why the president and his advisors responded in the way they did on that day and why they cannot come up with a consistent and credible account of their actions. No less odd is the media's almost complete willingness to let all the inconsistencies pass unexamined.

As Allan Wood and Paul Thompson describe on their extremely informative (and well-documented) Web site "An Interesting Day," many questions persist about George W. Bush's behavior on September 11, 2001. That morning he was paying a long-planned visit to the Emma E. Booker Elementary School in Sarasota, Florida. Reports differ about the precise moment when the president was informed of the crashes and whether it was explained to him that they were, in fact, attacks. Back in Washington, CIA chief George Tenet was notified within minutes of the first crash and is reported to have remarked to his breakfast partner, Senator David Boren, "You know, this has bin Laden's fingerprints all over it." The president's aides maintain that he was not told about the attack for more than fifteen minutes, long after viewers had seen it over and over on CNN, and even though he had interrupted his schedule to place a call to Condoleezza Rice upon leaving his limousine, which was after the first crash took place. In fact, many accounts have been offered of that morning's events by the White House, and they are almost all inconsistent with one another. On December 4, 2001, Bush himself was asked: "How did you feel when you heard about the terrorist attack?" He replied, "I was sitting outside the classroom waiting to go in, and I saw an airplane hit the tower—the TV was obviously on. And I used to fly, myself, and I said, well, there's one terrible pilot. I said, it must have been a horrible accident. But I was whisked off there, I didn't have much time to think about it." Bush repeated the same story on January 5, 2002, stating, "First of all, when we walked into the classroom, I had seen this plane fly into the first building. There was a TV set on. And you know, I thought it was pilot error and I was amazed that anybody could make such a terrible mistake."

In the first place, Bush is describing something that could not possibly have happened. Nobody watching television saw the first plane crash into the tower until the following day when a videotape of it turned up. Moreover, the president's memory not only contradicts every single media report of that morning, it also contradicts what he said on the very day of the attack. In his speech to the nation delivered that evening, Bush said, "Immediately following the first attack, I implemented our government's emergency response plans." This confusing statement has never been satisfactorily explained; no one other than Bush has ever spoken of these "emergency plans," and the very idea of their implementation is contradicted by Bush's stated belief that at the time, he believed the crash to have been a case of pilot error.

Other versions abound, circulated by both Bush himself and by top members of his staff. Bush told an interviewer that chief of staff Andrew Card had been the first person to let him know of the crash, explaining, "'Here's what you're going to be doing; you're going to meet so-and-so, such-and-such.' Then Andy Card said, 'By the way, an aircraft flew into the World Trade Center.'" Ari Fleischer repeated this same story, claiming that Card had told Bush about the crash "as the President finished shaking hands in a hallway of school officials." But other sources, including Bob Woodward's allegedly authoritative account, have Karl Rove telling Bush the news.

What we can say for certain is that whatever he knew, Bush continued to read to the children and pose for the cameras long after the Federal Aviation Administration (FAA), the North American Aerospace Defense Command (NORAD), the National Military Command Center (NMCC), the Pentagon, the White House, the Secret Service, and Canada's Strategic Command were all aware that three commercial jetliners had been hijacked. The president's entourage stayed at the school until 9:35 a.m., a full fifty minutes after CNN first broadcast the news of the initial crash.

White House staff members would claim that Bush remained with the children as long as he did so as not to "upset" or "alarm" them. This is a bewildering rationale, for if the country was under attack, the president, of all people, might be forgiven for upsetting a few schoolkids. If the president's life was in danger, then so was the life of every child in that room. At the time, fighter jets had been dispatched to defend New York City.

A panic motif runs through the president's actions for the remainder of the day. When the presidential motorcade did finally head for the airport, Bush is alleged to have spoken on the phone to Cheney and ordered all flights nationwide to be grounded. Transportation Secretary Norman Mineta has also tried to take credit for the order, but according to *Slate*, this, too, is false, though "FAA officials had begged [the reporter] to maintain the fiction." In fact, according to *USA Today*, it was FAA administrator Ben Sliney who issued this order. As he boarded *Air Force One*, nearly ninety minutes into the crisis, Bush had done nothing at all to take charge of the situation.

Four planes had been hijacked. The Twin Towers and the Pentagon were on fire. And George W. Bush was, in his own words, "trying to get out of harm's way." Amazingly, *Air Force One* took off without any military protection and remained unprotected in the sky for more than an hour, though Florida had many nearby air force bases with planes that are supposed to be on twenty-four-hour alert. If the president and his entourage were primarily concerned about Bush's own safety and ability to conduct operations, they could hardly have gone about a less effective way of ensuring it: remaining in a vulnerable school and then heading for the very plane that was said to be a target of the attack, unprotected.

Air Force One took off at approximately 9:55 a.m. for Barksdale Air Force Base near Shreveport, Louisiana, where Bush touched down to make a short set of remarks to the nation, which were considered halting and ineffective by most commentators, given the gravity of the situation. Bush then flew off to an underground bunker beneath the U.S. Strategic Command Center in Offutt, Nebraska. He finally landed at Andrews Air Force Base at 6:34 p.m., escorted by two F-15 fighters and one F-16. Bush gave his second televised speech of the day at 8:30, from the White House Oval Office; this one was widely seen to have repaired some of the damage of the earlier, uncertain, performance.

A minor controversy quickly arose as to why the president felt it necessary to fly around the country instead of returning home to reassure a frightened and shaken nation. "Stung," according to a *New York Times* report, "by suggestions that President Bush had hurt himself politically by delaying his return to Washington on Tuesday," White House officials tried to explain Bush's absence by insisting they were reacting to "hard evidence that he was a target of the terrorists who hijacked airliners and slammed them into the World Trade Center and the Pentagon." Karl Rove told reporters, "We are talking about specific and credible intelligence, not vague suspicions." Ari Fleischer added at a September 13 briefing that a threat "using code words" had been phoned in against *Air Force One*. He quoted the alleged caller, who was even said to know the proper code words, warning, "*Air Force One* is a target." But again, the official account is logically inconsistent. If the White House received a "credible" threat to *Air Force One,* why would the president and his men return to the target and take off unprotected? When questioned, Ari Fleischer originally tried to dodge and deny on his boss's behalf. Asked about his claim of "credible evidence" four days after the event, Fleischer replied, "We exhausted that topic about two days ago," and continued to stick to the story. Eventually, White House officials later explained that, despite the unambiguous claims of Rove and Fleischer, all that had really taken place was that White House telephone operators had "apparently misunderstood comments made by their security detail." There was, in fact, no threat to *Air Force One.*

Exactly how many of the contradictions in the many official stories offered by the White House—and generally accepted without question by the media—can be chalked up to understandable confusion, how many to panic or incompetence, and how many to a deliberate attempt to rewrite the historical record in an effort to present Bush as a powerful and calm force for a nation desperately in need of one is an issue not ever likely to be sorted out properly.

Whatever was cover-up and whatever genuine confusion, contrast Bush's behavior with that of New York mayor Rudy Giuliani, who displayed a combination of poise and courage on that fateful morning. The conservative television pundit Tucker Carlson made the damning comparison explicit:

> Rudy Giuliani was in midtown when the first passenger plane slammed into the World Trade Center. He made it to Barclay Street just in time to see the second plane hit. It was clear by this point that a coordinated terrorist attack was under way, but Giuliani didn't flee to a fortified bunker. He didn't argue that it was his duty to remain safe so he could continue to lead. He understood that the first requirement of leadership is being there, that nothing sends a stronger message to the troops than a general at the front. He understood that the symbolism is more important than any single decision a leader can make, more important even than the life of the leader.

A Brief Rebound

Bush soon recovered his political footing. Indeed, the media, and no doubt most Americans, were rooting hard for their president to rise to this gut-wrenching challenge. And Bush did rise quite admirably, at least after his initial stumbles. He gave a fine speech to the nation in which he outlined the nature of the al Qaeda network, promised unflinching determination to defeat it, and paused for a plea for tolerance for Islam and peaceful Muslims inside and outside the United States. On September 14 Bush delivered a moving tribute to the victims of the terrorist attacks at a memorial service at Washington's National Cathedral. He then flew to New York City, where he inspected the wreckage of the World Trade Center, using a bullhorn to address the rescue workers. When several of them shouted that they could not hear him, Bush replied, "I can hear you. The rest of the world hears you, and the people who knocked these buildings down will hear all of us soon!"

On September 20 the president made a forceful presentation to Congress, giving the Taliban regime in Afghanistan an ultimatum to turn the al Qaeda leadership over to the United States and close down its terrorist camps. Three weeks later, he gave an equally effective address to the United Nations. Most impressive to many was his October 11 prime-time news conference in the East Room of the White House. Here, for the first time, Americans saw their president capably answering the difficult questions put to him about the new war on terror with a degree of composure and competence that no doubt reassured millions of worried people. In part as a reflection of Americans' need to feel that their government was in good hands, and in part as a result of Bush's own personal and political growth in a time of profound crisis, his approval numbers reached 90 percent, the best showing of any president since presidential polling began.

No Nuance Need Apply

For all the horror, death, and destruction it caused, September 11 offered the Bush administration a rare opportunity to begin its foreign policy anew. Overnight Osama bin Laden and his fanatical followers had rewritten the rules of Atlantic engagement. Kyoto, the International Criminal Court, and Star Wars were forgotten. On September 12, the UN Security Council passed a resolution condemning those responsible for the attacks, as well as holding accountable "those responsible for aiding, supporting or harboring the perpetrators, organizers and sponsors of these acts," and authorizing "all necessary steps" to respond to the attacks. For the first time in that body's history, those present rose to stand together as they cast their votes—the better to demonstrate their unity with their host nation.

Nowhere were feelings stronger than in those European countries whose leaders had been at odds with the administration over the arrogance and unilateralism of its foreign policy. Formerly contentious Europe overflowed with spontaneous symbols of what German chancellor Gerhard Schröder called "unconditional solidarity." *Le Monde* ran a banner headline declaring *Nous Sommes Tous Americains* ("We Are All Americans"). Millions held vigils, rallies, and prayer services. Fantastic amounts of money were collected. The Stars and Stripes hung everywhere. For the first time in its history, the Atlantic Alliance invoked its solemn obligation to come to the defense of a fellow member, articulating what Michael Ignatieff termed "this sense of a common trans-Atlantic identity under attack."

Instead of accepting the world's—and most particularly its allies'—outstretched hands, Bush replied in deed if not in word: "Thanks, but no thanks." Europeans hoped that the now unquestionable need to fight a global terrorist menace "would turn the Bush administration toward greater multilateralism," as the editors of *The Economist* put it. It appears, however, to have had just the opposite effect. When U.S. deputy secretary of defense Paul Wolfowitz flew to Brussels to address the NATO defense ministers, he described the "wide-ranging, long-term approach the U.S. is adopting to combat terrorism" without even mentioning the extraordinary NATO offer. "He said very clearly that we don't need you," a European official at NATO later explained. The French strategist Jacques Rupnik characterizes the American attitude this way: "We decide what is good and we decide what is evil. If Europe wants to follow us, fine; if not, too bad for them."

The "correct" position as enunciated by Bush turned out to be one of never-ending war, based on the U.S. determination of who is a friend and who is a "terrorist." Lest this sound like hyperbole, consider the following statement: "Our war with terror begins with al Qaeda, but it does not end . . . until every terrorist group of global reach has been found, stopped and defeated." And what if America ends up alienating the entire world in the process? "At some point, we may be the only ones left," Bush told his closest advisors, according to an administration member who leaked the story to Bob Woodward. "That's OK with me. We are America."

Bush's simplistic nostrums about good and evil did not travel well. While many in Europe and elsewhere viewed the attacks on the towers to be unconscionable, they nevertheless understood the context in which they arose. Millions of Arabs were frustrated by their own lack of personal and political freedom, denied to them by autocratic and corrupt governments that maintained their despotic rule in part through their alliances with the United States. Israel was a particular source of grievance. Al-Jazeera broadcast daily the brutalities that the Likud government, armed with American weapons, visited upon the stateless Palestinians while settlers continued to occupy expropriated lands with the appearance of American forbearance, if not exactly its blessing. That these broadcasts ignored the Israeli argument that its violence was a response to Palestinian terrorism served only to multiply their inflammatory effect. In Saudi Arabia, home to the majority of the September 11 hijackers, U.S. troops protected a corrupt, feudal monarchy that lived lavishly on oil exports and controlled access to the holy Islamic cities of Mecca and Medina. Osama bin Laden drew sustenance from the wells of hatred these policies inspired.

Bush appeared to understand none of this. As noted earlier, he explained that "my job isn't to nuance, my job is to say what I think. I think moral clarity is important." Asked about the motivations of those across the Islamic world who "hated us," Bush blamed only America's virtues. "They hate our freedoms: our freedom of religion, our freedom of speech, our freedom to vote and assemble and disagree with each other." Once again, black and white were the only colors this president could see.

Their Terrorists . . . and Ours

No doubt that those who claim Bush grew in office following the attacks could make their case. The questions remains, however, "In what direction?" Considerable evidence demonstrates Bush simply grew into a more stubborn, determined, and single-minded version of his earlier self; "growing," if anything, less flexible, more unilateralist, and more deeply committed to his own belief in his righteousness. "Ambling through" his personal and professional life until September 11, to borrow the title of a best-selling examination of his character and political strategy, the attack on America seemed to imbue the president with eschatological purpose. "I'm here for a reason," Bush told Karl Rove shortly after the attacks, "and this is going to be how we're going to be judged." A close friend of Bush's told one reporter, "I think, in his frame, this is what God has asked him to do." And a "senior administration official," speaking to Bob Woodward, explained, Bush "really believes he was placed here to do this as part of a divine plan."

Bush didn't make the job of U.S. diplomats any easier by framing what he considered to be his holy war in the language of John Wayne movies. On September 15, 2001, he warned bin Laden: "If he thinks he can hide and run from the United States and our allies, he will be sorely mistaken." Two days later, he added, "I want justice. And there's an old poster out West, I recall, that says, 'Wanted: Dead or Alive.'" Immediately tabloid newspapers around the nation created exactly this poster, with bin Laden's menacing visage beneath Bush's boast.

The president apparently introduced a new "Bush Doctrine" for fighting terrorism, much as Ronald Reagan embarked on the "Star Wars" program in 1983, without having mentioned it in advance to his top foreign policy advisors, who might have pointed out some of its obvious pitfalls to the national security novice. When Bush pronounced, "We will make no distinction between the terrorists who committed these acts and those who harbor them," he did so apparently without seeking the counsel of Dick Cheney, Colin Powell, or Donald Rumsfeld.

On the very morning after September 11, however, U.S. deputy secretary of state Richard Armitage met with the head of Pakistan's Inter-services Intelligence (ISI), Lt. Gen. Mahmood Ahmed, who was visiting Washington to discuss Pakistani support for military operations in Afghanistan. The price, it later turned out, was an American agreement to turn a blind eye toward Pakistani support for Muslim terrorists fighting India in Kashmir. U.S. ambassador Wendy Chamberlain publicly stated, "We are keeping Kashmir out of this" to reassure Pakistan's military dictator, General Pervez Musharraf, that his military's strategic interests would not be compromised in return for his support for a quick U.S. victory in Afghanistan. According to the analysis of Husain Haqqani, a former Pakistani diplomat who served under prime ministers Nawaz Sharif and Benazir Bhutto, the dictator "managed to keep his intelligence and terrorism machine more or less intact, with U.S. support, in return for his cooperation in pulling down the Taliban regime." Thus, the cost of fighting terrorism in one place would mean supporting terrorism in another.

Harvard's venerable political scientist Stanley Hoffmann explained why the Bush tactic here was so clearly self-defeating. "Conceptually," Hoffmann wrote, "global terrorism is the sum of many individual terrorist acts (most of them local) with very different inspirations, dynamics and scopes. One size does not fit all. Indeed, some of our allies against al-Qaeda had been terrorists or had encouraged terrorists in the past—or even the present. Pakistan and Saudi Arabia had supported terrorism. Germany, Spain and the United States had all found reasons to tolerate them on their own soil, for reasons of political convenience." Hoffmann went on to point out yet another problem with the notion of an antiterrorism "war."

> The strategy posed yet another set of problems with nations that used the American war and its rhetoric as a pretext for getting dangerously tougher with their own enemies. These enemies were charged (often correctly) with terrorism, but their circumstances were radically different from those under which Osama bin Laden deployed his rabid theological and anti-Western global network. In the case of Kashmir, the cynical exploitation of the antiterrorist cause put the United States in an embarrassing position, especially given Pakistani President Gen. Pervez Musharraf's indispensable role in the assault on Afghanistan.

The hard-line neoconservatives in the Pentagon were more than eager to support Bush's post–September 11 plans. Paul Wolfowitz, number two man at the Pentagon, and the emerging guiding intellectual force behind America's aggressive new foreign policy, pledged that the United States would focus on "removing the sanctuaries, removing the support systems, ending states who sponsor terrorism." The link between terrorist organizations and state sponsors soon became the "principal strategic thought underlying our strategy in the war on terrorism," according to Douglas Feith, the Pentagon's number three, and a close ally of Wolfowitz and the right's foreign-policy Rasputin, Richard Perle. Congress went along as well, without much debate or even discussion. Ever since Pearl Harbor, the opposition party has rallied around the president in times of perceived crises in national security and allowed him to take pretty much whatever action he saw fit. In a measure that enjoyed all the vagueness and potential for abuse that the Gulf of Tonkin resolution had invited twenty-seven years earlier, Congress authorized the president "to use all necessary and appropriate force against those nations, organizations, or persons he determines planned, authorized, committed, or aided the terrorist attacks that occurred on September 11, 2001, or harbored such organizations or persons." In fact, Bush later admitted that Iraq had no such involvement, but somehow that information was largely ignored when it mattered.

War: What Is It Good For?

The Bush Doctrine, together with its accompanying policy of virtually endless war, would prove a historic mistake. While no serious American would argue that September 11 did not require a strong military response both to set an example to potential future terrorists and to punish those responsible for the cold-blooded murder of so many innocent people, the Bush administration erred profoundly in its choice of weapons. As the great

Oxford and Yale military historian Sir Michael Howard explained, the notion of a "war" on terrorism would prove an inappropriate and ultimately self-defeating concept.

> The British in their time have fought many such "wars," in Palestine, in Ireland, in Cyprus and in Malaya, to mention only a few. But we never called them "wars": we called them "emergencies." This meant that the police and intelligence services were provided with exceptional powers, and were reinforced where necessary by the armed forces, but all continued to operate within a peacetime framework of civil authority. If force had to be used, it was at a minimal level and so far as possible did not interrupt the normal tenor of civil life. The object was to isolate the terrorists from the rest of the community, and to cut them off from external sources of supply. They were not dignified with the status of belligerents: they were criminals, to be regarded as such by the general public and treated as such by the authorities.

Terrorism is merely a tactic, not a political, much less a religious, movement. (One might as well have followed up Pearl Harbor with a war on "sneak-attack-ism.") Fighting it requires, Howard notes, "secrecy, intelligence, political sagacity, quiet ruthlessness, covert actions that remain covert, above all infinite patience." But in wartime, "all these are forgotten or overridden in a media-stoked frenzy for immediate results, and nagging complaints if they do not get them." Moreover, he adds, "As we all know, one man's terrorist is another man's freedom fighter. Terrorists can be successfully destroyed only if public opinion, both at home and abroad, supports the authorities in regarding them as criminals rather than heroes."

It is exactly this trap into which Bush and the United States fell, however, by personalizing the fight with bin Laden and declaring "war" on a gang of criminals. Bin Laden became a hero to who knows how many more millions of Muslims as a result of the stature bestowed upon him by the leader of the most powerful nation in the world—one who, need we add, could not fulfill his empty boasts of capture, "dead or alive." This therefore already represented a kind of victory for America's enemies. Terrorists win, as Howard noted, "if they can provoke the authorities into using overt armed force against them. . . . Either they will escape to fight another day, or they will be defeated and celebrated as martyrs. In the process of fighting them a lot of innocent civilians will certainly be hurt, which will further erode the moral authority of the government."

Howard's warning proved prophetic, though it was predictably ignored by the Bush administration. The result was a presidential sleight of hand virtually every time the name "bin Laden" or "al Qaeda" was raised in his presence. When the U.S. military proved unable to capture bin Laden, or even, indeed, most of his top lieutenants, the president had no response for those who recalled his braggadocio. On March 8, 2002, Bush was still vowing: "We're going to find him." But just five days later, he tried to deflect attention from the subject. "[Bin Laden's] a person who's now been marginalized. . . . I just don't spend that much time on him. . . . I truly am not that concerned about him," Bush told reporters. By the winter of 2002 Bush had apparently forgotten all about bin Laden, and did not even mention him in his 2003 State of the Union address.

Such concerns are among the myriad reasons why war is simply not a terribly effective manner of addressing this problem, the considerable complicated moral calculations that are necessarily involved in the murdering of thousands of innocent civilians aside. While Americans have had little experience fighting a menace of this variety, the Europeans, whom Bush and Company continued to regard with impatience bordering on contempt, have had much. In this regard, the administration was replaying another of the mistakes made by the Kennedy-Johnson "best and the brightest" in Vietnam, who believed that the unhappy French colonial experience in Indochina had nothing to teach Americans. But as the veteran Spanish journalist Miguel Angel Aguilar explains, terrorism is an enemy "against which sheer military might is not going to help you." Spain, he notes, has fought a homegrown terrorist movement for thirty years. "Using the army turned out to be a disaster," Aguilar observes. "We were trying to kill mosquitoes with bombs. Innocents were killed and democracy suffered and we were no safer."

Even those American political scientists who view the problem from the traditional "realist"—as opposed to liberal or leftist—perspective reiterated the same warnings, again, much as their predecessors like Hans Morgenthau and George Kennan had done—unheeded—during Vietnam. *New Yorker* political reporter Nicholas Lemann surveyed a group of them at the outset of the conflict and came away with a remarkably consistent—and painfully prescient—set of analyses. "Military power is not necessary to wiping out al Qaeda," Stephen Walt of the Kennedy School at Harvard notes. "It's a crude instrument, and it almost always has effects you can't anticipate. . . . This is ultimately a battle for the hearts and minds of people around the world. When your village just got leveled by an American mistake, the conclusions you draw will be rather different from what we'd want them to be." Steven van Evera of MIT concurred: "A broad war on terror was a tremendous mistake. It should have been a war on al Qaeda. Don't take your eye off the ball. Subordinate every other policy to it, including the policies toward Russia, the Arab-Israeli conflict, and Iraq. Instead, the administration defined it as a broad war on terror, including groups that have never taken a swing at the United States and never will. It leads to a loss of focus. Al Qaeda escapes through the cracks. And you make enemies of the people you need against al Qaeda."

The actual operation—especially the bombing campaign—did indeed feed anti-American sentiments throughout the Muslim world. In a February 2002 Gallup poll of nine Muslim countries, 77 percent of respondents judged U.S. actions in Afghanistan to be unjustifiable; only 9 percent expressed support. Even in moderate Turkey, opinion ran 3 to 1 against, and in Pakistan the ratio was 20 to 1.

Meanwhile, George W. Bush continued on his chosen path, never giving the slightest indication that he had as much as considered the alternatives. But even if one accepted Bush's strategic choices, his execution of that strategy proved profoundly flawed. Despite the clear willingness of Americans to endure sacrifices in light of September 11, Bush chose to fight the war on the cheap. Ignoring decades of historical precedent, he cut taxes on the rich in wartime rather than raising them. He instituted no military call-ups, rationing measures, or even any actions to ensure a reduction in Americans' use of imported oil—clearly one of the indirect causes of the attack, since it necessitated the enormous U.S. presence in Saudi Arabia that bin Laden named as the inspiration for his murderous jihad. (In 2002, according to EPA figures, the average fuel economy of America's cars and trucks fell to its lowest level in twenty-two years.)

Furthermore, Bush expended zero political capital in Congress even to achieve so meager a goal as offering Pakistan a desperately needed relaxation of U.S. trade barriers on textile imports as a means of shoring up support for its fragile pro-American government in that strategically crucial, but politically precarious (and nuclear-armed), nation. A stand on behalf of open markets for Pakistani textiles would have been fully consistent with Bush's professed philosophy on free trade as well, though given his actions elsewhere in the free-trade arena, it is perhaps a bit much to ask Americans to take those proclamations seriously.

Finally, the Bush administration made a massive miscalculation in its choice of battlefield strategy, which would later ensure the failure of the United States to achieve its most important objective: the destruction of al Qaeda and assurance that Afghanistan could no longer provide a safe haven for Islamic terrorism. As Stephen Walt noted to Lemann, "While steadily laying out a case for something close to a world war, he has stationed fewer than ten thousand American troops in Afghanistan (many fewer than President Clinton stationed in the Balkans) and has deployed them sparingly in combat." The Carnegie Endowment's Thomas Carothers pointed out that the Pentagon's decision to rely on Afghan warlords as proxy fighters against al Qaeda "helped entrench the centrifugal politics that threaten Afghanistan's weak new government. Ironically, the strategy seems also to have been a partial military miscalculation, leading to the escape of a significant number of al Qaeda fighters at Tora Bora."

Though not well publicized, America's war suffered a grievous defeat at Tora Bora when, on November 15, 2001, U.S. generals could not or would not mass sufficient firepower, following a military victory, to prevent the escape of hundreds, and possibly thousands, of Taliban and al Qaeda fighters into Pakistan. The *Washington Post* later reported that "the Bush administration has concluded that Osama bin Laden was present during the battle for Tora Bora," along with al Qaeda's number two, Dr. Ayman al-Zawahiri, and that the failure to capture him was its gravest error in the war. The United States chose to bomb only one of two escape routes and allowed about six hundred of these fighters to leave unharassed by the unguarded route. It remained unguarded, moreover, for weeks afterward, which is when bin Laden is believed to have made his dash with another thousand or fifteen hundred of his followers. Barry Posen, another realist political scientist at MIT, sees Tora Bora as "a disaster, universally acknowledged as such, and never explained. . . . We couldn't have done a worse job. We should have put in every Ranger in range. There's no excuse. . . . So this is disturbing—a war on terror that doesn't focus on the terrorists."

Around the same period, beginning November 14, U.S. forces also allowed a series of rescue flights to arrive inside the Taliban stronghold of Kunduz, in northern Afghanistan, in order to evacuate Pakistanis fighting for the Taliban and return them to Pakistan. According to *The New Yorker*'s Seymour Hersh, Pakistan's president "Musharraf won American support for the airlift by warning that the humiliation of losing hundreds—and perhaps thousands—of Pakistani Army men and intelligence operatives would jeopardize his political survival." Large numbers of fighters also escaped on the backs of more than fifty trucks allowed into the region for the same purpose. As many as five thousand Taliban fighters may have escaped in this exodus, possibly including, Hersh reports, members of bin Laden's family. According to a CIA analyst, "Many of the people they spirited away were in the Taliban leadership," whom Pakistan wanted for future political negotiations. U.S. intelligence was "supposed to have access to them, but it didn't happen."

Meanwhile, Donald Rumsfeld demonstrated all too convincingly that the U.S. government could not be trusted to account for its actions in wartime. Asked by reporters about the airlift, Rumsfeld denied what a number of reporters had apparently witnessed. When asked about it on December 2, the U.S. defense secretary replied, "Oh, you can be certain of that. We have not seen a single—to my knowledge, we have not seen a single airplane or helicopter go into Afghanistan in recent days or weeks and extract people and take them out of Afghanistan to any country, let alone Pakistan." Rumsfeld had been no more forthcoming about Tora Bora, claiming he did not know at the time of the assault, "nor do I know today of any evidence that he [bin Laden] was in Tora Bora at the time or that he left Tora Bora at the time or even where he is today." As the U.S. officials transferred the focus of their attention to Iraq, it became clear that, as former CIA official Vincent Cannistraro told *The New Yorker*'s Jane Mayer, the search for bin Laden had "lost at least half of its original strength." He added, "Arabic speakers are in short supply. You still have some intelligence-collection assets in Afghanistan, but mostly it's just small teams looking for signals. That's because of Iraq." Many of the eight hundred special forces personnel who had been chasing al Qaeda were quietly brought back to the United States, where they rested, then were shipped to Iraq. Former NSC top counterterrorism official Rand Beers notes of the Bush team: "They didn't want to call attention to the fact that Osama was still at large and living along the Pakistan-Afghanistan border, because they wanted it to look like the only front was Iraq," he said. "Otherwise, the question becomes: If Afghanistan is that bad, why start another war?" "The reason these guys were able to get away," added a former Bush official speaking to *Time,* "was because we let up."

Any net assessment of the war in Afghanistan needs also to take into account its humanitarian costs. The most obvious of these is the immediate civilian toll of the bombing campaign, which probably exceeds a thousand fatalities. The war also produced five hundred thousand new Afghan refugees and displaced persons. But Bush demonstrated little patience for the hard work necessary to address either the political or human impact of these harsh consequences. When he signed the Afghanistan Freedom Support Act into law, the president authorized $3.3 billion in economic, political, humanitarian, and security assistance for Afghanistan over a period of four years. The White House spoke of "an Afghanistan that is prosperous, democratic, self-governing, market friendly and respectful of human rights." The United States, the president promised, would "give the Afghan people the means to achieve their own aspirations." But Bush had previously always spoken disdainfully of "nation-building," promising during the presidential campaign, "I think what we need to do is convince people who live in the lands they live in to build the nations. Maybe I'm missing something here. I mean, we're going to have kind of a nation-building corps from America? Absolutely not."

The results were all too predictable. One year after the joint U.S.–Northern Alliance overthrow of the Taliban, Afghanistan was teetering on the brink of chaos once again, the victim of the renewal of the previous U.S. policy of malign neglect. From the standpoint of the prevention of anti-American terrorism, the picture was only marginally more encouraging. The United States defeated the Taliban in significant measure by arming Afghanistan's warlords. Following the victory, it sat by and allowed these same warlords to return to the business of terrorizing the populace. While several of the warlords are still receiving direct U.S. assistance to ensure their cooperation in tracking down al Qaeda and Taliban remnants, the Taliban have already started regrouping in eastern and southern Afghanistan, along the Pakistan border, allegedly with some Pakistani help. In late June 2003 the Pakistan daily *The News* received an audiotape, deemed to be authentic, from the deposed leader of the Taliban, Mullah Omar, exhorting

Muslims to step up their jihad against U.S. forces in Afghanistan. Omar issued the tape from his hiding place in Afghanistan and has named a ten-member leadership council to organize the resistance. Soon, anti-Taliban mullahs began dying in assassinations and explosions at an alarming rate.

While the war was "won," the net result was a failure in many respects. The United States neither eliminated al Qaeda nor disarmed the Taliban. The task of dealing with al Qaeda in its mountain redoubts was assigned to warlords who took money from U.S. special forces to find the terrorists and then accepted cash bribes from some terrorists to let them go. U.S. inattention to the area—an unavoidable consequence of the Bush administration's obsession with Iraq—provided an opportunity for al Qaeda to regroup on its old home turf and begin to plan and execute more terrorist actions against the United States, its allies, and its interests.

The Saudis: Which Side Are They On?

As most readers of this book will already know—but most Americans do not—fifteen of the nineteen hijackers on September 11 were of Saudi origin. So, too, was much of the cash that made the operation—and others like it—possible; so, too, Osama bin Laden himself. One would think that our allies the Saudis—who enjoy the protection of U.S. military forces and whose regime the United States saved with the first Gulf War, which expelled Saddam Hussein from Kuwait in 1991—would provide a particularly rich source of intelligence for fighting and eventually destroying al Qaeda. Alas, one would be wrong.

In a bizarre event that still remains to be explained, members of the bin Laden family, under FBI supervision, were spirited out of the country on a private charter plane when airports reopened three days after the September 11 attacks. These flights, via Texas and Washington, D.C., took place before the nation's national air ban had been lifted. According to a report in the *Tampa Tribune,* on September 13 a Learjet left Tampa, Florida, carrying a Saudi Arabian prince, the son of the Saudi defense minister Prince Sultan, as well as the son of a Saudi army commander. It flew to Lexington, Kentucky, where the Saudis own racehorses, and its passengers were transferred to a private 747 out of the country. Top White House officials personally approved these extraordinary flights, even though these were exactly the kinds of people who might be able to provide the FBI with valuable information about bin Laden and his operations. But once they were back in Saudi Arabia, they were no longer available for questioning. Why the Bush administration allowed this operation to take place remains a mystery, as the administration continues to deny that it ever took place.

The Saudi government proved extremely reluctant to contribute to U.S. antiterrorism efforts. In Early December 2001 administration officials traveled to Saudi Arabia in what was a second attempt to convince the Saudi government to cooperate with the September 11 investigation. The Saudis had already proved unwilling to freeze assets of organizations linked to bin Laden. A former CIA agent, Bob Baer, charged at the time that U.S. intelligence agencies collect virtually no intelligence on the Saudis, nor do they receive any, a situation he blames on what he terms to be implicit orders from the White House that read: "Do not collect information on Saudi Arabia because we're going to risk annoying the royal family." On the very same news program, Saudi millionaire Yassin al Qadi, who is listed by the U.S. government as a terrorist, says, "I'm living my life here in Saudi Arabia without any problem" because he is being protected by the Saudi government. Al Qadi admits to giving bin Laden money for his "humanitarian" work. Meanwhile, the man in charge of investigating the September 11 attacks for the Saudi government, Interior Minister Prince Nayef, blames Zionists and Jews for them. He tells journalists, "Who has benefited from September 11 attacks? I think [the Jews] were the protagonists of such attacks." The Saudis also continue to refuse to grant permission to U.S. agents to talk to any family members of the hijackers.

The U.S. Treasury Department nevertheless continued to insist that the government "is pleased with and appreciates the actions taken by the Saudis" in the war on terror. When in November 2002 the United States tightened its immigration restrictions for eighteen countries, ensuring that all males over age sixteen entering the country from these nations register with the government and be photographed and fingerprinted at their local INS office, it amazingly left Saudi Arabia (and Pakistan) off the list. Both were finally added in December following a public outcry.

When the congressional committee of inquiry released its report in July 2003 virtually all of the material dealing with the Saudis' lack of cooperation with U.S. antiterrorism efforts was redacted, as was what a CIA memo termed "incontrovertible evidence" that individual Saudi officials provided financial assistance to al Qaeda operatives in the United States. New York senator Charles Schumer complained of a "systematic strategy of coddling and cover-up when it comes to the Saudis." And the word *cover-up* would indeed be hard to avoid with respect to the twenty-eight pages of the report dealing with Saudi connections to September 11 that were classified on alleged national security grounds. According to one official who read the redacted pages, they delineate "a coordinated network that reaches right from the hijackers to multiple places in the Saudi government. . . . If the people in the administration trying to link Iraq to al Qaeda had one-one-thousandth of the stuff that the twenty-eight pages has linking a foreign government to al Qaeda, they would have been in good shape." Forty-six Democratic senators asked that the deleted material be released, as did the Republican former chairman of the committee, Richard C. Shelby of Alabama. But the Bush administration refused.

What explains the incredible delicacy with which the Saudis were treated? For one thing, the Saudi billions that have been spread around Washington for decades have bought the country a great deal of sympathy. According to the conservative broadsheet, the *New York Sun,* the Saudis allocated more than $14.6 million to just one firm, Qorvis Communications, during just one six-month period in 2002, a figure termed to be "jaw-dropping" by the executive director for the Center for Public Integrity, Charles Lewis. "That's an astonishing amount of money for not just any foreign agent," Lewis added, "but for any PR firm to receive anywhere under any context." But for the Saudis, who set the previous record of $14.2 million to one firm in just one year decades ago, it is just a drop in the influence-buying bucket.

Their money has been quite strategically invested. Back in 1988 a failed Texas oil man by the name of George W. Bush found himself facing bankruptcy, as he had on three previous occasions, only to have been bailed out by friends. But this time, as his father ascended to the presidency, a group of Saudis bought a portion of his small company, Harken Oil. Later that year, Harken won itself its first overseas contract—in the Persian Gulf—and began, briefly, to prosper. At the time the *Wall Street Journal* wondered whether the arrangement might not "raise the question of . . . an effort to cozy up to a presidential son." Among the company's major investors, ironically, was Salem bin Laden, Osama bin Laden's oldest brother.

The Bush–bin Laden family connections span generations. In January 2000 former president George Bush met with the bin Laden family on behalf of the influence-peddling Carlyle Group; it was his second such meeting, though he denied the fact until a thank-you note turned up to confirm it. The extremely influential Carlyle Group has arranged similar gatherings during the previous fourteen years, beneath the radar of most of the mass media, between former politicians like Bush, James Baker, John Major, former World Bank treasurer Afsaneh Masheyekhi, and interested parties looking for some extremely expensive, high-powered lobbying services. On September 11, 2001, the Group happened to be hosting a conference at a Washington hotel. Among the guests of honor: investor Shafig bin Laden, another brother to Osama.

The Bush family's personal sympathy for the Saudis, however, may be offset in the administration by the extreme antipathy for the kingdom among the neoconservatives who determine most of the U.S. foreign policy. One of the most convincing arguments for the United States's invasion of Iraq was the desire of the neoconservatives to destroy the extraordinary leverage the Saudis enjoyed over U.S. foreign policy by virtue of their oil riches and strategic vulnerability. Bringing Iraq's tremendous oil reserves under the rubric of U.S. imperial rule would serve as a check to Saudi power and, hence, influence. Paul Wolfowitz told an interviewer as much in May 2003, when he admitted that "we settled on the one issue that everyone could agree on, which was weapons of mass destruction as the core reason," but admitted to his interviewer Sam Tanenhaus (in the latter's words) that "almost unnoticed but huge is another reason: removing Saddam will allow the U.S. to take its troops out of Saudi Arabia."

It would indeed be ironic if President Bush had been convinced by his neoconservative advisors to undertake an invasion of Iraq that had, as one of its main aims, the undermining of his friends in Saudi Arabia. That such a scenario is even thinkable is evidence of a lack of fundamental understanding of his own policies that ought to be unimaginable in an American president. But once again, we get ahead of ourselves. For the first two years after September 11, it was all the administration could do to try to secure any cooperation at all from its friends in the Saudi kingdom with regard to the joint threat the two nations faced together from al Qaeda and its Saudi-born leader, Osama bin Laden.

When al Qaeda attacked Saudi Arabia in spring 2003, Bush administration officials were heard to complain that the Saudis had ignored their repeated warnings and refused cooperation with their efforts to blunt the threat. One U.S. official, speaking on condition of anonymity to a *Washington Post* reporter, suggested that the CIA and other U.S. intelligence agencies were thwarted by the Saudis monitoring al Qaeda's operations in the kingdom. The Saudis finally relented and allowed their citizens to be questioned by American intelligence officials for the first time. It was more than a little late, however, and the level of cooperation offered may be too minimal to stave off the kingdom's overthrow, either through its internal weakness or through the machinations of Mr. Perle and his ambitious friends.

The Greatest Breach: Homeland Insecurity

Among the most egregious of the many disconnects between the Bush administration's rhetorical response to September 11 and its actual behavior has been its unwillingness to treat the problem of homeland security with any seriousness beyond its use as political symbolism. Here, as nowhere else, Dr. John DiIulio's diagnosis of what ails the administration has been borne out. A great deal of attention is paid to the politics of homeland security, but too little to the extremely daunting problem of actually addressing the nation's many critical vulnerabilities. What is truly incredible about its disinclination to improve America's security at home is that perhaps no issue anywhere on the political agenda—either foreign or domestic—commands as much political support.

Recall for a moment the degree of panic Americans experienced in the fall of 2001 following the initial attacks. In early October, the first of at least five envelopes containing deadly anthrax was opened at news organizations in New York and Miami. More mailings arrived at Capitol Hill later that month. Simultaneously, the media reported on possible al Qaeda plots to launch a "dirty bomb," or radiological weapon, in Washington, D.C. Twice that October the attorney general and FBI director went on national television to warn about the possibility of additional attacks.

With alarming consistency administration figures terrified Americans with near-certain, but curiously vague, warnings about upcoming attacks. Vice President Cheney explained that such an attack was "almost a certainty" and "not a matter of if, but when." A day later, FBI director Robert Mueller promised, "There will be another terrorist attack. We will not be able to stop it." On Tuesday, Defense Secretary Donald Rumsfeld added, "We do face additional terrorist threats. And the issue is not if but when and where and how." Rumsfeld also added that terrorists will "inevitably" obtain weapons of mass destruction. Director Mueller announced that more suicide bombings were "inevitable." US authorities issued separate warnings that al Qaeda might be planning to target apartment buildings nationwide, banks, rail and transit systems, the Statue of Liberty, and the Brooklyn Bridge. As a *Time* writer noted of the fearmongering: "Though uncorroborated and vague the terror alerts were a political godsend for an administration trying to fend off a bruising bipartisan inquiry into its handling of the terrorist chatter last summer. After the wave of warnings, the Democratic clamor for an investigation into the government's mistakes subsided."

Indeed, the national security historian John Prados found "ample reason to suspect that some of these recent warnings of terrorist threats have been made for political purposes." In the case of alleged "dirty bomber" Abdullah al Muhajir—a former Chicago gang member who was born Jose Padilla—Prados notes that the suspect was apprehended on May 8. "A desire to allay public fears should have led to an immediate announcement of the arrest. Instead the act was kept secret, allowing Donald Rumsfeld to have his cake and eat it too: The administration could raise the specter of al Qaeda nuclear attacks while not revealing that the man who constituted the threat was already in custody. Thus the arrest was only revealed when it offered maximum opportunity for turning attention away from inquiries into what went wrong before 9-11." The actual announcement of his arrest was another scene in what would be a comedy of errors were the consequences not so serious. Attorney General John Ashcroft revealed al Muhajir's arrest through a television hookup while he was on a visit to Moscow. In fact, al Muhajir had no nuclear materials when arrested or any immediate prospect of obtaining any, and the nuclear "plot" was actually just accounts of conversations between the suspect and another U.S. prisoner, Abu Zubaydah."

Yet another indication that the warnings were largely politically motivated was the fact that just as his administration was issuing them, Bush was telling the country not to take them too seriously. At one point, the president flew to Chicago and urged Americans to "get on board" airplanes and enjoy life "the way we want it to be enjoyed." Yet only three days later

Ashcroft warned of "a very serious threat" of additional terrorist activity, particularly if the United States launched a military retaliation.

Then there is the matter of a department of homeland security. After nine months of resisting the concept, preferring only a homeland security "advisor" without cabinet rank, Bush finally relented in June 2002. Working in secret with just a handful of advisors, he successfully co-opted Democratic demands for the creation of a Hart-Rudman–recommended department, designed to consolidate nearly 170,000 workers from twenty-two agencies, including the Coast Guard, the Secret Service, the federal security guards in airports, and the Customs Service. Of course, while it succeeded in shifting the focus from the administration's previous failures to protect the nation, the plan failed to address the primary source of those failures—that is, the dysfunctional cultures in the FBI and CIA, which are both purposely excluded from the new department. The new department's ineffectiveness was compounded, moreover, by its inability to synthesize intelligence data. Even once Homeland Security finally got up and running, in July 2003 its analysts stilled lacked computers capable of receiving any information classified higher than top secret, and the entire department had only three experts on biological terrorism, perhaps the most significant terrorist threat the nation faced. The entire operation, moreover, remains deeply understaffed, in part because potential recruits for top jobs are not interested in working for what is widely perceived to be an ineffective "government backwater," according to administration officials themselves.

But the department's political value was unquestionable. Although the idea received no more than "talking-points-caliber deliberation," according to John DiIulio, the administration was able to use its policy reversal in approving it to further its goals. The original Lieberman proposal, drawn from Hart-Rudman and so energetically resisted by the White House, offered workers in Homeland Security greater job protections than they had in other departments. The Bush version, however, took this and other civil service protections away and gave the president the ability to prevent these workers even from organizing themselves. When the Democrats stood their ground, for once, Bush immediately sought to exploit this dispute to question the patriotism of his opponents during the 2002 election, insisting that "the [then-Democratic-controlled] Senate is more interested in special interests in Washington and not interested in the security of the American people." Republican political ads went so far as to juxtapose photographs of Democratic senator Max Cleland, who lost three limbs in Vietnam, with those of Osama bin Laden and Saddam Hussein. It may have been morally (and logically) offensive, but it worked. Bush broke precedent and campaigned hard for his side, and Republicans were able to counter every political trend of the past hundred years, adding additional seats in virtually every category at the state and national level, despite a weak economy.

As if to demonstrate the administration's lack of seriousness when it came to the difficult business of actually providing Americans with improved security against terrorist attack, Republicans in Washington and Austin immediately seized on the new Homeland Security Department not to defend against any even remotely credible threats, but to track Texas Democratic legislators who left the state in May 2003 to block the railroading of Tom DeLay's unprecedented Republican redistricting plan. According to a report in the Fort Worth *Star-Telegram*, "The agency received a call to locate a specific Piper turboprop aircraft. It was determined that the plane belonged to former House Speaker Pete Laney." Laney is one of the Democrats who was fighting against the redistricting bill and hiding out at the time with his colleagues in Ardmore, Oklahoma, waiting for the session to end. The report continued, "Laney's plane proved to be a key piece of information because, [Republican House Speaker] Craddick said, it's how he determined that the Democrats were in Ardmore." In other words, instead of protecting Americans from terrorists, the department was being used by the Republicans to fight their local battles with the Democrats. In fact, the department failed to find them, but it is difficult to imagine a more offensive abuse of the September 11 tragedy and resultant efforts to address the terrorist threat, to say nothing of the political misuse of the government's police powers. (When Texas governor Rick Perry asked New Mexico to arrest any of the Democratic legislators who might have turned up there, that state's attorney general, Patricia Madrid, said, "I have put out an all-points bulletin for law enforcement to be on the lookout for politicians in favor of health care and against tax cuts for the wealthy.")

Immediately following the attacks, even as their own newsroom had been damaged by the attacks, the conservative ideologues at the *Wall Street Journal* editorial page were encouraging the Bush administration to go on the attack and take political advantage of the tragedy. "The assault on U.S. territory has altered the national dialogue in a way that makes Mr. Bush's agenda far more achievable," they exulted. Among the editors' recommendations for exploiting what it termed Bush's "windfall of political capital" were increased tax cuts, noting that "constraints on fiscal policy have fallen with the Trade Center towers," along with a push for "drilling for oil in Alaska," and greater action from Congress on free-trade treaties and judicial nominations.

George Bush and his aides repeatedly issued statements deploring the very idea of politicizing September 11 or the war on terror—at least they did so publicly. For instance the president claimed "no ambition whatsoever to use [the war on terror] as a political issue," and Ari Fleischer reported, "The President urges no one to politicize this [war] debate. This is a very serious matter, and it needs to be handled seriously by everybody." But behind the scenes and occasionally even in public, the Bush team took the *Journal*'s advice very much to heart. Not long after the tragedy, it was difficult to find any aspect of the administration's wish-list agenda that was not being justified as a means of fighting terrorism. Here are just a few of the most salient examples:

* George W. Bush on expanding his trade authority: "The terrorists attacked the World Trade Center, and we will defeat them by expanding and encouraging world trade."

* George W. Bush on drilling for oil in Alaska: "I urge the Senate to listen to the will of the senators and move a bill," the president told reporters after a cabinet meeting in the White House. "The less dependent we are on foreign sources of crude oil, the more secure we are at home."

* George W. Bush on the need for agriculture subsidies: "It's in our national security interests that we be able to feed ourselves."

* George W. Bush on taxes and spending: "The terrorists want us to stop flying, stop buying, but this great nation will not be intimidated by the evildoers."

* George W. Bush, in July 2003, on why he required $170 million to run, unopposed, for the Republican presidential nomination: "Every day, I'm reminded about what 9/11 means to America. . . . We're threatened."

A *Doonesbury* cartoon caught the mode perfectly: It showed Ari Fleischer making the following announcement to the assembled members of the White House press corps:

> Before we start today I have an announcement to make. I'm sure that all of you appreciate that national security is at the heart of all public policy. Therefore starting today and continuing through next year's election, the answer to any question posed to the White House will be "9/11." Whether the question is on foreign policy, the economy, tax cuts, energy, the environment, whatever, the answer will always be the same—"9/11."

This was clearly the result of an explicit strategy decision on the part of Bush and his advisors. In January 2002 Karl Rove told a Republican National Committee meeting, "We can go to the country on this issue because they trust the Republican Party to do a better job of protecting and strengthening America's military might and thereby protecting America." Rove even scheduled the Republican convention in New York City in September 2004, too late for Bush to be placed on the ballot in some states, but perfectly timed to exploit the anniversary of the attack in the city where it occurred. Bush and his party were not even averse to exploiting the attacks to line their own coffers when they sold photographs of George W. Bush allegedly in command on *Air Force One* on September 11 itself—an image filled with a great deal more irony than they were willing to admit—and sent out a letter to more than a million potential donors in which the president mentioned the war on terrorism alongside his request for campaign funds for an election that he warned "could be close."

Politics Before Protection

If indeed the public were to focus on Bush's actual record—as opposed to rhetoric—on homeland security, then he might not have a hope of re-election for any office at all, much less the presidency. The president has not merely ignored "homeland" protection, he has actively sabotaged it. To even utter these words is shocking, but the reader needn't take our words for it. A Council on Foreign Relations task force chaired by former senators Gary Hart and Warren Rudman warned in a report entitled *America—Still Unprepared, Still in Danger,* a sequel to their prescient 2001 report, that the country remains dangerously ill-equipped to prevent and respond to a catastrophic terrorist attack on U.S. soil. A January 2003 study by the venerable Brookings Institution offered up this extremely harsh (and strangely unpublicized) judgment: "President Bush vetoed several specific (and relatively cost-effective) measures proposed by Congress that would have addressed critical national vulnerabilities. As a result, the country remains more vulnerable than it should be today."

Manifestations of the administration's "politics before protection" attitude toward homeland security began almost immediately after September 11. As Frank Rich commented back in October 2001, when the country was in a panic over the possibility of a mass anthrax attack,

> airport security, which has been enhanced by at best cosmetic tweaks since Sept. 11, is also held hostage by campaign cash: As Salon has reported, ServiceMaster, a supplier of the low-wage employees who ineptly man the gates, is another G.O.P. donor. When anthrax struck, the administration's first impulse was not to secure as much Cipro as speedily as possible to protect Americans, but to protect the right of pharmaceutical companies to profiteer.

The list of those industries given special treatment at the expense of Americans' safety goes on and on. Power plants constitute obvious terrorist targets but are frequently operated by private or semiprivate corporations unwilling to pay to guard them. According to the Brookings study, the Bush administration did nothing—repeat, nothing—to help or encourage "private-sector firms—even ones that handle dangerous materials—toward improving their own security." In 2002 the Pittsburgh *Tribune-Review* discovered a frightening series of security lapses at three separate chemical plants in Houston and Chicago, which, if attacked, could endanger one million people in each case. The New York *Daily News* found one plant in East Rutherford, New Jersey, where an attack could threaten the lives of more than seven million people; it employed virtually no security at all. Spencer Abraham, Bush's energy secretary, worried in a March 2002 letter to then OMB director Mitch Daniels that firms "are storing vast amounts of materials that remain highly volatile and subject to unthinkable consequences if placed in the wrong hands." However, he added, owing to insufficient funding, "the Department now is unable to meet the next round of critical security mission requirements. . . . Failure to support these urgent security requirements," he concluded, "is a risk that would be unwise." Nevertheless, journalist Jonathan Chait reported, Bush agreed to propose a mere 7 percent of what Abraham said would be needed just to get started. And this was hardly an isolated case.

The Bush administration, moreover, worked hand in glove with its Republican allies in the Senate to defeat General Accounting Office–recommended legislation—offered by Democrat Jon Corzine and passed unanimously in the Senate—that would have required the industry to assess its vulnerability to terrorism and, where necessary, take corrective action. The administration's preference, Gary Hart noted, was an industry-backed bill that "provides for virtually no oversight or enforcement of safety requirements. It would not allow the government to demand emergency action by companies that it has reason to believe are terrorist targets, nor would it insist on government review of facility security plans." It would prohibit the federal agency with the most expertise on chemicals, the EPA, from involvement and would not even demand that companies replace dangerous chemicals even when safer technologies are available and affordable. Asked why the government had not moved to regulate security at chemical plants, Homeland Security czar Tom Ridge, on PBS's *NOW with Bill Moyers,* answered that on September 11, "it was not chemical plants that were blown up."

In 2002, in an attempt to demonstrate a brief move in the direction of fiscal responsibility, President Bush chose to impound $5.1 billion that had been included by Congress in an emergency measure; nearly $2.6 billion of these funds had been earmarked for homeland security and $500 million for first responders. Republican lawmakers literally pleaded with the president not to do so. But the arguments were of no avail. "I believe White House statements that Congress only provided $1.3 billion for first responders are factually inaccurate because you have narrowly chosen programs that only you believe will support the first-responder community," wrote House Appropriations Committee chairman C. W. Bill Young, a Florida Republican, in what a *Washington Post* reporter termed "an extraordinary departure from the public unity that has characterized White House relations with congressional Republicans."

In June 2003 the Council on Foreign Relations released the report of a commission chaired by Warren B. Rudman and Richard A. Clarke in which its members warned: "Although the American public is now better prepared in some respects to address aspects of the terrorist threat than it was two years ago, the United States remains dangerously ill-prepared to handle a catastrophic attack on American soil." It recommended that the nation spend $98 billion more than the Bush administration and the Republican Congress planned, or nearly five times current budget levels. Around the same time, yet another study, this one by the Partnership for Public Service, a nonprofit group founded in 2001 that seeks to attract more qualified people to government service, offered up a similar warning of the incompetence of Bush administration planning for the catastrophe its members frequently treat as inevitable. This study found that U.S. officials would likely be almost completely ineffective in the event of a bioterrorism attack on its population owing to poor planning, insufficient funding, and massive shortfalls in the kind of skilled medical and scientific personnel necessary to contain an outbreak of infectious disease. Reports by such well-respected organizations as the Centers for Disease Control, the RAND Corporation, and the National Association of School Resource Officers followed, all reiterating the sense of alarm. Bush ignored them all.

How to explain this? The National Nuclear Security Administration, the agency with perhaps the most important security job description imaginable—it protects our nuclear stockpile and weapons laboratories—was forced by Bush's brief pretense of deficit consciousness to announce a November 2002 hiring freeze despite an already serious shortage of security guards. Meanwhile, with so many Americans understandably losing sleep over the possibility of "loose nukes" falling into terrorist hands, the Bush administration even tried to cut overseas nuclear security funding by 5 percent.

Bush's 2004 budget also chose to squeeze the Coast Guard, which happens to be in charge of that most crucial area of people protection: port security. It also starves first responders—the very heroes of September 11 to whom he dishonestly promised so much. In addition, the Customs Service received not a single penny in new funding in the administration's budget. The Maritime Transportation Security Act of 2002 mandates extensive improvements but provides no money to meet the need, a deliberate omission repeated in Bush's 2003 budget. The 2002 maritime act also mandates vulnerability assessments at the nation's fifty-five largest ports, but at the current pace, slowed by lack of funds, the assessments won't be completed until 2009. As *Congressional Quarterly* reported, "The fact is, according to the administration's own budget documents, the Bush plan for funding first responders amounts to double-entry bookkeeping: changes in the ledger that would result in no net increase in the amount of federal funding flowing to cities, counties, and states." To add insult to injury, as the administration was budgeting more than $4 billion per month on security for Iraq, it was cutting back on air marshals for domestic flights, as it simultaneously issued a memo to all airlines warning of a new al Qaeda plan to hijack jets for additional suicide missions. In other words, the very threat that killed three thousand people and devastated lower Manhattan was being downgraded owing to what one bureaucrat termed "monetary concerns" and "budget realities" while the administration committed itself to an open-ended financial commitment to a voluntary war as well as the largest budget deficit in many decades. (This order was soon rescinded, following the bad publicity it received.)

It was presumably this very lack of seriousness by the Bush administration about the business of protecting the nation that led Rand Beers, a top White House counterterrorism advisor, to resign under protest over Bush administration policy. Beers, who served on the National Security Council under Presidents Ronald Reagan, George H. W. Bush, Bill Clinton, and George W. Bush, complained upon leaving the job he loved that "the difficult, long-term issues both at home and abroad have been avoided, neglected or shortchanged and generally underfunded." He was particularly critical of the Bush administration's enthusiasm for war with Iraq, given the massive challenge that lay before it vis-à-vis al Qaeda. "Why was it such a policy priority?" he asked. The war in Afghanistan, rather than destroying bin Laden's network, according to Beers, merely scattered it. "Terrorists move around the country with ease. We don't even know what's going on. Osama bin Laden could be almost anywhere in Afghanistan," he complained. Inside the United States, officials suffered from what he diagnosed as "policy constipation" in Beers's cogent phrasing. "Fixing an agency management problem doesn't make headlines or produce voter support. So if you're looking at things from a political perspective, it's easier to go to war." Beers's anger at the Bush administration for its fundamental failure in homeland security was so extreme that not only did he resign, he joined the presidential campaign of Senator John F. Kerry. "I can't think of a single example in the last thirty years of a person who had done something so extreme," Paul C. Light, a scholar with the Brookings Institution, told Laura Blumefeld of the *Washington Post.* "He's not just declaring that he's a Democrat. He's declaring that he's a *Kerry* Democrat, and the way he wants to make a difference in the world is to get his former boss out of office."

New York City, where both of the coauthors of this work happen to live, has also been asked to carry the brunt of the administration's penny-wise, pound-foolish parsimony. *The Economist* compared the city to Atlas, bearing the weight of the world on its shoulders. Already reeling from a massive deficit, declining income, and the economic aftershocks of the destruction of the Twin Towers on much of lower Manhattan, its residents must now pay an estimated $1 billion a year for emergency and counterterrorism costs owing to its rich endowment of potential targets. And yet as 2003 began, the city was already making do with four thousand fewer police officers than it had two years earlier, but was now forced to assign more than a thousand of those remaining to the terrorist beat. It was shuttering several fire companies. Layoffs, tax hikes, and cutbacks in every kind of social service were in the offing. After Bush's attempt to stiff New York entirely with his original 2004 allotment, Congress finally stepped in to increase the federal government's contribution to approximately $200 million. It was scarcely enough, but it would have to do. (Gotham was hardly alone: enhanced security measures cost the nation's cities an estimated $2.6 billion in the fifteen months after September 11.) And to top it all off, residents of the city learned that the Bush administration had deliberately misled them— together with the police, firefighters, and safety workers who risked their lives in the cleanup—about the health risk posed by the destruction of the World Trade Center. The EPA could not honestly say whether it was safe to breathe the air in lower Manhattan, but was instructed by the White House to say that it was indeed safe lest a wave of fear panic the stock market. Screaming phone calls were apparently exchanged by EPA professionals and the White House communications staff. The mind reels to imagine a greater injury heaped on the victims and heroes of September 11 than to be lied to by their own government in order that they might be induced to risk their own health and that of their children.

11. Invading Iraq

Operation Bait and Switch

✴

"You can't distinguish between al Qaeda and Saddam when you talk about the war on terror."

—President George W. Bush,
September 2002

"It's pretty interesting that all the generals see it the same way, and all the others who have never fired a shot, and are hot to go to war, see it another."

—Major General Anthony Zinni (ret.),
former chief of U.S. Central Command, October 2002

What really motivated George W. Bush to invade Iraq? Was it the intelligence he received regarding Iraq's weapons of mass destruction program, its nuclear research program, its potential threat to its neighbors, its alleged connections to al Qaeda? Was he genuinely hopeful of spreading democracy throughout the Arab world? Did he do it to thwart what he believed to be an imminent threat to America's safety and security? Was he moved to end the brutal repression of Saddam Hussein's Ba'ath regime of its own people? Did he wish to get his hands on that nation's enormous oil reserves and help out his (and Dick Cheney's) cronies in the energy business? Was he fooled by a conspiracy of his neoconservative advisors to do Israel's dirty work? Did the president share the view that Hussein had somehow been involved in September 11? Did Bush decide on the invasion because he wanted to secure access to military bases across the Middle East in order to expand America's military empire? Did he feel it important to do it merely to demonstrate to potential terrorists and other opponents that America was not a nation of wimps and would "fight back" whenever challenged? Did Bush decide on the invasion for domestic political reasons—to keep the country's mind off of his failure to make good on his boast to capture Osama bin Laden "dead or alive," or to distract attention from a failure to provide homeland security, or to deny civil liberties? Did Bush simply wish to continue to inspire a climate of fear in the nation, so helpful to Republican electoral ambitions and to Karl Rove's lifelong dream of a semipermanent Republican majority? Was it all of the above? None of them? Some but not others? Well, then, which ones?

Each of the above-described motivations for the invasion has been put forth as a hypothesis by the president himself, one of his admirers, one of his critics, or someone in between. But the only true answer is that we'll never know. During the course of the year in which his administration attempted to convince the rest of the world of the urgency of his quest, Bush offered a succession of ever-shifting justifications. No doubt his ultimate rationale grew out of some combination of these arguments, as well as some he may never have articulated. But what, if anything, proved to be the deciding factor is all but impossible to say. Even if one were (naively) to take the president at his word, the fact remains that his "word" kept changing all the time.

Still, one cannot help but wonder why it was that the Bush administration felt such urgency and was willing to expend its political capital and risk so much else—up to and including the entire presidency—to undertake this costly and dangerous invasion of a nation that, when all was said and done, could not credibly be said to threaten our own. Major General Anthony Zinni, who preceded General Tommy Franks as head of the U.S. Central Command and whom President Bush appointed to be his personal Middle East envoy—and who can hardly be painted as either a political adversary of either the administration or the U.S. military—said he considered Iraq to be a sixth-order security problem for the United States in the region. Asked how he would have prioritized U.S. commitments and initiatives in the period leading up to the war, General Zinni replied:

> First and foremost, the Middle East peace process and getting it back on track. Second, it is ensuring that Iran's reformation or moderation continues on track and trying to help and support the people who are trying to make that change in the best way we can. That's going to take a lot of intelligence and careful work. The third is to make sure those countries to which we have now committed ourselves to change, like Afghanistan and those in central Asia, we invest what we need to in the way of resources there to make that change happen. Fourth is to patch up these relationships that have

become strained, and fifth is to reconnect to the people. We are talking past each other. The dialogue is heated. We have based this in
things that are tough to compromise on, like religion and politics,
and we need to reconnect in a different way.

(After these remarks were reported, Zinni was informed that he "will never
be used by the White House again.")

And yet to George W. Bush, Iraq was not just a "first-order" priority but
at times his only priority. To ensure that he would succeed in convincing
the nation to go along with his invasion plan, Bush was willing to exagger-
ate the level of military threat Iraq could or did present to the United States;
to mischaracterize the evidence tying it to global terrorism; to minimize the
cost and difficulty of the military occupation he proposed; and to misstate
the potential for a democratic transformation not only of Iraq, but of the
entire Arab world. Just about every piece of evidence the administration
marshaled in support of its war would afterward be called into question, as
if the entire effort to convince the nation to undertake its first ever preventive war had been little more than one massive bait-and-switch operation.

What follows is an examination of President Bush's most frequently offered justifications for the invasion of Iraq.

The United States Faced a Threat from Iraq's Hidden Weapons of Mass Destruction

George W. Bush and his advisors allowed no room for doubt, in their
public presentations, that the Iraqi regime was in possession of a vast store
of potentially lethal "weapons of mass destruction" (WMD) and that it possessed not only the willingness but also the capability to use these weapons
against U.S. citizens on U.S. soil. In September 2002, at the side of British
prime minister Tony Blair, President Bush proclaimed, "I would remind
you that when the inspectors first went into Iraq and were denied—finally
denied access, a report came out of the Atomic—the IAEA [International
Atomic Energy Agency], that they were six months away from developing
a [nuclear] weapon. I don't know what more evidence we need." In fact the
estimate to which Bush was referring was more than a decade old and was
made before Iraq's military capabilities were decimated in the Gulf War. Ari
Fleischer tried to claim in a letter to the *Washington Post* that "it was in fact
the International Institute for Strategic Studies that issued the report concluding that Iraq could develop nuclear weapons in as few as six months."
But that report, which was unavailable at the time Fleischer made his claim,
did not support Bush's statement, either. In a speech to the nation, Bush
also added, "Iraq could decide on any given day to provide a biological or

chemical weapon to a terrorist group or individual terrorists," an alliance that "could allow the Iraqi regime to attack America without leaving any fingerprints." But this claim, too, was wholly unsupported and was contradicted by the CIA. Its report, declassified after Bush's speech, rated the possibility as "low" that Hussein would initiate a chemical or biological weapons attack against the United States but might take the "extreme step" of assisting terrorists if provoked by a U.S. attack.

In the same speech, Bush warned the nation that Iraq possessed a growing fleet of unmanned aircraft—"drones"—that could be used "for missions targeting the United States." But a CIA report suggested that the fleet was more of an "experiment" and "attempt" and labeled it a "serious threat to Iraq's neighbors and to international military forces in the region" but said nothing about its having sufficient range to threaten the United States. And the air force, which controls most of the American military's unmanned aircraft, believed the claim was nonsense as well. (Analysts at the Pentagon's Missile Defense Agency said the air force view was widely accepted at the time Bush made his claim.) In fact these drones were all directed at Iran.

In October 2002, in his first major speech devoted solely to the Iraqi threat, Bush told Americans, "Iraq possesses ballistic missiles with a likely range of hundreds of miles—far enough to strike Saudi Arabia, Israel, Turkey, and other nations—in a region where more than one hundred thirty-five thousand American civilians and service members live and work." This, too, was false. The missile under question, the Al Samoud-2, can actually travel less than two hundred miles, nowhere near far enough to reach these targets.

In his January 28, 2003, State of the Union address, Bush cataloged specific amounts of potentially lethal weapons with which he feared Saddam Hussein could threaten his neighbors and the United States itself. These included "biological weapons materials sufficient to produce over twenty-five thousand liters of anthrax—enough doses to kill several million people; materials sufficient to produce more than thirty-eight thousand liters of botulinum toxin—enough to subject millions of people to death by respiratory failure; the materials to produce as much as five hundred tons of sarin, mustard, and VX nerve agent. In such quantities, these chemical agents also could kill untold thousands; upwards of thirty thousand munitions capable of delivering chemical agents; several mobile biological weapons labs . . . designed to produce germ warfare agents." In each of these cases, Bush emphasized that Hussein had admitted to having such weapons in the past, but had failed to account for them in his declaration to the United Nations of the weapons he "currently" possessed. By asserting this, Bush completely discounted the Iraqis' explanation that the weapons in question had been destroyed in conjunction with the inspections regime that had been under way after the first Gulf War. There was, in fact, a consistent lack of any ambiguity at all to the Bush administration's claims:

* "Simply stated, there is no doubt that Saddam Hussein now has weapons of mass destruction." Dick Cheney, speech to VFW National Convention, August 26, 2002.

* "We know they have weapons of mass destruction. . . . There isn't any debate about it." Donald Rumsfeld, September 2002.

* "There is no doubt that the regime of Saddam Hussein possesses weapons of mass destruction." Gen. Tommy Franks, press conference, March 22, 2003.

* "We know where they are. They're in the area around Tikrit and Baghdad and east, west, south and north somewhat." Donald Rumsfeld, ABC interview, March 30, 2003.

* "I'm absolutely sure that there are weapons of mass destruction there and the evidence will be forthcoming. We're just getting it just now." Colin Powell, remarks to reporters, May 4, 2003.

It was statements like these, and many more, that enable those who favored immediate war in the debate on the matter to make contentions such as those by Robert Kagan and William Kristol, "No one disputes the nature of the threat" and "Nor is there any doubt that, after September 11, Saddam's weapons of mass destruction pose a kind of danger to us that we hadn't grasped before." Almost no one taken seriously in political discourse actually disputed the existence of these weapons; in fact, acknowledging them was viewed as the "price of admission" to be taken seriously at all. The only allowable points of discussion became to what degree they genuinely threatened American security and whether war was the only way to deal with them.

After defeating the Iraqis, occupying Baghdad, and sending seven "sensitive site teams," each consisting of twenty-five inspectors who visited about 330 target sites, none of the weapons cited was, at least as of our writing, ever found. In an attempt to pretend otherwise, President Bush, speaking in Krakow, Poland, on his way to a June 2003 G-8 meeting in Evian, France, referred to two trucks in Iraq that some U.S. intelligence officials believed might have been usable as mobile bioweapons laboratories. "For those who say we haven't found the banned manufacturing devices or banned weapons, they're wrong. We found them," the president claimed. In fact, the two mobile chemical labs and a dozen fifty-five-gallon drums of chemicals to which the president was referring had been immediately tested and "showed no positive hits at all" for chemical weapons. According to the official report of a British scientist who examined them for his government, "They are not mobile germ warfare laboratories. You could not use them for making biological weapons. They do not even look like them. They are exactly what the Iraqis said they were—facilities for the production of hydrogen gas to fill balloons." And while the CIA initially argued that the trailers may have been used as biological weapons laboratories, this conclusion was rejected by both the State Department's own Bureau of Intelligence and Research (INR) and engineering experts from the Defense Intelligence Agency (DIA) after extensive testing.

In early October 2003, David Kay, the Bush administration's chief investigator, formally told Congress that after searching for nearly six months, and spending more than $300 million, U.S. forces and CIA experts had found no chemical or biological weapons in Iraq, and had discovered that the nation's nuclear program was in only "the very most rudimentary" state. Incredibly, Bush continued to insist on this case even after his own weapons inspector dismissed it. "Iraq's WMD programs spanned more than two decades, involved thousands of people, billions of dollars, and was elaborately shielded by security and deception operations that continued even beyond the end of Operation Iraqi Freedom," Bush argued. "That is what the report said." The president seemed to think the mere existence of the program in past decades—though no one had ever disputed this and it apparently produced no usable weapons during the past decade—somehow justified the cost of war.

Lieutenant General James Conway, of the First Marine Expeditionary Force, told reporters at the end of May 2003 that the failure to find any WMD was certainly "not for lack of trying. We've been to virtually every ammunition supply point between the Kuwaiti border and Baghdad, but they're simply not there." Instead of discovering the vast stores of weapons the Bush administration insisted that Hussein was hiding, U.S. military forces, according to the *Washington Post*'s Barton Gellman, "dug a playground, raided a distillery, seized a research paper from a failing graduate student and laid bare a swimming pool where an underground chemical weapons stash was supposed to be."

One unnamed administration official attempted to explain the discrepancy between prewar certainty and postwar reality as follows. They were "not lying," he said. "But it was just a matter of emphasis." Speaking to *Vanity Fair* around the same time, Deputy Secretary of Defense Paul Wolfowitz also tried to minimize the importance of the WMD argument: "For bureaucratic reasons, we settled on one issue, weapons of mass destruction [as justification for invading Iraq] because it was the one reason everyone could agree on."

All of the above statements, however, beg the question of just what the top members of the administration knew and when they knew it. We can say, for instance, that Colin Powell, perhaps the most cautious and hence trustworthy member of the administration's foreign policy team, grew increasingly apprehensive about the veracity of the claims he was expected, as a good soldier, to support. At a meeting at the Waldorf-Astoria hotel just before he was to go before the United Nations to lay out the case for war, Powell complained to UK foreign secretary Jack Straw—according to a diplomatic source quoted by the *Guardian* who has read a transcript of the conversation—that the claims coming out of the Pentagon, particularly those made by Deputy Secretary Wolfowitz, could not be substantiated. Powell allegedly told the British foreign secretary that he had just about "moved in" with his intelligence staff to prepare for his speech before the UN Security Council but left his briefings "apprehensive," fearing that the evidence might "explode in their faces" once the facts were known. *US News and World Report* published a rather more lurid story, in which the U.S. secretary of state was seen throwing the documents he was being given into the air in fury, and declaring, "I'm not reading this. This is bullshit." Straw denied these reports, but Powell certainly did see these fears realized just a few days after his speech when the British foreign office was forced to admit that a considerable portion of its Iraq dossier—upon which Powell had decided to rely quite heavily—had been lifted, verbatim, from dated academic sources and even included a portion that was lifted from a twelve-year-old American doctoral dissertation.

Just about all of the rest of Powell's case soon collapsed as well. Charles J. Hanley, an Associated Press reporter, subjected Powell's claims to detailed scrutiny in light of what was known at the time as well as from later revelations and discovered the following:

★ Powell presented satellite photos of various buildings and vehicles in order to suggest that the Iraqis were shielding chemical and biological weapons, and the missiles with which to launch them. He insisted that the trucks at two such sites were really "decontamination vehicles" associated with chemical weapons. In fact, these very sites had undergone five hundred recent inspections. Chief UN inspector Hans Blix had explained a day earlier that no contraband was found and no signs that anything had been moved were detectable. Norwegian inspector Jorn Siljeholm told the Associated Press on March 19 that "decontamination vehicles" found by UN teams were actually fire trucks. No contrary evidence was ever found.

★ Powell played audiotapes of Arabic-speaking individuals discussing a "modified vehicle," "forbidden ammo," and "the expression *nerve agents.*" He said they were intercepts of Iraqi army officers, but there is no way to ascertain if any of this was true, as no context was provided. Meanwhile, if army sources were indeed searching for "forbidden ammo," it makes perfect sense, for the Iraqis had informed UN inspectors they would conduct exactly those searches. When these searches were completed, four stray, empty chemical warheads were turned over to the inspectors.

* Powell said "classified" documents found at a nuclear scientist's Baghdad home were "dramatic confirmation" of intelligence indicating that prohibited items were often concealed in that fashion. These items never materialized.

* Powell noted Iraq had declared it produced only 8,500 liters of anthrax before 1991, but UN inspectors had estimated the potential to make 25,000 liters. None of the supply, he argued, had been "verifiably accounted for." Yet no anthrax was ever found in Iraq after the invasion.

* Powell said defectors had reported "biological-weapons factories" on trucks and in train cars, and displayed artistic representations of them. These, too, never materialized, despite administration attempts to hype the discovery of what were later judged to be weather-balloon fueling stations. (See below.)

* Powell accused Iraq of creating four tons of the nerve agent VX. "A single drop of VX on the skin will kill in minutes." But the secretary neglected to note that most of the VX had been verifiably destroyed in the 1990s under UN supervision. The Iraqis showed inspectors where they had destroyed the rest, and chemical analyses undertaken by the United Nations generally confirmed this. An analysis by the International Institute of Strategic Studies in London found that all pre-1991 VX would probably have degraded, and none was ever found following the invasion.

* Powell claimed, "We know that Iraq has embedded key portions of its illicit chemical weapons infrastructure within its legitimate civilian industry." No evidence of this has yet been found. A September 2002 report by the Defense Intelligence Agency, which had always been available to Powell, indicated there was "no reliable information" on "where Iraq has—or will—establish its chemical-warfare-agent-production facilities."

* Powell claimed, "Our conservative estimate is that Iraq today has a stockpile of between one hundred and five hundred tons of chemical weapons agents." The source of this figure, too, remains a mystery, given the DIA's admitted lack of knowledge. In any case, none was ever found.

* Powell argued that 122-mm chemical warheads found by UN inspectors in January 2003 might be the "tip of an iceberg." He failed to note, however, that the warheads were empty and were assumed

by inspectors to be "debris from the past." No others have since been found.

* Powell claimed, "Saddam Hussein has chemical weapons. . . . And we have sources who tell us that he recently has authorized his field commanders to use them." Again, no such weapons were ever found, much less used.

* Powell claimed, "We have no indication that Saddam Hussein has ever abandoned his nuclear weapons program." But, of course, we had no real evidence that he had begun it, either. (See below.)

* Powell credited "intelligence sources" with discovering that Iraq possessed a secret force of up to a few dozen prohibited Scud-type missiles with a range of six hundred miles and was blocking its test facility from spy satellites. Nothing to support these claims was ever discovered.

Just as they had during the Gulf of Tonkin episode—when newspapers and newsweeklies published lurid accounts of a battle that never took place, based on fabricated stories passed along to them by the Johnson administration—many members of the news media were accomplices in this misinformation campaign, almost never questioning its credibility.

Gilbert Cranberg, former editorial page editor of the *Des Moines Register,* examined the media reaction to Powell's UN presentation, pointing out that the secretary "cited almost no verifiable sources. Many of his assertions were unattributed. The speech had more than forty vague references, such as 'human sources,' 'an eyewitness,' 'detainees,' 'an al Qaeda source,' 'a senior defector,' 'intelligence sources,' and the like." Nevertheless, surveying the coverage of an allegedly skeptical media from some forty papers from all parts of the country, he found the following conclusions:

> "a massive array of evidence," "a detailed and persuasive case," "a powerful case," "a sober, factual case," "an overwhelming case," "a compelling case," "the strong, credible and persuasive case," "a persuasive, detailed accumulation of information," "the core of his argument was unassailable," "a smoking fusillade . . . a persuasive case for anyone who is still persuadable," "an accumulation of painstakingly gathered and analyzed evidence," "only the most gullible and wishful thinking souls can now deny that Iraq is harboring and hiding weapons of mass destruction," "the skeptics asked for proof; they now have it," "a much more detailed and convincing argument than any that has previously been told," "Powell's evidence . . . was overwhelming," "an ironclad case . . . incontrovertible evidence," "succinct and damning evidence . . . the case is closed," "Colin

Powell delivered the goods on Saddam Hussein," "masterful," "If there was any doubt that Hussein . . . needs to be . . . stripped of his chemical and biological capabilities, Powell put it to rest."

Part of the explanation for the wholesale acceptance may be that Colin Powell is often credited with being the most believable and circumspect of administration members. Though Powell himself may have forgotten, he once knew better than to make the series of false claims he offered. Two years earlier, in February 2001 at a meeting with Egypt's foreign minister in Cairo, Powell defended the UN sanctions program against Iraq by noting how successful U.S. containment of Hussein had been. He explained of the sanctions, "Frankly, they have worked. He has not developed any significant capability with respect to weapons of mass destruction. He is unable to project conventional power against his neighbors." The rest of the Bush team joined the secretary of state in consistently making reference to intelligence information they claimed to have received that was either new or recently updated. They, too, got an easy pass from the media. For instance, in a speech before the Council on Foreign Relations, Paul Wolfowitz asserted that the administration's case for war "is a case grounded in current intelligence, current intelligence that comes not only from sophisticated overhead satellites and our ability to intercept communications, but from brave people who told us the truth at the risk of their lives. We have that; it is very convincing." George Tenet attested that U.S. intelligence "comes to us from credible and reliable sources." In fact, following the war's completion, most U.S. intelligence officials admitted they had been flying blind since 1998, when the United Nations inspections regime collapsed. "We were reduced to dead reckoning," a Pentagon official admitted.

The WMD argument was actually one of few relatively noncontroversial prewar claims Bush and Company made against the Iraqi regime. Most observers could easily imagine that the Iraqi dictator was hiding these weapons, and probably did not expect that Bush, Cheney, Powell, Rumsfeld, and the others would go quite so far out on their respective limbs without airtight evidence. And indeed, they benefited from the commonsense assumption that Hussein would not have been so intransigent with the UN inspectors unless he was trying to hide something.

But it may be that the dictator was merely trying to salvage his pride, or the intimidating image of his evil regime. He may also have suspected that Bush's cooperation with the inspections regime was itself a ruse and that the president intended to declare war on Iraq no matter what action Hussein took—short of resigning and going into exile.

Many alleged Iraqi weapons programs appear to have been nothing more than bluffs, according to the scientists who worked on them. "A lot of projects were just ink on paper," a former senior Iraqi intelligence officer explained. Many scientists contend that Hussein himself was fooled, while no new weapons were produced after the original destruction of the stocks in the early 1990s. A detailed *Wall Street Journal* examination of abandoned Iraqi efforts to manufacture the poison ricin as a weapon in 1990 paints a similar picture, despite specific administration claims that such a manufacturing process—complete with possible terrorist ties—was under way in 2003. Once again, the Americans insisted that the Iraqis had successfully completed what they had actually tried and failed to accomplish more than a decade earlier, before the first Gulf War.

Whatever Hussein's motivation, the question of whether he did have WMD or a program to develop them will likely remain one of history's great mysteries. Americans may count themselves as enormously fortunate that this was the case, for before the war began, according to a secret report released by the White House as part of its postwar propaganda offensive, the CIA and other agencies were perhaps most concerned with the danger that Iraq "probably would attempt clandestine attacks against the U.S. homeland if Baghdad feared an attack." The agency even believed that Hussein was likely to use biological weapons in this case and had instructed his intelligence service to do so. The Bushites went ahead with the war anyway, leading one to the conclusion that either they did not believe their own intelligence reports or they were so committed to attacking Iraq that they were willing to risk the possibility of biological attacks against the United States in order to achieve their aim.

Had the administration been less intent on forcing the available evidence to fit its preconceived notions, it could never have made its now apparently fantastic claims. What evidence it had at the time pointed to the accuracy of the conclusions drawn by the UN inspections team led by Hans Blix. He noted that the Iraqis had acknowledged that they did have some biological and chemical weapons and offered only incomplete documentation of their destruction. Some weapons and materials were bombed during the first Gulf War, and others were dismantled in the presence of international inspectors after the war. Overall, there was no reason to believe that substantial quantities remained, but no certainty, either.

Many in government were aware of how little they really knew about Iraq's WMD program, but these sources were at best ignored and at worst, quietly discredited. For instance, a secret September 2002 report of the Pentagon's Defense Intelligence Agency informed Secretary Rumsfeld, "There is no reliable information on whether Iraq is producing and stockpiling chemical weapons, or whether Iraq has—or will—establish its chemical warfare agent production facilities," according to U.S. officials interviewed by the *Los Angeles Times.* Yet even this did not prevent Powell from going to Congress and insisting that Hussein's "regime has amassed large, clandestine stockpiles of chemical weapons—including VX, sarin, cyclosarin and mustard gas."

And what has been the Bush administration's response to those who tried to hold it to its WMD-related word? According to Ari Fleischer, "I think the burden is on those people who think he didn't have weapons of mass destruction to tell the world where they are."

You can say that again.

A War Was Necessary to Prevent Iraq's Acquisition of Nuclear Weaponry

While the WMD argument was considered to be the most credible of all the Bush administration's many controversial contentions during the prewar period, it required a war itself to disprove. Others crumbled much more easily, and none more so than the administration's scare tactics regarding the alleged Iraqi nuclear program.

After the war Donald Rumsfeld contended, "I don't believe anyone that I know in the administration ever said that Iraq had nuclear weapons." The statement can only be considered true if one somehow defines Rumsfeld's mentor and political patron, Vice President Cheney, as either someone Rumsfeld never met or someone outside the administration. On *Meet the Press* in March 2002 Cheney clearly claimed that Iraq was already in possession of "reconstituted nuclear weapons."

The argument about Iraq's nuclear program in fact served as a constant drumbeat for the administration and convinced many people that war was the only prudent means to deal with its threat. And though one would have been hard-pressed to discern it from the credulous media coverage it received, the administration possessed virtually no credible evidence to back up its frightening claims. The *Washington Post*'s Walter Pincus tracked the progress of the incredibly disappearing evidence:

On August 26 Vice President Cheney got things going by telling a Veterans of Foreign Wars audience that "many of us are convinced that Saddam will acquire nuclear weapons fairly soon. Just how soon we cannot gauge." On September 8 the *New York Times* reported that Iraq had "embarked on a worldwide hunt for materials to make an atomic bomb" by trying to purchase "specially designed aluminum tubes" that unidentified administration sources believed were for centrifuges to enrich uranium. It added, as a statement of fact, "Mr. Hussein's dogged insistence on pursuing his nuclear ambitions along with what defectors described in interviews as Iraq's push to improve and expand Baghdad's chemical and biological arsenals, have brought Iraq and the United States to the brink of war." The same day, Condoleezza Rice confirmed the *Times* story on CNN's *Late Edition,* claiming that the tubes "are only really suited for nuclear weapons programs, centrifuge programs." She also added, "The problem here is that there will always be some uncertainty about how quickly he can acquire nuclear weapons, but we don't want the smoking gun to be a mushroom cloud."

Cheney made much the same claim on that very day, telling Tim Russert on NBC's *Meet the Press*, "We don't have all the evidence [but evidence] tells us that he [Hussein] is in fact actively and aggressively seeking to acquire nuclear weapons." In fact, these views were being fought over within the U.S. intelligence community and had been for more than a year. On September 7, 2002, when Bush appeared together with British prime minister Tony Blair at the White House, the president insisted that a "new" IAEA report stated that Iraq was "six months away" from building a nuclear weapon. "I don't know what more evidence we need," the president added, and Blair seconded this alarmist view with an "absolutely." In fact, no report and no evidence ever existed.

When the British dossier on Iraq's weapons program was published on September 24 it noted that "there is no definitive intelligence that it is destined for a nuclear program." Nevertheless Bush claimed in his October 7 speech that satellite photographs revealed that "Iraq is rebuilding facilities at [past nuclear] sites." He also cited Hussein's "numerous meetings with Iraqi nuclear scientists" as further evidence that the program was being reconstituted, along with Iraq's attempts to buy high-strength aluminum tubes "needed" for centrifuges used to enrich uranium. None of these claims stood the test of time. On January 27, as Pincus notes—the day before the State of the Union address—the head of the IAEA informed the UN Security Council that inspections had found that no prohibited nuclear activities had taken place at former Iraqi nuclear sites. Mohamed ElBaradei also told the Security Council that preliminary analysis suggested that the aluminum tubes, "unless modified, would not be suitable for manufacturing centrifuges." His even more strongly worded March 18 final report concluded: "The IAEA had found no evidence or plausible indication of the revival of a nuclear weapons program in Iraq." In fact, as the *Washington Post* reported after the war, the "closely held internal judgments of the Iraq Survey Group, overseen by David Kay as special representative of CIA director George J. Tenet, [were] that Iraq's nuclear weapons scientists did no significant arms-related work after 1991, that facilities with suspicious new construction proved benign, and that equipment of potential use to a nuclear program remained under seal or in civilian industrial use." Perhaps most significant, the report noted, the aluminum tubes were judged to be "innocuous," according to Australian brigadier general Stephen D. Meekin, commander of the Joint Captured Enemy Materiel Exploitation Center, the largest of a half-dozen units that report to Kay. The inspectors did not even bother to keep track of them after the war. "They weren't our highest priority," Meekin explained in late October 2003. "The thing's innocuous."

These conditions left only one tactic to the administration, and this was the story of alleged uranium purchases in Niger. In late September 2002 DCI George Tenet briefed both the Senate Select Committee on Intelligence and the Senate Foreign Relations Committee in executive session on

Iraqi military capabilities. Before the Intelligence Committee (where no staff members are allowed inside the room, hence making it easier to mislead senators), Tenet informed his audience, according to Seymour Hersh's reporting in *The New Yorker,* "that a shipment of high-strength aluminum tubes that was intercepted on its way to Iraq had been meant for the construction of centrifuges that could be used to produce enriched uranium." He added that no one could say for certain what the purpose of these tubes was, but in the Foreign Relations Committee briefing, Tenet added the shocking news that the CIA had allegedly discovered evidence that between 1999 and 2001 Iraq had attempted to buy five hundred tons of uranium oxide from the African nation of Niger. Here were all the ingredients of a recipe for nuclear weapons.

Shortly thereafter Colin Powell gave much the same testimony, while both Iraq and Niger denied the accusation. Two weeks after the Tenet-Powell appearances, Congress agreed to the president's request for the authority to go to war, with many members citing Iraq's alleged nuclear ambitions as their primary motivation. For instance, Congressman Henry Waxman, a liberal California Democrat, later explained that in his decision to support the war, "The most powerful argument that President Bush made to take the country to war was that Iraq was soon to become a nuclear power and that would change things dramatically—Saddam Hussein would have the ability to blackmail other countries in the region and it also meant that any other kind of military action we might have to take against them in the future would be far more serious. It was the reason, quite frankly, that brought me to vote for the resolution."

For nearly six months, the Niger story formed the backbone of administration efforts to convince the world of the imminent threat represented by the continuance of Saddam's regime. In December, for example, the State Department included the Niger claim in its public eight-point rebuttal to the 12,200-page arms declaration that Iraq had made to the United Nations two weeks earlier. But when the IAEA requested backup information, Washington gave it nothing. In January 2003 Donald Rumsfeld and Paul Wolfowitz both reiterated the claim. In a January 23 *New York Times* op-ed entitled "Why We Know Iraq Is Lying," Condoleezza Rice complained, "The declaration fails to account for or explain Iraq's efforts to get uranium from abroad." President Bush, as is now well known, made the case in his January 2003 State of the Union message, crediting the intelligence breakthrough to his partner Tony Blair's intelligence service, with the now-infamous sixteen words: "The British government has learned that Saddam Hussein recently sought significant quantities of uranium from Africa." Bush warned, "Saddam Hussein has not credibly explained these activities. He clearly has much to hide."

The campaign met with considerable success—at least, it would appear, with the U.S. public, which was initially quite skeptical of going it alone in

Iraq without the support of the Security Council. As a result of the enormous propaganda effort undertaken by the Bush administration, by November 2002 a Gallup poll found that 59 percent of Americans who were questioned supported an invasion, with only 35 percent opposed. A month later, a *Los Angeles Times* poll found 90 percent of Americans agreeing that Saddam was "currently developing weapons of mass destruction," while one month after that, an ABC/*Washington Post* poll discovered that 81 percent of those questioned believed Iraq posed a threat to the United States. Finally, by January 2003 a slim majority of Americans questioned—52 percent—favored a unilateral U.S. invasion of Iraq.

However powerful, the argument unfortunately rested on a foundation of falsehood. The Niger story had originated a year earlier; when someone in Cheney's office received a packet of documents from a British source— via Italy—allegedly proving the Iraq-Niger uranium deal. Cheney's office turned it over to the CIA, where Joseph C. Wilson, a former U.S. diplomat to various African nations as well as to Iraq, was asked to investigate. Wilson returned from Niger in February 2002 with the news that no such transaction ever took place. According to high-level intelligence sources speaking to Nicholas Kristof of the *New York Times,* while it was perhaps possible that CIA director George Tenet never informed President Bush that the Niger documents were bogus, "lower CIA officials did tell both the vice president's office and National Security Council staff members." In addition, Greg Thielmann, who had recently retired after spending twenty-five years in the State Department, the last four in INR, informed Kristof he was "quite confident" that these views were passed up all the way to Colin Powell. "Everyone knew" the documents "were not good," a senior administration decision maker who supported the war told the *Washington Post.* "The White House response has been baffling. This is relatively inconsequential. Why don't they tell the truth?"

Corroborating evidence was offered in a National Public Radio report in June, quoting sources inside the INR objecting to the Niger-related claims that were to appear in Bush's speech. "Earlier versions of the president's speech did not cite British sources," a senior intelligence official told NPR's Tom Gjelten. "They were more definitive, and we objected." The solution? White House officials said, "Why don't we say the British say this?" Later, CIA sources claimed to reporters that they had warned the British against using the information back in September.

The INR report warned: "[T]he claims of Iraqi pursuit of natural uranium in Africa are, in INR's assessment, highly dubious." Next it cast doubt on the very notion that Iraq was even trying to revive its nuclear program. "Lacking persuasive evidence that Baghdad has launched a coherent effort to reconstitute its nuclear weapons program, INR is unwilling to speculate that such an effort began soon after the departure of UN inspectors or to project a timeline for completion of activities it does not now see happening." In intelligence, as in life, the devil may be in the details, but when it came to making their case for war, according to a senior intelligence official, the president's advisors did not want "a lot of footnotes and disclaimers."

So once again, how exactly did the Niger connection make it into the non-fact-checking president's speech? When Bush was finally asked about his use of the discredited material, he at first responded with an assertion that appeared designed to raise questions about his fundamental competence as commander in chief. In response to the Niger allegations, Bush made the patently false claim that he did not decide to go to war until after he gave Saddam Hussein "a chance to allow the inspectors in, and he wouldn't let them in." Of course, the inspectors were inside Iraq at the very moment Bush announced his decision to go to war, rather than let them complete their work as virtually the entire world was requesting. The media decided to give the president a pass on this, however, because, as the usually tough-minded Dana Milbank of the *Washington Post* explained, "[P]eople basically decided this is just the president being the president. Occasionally he plays the wrong track and something comes out quite wrong. He is under a great deal of pressure."

Pressure or no pressure, it eventually became necessary to stem what was turning into a flood of stories about White House duplicity. After struggling to come up with a believable storyline with which to defend themselves, Bush aides ultimately did so by seeking to cast the blame on the CIA. Hours after the president complained that the allegation "was cleared by the intelligence services," Director of Central Intelligence George Tenet admitted in a prepared statement that the Niger story "did not rise to the level of certainty which should be required for presidential speeches and the CIA should have ensured that it was removed."

This is an old Washington trick and would have been more convincing had the president and his advisors not chosen the only high-level holdover from the Clinton administration still working for Bush to be the fall guy. Moreover, Tenet apparently had second thoughts about allowing the agency to take the fall, and in his congressional testimony that week reignited the controversy by noting that he had never actually been given the speech. This left Condoleezza Rice to resort to a dizzying series of arguments in what appeared to be a desperate attempt to blame the intelligence community and/or make the issue go away. Among them were:

* In his State of the Union address the president's claims regarding Niger were "technically accurate."

* The State Department's intelligence arm, the Bureau of Intelligence and Research (INR), "did not take a footnote to the consensus view that the Iraqis were actively trying to pursue a nuclear

weapons program," Rice insisted, speaking about the National In-telligence Estimate [NIE, which is the intelligence community's agreed-upon summary of the state of its knowledge]. "Now, if there were doubts about the underlying intelligence to that Na-tional Intelligence Estimate, those doubts were not communicated to the president, to the vice president, or to me." The truth, how-ever, was that INR *did* object, and these objections were contained in a portion of the NIE that Rice insists she never read. In fact, it was in the NIE's very first paragraph that INR stated there was not "a compelling case" and the government was "lacking persuasive evidence that Baghdad has launched a coherent effort to reconsti-tute its nuclear weapons program."

★ Information from other African nations—nations apparently never to be named—proved the case the administration had tried and failed to make with the phony Niger documents.

★ The whole ruckus was much ado about nothing. "It is unfortunate that this one sentence, this [*sic*] sixteen words," she complained two days after trying out the "other nations" rationale, "remained in the State of the Union. But this in no way has any effect on the president's larger case about Iraqi efforts to reconstitute the nuclear program and, most importantly, the bigger picture of Iraq's weapons-of-mass-destruction program."

What Dr. Rice ignores in her larger argument is that none of the rest of the Bush administration's allegation was found to be accurate, either. More-over, pleading ignorance in a case like this is tantamount to pleading in-competence. The Bush administration apparently boasts an NSC advisor who doesn't read her National Intelligence Estimates, a director of Central Intelligence who does not read the president's State of the Union address, a secretary of state who ignores his own intelligence bureau, and a president, vice president, and secretary of defense who claim to read almost nothing at all. When the *Washington Post* is able to report that "President Bush and his national security advisor did not entirely read the most authoritative prewar assessment of U.S. intelligence on Iraq, including a State Department claim that an allegation Bush would later use in his State of the Union address was 'highly dubious,'" one has to wonder about the credibility of anything these officials say.

Meanwhile, in seeking to defend his agency from attacks from the White House staff, and after deciding not to fall on his sword after all, DCI Tenet pointed his finger to a relatively anonymous NSC staffer named Robert Joseph, who had allegedly sought permission from a man named Alan Foley, a CIA expert on weapons of mass destruction, to include the phony material in the speech. But Joseph said he had no recollection of such a conversation, and White House communications director Dan Bartlett dismissed this as "a conspiracy theory." In open bureaucratic warfare with the CIA, the obsessively secretive White House then released the disputed NIE in the hopes of furthering its case. But that backfired as well, as apparently nobody had read it carefully before sending it out into the public. In subsequent days, however, memories were jarred, and memos discovered, and lo and behold, another national security staffer, Stephen J. Hadley, found a CIA memo about the Niger material dated October 6 and further recalled a phone call he received from Tenet a day later. The memo was directed to his boss, Dr. Rice, but Hadley, a good soldier, blamed only himself. "I am the senior-most official within the NSC staff directly responsible for the substantive review and clearance of presidential speeches," Hadley said. "The president and national security advisor look to me to ensure that the substantive statements in those speeches are the ones in which the president can have confidence. And it is now clear to me that I failed in that responsibility." Next, chief speechwriter Michael Gerson went back and found yet another warning dated October 5.

All of these findings, coupled with the fingers pointed in every direction in the ensuing weeks, not only contradicted past White House versions of events, but also raised the troubling question of just where "the buck stopped" in this administration. When questioned on this point directly, recently installed White House press secretary Scott McClellan could not bring himself to answer it, leading to an almost comical exchange in the briefing room that had more of a flavor of an Abbott and Costello routine than a reasoned discussion of the preparation of the president's most important speech of the year, and one in which he hoped to convince the nation to go to war. Bush finally said in a late-July press conference that he took "personal responsibility" for the content of the speech, but he again insisted that everything he did say had been justified, leaving the "taking of responsibility" to be yet another empty gesture in what had long since become an absurdist farce.

The question remains how Rumsfeld and Powell could continue to make their own incredible statements. Powell withdrew any mention of the Niger material from his February 5 UN presentation, so deeply unsatisfied was he with its provenance, despite its having been placed in the original draft, according to reports, by the vice president's and national security advisor's offices. Rumsfeld actually claimed to be unaware of the controversy over the material in early July, nearly six months after the IAEA and others had fully debunked the report. The Bush story seems to be that the Niger story was not good enough for a political speech in Cincinnati, but the CIA decided it would be okay for the State of the Union. Administration excuses also ignore the conclusions of yet another fact-finding trip, revealed after the Wilson story finally broke; this one was made by four-star marine general Carlton W. Fulford Jr., who also traveled to Niger in February 2002 and who came away "assured" of the security of that nation's uranium supply, and reported his findings back to the Joint Chiefs chairman, General Richard B. Myers.

Vice President Cheney's role is perhaps most mysterious of all. Circumstantial evidence points to a high level of knowledge on his part, and that of his chief staffer, I. Lewis Libby, throughout the affair. Indeed, it was his office that inspired the CIA investigation in the first place. "Who is it in the White House who was hell-bent on misleading the American people, and why are they still there?" asked Senator Richard Durban (D-IL). Perhaps they are still there, notes *Slate*'s Tim Noah, because they were elected—or at least putatively selected by the Supreme Court—to occupy the office of the vice presidency. Not many people in the administration have the kind of clout to go up against a secretary of state and a director of Central Intelligence, but Dick Cheney and his top deputy do. The only other real contenders are Rumsfeld, who seems to have been out of the loop on the matter; Rice, who would have been betraying her own boss and risking her job in doing so if she knowingly put false words in his mouth; and Powell. And yet the secretary of state insisted on scrubbing the Niger material from the draft of his February 5 speech that Libby, on behalf of Cheney, had tried to put in. Whether or not Cheney is responsible, virtually all the evidence points to Wilson's conclusion, offered to *The New Republic*'s John Judis and Spencer Ackerman: "They knew the Niger story was a flat-out lie."

After Ari Fleischer tried and failed to discredit Wilson's report, unnamed "administration officials" apparently decided to retaliate against Wilson by leaking to *Time* magazine and the right-wing columnist Bob Novak, as well as to five other journalists who did not use the story, the news that Wilson's wife, Valerie Plame, was "an Agency operative on weapons of mass destruction. Two senior administration officials told [Novak that] Wilson's wife suggested sending him to Niger to investigate." As Wilson noted at the time, this form of retaliation "compromised every operation, every relationship, every network with which she had been associated in her entire career. This is the stuff of Kim Philby and Aldrich Ames." Identifying such a person would also be a crime under the Intelligence Identities Protection Act of 1982, making it, in the words of Senator Carl Levin (D-MI), an act "that is not only a felony but directly can jeopardize lives." The cover of at least one CIA front company, where Ms. Plame was alleged to work, was blown by the leak. It was also rather nakedly hypocritical, given this administration's famous passion for secrecy with regard to national security matters, and therefore could only have been ordered by someone at the highest levels of authority. Vincent Cannistraro, former director of counterterrorism operations and analysis for the CIA, charged at a congressional hearing that Plame was "outed as a vindictive act because the agency was not providing support for policy statements that Saddam Hussein was reviving his nuclear program." The leak was undertaken to "demonstrate an underlying contempt for the intelligence community, the CIA in particular."

In one sense administration apologists were absolutely right: The Niger incident *was* much ado about nothing. It was a tiny part of a much larger campaign of deliberate deception, and given the fundamentally poor quality of the forged documents upon which it was based, all of the hand-wringing hardly seems to have been necessary. Mohamed ElBaradei, director-general of the IAEA, told the UN Security Council that he knew almost immediately upon viewing them that the documents were counterfeit. Dick Cheney responded by announcing on NBC's *Meet the Press* on March 16 that "I think Mr. ElBaradei frankly is wrong," and continued, without presenting any evidence, "I think, if you look at the track record of the International Atomic Energy Agency and this kind of issue, especially where Iraq's concerned, they have consistently underestimated or missed what it was Saddam Hussein was doing. I don't have any reason to believe they're any more valid this time than they've been in the past." Throwing all caution to the wind, Cheney then added, "We believe [Saddam] has, in fact, reconstituted nuclear weapons."

In fact, a senior IAEA official admitted, "These documents are so bad that I cannot imagine that they came from a serious intelligence agency." Indeed, one of the letters was signed with the name of a Nigerois minister of foreign affairs and cooperation who had been out of office for more than a decade. Another letter, allegedly from Niger's president, contained a signature that had obviously been faked and a text with inaccuracies so obvious that the same IAEA official observed that its counterfeit character "could be spotted by someone using Google on the Internet." The Italian journalists who first gave the documents to the U.S. embassy in Rome decided not to print the story. The journalist feared she might lose her job if she tried to pass this story off as genuine. Alas, the president of the United States—no fact-checker, he—was not so scrupulous.

The deception on the part of the Bush administration regarding Iraq's nuclear program appears to have taken place on two levels simultaneously. First, it misrepresented the likely use of Iraq's aluminum tubes and centrifuges, and second, it apparently ignored the information it received regarding the Niger forgeries in order to make an argument for a nuclear danger to the United States that did not, in fact, exist. What Bush knew and when he knew it are only partially the issue here. Another equally important question would be how and why a third-rate deception was able to make its way through the U.S. security establishment and all the way to the presidency. As of this writing, no one in the Bush administration has so far accepted responsibility for what everyone now understands to be false information passed along to Congress, the public, and the world and used as a key reason to launch a war. Moreover, just as they did with the September

11 investigation, and with greater success, the Bush administration, together with Republicans in Congress, resisted every conceivable attempt to get to the bottom of just how this catastrophic failure occurred—and how it might be prevented in the future.

Many in the intelligence community were understandably furious. One CIA analyst complained, "You had senior American officials like Condoleezza Rice saying the only use of this aluminum really is uranium centrifuges. She said that on television. And that's just a lie." *Time* quoted an army intelligence officer complaining that "Rumsfeld was deeply, almost pathologically distorting the intelligence." A Defense Intelligence Agency official told the *New York Times*, "The American people were manipulated."

Why did the intelligence community allow these deceptions to take place? In light of September 11, hadn't its members learned the importance of giving voice to uncomfortable truths, no matter whose feathers got ruffled in the process? Apparently its reluctance to speak out was born of the difficult experience of seeing the White House, together with the Pentagon, exert enormous pressure on its agents to come up with the kind of intelligence that would justify a war. For instance, Dick Cheney made numerous excursions across the bridge to Langley with the apparent aim of impressing upon CIA analysts the importance of finding evidence of Iraqi weapons programs and links to terrorists. The vice president's visits (in the company of his influential chief of staff, I. Lewis "Scooter" Libby) "sent signals," according to senior CIA employees, that "a certain output was desired from here," said another senior agency official. Other usual visitors included Deputy Secretary Wolfowitz and DOD's number three, Undersecretary of Defense for Policy Douglas Feith. "They were the browbeaters," said a former defense intelligence official who attended some of the meetings in which Wolfowitz and others pressed for a different approach to the assessments they were receiving. "In interagency meetings," he said, "Wolfowitz treated the analysts' work with contempt." Inside the State Department, Christian Westermann, the department's top expert on chemical and biological weapons, told congressional committees in closed-door hearings that he had been "pressed to tailor his analysis on Iraq and other matters to conform with the Bush administration's views," according to a number of congressional officials who attended the meeting. And there were rewards for work well done: One Energy Department intelligence officer who endorsed the White House view on the alleged Iraqi nuclear program found himself the recipient of more than twenty thousand dollars in bonuses in the period leading to the war.

Even when the intelligence community did provide solid, objective analysis, the administration tampered with it before releasing it to the public, thereby undermining its integrity and demonstrating the futility of undertaking the political risk of appearing to oppose a president. CIA director George Tenet appeared to have learned his lesson by October 2002, when, for the sake of public opinion, he produced a declassified report on Iraq's nuclear program that, as John Judis and Spencer Ackerman pointed out, "omitted the qualifications and countervailing evidence that had characterized the classified version and played up the claims that strengthened the administration's case for war." For instance, the authors note:

> The intelligence report cited the much-disputed aluminum tubes as evidence that Saddam "remains intent on acquiring" nuclear weapons. And it claimed, "All intelligence experts agree that Iraq is seeking nuclear weapons and that these tubes could be used in a centrifuge enrichment program"—a blatant mischaracterization. Subsequently, the National Intelligence Estimate (NIE) allowed that "some" experts might disagree but insisted that "most" did not, never mentioning that the DOE's expert analysts had determined the tubes were not suitable for a nuclear weapons program. The NIE also said that Iraq had "begun renewed production of chemical warfare agents"—which the DIA report had left pointedly in doubt. Graham demanded that the CIA declassify dissenting portions.

But even this pressure was insufficient. Defense Secretary Donald Rumsfeld went so far as to create his own intelligence analysis unit within the Pentagon—one that would more likely give him the answers he wished to hear rather than those that the professionals believed were warranted by the evidence. This office, self-mockingly termed "the Cabal," was located inside the Pentagon's Office of Special Plans (OSP). Originally a two-person operation, it soon ballooned to eighteen and relied heavily on information provided by the exile group headed by Ahmad Chalabi, the Iraqi National Congress (INC), and a group of still-unnamed Israelis. Funded and supported by the CIA and friendly American neoconservatives over the years, the INC naturally had a profound interest in encouraging a U.S. invasion of Iraq. A former CIA Middle East station chief told Hersh, "The INC has a track record of manipulating information because it has an agenda. It's a political unit—not an intelligence agency." Moreover, Chalabi himself—despite a history that included a conviction for the embezzlement of millions of dollars in Jordan, to say nothing of his absence from Iraq for a period of more than four decades—was the person chosen by the Defense Department to be the nation's new leader, if only everything had gone according to plan. During his decades in exile he had gotten to know, and reportedly impressed, not only Rumsfeld but also Wolfowitz, Feith, Libby, and former CIA director and Pentagon advisor R. James Woolsey, along with the "man behind the curtain," Richard Perle. What he and his associates did not get to know, however, was Iraq. And it showed.

After the war an inquiry led by Representative David Obey, senior Democrat on the Defense Appropriations Committee, found that the OSP refused to share its information "with established intelligence agencies [and this information] in numerous instances was passed on to the National Security Council and the president without having been vetted with anyone other than political appointees." Continuing the decades-long relationship between Perle and Feith on the one hand, and Israel's Likud Party on the other, it also apparently passed information to and from a similarly ad hoc operation inside Ariel Sharon's office, designed, analogously to the OSP, to bypass the experts in the Mossad and provide the administration with the kind of alarmist information that did not pass professional muster. Again, we are unlikely ever to know the full truth about this operation. In mid-July, during the outbreak of questioning regarding the Niger nuclear documents, Republicans beat back an attempt to appoint a nonpartisan congressional committee of inquiry on the misuse of the intelligence process to justify war.

Iraq Was in League with al Qaeda and May Have Been Involved in the September 11 Attacks

Almost from the moment the planes hit the towers on September 11, many people in and out of the Bush administration began thinking about how the tragedy could be used to advance their longtime goal of a U.S. invasion of Iraq. General Wesley Clark, who headed up the NATO war in Kosovo, reported that he got a call in his home on the very day of the attacks, telling him, "'You got to say this is connected. This is state-sponsored terrorism. This has to be connected to Saddam Hussein.'" When Clark replied, "I'm willing to say it, but what's your evidence?" he received none. What he heard instead was "a lot of pressure to connect this and there were a lot of assumptions made." When asked the source of these phone calls, Clark replied, "Well, it came from the White House, it came from people around the White House. It came from all over." (Clark later clarified his remarks to note that he received no calls from the White House itself.)

Meanwhile, four days after the attack, Vice President Cheney scribbled on his notepad, "Go massive. Sweep it all up. Things related and not." In a meeting of what would come to be called President Bush's "war cabinet," Deputy Defense Secretary Paul Wolfowitz made an argument for an immediate attack on Iraq. Why Iraq rather than Afghanistan, where al Qaeda originated and where its leader, bin Laden, was understood to be living and plotting? Wolfowitz replied, "Attacking Afghanistan would be uncertain. . . . Iraq was a brittle oppressive regime that might break easily. It was doable." Five days later, on September 20, forty neoconservatives, including such luminaries as then Defense Policy Board chair Perle, William Kristol, William Bennett, Norman Podhoretz, Jeane Kirkpatrick, and columnist Charles

Krauthammer, sent an open letter to the White House urging President Bush to attack Hezbollah, Syria, Iran, and Iraq. A failure to follow its advice, the letter warned, "will constitute an early and perhaps decisive surrender in the war on international terrorism."

According to Bob Woodward, Bush told his advisors, "I believe Iraq was involved, but I'm not going to strike them now. I don't have the evidence at this point." He instructed them to continue working on plans for an attack against Iraq but postponed his decision to do so until after dealing with the Taliban. "Start now," he ordered them, "it's very important to move fast." Defense Secretary Donald Rumsfeld all but confirmed this scenario when he explained, after the war, "the coalition did not act in Iraq because we had discovered dramatic new evidence of Iraq's pursuit of weapons of mass murder. We acted because we saw the existing evidence in a new light, through the prism of our experience on September 11."

The planned neoconservative war against Iraq had been brewing since 1991, when President George H. W. Bush, together with Generals Powell and Schwarzkopf, halted U.S. forces on the way to Baghdad after bloodying the Iraqi Republican Guard on the so-called Highway of Death. A series of massacres following U.S.-inspired uprising in the Kurdish north and Shiite south strengthened the moral case for another U.S. intervention on behalf of the people it had so frequently betrayed. Personal considerations were added when the CIA claimed to have detected an Iraqi plot to assassinate ex-president Bush while he was on a visit to Kuwait, though the evidence for this alleged attempt looks a great deal sketchier in retrospect. In 1992 Wolfowitz and Libby oversaw a draft for then defense secretary Cheney of a new Defense Policy Guidance (DPG) that contained implicit arguments for an invasion of Iraq (among other places), but it was ostentatiously rejected by President George H. W. Bush after a leak of its contents led to a public outcry among defense specialists.

Then, in 1996 Richard Perle and Douglas Feith authored a strategic study at the behest of Benjamin Netanyahu, the hard-line Likud ex–prime minister of Israel, in which they argued for an effort to "focus on removing Saddam Hussein from power in Iraq—an important Israeli strategic objective in its own right—as a means of foiling Syria" and remaking Syria. The report, entitled "A Clean Break," suggested that a new Iraqi regime, together with renewed pressure on Syria, could inspire Lebanese Shiite Muslims to reconnect with Iraqi Shiite religious leaders "to wean the south Lebanese [Shiites] away from Hezbollah, Iran and Syria." Like the 1992 DPG this was also rejected as too outlandish, even by so extreme a hawk as the former Israeli prime minister. In 1996 William Kristol and Robert Kagan penned "Toward a Neo-Reaganite Foreign Policy," the founding text of the Project for a New American Century (PNAC), a new think tank devoted to what Wesley Yang aptly terms "neoconservatism's maximalist adventurism." The authors demanded an eighty-billion-dollar increase in the size of the military

budget, with the capacity to intervene everywhere, unfettered by any restraints save those imposed by physics and the laws of nature. (Ironically,
Reagan's primary foreign policy achievement, embracing Mikhail Gor-
bachev's prophetic quest to end the Cold War, was bitterly opposed by
many of those claiming to conduct foreign policy in his name.)

In 1998, under the rubric of PNAC, ten members of the future Bush administration, including Wolfowitz, Rumsfeld, Perle, and Feith, signed a letter
arguing for a unilateral U.S. invasion of Iraq. According to the letter, dated
January 26, 1998, "the U.S. has the authority under existing UN resolutions
to take the necessary steps, including military steps, to protect our vital interests in the Gulf. In any case, American policy cannot continue to be
crippled by a misguided insistence on unanimity in the Security Council."
Indeed, Iraq was so central to the grand strategy mapped out by the PNAC
neoconservatives that they insisted on a lasting U.S. presence there. "While
the unresolved conflict with Iraq provides the immediate justification," the
group argued in a 2000 study signed by Wolfowitz, Libby, Kristol, and
Kagan, among others, "the need for a substantial American force presence
in the Gulf transcends the issue of the regime of Saddam Hussein."

After President Bush considered the Wolfowitz plan but decided to hold
off, Wolfowitz, working through Rumsfeld, almost immediately set out to
find some ammunition. He sent James Woolsey to Europe to investigate
murky reports of connections between al Qaeda and Iraqi intelligence, and
instructed officials on his staff to "get hold of Laurie Mylroie's book [*Study
of Revenge: The First World Trade Center Attack and Saddam Hussein's
War Against America*], which claimed Hussein was behind the 1993 bombing of the World Trade Center, and see if you can prove it." But they could
not do so; nobody could.

When he ultimately asked Congress for the authority to go to war with
Iraq, President Bush sent a letter in which he offered two justifications for
doing so. The first was that he had decided that further diplomacy would be
a waste of time. The second was that the United States was "continuing to
take the necessary actions against international terrorists and terrorist organizations, including those nations, organizations, or persons who planned,
authorized, committed, or aided the terrorist attacks that occurred on September 11, 2001." The language of Bush's letter echoed that of legislation
passed by Congress in October 2002 that gave the president the power to
go to war with Iraq should a link with the September 11 attacks be found.
The connection was never established, as Bush admitted much later. On
January 31, 2003, when a journalist inquired of both Bush and British prime
minister Blair, "Do you believe that there is a link between Saddam Hussein, a direct link, and the men who attacked on September the 11th?" Bush
replied, "I can't make that claim," to which Blair followed up, "That answers your question." (Bush made this admission more explicitly in September 2003.) Later British foreign secretary Jack Straw, who also favored

an invasion, admitted that while he did not rule out such a connection, he, too, had seen no evidence to substantiate it. Finally, when the congressional September 11 investigation was published in late July 2003, it denied any connection between Iraq and al Qaeda. As commission member former senator Max Cleland explained, "The administration sold the connection [between Iraq and al Qaeda] to scare the pants off the American people and justify the war. . . . What you've seen here is the manipulation of intelligence for political ends." Indeed, Cleland charged, "The reason this report was delayed for so long—deliberately opposed at first, then slow-walked after it was created—is that the administration wanted to get the war in Iraq in and over . . . before [it] came out. Had this report come out in January like it should have done, we would have known these things before the war in Iraq, which would not have suited the administration."

But the president and his advisors nevertheless did everything they could to convince Americans and the rest of the world that such a relationship existed, despite the fact that the secularist Hussein and the religious fundamentalist bin Laden were known to despise and frequently denounce each other. When bin Laden was interviewed for CNN in 1997, he was asked about Hussein. "He's a bad Muslim," bin Laden replied. "He took Kuwait for his own self-aggrandizement."

In his October 7 speech in Cincinnati, Bush claimed that high-level contacts between Hussein and al Qaeda "go back a decade." That statement may be (once again) technically accurate but it is also grossly misleading. The contacts in question took place in the early 1990s when the al Qaeda organization was in its infancy and the two men were largely allied against the Saudi monarchy. Bush informed his audience that leaders of al Qaeda had recently left Afghanistan for Baghdad and spoke of a "very senior al Qaeda leader who received medical treatment in Baghdad this year." In fact, the Jordanian Abu Mussab Zarqawi was not, according to U.S. intelligence, actually a member of the bin Laden organization but was the head of a different, unaffiliated group who traveled under many aliases and spent more time in Iran and Lebanon than in Iraq.

"We've learned," Bush continued, "that Iraq has trained al Qaeda members in bomb making and poisons and deadly gases." Again, he failed to mention that his only source was captured al Qaeda soldiers, no doubt eager to tell their captors whatever they wished to hear. Bush would further claim that "Iraq could decide on any given day to provide a biological or chemical weapon to a terrorist group or individual terrorists," and continued, "Alliance with terrorists could allow the Iraqi regime to attack America without leaving any fingerprints." Here, Bush ignored reports by the CIA and other intelligence sources that Hussein had no plans to attack the United States and might conceivably do so only if he was about to be overthrown. Similarly, the intelligence report indicated that Iraq was only likely to give away chemical or biological agents to terrorists as Hussein's "last chance to exact vengeance by taking a large number of victims with him"; even this would be considered an "extreme step." But Bush twisted this finding to imply that the United States would be attacked if it did *not* harm Hussein, a direct contravention of the CIA's finding.

Bush was frequently misleading on this topic without actually crossing over the line into what all would recognize as a lie. For instance, in his 2003 State of the Union, he claimed, "Evidence from intelligence sources, secret communications and statements by people now in custody reveal that Saddam Hussein aids and protects terrorists, including members of al Qaeda. . . . Secretly, and without fingerprints, he could provide one of his hidden weapons to terrorists, or help them develop their own." The theme of Hussein's training and funding of "al Qaeda–type organizations . . . al Qaeda and other terrorist organizations" was a constant feature of the president's speeches. Following a terrorist attack in Bali that left more than 180 people dead, Bush insisted that Hussein planned to employ al Qaeda as his own "forward army" against the West. In a speech to the United Nations on September 12, 2002, Bush charged: "Iraq continues to shelter and support terrorist organizations that direct violence against Iran, Israel, and Western governments. Iraqi dissidents abroad are targeted for murder. . . . And al Qaeda terrorists escaped from Afghanistan and are known to be in Iraq." With Americans he used simple scare tactics that had no basis in recent reality. "Imagine those nineteen hijackers with other weapons and other plans, this time armed by Saddam Hussein," he said in his 2003 State of the Union address. "It would take one vial, one canister, one crate slipped into this country to bring a day of horror like none we have ever known."

Though he never produced any evidence to support it, Bush didn't give up this particular line of argument. Just before the war began, he announced in similarly misleading terms, "The battle of Iraq is one victory in a war on terror that began on September 11, 2001, and still goes on." And in seeking to justify the war in its increasingly unpleasant aftermath before a July 4, 2003, audience of military families at Wright Patterson Air Force Base in Ohio, Bush fell back on his same rhetorical crutch: "Since that September day," he intoned, again making reference to the al Qaeda attack to justify his war against Iraq, "the United States will not stand by and wait for another attack or trust in the restraint and good intentions of evil men. We will not permit any terrorist group or outlaw regime to threaten us with weapons of mass murder."

Others in the administration naturally followed suit. Dick Cheney, for instance, asked the audience of a Sunday-morning talk show to imagine if, on September 11, al Qaeda had "had a nuclear weapon and detonated it in the middle of one of our cities, or if they had unleashed . . . biological weapons of some kind, smallpox or anthrax." He then tied that to evidence found in Afghanistan indicating that al Qaeda leaders "have done everything they could to acquire those capabilities over the years." Recall that he was doing so in support of a war not against al Qaeda, but Iraq. Condoleezza Rice claimed, "There clearly are contacts between al Qaeda and Iraq that can be documented." Well, then, asked Arianna Huffington quite logically, "Why not document them?"

In an address to the UN Security Council Secretary Powell made an elaborate case for what he termed to be a "potentially . . . sinister nexus between Iraq and the al Qaeda terrorist network, a nexus that combines classic terrorist organizations and modern methods of murder." Lacking any genuine evidence to support his position, Powell sought to create the impression of a close tie between the Iraqis and al Qaeda's Abu Musab al Zarqawi, who was supposed to have received medical treatment in Baghdad. Al Zarqawi, Powell said, ran a training camp inside Iraq that specialized in making poisons. But the area he described was in Kurdish-controlled northern Iraq, where Hussein could hardly be said to hold sway. Even if Powell's charges were accurate, it would demonstrate no connections between Hussein and al Qaeda. Moreover, reporters for the *Los Angeles Times* conducted their own apparently quite thorough investigation and found "no strong evidence of [al Qaeda] connections to Baghdad," nor even any evidence of "a sophisticated terrorist organization." They were, rather, another religious group who considered the secular Saddam Hussein to be "an infidel tyrant" and refused to fight under his "infidel flag." In late June 2003 members of a special UN terrorism committee investigating al Qaeda issued their own report. "Nothing has come to our notice that would indicate links between Iraq and al Qaeda," said Michael Chandler, the committee's chief investigator.

"The al Qaeda connection and nuclear weapons issue were the only two ways that you could link Iraq to an imminent security threat to the U.S.," explains Greg Thielmann, formerly INR director for strategic proliferation and military affairs, "and the administration was grossly distorting the intelligence on both things." According to the State Department's most recent annual report on the general subject, titled *Patterns of Global Terrorism,* Baghdad had no ties to al Qaeda or, for that matter, to any of the "al Qaeda–type organizations" operating in the Middle East and Africa. Although the report finds that Iraq has assisted "numerous terrorist groups," those outfits are all secular and "Marxist" or "socialist" in ideology—in other words, "infidels," the insult used by Osama bin Laden to describe Saddam Hussein. That same report, released last year, notes that the "main focus" of Saddam's terror expenditures has been on "dissident Iraqi activity overseas."

Rumsfeld, Wolfowitz, and company also placed their hopes on an alleged meeting between lead September 11 hijacker Mohamed Atta and an Iraqi intelligence official, Ahmed Khalil Ibrahim Samir al Ani, said to have occurred in Prague in April 2001. The claim, which was based on a single uncorroborated informant to Czech intelligence, was bandied about repeatedly in the media, with war supporters like William Safire calling it an "undisputed fact," and Vice President Cheney terming it "pretty well confirmed," even after President Havel informed President Bush that the meeting had almost certainly not taken place. In this regard, it is historically analogous to the alleged North Vietnamese attack on the *Turner Joy* and the *Maddox* in the Gulf of Tonkin, the reality of which was based on the word of a single, uncorroborated eyewitness.

When the high-level al Qaeda leader Abu Zubaydah was finally captured in March 2002 in Pakistan, he informed his captors that bin Laden had personally rejected the idea of any kind of alliance with Hussein. Zubaydah's explanation was later corroborated by testimony from top high-level al Qaeda agents captured later in the spring, including one of the key planners of the September 11 attacks, Khalid Shaikh Mohammed. Farouk Hijazi, a former Iraqi intelligence operative who U.S. officials allege met with al Qaeda operatives and perhaps bin Laden himself in the 1990s, has also denied any Iraq–al Qaeda ties, according to U.S. officials. U.S. military forces also captured Samir al Ani himself in July 2003, but he offered no evidence to support the administration's contention.

While no one could produce any credible evidence of an Iraqi-terrorist connection during at least the past decade, it did seem quite likely that Bush's proposed invasion would lead to a resurgence of anti-American terrorism rather than its diminution. The National Intelligence Estimate predicted that the scenario Bush claimed to be intervening to prevent might actually take place because of his invasion. It found that Hussein was then "drawing a line short of conducting terrorist attacks," but that if Hussein considered a U.S. invasion imminent "he probably would become much less constrained in adopting terrorist actions." It warned, "Saddam, if sufficiently desperate, might decide that only an organization such as al Qaeda could help him strike the U.S. homeland." He might take this "extreme step" of joining with al Qaeda in a terrorist attack against the United States if it "would be his last chance to exact vengeance by taking a large number of victims with him." And even if this worst-case scenario did not emerge, the United States might well increase terrorism in the long run with its unprovoked war.

General Wesley Clark predicted that the result of a unilateral U.S. invasion would be "to supercharge recruiting for al Qaeda." This view was echoed by Daniel Benjamin, who worked in the counterterrorism office in the Clinton administration, noting that the war would likely provide "the propaganda gains the jihadists will make in pointing to this as America attacking Islam. That will give them a big boost in recruiting and fund-raising. There are millions and millions of people whose hearts and minds are in play." Early in the war, a senior American counterintelligence official noted that "the invasion of Iraq is already being used as a recruitment tool by al Qaeda and other groups. . . . And it is a very effective tool." Indeed a surge in al Qaeda recruitment efforts was said to be noticeable in Germany, Britain,

Spain, Italy, and the Netherlands after the war began. "I can't use numbers, but we know the activity is increasing and the willingness to participate and to listen to radical messages is on the rise," added another member of the German interior ministry.

Soon after the major combat portions of the war ended, massive terrorist operations occurred in Saudi Arabia and Morocco. At the same time, foreign nationals from throughout the Arab world began to travel to Iraq to help with the violent resistance being mounted against the U.S. occupation. Saad al Faqih, head of the Movement for Islamic Reform in Arabia, a Saudi dissident group in London, told one interviewer that some three thousand young Saudis had entered Iraq to fight the Americans. He termed the war "a gift to Osama bin Laden." After the bombing of UN headquarters in August 2003 that killed twenty-three innocents and drove away many of the aid workers and volunteers needed to rebuild Iraq, army general John Abizaid, the head of the U.S. Central Command, termed these terrorists to be the "number-one security threat" in Iraq. The Bush administration had tried to hype a phony connection between Hussein and global terrorism before the war and was warned by its own intelligence agencies that while the connection didn't exist yet, the war Bush had planned just might cause one. And as Vincent Cannistraro told a Senate panel after the war, "There was no substantive intelligence information linking Saddam to international terrorism before the war. Now we've created the conditions that have made Iraq the place to come to attack Americans."

Yet Bush himself granted nothing on the issue. Asked by NBC's Tom Brokaw shortly after he prematurely declared victory, "Was the threat overstated?" the president replied, "No, not at all. As a matter of fact, I think time and investigation will prove a couple of points. One, that he did have terrorist connections. And secondly, that he had a weapons of mass destruction program. We know he had a weapons of mass destruction program." (Note the downsizing of Bush's claims here. No one disputes that Hussein *had* "terrorist connections" or that he once "had a weapons of mass destruction program." What they do question is whether either one remained sufficiently dangerous to justify an unprovoked war.)

Yet as late as September 2003, the administration was still peddling this dishonest line, albeit somewhat surreptitiously. Earlier NBC conducted a brief interview with Deputy Defense Secretary Paul Wolfowitz in which he warned of the continuing threat posed by al Qaeda and explicitly linked the ongoing conflict in Iraq to that threat. Several networks reported on growing concerns that al Qaeda may, in fact, have begun to operate in that country, but none saw fit to depict such developments as a consequence of a war that was sold to the public as a means of *preventing* al Qaeda from operating in Iraq. Condoleezza Rice made the original argument that we needed to go to war because Hussein posed a threat in "a region from which the 9-11 threat emerged." Meanwhile, Wolfowitz was proving no less disingenuous than Cheney on this issue. "We know [Iraq] had a great deal to do with terrorism in general and with al Qaeda in particular, and we know a great many of [Osama] bin Laden's key lieutenants are now trying to organize in cooperation with old loyalists from the Saddam regime," he told ABC on the second anniversary of the September 11 attacks. This was false, of course, and a day later Wolfowitz qualified his remarks, telling the Associated Press that he meant a single contact, Abu Musab Zarqawi—who may or may not even have been a member of al Qaeda. "[I] should have been more precise," Wolfowitz admitted. In fact, the reaction by the media to Cheney's misinformation in particular forced the administration to distance itself from his remarks. A couple of days later President Bush went so far as to admit that no evidence pointed to Iraqi involvement in the September 11 attacks, though he stuck to the "there's no question that Saddam Hussein had al Qaeda ties" line. (This too is false.)

Regrettably for the health of American democracy, a majority of Americans, according to polls, fell victim to their own government's serial deception. A February 2003 poll showed that 72 percent of Americans believed it was likely that Saddam Hussein was personally involved in the September 11 attacks. The validity of these figures is supported by a February 2003 Pew Research Center/Council on Foreign Relations survey, which found 32 percent of war supporters citing Saddam's alleged support for terrorists as their "main reason," while another 43 percent gave it as "one reason."

Even more disturbing, a January 2003 poll found that 44 percent of respondents said they thought "most" or "some" of the September 11, 2001, hijackers were Iraqi citizens. Only 17 percent of those polled were aware that none of them was. The answer shocked pollsters, as almost none of those questioned in the aftermath of the attack had cited an Iraqi connection. But the Bush administration had so hammered on this theme that Americans began to imagine something that even the administration had not been willing to argue; for example, a full 41 percent of those questioned believed that Iraq had already obtained the nuclear weapons the administration alleged it was merely pursuing. Later, as many as 69 percent of Americans questioned told pollsters they held Hussein responsible for September 11. Yet on the basis of such widespread misinformation, 66 percent of respondents claimed to have a "good understanding" of the arguments on either side. As Carroll Doherty, editor of the Pew Research Center, told *Editor and Publisher*'s Ari Berman, "There's almost nothing the public doesn't believe about Saddam Hussein."

Was this deception the administration's goal all along? Or did its members, as so many continue to argue, actually believe the misinformation they were passing along to the public in support of their desire to go to war? The available evidence points to deliberate deception, for if President Bush and his advisors were driven by a concern over Iraq's access to weapons of mass destruction—including, possibly, even nuclear weapons—and the likelihood that these weapons would be passed along to terrorist groups willing to use them against the United States and its interests abroad, then wouldn't one expect the first order of business of the invading force to be to secure these sites immediately upon gaining access to Iraq?

Inexplicably, given its own arguments, the Bush administration did not bother to either secure or even inspect those sites it had publicly identified to be the likely loci of nuclear weapons production. In Karbala, U.S. forces left canisters of radioactive material stored openly at a maintenance site completely unguarded. During the month between the beginning of the invasion and the American decision to undertake an investigation of their contents, local villagers plundered them, likely poisoning themselves and their families. Overall, fully seven separate sites said to be associated with the Iraqi nuclear program were left unguarded and unprotected by U.S. forces. As a result, it became impossible to identify, with any certainty, what kinds of materials were being produced and what might be missing.

Judging by their apparent lack of concern with their own credibility following the war, one can only conclude that Bush and his top advisors were willing to gamble that few Americans were likely to hold them responsible for trumping up the reasons for a war against so evil an enemy. A large segment of the media, in awe of the Bush propaganda machine, and concerned that conservatives not question their patriotism, chose to give the administration a pass for its deceptions. The editors of the *Washington Post,* for instance, opined, far too generously, "While the Bush administration may have publicly exaggerated or distorted parts of its case, much of what it said reflected a broad international consensus." Given the weakness of Democratic opposition to the war, coupled with Americans' historic distaste for refighting past battles and of the nonstop cavalcade of patriotic imagery to which they were subjected by the likes of Rupert Murdoch's Fox News Channel and an increasingly Foxified cable news universe, it probably was not that dangerous a gamble after all. Americans, like most people—perhaps even more than most people—are not inclined to decide their sacrifices were for naught unless faced with overwhelming evidence. And given the state of discourse in the United States in the year 2003, that evidence—no matter how bad things looked in postwar Iraq—was not likely to be forthcoming any time soon. Not surprisingly *Time* reported in late June 2003 that "Bush officials believe that time and history are on their side. They argue that now that Saddam is gone, Americans don't care very much about finding WMD." (And if the occupation had gone more smoothly, they may have been right.) While Tony Blair faced a near rebellion in his own party, his parliament, and his country's media, and a significant fall in his personal popularity over his inability to justify his prewar claims, Bush easily brushed off far more serious charges as mere "revisionist history." (And in doing so, he misused both the terms "revisionist" and "history.") "This isn't sticking," said one of Mr. Bush's top political strategists, "because people understand that the world is better off without Saddam Hussein." That was that.

The United States Had to Invade Iraq to Protect Human Rights in Iraq and Defend the Will of the "World Community"

It's certainly true that Saddam Hussein was a murderous dictator and the Iraqi people will one day be better off for his overthrow. But while the president and his underlings made frequent reference to Hussein's brutalities, no serious analyst can claim that these are what ultimately motivated the U.S. invasion.

In his 2003 State of the Union address Bush charged, "The dictator who is assembling the world's most dangerous weapons has already used them on whole villages, leaving thousands of his own citizens dead, blind or disfigured." Yet the United States tolerated Hussein's brutality for decades, going so far as to supply him with weapons, intelligence, and other resources needed to carry it out during his war with Iran and removing him from the State Department's list of terrorist states to make all this more convenient. Moreover, many of the same people who promoted Bush's war—including Cheney, Perle, Wolfowitz, and others—served in the Reagan-Bush Defense Department while this ad hoc alliance was under way. Donald Rumsfeld, like former Republican presidential nominee Robert Dole, personally visited Hussein in Baghdad in December 1983, during the period of gassing, as a special emissary of President Ronald Reagan and managed to avoid the distasteful topic. (Talking points and minutes of the meeting demonstrate that Rumsfeld's primary concern was keeping Hussein informed about America's changing Middle East policy. He also wished to discuss a proposal by the Bechtel Corporation to build an oil pipeline from Iraq to Aqaba, in Jordan, as well as to make sure that Iraq not attack Iran's oil facilities.) Moreover while Dick Cheney was CEO of Halliburton, one of its subsidiaries, Ingersoll Dresser Pump, signed contracts with Hussein's regime—a deal later blocked by the Clinton administration—to rebuild the very oil facilities that Cheney had ordered destroyed when he was George H. W. Bush's defense secretary.

If Iraq had been invaded merely on the basis of its human rights record, it would have had to join an extremely long list of human rights abusers, one that includes nations that have traditionally relied on the U.S. government for support. More than 3 million people are estimated to have died in the current civil war in the Democratic Republic of the Congo, for example, a nation Bush pointedly avoided during his July 2003 trip to Africa. The Congo, a traditional Cold War ally with a longtime dictatorship propped up by Washington for so-called strategic reasons, joins Rwanda, Uganda, Ethiopia, Liberia, Sierra Leone, Zimbabwe, and Eritrea among African countries that come immediately to mind when considering which areas are in most dire need of sustained humanitarian intervention from the world's only hyperpower. Merely to raise this possibility is to demonstrate how empty is the argument that the Bush administration's primary motivation in Iraq was humanitarianism.

Nor can George W. Bush argue—as his father did in 1991—that he was acting on behalf of the "international community"—or as he calls it, "the world." While Saddam Hussein had repeatedly violated UN resolutions calling on his regime to disarm, as administration members kept insisting, U.S. efforts to secure UN assent to its invasion proved to be an embarrassing failure. Diplomatic ambiguity has its purposes, to be sure, but one of them is not to secure global support for an unpopular, unprovoked war. The one measure for which U.S. negotiators were able to garner support—Security Council Resolution 1441, passed with great fanfare in September 2002— contained only vague definitions of what would constitute the desired casus belli, and administration members quickly realized that it did not contain the invasion trigger they sought. The United States's UN ambassador, John Negroponte, admitted on the day the resolution passed, "There's no 'automaticity,' and this is a two-stage process. . . . Whatever violation there is, or is judged to exist, will be dealt with in the council, and the council will have an opportunity to consider the matter before any other action is taken."

Without much hope of Security Council assent, the Bush administration held out an enormous number of diplomatic carrots and sticks in an attempt to enlarge its coalition against Iraq to a remotely respectable number of nations. But despite the billions in bribes and punishments, it almost always came up empty-handed. Not merely "Old Europe" refused to go along, but even such traditional American supporters as Mexico and Chile would not be swayed. Turkey turned down a sixteen-billion-dollar payoff, and an offer by the Americans to sell out the Kurds to appease Turkish concerns about their own population. While only England and Australia were in the end willing to commit troops, materiel, or medical teams—compared with thirty-four legitimate nations in George H. W. Bush's 1991 campaign—not a single nation's population, save that of Israel, supported the war, either before or after the invasion. Even in so-called New Europe, where some governments offered public support for the war, between 70 and 80 percent of the Hungarian, Czech, and Polish populace was opposed, a proportion comparable to those found in the "old" parts of the continent.

If George Bush truly intended to act on behalf of the "international community," as he so frequently insisted, he would have found an alternate method of dealing with the problem of containing Iraq, one that enjoyed the support not merely of the Security Council but also of a significant proportion of the world's population. As Frankfurt School philosopher Jürgen Habermas notes, Bush's "'coalition of the willing' confirmed this failure performatively as it initially sought a 'second' resolution, but in the end refused to bring the motion to a vote because it could not even count on the 'moral' majority of the Security Council not to veto. The whole procedure turned to farce."

Part of the problem was professional incompetence on the part of the Bush team, for the president and his senior advisors eschewed foreign travel or even keeping up reasonable lines of communication. In 1990 George H. W. Bush telephoned the Turkish leader fifty-five to sixty times after Turkey agreed to shut down an oil pipeline to Iraq before the Persian Gulf War began, according to then U.S. ambassador to that nation, Morton Abramowitz. His secretary of state, James A. Baker, made three trips to Turkey in five months in an effort to have Turkish bases opened to the United States after the bombs began to fall. For the current war effort the United States sought to insert sixty-two thousand troops in Turkey, a much more sensitive undertaking, yet Secretary Powell did not pay a single visit to Turkey during this period, while President Bush made a total of three phone calls toward the effort. When the Turks balked at Bush's terms for the deal, Paul Wolfowitz implicitly threatened Turkey's fragile democratic government with a U.S.-supported military coup. He all but admitted as much when he later told CNN, "I think for whatever reason, they [Turkey's generals] did not play the strong leadership role that we would have expected." The threat shocked many democrats, in the United States and abroad. "For a high-ranking American official to urge the undermining of democratic decision-making by military intervention is appalling in any case," said Representative Barney Frank on the floor of the House of Representatives. "It is particularly disturbing in this instance." He went on to call for Wolfowitz's resignation.

Meanwhile, during the lead-up to the final Security Council showdown, the international media were filled with diplomatic complaints over the strong-arm tactics of the Bush team. A former Conservative cabinet minister termed Bush "like a child running around with a grenade with the pin pulled out." "There have been really aggressive battles that have got people's backs up," was the assessment of yet another diplomat whose government publicly supported the U.S. invasion. "People feel bullied, and that can affect the way you respond when someone makes a request."

One of the great ironies of the Bush administration's behavior was that had it been a bit more patient—and diplomatically savvy—it might have gotten its war *and* the assent of the UN Security Council. Although Colin Powell told the world that French president Jacques Chirac had announced that France would refuse to go to war "under any circumstances," the Harvard French scholar Stanley Hoffmann contends that this was yet another purposeful Bush administration misrepresentation. The French president, he reported, had earmarked his country's forces for war "if the inspectors, after a limited number of weeks and after having followed a series of 'benchmarks' not dissimilar from those Tony Blair had demanded, concluded that Iraq did have forbidden weapons and could not be disarmed peacefully." Chirac's demurral therefore referred not to war in general but only to the U.S.-British text of the second resolution, drafted for submission to the Security Council and then withdrawn. On March 16 the administration refused Chirac's proposal to consider the use of force should the inspectors have reached an impasse at the end of a thirty-day deadline. Speaking to Cristiane Amanpour on CBS's *60 Minutes,* Chirac allowed if "our strategy, inspections, were failing, we would consider all the options, including war." On the op-ed page of the *New York Times,* the political philosopher Michael Walzer invited Bush to test French intentions with just such a proposal days before the war began, but it was a no go.

Administration figures occasionally pretended to prefer a peaceful settlement to war. Condoleezza Rice would frequently claim that war remained a last resort. In October 2002 she announced, "We're going to seek a peaceful solution to this. We think that one is possible." Then in November 2002 she said, "We all want very much to see this resolved in a peaceful way." In March 2003 she claimed, "We are still in a diplomatic phase here." However, when asked when he learned that war was a certainty, Richard Haas, who had then been Bush's director of policy planning at the State Department, explained, "The moment was the first week of July [2002], when I had a meeting with Condi. I raised this issue about were we really sure that we wanted to put Iraq front and center at this point, given the war on terrorism and other issues. And she said, essentially, that that decision's been made, don't waste your breath."

No doubt the Bush administration's actions—independent of its policies—not only frustrated the achievement of its own aims, but also contributed to what were widely viewed to be the largest worldwide protests against any government in human history. One U.S. ambassador based in an allied nation cabled home, "Bush has become the enemy." "The debate [overseas] has not been about Iraq," added another State Department official. "There is real angst in the world about our power, and what they perceive as the rawness, the arrogance, the unipolarity" of the administration's position. Perhaps never in its entire history had the United States—with the support of only the population of Israel across the entire globe—been so isolated as it was in the moment that George Bush decided to take it to war, world opinion be damned.

The War and Occupation Would Be Easily Affordable and Welcomed by Iraqis as the "Liberation"

Among the many silences of the Bush administration during the debate over the war, one of the most curious related to its projected cost. The administration consistently refused to offer any reasonable estimates of how much U.S. taxpayers would be asked to lay out for the invasion—not to mention the occupation of Iraq, nor for its subsequent reconstruction. President Bush himself addressed the matter only in clichés, promising U.S. troops would not remain in the region "for one day longer than is necessary."

His chief economic advisor, Lawrence B. Lindsey, was forced out of office in late 2002 after he gave what he thought was an honest—and rather conservative—assessment of $100 billion to $200 billion. When army chief of staff General Eric K. Shinseki accurately suggested that the occupation of Iraq would likely require "something on the order of several hundred thousand soldiers," he spoke with some authority. In 1999 the Pentagon had set up an Iraq war game called "Desert Crossing," which recommended a force of four hundred thousand troops to be ready not only to invade Iraq but also to stabilize it in the postinvasion period. (And, indeed, had the model of peacekeeping deployed in Kosovo been employed for Iraq, the number of troops necessary would have risen to five hundred thousand.) But the neoconservatives—who wanted to keep troops available for future military adventures, as well as to downplay the potential costs of Iraq itself—dismissed the exercise. Deputy Secretary Wolfowitz termed its estimate to be "wildly off the mark," adding, "It's hard to conceive that it would take more forces to provide stability in post-Saddam Iraq than it would to take to conduct the war itself and secure the surrender of Saddam's security forces and his army." In fact, to pick just one example of many, far more troops were required to restore order to Kosovo than were required to conquer it. A commitment to a comparable level of troops for a nation the size of Iraq would require a force of 526,000 through the year 2005.

Ignoring the lessons of past occupations, as well as the strong recommendations of Bush's special envoy to post-Taliban Afghanistan, James Dobbins, prewar Pentagon estimates used a figure of only fifty thousand U.S. soldiers remaining in the region. But as Dobbins has observed, "Only when the number of stabilization troops has been low in comparison to the population"—such as in Somalia, Afghanistan, and now Iraq—"have U.S. forces suffered or inflicted significant casualties." By contrast, in Germany, Japan, Bosnia, and Kosovo—where troop levels were high—Americans suffered *no* postwar combat deaths.

But based on the kind of wishful thinking that characterized so much of U.S. planning, Wolfowitz asserted, "I am reasonably certain that they will greet us as liberators, and that will help us to keep requirements down." But on July 1, 2003, as chaos continued to reign nationwide, U.S. commander in Iraq Tommy Franks acknowledged the accuracy of Shinseki's judgment, admitting to the House Armed Services Committee that 147,000 troops would likely remain in Iraq "for the foreseeable future." As Franks said, "Whether that means two years or four years, I don't know."

Yet another ingredient in the boiling cauldron of voodoo economic assumptions that characterized administration planning was Wolfowitz's prewar argument that thanks to Iraq's oil supplies, "We're dealing with a country that can really finance its own reconstruction, and relatively soon." But a prewar study prepared for the Council on Foreign Relations and the James A. Baker III Institute for Public Policy at Rice University placed reconstruction costs at $30 billion to $40 billion just for the oil industry alone. When other reconstruction costs are factored in, $100 billion is not an outrageous estimate, and even this figure does not include the $4 billion to $5 billion per month the United States will be forced to spend on maintaining order and basic services. Meanwhile, profits from Iraqi oil sales cannot realistically be estimated to amount to more than $20 billion a year and are likely to be a great deal less. Paul Bremer admitted this shortly after the war, noting, "We are going to have to spend a lot more money than we are going to get revenue, even once we get oil production back to prewar levels." As the conservative *Economist* points out, "Wolfowitz is either innumerate (unlikely), or is being economical with the truth." What's more, Wolfowitz and Company should certainly have known this. After the war, in October 2003, the *New York Times* discovered that a government task force assembled to look at this very question and based inside the Pentagon produced a lengthy report that offered evidence of the sustained damage to the Iraqi oil industry, making it unlikely that it would be able to produce anything near what Wolfowitz and Rumsfeld were projecting to Congress. Meanwhile, Iraq is stuck with an enormous amount of foreign debt—roughly $350 billion.

In addition to its overestimation of the Iraqi contribution, the Bush administration refused to provide any prewar cost estimates whatsoever, whether for the war, the occupation, or the reconstruction. This left Congress facing what even the hawkish *Washington Post* editorial board termed "a surreal timetable" that demanded that both the Senate and House approve budget resolutions locking in massive tax cuts for Americans, without "setting aside a penny for war in Iraq." "If you don't know if it's going to last six days, six weeks or six months, how in the world can you come up with a cost estimate?" Donald Rumsfeld insisted. In fact, Rumsfeld had already estimated the costs for the first phase of the war, based on the $80 billion figure (in current dollars) for the previous Gulf War, as well as the cost of the Kosovo bombings. These were presented to Congress shortly after it began. What's more, such amounts were not so difficult to estimate. In November 2002 journalist James Fallows interviewed a group of spies, Arabists, oil-company officials, diplomats, scholars, policy experts, and many active-duty and retired soldiers and managed to project the financial implications of the coming U.S. invasion in a fashion that the U.S. government insisted was beyond its capabilities. Likewise, Yale University economist William D. Nordhaus analyzed the overall effect of a war, both in terms of direct costs and its impact on the U.S. economy. Under one scenario expenses were assessed to be a likely $99 billion over the next decade. But Nordhaus offered a second scenario in which the figure rose as high as $1.9 trillion, which included the cost of a lengthy postwar occupation ($500 billion) and an economic downturn ($391 billion). In late October 2003, the nonpartisan Congressional Budget Office issued an estimate of a cost of $85 billion over four years to $200 billion over ten years for the occupation, not including costs to the U.S. and world economies for slower growth. Nor did they include the soaring costs of reconstruction.

Had the administration been more honest about this whole host of issues, Americans would not have experienced the "sticker shock" they endured when President Bush announced an $87 billion price tag on aid to Iraq in September 2003. This figure was in addition to the $79 billion Congress had approved for the war, bringing the initial down payment on the war to $166 billion. And this total didn't include any money for reconstruction—estimated to cost another $55 billion. Even without the latter investment, owing to President Bush's inability to secure any significant foreign help, the number came to more than twenty-five times the $6.4 billion his father's war had cost Americans. And even the $166 billion, observed Rachel Bronson, director of Middle East Studies at the Council on Foreign Relations, was "probably on the low side of what's needed," though she credited the administration with "finally" entering the "realm of realism."

Before the war, Bush and Company appear to have sidestepped any accusations of hiding their plans for postwar Iraq by simply avoiding almost any recognizable planning. Amazingly, as *The Nation*'s Robert Dreyfuss points out, the administration "did not even bother to prepare and internally publish an intelligence estimate about postwar Iraq." The first such government-wide planning meeting was not even held until February 21, as over one hundred thousand troops were already deployed on Iraq's borders, ready to invade within a month. "The messiah could not have organized a sufficient relief and reconstruction or humanitarian effort in that short a time," Judith Yaphe, a former CIA analyst who attended the session, later explained. (In contrast, U.S. planning for the occupation of Germany had begun a full three years before the end of World War II.)

In a leaked report, and one apparently entirely ignored by the top administration planners, analysts for the U.S. Army War College's Center for Strategic Leadership predicted low-end manpower requirements for a military occupation expected to last not a matter of months, but a minimum of five years and possibly as many as ten. The study, entitled "The Day After: The Army in a Post-Conflict Iraq," published in February 2003, predicted many of the very same problems that resulted from the Pentagon's poor planning and rose-tinted assumptions. It warned, "Without an overwhelming effort to prepare for occupation, the U.S. may find itself in a radically different world over the next few years, a world in which the threat of Saddam Hussein seems like a pale shadow of new problems of America's own making."

Its authors forecast the post-Saddam environment for U.S. troops as "very unstable." Such crucial institutions as the police and judiciary were deemed to be "dysfunctional due to the purging of the top leadership and no replacements." U.S. soldiers, it predicted, would find themselves constantly endangered as "some Iraqi military units are operating at will and conducting guerrilla attacks throughout the country. Sunni, Shiite, and Kurdish tribal leaders are ruling respective areas and are initiating frequent skirmishes in an effort to expand their power base."

The report continued, "In many cases, the army will be the only entity capable of providing much needed assistance and the required security aspects of the relief effort." These challenges—and many others rarely discussed by the Bush administration or in the mainstream media—demonstrated to its authors that "post-conflict Iraq security tasks may include control of belligerents, territorial security, protection of the populace, protection of key individuals, infrastructure and institutions, and reform of all indigenous security institutions," and would require "well over one hundred essential services that the army must provide or support." The "resultant stress on the army mobilization function" could, the report predicted, be overwhelming. A CIA study reached similar conclusions and warned that the Iraqis "would probably resort to obstruction, resistance and armed opposition if they perceived attempts to keep them dependent on the United States and the West." According to one senior administration official, the agency was "utterly consistent in arguing that reconstruction rather than war would be the most problematic segment of overthrowing Saddam." But Pentagon planners, relying on Chalabi and their own coterie of intelligence analysts and the dictates of their ideological obsessions, ignored such advice. "We fooled ourselves into thinking we would have a liberation over an occupation," admitted a U.S. official stationed in Baghdad. "Why did we do that?" One answer came from the State Department: "The problems came about when the office of the secretary of defense wouldn't let anybody else play—or play only if you beat your way into the game," a State Department official said. "There was so much tension, so much ego involved."

After rejecting nine State Department nominees Rumsfeld gave the top job of running Iraq to former lieutenant general Jay M. Garner, who had also been president of SY Technology, a southern California defense contractor. There, Garner grew close to the Israelis while working on that nation's $2 billion Arrow missile-defense system. Because of these sympathies, he may have been attractive to the administration neoconservatives, but his views were hardly likely to endear him to Iraq's virulently anti-Israel population. In any case, Garner did not appear to be up to the job, though to be fair, he was also hampered by the behavior of those who supported him. Fully sixteen of his chosen appointments were vetoed by Donald Rumsfeld as, according to *Newsweek,* "Arabist apologists, or squishy about the United Nations, or in some way politically incorrect to the right-wing ideologues at the White House or the neocons in the office of the Secretary of Defense. The vetting process 'got so bad that even doctors sent to restore medical services had to be anti-abortion,' recalled one of Garner's team." Not even the official who oversaw the State Department's yearlong postwar planning initiative and predicted many of the horrific consequences of the invasion, Tom Warrick, made the cut. And this despite an almost total lack of expertise on Garner's team, save the fantasy-riddled hopes of their chosen Iraqi exiles. Garner was replaced almost as quickly as he was appointed.

A second oddity of the administration's postwar lack of planning was its original choice for the new Iraqi leader, indicted embezzler Ahmad Chalabi. In selecting the mercurial Chalabi—who was known primarily for his reputation as a snappy dresser and a first-class schmoozer in London, and who had not set foot in Baghdad in roughly four decades—Pentagon officials ignored the War College report's estimation that "it is doubtful that the Iraqi population would welcome the leadership of the various exile groups after Saddam's defeat. . . . Iraqi citizens who have suffered under Saddam could well resent Iraqis coming from outside the country following a war and claiming a disproportionate amount of power." But like Garner, Chalabi was favored by neoconservatives and other supporters of Israel's Likud government. According to Richard Perle, "Chalabi and his people have confirmed . . . that they would recognize the state of Israel."

Early in the war U.S. military planes flew Chalabi, joined by Harold Rhode, a top aide to Undersecretary of Defense for Policy Douglas Feith, together with seven hundred troops into Nasiriyah to be integrated into the U.S. command structure. But according to the AP's Jonathan Landay, "Chalabi had had difficulty recruiting enough forces to go into southern Iraq and may have tapped the discredited Badr Brigade, an Iranian-backed Shiite Muslim group." In other words, not only was he regarded as extremely sympathetic to Israel, he may also have been working with the enemy, Iran. Upon arriving in Iraq with the American stamp of approval, Chalabi received virtually no visible support from the nation to whose leadership he pretended. Like Garner he was quickly shoved aside by U.S. officials looking for credible Iraqi authority figures to whom to entrust even a temporary administration. President Bush never said truer words than those he is quoted as having uttered by a former senior White House official: "The future of this country . . . is not going to be charted by people who sat out the sonofabitch in London or Cambridge, Massachusetts." And yet, though the president may not have known it, it was upon the unreliable intelligence provided by exactly those exiles "who sat out the sonofabitch" in the comfort of London and Cambridge that he and his advisors made the ultimate decision to go to war.

Whatever the relative honesty, or lack thereof, of its prior justification, Bush's war must ultimately be judged, like most endeavors, on the basis of costs and benefits. The latter are obvious and are given voice on a daily basis by the administration and its supporters: A vicious dictator was removed from power and no longer threatened either his own population or those in neighboring nations. Eventually, Iraqis may be free to choose their own form of government and create a society consistent with their own principles and desires.

But the invasion's debits continue to mount at a rather alarming rate. Of course, there are the obvious ones: death and destruction. Because the U.S. military has no interest in such statistics, however, we will never be able to estimate the true extent of the number of Iraqi civilians or soldiers killed in the war. Despite the use of precision-guided munitions and "smart bombs," at least seventeen hundred Iraqi civilians died and more than eight thousand were injured in Baghdad alone, according to a *Los Angeles Times* survey of records from twenty-seven hospitals in the capital and its outlying districts. Undocumented civilian deaths in Baghdad may reach one thousand according to Islamic burial societies and humanitarian groups. (The best estimate the Bush administration could give, as it kept no records, was Paul Bremer's description of the number as "really very low.") The Iraqi public health predicament appeared to be complicated by the Bush administration's decision to allow the military to employ weapons that made use of depleted uranium, a low-level radioactive waste byproduct of the nuclear weapons manufacturing process. Extremely effective from a military perspective, the weapon appears also to be vastly increasing the number of congenital birth defects and leukemia cases among Iraqi children since its first use during the 1991 Gulf War. In addition, according to the Baghdad representative of UNICEF, the chaos engendered by the U.S. invasion and failure to maintain stability afterward had the effect of endangering the lives of more than three hundred thousand Iraqi children. Twice as many children under age five in urban centers were believed to be suffering from acute malnutrition than was the case a year earlier.

The Pentagon also rebuffed efforts by archaeological experts to meet with those planning the invasion in the hopes of minimizing the degree of destruction to much of humankind's heritage, as ancient Mesopotamia happened to be located within modern-day Iraq. While the extent of the looting of the national museum—left unguarded by U.S. troops stationed nearby in the oil ministry—did prove exaggerated by early media reports, this unfortunately did not prove to be the case nationally, according to a group of American archaeologists who undertook a systematic assessment of the damage. University of Michigan anthropologist Henry T. Wright, who led the team of scientists, found sites "ripped from the ground in the same way as you tear pages of history." These artifacts, not yet cataloged or studied, contained cuneiform tablets that, in the ensuing chaos, were pillaged and destroyed by looters. And the damage that resulted from the looting of the museum was hardly trivial. According to its director, Dr. Nawalaal Mutawalli, a preliminary search found that some thirteen thousand objects were missing from its collection and forty-seven pieces had been taken from its exhibition room, with seven described as "very important masterpieces."

Much of the chaos on the ground in Iraq was directly attributable to the aversion shared at the top levels of the Bush war-planning team for what they derisively term "nation-building." Like Afghanistan, postwar Iraq quickly reverted to a kind of Hobbesian state of nature with marauding bandits, no recognized civil authority, mass rape and pillaging, with only intermittent water and electricity. The city of Basra lacked a functioning health ministry to procure drugs. Water shortages led to cholera as residents were forced to drink from rivers that doubled as sewers. The number of reported gun-related killings in Baghdad has increased since President Bush declared an end to major combat May 1—from an average of 20 deaths a month in prewar times to 872 deaths in August 2003. "It presented us with a hard problem," Garner later admitted. "Our plan was to immediately stand up twenty of twenty-three existing ministries," he says. "But seventeen of them had been vaporized."

U.S. troops soon found themselves beset by guerrilla attacks of an increasingly brazen nature. So, too, did Iraqis who cooperated with the occupational forces: Members of the first class of Iraqi policemen were murdered during their graduation ceremony. And because of Bush's snubbing of the United Nations, the American officials found themselves facing this nightmarish situation with the sole assistance of the British. As late as October 2003, few if any of these problems had been solved. Resistance among Iraqis was increasing; retaliation against those who cooperated with U.S. authorities grew more brutal, and longtime military officers began to speak more and more of Vietnam. Finally, in October 2003, the White House once again attempted to reorganize its efforts in order to bring a measure of minimal coherence to its various policies in Iraq. "The president knows his legacy, and maybe his re-election, depends on getting this right," an administration official was quoted as saying. "This is as close as anyone will come to acknowledging that it's not working." Incredibly, in the midst of what nearly all disinterested observers were being forced to admit was a rapidly deteriorating catastrophe—and on a day when Iraqi guerrillas managed to kill 45 people and wound another 250—George Bush offered this nakedly Orwellian defense of the U.S. incursion. "There are terrorists in Iraq who are willing to kill anybody in order to stop our progress. The more success-ful we are on the ground, the more these killers will react." By this logic, if all Iraqis and American soldiers are eventually killed, the entire operation may be judged a total success. It led the former Vietnam War POW, Republican senator, and strong war supporter John McCain (R-AZ) to observe, "This is the first time that I have seen a parallel to Vietnam, in terms of information that the administration is putting out versus the actual situation on the ground.

The chaos engendered by America's inability to make good on its promises to the Iraqi people provided an opportunity for exactly the kinds of terrorists to take root that the United States claimed to be invading Iraq to root out. The notorious Hezbollah was reported to be forming a branch in Baghdad. Armed militias sprouted up, ranging in size, according to *The New Republic,* from five hundred men for Hizb Al Dawa, a leading theocratic Shia group, to more than two thousand fighters for SCIRI, whose armed wing is called the Badr Brigade. SCIRI, like several of these organizations, allegedly received training for its militias from Iran's Revolutionary Guards. Another group, made up of former Ba'athists, was also reported to be creating a militia of Saddam loyalists, no doubt spurred on by Al-Jazeera's broadcast of an audiotape deemed by the CIA likely to be that of Hussein himself, urging resistance.

The editors of the *Financial Times* in London observed prematurely in July 2003, "It has now dawned on the United States that its massive military machine may be sufficient to conquer a country but not necessarily to hold or police it." And yet despite all the amassed evidence that its team was not up to the job of policing postwar Iraq—much less restoring some normalcy to civilian life—the Bush administration stuck with its stubborn "We'll go it alone" policy. "We're utterly surprised," a senior UN diplomat told Fareed Zakaria. "We thought that after the war, the United States would try to dump Iraq on the world's lap and the rest of the world would object, saying, 'This is your mess, you clean it up.' The opposite is happening. The rest of the world is saying, 'We're willing to help,' but Washington is determined to run Iraq itself." Even when President Bush came to the UN to ask for help, he admitted no mistakes and offered no concessions whatsoever. As a result, he secured no assistance from the rest of the world, and nothing but enmity from the rest of the Security Council, many of whose nationals had been killed during the bombing of Iraq's UN headquarters. As France's *Le Figaro* reported, "not one of the 191 countries represented there had responded to his appeal for help with a concrete promise, whether in the form of a financial contribution or by placing troop contingents at his disposition. The UN even decided to withdraw part of their expatriate personnel in Iraq, undermining American normalization efforts a little more." Virtually the entire cost of the war and the ensuing reconstruction would be borne by the American taxpayer.

Meanwhile, efforts to involve the Iraqis in their own governance had to be repeatedly postponed. In late June Bremer ordered an end to elections and self-rule in provincial cities across Iraq. The combination of apparently unending chaos, incompetence, occupation, and increasing violence probably caused whatever goodwill Americans might have earned for their toppling of Hussein's dictatorship to largely dissipate. In Najaf, for instance, masses of demonstrators joined together to demand elections, with banners reading, "Canceled elections are evidence of bad intentions" and "O America, where are promises of freedom, elections, and democracy?" The military proved to be hardly the proper tool to deliver to the Iraqis what they needed in the aftermath of the wholesale destruction of their society. Captain James Ogletree, a marine civil-affairs officer in Karbala, says his units receive orders like: "'See how many orphanages there are in the city and what they need.'" He carries these out as far as possible, with the result that "marines who pull triggers are going into schools and saying 'OK, it needs this many windows?'"

As a result of decisions like those just described—and many more too numerous to catalog—a dynamic containing most identifiable characteristics of a quagmire soon asserted itself on the ground in Baghdad, as violence and chaos begat more violence and chaos. "Over the next months, I expect a vicious cycle in which force-protection measures will alienate the population and create more opposition to the occupation, with rising casualties," predicted Laurence Pope, a retired State Department expert on the Arab world who served as a political advisor at the Central Command. In mid-July 2003 General John P. Abizaid, America's new commander of allied forces in Iraq, admitted that Iraqis were "conducting what I would describe as a classical guerrilla-type campaign against us. . . . It's low-intensity conflict, in our doctrinal terms, but it's war, however you describe it." A bitter Lieutenant Colonel Karen Kwiatkowski, who had worked in the office where the plans were drafted before her retirement, blamed "the key decision-makers in the Pentagon" for "the odd set of circumstances that placed us as a long-term occupying force in the world's nastiest rat's nest, without a nation-building plan, without significant international support and without an exit plan." She worried that they would "[n]ever be required to answer their accusers, thanks to this administration's military as well as publicity machine, and the disgraceful political compromises already made by most of the Congress."

Naturally, the strain on the soldiers asked to serve in these conditions proved considerable. "It's like we won the Super Bowl," complained one, "but we have to keep on playing." "Make no mistake, the level of morale for most soldiers that I've seen has hit rock bottom," added another, an officer from the army's 3rd Infantry Division. "Faced with continued resistance, Department of Defense now plans to keep a larger force in Iraq than anticipated for a period of time," Major General Buford Blount, commander of the 3rd Infantry Division, eventually explained in a statement to soldiers' families in June 2003. "I appreciate the turmoil and stress that a continued deployment has caused." President Bush responded to the increasing sense of crisis with what *New York Times* editors generously termed "misplaced bravado": "There are some who feel that conditions are such that they can attack us there," he announced to reporters at the White House in late June. "My answer is bring 'em on." On the following day twenty U.S. soldiers were wounded in attacks across Iraq. Two weeks later Minnesota Public Radio quoted Mary Kewatt, the aunt of a soldier killed in Iraq, as follows: "President Bush made a comment a week ago, and he said 'bring it on.' Well, they brought it on, and now my nephew is dead."

The White House reaction? First it ordered severe punishments for the soldiers who shared their thoughts with reporters. "It was the end of the world," said one officer. "It went all the way up to President Bush and back down again on top of us. At least six of us here will lose our careers." Presaging its campaign against Joseph Wilson, next it passed along a leak to cybergossip Matt Drudge, resulting in the screaming headline on *The Drudge Report,* "ABC NEWS REPORTER WHO FILED TROOP COMPLAINTS STORY— OPENLY GAY CANADIAN," as if this news somehow discredited his report. Could Joe McCarthy himself have been any more efficient?

A U.S. Invasion Will Create the First Arab Democracy and Therefore Inspire the Arab World to Embrace Western Values

Perhaps the most genuinely idealistic reason to have supported George Bush's war in Iraq was the hope of many that Paul Wolfowitz and others were serious when they predicted that Iraq would become "the first Arab democracy" and that even modest democratic progress in Iraq would "cast a very large shadow, starting with Syria and Iran but across the whole Arab world." William Kristol went so far as to suggest before the Senate Foreign Relations Committee that "reconstructing Iraq may prove to be a less difficult task than the challenge of building a viable state in Afghanistan," which, given the state of things in that benighted nation, turned out to be a modest boast.

These views, to the degree that they were seriously considered at all, can be argued to have proceeded from dangerously ahistorical assumptions, for history demonstrates just how difficult democracy is to export even under the best of circumstances. A recent study by the Carnegie Endowment for International Peace found a meager 25 percent success rate for the United States during the past century in sixteen such attempts. And in each of the successful cases—Germany, Grenada, Japan, and Panama—the barriers were nowhere near as formidable as in Iraq, whose people have had no experience whatever with the practice of democracy and few of what most political scientists consider its necessary preconditions. A study by several World Bank economists, led by Oxford University professor Paul Collier, notes that developing nations with significant natural resources often experience intense violent internal conflict, as we have seen in Angola, Congo, Indonesia, Nigeria, and Sierra Leone, among many others. With the diversity of its religious and ethnic groups, violently oppressed by decades of brutal Ba'ath rule, it hardly seems a stretch to imagine a similarly unhappy path for postwar Iraq. Indeed, a secret CIA report preceding the invasion judged the alternative to be, in all likelihood, "impossible."

Yet here again, administration planners preferred to ignore the internal guidance they received. A classified State Department study reportedly questioned many of their assumptions well before the invasion, arguing that Iraq's enormous economic and social problems would likely undermine basic stability in the region for years, much less serve as fertile ground for a stable democracy. And even if one did somehow come into being, anti-American sentiment was considered to be so pervasive that truly democratic elections in the short term could lead to the rise of an Islamic republic consumed with hatred for the United States.

The country's problems are also deeply interwoven. Noting that "Iraqi political values and institutions are rooted in a tortured history that must be understood before it is possible to consider the rehabilitation of Iraqi society," the report summarized hundreds of years of Iraq's violent tribal history before concluding, "The establishment of democracy or even some sort of rough pluralism in Iraq, where it has never really existed previously, will be a staggering challenge for any occupation force," particularly given a society "where anti-democratic traditions are deeply ingrained." This view was seconded by the previously mentioned Army War College report, whose authors warned, "U.S. policymakers sometimes assume that a democratic government will be friendly to U.S. policies in the Middle East. This cannot," the report states, "be assumed in the case of Iraq." The same conclusion was reached by knowledgeable observers outside the administration, had the Bush team been paying attention.

While no one could foresee with any certainty the future of a liberated Iraq, useful precedents allowed for intelligent predictions. Sunni Arabs, who controlled the country through its Ba'ath Party, make up only 17 percent of the Iraqi population, with the Shiites and Kurds making up roughly three-quarters. The Iraqi exile Kanan Makiya viewed the post-1991 chaos in Iraq, when Kurds in the north and Shiites in the south rose up against Saddam, to be so extreme that he spoke of a "basic nihilistic impulse." Former Senate aide Peter Galbraith, who had devoted a considerable portion of his life to helping to secure protection for the Kurds, told a journalist, "A unified and democratic Iraq is an oxymoron. The important point about the north is that the Iraqi identity is disappearing there." Author George Packer pointed out that "Iraq's Shiites—the most disenfranchised group, with the freshest grievances and the strongest claim on a share of power—will challenge the policing and diplomatic skills of an army of occupation," even assuming the most optimistic of scenarios. Outside Iraq Iran was poised to exploit the situation to its benefit, with its Shiite-driven fundamentalist revolution and potentially expansionist claims. And then there was Turkey to the north, worried about the potential creation of a de facto independent Kurdistan on its vulnerable border and the effects this could have on its own independence-seeking Kurdish population.

Even less credible than the administration's belief in the creation of a generation of Iraqi Jeffersons and Madisons were its intimations that much of the rest of the Arab world was poised to embrace democracy as well. David Frum offered a typical expression of this naive faith in his memoir, *The Right Man:* "American-led overthrow of Saddam Hussein—and a replacement of the radical Ba'athist dictatorship with a new government more closely aligned with the United States—would put America more wholly in charge of the region than any power since the Ottomans, or maybe the Romans." This, presumably, would lead to what administration officials claimed would be a "democracy domino" effect, with, as Packer described it, "tyrannies collapsing on top of one another." According to Richard Perle, the U.S. invasion had "the potential to transform the thinking of people around the world about the potential for democracy, even in Arab countries where people have been disparaging of their potential." William Kristol even suggested that a U.S. invasion would inspire "the principles of liberty and justice in the Islamic world" generally.

This was what one analyst termed "magical realism, Middle East–style." William F. Schulz, head of Amnesty International, describes the Bush-neoconservative policy only partially in jest as "become a democracy tomorrow or we bomb the shit out of you." And indeed, examined closely, the belief in the creation of an Arab democratic revolution, inspired from without by means of a war that is universally opposed within the region and by a power that is everywhere feared, despised, or both, collapses almost instantly. During the period of the run-up to the war and its aftermath, human rights advocates and honest journalists were being rounded up and jailed in U.S.-friendly nations like Saudi Arabia and Egypt. The former was shutting down independent newspapers; the latter continued to operate under the emergency laws in effect since the 1967 Six-Day War. In Jordan democracy advocates were barred from running for the (until recently, dissolved) legislature. And these countries—unlike Syria, Iran, or Iraq—are considered to be the relatively easy cases, the nations open and sympathetic to Western influence and ideas. Surveying the rest of the Arab world, Ken Jowitt acknowledged in the journal *Policy Review,* which is published by the extremely conservative and prowar Heritage Foundation:

> It is true that a more democratically inclined Iranian middle class exists. The problem? Most of it lives in Los Angeles. As for the part remaining in Iran, unlike the Polish middle class at the time of Solidarity's revolution against the Communist Party, the Iranian middle classes have no experience organizing against or fighting the regime. Even Iranian students who have a much more favorable base for organizing have been singularly ineffectual in their demands for a more moderate mode of rule.
>
> In Syria, efforts at liberalization will immediately threaten the rule of Bashar al Assad, his family, the group of generals that support him, the merchants that depend on him, and most of all the minority group that rules Syria, the Alawis, a quasi-Muslim sect that the Sunni majority regard as heretics and unbelievers. Should the Assad regime fall, his family and fellow Alawis would be exposed to widespread murderous violence.
>
> The majority of Jordan's population is Palestinian, not Hashemite, Bedouin, and Circassian. How will democracy square with the direct electoral threat it poses to the Hashemite dynasty in general and to King Abdullah's family rule in particular? In a similar fashion, democratization, even liberalization, directly threatens Mubarak's determined efforts to groom his son Gamal as successor and guarantor of his authoritarian family rule in Egypt.
>
> And Saudi Arabia, far from becoming an isolated Arab "North Korea" in the allegedly democratic Middle East that will follow regime change in Iraq, the al-Saud family will maintain enormous economic leverage, even after "democratic" oil flows from Iraq and the Caspian. And if, as I am suggesting, authoritarian family rule is the defining feature of the Middle East, how likely is it that a family like the al-Saud will look to Great Britain or Norway as a model for their family and kingdom?

There are those who hopefully compare the situation in Iraq to the post–World War II U.S. occupation of Japan—where, like Iraq (and unlike Germany), no democracy existed until the United States created it. The preeminent historian of the Japanese occupation, John Dower, discredits that notion rather quickly. "We do not have the moral legitimacy we had then," he notes, "nor do we have the other thing that was present when we occupied Japan—the vision of the American public that we would engage in serious and genuinely democratic nation-building and that we would do this in the context of an international order." In January 2003 Dower joined thirty-five of his colleagues among scholars of the occupation to denounce the notion that the two examples were, in any remote fashion, analogous.

Why, Really?

Ultimately, George W. Bush had any number of reasons to want to invade Iraq, but the most compelling ones seem to have been the most personal. At a September 2002 Republican fund-raiser in Houston, he justified his desire to go to war because Saddam Hussein was "the guy who tried to kill my dad." According to a translation of minutes of a meeting between Palestinian factions in the spring of 2003, published in the Israel newspaper *Ha'aretz,* Bush informed Palestinian prime minister Mahmoud Abbas, "God told me to strike at al Qaeda and I struck them, and then he instructed me to strike at Saddam, which I did." (The White House denied this statement.) White House sources told the *Financial Times* that for Bush, the determination to take the United States to war was largely a matter of personal pique: "A tinpot dictator was mocking the president. It provoked a sense of anger inside the White House." Coupled with the fact that the decision was never vetted by the typical bureaucratic procedures—according to Condoleezza Rice, Bush literally stuck his head inside her door in July 2002 and informed her, "Fuck it, we're taking him out"—the entire process strikes one as so fantastic as to be hard to synthesize.

John Brady Keisling, a veteran and much-decorated U.S. foreign service officer who resigned over the deceptions of the war, believes that the president himself was "easy to convince." Keisling sees Bush as "a politician who badly wants to appear strong but in reality is very weak," and therefore "blindly believed Rumsfeld's assurances that the occupation of Iraq would pay for itself." Again, this is ultimately unknowable, but it so happens that the man whom Donald Rumsfeld and Paul Wolfowitz chose to provide their president with exactly the kind of intelligence they needed to justify an invasion, Abram M. Shulsky, is, like Wolfowitz and many other neoconservatives, an admirer of the movement's founding father, the late political philosopher and refugee from Nazi Germany Leo Strauss. Together with PNAC head Gary Schmitt, Shulsky authored an essay published in 1999 entitled "Leo Strauss and the World of Intelligence (By Which We Do Not Mean Nous)." In it, the authors argue that Strauss's idea of hidden meaning "alerts one to the possibility that political life may be closely linked to deception. Indeed, it suggests that deception is the norm in political life, and the hope, to say nothing of the expectation, of establishing a politics that can dispense with it is the exception."

Robert Pippin, the chairman of the Committee on Social Thought at the University of Chicago and a critic of Strauss, said, "Strauss believed that good statesmen have powers of judgment and must rely on an inner circle. The person who whispers in the ear of the king is more important than the king. If you have that talent, what you do or say in public cannot be held accountable in the same way." NYU law professor Stephen Holmes added, "They believe that your enemy is deceiving you, and you have to pretend to agree, but secretly you follow your own views." He continued, "The whole story is complicated by Strauss's idea—actually Plato's—that philosophers need to tell noble lies not only to the people at large but also to powerful politicians." Even Strauss's admirers do not hesitate to grant this essential point with regard to the founding father of neoconservatism. Joseph Cropsey, Strauss's close friend and colleague at the University of Chicago as well as the editor of his work, explains that in Straussian thought, a degree of public deception is considered absolutely necessary. "That people in government have to be discreet in what they say publicly is so obvious—'If I tell you the truth I can't but help the enemy.'"

The neoconservatives who provided the intellectual stimulus for the Bush administration's foreign policies had an armada of what they believed to be good reasons to promote within the administration an invasion of Iraq. Their formal reasoning was laid out consistently and without apology in such documents as the Libby-Wolfowitz 1992 strategy document, authored for Dick Cheney and George H. W. Bush; the 1996 Perle-Feith study for Benjamin Netanyahu; the Kristol-Kagan 1996 "Toward a Neo-Reaganite Foreign Policy" essay; the Wolfowitz-Rumsfeld-Perle-Feith letter calling for an invasion published the same year; and the PNAC "Rebuilding America's Defenses" policy statement published in 2000, signed by Wolfowitz, Libby, Bolton, and others. This strategic kibitzing was finally codified as official U.S. government policy in September 2002, with the release of "National Security Strategy of the United States," which adopted many of the strategic imperatives and policy priorities for which the neocons had been agitating, even echoing the above documents' language and emphases. It's hard to know how seriously to take a strategy that commits the United States to "rid the world of evil," but of course, with good Straussians, we can neither credit nor discount formal policy statements, as they may contain nothing more than "noble lies."

But an invasion of Iraq presented any number of opportunities and potential benefits from an ideological perspective that could not be honestly and openly identified in official policy documents. It removed a significant threat to Israel and, once all went according to plan, would also help to demoralize the Palestinians and force them to accept their lot in life as an occupied people with reduced resistance. This was explicit in the Perle-Feith document prepared for Netanyahu and was undoubtedly implicit in the planning for the Iraq war. The war also provided the United States with an occasion to show the Arab world that it was willing to respond accordingly if they behaved offensively. Dismissing Bush administration rhetoric as offered "for PR reasons" in a column entitled "Because We Could," prowar columnist Thomas Friedman posits this as the "real" reason for the war.

"After 9/11 America needed to hit someone in the Arab-Muslim world," he writes. Olivier Roy, a specialist on the Islamic world at the Centre National de la Récherche Scientifique, described this argument as follows:

> The rationale for the military campaign in Iraq was not that Iraq was the biggest threat but, on the contrary, that it was the weakest and hence the easiest to take care of. The invasion was largely aimed at demonstrating America's political will and commitment to go to war. Reshaping the Middle East does not mean changing borders, but rather threatening existing regimes through military pressure and destabilizing them with calls for democratization. After Baghdad's fall, Teheran, Damascus and Riyadh should understand that America is back.

This rationale is consistent with Undersecretary of Defense Douglas Feith's argument that Iraq itself was never really so critical an issue. "Can you imagine what our enemies think of us right now?" asked Feith. "The deterrent value of what we've accomplished far overshadows the direct results."

Then there's the oil. It's not merely a matter of Bush and Cheney distributing favors to their former cronies, friends, and business associates in the energy industry, though they were no doubt pleased to be able to do so. Rivals did not even bother bidding after the Cheney home team, Halliburton, won the lion's share of a billion-dollar rebuilding contract for the Iraqi oil industry in what looked to many to be a nakedly rigged process. And this practice was hardly an isolated one. The United States's takeover of Iraq also had the effect of vastly reducing the power and influence of the Saudis—whom, as we have seen, the Bushes appear to find quite sympathetic, but the neocons find repugnant—to keep our foreign policy, as it were, over a barrel.

In May 2003 crude oil imports to the United States reached a record high for the third straight month, as just more than 320 million barrels. According to Vice President Cheney's National Energy Policy Development Group, U.S. oil production is expected to fall by 12 percent during the coming two decades. The Saudis, meanwhile, are currently understood to be in possession of about 250 billion barrels, or a quarter of the world's oil reserves. Given America's apparently incurable oil-dependency—and the Bush administration's aversion to conservation—the Saudis therefore enjoy enormous political influence over Washington, despite the blind eye they have traditionally turned toward anti-American terrorism and their apparent role in encouraging bin Ladenism and Arab hatred for both the United States and Israel. It is hardly good policy for the world's most powerful nation to ally its fate to a deeply corrupt and reactionary, theocratic "royal family" like that in power in the Saudi kingdom. Moreover, U.S. troops protecting Saudi Arabia are understood by all to be one of the primary motivations for bin Laden's jihad. Paul Wolfowitz himself termed them to be "a huge recruiting device for al Qaeda," and their removal, therefore, according to Wolfowitz, would be a "huge improvement" over the previous situation. "We have a new ally in the Middle East and one that is secular, modern, and pro–free market," announced Francis Brooke, an American political advisor to Ahmad Chalabi. "It's time to replace the Saudis with the Iraqis."

With its 112 billion barrels in proven reserves and a potential for anywhere from 200 billion to 300 billion barrels, Iraq just happens to be the only nation on earth graced with a supply of oil reserves comparable to—and possibly even in excess of—those in Saudi Arabia. Iraqi oil is also wonderfully inexpensive to extract. Because it is trapped at such a high level of pressure in the ground, it does not require the "noodling donkeys" necessary to force it from the ground, as in places like Texas or Oklahoma. With the additional advantage of extremely cheap labor, Iraqi oil is just about the least expensive oil to produce on the planet. But although its production cost is a mere two dollars per barrel—compared with roughly six dollars in Texas—it sells for the same twenty-seven dollars per barrel on the open market. Clearly these factors contributed to the attractiveness of war with Iraq, rather than, say, Iran, Syria, or North Korea.

Control over Iraq's reserves would enable a U.S. president to get tough with the Saudis in a way that none have been able to imagine since the first Arab oil embargo of 1973. It would also help the U.S. economy over the long term by providing a stable supply at stable prices. The United States could even order the Iraqis to withdraw from OPEC, possibly crippling that body's power to set global oil prices and the terms of its supply. Even apart from their economic value per se, the oil reserves may have proved irresistible to the neoconservative crusade as their fledgling empire's "center of gravity," giving the United States the power and influence to determine much about the future strategic shape of the Persian Gulf and the entire Middle East. The 2000 PNAC report that provided the blueprint for the administration's *National Security Strategy of the United States* speaks of the need for Iraq-based "forward-based forces in the region" as an "essential element in U.S. security strategy given the long-standing American interests in the region." The 1992 Cheney-Libby-Wolfowitz DPG draft was even more explicit in its discussion of the need to assure "access to vital raw material, primarily Persian Gulf oil."

It's not necessary that any one of the administration's motivations be its only, or even primary, inspiration. This is the fallacy of those at antiwar rallies who chant, "No blood for oil" and other such slogans. All that is necessary is that the calculus of Bush administration officials favored war, on balance, over peace; that they believed that the risks and costs that they were undertaking were justified by the potential benefits they expected to reap. It would have been an argument worth having before taking America on its unprecedented adventure into its first ever preventive war against an enemy six thousand miles away. But the president and his top advisors did not trust Americans to judge their arguments regarding risks and rewards and reach the conclusions they desired. And so they misled them, instead.

"Mission Accomplished"?

In the end, nothing spoke more eloquently about the Bush administration's contempt for the complexity of the task it set for itself than the manner in which it tried to turn the military's victory in Iraq into a political commercial for the president and the Republican Party. Shortly after the troops arrived in Baghdad, and just before they started to become targets for guerrilla attacks, Bush and Company arranged for the president to don the costume of a fighter pilot—the only identifiable moment in all U.S. history that a sitting president decided to dress up as soldier—and fly a jet onto the *Abraham Lincoln,* an aircraft carrier that was transporting returning soldiers. In order to make this complicated photo-op work, the navy was forced to slow down the carrier and extend by a day the sailors' almost ten-month deployment at sea, the longest by a carrier in thirty years. Originally, White House officials insisted that Bush made the dramatic trip by fighter jet because the ship was too far out to sea to be reached by helicopter. But even with the intentional delay in its return, the carrier was a mere thirty miles from shore by the time Bush arrived—well within reach of a helicopter, and without call for Bush to dress up like Tom Cruise for the cameras.

In a maneuver so transparent as to flirt with self-parody, when the "Mission Accomplished" photo-op started to look like a political albatross as the quagmire deepened in late October, Bush tried to shift responsibility for the banner to the enthusiasm of the sailors, away from his own overeager communications staff. It "was suggested by those on the ship," he said. "They asked us to do the production of the banner, and we did. They're the ones who put it up." At the time of the event, however, White House aides were happy to take full credit, telling reporters that the now disavowed slogan was chosen in part to "mark a presidential turn toward domestic affairs as his campaign for reelection approaches." As General Wesley Clark quipped in response, "I guess the next thing we are going to hear is that the sailors told him to wear the flight suit and prance around on the aircraft carrier."

While it may have escaped the notice of many of the awed reporters who covered Bush's trip, the stunt was positively pregnant with irony. This was, after all, a president who had avoided the war when, as a young man, he was given the chance to fight in one. As Bush told a reporter of his cushy stint flying airplanes at home during Vietnam, "I was not prepared to shoot my eardrum out with a shotgun in order to get a deferment. Nor was I willing to go to Canada. So I chose to better myself by learning how to fly airplanes." And even with that good fortune, made possible by special treatment accorded to him by his famous father's friends, Bush managed to disappear from his reserve unit for his final eighteen months of service. Normally this would be called a "desertion," but with Bush it is usually treated by a compliant media as nothing more than a curious gap in his autobiography as well as the record-keeping abilities of the U.S. military.

More significant for the nation than his own mysterious past as pilot, however, was the course of the war in which he was now prematurely declaring victory. An attentive press corps might have pointed out that when the Bush banner aboard ship read "Mission Accomplished," America's mission in Iraq was anything but. Within only a few short weeks more American servicemen would die in Iraq after the pronouncement than during the combat itself. The soldiers who provided the backdrop for this campaign visual did not, in truth, have much reason to express their gratitude. Not only was Bush taxing the military's capabilities near to its likely breaking point—with 185,000 troops deployed in and around Iraq, an additional 10,000 in Afghanistan, 25,000 and 5,000 in the Balkans, to say nothing of the 175,000 or so in Europe and Japan, it was a far larger and more diverse deployment than that which garnered so much criticism from George Bush and Dick Cheney during the Clinton administration—his budget was also quietly slashing their benefits over the next decade by nearly $29 billion. At the same time, his administration was restricting soldiers' medical care in the service of giving a tax break to the wealthiest Americans. On Monday, July 14, the Pentagon announced that "due to the uncertainty of the situation in Iraq and the recent increase in attacks on the coalition forces," the 3rd Infantry Division—which had suffered thirty-six deaths, with many of its troops having been stationed in the region since September—would have to remain in Iraq and continue fighting. Rotations were being canceled and "in-country" tours were being extended to a full year. No wonder that half of nearly 2,000 Iraq-stationed soldiers questioned in October 2003 by *Stars and Stripes* newspaper described their unit's morale as low and their training as insufficient, and admitted that they had no plans for reenlistment.

Meanwhile the outsourcing of many of the tasks of providing for the troops to private companies—consistent with the administration's business-first ideology—had resulted in poor living conditions, contaminated drinking water, and malnutrition among the troops. A few of them decided they really didn't want to serve in a war zone, after all. One of the soldiers, openly interviewed on television, was so distraught that he said, "If Donald Rumsfeld were here, I'd ask him for his resignation."

The invasion of Iraq was turning into a disaster for the nation and much of the world, but it was the men and women of the military who had the right to be most bitter—they had been to this movie before and it nearly destroyed them. As General Zinni told one reporter, "It reminds me of Vietnam. Here we have some strategic thinkers who have long wanted to invade

Iraq. They saw an opportunity and they used the imminence of the threat and the association with terrorism and the 9/11 emotions as a catalyst and justification. It's another Gulf of Tonkin."

Let's give the final word to a perspicacious statesman, George H. W. Bush, who together with former advisor Brent Scowcroft wrote the following in *A World Transformed,* the former president's 1998 foreign policy memoir of the first Gulf War:

> Trying to eliminate Saddam, extending the ground war into an occupation of Iraq, would have violated our guideline about not changing objectives in midstream, engaging in "mission creep," and would have incurred incalculable human and political costs. Apprehending him was probably impossible. . . . We would have been forced to occupy Baghdad and, in effect, rule Iraq. The coalition would instantly have collapsed, the Arabs deserting it in anger and other allies pulling out as well. Under those circumstances, there was no viable "exit strategy" we could see. . . . Had we gone the invasion route, the United States could conceivably still be an occupying power in a bitterly hostile land. It would have been a dramatically different—and perhaps barren—outcome.

12. The "Bungling Bully"

The "Ruin"
of U.S. Foreign Policy

*

Writing in the *Financial Times* in April 2003, Jeffrey Sachs, Columbia economics professor and president of its Earth Institute, observed, "President George W. Bush is presiding over the ruin of U.S. foreign policy. A world united against the war in Iraq is only the start, since U.S. diplomatic failure and neglect extend to virtually every area of foreign policy."

Three years into Bush's disputed presidency, his administration policy "groaned," in Sachs's words, "under the weight of extremism, cynicism, ignorance and the obsession over Iraq." The costs were everywhere evident. Not only were both Iraq and Afghanistan—the loci of the administration's two most significant foreign policy efforts—descending into murderous chaos, but relations with our European allies had reached a postwar nadir. New nuclear threats were emerging from both Iran and North Korea only to be either ignored, exacerbated, or both. As Africa descended into a nightmare of an exploding AIDS pandemic, civil war, and starvation, the most powerful group of men and women in human history largely stood by and averted their eyes to what historians may one day view as the single greatest humanitarian disaster in the history of modern mankind. And as Sachs pointed out, in Latin America, "The U.S. administration has proved to be incapable of even the simplest responses to a profound crisis engulfing the region."

Professor Sachs may be considered a moderate liberal, but his assessment was hardly unique to those of his political persuasion. In July 2003 the editors of the *Financial Times,* citing the combination of Bush's "incompetence" and "ham-fisted tactics," termed the president a "Bungling Bully." This was not Noam Chomsky or *The Nation* magazine speaking; it was perhaps the most distinguished *conservative* newspaper in the English language and one based in the only nation that had been willing to join—in a significant fashion—the United States in its military adventure in Iraq. In France the journal *Le Débat* published an editorial that, while taking the U.S. position in the Iraq debate against that of its own government, nevertheless felt compelled to distance itself from an administration it termed "perhaps the worst in American history."

To the Allies: "Here's More Sand in Your Eye"

After the invasion of Iraq it would have been logical for George W. Bush to begin the hard work of repairing alliances and trying to undo some of the damage caused both by the invasion itself and by the manner in which it was carried out. After all, for half a century NATO had proved to be the foundation of security arrangements not only for the United States but for the world. Without it, and without an effective UN Security Council, the world would lack a formal structure to keep the peace and enforce good behavior on nation-states. Another consideration was that the reconstruction of Iraq was proving far more difficult—and expensive—than just about anyone in the Bush administration had anticipated. Even before any of the "staggering"—to borrow Paul Bremer's descriptive term—reconstruction costs had begun to be tallied, in July 2003 the occupation was already costing the United States more than a billion a week merely to try to police the country, and this effort could hardly be said to be going smoothly.

It could only be to the administration's advantage, one would have imagined, to invite its allies and the members of the UN Security Council to accept some of this enormous responsibility and bear some of the burden of remaking what American and British bombers had so effectively destroyed. Instead, it rejected substantive concessions to the Security Council and actually went out of its way to instigate additional conflicts with its erstwhile allies, make new enemies, and increase the difficulty of achieving its ambitious aims. By the unique logic that had characterized so much of U.S. foreign policy as it related to Iraq, one senior official told a reporter, "We really need to make Iraq an international operation. . . . You can make a case that it would be better to do that, but right now the situation in Iraq is not that dire." He uttered these words just days before a car bomb blew up UN headquarters in Baghdad, killing the distinguished diplomat Sergio Vieira de Mello, together with twenty-two others.

Most of the administration's ire appeared focused on France. As *The New Republic*'s Peter Beinart pointed out, "Almost as soon as the fighting stopped, the French government started trying to mend fences." The French gave up their opposition to NATO control over the peacekeeping force in Afghanistan, and unlike Putin's Russia, they agreed to suspend (though not remove) UN sanctions on Iraq. French president Chirac warned Syria not to harbor Iraqi officials and broke the high-level silence with the United States by telephoning President Bush. Jean-David Levitte, France's ambassador to the United States, spoke of the need to "turn this bitter page and think positively about what we have to do together."

The French received their public answer from Secretary Powell. Asked by talk show host Charlie Rose whether France could expect punishment for its role as leader of the opposition to the invasion, the general replied simply yes, and indeed, White House meetings were called for just this purpose. Apparently, among the brilliant ideas offered at one such gathering was a campaign of anonymous intrigue to try to ruin France's reputation as a dependable ally to the West in the fight against terrorism. Reports began cropping up in the U.S. media accusing the French of all manner of malfeasance: selling Iraq spare parts for nuclear weapons construction and other military programs before the war, providing fake passports to Iraqi officials afterward, and even hiding smallpox pathogens in secret laboratories. All of these fantastic stories shared the characteristics that they were vehemently denied by the French government and based on information from "anonymous administration officials."

France, though perhaps the most high-profile of the administration's post-Iraq punishment campaigns, was hardly alone; among the others that felt the lash of the administration's anger was Chile. As the editors of the *Washington Post* pointed out, Chile was "far and away the leader of the Latin American movement toward free-market economic policies and the clearest success story; for the past dozen years it has also been a model of moderate and stable democratic politics." The United States had planned to sign a free-trade pact with Chile designed not only to reward that behavior but also to demonstrate to its neighbors, including regional powers Argentina and Brazil, that adherence to the kinds of policies preached by American leaders abroad would draw them closer to the United States and earn them similar treatment in the future. But when 85 percent of Chileans opposed a war in Iraq, their government responded by supporting a compromise in the Security Council that was intended to delay the war while making possible its eventual endorsement. In response the United States punished the Chileans by refusing to set a date to sign a free-trade agreement whose terms had been completed in 2002, demonstrating to the rest of Latin America just where its priorities lay.

The administration gave every impression of wishing to go out of its way to chastise any number of its long-standing friends and allies who acceded to the democratic wishes of their own people vis-à-vis its war with Iraq. White House envoy to the Americas Otto Reich warned of "consequences" for these nations, and as if to prove that its pettiness knew almost no limits, the Bush team even sought to teach Mexican president Vicente Fox a lesson by canceling its annual Cinco de Mayo celebration, as well as canceling a planned presidential trip to Canada. In May 2003 U.S. trade representative

Robert Zoellick informed New Zealand that it could forget about its bilateral trade deal for a while owing to "recent actions" by its government. This was in contrast to neighboring Australia—together with Britain, the only nation to provide troops for the conflict—where an administration official was quoted as saying that a U.S.-Australia pact would be moved up from its original deadline. He explained his reasoning in a speech to the Institute for International Economics, in which he stipulated Washington's expectation of "cooperation—or better—on foreign policy and security issues" for those nations expecting to enjoy healthy trade relations.

In July 2003 Bush decided to freeze military aid to thirty-five nations that had refused to exempt U.S. soldiers from the jurisdiction of the International Criminal Court (ICC). These nations could expect to forfeit millions for military equipment and training programs if they failed to accede to U.S. demands. Included in this group, amazingly, were new NATO member Lithuania, which was proudly "standing along with the United States in [its] fight against terrorism and sending troops to Afghanistan and Iraq," and Bosnia, despite America's enormous investment in trying to keep it afloat during the 1990s. That nascent nation's foreign minister, Mladen Ivanic, explained that the United States had warned that it would be "very difficult to continue military and other assistance" if Bosnia did not capitulate. The United States promised to review "dispensable programs," including economic aid. Bush was in effect threatening to withdraw exactly the military assistance necessary to help these nations meet the qualifications for the NATO membership he deemed so important to the peace of Europe and the world.

A June 2003 global survey by the nonpartisan Pew Research Center for the People and the Press found an astonishing level of hostility directed against America by traditionally friendly nations. In Germany, for example, only 25 percent of respondents offered a favorable opinion of the United States, down from 61 percent a year earlier. In France, the number fell from 63 percent to 31 percent. The numbers were the same in Italy, where favorable views dropped from 70 percent to just 34 percent.

Among nations with whom the United States has not been traditionally allied—but has nevertheless sought cooperative, mutually beneficial relations—the number of people who viewed America as a threat during this period likewise skyrocketed: 74 percent of Indonesians questioned said they were "very or somewhat worried" that the United States could become a threat to their country, as did 72 percent of Nigerians and 71 percent of both Russians and Turks. And for the first time since the Vietnam War, United States corporate brands began registering negative images with global consumers. Companies as diverse as Nike, MTV, Disney, Microsoft, McDonald's, Yahoo!, and Citibank all saw their brand identification suffer with the global rise in resentment of the United States in what Tom Miller, the managing director of RoperASW, called "an early-warning sign" of a possible historical turnaround in the positive perception of U.S.-based businesses.

Axis Me No Questions

Faced with one war blazing in Afghanistan and enmeshed in the early planning stages of yet another in Iraq in late 2001, the Bush administration apparently decided that a few more potential adversaries might be useful and so quite casually added Iran and North Korea to the mix. As the president announced in his January 2002 State of the Union address:

> States like these [Iraq, Iran, and North Korea], and their terrorist allies, constitute an axis of evil, arming to threaten the peace of the world. By seeking weapons of mass destruction, these regimes pose a grave and growing danger. They could provide these arms to terrorists, giving them the means to match their hatred. . . . The United States would not stand still as the danger posed by this threat continued to grow. Time is not on our side. I will not wait on events, while dangers gather. I will not stand by, as perils draw closer and closer. The United States of America will not permit the world's most dangerous regimes to threaten us with the world's most destructive weapons.

In England the liberal *Guardian* reacted by coining the phrase "Hate of the Union," but even Jörg Lau, a *Die Zeit* correspondent in Berlin who is quite sympathetic to the United States, ruefully noted that the speech was "unanimously unpopular" in Europe. "It was just so stupid; they are always talking about good and evil, in quasi-religious terms, and it gives us a strange sense of relief. Bush is always showing himself to be utterly stupid. . . . And we just sit back and wait for him to do it. It's unhealthy."

David Frum, a former staffer of William Kristol's at the *Weekly Standard,* was the original author of the "axis of evil" phrase during his fourteen-month sojourn as a White House speechwriter. But later, in his score-settling memoir, *The Right Man*, Frum explained that he originally came up with the term "axis of hatred," which was later massaged by chief speechwriter Michael Gerson in order to employ "the theological language that Bush had made his own since September 11." Frum had in fact been assigned by Gerson to come up with a justification for war with Iraq, which in itself is alarming, for Frum was a relatively junior speechwriter with no experience in foreign affairs. His solution was an analogy between Iraq, Iran, and North Korea and Hitler's Germany, Mussolini's Italy, and Tojo's Japan, that, to put it generously, made no historical sense whatsoever.

But presidential ideas—even incoherent ones—have consequences.

Knowledgeable critics immediately identified two obvious dangers from the White House's casual decision to make these implied threats to Iran and North Korea. Unlike Iraq, Iran really *was* supporting terrorism across the world, including the notorious Hezbollah, and possibly al Qaeda as well, while simultaneously seeking to become a nuclear power. A three-month investigation by the *Los Angeles Times* discovered that Iran had been in "a pattern of clandestine activity that has concealed weapons work from international inspectors" and named Russia, China, North Korea, and Pakistan as the nations that had provided the science and technology to advance Iran's nuclear weapons program much closer to completion than Iraq's ever was. The French warned other governments to exercise "the most serious vigilance on their exports to Iran and Iranian front companies."

This report was corroborated by others, yet was all but ignored by a Bush administration that sought to focus all attention on Iraq. United Nations inspectors found enriched uranium in environmental samples taken in Iran, implying that Tehran was secretly enriching uranium. The level of enrichment, according to diplomats who spoke to the Reuters news service, was consistent with an attempt to make weapons-grade material and high enough to cause concern at the International Atomic Energy Agency (IAEA). In early 2003 Iranian authorities admitted the existence of these facilities and invited the IAEA to inspect them, thereby confirming their ability to complete the nuclear fuel cycle. Intelligence services had reportedly observed "extensive digging" in Iran as nuclear engineers hurried to hide their production facilities. "We know that they're going deep and clandestine," a former Pentagon official told *The New Yorker's* Seymour Hersh. An Israeli official confirmed that the hidden sites "are spread all around the country," thereby complicating any possible military action to eliminate them. In July the Iranians confirmed that they had tested a ballistic missile with sufficient range to hit Jerusalem and Tel Aviv.

Meanwhile, the Bush administration also sought to cut the Clinton administration's program designed to safeguard the Russian nuclear stockpile that has proven so useful a source of knowledge and material to the Iranians. It has also resisted putting any diplomatic pressure on Russian president Vladimir Putin to end these practices—and this despite his intense opposition to the war in Iraq. What explains the free pass for the former KGB henchman while allies France and Germany are punished and shunned? Recall that Bush told reporters he had looked into his "friend" Putin's soul and found a man who believed in God. After the Iraq war, when Putin continued to resist Bush's polite requests, Bush laughed off the matter. He termed his dealings with Putin as part of "a trustworthy relationship," adding, "Plus, I like him, he's a good fellow to spend quality time with."

Nevertheless the problem of Iran refused to go away. In most formal documents, U.S. intelligence depicted Iran as a more significant threat—both in terms of nuclear proliferation and support for terrorism—than Saddam Hussein's Iraq.

But the announcement of the imaginary axis proved counterproductive on all counts. The September 11 attacks had been denounced by Iran's hard-line clergy as well as its democratic leadership, and many Iranian cities saw mass demonstrations of sympathy for the nation once denounced as "the Great Satan." The United States could have reached out to Iran and thereby strengthened its moderate, secular leadership in its struggle with the fundamentalist inheritors of the country's Islamic revolution. Yale historian Abbas Amanat warned shortly after the axis announcement that such rhetorical saber-rattling would likely accomplish exactly the opposite: strengthening the mullahs vis-à-vis the progressive, democratic forces that are seeking to open that nation up to U.S.-Western influence. The easiest excuse for tyrants looking to quash a democratic protest movement is the alleged presence of hostile foreign agents. Bush's careless rhetoric provided the Iranian hard-liners with a ready-made justification for exactly those activities that threaten the nation's—and the world's—security: nuclear proliferation, encouragement of terrorism, and suppression of democracy.

Keystone Kops and the Korean Conundrum

The Bush administration appeared no less counterproductive in its dealings with the third leg of its imaginary axis, North Korea, perhaps the most worrisome of its many misadventures. As former ambassadors Morton Abramowitz and James Laney warned at the moment of Bush's carelessly worded "Axis of Evil" address, "Besides putting another knife in the diminishing South Korean president," the speech would likely cause "dangerous escalatory consequences [including] . . . renewed tensions on the peninsula and continued export of missiles to the Mideast." North Korea called the Bush bluff, and the result, notes columnist Richard Cohen, was "a stumble, a fumble, an error compounded by a blooper. . . . As appalling a display of diplomacy as anyone has seen since a shooting in Sarajevo turned into World War I."

Bush made a bad situation worse when, in a taped interview with Bob Woodward, he insisted, "I loathe Kim Jong Il!" waving his finger in the air. "I've got a visceral reaction to this guy, because he is starving his people." Bush also said that he wanted to "topple him," and that he considered the leader to be a "pygmy." Woodward wrote that the president had become so emotional while speaking about Kim Jong Il that "I thought he might jump up."

Given what a frightful tinderbox the Koreas have become, Bush's ratcheting up of the hostile rhetoric could hardly have come at a worse time. In December 2002 the North Koreans shocked most of the world by ordering the three IAEA inspectors to leave the country, shutting down cameras monitoring the nuclear complex in Yongbyon and removing the IAEA seals in their nuclear facilities. The following month, Pyongyang announced it had withdrawn from the nuclear Non-Proliferation Treaty (NPT), restarted its small research reactor, and began removing spent nuclear fuel rods for likely reprocessing into weapons-grade plutonium. In October 2003, it announced that it had finished reprocessing spent fuel rods into plutonium and now possesses "nuclear deterrence"—another way of saying it has the bomb. No independent confirmation was available.

Even including Iraq and Iran, the Korean peninsula is probably the single most dangerous and possibly unstable situation on Earth. As Jonathan Pollack, chairman of the Strategic Research Department of the Naval War College, observes, "If you wanted a case of imminent threat and danger, according to the principles enunciated in the National Security Strategy document, then North Korea is much more of a threat than Iraq ever was in the last few years."

Bush had already undermined the extremely sensitive negotiations under way to bring the North Korean regime into the international system. When South Korean president (and Nobel laureate) Kim Dae Jung visited Washington six weeks after Bush took office, Bush humiliated both his guest and his own secretary of state by publicly repudiating the negotiations after both had just publicly endorsed them. (Powell had termed their continuation "a no-brainer.") One suspects the president's decision was motivated by a combination of unreflective machismo and a desire to provide military planners with an excuse to build a missile-defense system. But in doing so, he displayed a disturbing lack of familiarity with the details of the negotiations he purposely sabotaged. "We're not certain as to whether or not they're keeping all terms of all agreements," he said at the time. But at the time, these "agreements" numbered just one: the 1994 "Agreed Framework," which froze North Korea's enormous plutonium-processing program—one that was bigger, at the time, than those of Israel, India, and Pakistan combined—in exchange for economic aid. Bush aides were later forced to admit they could find no evidence to support the president's accusation. (A White House official tried to clear up the matter by explaining: "That's how the president speaks.")

General Wesley Clark described the result of the Bush policy as follows:

> The red line's already been crossed in North Korea, to be honest. That red line was crossed while we were engaged with Iraq. And North Koreans have told us, and I don't have any information that would contradict this, that they've begun reprocessing the plutonium and that it's mostly completed in the reprocessing. This was what we tried to prevent starting in 1994, and we had it frozen for several years. But if they've moved it, if it's reprocessed, if it's out in the system, then what it means is that even a preemptive strike on

that facility won't necessarily get the nuclear material, and you have to live with the consequences of that.

"Dealing" with it, as Clark recommends, would not be easy. Much of what President Bush falsely claimed about Iraq turns out to be true of North Korea. "We see a country that is designing and selling its ballistic missiles around the world," explained an American diplomat in January 2002. "We see a country that might export nuclear weapons."

No sensible military options exist to deal with the North Koreans when they promise "total war" in the event of a U.S. attack on their nuclear facilities. While the United States does have thirty-seven thousand troops stationed on the other end of the DMZ, the North Koreans have eleven thousand artillery guns, some possibly chemically tipped, within fifty miles of Seoul. In addition they have roughly thirty-seven hundred tanks and seven hundred Soviet-built fighter jets of uncertain vintage, but no doubt sturdy enough to make it to Seoul for devastating bombing missions. With about a million soldiers and another seven million reserves, North Korea has the fourth or fifth largest standing army on Earth. In a best-case scenario, with a surgical strike against the nuclear plant itself and no attendant radiation effects, thousands of U.S. troops and tens of thousands of South Korean troops would probably still be killed, and millions of refugees would be created. Clearly no responsible leader can willingly risk such a catastrophe.

But choosing not to deal with the problem of North Korea presents the world with two profoundly worrying prospects. The first is that North Korea will make one of its bombs available to a party that would in fact like to use it—perhaps even al Qaeda. (U.S. weapons inspector David Kay claimed to discover a $10 million deal for just such a transfer between North Korea and Iraq, though the former kept the money and did not deliver the material, insisting that U.S. pressure made it impossible.) Second, a spiraling collapse of the regime could lead to a last-ditch attack on Seoul, with both conventional and nuclear weapons. As one U.S. official put it, toleration of a nuclear North Korea sends the same message to Iran that the invasion of Iraq sent to North Korea: "Get your nuclear weapons quickly, before the Americans do to you what they've done to Iraq, because North Korea shows once you get the weapons, you're immune."

Those who have long dealt with the Korean problem began, in mid-2003, to express alarm at the consequences of Bush's mishandling of it. "I think we are losing control," worried former secretary of defense William Perry. "The nuclear program now under way in North Korea poses an imminent danger of nuclear weapons being detonated in American cities." Only six months earlier Perry had been arguing in public that the problem was addressable, "if we did the right things." Now, however, he worried that "time is running out, and each month the problem gets more dangerous." His sense of alarm is seconded by a report by the International Crisis Group, which warns, "Time is slipping away for a peaceful resolution of the nuclear crisis on the Korean peninsula. . . . North Korea has the materials and the capability to develop nuclear weapons—more than two hundred of them by 2010."

The administration describes its current policy toward North Korea as one of "tailored containment," which a senior administration official explains to mean: "It is a lot about putting political stress and putting economic stress. It also requires maximum multinational cooperation." The Bush plan seems to be to persuade several key Asian countries that now provide cash and assistance to Pyongyang to turn off the taps and stand by as its people starve and the nation—with its nukes—implodes.

But those upon whose cooperation the policy rests appear to have little inclination to support the plan. South Korea's population, like that of most of the world, has grown increasingly distrustful of the Bush administration's behavior and is far less eager to follow the U.S. lead. Its current president, Roh Moo Hyun, won his office by following the German pattern, with a campaign that stressed his independence from the United States and its martial declarations. The Chinese remain by far the North Koreans' most important trading partner, supplying for instance 70 percent of its crude oil needs and much of its foodstuffs. Its leadership has shown no interest in doing Bush's bidding or participating in a strategy that appears designed to create political change through mass starvation. And the last thing Japan wants to see is the collapse of the regime, thereby finding itself facing a nuclear-armed, unified Korea on its borders.

The obvious solution—both to the strategic problem and to the humanitarian crisis—is clearly some sort of negotiated buyout, along the lines that the Clinton administration began, but fumbled. Under the terms of that deal, North Korea was to freeze and eventually eliminate its nuclear program while the United States spearheaded an international effort to provide fuel and light-water (non-weapons-producing) nuclear reactors. The Clinton administration also tried to negotiate an accord whereby the North would have forfeited its long-range missiles and terminated all missile exports. But hopes of concluding the deal—which would have required a presidential trip to Pongyang—collapsed when Clinton decided in the final weeks of his administration to table the trip in favor of trying, unsuccessfully, to negotiate a Middle East peace deal.

Perhaps because such talks were associated with his predecessor, and no doubt because he wished to keep the focus on Iraq, Bush refused to carry out this plan and instead sought to play down the sense of crisis. "It's a diplomatic issue, not a military issue," he insisted in early 2003. When Bush advised Americans to "learn the lessons of the Korean peninsula and not allow an even greater threat to rise up in Iraq," he appeared to be arguing that the United States should have invaded those nations as well, when it still had the chance. "But as Bush sets it out," Michael Kinsley notes, "the 'lesson' of Korea seems to be that if you don't go to war soon enough, you might have a problem years later that can be solved through regional discussions. That doesn't sound so terrible, frankly." Secretary Powell justifies the blasé attitude toward North Korea on the grounds that "you can't eat plutonium." But as Brookings analysts Ivo H. Daalder and James M. Lindsay are quick to respond, "Of course, you can sell it and use the proceeds to buy a very nice meal."

Both the Korea and the Iran problems point to yet another weakness of the Bush security policy: its inability to reign in the nuclear supermarket being run out of Pakistan, which has offered significant aid to both. While the Musharaff government is almost certainly too weak to deal with the al Qaeda terrorists who operate with impunity on Pakistani territory, that weakness should not be used as an argument to turn a blind eye to its nuclear adventurism—particularly the role it has played in both the Iranian and North Korean nuclear programs. While the Bush administration hid this information during the run-up to its war with Iraq, it became clear that Pakistan was eager to supply a decade's worth of research, including sophisticated technology, warhead-design information, and weapons-testing data—just about anything the market would bear, regardless of the peril in which it placed the rest of the world. Like both Iran and North Korea, the situation in Pakistan creates far more serious concerns for the United States than did Iraq. But the administration proved so obsessive during the period when it was trying—and failing—to whip up support for its war that it allowed these problems to fester and become even more serious.

Africa's Agony, America's Indifference

The same Bush policy of malign neglect extended toward most of the world's non-Iraqi population manifested itself as well on the increasingly beleaguered continent of Africa. Emblematic of America's new status under Bush as a nation to be feared and endured rather than admired and embraced was a short trip that the president took to Africa in the summer of 2003. Much of the continent was, at the time, in the midst of a horrific humanitarian crisis, with problems ranging from murderous civil wars, in which millions have been killed over the past decade, to mass starvation, continued vitamin E deficiency, and of course the raging AIDS pandemic. Before leaving the United States, Bush proclaimed, "We care deeply about the plight of the African citizen. . . . When we see starvation, we don't turn our back, we act."

In fact, the United States is just about the least generous wealthy nation on the planet, save Japan. It placed at number twenty out of twenty-one ranked nations, according to a complicated formula (developed in 2003 by the

Center for Global Development and *Foreign Policy* magazine) which encompasses not only development aid but also trade, environmental, investment, migration, and peacekeeping policies. (If development aid is ranked alone, as is typically done, then Japan leaves the United States in the cellar.)

The president made two major proposals for Africa before his visit there. First was a $15 billion initiative, originally presented in his 2003 State of the Union, to attack the AIDS crisis with a flood of antiretroviral treatments and prevention funds. And he offered up a $10 billion program termed the Millennium Challenge Account, to provide poor nations with the opportunity to compete with one another for grants in order to inspire the new race toward development efficiency.

But as so many millions of vulnerable and dependent Americans had already learned, what the president says and what the president does are not always equivalent. In this case, the money disappeared from the table even before Bush left for Africa, and his request for a 2004 budget for the Millennium Challenge Account had shrunk to just $1.3 billion. (Recall that that figure is the high point of the congressional appropriations process.) And instead of the $3 billion Bush promised per year over five years for the AIDS initiative, the White House's 2004 budget request asked Congress for only $1.9 billion annually. But even that sum was something of a mirage, as it appears to have been based on a mere reshuffling of related accounts. The Global Fund to Fight AIDS, Tuberculosis and Malaria—much of which is designated for Africa—for instance, received a $150 million cut from the previous year. (Moreover, Congress mandates that even this money will not be spent unless the Europeans match the U.S. contribution.) USAID's budget for infectious disease programs, much of which is earmarked for Africa, fell 32 percent from the previous year, while the funding levels for child survival/maternal health funds dropped by 12 percent. To add the final insult to the various injuries it had already inflicted, in August 2003 the administration also discontinued financing for a small but extremely highly regarded AIDS program for African and Asian refugees, alleging that one of the groups involved in the project supports forced abortions and involuntary sterilization in China. The administration admitted, however, that it had no actual evidence that the Reproductive Health for Refugees Consortium had actually participated in any such activities. Its weakened financial state will almost certainly result in the necessity of more abortions—as well as more unnecessary AIDS deaths.

Finally, other than the Global Fund monies, most of the new funds Bush did pledge but so far has refused to deliver will not be going directly to the kinds of recipients who can provide the necessary services but to bilateral trade programs designed to promote U.S. companies through the purchase of their goods and services. This program is to be coordinated by Randall Tobias, a former CEO of Eli Lilly and a major Republican donor.

Then there's Liberia. A nation founded by former American slaves and caught between rival gangs of thugs, Liberia was desperate for a U.S. military intervention at the time of Bush's summer visit to the continent. Just before he left for Africa, Bush spoke of America's "special ties to Liberia," adding that he was "determined to help the people of Liberia find the path to peace." The president committed himself to "a willingness to look at all the options to determine how best to bring peace and stability," and told UN secretary general Kofi Annan that the United States would "participate with the troops."

While those initial pledges were met with joy in the streets, Donald Rumsfeld objected to the plan, and Bush did next to nothing, authorizing only ten marines to go ashore from an offshore deployment of twenty-three hundred. As the *Washington Post* reported, the president "made no provision for reining in the rape, looting and gunfire that are terrifying residents of the capital, Monrovia."

Pentagon opposition to the deployment of U.S. troops was not surprising, as the top brass was understandably concerned about the stretching of U.S. troops around the world beyond their breaking point, another legacy of Bush's misguided priorities. As one official puts it, "There is extreme reluctance to get into something that just becomes a sinkhole." Pentagon officials went so far as to quash a report to the president that they themselves ordered up just before his African trip because it recommended that "the U.S. should provide and/or support a security force which will ensure safe access of NGO/IOs [nongovermental organizations and international organizations] to needy populations and protect civilians from human rights violations." Nigerian president Olusegun Obasanjo, whose nation provided the initial force of fifteen hundred peacekeepers, compared the U.S. offer of help to a fire brigade standing outside a burning house and using its hoses only after the fire was out. The tiny contingent of U.S. soldiers remained in the country a mere eleven days before retreating to the safety of their warships off the coast, leaving Liberians to their anguish. Robert Warwick, the International Rescue Committee's West Africa director, noted following the much-delayed departure of the Liberian despot, Charles Taylor, "The U.S. squandered their opportunity. . . . There was a moment when it seemed like all of the players, even the rebels, were willing and anxious for the United States to get involved. An earlier intervention would have stemmed the loss of more than a thousand lives from fighting and illnesses, and the looting of food and supplies." As a result, the various aid groups working there have had their supplies and equipment stolen, making it much more difficult to respond to an already dire humanitarian crisis. "It baffles Liberians," wrote reporter Robin Wright, "that American soldiers would interfere where they are not wanted, and stay away from where they are."

The humanitarian crisis in Liberia was far worse than Iraq. Monrovia, for example, has had no running water or electricity for seven years. Taylor, too, exhibited many of the same qualities that gave rise to Bush's various warnings about Saddam Hussein. Foreign correspondent Douglas Farah described Taylor as follows:

> The despotic president, indicted by a U.N.-backed tribunal for crimes against humanity, came to power by forcibly recruiting young boys and turning them into killers. His troops manned checkpoints lined with human skulls, where the roadblocks were made out of human intestines, the disemboweled victims left by the roadside. For a decade this despot has systematically pocketed the wealth of his country, leaving his people in abject poverty. He has done millions of dollars' worth of business with al Qaeda and Hezbollah. His son is a brutal thug, feared for his executions and proclivity for kidnapping young women and raping them.

Part of the problem for Bush here may have been the support that Taylor received right up until his bloody end from key members of the Republican political coalition. The most prominent of his supporters was undoubtedly the Reverend Pat Robertson, owner of the Christian Broadcasting Network and host of *The 700 Club*, and a man of absolutely vital importance to the Karl Rove strategy of always keeping the religious right happy. Robertson has invested more than $8 million in a gold mine in Liberia under Freedom Gold Limited, registered in the Cayman Islands. He considers Taylor to be a "fellow Baptist" and a "fine Christian" and told a reporter that Taylor's indictment "is nonsense and should be quashed." (Robertson has in fact never visited Liberia or laid eyes on Taylor.)

Just how low America's reputation had sunk under Bush's leadership was evident when he finally did arrive in Africa. South Africa's Nelson Mandela, perhaps the single most revered and admired individual on the planet, happened to be away on the day Bush came to Cape Town. Mandela's successor as president, Thabo Mbeki, left the country after just a half day with Bush as well. The nation's key political party, the African National Congress, greeted Bush with a two thousand-person protest march. Bush's reception could hardly have contrasted more profoundly with the enormous and enthusiastic crowds that came to meet Bill Clinton in 1998, a time when at least some Africans believed that America was on their side in their daunting struggles. But as Gitau Warigi observed in *The Nation* (Nigeria) during the president's brief trip, "Bush's singular achievement has been to make America resented in Africa—and elsewhere—to an unprecedented degree. America's unilateralist behavior under Bush has messed up much of the goodwill America used to enjoy here. . . . In Kenya especially, America has become a dirty word."

Endless War

Is the Bush foreign policy fundamentally a formula for endless war in the service of a global empire? Administration sources don't like to be quoted on this point, but it seems a fair bet that Iraq was intended to be merely the first step on an extended journey. Neoconservatives who do not serve in the administration are freer to give voice to its long-term strategic aims, and among the most honest is William Kristol, who notes, "President Bush is committed, pretty far down the road. The logic of events says you can't go halfway. You can't liberate Iraq, then quit." Defense Policy Board ex-chair and member Richard Perle agrees. "This is total war," he says. "We are fighting a variety of enemies. There are lots of them out there. All this talk about first we are going to do Afghanistan, then we will do Iraq . . . this is entirely the wrong way to go about it. If we just let our vision of the world go forth, and we embrace it entirely and we don't try to piece together clever diplomacy, but just wage a total war . . . our children will sing great songs about us years from now."

An ideological argument is also being prepared by these same neocons, designed to encourage Americans to abandon their traditional notions of security in favor of one in which endless war necessarily involves endless casualties and terrorist incidents as a permanent state of affairs. At one of the lowest ebbs in what was clearly turning into a quagmire in Iraq, shortly after the destruction of UN Headquarters in August 2003, DPB board member Kenneth Adelman suggested to a reporter, "We should not try to convince people that things are getting better. Rather, we should convince people that ours is the age of terrorism." Perle added, "It may be a very long time before we've so substantially eliminated the source of terror that we can pronounce that we are safe."

Similar hints, warnings, and musings can be found attributed to Bush administration sources as well, though rarely quite so openly stated. One senior British official remarked of U.S. policy just before the war: "Everyone wants to go to Baghdad. Real men want to go to Tehran." A single *Newsweek* article claimed to find advocates within the administration for attacks on Saudi Arabia, Iran, North Korea, Syria, Egypt, and Burma. In February 2003 Undersecretary of State John Bolton told Israeli officials that he expected the nation to deal with threats from Syria, Iran, and North Korea after it addressed Hussein's Iraq. Bolton gave a speech in Seoul in August 2003 in which he attacked North Korea as a "hellish nightmare" and called on the world to "send a clear message to dictators like Kim Jong Il" with a plan to interdict trade for the purposes of finding weapons shipments. (This led the North Koreans to term Bolton "human scum and [a] bloodsucker," characterized by "political vulgarity and [a] psychopathological condition"; they insisted that he not be included in any talks.) Meanwhile, back in Washington, Bolton went before Congress to argue that

Syria's development of chemical and biological weapons had progressed to the point that they posed a threat to stability in the Middle East. The Bush administration was so eager to paint Syria in the "against" column when it comes to potential enemies that it rejected its cooperation in the war with al Qaeda. The Syrians had been willing to share intelligence, but according to one CIA official, the offer was deliberately rejected because "they"—meaning Donald Rumsfeld and his neoconservative advisors—"want to go in there next."

Rumsfeld envisions a force that will rotate through a large number of bases scattered throughout the world, in places like Kyrgyzstan, the Philippines, Singapore, the Horn of Africa, and Eastern Europe. This is in addition, one hesitates to add, to any potential plans for Iran, North Korea, Syria, or even Saudi Arabia. No doubt the failure to secure Iraq long after President Bush declared "mission accomplished" put the brakes on any immediate plans to begin a third or fourth war during the president's first term in office. But such actions are certainly implied in the PNAC strategic documents, as well as in the language of the president's *National Security Strategy*. They also explain the unwillingness of Donald Rumsfeld to commit sufficient troops to the occupation of Iraq to maintain security there; those troops might become "less usable" elsewhere in the world if bogged down in Iraq.

The mismatch between administration theory and Iraqi reality demonstrates just how disastrous a path lay in store for the United States should it seek to reorder the world according to the ideological preferences of its current leaders. It has also revealed how unprepared, if only in sheer military terms, the United States is to assume this burden. Even with the extended stays that the Pentagon is demanding of current enlistees, and with Rumsfeld's decision to deploy only the absolute minimum number of troops there, the military is badly overstretched. According to Michael O'Hanlon of Brookings, without a significant commitment of international troops to Iraq, the United States will have to take the "unthinkable" step of rotating troops back into Iraq within a year of their return home. That would almost certainly destroy reenlistment incentives, given the burden it places on already overburdened military families. (This is in addition to cutting their pay and medical benefits.) Without a significant expansion of the military, coupled with a significant improvement in the Iraqi situation—to say nothing of that in Afghanistan—any future invasions are about as likely as an invasion of Mars.

A First: Isolationist Interventionists

Back in 1986 Irving Kristol, the "godfather" of neoconservatism—and actual father of William Kristol—proposed the doctrine of "global unilateralism." He argued that America would be better off acting alone in the world rather than allowing its interests to be compromised by the pusillanimity of its allies, who were hampered by a failure of will, a loss of faith in their own values, and a barely submerged hostility toward Jews—which they manifested in an incurable hostility to Israel. As a result, Kristol argued, the United States needed to adopt a posture that is less risk averse. "In the years ahead, the United States will be far less inhibited in its use of military power," he advised. Sounding very much as if he were talking about al Qaeda and the threat of Islamic fundamentalism rather than a dying Communist empire, he stated that, unless the enemy was willing to transform "its secular, political messianism into a stable orthodoxy," the United States could expect a period of conflict, "political, economic, and military, though always short of nuclear war."

Kristol and his fellow neoconservatives represented a new development in American ideological history. As Theodore Draper ruefully observed, "We have had isolationists. We have had interventionists; we have never had isolationists who were also interventionists. This abnormal crossbreeding of isolationism and interventionism has produced the new species of global unilateralists. They are global in their intervention and unilateral in the way they wish to go about it."

What sounded outrageous in 1986 became the official doctrine of the United States in 2002, though its target now was not communism but "terrorism," extremely loosely defined. The pressure for a policy of assertive unilateralism has been intense for more than twenty years, and it grew in influence in conjunction with the electoral success of the Reagan administration, and later, with the Gingrich–DeLay–George W. Bush takeover of the Republican Party. In the media, the neoconservatives established their primacy in the foreign policy debate through their prominence on the op-ed pages of key newspapers, in opinion magazines like *The New Republic* and the *Weekly Standard*, and virtually everywhere on cable TV. As a result of growing neoconservative political and intellectual influence, even liberal-minded internationalist politicians—including Presidents Clinton and Bush 41—were forced to accommodate its demands.

It was during the Clinton administration, after all, when French foreign minister Hubert Védrine proclaimed the United States to be a "hyper-puissance," a power that "today predominates on the economic, monetary [and] technological level, and in the culture area. . . . In terms of power and influence, it is not comparable to anything known in modern history." Still, the Clinton administration was committed to doing whatever possible to maintain the sanctity of the NATO alliance. The war in Kosovo was ostensibly a NATO effort, even though U.S. bombers bore the brunt of the responsibility and pretty much insisted on the right to call the shots. Quite a few generals were heard to grumble that the entire operation would have gone more smoothly if the other NATO nations had not had to be brought into every decision. For their part, the Europeans were not thrilled with their position as America's junior partner. But neither were they willing to devote anything like the proportion of their resources to military spending that had bought the United States its unchallenged superiority on the battlefield and provided, in American eyes, the price of a ticket for admission to NATO's top table. As a result, as Europeans frequently put it, when it came to military operations, "America cooks the meal and Europe does the dishes."

American defense spending levels only continued to climb—skyrocketing after September 11. The George W. Bush who had campaigned on the basis of a humble foreign policy had disappeared into history, and the neocon contempt for Europe began to creep into official policy-making circles. Even such famous pro-American voices as Chris Patten, the much-admired conservative former governor of Hong Kong—now EU commissioner for External Relations—have taken to complaining about the Bush administration's launch into "unilateralist overdrive," with its "absolutist" approach to world affairs. Frankfurt School philosopher Jürgen Habermas, the titanic figure of the European democratic (and pro-American) left, warns, "Many Americans do not yet realize the extent and the character of the growing rejection of, if not resentment against, the policy of the present American administration throughout Europe, including in Great Britain. The emotional gap may well become deeper than it has ever been since the end of World War II. . . . The world has grown too complex for this barely concealed unilateralism."

The Bush administration's demand for war against Iraq, despite an overwhelming worldwide preference for the reinvigoration of the UN inspections-containment regime, proved the catalyst for what appears to be the slow-motion dissolution of the post–World War II global security system, a system that began with the 1941 Atlantic Charter and blossomed into the United Nations, the Bretton Woods accords, the IMF, the World Bank, and assorted international institutions devoted to arms control, peacekeeping, human rights, and the like. These institutions were designed explicitly with horrid memory of the calamities of two world wars in mind and served to limit conflict, however imperfectly, for more than half a century. As *The Guardian*'s Jonathan Friedland notes, "It's easy to forget this now, as U.S. politicians and commentators queue up to denounce international institutions as French-dominated, limp-wristed, euro-faggot bodies barely worth the candle, but those bodies were almost all American inventions."

Many neocons argue—together with Secretary Rumsfeld—that the United States is better off replacing "old" Europe with the "new." This wistful notion is riddled with flaws and inconsistencies. First, "new" populations are hardly more sympathetic to America's global unilateralism than are their "old" European counterparts. In no nation did a major opposition party score points against the other by supporting the war, or criticizing its lack of enthusiasm. The primary difference between "old" and "new" Europe in this regard was the latter's willingness to act in an undemocratic fashion against the expressed opinions of its people. Second, these nations are of limited value when it comes to military action, in any case. Denmark spends just 1.6 percent of its GNP on defense; Italy, 1.5 percent; and Spain, 1.4 percent, which is not quite half what that old European warhorse, France, puts up. Third, the countries of "new Europe" are not exactly bellicose nations. As one Central European foreign minister said during the Kosovo intervention, "We didn't join NATO to fight wars." An early 2003 survey found that 69 percent of Poles, along with 63 percent of Italians, oppose any increase in their military spending. If the neocons now regard Poland, Britain, and Italy as the nation's chief European allies, then as Judt observed, "Tony Blair apart—America is leaning on a rubber crutch."

The belief that the United States can assure its own safety and security—much less prosperity—more effectively without the support of its allies is simply belied by reality. It is not even true in the extremely narrowly drawn confines of the war against terrorism. In Afghanistan, for instance, Europe took the lead in providing security and funds for reconstruction absent a serious commitment by the Bush administration. When the chairman of the Senate Armed Services Committee, John Warner, dropped in on Kabul in early 2003, he was surprised to be greeted there by a French officer. "What are they doing here?" he demanded of his U.S. military escort. "They muckin' things up again?" The answer he got was, "If they weren't here, we'd be failing." When the United States refused to do so, France picked up the monthly payroll for the training of Afghan officers. Meanwhile, Germany boasts a contingent of about twenty-three hundred troops. Chancellor Gerhard Schröder—another of the Bush administration's great bugaboos—risked a no-confidence vote, winning by a margin of just two, to deploy German troops into this political (and literal) minefield. But in an early June 2003 speech, given on German soil, Secretary Rumsfeld ignored his host's participation—and of course those feckless French—and chose instead to salute Romania and Albania. In fact, the ten nations stretching from Albania to Estonia have managed to contribute a grand total of about 170 soldiers to the entire effort.

The story is similar elsewhere in the world. In Bosnia, Europeans are taking over the burden left by departing U.S. troops. In Kosovo, the United States is down to a force of twenty-seven hundred, while France and Germany have approximately four thousand troops each. France has also taken up much of the slack in the Congo, whose murderous civil war has gone all but ignored by the Bush administration, as well as the Ivory Coast. The French even evacuated one hundred Americans from Liberia. But to the Bush administration, it is they who are considered the enemy.

The situation is even more pronounced in Iraq. The United States may have been able to win a war there on its own, but it cannot win the peace. "There are just too many players in this game," in the words of the extremely pro-American editor of *Die Zeit,* Josef Joffe, "who would love to see the United States and Britain fail, starting with the remnants of the Baathist regime and continuing with Iran, the Arab dictatorships and the Palestinians. . . . The long and the short of this is: The most sophisticated military panoply in history cannot quite substitute for international legitimacy." Joffe, known as one of the few intellectuals in Europe sympathetic to the neocon worldview, notes that its failure in Iraq is likely to be generalized to the rest of the world:

> The most interesting issues in world politics cannot be solved even by an Über-Gulliver acting alone. How shall we count the ways? Nuclear proliferation in Iran and North Korea, international terrorism, free trade, global financial stability, mayhem in places like Liberia, the Congo or the Sudan, climate control, the AIDS epidemic in Africa, China's transition from totalitarianism to the rule of law and perhaps even democracy, the political pathologies of the Arab Middle East that gave us al Qaeda. These are all issues that, almost by definition, require collective responses.

The inexorable indivisibility of international security in an era of cheap, easily transportable weaponry and inescapable vulnerability was a lesson that both recent and historic experience had taught just about everyone— except the people making U.S. foreign policy.

Empire of Ignorance?

One hopes that all of the above will serve as a caution, as well as a practical inconvenience. Aboard the USS *Abraham Lincoln* Bush insisted, "Other nations in history have fought in foreign lands and remained to occupy and exploit. Americans, following a battle, want nothing more than to return home." A few days earlier, Secretary Rumsfeld told Al-Jazeera, "We're not imperialistic. We never have been."

Once again, watch what they do. Ever since September 11 conservative foreign policy analysts centered in places like the *Weekly Standard,* the *National Review,* the *Wall Street Journal* editorial board, the American Enterprise Institute, the Heritage Foundation, and even the Council on Foreign Relations began to call openly for the creation of a formal U.S. military empire, on the order of the lost glory that was England. Writing in the flagship journal of the foreign policy establishment, *Foreign Affairs,* PNAC senior fellow Thomas Donnelly argued that "American imperialism can bring with it new hopes of liberty, security, and prosperity." And the *Weekly Standard* featured a cover story by Max Boot offering up a rousing call for Americans "unambiguously to embrace [America's] imperial role."

Even leaving the debacle of Iraq aside, dreams of a new American empire are bound to be just that. As the economist James Galbraith points out:

> Empire is an economic system. But it is a system that works only in the presence of an overwhelming advantage of force, a general acquiescence of the regional leadership, large local security forces, and an absence of determined opposition. The British held India because, and only so long as, they enjoyed these advantages. In the Sudan, the matter was already different as early as the 1880s. The outcome against the Mahdi at Omdurman was only because, as Hillaire Belloc put it: "Whatever happens, we have got the Maxim Gun, and they have not." But in modern conditions the correlation of forces does not lie with the imperial power. Explosives, mines, booby traps, rockets and similar weapons of resistance are too cheap and too effective.

The problem for an American empire is not just in the difficulty (and costliness) of its conduct, but also in the opposition it inspires not merely in its subjects but also—almost unavoidably—in the policies of those nations with the resources to resist its imposition. In recent elections in countries as diverse as Belgium, Germany, Spain, South Korea, and Pakistan, the parties most identified with opposition to the U.S. foreign policy have proved victorious. They are likely to join in economic and diplomatic actions designed to frustrate U.S. purposes in those bodies the Bush administration has been unable to dominate. Effective opposition to Bush's tariffs on steel within the World Trade Organization led to its ruling them illegal. The EU has refused to reconsider its ban on genetically modified food, almost all of which is produced in the United States. The Europeans also effectively sabotaged the February 2003 round of World Trade talks in Tokyo. In addition, Cox News reports, "Many Muslim clerics [have begun] demanding that Arab countries sell oil for euros, not dollars," a subject that is said to be already under discussion in Russia and Iran. Should this take place, it could profoundly affect U.S. fiscal policy as the nation's enormous budget deficits have historically been financed by oil exporters willing to deploy their massive surpluses to sweep up Treasury notes.

Writing in Munich's *Süddeutsche Zeitung*, Richard Rorty, America's most distinguished philosopher, warned that America's current ambitions might not only create additional terrorists worldwide but could, in extremis, even lead to a nuclear confrontation with China or Russia. Rorty called upon Europe to take definite steps to frustrate the hegemony enjoyed by the Bush team, for the sake of both America and her alleged adversaries and enemies. These steps included "the eradication of founding nations' veto power in the UN; the transformation of that institution into a global parliament with an effective military; and worldwide, UN-enforced nuclear disarmament even of NATO powers." Meanwhile in late May 2003, the two most influential philosophers on the continent, Jürgen Habermas and Jacques Derrida, issued a joint declaration, "After the War: The Rebirth of Europe," in which they managed to cast aside their many significant doctrinal disagreements to come together to call for a unified European response "to balance out the hegemonic unilateralism of the United States." They proposed February 15, 2003—the date when millions of demonstrators took to the streets in Europe and America to protest the looming military action in Iraq—as the historic birth of the beginning of Europe's political and intellectual independence from the United States.

These are mere dreams at the moment, but they continue to grip Europe's thinkers and inspire its institutions. France's leading think tank, the Institut Français des Rélations Internationales, has warned that, if Europe doesn't want to be dominated by the United States, it must create an economic bloc that would stretch to Russia in the east and to Arab North Africa in the south. Such a bloc would enjoy natural resources and a pool of well-educated professionals and low-wage service workers. Eventually, such efforts must take on a military component as well, as European nations begin to realized that this will be the price of having the United States take their voices into account before embarking on its next imperial adventure. Even Tony Blair, Bush's only significant supporter in the world of great-power politics, appears to be distancing himself from U.S. foreign policy and moving closer to France and Germany in the war's aftermath. Britain has not participated in a meaningful way in the occupation, and Downing Street recently endorsed an EU proposal speeding up a plan of "structured cooperation" on the military that may lead eventually to the creation of a European Army. "A military, as well as economic, alliance between Western Europe and nuclear-armed Russia," John Judis predicts, "could one day pose a real threat to U.S. dominance. Together with the inevitable growth of China as an economic and military power, it could lead to a world divided into hostile U.S., Euro-Russian, and Chinese power blocs."

Finally, even if all of the above fails to materialize, it is not in the fundamental nature of Americans to seek empire. It is rather ironic to turn to a foreign source to point this out to überpatriots like Bush and Cheney, but they would do well to ponder the words of the conservative *Economist* magazine:

> Imperialism and democracy are at odds with each other. The one implies hierarchy and subordination, the other equality and freedom of choice. People nowadays are not willing to bow down

before an emperor, even a benevolent one, in order to be democratized. They will protest, and the ensuing pain will be felt by the imperial power as well as by its subjects.

For Americans, the pain will not be just a matter of budget deficits and body bags; it will also be a blow to the very heart of what makes them American—their constitutional belief in freedom. Freedom is in their blood; it is integral to their sense of themselves. It binds them together as nothing else does, neither ethnicity, nor religion, nor language. And it is rooted in hostility to imperialism— the imperial rule of George III. Americans know that empires lack democratic legitimacy. Indeed, they once had a tea party to prove it.

13. Conclusion

The Messianic Man

★

"The president of the United States is not a fact-checker."
—Senior White House advisor, July 2003

In January 2001 George Bush swore the oath of office to lead a country that was at the time enjoying peace, prosperity, and a sense of well-being such that 47 percent of voting Americans were willing to take a flier on someone with little experience and only sketchily enunciated views.

And why not? During the Clinton administration, median household income had reached an all-time high; the unemployment rate was at its lowest point in three decades; the rate of violent crime was down; and the once cavernous deficit had become a mountainous surplus. The job-producing capacities of the American economy—though beginning to sputter—remained the envy of the world. Abroad, allied unity had just been strengthened by the successful prosecution of a collective effort to free Kosovo from the yoke of Serbian oppression and without a single combat loss of American life. But candidate Bush, who was to inherit such favorable conditions, was, as *New York Times* editors noted, "a man who was reared in privilege, who succeeded in both business and politics because of his family connections." The question, never fully answered during his presidential campaign, was "whether he was anything more than just a very lucky guy."

Today we have our answer. George W. Bush is much, much more than "just a very lucky guy." He is, as we have discovered, also a very determined guy. The problem is that he is determined to serve his political base—extremist elements of the Republican Party—the religious right, *Fortune* 500 CEOs, especially those from the oil patch, and neoconservative ideologues—

at the expense of the rest of the nation. While it has become a cliché to observe that President Bush talks "compassion" but governs "conservative," his more honest supporters can be depended upon to convey the true agenda of the administration. His appointee to oversee the American justice system, for example, Attorney General John Ashcroft, likens civil libertarians to terrorist sympathizers. His education secretary, Rod Paige, lauded private schools with "Christian values" over the public schools his department was created to improve. Meanwhile, the influential Republican organizer Grover Norquist, who meets regularly with Karl Rove to plot political strategy, says that "bipartisanship is another name for date rape." Rev. Franklin Graham, the son of Billy Graham, who gave the invocation at President Bush's inauguration, later called Islam "a very evil and wicked religion"—and he not only met with no presidential rebuke, but was shortly thereafter invited to address troops at the Pentagon. Even this paled, however, compared to the administration's unwillingness to fire Lt. Gen. William Boykin of the army, deputy undersecretary of defense for intelligence and war-fighting support, who gave a speech in an evangelical church in which he portrayed the war in Iraq as one against "Satan," disparaging all Muslims with his claim that "my God was bigger than his," and "I knew that my God was a real God, and his was an idol."

What we have sought to do in *The Book on Bush* is separate the rhetoric from the policy to illustrate the costs to America and the world of allowing hard-right radicals to continue their misrule over the world's most powerful nation. The great disadvantage the mass media have in covering this administration is that they must take its words as seriously as its deeds; more seriously, in fact, because words are public and deeds are largely private and/or too complex for coverage. Add to this mix an increasingly vocal and well-funded conservative media operation that dominates cable TV news and talk radio, combined with a dumbing down/tabloidization of so many journalistic enterprises, and we find precious little attention paid to the actual consequences of the Bush administration's assault on most Americans' interests and beliefs.

We do not doubt that some Americans have benefited from the priorities of the current presidency. It is clearly "Morning in America" again for the superrich. After two years of declines, *Forbes* reported in 2003, the total net worth of America's four hundred richest people rose 10 percent to $955 billion in September 2003. With the top 1 percent receiving as much as the bottom 60 percent in Bush's tax breaks this coming decade, the gap between the rich and everyone else will only grow. But the progress that most Americans were making during the Clinton-Gore administration came to an almost immediate halt during the Bush presidency. As chapter 3 discussed, Census Bureau data released in September 2003 show that under George W. Bush, the number of Americans living in poverty saw its largest increase in more than forty years, median household income declined, and the number of Americans living without health insurance spiked upward, together with unemployment. Meanwhile, the government's fiscal position, which improved every year under Bill Clinton finally reaching a record surplus, collapsed into a projected deficit approaching $500 billion, and even this astronomical figure excluded the costs of the Iraq war, already in the hundreds of billions. While a portion of these unhappy trends can be attributed to structural changes in both the United States and the global economy—for instance, the flight of manufacturing jobs to low-wage, low-rights countries—almost all were exacerbated by Bush administration policies.

In the crucial area of security in the post–September 11 era, the administration surely talked tough, but inspired threats to Americans where none existed before. The Bush invasion of Iraq solved no security problems facing the United States; our nation's homeland remains dangerously vulnerable to potentially catastrophic terrorist attack, especially from containers on entering vessels. Osama bin Laden and his al Qaeda cronies remain at large in part because of the administration's miscalculation when it refused to send in even a fraction of the number of soldiers it later deployed to Iraq, thus allowing the real perpetrators of September 11 to elude capture after being cornered in Tora Bora. Indeed, al Qaeda is armed with fresh recruits inspired by the U.S. invasion and a new base of operations amid the chaos in Baghdad. Bush's invasion of Iraq may one day be studied by future historians as among the most costly self-inflicted injuries ever to befall a democratic nation.

The Iraq obsession also distracted the administration from addressing genuine threats emanating from Iran and North Korea, where, deaf to Bush's entreaties, the president's "friend," Russia's Vladimir Putin, is engaged in helping these "axis of evil" members achieve their nuclear ambitions.

A related international cost of the Bush presidency is the intense hostility it has inspired against Americans in virtually every nation on earth.* While Presidents Kennedy and Clinton were usually lionized abroad, and even Ronald Reagan had his overseas admirers, George W. Bush dare not show his face in public on the European continent or, indeed, almost anywhere in public where a large and probably angry crowd might gather. On the second anniversary of September 11, the *New York Times* reported that "in Europe overall, the proportion of people who want the United States to maintain a strong global presence fell nineteen points since a similar poll last year, from 64 percent to 45 percent, while 50 percent of respondents in Germany, France, and Italy express opposition to American leadership." In numerous nations, including many allies, respondents told pollsters they feared George W. Bush more than Saddam Hussein or even Osama bin Laden. "The war has widened the rift between Americans and Western Eu-

---

*The only exception being Israel.

ropeans," concluded Pew Research Center director Andrew Kohut, "further inflamed the Muslim world, softened support for the war on terrorism and significantly weakened global public support for the pillars of the post–World War II era—the UN and North Atlantic Alliance today." The White House's own "Advisory Group on Public Diplomacy for the Arab and Muslim World" found hostility toward the United States under George W. Bush reaching what it termed "shocking levels."

The point is not that these more extreme sentiments should be considered in any way sensible; rather they are a clear measure of Bush and Company's failure. For such hostility will surely be costly when America needs to share military burdens, exchange intelligence data about global terrorism, and arrive at economic policies that strengthen the global economy. The revulsion of the international community to both the substance and style of U.S. policies is already costing American taxpayers, since these nations have no interest whatsoever in helping a Bush who cried wolf bear the burden for the occupation of Iraq. As one UN official put it to a *Washington Post* reporter, "They're on their own [in Iraq]. It's just between them and the American taxpayer."

In documenting the arguments in this book, we have not selected isolated examples of Bush malfeasance. Virtually every area of policy contains the patented Bush administration admixture of false claims, irresponsible policies, a recalcitrance that passes for resolution, and a blind confidence that brings to mind the British aphorism, "Perhaps wrong but never in doubt."

We leave it to others to explain what factors in Mr. Bush's biography or past life experiences account for his conversion to and stubborn embrace of so extreme a political path. What interests us are the policies themselves and the manner in which they have been pursued. Indeed, Bush sometimes gives the impression of being willing to say or do almost *anything* to achieve his political goals. That includes exploiting the understandable fear of terrorism for political gain—"Every day, I'm reminded about what 9/11 means to America," Bush responded (as previously noted) when asked in July 2003 about the $170 million budget for his unopposed primary campaign, adding "we're still threatened." Here Bush is fulfilling the joking observation of E. J. Dionne that W.'s slogan seems to be "The only thing we have to fear is the loss of fear itself."

How does he get away with it? Again, this is a topic for another book, but a few explanations strike us as obvious. For much of his presidency—during the early "honeymoon" period and in the aftermath of September 11 and the two wars that followed—most Democrats were disinclined to give Mr. Bush any trouble on almost anything. And the adversarial image of the Fourth Estate glorified in *All the President's Men* is about as current as the bell-bottoms Robert Redford wore on-screen. Given the perception of Bush's enormous "wartime" popularity, few in the mainstream media felt inclined to subject the president to much critical scrutiny without an opposition figure to whom they might attach the story. It was revealing that until his now famous "sixteen words" about Iraq-Niger were shown to be false in 2003, the American media spent far more space writing about the serial dissembling of one reporter named Jayson Blair (which was spectacular) than the serial dissembling of one president named George W. Bush (which was far more consequential).

Those reporters who did keep asking tough questions or writing critical stories suddenly found themselves sitting in back rows, not called on or not called back. How many journalists are willing to write an article exposing Bush's disinformation knowing that an owner or editor may frown on it, the White House may retaliate, Bill O'Reilly may attack it as unpatriotic, and he or she will be unable to keep writing about them in any event because repeated misstatements by definition aren't "new," hence not news? Bush's infrequent press conferences hardly invite candid exchanges. It was so obvious at his pre–Iraq invasion press conference that he was calling on preselected reporters that even Bush joked that "this is scripted." Journalist Lawrence McQuillam, a veteran of six White Houses, sat in the front rows and quickly understood what was happening. "Eventually futility sinks in," he told *The American Prospect.* "I've just never been to a press conference where the president never looked at the audience to see if anybody was raising a hand to ask a question."

The predominance of the Bush version of reality was strengthened by the undeniably powerful right-wing attack machine that conservatives have constructed during the past three decades. Should any prominent individual— say, Al Gore or Tom Daschle—risk raising his voice to point out that the president said "black" to describe "white," he could expect to witness an immediate partisan character attack echoing through a dizzying array of media outlets: in print, on network and cable TV, on talk radio, and on the Internet.

It must be added that even though we all know "politics ain't beanbag," the Bush team plays awfully dirty. On Washington's K Street, GOP officials demand that corporations fire their longtime lobbyists and hire loyal Republicans instead. "There is a perception among some business interests there could be retribution if you don't play ball on almost every issue that comes up," Representative Calvin Dooley (D-CA) explains. On issue after issue, the White House and its allies play hardball while others play stickball.

When former ambassador Joseph Wilson went public to reveal the truth about Bush's discredited claim about Iraq-Niger weapons-grade uranium, two senior Bush administration officials apparently retaliated by leaking the name of his wife, a longtime CIA agent, to six separate journalists, endangering both U.S. intelligence operations and possibly the lives of agents and serving notice as well to those who step out of line. (Revealing the identities of covert officials is a violation of two laws, the National Agents' Identity Act and the Unauthorized Release of Classified Information Act.)

After a congressional ally said that the Bush White House's response to Wilson would be to "slime and defend," John Dean remarked, "If I thought I had seen dirty political tricks as nasty and vile as they could get at the Nixon White House, I was wrong. Nixon never set up a hit on one of his enemy's wives."

On Capitol Hill, Democratic senators who opposed Bush's judicial nominations, some of whom were Catholic, found themselves systematically attacked as "anti-Catholic" by a group set up by C. Boyden Gray with White House coordination. This tack surely surprised such Catholic senators as Edward Kennedy and Patrick Leahy, the latter denouncing it as "religious McCarthyism." When Senator Richard Durbin (D-IL) consistently criticized administration policy in Iraq, the White House floated, said Durbin, a bogus story that he had disclosed confidential information and might be removed from the Senate Intelligence Committee as a result. "If any member of this Senate questions this White House policy," said an angry Durbin on the Senate floor, "be prepared for the worst." The worst may well have been how the White House allowed Republican campaign officials to attack the patriotism of Senator Max Cleland, a triple amputee and Vietnam war hero, in pursuit of its goal of a Republican victory in 2002.

The John DiIulio incident also shows how effectively muscular the Bush team can be. After this aide wrote a seven-page, on-the-record letter to a journalist detailing a White House that was all-politics, all-the-time, within days DiIulio had been forced to abjectly apologize. His office at the University of Pennsylvania distributed this statement: "John DiIulio agrees that his criticisms were groundless and baseless due to poorly chosen words and examples. He sincerely apologizes and is deeply remorseful." The same day, press spokesman Ari Fleischer was saying, "any suggestion that the White House makes decisions that are not based on sound policy reasons is baseless and groundless." Is the use of the same words a coincidence or a show trial?

The politics of vindictiveness also governs international relations. When Bush's good friend Mexican president Vicente Fox hesitated to support the U.S. resolution in the Security Council to invade Iraq, a U.S. diplomat warned that its demurral could "stir up feelings" against Mexicans in the United States, and, referring to the internment of Japanese-Americans in 1942, asked whether Mexico "wants to stir the fires of jingoism during a war." And President Bush said of countries who opposed the final U.S. war resolution (which included a large majority of the Security Council), "there will be a certain sense of discipline."

Finally, the willingness of so many administration members to lie outright about the most somber—even sacred—matters of state, such as war, caught many Americans and much of the media off guard. "Everyone makes mistakes when they open their mouths and we forgive them," said Brookings Institution scholar Stephen Hess, a former Eisenhower speechwriter. "What worries me about some of [Bush's] mistakes is that they appear to be with foresight. This is about public policy in its grandest sense, about potential wars and who is our enemy, and a president has a special obligation to getting it right." Indeed, how else to explain the amazing statistic that 70 percent of Americans believe Saddam Hussein was the cause of the September 11 attack other than W.'s repeated dissembling about Saddam and 9/11?

In September 2003 Bush finally admitted that, "there is no evidence that Hussein was involved with September 11," an inconvenient acknowledgment that came only after a war and occupation based largely on false pretenses. Previously, when the truth was critically important, the president told the nation: "You can't distinguish between al Qaeda and Saddam when you talk about the war on terror." Indeed, Bush even justified the war to Congress on this basis when he asserted his legal right to begin it because of legislation passed by Congress that authorized force against "nations, organizations, or persons who planned, authorized, committed, or aided the terrorist attacks that occurred on September 11, 2001." Incredibly, even after President Bush himself had begun discrediting the Saddam–9/11 link, Vice President Cheney was still trying to sow confusion on this crucial point. Speaking on NBC's *Meet the Press*, Cheney described Iraq as "the geographic base of the terrorists who have had us under assault for many years, but most especially on 9/11."

Perhaps most egregious—at least in the eyes of these two New Yorkers—was the Bush administration's willingness to lie to the heroic safety workers and traumatized citizens in the aftermath of September 11 about contamination levels near Ground Zero. Can there be a greater violation of public trust than to knowingly manipulate data in order to endanger first responders and citizens still reeling from the shock of a horrific terrorist attack?

The Bush administration's penchant to tell "stretchers," in Mark Twain's word, not only puts people's lives at risk, but it also corrodes and ultimately destroys our democracy's most precious asset—the public trust. In her 1986 book *Lying: Moral Choices in Public and Private Life,* the philosopher Sissela Bok wrote:

> Imagine a society, no matter how ideal in other respects, where word and gesture could never be counted upon. Questions asked, answers given, information exchanged—all would be worthless. A warning that a well was poisoned or a plea for help in an accident would come to be ignored unless independent confirmation could be found. . . . Trust is a social good just as much as the air we breathe or the water we drink.

Among the angriest victims of the administration's dishonesty are America's soldiers themselves. Told to expect wine and roses from a population cheering its "liberation," they now find themselves targets of hatred and persistent guerrilla attacks. These men and women are, in the words of reservist Richard Murphy, being asked to "get shot at regularly, endure searing heat and live in less than desirable conditions." They have been told by their superiors to expect at least one twelve-month rotation in Iraq and possibly more. Because the military is undermanned and the Bush-Rumsfeld foreign policy underplanned, it is "grunts" like Murphy who, more than anyone, are being forced to bear the brunt of the administration's failure to prepare for the occupation and reconstruction of Iraq beyond any contingency envisioned by its improbably rosy scenarios.

And yet Bush continues on his chosen path, unmoved, unconcerned, and perhaps even unaware. The president told Fox News interviewer Brit Hume in September 2003 that rather than read a complete newspaper story, he merely "glance[s] at the headlines just to [get a] kind of a flavor for what's moving. I rarely read the stories." When Hume asked how long he'd been doing this as president, Bush replied, "Practice since day one"—and Hume emitted a surprised, "Really?" Bush does so, he says, because "the most objective sources I have are people on my staff who tell me what's happening in the world." (Probably without any ironic self-awareness, W. complained in the fall of 2003 about a press "filter" that kept the good news about the American occupation of Iraq from reaching the public without realizing how the word could also refer to staff who "filtered" out news that might displease the boss.) In other words, he lives inside an information bubble, fed only by faithful aides, telling him what he wants to hear, when he wants to hear it.

The problem, ultimately, is a president who is both messianic and radical. Bush himself in the past has shrewdly called the first Tuesday in November "Reality Day" because talk ends when there is a real result. So what happens on presidential "reality days" when the results are the opposite of wishful assertions—for example, when Iraq has no nuclear weapons program or cheering crowds, when tax cuts cause deficits to skyrocket, when there are too few stem cell lines for scientific research, when global warming heats up, when poor children are left behind in school, when AmeriCorps does not grow by 20,000 volunteers but shrinks by 20,000, when hero cops and firefighters get seriously ill after they were assured that the Ground Zero air was safe, when allies and the UN shun your call to share the burdens of occupying Iraq because they regard you as a "bungling bully," or when a Supreme Court of mostly Republican appointees rules that affirmative action is not "quotas" but desirable? Does George W. Bush then exit his bubble called denial, and later change course—as Reagan and Bush 41 did when they raised taxes in their third years to avoid ruinous deficits—or keep flying on just a right wing and a prayer?

"My faith frees me," Bush has claimed in his (ghostwritten) autobiography. "Frees me to make the decisions that others might not like. Frees me to try to do the right thing, even though it may not poll well. Frees me to enjoy life and not worry about what comes next." These may be admirable qualities in a parson or preacher, but for a president of the United States who combines ideological extremism with intellectual laziness, and tops them off with serial dishonesty, this type of "faith" is a recipe for disaster. It is America's peculiar burden at the dawn of the new century that its citizens— a majority of whom did not even choose to elect Mr. Bush to be their president in the first place—must now reap what he has sown.

Acknowledgments

*

R eaders should know what all authors do—that while writing is a solo experience, publishing requires a collaboration. Winston Churchill may have been able to simply dictate his histories, but we could not. Instead, each of us is deeply grateful to family, friends, and colleagues who were indispensable to *The Book on Bush*.

Eric: I would like to thank my amazing girls, Diana Roberta Silver and Eve Rose Alterman, for making life between deadlines their patented mixture of joy and exasperation. Life would hardly be worth living without the *mishegas* that mother and daughter regularly inject into an otherwise empty existence. In addition to the work of my coauthor—and to the many reporters and scholars cited in the text and footnotes—I owe a special debt to my friend Husain Haqqani of the Carnegie Endowment for International Peace, who helped explain to me the history and geopolitics of southern Asia. I would also like to express my gratitude to longtime basketball/poker buddies, Isaac Shapiro and Joel Friedman of the Center on Budget and Policy Priorities, who together with the no-less-generous Jeff Madrick of the Cooper Union, dropped everything to offer extremely valuable expertise on an extremely tight schedule. Finally, this same tight publication schedule has led me to an even greater appreciation of my great good fortune to be able to rely on the genius and professionalism of my longtime editor, Rick Kot, and much-beloved agent, Tina Bennett. Writing books is tedious work, and knowing that I had Rick and Tina on my side improves not only the final product, but also my (generally grumpy) mood in trying to produce it. It is with the deepest gratitude for their support and expertise in the past that I dedicate my portion of this work to Rick and Tina.

Mark: I express special appreciation to the New Democracy Project and NYU Law School—most notably to President John Sexton for the faculty appointment that helped spawn this baby. Chief editorial assistant Jenny Stepp of NDP kept the trains on their tracks with equanimity and intelligence. Longtime colleague Glenn von Nostitz and five law students brilliantly explored the policies of Bushworld, helping explain the gap between word and deed—David Berger, Warren Braunig, Peter Lallas, Ashika Singh, and Matthew Trokenheim. Others providing valuable research and/or logistical support at NDP included Leora Hanser, Patrick Low, Mark Silverbush, Jon Brody, Tara Ochman, and Heather Austin.

Friends and scholars generously helped by reviewing chapters in their areas of knowledge and have earned my deep gratitude—Mike Barnes, Gary Bass, Muzaffar Chishti, Charlie Cray, Marie Filbin, George Frampton, Janna Freed, Jamie Galbraith, Marcela Howell, Nancy Keenan, Kirsten Moore, Tony Orza, Ron Pollack, and Michael Waldman.

Last, a special hug to Deni, Jenya, and Jonah, who are as critical privately as they are loyal and loving publicly—and astonishingly understanding as their husband or father goes from deadline to deadline, whether literary or political. And I dedicate my share of the book to Steve, for continuing to educate, with wisdom if not patience, his younger brother.

ERA
MJG
November 1, 2003

Notes

*

1. Introduction

1 **"All public policy . . ."**: Bill Minutaglio, *First Son: George W. Bush and the Bush Family Dynasty* (New York: Three Rivers Press, 1998), 277 (hereafter cited as *First Son*).

2 **Senator Moynihan:** R. W. Apple Jr., "Bush Sues to Halt Hand Recount in Florida; The Limits of Patience," *New York Times,* November 12, 2000.

2 **Klein:** Quoted in Jonathan Chait, "Mad About You," *The New Republic,* September 29, 2003, 20.

2 **Bruce Buchanan:** Ronald Brownstein, "Bush Moves by Refusing to Budge; Seen as a Centrist While Governor of Texas, He Is Testing the Limits of Consensus as President," *Los Angeles Times,* March 2, 2003.

3 **Frank Bruni:** Frank Bruni, "White House Memo: Presidency Takes Shape with No Fuss, No Sweat," *New York Times,* February 10, 2001.

3 **"Bush Charm Offensive":** Judy Keen, "Bush Charm Offensive Gains Ground; The President's Efforts to Reach Out to Friend and Foe Have Softened Post-Election Rancor," *USA Today,* February 2, 2001.

3 **"We're not serious readers":** *First Son,* 86.

3 **Tucker Carlson:** Tucker Carlson, *Talk,* September 1999.

3 **"policy time" sessions:** Steven Brill, *After: How America Confronted the September 12 Era* (New York: Simon & Schuster, 2003), 376.

3 **Richard Perle:** Sam Tanenhaus, "Bush's Brain Trust," *Vanity Fair,* July 2003.

4 **Jonathan Pollard:** Jonathan Chait, "Mad About You," *The New Republic,* September 29, 2003, 20.

4 **"don't second-guess":** Elisabeth Bumiller, David E. Sanger, and Richard W. Stevenson, "The President: How Three Weeks of War in Iraq Looked From the Oval Office," *New York Times,* April 14, 2003.

4 **David von Drehle:** David von Drehle, *Washington Post,* "A Bush Trademark: Sticking to the Plan," April 6, 2003.

5 **Dr. Richard Land:** Elisabeth Bumiller, "Evangelicals Sway White House on Human Rights Issues Abroad," *New York Times,* October 26, 2003.

5 **"Karl Rove would likely rather risk":** Michele Cottle, *The New Republic,* April 21 and 28, 2003, 16.

7 **Arthur Miller:** "The Nation's 137th Anniversary Celebration," December 8, 2002.

7 **Stem cell "compromise":** David Frum, *The Right Man: The Surprise Presidency of George W. Bush* (New York: Random House, 2003), 110.

7 **"confidently expressed":** Joshua Micah Marshall, "The Post-Modern President," *Washington Monthly,* September 2003, 22.

8 **"hypnotize the American people":** Editorial, "Sidestepping on Iraq," *New York Times,* July 31, 2003.

8 **Renana Brooks:** Renana Brooks, "A Nation of Victims," *The Nation,* June 30, 2003.

8 **Presidential circumlocutions:** Dana Milbank, "For Bush, Facts Are Malleable: Presidential Tradition of Embroidering Key Assertions Continues," *Washington Post,* October 22, 2002.

9 **media filter:** ABC News, "The Note," September 3, 2002, at http://www.abcnews.go.com/sections/politics/DailyNews/TheNote.html.

9 **"lying by reflex":** Michael Kinsley, "87 Billion Apologies," *Slate*, September 11, 2003.

10 **"more important things to do than worry about":** Michael Kinsley, "Lying in Style," *Slate*, April 18, 2002.

10 **labor defenestration:** William Grieder, "Rolling Back the 20th Century," *The Nation*, May 12, 2003.

2. Drill and Cough

12 **A comprehensive 2000 survey:** Surveys by National Opinion Research Center-General Social Survey, February 1-June 25, 2000, and Roper Organization, September 2001.

12 **He even promised:** George W. Bush, "A Comprehensive National Energy Policy," September 29, 2000, Saginaw, Michigan.

13 **"unable to fend":** Thomas J. Bray, "Conservatives Worry Bush Is Too Green," *Detroit News*, October 25, 2000.

13 **Whitman quote:** Eric Pianin, "EPA Mulls Limits for Power Plant Emissions," *Washington Post*, February 28, 2001.

13 **O'Neill:** Julian Borger, "Bush Drops Pledge on Cutting CO_2," *The Guardian (London)*, March 15, 2001.

14 **Bush himself argued:** Bennett Roth, "Bush Defends Reversal of Gas Limits," *Houston Chronicle*, March 15, 2001; Bruce Reed, "Monkey Do: Similarities Between Presidencies and Management Decisions on President George W. Bush and President Bill Clinton," *Washington Monthly*, June 1, 2001.

14 **"profoundly shortsighted":** Resignation letter from Jane Hughes Turnbull to Energy Secretary Spencer Abraham, March 16, 2001.

14 **$3 million in campaign contributions:** Center for Responsive Politics Web site, http://www.opensecrets.org/2000elect/sector/AllCands.htm; Federal Election Commission data.

14 **emissions will actually *increase:*** Editorial, "Weak Response on Global Warming," *New York Times*, February 14, 2003; Natural Resources Defense Council, "Untangling the Accounting Gimmicks in White House Global Warming, Pollution Plans," February 2002.

14 **"There's no evidence":** Interview with Howard "Bud" Ris, March 4, 2003.

14 **Edison Electric:** Elizabeth Shogren, "13 Industries Set Emissions Targets as Part of Bush Initiative," *Los Angeles Times*, February 13, 2003.

15 **In the international press:** James Graff, "Bad Air over Kyoto," *Time (Int'l. Edition)*, April 9, 2001, 18; Rob Edwards, "Dubya Steps on the Gas and Leaves the World Fuming," *(Scottish) Sunday Herald*, April 1, 2001, 13.

15 **"We're absolutely sure":** John Harries, in Julian Borger, "Bush Drops Pledge on Cutting CO_2," *The Guardian (London)*, March 15, 2001.

15 **warmest in a thousand years:** Andrew C. Revkin, "Temperatures Are Likely to Go from Warming to Warmer," *New York Times*, December 31, 2002.

15 **two of the three:** Eric Pianin, "Reductions Sought in Greenhouse Gases: Criticizing Bush, Senators Would Set Deadlines," *Washington Post*, January 9, 2003.

15 **British scientists:** Juliette Jowit, "Official: Earth Is Hotter and It's Our Fault," *The Observer*, July 27, 2003.

15 **Temperatures in the Arctic:** Intergovernmental Panel on Climate Change, "Climate Change 2001: Impacts, Adaptation and Vulnerability," 2001.

15 **glaciers of the Andes:** Juan Forero, "As Andean Glaciers Shrink, Water Worries Grow," *New York Times*, November 24, 2002.

16 **spent $18 billion:** George W. Bush, "President Bush Discusses Global Climate Change," White House release, June 11, 2001.

16 **"The administration has fallen":** Interview with Howard "Bud" Ris, March 5, 2003.

16 **In 2001 additional reports:** Intergovernmental Panel on Climate Change, "Climate Change 2001: IPCC Third Assessment Report, 2001," www.grida.no/climate/ipcc_tar/index.htm; National Research Council, "Climate Change: An Analysis of Some Key Questions," 2001, at http://books.nap.edu/books/0309075742/html/index.html.

16 **Watts quote:** *Business Respect*, no. 52 (March 14, 2003).

16 **"incomplete state of scientific":** James Graff, "Bad Air Over Kyoto," *Time (Int'l. Edition),* April 9, 2001, 18.

16 **deleted the entire global warming section:** Katharine Q. Seelye and Jennifer 8. Lee, "E.P.A. Calls U.S. Cleaner and Greener Than 30 Years Ago," *New York Times,* June 24, 2003.

16 **Internal EPA memo:** The memo, dated April 29, 2003, can be found in the News Release Archives section of the National Wildlife Federation's Web site, www.nwf.org.

17 **The Luntz report:** Jennifer Lee, "A Call for Softer, Greener Language: G.O.P. Adviser Offers Linguistic Tactics for Environmental Edge," *New York Times,* March 2, 2003. To read the Luntz report, go to www.ewg.org/briefings/luntzmemo/pdf/LuntzResearch_environment.pdf.

17 **Of the 400 organizations:** Don Van Natta Jr. and Neela Banerjee, "Top G.O.P. Donors in Energy Industry Met Cheney Panel," *New York Times,* March 1, 2002.

17 **Kelliher e-mail:** Natural Resources Defense Council, Press Release, April 26, 2002, at www.nrdc.org/media/pressreleases/020426.asp.

18 **A March 22, 2001, e-mail:** E-mail from Bob Slaughter to Joseph Kelliher, March 22, 2001, at www.nrdc.org/air/energy/taskforce/doc6368.html.

18 **Among oil and gas:** Center for Responsive Politics Web site, www.opensecrets.org; Federal Elections Commission data.

18 **Data on contributions and visits:** NRDC Press Release, May 21, 2002.

18 **Enron donation figures:** American Family Voices Special Report, "Time for an Independent Counsel: Enron's Shadow Government," March 12, 2002; Center for Responsive Politics, at www.opensecrets.org; Federal Elections Commission data.

19 **seventeen different policy initiatives:** American Family Voices, "Enron's Legacy: Letting the Big Dogs Run"; American Family Voices Special Report, "Time for an Independent Counsel: Enron's Shadow Government," March 12, 2002. Both are published at www.thedailyenron. com.

19 **Palmer quote:** Don Van Natta Jr. and Neela Banerjee, "Top GOP Donors in Energy Industry Met Cheney Panel," *New York Times,* March 1, 2002.

19 **"Real men don't build windmills . . .":** Carl Pope in Amy Standen, "Interview with Carl Pope," *Salon.com,* April 29, 2002.

19 **"Virtually all of":** Vice President Dick Cheney, *Face the Nation,* CBS, May 20, 2001.

19 **Bush's $28 billion in subsidies:** Green Scissors Report, "Running on Empty: How Environmentally Harmful Energy Subsidies Siphon Billions from Taxpayers," 2002, at www.greenscissors. org/publications/runningonempty.pdf. This is just one of many reports that attempt to add up and detail the energy subsides. The nonpartisan Joint Committee on Taxation and the U.S. Energy Information Administration estimate the total at $29 billion, while the Special Investigation Division for the U.S. House of Representatives Committee on Government Reform, in its report "Hitting the Jackpot: How the House Energy Bill Rewards Millions in Contributions with Billions in Returns," calculated the total at $36 billion.

19 **Cheney also claimed:** Vice President Dick Cheney, *Face the Nation,* CBS, May 20, 2001. For a comparison of the Cheney plan and the Sierra Club plan, go to www.sierraclub.org/energy/bush_plan/12pointsofenergy.pdf.

19 **the Sierra Club's response:** Andrew Goldstein and Matthew Cooper, "How Green Is the White House?" *Time,* April 29, 2002.

20 **Pope describes the meeting:** Amy Standen, "Interview with Carl Pope," *Salon.com,* April 29, 2002.

20 **Bush had declared, "To enhance America's":** Robert Kuttner, "The Ideological Impostor," *American Prospect,* June 3, 2002.

20 **the budget he submitted:** Department of Energy, FY2004 budget.

20 **Frank Luntz memo:** Evan Ratliff, "The Art of Doublespeak," *OnEarth Magazine,* Summer 2003, p. 30.

20 **"The House knows":** Spencer Abraham, "Drill ANWR Now," *Wall Street Journal,* November 8, 2001.

21 **the weeks after:** Colin Sullivan, "ANWR: Republicans Still Scoping Daschle's Compromise," *Greenwire,* October 15, 2001.

21 **63 percent of voters:** Mellman Group, January 2002, reported in "U.S. Majority Not Keen on Bush's Plan," *Inter News Service,* January 26, 2002.

21 **A year later:** Liz Ruskin, Wilderness Society Poll, "Poll Finds Majority Against ANWR," *Anchorage Daily News,* February 1, 2003.

21 **The panel reported:** Andrew C. Revkin, "Experts Conclude Oil Drilling Has Hurt Alaska's North Slope," *New York Times,* March 5, 2003.

21 **they warned that current:** Ibid; Editorial, "Cautionary Notes from Alaska," *New York Times,* March 10, 2003.

21 **"the equivalent of":** Spencer Abraham, "Drill ANWR Now," *Wall Street Journal,* November 8, 2001.

21 **Bush later claimed:** H. Josef Hebert, "Energy Prices Boost Arctic Drilling Plan," Associated Press, March 12, 2003.

21 **"Technically recoverable oil":** U.S. Geological Service, "Arctic National Wildlife Refuge, 1002 Area Petroleum Assessment, 1998, Including Economic Analysis," 1998.

22 **Based on EIA data:** Energy Information Administration/Monthly Energy Review, Table 1.8, Overview of U.S. Petroleum Trade, February 2003.

22 **Fineberg quote:** Diane Feen, "War on Terror Boosts Bush's Popularity, Worries 'Greens,'" *O'Dwyer's PR Services Report,* February 2002.

22 **a 0.4 mpg improvement:** Amory B. Lovins and L. Hunter Lovins, "Frozen Assets: Alaskan Oil's Threat to Energy Security," Rocky Mountain Institute Report, 2001.

22 **the $1.9 million:** Center for Responsive Politics Web site, http://www.opensecrets.org/2000elect/select/AllCands.htm; Federal Election Commission data.

22 **automakers already have the technology:** National Research Council, "Effectiveness and Impact of Corporate Average Fuel Economy (CAFE) Standards," 2002.

22 **adamantly opposing:** Jeff Plungis, "Automakers Support Alternate CAFE Proposal," *Detroit News,* March 11, 2002.

22 **"If the vehicles":** Daniel Becker, in James Ridgeway, "Forget Your Problems, We're Preparing for War," *Village Voice,* January 29, 2003.

22 **"The degree of duplicity":** Interview with Daniel Becker, April 2, 2003.

23 **Ris on hydrogen car project:** Interview with Howard "Bud" Ris, March 4, 2003.

23 **"Hummerdinger" giveaway:** Danny Hakim, "Bush Proposal May Cut Tax on S.U.V.'s for Business," *New York Times,* January 21, 2003; see also Al Kamen, "A Hummerdinger of a Tax Loophole?," *Washington Post,* September 26, 2003.

23 **contributing $2.7 million:** Center for Responsive Politics Web site, http://www.opensecrets.org/industries/indus.asp?ind=T2100; Federal Election Commission data.

24 **Numerous studies have:** Abt Associates, "The Particulate-Related Health Benefits of Reducing Power Plant Emissions," October 2000, Exhibit 6-1, 6-4.

24 **"We must seek":** President George W. Bush, Sequoia National Park, May 30, 2001.

24 **"Clear Skies will reduce":** President George W. Bush, "Announcement of Clear Skies Initiative," July 1, 2002.

24 **Bush's EPA had a meeting:** U.S. EPA, "Discussion of Multi-Pollutant Strategy: Comparison of Requirements Under Business-as-Usual and the Straw Proposal." Meeting with EEI, September 18, 2001, p. 10. Available at www.cleartheair.org/currentstatus.pdf.

24 **Side by side:** "The Bush Administration's Air Pollution Plan Hurts Public Health, Helps Big Polluters, Worsens Global Warming." Report published by 14 nonprofit organizations, including the American Lung Association, Physicians for Social Responsibility, the Sierra Club, and the League of Conservation Voters, February 2003. The report can be found online at www. nrdc.org/air/pollution/fclearsk.asp.

25 **a 2003 EPA report:** Environmental Protection Agency, "America's Children and the Environment," 2003; Chris Holly, "EPA Reports Heats Up Utility Mercury Debate," *Energy Daily,* February 26, 2003.

25 **the overall emissions:** Gary C. Bryner, "The National Energy Policy: Assessing Energy Policy Choices," *Colorado Law Review* 73 (Spring 2002): 341, 376.

25 **responsible for 5,000 deaths:** Clean Air Task Force, "Power to Kill: Death and Disease from Power Plants Charged with Violating the Clean Air Act," July 2001, at www.catf.us/publications/reports/power_to_kill.php.

25 **"EPA was finally":** Interview with Eric Schaeffer, February 25, 2003.

25 **Southern Company memo:** Memo from Michael J. Riith to Joseph Kelliher, "NSR and Energy Strategy," March 23, 2001, NRDC Web site at www.nrdc.org/air/energy/taskforce/doc150.html and doc151.html.

26 **The Task Force included:** Michael Kilian, "EPA Softens Rules to Allow More Emissions," *Chicago Tribune,* August 28, 2003.

26 **Bush rule would allow:** Eric Pianin, "Clean Air Rules to Be Relaxed: EPA Will Ease Power Plants' Requirements," *Washington Post,* August 23, 2003; Katharine Q. Seelye, "Draft of Air Rule Is Said to Exempt Many Old Plants," *New York Times,* August 22, 2003.

26 **Bush made the New Source Review announcement:** Dana Milbank, "Bush Lauds Michigan Power Plant as Model of Clean Air Policy," *Washington Post,* September 16, 2003.

26 **1.4 million tons:** The Associated Press, "Two Studies Contradict EPA on New Rules," October 23, 2003.

26 **"The rule change . . .":** Editorial, "EPA Issues License to Pollute," *New York Daily News* August 31, 2003.

26 **Bush's 2003 EPA budget:** Natural Resources Defense Council, "Rewriting the Rules: Year-End Report 2002," January 2003.

26 **Since Bush took office:** Elizabeth Shogren, "Environmental Penalties Down Under Bush, Data Show; Administration Critics See a Smoking Gun, but Officials Say Spending on Forced Cleanups Is Up," *Los Angeles Times,* January 31, 2003.

27 **"What often happens":** Ari Fleischer, White House press briefing, June 13, 2002.

27 **"The data to defend":** Interview with Greg Wetstone, March 11, 2003.

27 **Sansonetti acknowledged:** Michael Schmidt, "Senate Democrats Grill Bush Officials Over NSR Changes," *Inside Energy,* July 22, 2002, 6.

27 **"literally written by":** Kennedy, Jim E., internal memo, DuPont Corporation, June 20, 1997. Published on TomPaine.com at www.tompaine.com/feature.cfm/ID/3126.

27 **"biggest environmental achievement":** Ken Silverstein, "The Polluters' President," *Sierra,* November 1, 1999.

27 **fewer than 10 percent:** Laura Elder, "No More Loopholes," *Corpus Christi Caller-Times,* June 10, 2001.

28 **less than 3 percent:** "The Lone Smog State," *The Economist,* July 22, 2000.

28 **Texas replaced voluntary program:** Laura Elder, "No More Loopholes," *Corpus Christi Caller-Times,* June 10, 2001.

28 **grandfathered companies contribute:** Peggy Fikac, "Limits on Campaign Finance Sought to Fight Air Pollution, *Austin American-Statesman,* June 10, 1998; Yuval Rosenberg, "What's the Truth About Bush's Environmental Campaign Claims?," *Newsweek,* October 19, 2000.

28 **"We need to make sure":** George W. Bush, presidential debate, October 11, 2000.

28 **535,000 children:** Laura Parker, "Lead Testing Policy May Change," *USA Today,* April 17, 2002.

29 **disavowed the plan:** Ceci Connolly, "Plan to Ease Lead Testing Regulations Disavowed: U.S. Backs Screening of Poor Children," *Washington Post,* May 15, 2002.

29 **"our lakes and rivers":** George W. Bush, Sequoia National Park, May 30, 2001.

29 **"Bush administration redefined":** John B. Judis, "King Coal," *The American Prospect,* December 16, 2002.

29 **Coal companies' support for Republicans:** Center for Responsible Politics Web site, www.opensecrets.org/industries/indus.asp?ind=E1210; Federal Elections Commission.

29 **"mining in the western United States":** John B. Judas, "King Coal," *The American Prospect,* December 16, 2002.

29 **Whitman's EPA deserves:** Michael E. White, "Whitman's EPA Could Have Been Worse, Right?," *Newsday* (op-ed), May 29, 2003.

30 **2003 report:** "Did EPA Mislead Public After 9/11?" CBSNews.com, August 9, 2003.

30 **asbestos levels were three times higher:** Laurie Garrett, "A Stink Over Air Quality," *(New York) Newsday,* August 23, 2003.

30 **"gave off gases . . .":** Ellen Wulfhorst, "Study Finds WTC Fires Spewed Toxic Gases for Weeks, *Reuters News Service,* September 12, 2003.

30 **May 2003 poll:** Pete Bowles, "Shock, Outrage from Residents," *(New York) Newsday,* August 23, 2003.

30 **Toxic waste/Superfund paragraph:** Natural Resources Defense Council, "Rewriting the Rules, Year End Report 2002," January 2003, p. 20; Katharine Q. Seelye, "Bush Proposing Policy Changes on Toxic Sites," *New York Times,* February 24, 2002.

31 **environmental regulation:** DuPont memo; see www.tompaine.com/feature.cfm/ID/3126.

31 **"If confirmed":** Gale Norton, testimony before the Senate Energy and Natural Resources Committee, January 26, 2001.

31 **2.6 million acres:** Editorial, "The End of Wilderness," *New York Times,* May 4, 2003.

31 **"took 40 million":** George W. Bush, presidential debate, October 11, 2000.

31 **six hundred public hearings:** Sam Parry, "Bush's Life of Deception," *Consortiumnews. com,* November 4, 2002.

31 **strongly confirmed:** *Kootenai Tribe of Idaho v. Veneman,* 313 F.3d 1094, 1121 (9th Cir. 2002). The court's opinion reads: "Members of the public had every right and ability after publication of the FEIS on November 13, 2000, to comment further before adoption of the final Rule on January 12, 2001. . . . Mere griping or even serious complaints from a segment of the public are not sufficient to justify a judicial negation of the entire rulemaking process."

31 **"contains nearly 30 percent":** Dana Milbank, "White House Won't Bar Logging on Alaska Land," *Washington Post,* March 1, 2003.

32 **would consider requests:** Paula Dobbyn, "Roadless Rule Exemptions Sought," *Anchorage Daily News,* June 10, 2003.

32 **"This isn't a chance":** George W. Bush, "President Announces Healthy Forests Initiative," Central Point, Oregon, August 22, 2002.

32 **Hayden quote:** "Bush Plan Leaves Forest Care to Timber Companies," *The Olympian (WA),* March 9, 2003.

32 **Even the study cited:** Ibid.

33 **In a telling gesture:** Jeff Mapes, "Support for Forest-Thinning Steps Up," *(Portland) Oregonian*, March 9, 2003.

33 **Bush's proposal would allow:** Douglas Gantenbein. "Dead Wood," *Slate.com*, December 4, 2002; Robert Pear, "Bush Plan Gives More Discretion to Forest Managers on Logging," *New York Times*, November 28, 2002; J. R. Pegg, "Bush Rewrites National Forest Management Plan," *Environment News Service*, November 28, 2002.

33 **"We have a problem":** George W. Bush, "President Announces Healthy Forest Initiative," Central Point, Oregon, August 22, 2002.

33 **A 2003 GAO report:** Zachary Coile, "Appeals Don't Stall Most Foreign Thinning Projects," *San Francisco Chronicle*, May 15, 2003.

33 **Griles and Powder River Basin:** Natural Resources Defense Council, "Rewriting the Rules, Year End Report 2002: The Bush Administration's Assault on the Environment," January 2003, 3.

34 **Myers and grazing rules:** Jonathan Chait, "Special K," *The New Republic*, December 30, 2002.

34 **Smith and oil and gas:** Ibid.

34 **Becker quote:** Interview with Dan Becker, April 2, 2003.

34 **pushed for drilling in Utah … Texas … California:** Natural Resources Defense Council, "Rewriting the Rules: Year-End Report 2002," January 2003.

34 **virtually every Republican:** Katherine Mieszkowski, "Bush to California: Choke on This," *Salon.com*, December 16, 2002.

34 **Bush was kinder:** Douglas Jehl, "On Environmental Rules, Bush Sees a Balance, Critics a Threat," *New York Times*, February 23, 2003.

34 **80 percent of these:** Eric Pianin, "U.S. Policy on Wetlands Redefined: Administration Stresses How, Not How Much, to Protect," *Washington Post*, December 28, 2002; Lindsay Riddell, "Wetland Guidelines Remove Some Protection," *Chattanooga Times Free Press (Tennessee)*, January 25, 2003; Damon Franz, "Data Lacking on Mitigation Projects, Experts Say," *Land Letter*, March 21, 2002.

35 **"Our lakes and rivers":** George W. Bush, "President Bush Announces National Parks Legacy Project," May 30, 2001.

3. Déjà Vu-doo Economics

36 **"from bitter experience" and 1984 polling data:** Quoted in Mark Mellman, "2004 Election: It's Still the Economy Stupid," TheHill.com, June 11, 2003.

37 **"no supply-side revolution":** Will Hutton, *A Declaration of Interdependence* (New York: W. W. Norton, 2003), 88-89.

37 **excess inventories:** Louis Uchitelle, "U.S. Overcapacity Stalls New Jobs," *New York Times*, October 19, 2003.

38 **income data:** See both Kevin Phillips, *Wealth and Democracy* (New York: Broadway Books, 2002), 121, and Edmund Andrews, "Heart of the Tax Debate: Who Benefits the Most?," *New York Times*, January 14, 2003.

38 **CEO and worker pay increases:** Kevin Phillips, ibid., 153.

38 **1 percent own about 50 percent:** Gar Alperovitz, "Tax the Plutocrats," *The Nation*, January 27, 2003, 15.

38 **black and Latino households:** Ray Boshara, "The $6,000 Solution," *Atlantic Monthly*, January-February 2003, 87.

38 **1900 compared to 2000:** Steven Weisman, *The Great Tax Wars* (New York: Simon and Schuster, 2002), 179.

39 **ten times more likely:** Speech by Will Hutton to Open Society Institute, April, 2003.

39 *Economist:* "Liberty's Great Advance," *The Economist*, June 28, 2003, 7.

39 **"largest rich-poor gap":** Phillips, *Wealth and Democracy*, xviii.

39 **tax "saving the Union":** Weisman, *The Great Tax Wars*, 252.

39 **John D. Rockefeller:** Ibid.

40 **"sunrises and sunsets":** Allan Sloan, "The Levitating Economy," *Newsweek*, July 7, 2003, 35-36.

42 **"making people struggle . . ."** Elizabeth Shogren, "Tighter Rules Likely for Welfare Families," *Los Angeles Times,* September 11, 2003.

43 **Ari Fleischer on taxes:** Quoted in Richard W. Stevenson, "Democrats See Opening for Attack on Economy," *New York Times,* July 4, 2003.

43 **Fleischer and RNC Web site:** David Firestone, "Second Study Finds Gaps in Tax Cuts," *New York Times,* June 1, 2003.

43 **non-married without children:** Robert S. McIntyre, "Third Time's No Charm," *The American Prospect,* July-August 2003, 23.

43 **$227, $20,762 and $89,509 numbers:** See tables 1.1 and 1.2 at www.taxpolicycenter.org/commentary/alumni_dist_inc.cfm#inc.

43 **"lucky duckies":** Editorial, "The Non-Taxpaying Class: Those Lucky Duckies," *Wall Street Journal,* November 20, 2002.

44 **". . . children":** Editorial, "Children Left Behind," *Washington Post,* June 2, 2003.

44 **15 percent and 7 percent:** www.ctj.org/pdf/allbushcut.pdf.

45 **"savings" of top officials:** See House Committee on Government Reform, minority staff release of June 2, 2003.

45 **small business taxes:** Center on Budget and Policy Priorities.

45 **McCain:** John McCain, interview by Katie Couric, *Today,* NBC, January 7, 2003.

45 **"can't miss":** Notebook, *The New Republic,* February 24, 2003, 8-9.

46 **Bush and start of recession:** See Dana Milbank, "As 2004 Nears, Bush Pins Slump on Clinton," *Washington Post,* July 1, 2003.

46 **Ten-year deficits:** See Richard Kogan, "401 Billion vs. 455 Billion: Good News, Bad News, or No News?" Center on Budget and Policy Priorities, August 13, 2003; also see, Jonathan Weisman, "2004 Deficit to Reach $480 Billion, Report Forecasts," *Washington Post,* August 27, 2003.

47 **Social Security and Medicare growth:** Jeff Madrick, "The Iraqi Time Bomb," *New York Times Magazine,* April 6, 2003, 48-51.

48 **deficit hypocrites:** See Peter Beinart, "Unbalanced," *The New Republic,* May 26, 2003, 6; David Firestone, "Conservatives Now See Deficits as a Tool to Fight Spending," *New York Times,* February 11, 2003.

48 **Hubbard's textbook and Snow and Mankiw:** *Money, the Financial System and the Economy;* see also Edmund L. Andrews, "A Salesman for Bush's Tax Plan Who Has Belittled Similar Ideas," *New York Times,* February 28, 2003; Greg Ip, "New Advisors' Deficit Dilemma," *Wall Street Journal,* January 29, 2003.

48 **deficits and interest rates:** See Gene Sperling, "The Long-Term Perils of Short-Term Tax Cuts," *Financial Times,* January 6, 2003, and Jonathan Chait, "Bad Debt," *The New Republic,* January 13, 2003, 12.

49 **Thomas L. Friedman:** "Read My Lips," *New York Times,* June 11, 2003.

49 **Center on Budget:** Robert Greenstein and Robert Kogin, "Cutting $10 Billion in Appropriations for Poverty and Other Programs . . . While Promoting a $670 Billion Tax Cut," Center on Budget and Policy Priorities, January 21, 2003.

49 **Over the decade:** Jeff Madrick, "The Iraqi Time Bomb," *New York Times Magazine,* April 16, 2003, 48-51.

49 **Examples of lauding and cutting:** Jason Miner, Democratic National Committee, "Bush's Budget Kiss of Death: Travel to a Venue; Cuts Its Funding," 2003.

50 **cotton subsidies:** Peter Beinart, "Grain of Salt," *The New Republic,* June 9, 2003, 6.

50 **Shifts in spending:** David Pace, "GOP Shifted Billions to Districts," Associated Press State and Local Wire, August 5, 2002.

50 **Milton Friedman:** "What Every American Wants," *Wall Street Journal,* January 15, 2003.

51 **Allen Schick:** "Bush's Budget Problem," at "The George W. Bush Presidency: An Early Assessment," Princeton University, April 25, 2003, 7.

51 **Senator Conrad:** Quoted in Eleanor Clift, "What Is He Thinking?," *Newsweek,* February 7, 2003.

51 **Broder:** "It Reeks of Politics," *Washington Post,* January 12, 2003.

52 **Akerlof:** Quoted on CBS. Marketwatch.com, August 14, 2003.

52 **workers pay many taxes:** Daniel Altman, "Doubling Up Taxation Isn't Limited to Dividends," *New York Times,* January 23, 2003.

52 **$60,000 family:** Donald L. Bartlett and James B. Steele, "The Really Unfair Tax," *Time,* February 3, 2003, 46.

52 **nearly 8 million:** Ibid.

52 **40 percent to 2.5 percent:** Joel Friedman, "Impact of the Dividend Tax Cut on the Elderly," Center on Budget and Policy Priorities, January 7, 2003.

53 **Declining and avoided corporate taxes:** See both Gar Alperovitz, "Tax the Plutocrats!," *The Nation,* January 27, 2003, 15-16, and Robert S. McIntyre, "Reality Check: Why the Bush Trea-

sury Department's Line on Corporate Taxes Doesn't Track," *The American Prospect*, December 30, 2002, 19.

53 **wars and inheritance taxes:** Weisman, *The Great Tax Wars*, 177-79, 201, 254.

54 **467 estates:** Discussed in Paul Krugman, "The Disappearing Middle," *New York Times Magazine*, October 20, 2002, 62.

54 **"Every family":** William Saletan, "Age Before Booty," Slate, January 7, 2003, at www.slate.com.

54 **Gates Sr. and United for:** See Bill Gates Sr. and Chuck Collins, *Wealth and Our Commonwealth: Why America Should Attack Accumulated Fortunes* (Cambridge: Beacon Press, 2003).

55 **Warren Buffett:** Warren Buffett, "Billionaires Don't Need Yet Another Tax Break," *(New York) Newsday*, May 25, 2003.

56 **Hassett:** Dana Milbank and Jonathan Weisman, "Middle Class Tax Share Set to Rise," *Washington Post*, June 4, 2003.

56 **Caldwell:** "Bush's Tax Cut is Unconservative," *Financial Times*, January 8, 2003.

56 **Citizens for Tax Justice:** "We're Paying Dearly for Bush's Tax Cuts," September 12, 2003.

57 **"intergenerational losing streak":** Ron Brownstein, "Like Father, Like Son," *Los Angeles Times*, September 30, 2002.

57 **Eighteen percent lost jobs:** K. A. Dixon and Carl E. Van Horn, "The Disposable Worker: Living in a Job-Loss Ecionomy," John Heldrich Center for Workforce Development at Rutgers, July 2003.

57 **job market downturn:** "Why for Many This Recovery Feels More Like a Recession," *Wall Street Journal*, May 29, 2003.

57 **low-wage data:** See Beth Shulman, "Four Myths, 30 Million Potential Votes," *Washington Post*, August 17, 2003; Randi Marshall, "Job Loss Anxiety Highest in Years," *(New York) Newsday*, July 29, 2003; and Abby Ellin, "For Many, Full-Time Work Means Part-Time Benefits," *New York Times*, August 17, 2003.

58 **Governor Riley:** Dale Russakoff, "Alabama Tied in Knots by Tax Vote," *Washington Post*, August 17, 2003.

58 **Governor Huckabee:** David Ignatius, "Bush's Neverland Economics," *Washington Post*, August 19, 2003.

59 **Bronx cheer:** "Americans' Views on Taxes," NPR, April 2003 and Dana Milbank and Dan Balz, "GOP Eyes Tax Cuts as Annual Events," *Washington Post*, May 11, 2003.

59 **partyology:** Jack Tapper, "Painting the Country Red," *Salon.com*, May 15, 2003.

59 **money shouts:** See, generally, Mark Green, *Selling Out: How Big Corporate Money Buys Elections, Rams Through Legislation and Betrays Our Democracy* (New York: ReganBooks, 2002).

60 **"is all about":** Ronald Brownstein, "President's Dramatic Reagan-esque Proposals Sharpen His Differences with Democrats," *Los Angeles Times*, January 8, 2003.

60 **Of some 40 million:** Jim Pinkerton, "Bush's Tax Cut Plan Figures to Win Him Votes," *(New York) Newsday*, January 9, 2003.

60 **Mitch Daniels:** Robin Toner, "For Republicans, Deficits Are Nothing to Be Ashamed Of," *New York Times*, February 9, 2003.

60 **Forums of economists:** Daniel Altman, "Divided Economic Advice and the Lure of Politics," *New York Times*, April 12, 2003.

4. *When Laissez Isn't Fair*

62 **"It solved my biggest":** Bill Minutaglio, *First Son: George W. Bush and the Bush Family Dynasty* (New York: Three Rivers Press, 2001), 241.

63 **MBNA, Bush's largest donor during 2000 election:** Center for Responsive Politics, at www.opensecrets.org.

63 **Eli Lilly and Homeland Security:** Bob Herbert, "Whose Hands Are Dirty?," *New York Times*, November 25, 2002.

64 **William Safire:** William Safire, "The Great Media Gulp," *New York Times*, May 22, 2003.

64 **Michael Copps:** Marilyn Geewax, "FCC's Action Under Attack; Battle Lines: Some in Congress Consider Trying to Undo New Media Rules," *Atlanta Journal-Constitution*, June 5, 2003.

64 **Over 750,000 citizens:** John Nichols, "FCC Rejects Public Interest," *The Nation* online, June 2, 2003, at www.thenation.com.

64 **Clear Channel ownership:** Eric Boehlert, "Clear Channel's Big, Stinking Deregulation Mess," *Salon.com,* February 19, 2003, at www.salon.com/tech/feature/2003/02/19/clear_channel_deregulation.

64 **Texas Rangers:** Paul Krugman, "Channels of Influence," *New York Times,* March 25, 2003.

64 **"the Administration . . . landscape":** Reuters, "White House Threatens Veto on Media-Ownership Cap," FindLaw, July 22, 2003, at www.findlaw.com.

65 **Bush on Powell decision:** George W. Bush, interview by Brit Hume, Fox News, September 23, 2003, at www.foxnews.com/story/0,2933,98111,00.html.

65 **"a stay is warranted":** Stephen Labaton, "U.S. Court Blocks Plan to Ease Rule on Media Owners," *New York Times,* September 4, 2003.

65 **Postwar cleanup will cost $100 billion:** Naomi Klein, "Privatization in Disguise," *The Nation,* April 28, 2003.

65 **Six companies gave more than $3.5 million:** Sheryl Fred, "Postwar Profits: How a Handful of Construction Firms Got an Early Invitation to Rebuild Iraq," Capital Eye, March 12, 2003, at www.capitaleye.org.

65 **Cheney denies financial ties to Halliburton:** Quoted in Mike Allen, "Cheney's Ties to Halliburton; Deferred Compensation Package Counts, Report Indicates," *Washington Post,* September 26, 2003.

65 *New York Times* **on Cheney-Halliburton:** Editorial, "The Iraq Reconstruction Bonanza," *New York Times,* October 1, 2003.

66 **Halliburton and $7 billion contract:** Joshua Chaffin, "Halliburton 'Reaps Nearly $500 m' from Iraq-Related Projects," *Financial Times,* May 30, 2003.

66 **Bechtel's eighteen-month contract and campaign contributions:** Ibid.

66 **MCI/WorldCom contract:** "Report Exposes Undemocratic Record of U.S. Corporations Operating in Iraq," U.S. Labor Against the War, June 15, 2003, at www.uslaboragainstwar.org.

66 **Only MCI can provide cell phone service:** Paul Krugman, "Who's Sordid Now?," *New York Times,* September 30, 2003.

66 **MCI/WorldCom political contributions:** www.opensecrets.org.

67 **"[N]ot in memory":** Kevin Phillips, "The Company Presidency," *Los Angeles Times,* February 10, 2002.

Secretary of the Army Thomas White was the vice chairman of Enron Energy Services; Trade Representative Robert Zoellick was an advisor to the company; Deputy Attorney General Larry Thompson, who is overseeing the Justice Department investigation of Enron, worked at the law firm that represents Enron; Attorney General John Ashcroft recused himself from the Enron investigation because of $61,000 worth of campaign contributions he had accepted during his 2000 campaign for governor of Missouri; White House counsel Alberto Gonzalez worked at Vinson and Elkins, the law firm that represented Enron; Bush's choice for Republican National Committee chairman, Marc Racicot, was Enron's lobbyist in Washington; Ken Lay was a member of Bush's transition team; Fifth Circuit judicial nominee Priscilla Owen took contributions from Enron for her Texas State Supreme Court run but failed to recuse herself from a case involving Enron. More than forty appointments spanning several cabinet departments are significant shareholders, including Bush political advisor Karl Rove; who continued to hold shares of Enron while participating in formulation of energy policy.

67 **"Lindsay described Lay's contribution as key":** Dana Milbank and Glenn Kessler, "Enron's Influence Reached Deep into Administration; Ties Touched Personnel and Policies," *Washington Post,* January 18, 2002.

67 **Enron jets used by Bush campaign during Florida recount:** "Bush Campaign Hired Jets from Enron, Halliburton," Reuters, August 3, 2002.

67 **Appointments to the FERC:** Lowell Bergman and Jeff Gerth, "Power Trader Tied to Bush Finds Washington All Ears," *New York Times,* May 25, 2001.

68 **"whose bonuses were tied to performance":** Joshua Green, "The 'Gate-less' Community," *Washington Monthly* (July/August 2002).

68 **Enron accounting practices:** Lee Romney, "Waxman Says Video Contradicts Skilling," *Los Angeles Times,* February 26, 2002.

68 **shifting profits to reserve accounts:** "Energy Markets: Enron Used Reserves to Hide $1.5B During Calif. Crisis, Former Execs Say," Greenwire, June 24, 2002, at www.greenwire.com; "Claims of Enron's Profits Hidden in Reserves Denied," *Houston Chronicle,* June 23, 2002.

69 **Enron profits from FERC inaction:** "Chronology of Enron's Influence, Rise and Fall," Public Citizen, at www.citizen.org.

69 **Cheney collects Enron's bills from Indian government:** Timothy J. Burger, "Veep Tried to Aid Firm; Key Role in India Debt Row," *(New York) Daily News,* January 18, 2002.

69 **White House withdraws support for cracking down on tax havens:** "A Retreat on Tax Havens," *New York Times,* May 26, 2001.

69 **Halliburton subsidiaries:** Editorial, "Why Legal Isn't Always Ethical," *Washington Post,* August 13, 2002.

69 **"I think we ought to":** George W. Bush, "President Discusses Economy, Middle East Following Cabinet Meeting," White House press conference, July 31, 2002, at www.whitehouse.gov.

69 **"Companies come and go":** Treasury Secretary Paul O'Neill, interview by Tony Snow, *Fox News Sunday,* Fox, January 13, 2002.

69 **No one told Bush about Enron's troubles:** Ari Fleischer, White House press briefing, January 10, 2002, at www.whitehouse.gov.

69 **Spectrum 7 and Enron:** David Corn, "W's First Enron Connection: Update on the Bush-Enron Oil Deal," *The Nation,* March 4, 2002, at www.thenation.com.

69 **Bush helps Enron with Argentine pipeline:** Kevin Phillips, "The Company Presidency," *Los Angeles Times,* February 10, 2002.

69 **"was a supporter of Ann Richards":** George W. Bush, remarks by the president in meeting with his economic team, January 10, 2002.

70 **"I'd worked very closely":** "Despite President's Denials, Enron and Lay Were Early Backers of Bush," Texans for Public Justice, a nonpartisan nonprofit research group studying campaign finance in Texas, January 11, 2002, at www.tpj.org.

70 **Lay gave three times more money to Bush:** Richard A. Oppel Jr. and Don Van Natta Jr., "Enron's Collapse: The Relationships; Bush and Democrats Disputing Ties to Enron," *New York Times,* January 12, 2002.

70 **Enron contribues more to Bush than Richards:** "Despite President's Denials, Enron and Lay Were Early Backers of Bush," Texans for Public Justice, January 11, 2002, at www.tpj.org.

70 **Bush director of bank that gave him loan for Rangers deal:** Michael Kranish and John Aloysius Farrell, "Bush's Business Career a Study in Using Connections; Critics Look Anew at Bush's Dealings," *Boston Globe,* July 12, 2002.

70 **Chronology of the Harken stock sale:** Anthony York, "Memos: Bush Knew of Harken's Problems," *Salon.com,* July 12, 2002, at www.salon.com; John Aloysius Farrell, "Papers Show Bush Knew of a Crisis as He Sold Stock; Investigators Decided in 1991 That He Had No Intent to Defraud," *Boston Globe,* July 13, 2002; Michael Kranish and Beth Healy, "Harvard Invested Heavily in Harken," *Boston Globe,* October 30, 2002.

71 *Boston Globe* **articles on Harken and Bush:** Michael Kranish, "Harvard Role in Harken Called Deeper; Group Said Partnership Kept Bush Firm Afloat," *Boston Globe,* October 9, 2002; Michael Kranish and Beth Healy, "Harvard Invested Heavily in Harken," *Boston Globe,* October 30, 2002.

72 **"that fact came up after I sold the stock":** George W. Bush, press conference by the president, July 8, 2002, at www.whitehouse.gov.

72 **Bush not exonerated by SEC:** Anthony York: "Memos: Bush Knew of Harken's Problems," *Salon.com,* July 12, 2002, at www.salon.com.

72 **Bush's personal lawyer was general counsel at the SEC:** Harold Evans, "Why US Press Didn't Give Bush a Burning: The Papers Knew About Dubya's Deals in 2000. Strangely, They Kept Quiet," *The Observer,* July 14, 2002.

72 **"the people at Enron":** Warren Vieth, "As Board Member, Bush Okd a Deal Like Enron's," *Los Angeles Times,* July 12, 2002.

72 **Bush claims to vote against Cayman tax shelter:** Ari Fleischer, White House press briefing, July 31, 2002, at www.whitehouse.gov.

72 **Bush votes for Harken's Cayman tax shelters:** "More Harken Energy Corporation Documents," Center for Public Integrity, at www.public-i.org.

73 **White House keeps Harken records out of reach:** Mike Allen, "Bush Took Oil Firm's Loans as Director," *Washington Post,* July 11, 2002.

73 **"a great success story":** Laurence McQuillan, "Investigations Pry Into Cheney's Business," *USA Today,* June 10, 2002.

73 **Cheney and Arthur Andersen:** Bridget Gibson, "The Party of Excess," Democratic Underground, July 13, 2002, at www.democraticunderground.com.

74 **Cheney aware of accounting changes at Halliburton:** Dana Milbank, "For Cheney, Tarnish From Halliburton; Firm's Fall Raises Question's About Vice President's Leadership There," *Washington Post,* July 16, 2002.

74 **Judicial Watch files suit against Halliburton and Cheney:** "Cheney Sued by Group," *(New York) Newsday,* July 11, 2002.

74 **Cheney refuses to answer questions on Halliburton:** Allan Sloan and Johnnie L. Roberts, "Sticky Business," *Newsweek,* July 22, 2002, 26.

74 **Halliburton employees:** Dana Milbank, "Democrats Urge Cheney to Aid Ex-Employees," *Washington Post,* September 11, 2002, A3; Dave Zweifel, "Workers' Benefit Loss Is Cheney's Gain," *Capital Times* (Madison, WI), September 23, 2002.

74 **"the government had absolutely nothing to do with it":** Dick Cheney, 2000 vice presidential debate, www.c-span.org, October 5, 2000.

74 **Halliburton wins government business:** Pratap Chatterjee, "Dick Cheney: Soldier of Fortune," May 2, 2002, www.corpwatch.org.

75 **"Bush is dreaming":** Michael Kramer, "Step One: Limit All Those Options," *(New York) Daily News,* July 10, 2002.

75 **CEOs' reaction to the Wall Street speech:** Ellis Henican, "Don't Believe Tough Talk," *Newsday,* July 10, 2002.

76 **"[h]e mentioned a lot of things":** Ben White, "Bush Draws Little Wall Street Reaction; Traders Pay Little Attention; Executives Reluctant to Comment," *Washington Post,* July 10, 2002.

76 **"There's no additional funding or staff":** Charlie Cray and Lee Drutman, "Bush: Corporate Confidence Man," CorpWatch, July 10, 2002, www.corpwatch.org.

77 **"the far-too-interlocking relationship":** Editorial, "What the President Should Have Said; Yes, Catch Corporate Crooks, But Fix Auditing System Too," *(New York) Newsday,* July 14, 2002.

77 **"is backed by the accounting firms":** Eric Rauchway, "A Century of Corporate Crime: If George Bush Wants to Match Theodore Roosevelt's Efforts He Must Increase Government Regulation," *Financial Times,* July 12, 2002.

77 **"Bush's plan wouldn't create":** Ryan Lizza, "World Away; White House Watch," *The New Republic,* July 22, 2002, 24.

78 **"My administration pressed for greater corporate integrity":** George W. Bush, Remarks by the President at Signing of the Sarbanes-Oxley Act of 2002, July 30, 2002, www.whitehouse.gov.

78 **"A widespread belief":** Joel Seligman, "No One Can Serve Two Masters: Corporate and Securities Law after Enron," *Washington University Law Quarterly* (Summer 2002), 449-536.

78 **Members of Congress who lobbied against Levitt received contributions from accounting industry:** "Accounting Industry," Center for Responsive Politics, at www.opensecrets. org/news/accountants/index.asp.

78 **"[E]ach firm would customize":** Arthur Levitt quoting Harvey Pitt, *Take On the Street: What Wall Street and Corporate America Don't Want You to Know* (New York: Pantheon, 2002), 119.

78 **"the system itself needs a major overhaul":** Roderick Hills, Senate Committee on Banking, Housing and Urban Affairs, *Oversight Hearing on "Accounting and Investor Protection Issues Raised by Enron and Other Public Companies,"* February 12, 2002.

79 **"The problem is not":** Jonathan Alter, "Whose Side Is Bush On?," *Newsweek,* July 22, 2002, 25.

80 **"his SEC colleagues were embarrassed":** Jeffrey Birnbaum, "It's Time For Him to Go: The Securities and Exchange Commission Is Desperate for Strong Leadership—And Harvey Pitt Isn't Providing It," *Fortune,* October 13, 2002, at www.fortune.com.

80 **Pitt and Webster resign:** Stephen Labaton, "Government Report Details a Chaotic SEC Under Pitt," *New York Times,* December 20, 2002.

80 **2001, 2002 SEC budget:** Colleen Marie O'Connor, "SEC Faces Cuts in Bush Budget Proposal," *Investor Relations Business,* April 30, 2001.

80 **"[u]nfortunately, and perhaps ironically":** Laura Unger, acting chair, U.S. Securities and Exchange Commission, Senate Subcommittee on Commerce, Justice, State, and the Judiciary Committee on Appropriations, *Testimony Concerning Appropriations for Fiscal Year 2002,* June 28, 2001, at www.sec.gov/news/testimony/062801tslu.htm.

80 **2002 SEC budget:** "SEC Budget History vs. Actual Obligations," at www.sec.gov/foia/docs/budgetact.htm.

81 **SEC budget increases vs. NYSE trading increases:** Christopher Byron, "Lean Sweep at SEC; Budget Still Too Small for Wall Street Housecleaning," *New York Post,* January 6, 2003.

5. Secrecy and Civil Liberties

83 **"Secrecy is for losers":** Daniel Patrick Moynihan, *Secrecy* (New Haven: Yale University Press, 1998), 227.

83 **Labor Department's response:** "Gov't Drops Monthly Mass Layoff Report: Labor Department Drops Monthly Report of Mass Layoffs; Lack of Funds Cited," Associated Press, January 3, 2003.

84 **"fatal to its ability to perform functions":** As quoted in Dana Milbank, "GAO Ends Fight with Cheney Over Files," *Washington Post,* February 8, 2003.

84 **only 29 with identified non-industry groups:** NRDC press release, May 21, 2002.

84 **"I worked for Richard Nixon":** John W. Dean, "GAO v. Cheney is Big-Time Stalling," February 1, 2002, at www.truthout.org.

84 **squabble over the Energy Task Force is only the "tip of the iceberg":** John Dean, "The Nixon Shadow that Hovers over the Bush White House," *History News Network,* January 6, 2003.

84 **"even Congress isn't entitled to know":** As quoted in Daniel Franklin, "Official Secrets: Is the Bush Administration Using Terrorism Fears to Shield Government—and Business—from Public View?," *Mother Jones,* January 1, 2003.

85 **"that information ought to be shared":** As quoted in Bob Herbert, "What Is It Good For?," *New York Times,* April 21, 2003.

85 **"more . . . open than many previous administrations":** As quoted in Adam Clymer, "Government Openness at Issue as Bush Holds on to Records," *New York Times,* January 3, 2003.

86 **"an affirmative duty to make such records available":** 44 U.S.c. 2203 (2003).

86 **"jeopardize, say, the national security of this country":** As quoted in Mike Allen and George Lardner Jr., "A Veto over Presidential Papers; Order Lets Sitting or Former President Block Release," *Washington Post,* November 2, 2001.

86 **lauding the EO as an "orderly process":** Ari Fleischer, White House press briefing, November 1, 2001.

86 **"enable historians to do their job":** White House press conference, November 2, 2001.

86 **"this order sets up a minefield":** Anna K. Nelson, as quoted in Bruce Craig, *NCC Washington Update,* National Coordinating Committee for the Promotion of History (NCCPH), vol. 7, no. 46 (November 9, 2001).

86 **a right that has no basis in the law or the Constitution:** John Dean, "Hiding Past and Present Presidencies," *Washington Post,* November 9, 2001.

87 **"ensuring some understanding of what's happening in our communities":** Interview with Gary Bass, New York, March 11, 2003.

87 **"to stonewall or deny requests whenever possible":** As quoted in Mark Helm, "Quietly, Feds Alter Rules on Public Files; Reporters Protest," *San Antonio Express-News,* November 18, 2001.

88 **"a loophole big enough to drive any corporation and its secrets through":** As quoted in Sarah D. Scalet, "Everything You Ever Wanted to Know About FOIA but Were Afraid to Ask," *CSO Magazine,* November 2002.

88 **"therefore we need to get additional protection":** Ibid.

88 **"This is a proposal born in secrecy":** Testimony before the Senate Judiciary Committee, 107th Congress, June 26, 2002.

89 **"democracies die behind closed doors":** *Detroit Free Press v. Ashcroft,* 303 F.3d 681, 683 (6th Cir. 2002).

89 **"the Pentagon does not lie":** As quoted in Mike Allen, "White House Angered at Plan for Pentagon Disinformation," *Washington Post,* February 25, 2002.

89 **"the blackest of black programs to the whitest of whites":** As quoted in Maureen Dowd, "Office of Strategic Mendacity," *New York Times,* February 20, 2002.

90 **"but not necessarily government":** As quoted in E. J. Dionne, "In Search of George W.," *Washington Post,* September 19, 1999.

90 **"giving the states all power not specifically granted to the federal government":** Ibid.

91 **the new rules were never made public:** Charles Levendosky, "Bush Needs a Lesson in Law, Liberty," *Ventura County Star,* September 12, 1999.

91 **Ashcroft pushing the changes incorporated in the Patriot Act:** Remarks of U.S. attorney general John Ashcroft to the U.S. Attorney's Conference, October 1, 2002.

91 **the Patriot Act does take several useful steps:** David Cole and James X. Dempsey, *Terrorism and the Constitution: Sacrificing Civil Liberties in the Name of National Security* (New York: The New Press, 2002), 148.

92 **Bryant defended this FBI power:** As quoted in Nat Hentoff, "Vanishing Liberties," *Village Voice,* April 16, 2003.

92 **"It feels like Big Brother":** As quoted in Rene Sanchez, "Librarians Make Some Noise Over Patriot Act; Concerns About Privacy Prompt Some to Warn Patrons, Destroy Records of Book and Computer Use," *Washington Post,* April 10, 2003.

92 **"hysteria" . . . check library records:** Remarks of Attorney General John Ashcroft, Milwaukee, Wisconsin, September 22, 2003, available at http://www.usdoj.gov/ag/speeches/2003/092203milwaukee.htm.

92 **"because they're prevented by law":** Anne Klinefelter, as quoted in Bonnie Rochman, "Triangle Librarians Lament Patriot Act," *(Raleigh) News Observer,* September 28, 2003.

92 **Justice Department spokespeople have repeatedly asserted:** *Seeking Truth from Justice, Volume One: Patriot Propaganda: The Justice Department's Campaign to Mislead the Public About the USA Patriot Act.* July 2003, American Civil Liberties Union, 2-4.

92 **"lower than probable cause":** House Committee on the Judiciary, Oversight Hearing on the U.S. Department of Justice, June 5, 2003. Transcript available at http://www.house.gov/judiciary:/fulltrans060503.htm.

92 **"Our prevention strategy targets the terrorist threat":** Testimony of Attorney General John Ashcroft, Senate Committee on the Judiciary, 107th Congress, December 6, 2001.

93 **Justice Department guide and report:** Eric Lichtblau, "U.S. Uses Terror Law to Pursue Crimes from Drugs to Swindling," *New York Times,* September 28, 2003.

93 **FISA "is not to be used as an end run around the Fourth Amendment's prohibition":** *United States v. Johnson,* 952 F.2d 565, 572 (9th Cir. 1992).

93 **Section 213 authorizes sneak and peek searches:** 18 U.S. 3103a.

94 **"seems to be running amok":** As quoted in Jeffrey Rosen, "Civil Right: Thank Goodness for Dick Armey," *The New Republic,* October 21, 2002, 15.

94 **Ashcroft himself, as a senator:** Editorial, *Las Vegas Review-Journal (Nevada),* December 29, 2000.

94 **return the nation to the "culture of inhibition":** Remarks of Attorney General John Ashcroft, U.S. Attorney's Conference, New York City, October 1, 2002.

94 **"we do not destroy the freedoms that we cherish":** Congressional Record, Senator Patrick Leahy, S10366, 107th Congress, October 9, 2001.

94 **none of the sixty-eight programs for which Ashcroft requested spending increases:** Jeffrey Toobin, "Ashcroft's Ascent: How Far Will Attorney General Go?," *New Yorker,* April 15, 2002.

94 **despite the advice of outgoing National Security Advisor Sandy Berger:** Michael Elliot, "They Had A Plan; Long Before 9/11, the White House Debated Taking the Fight to al-Qaeda. By the Time They Decided, It Was Too Late. The Saga of a Lost Chance," *Time,* August 2, 2002.

95 **legislators told that no such legislation was in the pipeline:** Charles Lewis and Adam Mayle, "Justice Dept. Drafts Sweeping Expansion of Anti-Terrorism Act," Center for Public Integrity, February 7, 2003.

95 **"we're supposed to roll over and play dead and just pass it":** As quoted in Eric Lichtblau with Adam Liptak, "On Terror, Spying and Guns, Ashcroft Expands Reach," *New York Times,* March 15, 2003.

95 **"the strongest commitment to our Constitution and civil liberties":** As quoted in Adam Clymer, "Justice Department Draft on Wider Powers Draws Quick Criticism," *New York Times,* February 8, 2003.

95 **Victory Act:** Dan Eggen, "GOP Bill Would Add Anti-Terror Powers," *Washington Post,* August 21, 2003.

95 **Other provisions:** Errol Louis, "Ashcroft's Victory Act," *New York Sun,* August 22-24, 2003.

96 **"we've been asking for this for a long time":** As quoted in Jeffrey Rosen, "Civil Right: Thank Goodness for Dick Armey," *The New Republic,* October 21, 2002, 16.

96 **"we may place upon the statute books":** Charles S. Thomas, as quoted in Daniel Patrick Moynihan, *Secrecy* (New Haven: Yale University Press, 1998), 93.

96 **"The state's interest in crime-fighting":** As quoted in Nat Hentoff, "The Death of Operation TIPS," *Village Voice,* December 18, 2002.

96 **"useful for preemption":** IAO Mission, at www.darpa.mil/iao/.

97 **"Admiral Poindexter ... an outstanding American":** As quoted in Joe Conason, "Disgraced Admiral Now Super-Spy," *New York Observer,* November 25, 2002.

97 **to encourage ordinary Americans:** "President Creates Citizen Corps," White House press release, January 2002.

97 **"a unique position to see potentially unusual or suspicious activity":** As quoted in Dan Eggen, "Proposal to Enlist Citizen Spies was Doomed from the Start," *Washington Post,* November 24, 2002.

97 **"government-sanctioned Peeping Toms":** As quoted in ibid.

97 **"That's what the President is going to make certain what [*sic*] is done":** Press Gaggle by Ari Fleischer, November 22, 2002.

98 **if an individual has been inaccurately or unfairly scored:** EPIC, "Passenger Profiling," www.epic.org/privacy/airtravel/profiling.html.

98 **Jan Adams and Rebecca Gordon:** *Caught in the Backlash: Stories from Northern California,* American Civil Liberties Union of Northern California report, 2002.

98 **"People don't know why their names were put on this list,":** Ibid.

98 **Ashcroft told the Senate Judiciary Committee:** Testimony to the Senate Judiciary Committee, 107th Congress, September 25, 2001.

98 **Constitution "is not a suicide pact":** *Kennedy v. Mendoza Martinez,* 372 U.S. 144 (1963).

98 **"we live in a country that wants to protect basic civil liberties":** In a speech to the American Society for International law, as quoted in "High Court Prepares for Anti-Terrorism Cases," Associated Press, April 5, 2003.

98 **died of a heart attack in jail:** Ralph Temple, "The Sorry and the Pity of Racial Profiling," in *It's a Free Country: Personal Freedom in America After September 11,* eds. Danny Goldberg, Victor Goldberg, and Robert Greenwald (New York: RDV Books, 2002), 69-75.

99 **inconsistent with the Immigration and Naturalization Act:** James Zigler, talk at New York University, April 21, 2003.

99 **clues as to how the United States conducts counterterrorism investigations:** Neil A. Lewis, "U.S. Says Revealing Names Would Aid Al Qaeda," *New York Times,* November 18, 2002.

99 **secrecy was necessary to protect the detainees' privacy:** Department of Justice: Attorney General Ashcroft Provides Total Number of Federal Criminal Charges and INS Detainees, November 27, 2001.

99 **"the right to contact their lawyers and their families":** Testimony of Attorney General John Ashcroft, Senate Committee on the Judiciary, 107th Congress, December 6, 2001.

99 *60 Minutes* **and Hady Omar:** *60 Minutes* transcript, April 6, 2003.

99 **her children ask every day:** "Guilty Until Proven," CBSnews.com, April 6, 2003.

99 **inundated with allegations of comparable civil rights abuses:** Jim Mcgee, "Internal Justice Probe Examines Handling of Post-9/11 Roundups," *Congressional Quarterly,* February 10, 2003.

100 **"what happened to Hady Omar":** *60 Minutes* transcript, April 6, 2003.

100 **"about 97 percent" of the people detained:** Department of Justice: Attorney General Ashcroft Provides Total Number of Federal Criminal Charges and INS Detainees, November 27, 2001.

100 **100 percent:** Interview with Muzaffer Christi, Migration Policy Institute, NYU, June 29, 2003.

100 **"It's wrong and we will end it in America":** Address to Congress, February 27, 2001.

100 **"Arab-Americans are racially profiled":** *New York Times* transcript, presidential candidates debate, October 11, 2000.

101 **"we obviously have lost that moral footing":** "Guilty Until Proven," CBSnews.com, April 6, 2003.

102 **"suspending habeas corpus for 20 million people":** William Safire, "Voices of Negativism," *New York Times,* December 6, 2001.

102 **"the Supreme Court has never held that any Congress may limit it":** Testimony before the Senate Committee on the Judiciary, 107th Congress, December 6, 2001.

103 **seeking a fundamental shift in the legal system:** Jeffrey Toobin, "Ashcroft's Ascent: How Far Will Attorney General Go?," *New Yorker,* April 15, 2002.

103 **"encourage people of good will to remain silent in the face of evil":** Testimony of Attorney General John Ashcroft, Senate Committee on the Judiciary, 107th Congress, December 6, 2001.

103 **"because he bombs people all over the world for profits":** *Caught in the Backlash: Stories from Northern California,* ACLU of Northern California Report, 2002.

103 **Americans harassed for participating in legitimate First Amendment activity:** Ibid.

104 **"these were sorry historical embarrassments":** Stephen J. Schullhofer, "At War with Liberty: Post 9-11, Due Process and Security Have Taken a Beating," *The American Prospect,* March 1, 2003.

104 **right to a public hearing upon arrest exists:** David Cole, "Enemy Aliens and American Freedoms," *The Nation,* September 23, 2002.

104 **"to save innocent lives from further acts of terrorism":** Testimony of Attorney General John Ashcroft, Senate Committee on the Judiciary, 107th Congress, December 6, 2001.

6. Mismanaged Health Care

105 **Poll on health care system:** Harris Interactive, "Attitudes Toward the United States' Health Care System: Long Term Trends," *Health Care News,* August 21, 2002.

105 **Bush on government role:** Public Papers of the Presidents, speech at the Medical College of Wisconsin, February 11, 2002.

106 **Bush Medicare promises:** Ibid.

106 **Seniors without drug coverage:** Raja Mishra, "Specialists Are Wary of Medicare Overhaul," *Boston Globe,* January 28, 2003.

106 **Portion Medicare recipients uncovered:** Todd J. Gillman, "Spiraling Drug Costs Lead Bush, Gore to Seek Relief; Older Voters Concerned over Rising Bills Driving Presidential Medicare Debate," *Dallas Morning News,* May 21, 2000.

106 **Bush's promise to cover all seniors:** Federal News Service, *Election 2000 Presidential Debate Between Democratic Candidate Vice President Al Gore and Republican Governor George W. Bush,* October 3, 2003.

107 **Percentage who stayed with traditional Medicare:** Source: Medicare Rights Center.

107 **Marilyn Moon on Medicare+Choice:** Testimony before the U.S. House of Representatives Committee on Ways and Means, Subcommittee on Health, May 2, 2001.

108 **Thompson on the $400 billion:** Steve Schultze, "Thompson Talks Medicare: Bush Reform Would Be Important First Step, He Says," *Milwaukee Journal-Sentinel,* March 12, 2003.

108 **Marilyn Moon drug expenditure estimate:** Interview, New York City, April 9, 2003.

108 **Thompson on privatization:** Steve Schultze, "Thompson Talks Medicare," *Milwaukee Journal-Sentinel,* March 12, 2003.

108 **Medicare's share of drug costs:** U.S. Centers for Medicare and Medicaid Services.

108 **Bush-Gore comparison:** The Center for Responsive Politics, at www.opensecrets.org.

109 **GOP's share of drug industry money:** Public Citizen, *The Other Drug War, Big Pharma's 625 Lobbyists,* 9-10.

109 **Health services and HMO industry contributions:** Center for Responsive Politics, at www.opensecrets.org.

109 **Sherrod Brown on administration's goal:** Interview, New York City, April 11, 2003.

110 **PhRMA expenditures:** Robert Pear, "Drug Companies Increase Spending on Efforts to Lobby Congress and Governments," *New York Times,* June 1, 2003.

111 **Families USA on generic drugs regulation:** Families USA, "Administration's Generic Drug Rules Provide Weak, Diluted Relief for America's Consumers," press release, October 21, 2002.

111 **Holmer on price controls:** As cited by Arthur Levin, president, Center for Medical Consumers, "High Cost of Drug Research a Myth," August 2001, at www.medicalconsumers.org.

111 **Marketing and advertising expenditures:** Interview with Arthur Levin, president, Center for Medical Consumers, March 17, 2003.

111 **spending on marketing and research:** Families USA, "Profiting from Pain: Where Prescription Drug Dollars Go," self-published report, July 2002, 5, at www.familysusa.org/site/DocServer/PPreport.pdf?docID-249.

111 **Bush and drug industry wish list:** Examples provided by Rep. Henry Waxman (D-CA), interview, April 16, 2003.

112 **Fitzgerald on House HMO bill:** As quoted in Robert Pear, "States Dismayed by Federal Bill on Patient Rights," *New York Times,* August 13, 2001.

113 **Bush on HMO lawsuits in federal court:** Public Papers of the Presidents, March 26, 2001, remarks at the American College of Cardiology Convention in Orlando, Florida, March 21, 2001.

113 **HMO lawsuits in Texas:** Craig Gunsauly, "Texas Legislation May Provide a Model for Patients' Rights," *Employee Benefit News,* April 1, 2001.

113 **Bush on Kennedy-McCain:** Robert Pear and Robin Toner, "Bush Demands Senate Changes on Patient Bill," *New York Times,* June 22, 2001.

114 **Business gubernatorial campaign contributions:** "The Governor's Gusher: Sources of George W. Bush's $41 Million Texas War Chest," at www.tpj.org.

114 **Bush in Mississippi:** Patrice Sawyer, "Derail 'Lawsuit Industry,'" *The Clarion Leader (Jackson, Mississippi:),* August 8, 2002.

114 **Malpractice lawsuit award myths:** "A Second Opinion on the Malpractice Plague," *Business Week,* March 3, 2003, 98.

114 **Pennsylvania jury awards:** Public Citizen Congress Watch, *Medical Misdiagnosis in Pennsylvania, Challenging the Medical Malpractice Claims of the Doctors' Lobby,* January 2003, p. 2

115 **Bush on lawsuits' impact:** Official Transcript, Medicare Payment Advisory Commission, Public Meeting, December 12, 2002.

115 **Medical malpractice insurance premiums:** Calculations by Public Citizen's Congress Watch from the Bureau of Labor Statistics, Medical Services CPI, and Best's Aggregates and Averages, March 4, 2003.

115 **Doctor expansion in Mississippi:** Joey Bunch, "Crisis or PR Campaign; Pro and Con Forces Seek to Win Hearts and Minds of Mississippians," *Biloxi Sun Herald,* August 11, 2002.

115 **GAO report:** U.S. General Accounting Office, *Medical Malpractice—Implications of Rising Premiums on Access to Health Care,* August 2003.

115 **Daily value of $250,000 cap:** Interview, April 30, 2003.

116 **Number of medical error deaths:** Roni Rabin, "Quest for Answers; Renewed Scrutiny of Suspected Medical Errors," *(New York) Newsday,* March 16, 2003.

116 **Hospital preventable accident deaths:** Jim Ritter, "155,000 Die Every Year from Medical Errors: Study," *Chicago Sun Times,* February 10, 1992.

117 **Bush on the uninsured:** Presidential debate of October 17, 2000, CBS News transcripts.

118 **"I wish I could wave a wand":** Frank Bruni, "The 2000 Campaign: The Texas Governor, Bush left in Want of a Wand as Questioner Asks for Help," *New York Times,* February 15, 2000.

118 **Pollack on tax credits:** Ron Pollack, interview, June 20, 2003.

119 **Bush on AHPs:** Remarks at the Summit on Women Entrepreneurship in the Twenty-first Century, Ronald Reagan Building and International Trade Center, Washington, D.C., March 25, 2002.

119 **Bush administration Medicaid goals:** Weekly radio address, Saturday, August 4, 2001.

The plan would raise the federal Medicaid contribution by $12.7 billion over the first seven years, but provide less money during the eighth through tenth years. Net effect would be no increase over ten years.

120 **Thompson on Medicaid rules:** Robert Pear, "Medicaid Proposal Would Give States More Say on Costs," *New York Times,* February 1, 2003.

120 **Jeb Bush on Medicaid plan:** Robert Pear, "Governors Resist Bush Plan to Slow Costs of Medicaid," *New York Times,* May 25, 2003.

120 **Sherrod Brown Medicaid prediction:** Interview, April 11, 2003.

121 **Bush on privacy:** Michael J. Miller, Forward Thinking, *PC Magazine,* February 6, 2001, 7. Toward the end of the campaign, the magazine had asked Bush about privacy.

121 **Bush says he is a "privacy-rights person":** Interview on May 11, 2000, *Business Week Online,* "Surprise! Bush Is Emerging as a Fighter for Privacy on the Net," June 5, 2000.

121 **Rep. Henry Waxman:** Interview, April 16, 2003.

123 **U.S. reversed itself and opposed banning descriptive terms condemned by the National Cancer Institute:** Barry Yeoman, "Secondhand Diplomacy," *Mother Jones,* March/April 2003.

123 **U.S. reverses itself and agrees to now-watered-down treaty:** Rob Stein and Marc Kaufman, "U.S. Backs Pact Curbing Tobacco Use Worldwide," *Washington Post,* May 19, 2003.

123 **Number of tobacco deaths will double and most of that increase will come from the developing world:** Ibid.

7. Race

125 **"there's a record":** Third presidential debate, October 17, 2000, at www.debates.org/pages/trans2000c.html.

125 **"reaching out":** Address by Colin Powell at the 2000 Republican National Convention, at www.cnn.com/ELECTION/2000/conventions/republican/transcripts/u000731.html

125 **"bigotry disfigures the heart":** Address by George W. Bush at the Republican National Convention, at www.cnn.com/ELECTION/2000/conventions/republican/transcripts/bush.html.

126 **"benign conservative":** Robert A. George, "Lott's Mississippi Ghosts," *New York Post.* Lott's uncle later stated that Lott knew well what the CCC was all about.

126 **Reagan preached his support for "states' rights":** Dan Goodgame and Karen Tumulty, "Tripped Up by History," *Time* 27.

126 **"virulently racist":** Interview with Julian Bond, March 3, 2003.

126 **"conservative philosophy":** William Saletan, "Defining W. Down," Slate.com, February 22, 2000, at www.slate.msn.com/id/75570/.

126 **"cults which call themselves Christian":** "Bob Jones Bites Back: Controversial School Founder Defends Policies," Associated Press, March 3, 2000, at www.abcnews.go.com/sections/politics/DailyNews/bobjones000303.html.

126 **"causing needless offense":** www.issues2000.org/George_W_Bush_Civil_Rights.htm.

126 **"people of South Carolina's decision":** Mike Allen and Dana Milbank, "Bush Won't Resist Leadership Change; President's Agenda Feared in Jeopardy," *Washington Post,* December 17, 2002.

127 **"I am a uniter":** George W. Bush, "Why You Should Vote For Me," *USA Today,* November 7, 2000, at www.usatoday.com/news/opinion/ncguest3.htm.

127 **"looking at Colin Powell and Condi Rice":** Mike Allen and Dana Millbank, *Washington Post,* December 17, 2002.

127 **"If affirmative action means quotas":** www.debates.org/pages/trans2000c.html.

127 **amounted to a "quota system":** "President Bush Discusses Michigan Affirmative Action Case," January 15, 2003, at www.whitehouse.gov/news/releases/2003/01/20030115-7.html.

127 **no such set-asides:** Editorial, "An Anti-Quota Smoke Screen," *New York Times,* January 18, 2003.

127 **percentage of minority students varied:** Editorial, "Bush's Negative Action," *Boston Globe,* January 17, 2003.

127 **"overwhelming consideration":** Neil A. Lewis, "U.S. Says Michigan System Is Equivalent to a Quota," *New York Times,* January 17, 2003.

127 **"I'm not sure I would say it is a quota system":** Interview with Ken Starr, New York, March 7, 2003.

128 **full force today:** Daniel Golden, "Family Ties: Preference for Alumni Children in College Admissions Draws Fire," *Wall Street Journal,* January, 15, 2003.

128 **"especially hypocritical":** Interview with Wade Henderson, April 4, 2003.

128 **"amorphous advantages":** Michael Kinsley, "How Affirmative Action Helped George W. All Politics," January 20, 2003, at www.cnn.com/2003/ALLPOLITICS/01/20/timep.affirm.action.tm/.

128 **"method . . . is fundamentally flawed":** "President Bush Discusses Michigan Affirmative Action Case," January 15, 2003, at www.whitehouse.gov/news/releases/2003/01/20030115-7.html.

128 **"modus operandi":** Adam Nagourney, "With His Eye on Two Political Prizes, the President Picks His Words Carefully," *New York Times,* January 16, 2003.

128 **"great stumbling block":** Lani Guinier, "The 'Quota' Smokescreen," *The Nation,* February 10, 2003, 4.

129 **drive to the right:** Adam Nagourney, "With His Eye on Two Political Prizes, the President Picks His Words Carefully," *New York Times,* January 16, 2003.

129 **"considerable fanfare":** Howard Fineman and Tamara Lipper, "Spinning Race," *Newsweek,* January 27, 2003, 27-29.

129 **"labeled it affirmative access":** www.debates.org/pages/trans2000c.html.

129 **"promoted educational diversity":** "Excerpts from Administration Briefs on Michigan Affirmative Action," *New York Times,* January 17, 2003.

129 **according to a 2003 study:** Brian Bucks, "Affirmative Action versus Affirmative Access: How Have Texas' Race-Blind Admissions Effected College Outcomes?" at www.utdallas.edu/research/greenctr/Papers/pdfpapers/paper33.pdf.

129 **top 10 percent:** Benjamin Forest, "A Policy that Depends on Segregation," *New York Times,* March 29, 2003.

130 **"appeal to a variety of consumers":** Roger O. Crocket, "Memo to the Supreme Court: "Diversity Is Good Business," *Business Week,* January 27, 2003.

130 **The secretary . . . delivered a ten-minute soliloquy:** Interview with David Berger, student questioner, May 6, 2003, Washington, D.C.

130 **14.5 percent to 4 percent:** Editorial, "A Win for Affirmative Action," *New York Times,* June 24, 2003.

130 **"resegregation":** Lee Bollinger, interview by Charlie Rose, *Charlie Rose,* PBS, June 24, 2003.

130 **"applauded" the Court:** "President Applauds Supreme Court for Recognizing Value of Diversity," Statement by the President, June 23, 2003, at http://www.whitehouse.gov/news/releases/2003/06/20030623.html.

131 **"problems over all these years":** Stephen Dinan, " 'Forgive Me' for Remarks, Lott Asks," *Washington Times,* December 14, 2002, at www.washtimes.com/national/20021214-17907952.htm.

131 **"ludicrous":** Douglas Kiker, "A Whole Lott-a' Trouble," CBSNEWS.com, December 11, 2002, at www.cbsnews.com/stories/2002/12/11/politics/main532739.shtml.

131 **"final word":** Ari Fleischer, press conference, December 10, 2002, at www.whitehouse.gov/news/releases/2002/12/20021210-11.html.

131 **"apologized and rightly so":** "Bush Calls Lott Comment Offensive: GOP Leader Faces Pressure for Further Explanation," CNN.com, December 13, 2002, at www.cnn.com/2002/ALLPOLITICS/12/12/lott.comment/.

131 **"president doesn't think Trent Lott needs to resign":** Joe Conason, "Lott's Departure Won't Be Enough," *New York Observer,* December 26, 2002; www2.observer.com/observer/pages/conason.asp.

131 **"surgeon's skill":** Elisabeth Bumiller, "With Signals and Maneuvers, Bush Orchestrates an Ouster," *New York Times,* December 21, 2002.

131 **Bill Back:** Thomas B. Edsall, "White House Silent On Racial Controversy: GOP Official Expresses Regret Over Distributing Article Critical War Outcome," *Washington Post,* January 5, 2003.

132 **"Let's Not Embarrass the Governor":** Molly Ivins, "A Little Background on that Hate Crimes Bill," *Star-Telegram,* October 30, 2000.

132 **"it's all a ploy":** Jake Tapper, "Bush Anger's Slain Man's Family," *Salon.com,* October 16, 2000, at archive.salon.com/politics/feature/2000/10/16/byrds/print.html.

133 **"repeatedly offered a platform":** "Bush's 'Close Ties' to Neo-Confederate Groups Questioned," Press Release of the journal *Southern Exposure,* February 18, 2000, at www. commondreams. org/news2000/0218-04.htm (last visited December 29, 2002).

133 **Richard T. Hines ... "most outspoken":** Sean Wilentz, "Inveterate Confederates: The Southern Skeletons in the Bush Administrations Closet," December 20, 2002, at www.prospect. org/webfeatures/2002/12/wilentz-s-12-20.html.

133 **close friend ... of Karl Rove:** Sean Wilentz, "Lott, GOP, and the Neo-Confederacy: No Surprise in the Senator's Remarks. It's Just the Latest in an Old Story," *Philadelphia Inquirer,* December 20, 2002.

133 **"debunk our heritage":** Anthony York, "Confederates in the Attic," *Salon.com,* December 20, 2002.

133 **"active voice in the current Bush administration":** www.rthconsulting.com/richard_bio.html (last visited February 18, 2003).

133 **crucial to Bush's victory:** "In Final Days, Candidates Could Trip on Confederate Flag Issue," October 26, 2000 at www.confederate.org/publish/100022.html (last visited December 29, 2002).

133 **"civil rights for all citizens":** Allison Mitchel, "The 43rd President: The Context; Bush's Latest Appointments Elate Right; Left Begins to Mobilize Opposition," *New York Times,* December 23, 2000.

133 **racist *Southern Partisan:*** A 1984 *Southern Partisan* argued that "Negroes, Asians, and Orientals; Hispanics, Latins, and Eastern Europeans; have no temperament for democracy, never had, and probably never will." A 1996 *Southern Partisan* article argued that "slave owners ... did not have a practice of breaking up slave families. If anything they encouraged strong slave families to further the slaves' peace and happiness." The magazine has even called David Duke "a candidate concerned about 'affirmative' discrimination, welfare prolifigacy [*sic*], the taxation holocaust ... a Populist spokesperson for a recapturing of the American ideal"; Joshua Micah Marshall, "John Ashcroft's Rebel Yell," Slate.com, December 26, 2000.

133 **"perverted agenda":** Interview of John Ashcroft in *Southern Partisan,* Second Quarter, 1990.

133 **"consensus on divisive issues":** "The 43rd President; Remarks at Announcement of Bush's Choices for 4 Cabinet Secretaries," *New York Times,* December 30, 2000.

133 **"we lost too much":** Martin Kettle, "Echoes of Slavery as Bush Nominees Back Confederacy," *The Guardian,* January 1, 2001.

134 **"single nation of justice":** Carter M. Yang, "On the Homefront," abcnews.com, April 24, 2001, at www.abcnews.go.com/sections/nightline/DailyNews/100days_domestic.html.

134 **"see him the night before":** Statement of Mississippi senator Theodore Bilbo, a Democrat, in 1946, as reported in Merida, Kevin, "Consonants and a Disavowal: The More You Ask Trent Lott About His Ties to the White-Supremacist CCC, the less he has to say," *Washington Post,* March 29, 1999.

134–35 **"gotta go home":** Marie Cocco, "Republicans Are Still Playing the Race Card," *(New York) Newsday,* December 19, 2002.

135 **"spotters" in Detroit:** Ibid.

135 **votes would no longer count:** "Chairman McAuliffe Calls on Bush to Stop Republican Voter Suppression Tactics," October 29, 2002, at www.democrats.org/news/200210300001.html.

135 **"don't expect us":** Marie Cocco, "Republicans Are Still Playing the Race Card," *(New York) Newsday,* December 19, 2002.

135 **"tacit sanction":** Interview with Wade Henderson, April 4, 2003.

136 **"rules are consistently applied":** "President Signs Historic Election Reform Legislation into Law: Remarks by the President at Signing of H.R. 3295, Help America Vote Act of 2002," October 29, 2002, at www.whitehouse.gov/news/release/2002/10/20021029-1.html.

136 **harder to vote:** McDonald, Laughlin, "The New Poll Tax: Republican-sponsored Ballot-security Measures Are Being Used to Keep Minorities From Voting," *The American Prospect,* December 30, 2002, 26.

136 **Fraction of the $3.9 billion that the act authorizes:** Interview with Steven Carbo, New York, April 11, 2003.

136 **"deal with some of the people":** Steve Miller, "Jackson Raps Bush, Ashcroft," *Washington Times,* July 9, 2002, www.washtimes.com/national/20020709-85173940.htm.

8. Reality Bites

Education

138 **speech a week:** Molly Ivins and Lou DuBose, *Shrub: The Short but Happy Political Life of George W. Bush* (New York: Vintage Books, 2000).

138 **H.B. 72:** Melanie Markley, "Texas a Qualified Number 1 in U.S. Education Study," *Houston Chronicle,* July 26, 2000.

139 **RAND corporation:** David W. Grissmer et al., *Improving Student Achievement: What State NAEP Test Scores Tell Us* (Santa Monica, California: Rand Publications, 2000).

139 **"Testing is the cornerstone of reform":** Governor George Bush and Vice President Al Gore, the first Gore-Bush presidential debate, October 3, 2000, Boston.

139 **High-stakes testing was not critical factor:** David W. Grissmer et al., *Improving Student Achievement: What State NAEP Test Scores Tell Us* (Santa Monica, California: Rand Publications, 2000).

139 **TAAS ratings:** "Report: Two Dallas Schools Cheated on TAAS," *Austin-American Statesman,* May 19, 1999.

139 **"bipartisan education reform":** President George W. Bush, "Foreword by President George W. Bush," *Transforming the Federal Role in Education So That No Child Is Left Behind,* January 23, 2001.

139 **"deep passion" . . . "most meaningful":** George W. Bush, "President Celebrates First Anniversary of No Child Left Behind, Remarks by the President on the First Anniversary of the No Child Left Behind Act," January 8, 2003.

140 **"if you receive federal money":** Governor George Bush and Vice President Al Gore, the first Gore-Bush presidential debate, October 3, 2000, Boston.

140 **test students:** Fact Sheet: The No Child Left Behind Act, at www.whitehouse.gov.

140 **transfer requests:** "Title I: Improving the Academic Achievements of the Disadvantaged: Final Regulations," The No Child Left Behind Act, November 26, 2002, at www.ed.gov.

141 **"The new role of the federal government":** President George W. Bush, "President Signs Landmark Education Bill," January 8, 2002, Hamilton, Ohio.

141 **one-year anniversary:** Representative George Miller, "Press Conference on the NCLB One Year Anniversary Funding Shortfalls, Implementation Problems Threaten Law's Success," Statement by the Honorable George Miller, January 8, 2003.

141 **$4 billion short:** Democratic Staff of the Committee on Education and the Workforce with the U.S. House of Representatives, "Shortchanging Education Reform," FY 2004 Bush Budget, February 3, 2003.

141 **"Part of the issue":** Phone interview with Alex Knox.

141 **$6 billion short:** Diana Jean Schemo, "The President's Budget Proposal: Education: Critics Say Money for Schools Falls Short of Promises," *New York Times,* February 5, 2003.

142 **K-12 funding:** "State Budget Shortfalls at $27 Billion: 40 States Project Budget Cuts This Year," *NCSL News,* April 16, 2002; "Three Years Later, State Budget Gaps Linger: Total Gap Grows to $200 Billion Since FY 2001," *NCSL News,* April, 24, 21003, at www.ncsl.org/programs/press; Pamela M. Prah and Jason White, "Education Feels States' Financial Squeeze," Stateline.org, March 26, 2003; and Greg Toppo, "States Strain to Keep Up with 'No Child Left Behind,'" *USA Today,* January 29, 2003.

142 **20 percent of their Title I:** President George W. Bush, "Executive Summary," The No Child Left Behind Act, January 2001, at www.ed.gov.

142 **"the modest 2.8 percent increase":** Center on Education Policy, *From the Capital to the Classroom: State and Federal Efforts to Implement the No Child Left Behind Act,* January 2003, 22.

142 **"better schools":** Office of the Press Secretary, "Remarks by the President and Michele

Forman, Teacher of the Year, in Presentation of National Teachers of the Year Awards," April 23, 2001, at www.whitehouse.gov.

142 **"pumping gas into a flooded engine":** Office of the Press Secretary, "Remarks by the President to 2001 National Urban League Conference," August 1, 2001, at www.whitehouse.gov.

142 **one-third of the children eligible:** National PTA, "Title I of the Elementary and Secondary Education Act," www.pta.org/ptawashington/issues/titleone.asp.

143 **"low expectations":** Office of the Press Secretary, "Remarks by the President at Central Connecticut State University," April 18, 2001, at www.whitehouse.gov and Office of the Press Secretary; "Remarks by the President on Education Reform," July 5, 2001, at www.whitehouse.gov.

143 **"Schools used to say":** Governor George Bush and Vice President Al Gore, the first Gore-Bush presidential debate, October 3, 2000, Boston.

143 **"thermometers to reduce fevers":** Gary Orfield and Johanna Wald, "Testing, Testing," *The Nation,* June 5, 2000, at www.thenation.com.

143 **study on . . . high-stakes tests:** Audrey L. Amrein and David C. Berliner, *The Impact of High-Stakes Tests on Student Academic Performance: An Analysis of NAEP Results in States with High-Stakes Tests and ACT, SAT, and AP Test Results in States with High School Graduation Exams,* Education Policy Research Unit of Arizona State University, December 2002.

144 **"that's the expensive route":** Phone interview with Audrey Amrein, February 27, 2003.

144 **"Head Start ought to be moved" . . . "first and foremost":** Office of the Press Secretary, "Remarks by the President to Teachers and Students," February 21, 2001; Office of the Press Secretary, "Remarks by the President to Parents and Teachers," February 20, 2001.

144 **"dilutes and takes away the mission":** Interview with Sarah Greene.

144 **"My reading of the by-now voluminous evidence":** National Head Start Association Hearing, 108th Congress, January 29, 2003.

145 **Republican Senate . . . House:** Andrew Mollison, "Head Start Enthusiasts Target Tests, Spending," *Atlanta Journal-Constitution,* January 27, 2003.

145 **"during the first two years":** Interview with Sarah Greene.

145 **2001 poll conducted:** Karla Scoon Reid, "Poll Finds Support for Vouchers Wanes if Public Schools Affected," *Education Week,* October 3, 2001.

145 **49 percent to 47:** National School Boards Association/Zogby International Poll, "School Vouchers: What the Public Thinks and Why."

145 **negative side effects:** V. Martinez et al. "The Consequences of School Choice: Who Leaves and Who Stays in the Inner City," *Social Science Quarterly* (1995); and Stearns, "School Reform: Lessons from England, *Social Science Quarterly* (1996).

145 **"facilitate the capacity of parents" . . . "parents must be empowered":** Office of the Press Secretary, "Remarks by the President on Education Implementation," September 4, 2002; Office of the Press Secretary, "President Outlines Education Reform in Boston Speech," January 8, 2002.

146 **"see the educational entrepreneurial spirit":** Jay Matthews, "Bush Pushes Vouchers, D.C. Charters; Educational Options Touted as Ways to Make City a 'Model of Excellence.'" *Washington Post,* July 2, 2003.

146 **voted 209 to 208:** Spencer S. Hsu and Justin Blum, "D.C. School Voucher Bill Passes in House by 1 Vote; Grant Plan for at Least 1,300 Students Goes to Senate," *Washington Post,* September 10, 2003.

146 **"When this administration underfunds public schools":** Phone interview with Nancy Keenan, March 18, 2003.

146 **"vehicle for vouchers":** Phone interview with Noreen Connell.

146 **"there are a lot, a lot of technical implementation issues":** Ibid.

Science

147 **"[W]e do not know how much effect":** Office of the Press Secretary, "President Bush Discusses Global Climate Change," June 11, 2001.

148 **Exxon contacted the Bush White House:** Brad Foss, "Group: Exxon Pressured White House," Associated Press, April 3, 2002.

148 **"the report put out by the bureaucracy":** Katharine Q. Seelye, "President Distances Himself from Global Warning Report," *New York Times,* June 5, 2002.

148 **deleted by top officials at the EPA:** Andrew C. Revkin, "With White House Approval, E.P.A. Pollution Report Omits Global Warming Section," *New York Times,* September 15, 2002.

148 **"ignored a decade of peer-reviewed science":** Natural Resources Defense Council,

"Rewriting the Rules, Year-End Report 2002: The Bush Administration's Assault on the Environment," January 2003, 11.

148 **"real disregard for the science":** Phone interview with Bud Ris, New York, January 12, 2002.

148 **"the White House directing the secretary of labor":** Andrew C. Revkin and Katharine Q. Seelye, "Report by E.P.A. Leaves Out Data on Climate Change," *New York Times,* June 19, 2003.

149 **cells . . . can . . . become any type of cell in the human body:** Office of the Press Secretary of President George W. Bush, "Fact Sheets: Embryonic Stem Cell Research," August 9, 2001.

149 **The mass of stem cells is created:** Jerome Groopman, "Holding Cell: Why the Cloning Decision Was Wrong," *The New Republic,* August 5, 2002, 14.

149 **"As a result of private research":** President George W. Bush, "Remarks by the President on Stem Cell Research," August 9, 2001, Crawford, Texas.

149 **stem cell research to Nazi murders:** Tom Strode, "Pro-Lifers Condemn Creation of Embryos Only for Research," *Southern Baptist Press News,* July 16, 2001.

149 **"implied that life begins at conception":** Michael Foust, "Mohler: Bush Decision Has Much for Pro-Life Community to Applaud," *Southern Baptist Press News,* August 10, 2001.

150 **"the biggest political victory the pro-life movement has had in years":** David Frum, "It's His Party," *New York Times,* January 5, 2003.

150 **"generally favorable," "advocates of" and "pro-lifers should be":** Tom Strode, "Pro-lifers Give Favorable Marks to Bush's Bioethics Appointees," *Southern Baptist Press News,* January 18, 2002.

150 **"virtually every new reproductive technology":** Chris Mooney, "Irrationalist in Chief," *The American Prospect,* September 24, 2001.

150 **He opposed:** Ibid.

150 **"the entire decade of their twenties":** Leon Kass, "The End of Courtship," *The Public Interest,* summer 2003.

150 **"more than twice the number":** Gretchen Vogel, "Bush Squeezes Between the Lines on Stem Cells: Not All Stem Cell Lines Common Knowledge," *Science,* August 17, 2001, 1242.

150 **NIH . . . reduced the number of . . . lines to . . . *eleven:*** Elias Zerhouni, Testimony Before the Senate Committee on Appropriations, Subcommittee on Labor, Health and Human Services, and Education, Federal Funding for Stem Cell Research, 108th Congress (May 22, 2003).

150 **Stephen Hall:** Stephen S. Hall, "Bush's Political Science," *New York Times,* June 12, 2003.

150 **"have the ability to regenerate":** President George W. Bush, "Remarks by the President on Stem Cell Research," August 9, 2001, Crawford, Texas.

151 **Pedersen explained:** Rick Weiss, "Scientists Say Access to Embryo Stem Cells Lacking," *Washington Post,* September 26, 2002.

151 **"[e]mbryonic stem cell research is crawling":** Ibid.

151 **projects . . . must be approved:** Peter Ford, "Europe Is Speeding Up Stem-Cell Research," *Christian Science Monitor,* July 19, 2001.

151 **Kinsley on stem cell decision:** Michael Kinsley, "Taking Bush Personally," *Slate,* October 23, 2003.

152 **Bush . . . comes from a pro-choice family:** David Corn, "Loyal Opposition: George Bush's Secret Abortion Views," *Tom Paine,* June 16, 2000, at www.tompaine.com.

152 **that position . . . changed:** During the presidential campaign, David Corn reported that even Bush Jr. had "flip-flopped" on the abortion issue, citing a 1978 article where George W.—while opposed to the federal funding of abortion—said he believed it should be up to "a woman and her doctor" to decide whether abortion was the best option for that individual.

152 **"You may have noticed":** Joe Klein, "Too Personal for Comfort," *Time,* January 27, 2003, 21.

152 **Dr. David Hager:** Associated Press, "Abortion Opponent Is Named to Panel on Women's Health," *Washington Post,* December 31, 2002.

152 **NCI removed fact sheet:** Sally Squires, "Study Discounts Link Between Abortion, Breast Cancer Risk," *Washington Post,* February 28, 2003.

152 **"the scientific evidence does not support":** American Cancer Society, "Ask the Expert," at www.cancer.org.

152 **that hazy formulation is also untrue:** Mads Melbye et al., "Induced Abortion and the Risk of Breast Cancer," *New England Journal of Medicine* 336:2 (January 9, 1997): 81-85.

152 **accurate fact sheet:** "Cancer Facts: Abortion, Miscarriage and Breast Cancer Risks," NCI, May 30, 2003; http://cis.nci.nih.gov./fact/3_75.htm.

152 **steadily dropping since 1990:** Lawrence B. Finer and Stanley K. Henshaw, "Abortion Incidence and Services in the United States in 2000," *Perspectives on Sexual and Reproductive Health* (January/February 2003): 6-15.

153 **"You know, I've heard all the talk"**: President George W. Bush, "President Urges Senate to Pass Compassionate Welfare Reform Bill," July 29, 2002, Charleston, South Carolina.

153 **sex outside of marriage**: J. A. Grunbaum et al., "Youth Risk Behavior Surveillance," *MMWR CDC Surveillance Summaries,* 2001, 51 (SS-4): 1-64; National Center for Health Statistics, *Fertility, Family Planning, and Women's Health: New Data from the 1995 National Survey of Family Growth,* Vital & Health Statistics, Series 23, no. 19 (Hyattsville, MD: U.S. Dept. of Health & Human Services, 1997).

153 **"backfire"**: Phone interview with Adrienne Verrilli, August 2002.

153 **discuss contraceptives**: Advocates for Youth, "Will Ideology Trump Science in Deciding Public Health Policy? Drive to Promote Only Abstinence Undermines Efforts to Prevent HIV/ AIDS, STDs, and Teen Pregnancy in U.S. and Abroad."

153 **"deathstyle" . . . "gay plague"**: Maggie Fox, "Scientists Question Bush Panel Appointments," Reuters, January 24, 2003.

154 **eliminate . . . "reproductive health services and education"**: Doug Ireland, "Bush's War on the Condom: U.N. Report Documents the Failures to Curb AIDS," *L.A. Weekly,* December 6, 2002, 23.

154 **"sensitive language"**: Erica Goode, "Certain Words Can Trip Up AIDS Grants, Scientists Say," *New York Times,* April 18, 2003.

154 **Alfred Sommer**: Ibid.

154 **acceptable level of lead**: Dan Ferber, "Overhaul of CDC Panel Revives Lead Safety Debate," *Science,* October 25, 2002, 732.

154 **William Banner . . . Joyce Tsuji**: Ibid.

154 **contacted . . . by lead-industry**: Jonathan Cohn, "Toxic: The Lead Industry Gets Its Turn," *The New Republic,* December 23, 2002, 17.

155 **Gold and Paustenbach**: Rick Weiss, "HHS Seeks Science Advice to Match Bush Views," *Washington Post,* September 17, 2002.

155 **William Miller**: Aaron Zitner, "Advisors Put Under Microscope: The Bush Team Is Going to Great Lengths to Vet Members of Scientific Panels; Credentials, Not Ideology, Should Be the Focus, Critics Say," *Los Angeles Times,* December 23, 2002; Nicholas Thompson, "Science Friction: The Growing—and Dangerous—Divide Between Scientists and the GOP," *Washington Monthly,* July 1, 2003, 11.

155 **American Public Health Association . . . policy statement**: American Public Health Association, "Ensuring the Scientific Credibility of Government Public Health Advisory Committees," 2002 at www.alpha.org/legislative/policy/2002/LB02-2-scicred,pdf.

155 **"Advice Without Dissent'**: David Michaels et al., "Advice Without Dissent," *Science,* October 25, 2002, 703.

155 **relationship between federal science agencies and the scientific community**: Phone interview with Lynn Goldman, April 9, 2003.

156 **"That is what they're thinking"**: Ibid.

156 **"Expert committees need to be filled"**: Editorial, "Keeping Scientific Advice Non-Partisan," *The Lancet,* November 16, 2002, 1525.

The Right Judges . . . ?

156 **"The role of a judge"**: "Remarks by the President During Federal Judicial Appointments Announcement," May 9, 2001, at www.whitehouse.gov/news/releases/2001/05/print/20010509-3.html.

156 **"most important reason" . . . "govern for a generation"**: E. J. Dionne, "Payback in Judges," *Washington Post,* January 10, 2003.

157 **parental consent statutes**: *Planned Parenthood of Southeastern Pennsylvania v. Casey,* 505 U.S. 833, 898 (1992); *Ohio v. Akron Center for Reproductive Health,* 497 U.S. 502, 510-519 (1990) (Akron II); *Hodgson v. Minnesota,* 497 U.S. 417, 461 (1990) (J. O'Connor, concurring in part and concurring in the judgment in part); *City of Akron v. Akron Center for Reproductive Health,* 462 U.S. 416, 440 (1983) (Akron I); *Bellotti v. Baird,* 443 U.S. 622, 643-644 (1979) (plurality opinion) (Bellotti II).

157 **Texas law instructs**: Texas law permits a court to bypass the parental consent requirement if the girl is sufficiently mature and well informed; if notification is not in her best interest; or if notifying her parent(s) might lead to physical, sexual, or emotional abuse. Tex. Fam. Code 33.003(i).

157 **"aware of . . . religious arguments"**: *In re Jane Doe 1 (I),* 19 S.W.3d 249, 264-5 (Tex. 2000) (J. Owen, concurring).

157 **Owen's reading:** The Texas Supreme Court has interpreted the phrase to require the minor to demonstrate she "is capable of reasoned decision-making." *In re Jane Doe I (I),* 19 S.W.3d 249, 255 (2000).

157 **"unconscionable act":** *In re Jane Doe 1 (II),* 19 S.W.3d 346, 376 (Tex. 2000) (J. Owen dissenting).

158 **"unfairness against qualified women":** Marianne Means, "Fight over Texas Judge a Taste of More to Come," *Houston Chronicle,* September 15, 2002.

158 **Rove . . . was paid:** Priscilla Owen, Texas Ethics Commission Candidate Officeholder Report of Contributions, Expenditures, and Loans, January 1, 1994 through December 31, 1994.

158 **couldn't think of one:** Senate Committee on the Judiciary, Judicial Nominations, 107th Congress, 2nd sess., 2002.

159 **"inappropriate" . . . memberships:** Dana Priest, "Judiciary Panel Warns About Clubs; Membership in Discriminatory Organizations Called 'Inappropriate,'" *Washington Post,* August 3, 1990.

159 **"could think of three":** Tim O'Brien, "Democrats Begin Filibuster Against Estrada," Cnn.com, February 13, 2003, at www.cnn.com/2003/allpolitics/02/13/senate.estrada/index.html.

159 **"right-wing ideologue":** David G. Savage and Janet Hook, "Stakes Are High in Push for Latino Court Nominee," *Los Angeles Times,* April 11, 2002.

159 **"stealth nominee":** Neil Lewis, "A Once-Doomed Nomination Wins Senate Panel Approval," *New York Times,* January 31, 2003.

159 **"help us with Hispanic voters":** Carl Hulse, "Strategists See Victory in Stalemate over Nominee," *New York Times,* February 27, 2003.

159 **"ashamed to discuss their views":** Janelle Carter, "Bush Aide Sees Double Standard for Hispanic Nominee," *Philadelphia Inquirer,* February 24, 2003.

159 **"Form over substance":** Carl Hulse, "Strategists See Victory in Stalemate over Nominee," *New York Times,* February 27, 2003.

160 **"pack our courts":** E. J. Dionne, "They Started It," *Washington Post,* February 21, 2003.

160 **"extreme civil rights rulings":** Alliance for Justice, "The Case Against the Confirmation of Charles W. Pickering, Sr. to the U.S. Court of Appeals for the 5th Circuit," January 23, 2003, at www.allianceforjustice.org/judicial/research_publications/research_documents/Pickering_Full_Report.pdf.

160 **published only ninety-five decisions:** Senate Committee on the Judiciary, Judicial Nominations, 107th Congress, 1st sess., 2001, 40-41.

161 **Edwards . . . expressed concern:** Jonathan Groner, "New Line of Questioning at Pickering Hearing," *Legal Times,* February 11, 2002, 6.

161 **experts on judicial ethics:** Edward M. Kennedy, "Statement of Senator Edward M. Kennedy Regarding the Nomination of Judge Charles W. Pickering to the Fifth Circuit Court," March 14, 2002, at www.kennedy.senate.gov/~kennedy/statements/02/03/2002315B48.html.

161 **Pickering's . . . history:** See Sean Wilentz, "The Racist Skeletons in Charles Pickering's Closet," *Salon.com,* at www.salon.com/news/features/2003/05/12/pickering; Neil A. Lewis, "A Judge, a Renomination and the Cross-Burning Case that Won't End," *New York Times,* May 28, 2003.

161 **"never had any contact":** Senate Committee on the Judiciary, Federal Appointments, 101st Congress, 2nd sess., 656, 657.

161 **voted to provide public funding:** See *Journal of the Senate of the State of Mississippi,* Regular Session Commencing January 4, 1972, at 1165 (vote on H.B. No. 1294); See *Journal of the Senate of the State of Mississippi,* Regular Session Commencing 2 January 1973, at 948 (vote on H.B. No. 1273).

161 **Pickering was "very interested":** Memorandum from Edgar C. Fortenberry to W. Webb Burke (January 5, 1972), in Ralph Neas, "Report of People for the American Way Opposing the Confirmation of Charles W. Pickering, Sr. to the U.S. Court of Appeals for the Fifth Circuit," January 24, 2002, 10, at www.pfaw.org/pfaw/dfiles/file_53.pdf.

161 **"perilously close to lying under oath":** Joe Conason, Joe Conason's Journal, *Salon.com,* January 9, 2003, at www.salon.com/opinion/conason/2003/01/09/bush/index.html.

162 **"play the race card":** "NAACP Calls on Senate to Oppose Pickering and Owen Nomination to Federal Appeals Court," January 9, 2003, at www.naacp.org/news/releases/pickering01903.shtml.

162 **"wife is to subordinate herself" . . . "conceptions from rape":** Jennifer Lee, "Attack on Judicial Nominee Leads Panel to Delay Vote," *New York Times,* April 11, 2003.

162 **It snowed once in Miami:** See Jeffrey Toobin, "Annals of Law: Advice and Dissent," *New Yorker,* March 26, 2003, 42.

162 **"worst abomination" . . . "political battlegrounds":** Editorial, "Unfit to Judge," *Washington Post,* April 11, 2003.

162 **"There is no question":** Alliance for Justice press release, "Alliance for Justice Calls for Withdrawal of Alabama Attorney General's Nomination to 11th Circuit," July 17, 2003.

162 **"probably the most doctrinaire":** National Public Radio, *Morning Edition,* June 11, 2003.

163 **Sunstein told a group:** Jeffrey Toobin, "Advice and Dissent: The Fight Over the President's Judicial Nominations," *The New Yorker,* May 26, 2003, 42.

163 **61 percent:** People for the American Way, "The Senate, the Courts, and the Blue Slip," at www.pfaw.org/pfaw/general/default.aspx?oid=7623.

163 **days for an appeals court judge:** People for the American Way, "President Bush, the Senate and the Federal Judiciary: Unprecedented Situation Calls for Unprecedented Solution," at www.pfaw.org/pfaw/general/default.aspx?oid=632.

Poverty

165 **"help people help themselves":** "Remarks at a Reception for Gubernatorial Candidate Bill Simon in Dana Point, California," September 2, 2002.

165 **"little girl from New York":** "Remarks at Boston Latin School in Boston, Massachusetts," January 14, 2002.

165 **"fight for things":** "Remarks Following a Cabinet Meeting on the Administration's Agenda," August 6, 2001.

165 **"every child is educated":** "Remarks to Catholic Leaders," March 26, 2001.

165 **"in my heart a prayer":** "Remarks at the National Prayer Breakfast," February 5, 2001.

165 **"when I speak, you will know my heart":** www.cnn.com/ELECTION/2000/conventions/republican/transcripts/bush.html.

166 **"support the heroic work":** www.cnn.com/ELECTION/2000/conventions/republican/transcripts/bush.html.

166 **"man of action":** "Remarks of the President at the Capital Area Food Bank," December 19, 2002, at www.usafreedomcorps.gov/about_usafc/whats_new/speeches/20021219.asp.

166 **"terminate heating":** Molly Ivins, "Bush Discovers Hunger and Looks the Other Way," *Chicago Tribune,* December 26, 2002, at www.chicagotribune.com/news/opinion/oped/chi0212260202dec261,7772200.story?coll+chi%2Dnewsopinioncommentary%2Dhed.

166 **bottom three-fifths:** "Census Data Show Increases in Extent and Severity of Poverty and Decline in Household Income: Income Disparities At Record Levels," Center for Budget and Policy Priorities, press release, September 24, 2002, at www.cbpp.org/9-24-02pov.htm.

166 **"We want to help people":** "President's Welfare Reform Package Strengthens Families," January 14, 2003, at www.whitehouse.gov/news/releases/2003/01/20030114-6.html.

166 **"applied carefully and compassionately":** "Radio Address by the President to the Nation," May 11, 2002, at www.whitehouse.gov/news/releases/2002/05/20020511.html.

167 **welfare reform increased employment:** Stephanie Mencimer, "Children Left Behind: Why We Need a National Child-Care Program, Now More Than Ever," *The American Prospect,* December 30, 2002, 29.

167 **"If more people . . . are poor":** Ruth Brandwein, "It's Getting Worse for Poor Families," *(New York) Newsday,* October 1, 2003.

167 **block grants:** Jennifer Foote Sweeney, "The Cruelty of Compassionate Conservatism: Bush Hacks at Programs to Aid Children, Leaving the Battered, the Ill and the Poor Behind," *Salon.com,* March 23, 2001; Stephanie Mencimer, "Children Left Behind: Why We Need a National Child-Care Program, Now More Than Ever," *The American Prospect,* December 30, 2002, 29.

167 **"fully fund all of these programs":** David Broder, "Cutbacks to Our Children," *Washington Post,* March 23, 2003.

167 **"I don't even want to truly think about it":** Jonathan Weissman, "Some Jobless May Lose Benefits in Dec.; House Has Last Chance to Break Impasse on Extending Insurance Program," *Washington Post,* November 22, 2002.

168 **"drop their opposition":** Ibid.

168 **"bring some comfort":** "Bush Signs Unemployment Benefits Bill: Measure Sails Through Congress," CNN.com, January 8, 2003, at www.cnn.com/2003/ALLPOLITICS/01/08/congress.unemployment/.

168 **still unemployed:** Wendell Primus, Jessica Goldberg, and Isaac Shapiro, "New Unemployment Insurance Proposal Neglects One Million Jobless Workers Who Have Run Out of Federal Unemployment Benefits," January 14, 2003, at www.cbpp.org/1-6-03ui.htm.

168 **"dividends received":** Report of the Minority Staff of the House Appropriations Committee, "Eight Years of Progress in Fighting Long-Term Unemployment Is Lost in Only Twenty-Four Months," January 30, 2003.

168 **"fully fund LIHEAP":** Second presidential debate, Boston, October 30, 2000.

168 **"heat and cool their homes"**: "Remarks During a Tour of the Youth Entertainment Academy and an Exchange with Reporters in Plainfield, New Jersey," March 19, 2001.

169 **"third-world situation"**: John W. Fountain, More Families Face Loss of Heat with Public Aid Scarce," *New York Times,* December, 5, 2002.

169 **Olasky:** James Moore and Wayne Slater, *Bush's Brain: How Karl Rove Made George W. Bush Presidential* (Hoboken, NJ: John Wiley & Sons, 2003), 202.

169 **"emphasis on results"**: Marvin Olasky, "Coming in From the Cold," January 29, 2001, at www.olasky.com.

169 **"one soul at a time"**: "President Bush Implements Key Elements of His Faith-Based Initiative," December 12, 2002, at www.whitehouse.gov/news/releases/2002/12/20021212-3.html.

169 **"government should welcome faith-based groups"**: "President Bush Discusses Faith-Based Initiative in Tennessee," February 10, 2003, at www.whitehouse/gov/news/releases/2003/02/20030210-1.html.

170 **DiIulio:** Ron Suskind, "Why Are These Men Laughing?," *Esquire,* January 2003.

170 **"winked at the most far-right"**: Ibid.

170 **"'F in terms of legislation"**: Dana Milbank, "President's Compassionate Agenda Lags: Bush's Legislative Record for Disadvantaged Wanting," *Washington Post,* December 26, 2002.

170 **religiously based services:** Editorial, "Using Tax Dollars for Churches," *New York Times,* December 30, 2002.

170 **"program is funding treatment"**: Alan Cooperman, "2 Faith-Based Proposals May Face Legal Challenge," *Washington Post,* January 30, 2003.

171 **"The line can't be blurred"**: Eric Lichtblau, "Bush Plans to Let Religious Groups Get Building Aid," *New York Times,* January 23, 2003.

171 **Federal funding for Medicaid:** David S. Broder, "A Budget of Dire Consequences," *Washington Post,* March 31, 2003.

171 **"flesh on the bones"**: Ron Suskind, "Why Are These Men Laughing?," *Esquire,* January 2003.

171 **"This 'compassionate conservatism'"**: Richard Benedetto, "Clinton Jeers Bush's 'Compassion Theme'," *USA Today,* July 15, 1999.

172 **"over your lifetime"**: "President Launches USA Freedom Corps," January 30, 2002, at www.whitehouse/gov/news/releases/2002/01/20020130-12.html.

172 **"good works deserve our praise"**: "President Delivers 'State of the Union,'" January 28, 2003, at www.whitehouse/gov/news/releases/2003/01/20030128-19.html.

172 **"I don't understand"**: Elisabeth Bumiller, "Bush 'Compassion' Agenda: An '04 Liability?," *New York Times,* August 26, 2003.

Crime and Punishment

172 **"should not respond"**: "Remarks by the President at the National Republican Senatorial Committee Annual Dinner," September 25, 2002, at http://www.whitehouse.gov/news/releases/2002/09/20020925-6.html.

172 **"enforce the"**: George W. Bush, "President Says U.S. Attorneys on Front Line in War," November 29, 2001, at http://www.whitehouse/gov/news/releases/2001/11/20011129-12.html.

172 **"violent criminals"**: "Your Turn: A Reader Asks Governor Candidates," *Houston Chronicle,* September 14, 1994.

172 **"this is a society"**: "Transcript of Presidential Debate at Wake Forest University," C-SPAN, October 11, 2000, at http://www.c-span.org/campaign2000/transcript/debate_101100.asp.

173 **208 gun deaths:** Colin Greenwood, "Cross-Sectional Study of the Relationship Between Levels of Gun Ownership and Violent Deaths," *Firearms Research and Advisory Service,* March 2000, 12.

173 **"we'll have a president"**: Carter M. Yang, "Gore Rips Bush on Guns," ABCNews.com, May 5, 2000.

173 **A rating:** Donna Ladd, "'Puke and Shoot': Gun Champs Win Congress, Fight for Bush," *Village Voice,* November 21, 2000.

173 **"a dream come true"**: Laura A. Kiernan, "Signs Were There Before Dole Quit," *Boston Globe,* October 24, 1999.

173 **two to three times:** Juliet Eilperin, "A Pivotal Election Finds NRA's Wallet Open," *Washington Post,* November 1, 2000.

173 **more than $4 million into Republican:** "Gun Rights: Long-Term Contribution Trends," *Center for Responsive Politics,* at http://www.opensecrets.org/industries/indus.asp?Ind=Q13.

173 **"Supreme Court that will":** Laura Meckler, "Gun Politics Hits Airwaves as Bush and Gore Trade Barbs," Associated Press, May 4, 2000.

173 **1939 Supreme Court ruling:** "The Second Amendment," *Brady Campaign to Prevent Gun Violence,* at http://www.bradycampaign.org/facts/issuebriefs/second.asp.

173 **"I can't think of any":** Jake Tapper, "Gunning for the Center," *Salon.com,* May 17, 2000.

173 **"refused to let Texans":** "A Reader Asks Governor Candidates," *Houston Chronicle,* September 19, 1994.

174 **"frivolous lawsuits":** Scott S. Greenberger, "Texas' Gun Bent Could Plague Bush Campaign," *Austin American-Statesman,* June 18, 1999.

174 **"nearly fifty thousand people have been killed":** "Targeting Safety," *Center to Prevent Handgun Violence,* 2001.

174 **never seriously advocated:** Anna Quindlen, "Tort Reform at Gunpoint," *Newsweek,* May 5, 2003, 72.

174 **would prevent gun-violence victims:** "The U.S. Senate Is on the Verge of Voting to Let Reckless Gun Dealers Get Away With Murder," Million Mom March, at http://www.mmm2004.com/site/DocServer/AA_pdf_reckless_gun.pdf.

175 **"supports the reauthorization:** "The Gun-Control Issue," *Washington Times,* April 27, 2003.

175 **"America's economy" . . . "priority":** "Press Briefing by Ari Fleischer," November 6, 2002, at http://www.whitehouse.gov/news/releases/2002/11/20021106-1.html.

175 **"the president will never":** Karen MacPherson, "Bush Holds Key to Assault Weapon Ban," *Pittsburgh Post-Gazette,* May 25, 2003.

175 **"true to his" and "good cop":** Editorial, "An Assault on Common Sense," *(New York) Daily News,* May 25, 2003.

175 **barred the FBI and issued warnings:** Don Thompson, "State to Continue Gun Checks Despite Warning," *San Diego Union-Tribune,* March 1, 2003.

175 **"prevent private citizens":** "President Bush's 2001 U.N. General Assembly Speech," U.S. Dept. of State, November 10, 2001, at http://usinfo.state.gov/topical/pol/terror/01111001.htm.

175 **65 to 75 percent majorities:** Fox News Poll found that 69 percent of Americans favor the death penalty for those convicted of premeditated murder, a drop of 7 percentage points since 1997. Fox News, June 10, 2003, at http://www.deathpenaltyinfo.org/article.php?did=619&scid=64. An ABC News/Washington Post poll found that 64 percent of Americans support the death penalty when no other alternative is offered. When given a choice, 49 percent choose the death penalty and 45 percent choose life in prison, ABC News.com, January 24, 2003, at http://www.deathpenaltyinfo.org/article.php?scid=23&did=210.

176 **"always believed that" . . . "All I can tell you is":** Charles Zewe, "Texas Prepares to Execute Woman," CNN.com, January 15, 1998, at http://www.cnn.com/US/9801/15/texas.execution/; Jim Yardley, "Bush and the Death Penalty; Texas' Busy Death Chamber Helps Define Bush's Tenure," *New York Times,* January 7, 2000.

176 **"relatively removed posture" . . . "paroles board stands between him and the process":** Jim Yardley, "Bush and the Death Penalty, Texas' Busy Death Chamber Helps Define Bush's Tenure," *New York Times,* January 7, 2000.

176 **overriding local prosecutors:** Aitan Goelman, "Let the Prosecutor Decide," *The National Law Journal,* June 2, 2003.

177 **"promised to testify":** Joseph Rosenbloom, "No Death-Penalty Doubts at Justice; DNA Testing and Racial Bias Raise Questions of Fairness—but Not with Ashcroft," *The American Prospect,* March 2003.

177 **"To many federal prosecutors . . . it appears":** Aitan Goelman, "Let the Prosecutor Decide," *The National Law Journal* (June 2, 2003).

177 **Michigan (capital punishment banned):** Viveca Novak, "Putting the Death Penalty to Work," CNN.com, April 15, 2002, at http://www.cnn.com/ALLPOLITICS/time/2002/04/22/death.html;

177 **Puerto Rico (whose constitution)** "Puerto Rico and the Death Penalty," Death Penalty Information Center, at http://www.deathpenaltyinfo.org/article.php?scid=11&did=670 (citing article from *Los Angeles Times,* June 9, 2003).

177 **"We don't believe in capital punishment":** Ibid.

177 **Bush signed a military order:** Amnesty International—Campaigns—Death Penalty Developments in 2002, at http://web.amnesty.org/pages/deathpenalty-developments-eng.

177 **more documented executions of child offenders . . . head of a list:** Amnesty International, "Children and the Death Penalty—Executions Worldwide Since 1990." at http://web.amnesty.org/library/print/ENGACT500072002.

177 **"Guess what?":** Bob Herbert, "The Death Capital: Exposing Texas' Unjust System," *New York Times,* October 16, 2000.

177 **"Please, Bush whimpers":** Tucker Carlson, "Devil May Care," *Talk,* September 1999.

178 **48 percent to 101 percent higher:** Amnesty International, "Death Penalty Facts," Deterrence, at www.amnestyusa.org/abolish/deterrence.html.

178 **inconsistent standards and underfunding:** "A State of Denial: Texas Justice and the Death Penalty," Chapter Six—The Right to Counsel in Texas: You Get What You Pay For, *Texas Defender Services,* 80-81.

178 **"dozed and actually":** Editorial, "Only in Texas," *Washington Post,* January 20, 2002.

178 **"America will always stand firm":** Nat Hentoff, ". . . But Objections Don't Sway Supreme Court, President," *Chicago Sun-Times,* June 1, 2003.

178 **80 percent of those executed since 1977:** "Death by Discrimination—The Continuing Role of Race in Capital Cases," Amnesty International.

179 **123 people:** Dan Eggen, \$1 Billion Proposed for DNA Testing: Administration Seeks to Clear Backlog of Analysis in Criminal Cases," *Washington Post,* March 12, 2003.

179 **no biological evidence available:** "Innocents Exonerated by DNA . . . But What If There Is No DNA? Have Innocents Been Put To Death?" Forensic-Evidence.com, at www.forensic-evidence.com/site/EVID/DNAexonerations.html.

179 **"there's no doubt":** Interview with Barry Scheck, November 5, 2003.

179 **commuted the death sentences of 167 people:** Robert E. Pierre and Kari Lydersen, "Illinois Death Row Emptied; Citing 'Demon of Error,' Ryan Commutes Sentences," *Washington Post,* January 12, 2003.

179 **"Our capital system is haunted":** Associated Press, "ILL Gov. Ryan clears death row inmates," USATODAY.com, updated January 12, 2003, at www.usatoday.com/news/nation/2003-01-11-illinois-death-penalty_x.htm.

179 **never intended to be activist . . . "I have always reserved":** Governor George H. Ryan Address, Northwestern University School of Law, January 11, 2003, at www.law.northwestern.edu/depts/clinic/wrongful/RyanSpeech.htm.

Labor Pains

180 **Ergonomic . . . hazards:** General Accounting Office, "Worker Protection: Private Sector Ergonomics Programs Yield Positive Results," footnote 2, August 1997, at frwebgate.access.gpo.gov/cgi-bin/useftp. cgi?IPaddress=162.140.64.21&filename=he97163.pdf&directory=/diskb/wais/data/gao.

180 **most widespread:** House Committee on Small Business Subcommittee on Regulatory Reform and Paperwork Reduction, *Hearing on OSHA's Proposed Ergonomics Standard: Its Impact on Small Business,* 106th Congress, 2nd sess., 2000.

180 **"It's just rhetoric":** Telephone interview with David LeGrande, March 12, 2003.

180 **more than \$9 billion:** Nick Anderson, "OSHA Scales Back Its New Workplace Safety Plan," *Los Angeles Times,* November 23, 1999.

180 **Companies that have implemented ergonomic standards:** Senate Committee on Appropriations, *Workplace Safety and the Ergonomics Rule,* 107th Congress, 1st sess., 2001.

181 **reduced their annual workers' compensation costs:** House Committee on Small Business Subcommittee on Regulatory Reform and Paperwork Reduction, *Hearing on OSHA's Proposed Ergonomics Standard: Its Impact on Small Business,* 106th Congress, 2nd sess., 2000.

181 **In a report:** National Academy of Sciences, *Musculoskeletal Disorders and the Workplace* (Washington: National Academy Press, 2001).

181 **"see unions":** Interview with Dennis Hughes, New York, March 10, 2003.

181 **"For Bush":** Robert Borosage, "Class Warfare, Bush-style," *The American Prospect,* March 1, 2003.

181 **rejected three nominees . . . "offended":** Dan Ferber, "HHS Intervenes in Choice of Study Section Members" *Science,* November 15, 2002.

181 **"To stack [these] panels":** Aaron Zitner, "Advisors Put Under a Microscope," *Los Angeles Times,* December 23, 2002.

182 **Mine Safety and Health Administration:** David Corn, "W. and the Coal Miners: Photo-op Cover for Anti-worker Policies," *The Nation,* August 6, 2002.

182 **add . . . mining inspectors:** The Associated Press, "National Briefing: Washington," January 28, 2003.

182 **close examination of the agency's budget:** Telephone interview with Joe Main, March 12, 2003.

182 **"eliminating many worker rights"**: Christopher Lee and Sara Kehaulani Goo, "TSA Blocks Attempt to Unionize Screeners," *Washington Post,* January 10, 2003.

183 **"role as union leader"**: Brian Friel, "Labor Pains," *Government Executive,* October 1, 2002.

183 **employees may quit**: Mimi Hall, "New Homeland Security Dept. Faces Challenges; Unions, Budget and Computers Among Concerns," *USA Today,* November 26, 2002.

184 **"Chao obviously"**: Interview with Denis Hughes, New York, March 10, 2003.

184 **8 million Americans**: Ross Eisenbrey and Jared Bernstein, "Eliminating the Right to Overtime Pay," at www.epinet.org/content.cfm/briefingpapers_flsa_jun03.

184 **Almost 80 percent**: U.S. Department of Labor, *The "New Economy" and Its Impact on Executive, Administrative, and Professional Exemptions to the Fair Labor Standards Act (FLSA)* (Washington, D.C., 2001); Ross Eisenbrey and Jared Bernstein, "Eliminating the Right to Overtime Pay," at www.epinet.org/content.cfm/briefingpapers_flsa_jun03.

184 **"vastly misleading"**: Jared Bernstein, "New Overtime Rules," *New York Times,* July 3, 2003.

184 **labor unions**: Brian Friel, "Labor Pains," *Government Executive,* October 1, 2002.

9. Rules for Hyperpowers

185 **"Look, I know what I believe"**: Kathleen Maclay, "Researchers Help Define What Makes a Political Conservative," *UC Berkeley News,* July 22, 2003, at www.berkely.edu/news/media/releases/2003/07/22_politics.shtml.

185 **reporters . . . followed . . . Fleischer's lead**: Dana Milbank, "A 10-Minute Test of Mending Fences, Claiming Mandate," *Washington Post,* January 19, 2001.

185 **"media coverage of Bush's inauguration"**: Fred I. Greenstein, "The Leadership Style of George W. Bush," paper presented at the conference on the Bush Presidency: An Early Assessment, Princeton University, Princeton, New Jersey, April 25-26, 2003.

186 **Foreign policy in Bush's Inaugural Address**: President George W. Bush, "President George W. Bush's Inaugural Address," the White House, January 20, 2001, at www.whitehouse. gov/news/inauguraladdress.

186 **"overcommitting our military"**: George W. Bush, "The Second 2000 Gore-Bush Presidential Debate," Commission on Presidential Debates, October 11, 2000, at www.debates.org/pages/trans2000b.html.

186 **U.S. fighters and bombers**: Gregg Easterbrook, "Out on the Edge: American Power Moves Beyond the Mere Super," *New York Times,* April 27, 2003.

186 **military budget numbers and comparative size**: Steve Lopez, "Just How Big Does the World's Biggest War Machine Need to Be?" *Los Angeles Times,* May 9, 2003.

187 **Paul Kennedy**: Paul Kennedy, "The Eagle Has Landed," *Financial Times,* February 2, 2002.

188 **"I do need somebody to tell me where Kosovo is"**: John Young, "Quick, Bush, Give Reporters Some Other Substance to Report," Cox News Service, August 26, 1999.

188 **Taliban and "some band"**: Ivo H. Daalder and James M. Lindsay, "The Bush Revolution: The Remaking of America's Foreign Policy," Brookings Institution, April 2003.

188 **Rice on Bush's "on-the-ground experience" and "American values"**: James Traub, "W's World," *New York Times Magazine,* January 14, 2001, 28.

188 **"My job isn't to nuance"**: Stanley Hoffmann, "America Alone in the World," *The American Prospect,* September 23, 2002.

189 **Bush's "laid-back" reign as governor**: Alan C. Miller and Judy Pasternak, "Records Show Bush's Focus on Big Picture," *Los Angeles Times,* August 2, 2000.

189 **President shows "little interest" in complexity**: Glenn Kessler, "Bush Sticks to the Broad Strokes in Mideast Peace Push, President Wary of Details and Deep Intervention," *Washington Post,* June 3, 2003.

189 **Bush believes he was "called by God"**: Judy Keen, "Strain of Iraq War Showing on Bush, Those Who Know Him Say," *USA Today,* April 2, 2003.

189 **David Gergen**: CNBC's *Capital Report,* February 18, 2003 (author present).

190 **"attendance at Bible study"**: David Frum, *The Right Man: The Surprise Presidency of George W. Bush* (New York: Random House, 2003), 272.

190 **Brookhiser on Bush**: Richard Brookhiser, "What Makes W. Tick?" Atlantic Unbound, March 11, 2003, at www.theatlantic.com/unbound/interviews/int2003-03-11.htm.

190 **Powell disagreed**: Alan Sipress and Steven Mufson, "Powell Takes the Middle Ground" *Washington Post,* August 26, 2001.

190 **Bush on Putin:** Thomas L. Friedman, "Soul Brother," *New York Times*, June 29, 2001.

190 **Rice on Russia:** "Entretien avec Condoleezza Rice," *Politique Internationale* 10 (2000): 30, cited in Ivo H. Daalder and James M. Lindsay, "The Bush Revolution: The Remaking of America's Foreign Policy," paper presented at The George W. Bush Presidency: An Early Assessment, Princeton University, Princeton, New Jersey, April 25, 2003.

191 **Ramesh Ponnuru:** Rich Lowry, "It's Not Personal, Mr. Bush," *Washington Post*, July 1, 2001.

191 **Bush and Vicente Fox press conference:** Karen DeYoung and Mike Allen, "Bush's Efforts on Iraq, N. Korea Flag," *Washington Post*, October 27, 2002.

191 **"Que bueno":** Maureen Dowd, "W.'s Spaghetti Western," *New York Times*, May 29, 2002.

191 **Anne Applebaum:** Anne Applebaum, "Memo to Bush: Europe Is Listening," *Washington Post*, May 28, 2003.

191 **Putin and "bad companions":** Carla Anne Robbins and Jeanne Cummings, "In President's Postwar Vision, Small Allies Play a Large Role," *Wall Street Journal*, May 30, 2003.

192 **Secular Schröder:** Bill Keller, "God and George W. Bush," *New York Times*, May 17, 2003.

192 **Bush tries to pray with Saudi prince and guests:** Elsa Walsh, "The Prince: How the Saudi Ambassador Became Washington's Indispensable Operator," *New Yorker*, March 24, 2003, 48.

193 **"everything . . . run by the political arm":** Ron Suskind, "Why Are These Men Laughing?," *Esquire*, December 2002.

193 **Cheney in charge of sensitive projects:** James A. Barnes, "Politics: The Imperial Vice Presidency," *National Journal*, March 17, 2001; Carl M. Cannon, "Politics: The Point Man," *National Journal*, October 11, 2002.

194 **Cheney's secret energy-policy meetings:** Harold Meyerson, "The Most Dangerous President Ever: How and Why George W. Bush Undermines American Security," *The American Prospect*, May 1, 2003.

194 **Wolfowitz and Powell:** Johanna McGeary, "Odd Man Out," *Time*, September 10, 2001, 28.

194 **"suggestion that imminent negotiations are about to begin":** Jane Perlez, "Washington Memo: Divergent Voices Heard in Bush Foreign Policy," *New York Times*, March 12, 2001.

194 **"I got a little far forward on my skis":** Johanna McGeary, "Odd Man Out," *Time*, September 10, 2001, 30.

195 **Kissinger on Powell and advisors:** Steven R. Weisman, "What Rift? Top Aides Deny State Dept.–Pentagon Chasm," *New York Times*, May 31, 2003.

195 **Rice on failures of Clinton administration policies:** Condoleezza Rice, "Promoting the National Interest," *Foreign Affairs*, January/February 2000.

195 **Baker and "jobs, jobs, jobs":** James A. Baker III, with Thomas M. DeFrank, *The Politics of Diplomacy: Revolution, War and Peace, 1989-1992* (New York: Putnam 1995), 336-37.

195 **Negroponte and Sandinistas:** Sarah Wildman, "Contra Aide: W. Picks an Amoralist for the United Nations," *The New Republic*, March 19, 2001, 20; Maggie Farley and Norman Kempster, "Bush's U.N. Pick Faces Battle Over Contra Role: Critics Raise Questions About John Negroponte's Actions as Ambassador to Honduras and His Knowledge of a CIA-Backed Death Squad," *Los Angeles Times*, March 25, 2001.

196 **Otto Reich:** *The Iran-Contra Scandal: The Declassified History*, eds. Peter R. Kornbluh and Malcolm Byrne (New York: The New Press, 1993); Theodore Draper, *A Very Thin Line: The Iran Contra Affairs* (New York: Hill and Wang, 1991), 200; Karen DeYoung, "Anti-Castro Figure Named to State Dept: Critics Vow to Block Bush Nominee, Citing Conflict of Interest, Iran-Contra Ties," *Washington Post*, April 15, 2001.

196 **Elliott Abrams:** "Iran-Contra Figure Back at White House," *New York Times*, June 30, 2001; David Greenberg, "Back, But Not by Popular Demand," *Washington Post*, December 8, 2002.

196 **John Poindexter:** John Markoff, "Chief Takes Over at Agency to Thwart Attacks on U.S.," *New York Times*, February 13, 2002.

197 **Defense Planning Guidance Draft:** Dick Polman, "Neo Conservatives," *Philadelphia Inquirer*, May 4, 2003.

197 **Final Defense Planning Guidance Draft repudiated by Bush Sr. White House:** Jay Bookman, "The President's Real Goal in Iraq," *Atlanta Journal-Constitution*, September 29, 2002; Ronald D. Asmus, *The New U.S. Strategic Debate* (Santa Monica: Rand, 1994); Barton Gellman, "Keeping the U.S. First; Pentagon Would Preclude a Rival Superpower," *Washington Post*, March 11, 1992; Andrew Goldberg, "Selective Engagement: US National Security Policy in the 1990s," *Washington Quarterly* (Summer 1992).

197 **Project for a New American Century:** "Rebuilding America's Defenses: Strategy, Forces and Resources For a New Century," a report of The Project for the New American Century, Washington, September 2000.

197 **"High Noon" and "Gary Cooper":** Jay Bookman, "The President's Real Goal in Iraq," *Atlanta Journal-Constitution*, September 29, 2002.

197 **"Without 9/11, Bush might have been off wandering in the desert":** Dick Polman, "Neo Conservatives," *Philadelphia Inquirer,* May 2, 2003.

198 **U.S. would do "whatever it took" to defend Taiwan from Chinese attack:** Neil King Jr., "Bush Leaves Taiwan Policy in Confusing Straits," *Wall Street Journal,* April 26, 2001.

198 **"It will . . . further damage U.S.-China relations":** Philip Pan, "China 'Concerned' by Bush Remarks," *Washington Post,* April 27, 2001.

198 **"President Bush has revealed weakness":** Robert Kagan and William Kristol, "A National Humiliation," *Weekly Standard,* April 16/April 23, 2001.

199 **Donald Rumsfeld and Al Capone:** Fareed Zakaria, "The Arrogant Empire," *Newsweek,* March 24, 2003.

199 **Frum on Bush's response to international criticism:** Frum, *The Right Man,* 240.

199 **Bush's limited interaction with other state leaders:** Fareed Zakaria, "The Arrogant Empire," *Newsweek,* March 24, 2003.

199 **Powell on President Bush:** "Old Friends and New," *Economist,* May 30, 2002, 28.

200 **Rice informed EU deal was "dead":** Jeffrey Kluger, "A Climate of Despair," *Time,* April 9, 2001, 30.

200 **"all they need to do is look at home":** Eric Alterman, *Altercation,* MSNBC, April 27, 2001, at www.msnbc.com/news.

200 **The idea . . . "does not make economic sense for America":** David E. Sanger, "Leaving for Europe, Bush Draws on Hard Lessons of Diplomacy," *New York Times,* May 22, 2002.

200 **"I went to dinner . . . with fifteen leaders of the EU":** Peggy Noonan, "A Chat in the Oval Office," *Wall Street Journal,* June 25, 2001.

201 **Powell, Whitman, and O'Neill all ignored on Kyoto:** Ivo H. Daalder and James M. Lindsay, "The Bush Revolution: The Remaking of America's Foreign Policy," Brookings Institution, April 2003.

201 *The Independent* **and American verification:** Thomas L. Friedman, "Noblesse Oblige," *New York Times,* July 31, 2001.

201 **ICC jurisdiction:** Michael Hirsh, "Bush and the World," *Foreign Affairs* (September/ October 2002).

202 **Half a million people die each year:** Colum Lynch, "U.S. Fights U.N. Accord to Control Small Arms: Stance on Draft Pact Not Shared by Allies," *Washington Post,* July 10, 2001.

202 **"funding issues are too complex for the pact":** Bob Davies, "U.S. Battles Europe to Narrow a Treaty Banning Corruption," *Wall Street Journal,* June 17, 2003.

202 **"reached preliminary agreement":** Bob Davis, "The U.S. Nears a Pact on Corruption Treaty," *Washington Post,* August 13, 2003.

203 **pharmaceutical industry spent more than $50 million to help Republicans:** Roger Thurow and Scott Miller, "As U.S. Balks on Medicine Deal, African Patients Feel the Pain," *Wall Street Journal,* June 2, 2003.

203 **"HIV prevalence":** "AIDS Epidemic Update," UNAIDS, December, 2002, p. 16, at www.unaids.org/worldaidsday/2002/press/update/epiupdate_en.pdf.

204 **Bush on free trade:** Governor George W. Bush, "A Distinctly American Internationalism," Ronald Reagan Library, Simi Valley, California, November 19, 1999, at www.mtholyoke.edu/acad/intrel/bush/wspeech.htm.

204 **"free markets and trade have helped defeat poverty":** Mike Allen and Karen DeYoung, "Bush Calls Trade Key to Mideast: President Launches Plan for U.S. Pact in Region," *Washington Post,* May 10, 2003.

205 **"false comfort of protectionism":** Steven Pearlstein and Clay Chandler, "Reaction Abroad on Steel Is Harsh: Bush Decision to Impose Tariffs Called Setback to Free-Trade Effort," *Washington Post,* March 7, 2002.

205 **farm subsidies:** William Finnegan, "The Economy of Empire," *Harper's,* May 2003, 50.

205 **"I'll sure remember Bush":** Francis X. Clines, "In Grateful Big Steel States, the Bush Democrat May Be Born," *New York Times,* March 8, 2002.

205 **George Will on steel tariff:** George F. Will, "Bush Swaps Principles for Politics: Protecting Steel Hurts Car Buyers, Companies and President's Integrity," *Chicago Sun-Times,* March 7, 2002.

205 **Blair on steel tariff:** Francis X. Clines, "In Grateful Big Steel States, the Bush Democrat May Be Born," *New York Times,* March 8, 2002.

205 **Robert Zoellick:** Paul Krugman, "Testing His Metal," *New York Times,* March 8, 2002.

205 **tariffs were illegal:** Elizabeth Becker, "U.S. Tariffs on Steel Are Illegal, World Trade Organization Says," *New York Times,* November 11, 2003.

205 **administration officials let it be known:** Mike Allen and Jonathan Weisman, "Steel Tariffs Appear to Have Backfired on Bush," *Washington Post,* September 19, 2003.

206 **Fleischer refuses to call Chavez ouster a "coup":** Christopher Marquis and Peter Slevin, "U.S. Cautioned Leader of Plot Against Chavez," *Washington Post,* April 17, 2002.

206 **U.S. ambassador chastised OAS members at meeting:** Karen DeYoung, "U.S. Seen as Weak Patron of Latin Democracy," *Washington Post,* April 16, 2002.

206 **Jorge Montano on Bush administration:** Glenn Kessler, "Swell of Foreign Support Goes Flat: Between U.S. Allies, Diplomatic Gap Grows," *Washington Post,* September 1, 2002.

206 **Rice warned Chavez:** www.slate.com, April 18, 2002.

206 **"left many here and in Venezuela scratching their heads":** Karen DeYoung, "Recent Statements Muddle U.S. Stance on Venezuela, Confusing Remarks a Symptom of Iraq Focus, Some Say," *Washington Post,* December 21, 2002.

207 **Bush signaled plans to build missile defense system:** www.whitehouse.gov, May 1, 2001.

207 **more than $70 billion on missile system:** Frances FitzGerald, *Way Out There in the Blue* (New York: Simon & Schuster, 2000), 258-59.

207 **missile system safety:** Michael R. Gordon with Steven Lee Myers, "The Nuclear Shield: Looking for Cover, Politics Mixes with Strategy in Plan for Antimissile System," *New York Times,* June 23, 2000; Eric Alterman, "Hey Buddy, Wanna Buy a Bridge?" *The Nation,* August 6, 2001. For background see FitzGerald, *Way Out There in the Blue* and Gordon R. Mitchell, *Strategic Deception: Rhetoric, Science and Politics in Missile Defense Advocacy* (East Lansing: University of Michigan Press, 2000).

207 **components "that have not been demonstrated as mature and ready":** Bradley Graham, "GAO Cites Risks in Missile Defense," *Washington Post,* June 5, 2003.

207 **"The final architecture is not knowable":** Fred Kaplan, "More Missile-Defense Madness: Bush's Latest Ploy for a System We Don't Even Need," *Slate,* February 20, 2003, at www.slate.com.

207 **weapons ineffective against solid-fueled missiles:** Bradley Graham, "Questions on Missile Defense Plans: Scientists' Report Questions Technology's Effectiveness," *Washington Post,* July 16, 2003.

208 **"not mature enough":** See Fred Kaplan, "Shooting Down Missile Defense," *Slate,* August 7, 2003, at www.slate.com.

208 **intermediate-range missiles:** Joseph Cirincione, "A Much Less Explosive Trend," *Washington Post,* March 10, 2002.

208 **"Victory Is Possible":** Colin S. Gray and Keith Payne, "Victory Is Possible," *Foreign Policy* (Summer 1980) at http://foreignpolicy.com/pdf/victory_is_possible.pdf.

208 **Payne on "multiple nuclear strikes":** Keith B. Payne, "Nuclear Weapons, Ours and Theirs," paper presented at "Nuclear Weapons, How Low Can We Go?" The Cato Institute Public Policy Forum, Washington, D.C., May 7, 1999.

208 **six thousand nuclear warheads eliminated from Russian arsenal:** Editorial, "Destroy Russia's Weapons," *Washington Post,* July 11, 2003.

209 **Turner and Buffett secure facility in Belgrade:** See Molly Ivins and Lou Dubose, *Bushwhacked: Life in George W. Bush's America* (New York: Random House, 2003), 265.

209 **Kaplan on anti-aircraft protection:** Fred Kaplan, "Homeland Insecurity: What Are the Feds Doing About Domestic Terrorism? Not Enough," *Slate,* June 6, 2003, at www.slate.com.

210 **Bush rejects money for the Department of Homeland Security:** Fred Kaplan, "More Missile-Defense Madness: Bush's Latest Ploy for a System We Don't Even Need," *Slate,* February 20, 2003, at www.slate.com.

210 **FitzGerald on American preparation for missile attack:** Frances FitzGerald, *Way Out There in the Blue: Reagan, Star Wars and the End of the Cold War* (New York: Simon and Schuster, 2000).

210 **RAND study:** Lawrence F. Kaplan, "Why the Best Offense Is a Good Missile Defense," *The New Republic,* March 12, 2001.

211 **"undermined the atmosphere for dialogue":** Roger Cohen, "America the Roughneck (Through Europe's Eyes)," *New York Times,* May 7, 2001.

211 **public support for strengthening international institutions:** See Craig Kennedy and Marshall M. Bolton, "The Real Transatlantic Gap," *Foreign Policy* (November-December 2002), based on a recent survey by the Chicago Council on Foreign Relations and the German Marshall Fund. For American views, see www.gallup.com/poll/releases/pr030228.asp.

211 **Bush actions repeatedly contradicted wishes of American citizens:** For a discussion of this issue, see Eric Alterman, *Who Speaks for America? Why Democracy Matters in Foreign Policy* (Ithaca, N.Y.: Cornell University Press, 1998).

211 **polls on American foreign policy issues:** Ivo H. Daalder and James M. Lindsay, "The Bush Revolution: The Remaking of America's Foreign Policy," paper presented at The George W. Bush Presidency: An Early Assessment, Princeton University, Princeton, New Jersey, April 25, 2003.

10. A Nation Transformed, a Tragedy Exploited

212 **"responsibility era"**: Dana Milbank, "Responsibility: A Capital Minuet," *Washington Post,* July 29, 2003.

212 **"terrorism on our soil"**: Associated Press, "Before 9-11, Terror Was Low Priority for Bush Administration," *New York Times,* June 29, 2003.

213 *Cole* **bombers and al Qaeda:** Michael Hirsh and Michael Isikoff, "What Went Wrong?," *Newsweek,* May 27, 2003, 28.

213 **no review ever took place:** Barton Gellman, "A Strategy's Cautious Evolution," *Washington Post,* January 20, 2002.

213 **two meetings:** Michael Elliot, "They Had a Plan," *Time,* August 4, 2002.

213 **"The administration actually"**: Robert Parry, "The Training Wheel President," Consortium News, May 2002, at www.consortiumnews.com/2002/052002a.html.

214 **"Never"**: Paul Thompson, "Cover-up, Lies, and/or Contradictions," Center for Cooperative Research, at www.cooperativeresearch.org/timeline/main/AAcoverup.html.

214 **McCain:** John McCain, "Probe Deep, and Fairly," *Washington Post,* May 22, 2002.

214 **"flying bombs"**: Nicholas Rufford, "MI6 Warned of Al Qaeda Attacks," *(London) Times,* June 9, 2002.

214 **"American and Israeli"**: "Hints for Months: Experts Talk About 'Failure of the Secret Service,'" *Frankfurter Allgemeine Zeitung,* September 11, 2001.

214 **plane-as-weapon:** Jon Bonne, "Suicide Scenario Was Nothing New; U.S. Officials Had Heard of Possible Attacks Similar to 9/11," MSNBC, May 17, 2002.

214 **Six years later:** John McCain, "Probe Deep, and Fairly," *Washington Post,* May 22, 2002.

214 **FBI and FAA:** Senate Select Committee on Intelligence, *Joint Inquiry Staff Statement, Part 1,* report prepared by Eleanor Hill, 107th Congress, September 18, 2002, 15, 27 at http://intelligence.senate.gov/0209hrg/020918/hill.pdf.

214 **New York and Washington:** Ibid., 15, 27.

214 **French commandos:** Ibid., and James Risen, "Threats and Responses: The Investigation; U.S. Failed to Act on Warnings in '98 of a Plane Attack," *New York Times,* September 19, 2002; Dana Priest and Dan Eggen, "9/11 Probers Say Agencies Failed to Heed Attack Signs," *Washington Post,* September 19, 2002.

214 **Philippines:** Gene Lyons, "A Self-Made Crisis," *Arkansas Democrat-Gazette,* May 22, 2002.

214 **Western leaders:** "Genoa set for summit onslaught," BBC News, July 18, 2001, at http://news.bbc.co.uk/2/hi/europe/1444922.stm.

215 **offshore carrier:** "Genoa Braces for G8 Summit," CNN, July 18, 2001, at www.cnn.com/2001/WORLD/europe/07/17/genoa.security/.

215 **"Plans to hijack"**: House Permanent Select Committee on Intelligence and Senate Select Committee on Intelligence, *Report of the Joint Inquiry into the Terrorist Attacks of September 11, 2001,* 107th Congress, 2nd sess., 2002, S. Rept. No. 107-351, H. Rept. No. 107-792, at http://news.findlaw.com/hdocs/docs/911rpt/911report72403.pdf; and David Johnston, "Report of 9/11 Panel Cites Lapses by CIA and FBI," *New York Times,* July 25, 2003.

215 **memo on al Qaeda:** Bob Woodward and Dan Eggen, "August Memo Focused on Attacks in U.S.; Lack of Fresh Information Frustrated Bush," *Washington Post,* May 18, 2002.

215 **Rice and likelihood of overseas attack:** Suicide Scenario Was Nothing New; U.S. Officials Had Heard of Possible Attacks Similar to 9/11," MSNBC, May 17, 2002; David Sanger, "Bush Was Warned Bin Laden Wanted to Hijack Planes," *New York Times,* May 16, 2002; and Oliver Schröm, "Deadly Mistakes," *Die Zeit,* October 1, 2002.

215 **warnings to Bush:** See the compilation of warnings (and sources) posted by the Center for Cooperative Research at www.cooperativeresearch.org/wot/sept11/explicitwarnings.html.

215 **memo on plans of bin Laden supporters:** Senate Select Committee on Intelligence, Joint Inquiry Staff Statement, Part 1, September 18, 2002, at http://intelligence.senate.gov/0209hrg/020918/hill.pdf.

215 **"Something really spectacular is going to happen"**: Dan Eggen and Bill Miller, "Bush Was Told of Hijacking Dangers; August Report Had No Details on September Plot," *Washington Post,* May 16, 2002.

215 **no alerts for airline carriers:** "Suicide Scenario Was Nothing New; U.S. Officials Had Heard of Possible Attacks Similar to 9/11," MSNBC, May 17, 2002.

216 **redactions from report on congressional inquiry:** House Permanent Select Committee on Intelligence and the Senate Select Committee on Intelligence, *Report of the Joint Inquiry into the Terrorist Attacks of September 11, 2001,* 107th Congress, 2nd sess., 2002; and S. Rept. No. 107-351, 107th Congress, 2nd sess., H. Rept. No. 107-792, *Joint Inquiry into Intelligence Community Activities Before and After the Terrorist Attacks of September 11, 2001; Report of the U.S. Senate Select Committee on Intelligence and U.S. House Permanent Select Committee on Intelligence Together with Additional Views,* December 2002; and S. Rept. No. 107-351, 107th Congress, 2nd sess., H. Rept. No. 107-792, *Joint Inquiry into Intelligence Community Activities Before and After the Terrorist Attacks of September 11, 2001;* and *Report of the U.S. Senate Select Committee on Intelligence and U.S. House Permanent Select Committee on Intelligence Together with Additional Views,* December 2002, at http://news.findlaw.com/hdocs/docs/911rpt/911report72403.pdf.

216 **al Qaeda a "tremendous threat":** Bob Woodward, *Bush at War* (New York: Simon & Schuster, 2002), 34.

216 **Berger warned Rice:** Daniel Benjamin and Steven Simon, *Age of Sacred Terror: Radical Islam's War Against America* (New York: Random House, 2002), 328.

216 **Bush administration decided to conduct its own review:** Michael Elliot, "They Had a Plan; Long Before 9/11, the White House Debated Taking the Fight to Al Qaeda. By the Time They Decided, It Was Too Late. The Saga of a Lost Chance," *Time,* August 12, 2002, 28.

216 **Rice demoted Clarke:** Daniel Benjamin and Steven Simon, *The Age of Sacred Terror* (New York: Random House, 2002), 335.

217 **"farther to the back burner":** Ibid.

217 **Saudi billionaires transferring money to al Qaeda:** Jack Kelley, "Saudi Money Aiding bin Laden," *USA Today,* October 29, 1999.

217 **"name and shame":** Rob Garver, "Task Force Asked to Give Terrorists No 'Safe Harbor,'" *American Banker,* October 30, 2001.

217 **Bush administration and FATF:** Molly Ivins, "U.S. Washes Hands of Anti-Crime Effort," *Dayton Daily News,* July 7, 2001.

217 **U.S. cooperation "under review":** William Wechsler, "Follow the Money," *Foreign Affairs,* July 1, 2001.

217 **Predator:** Michael Hirsh and Michael Isikoff, "What Went Wrong?," *Newsweek,* May 27, 2002, 28.

218 **"Everyone seemed to have an excuse":** Jane Mayer, "The Search for Osama," *The New Yorker,* August 4, 2003.

218 **"We are at war":** Michael Duffy, "Could It Happen Again?" *Time,* July 27, 2003.

218 **"CIA ended Fiscal Year 2001 with . . . money left *unspent*":** Fred Kaplan, "How Not to Stop the Next 9/11: Congress' Pointless Plan for Preventing Terrorism," *Slate,* July 25, 2003, at http://slate.msn.com/id/2086113/.

218 **"Ashcroft didn't want to hear about it":** Michael Hirsh and Michael Isikoff, "What Went Wrong?," *Newsweek,* May 27, 2002, 28.

218 **fewer agents working on terrorism on September 11 than August 1998:** House Permanent Select Committee on Intelligence and the Senate Select Committee on Intelligence, *Report of the Joint Inquiry into the Terrorist Attacks of September 11, 2001,* 107th Congress, 2nd sess., 2002; S. Rept. No. 107-351, 107th Congress, 2nd sess., H. Rept. No. 107-792, *Joint Inquiry into Intelligence Community Activities Before and After the Terrorist Attacks of September 11, 2001; Report of the U.S. Senate Select Committee on Intelligence and U.S. House Permanent Select Committee on Intelligence Together with Additional Views,* December 2002; and S. Rept. No. 107-351, 107th Congress, 2nd sees., H. Rept. No. 107-792, *Joint Inquiry into Intelligence Community Activities Before and After the Terrorist Attacks of September 11, 2001;* and *Report of the U.S. Senate Select Committee on Intelligence and U.S. House Permanent Select Committee on Intelligence Together with Additional Views,* December 2002, at http://news.findlaw.com/hdocs/docs/911rpt/911report72403. pdf.

218 **number of analysts working on al Qaeda at the Counter-Terrorism Center:** Fred Kaplan, "How Not to Stop the Next 9/11: Congress' Pointless Plan for Preventing Terrorism," *Slate,* July 25, 2003, at http://slate.msn.com/id/2086113/.

218 **FBI agent Robert Wright:** Nicholas M. Horrock, "FBI Agent: I Was Stymied in Terror Probe," UPI, May 30, 2002.

219 **"a significant al Qaeda attack is in the near future":** Barton Gellman, "Before Sept. 11, Unshared Clues and Unshaped Policy," *Washington Post,* May 17, 2002.

219 **Kenneth Williams and Bill Kurtz:** David Johnston and Don Van Natta Jr., "Traces of Terror: The FBI Memo; Ashcroft Learned of Agent's Alert Just After 9/11," *New York Times,* May 21, 2002.

219 **Minneapolis agents refused warrant:** David Johnston and Neil A. Lewis, "Whistle-Blower Recounts Faults Inside the FBI," *New York Times,* June 7, 2002.

220 **Nawaf Alhazmi and Khalid Almihdhar tracked to Los Angeles:** Michael Isikoff and Daniel Klaidman, "The Hijackers We Let Escape," *Newsweek*, June 10, 2002.

220 **hijackers in contact with subjects of previous FBI investigations:** Susan Schmidt and David Von Drehle, "Hill's 9/11 Probe Finds Multiple Failures; Congressional Inquiry Faults FBI Monitoring of Hijackers," *Washington Post*, July 25, 2003.

220 **"What is al Qaeda?":** Fred Kaplan, "How Not to Stop the Next 9/11: Congress' Pointless Plan for Preventing Terrorism," *Slate*, July 25, 2003, at http://slate.msn.com/id/2086113/.

220 **Mueller claimed "there were no warning signs":** "Attorney General John Ashcroft Remarks: Press Briefing with FBI Director Robert Mueller," Department of Justice, September 17, 2001, at www.usdoj.gov/ag/speeches/2001/0917pressbriefingfbi.htm.

220 **"There were no warning signs":** Timothy Noah, "Whopper of the Week: Robert Mueller; He Knew More Than He Said About 9/11," *Slate*, May 17, 2002, at http://slate.msn.com/id/2065954/.

220 **lack of accountability:** Jeff Gerth, "Officials Who Failed to Put Hijackers on Watch List Not Named," *New York Times*, May 15, 2003.

220 **Bush and Cheney on U.S. vulnerability to September 11 attacks:** Elisabeth Bumiller, "New Tone, Old Goal," *New York Times*, June 6, 2002.

221 **Laura Bush on questioning the administration about September 11:** Howard Kurtz, "As Reporters Seek Details, the Media Climate Shifts," *Washington Post*, May 17, 2002.

221 **Senator Bob Graham on prevention of September 11 attacks:** David Johnston, "Report of 9/11 Panel Cites Lapses by C.I.A. and F.B.I.," *New York Times*, July 25, 2003.

221 **"There is no question but that there were failures":** William Safire, "The Williams Memo," *New York Times*, May 20, 2002.

221 **administration has thwarted investigations of September 11 attacks:** David Corn, "The 9/11 Investigation," *The Nation*, August 4, 2003.

212 **General Wesley Clark:** Transcript, *Meet the Press*, NBC, June 16, 2003.

221 *eight* **government-led investigations into Pearl Harbor:** Eric Boehlert, "Bush's 9/11 coverup?" *Salon.com*, June 18, 2003, at www.salon.com.

222 **DeLay and an "after-action report" for the terrorists:** E. J. Dionne Jr., "Freedom-Fried Republicans," *Washington Post*, April 25, 2003.

222 **Fleischer and "One hundred percent attention" on the war:** Richard S. Dunham, "Washington Watch," *Business Week*, May 20, 2002.

222 **Bush saw no need for investigation into FBI or CIA:** "Bush Opposes 9/11 Query Panel," CBS News, May 23, 2002, at www.cbsnews.com/stories/2002/05/15/attack/main509096.shtml.

222 **Cheney intervened to prevent congressional compromise:** Carl Hulse, "Threats and Responses: The Inquiry; How a Deal Creating an Independent Commission on September 11 Came Undone," *New York Times*, November 2, 2002.

222 **"Who better to investigate":** Maureen Dowd, "He's Ba-ack," *New York Times*, December 1, 2002.

222 **White House agreed to $9 million for commission:** Editorial, "Undercutting the 9/11 Inquiry," *New York Times*, March 31, 2003.

223 **"Bush has done everything in his power to squelch this commission":** Eric Boehlert, "Bush's 9/11 coverup?" *Salon.com*, June 18, 2003, at www.salon.com.

223 *Fortune* **and Kean:** Nicholas Stein, "Five Degrees of Osama," *Fortune*, January 22, 2003, at www.fortune.com/fortune/print/0,15935,410237,00.html.

223 *Fortune* **and Hess:** Ibid.

223 **Kean's ties to Delta Oil:** Laurence Arnold, "September 11 Panel Faces Pressures of Time, Money, High Expectations," Associated Press, January 20, 2003.

223 **Zelikow and Rice study:** Philip Zelikow and Condoleezza Rice, *Germany Unified and Europe Transformed: A Study in Statecraft* (Cambridge, MA: Harvard University Press, 1995).

223 **families of victims ask that Zelikow recuse himself:** Dan Eggen, "Sept. 11 Panel Defends Director's Impartiality," *Washington Post*, October 14, 2003.

224 **commission slowed by White House:** Scot J. Paltrow, "White House Hurdles Delay 9/11 Commission Investigation," *Wall Street Journal*, July 8, 2003.

224 **Administration concerned report named "senior officials" who ignored al Qaeda briefings:** Michael Isikoff and Mark Hosenball, "The Secrets of September 11," *Newsweek*, April 30, 2003, at www.msnbc.com/news/907379.asp?0cv=KA01.

224 **"Weakness, vacillation, . . . that is provocative":** Vice President Dick Cheney interview by Tim Russert, *Meet the Press*, NBC, March 16, 2003.

224 **Libby blames Clinton administration:** Richard Cohen, "Answers, Not Scapegoats," *Washington Post*, May 21, 2002.

225 **Korb credits Clinton:** Lawrence J. Korb, "Thank Clinton for a Speedy Victory in Iraq," *Boston Globe*, May 13, 2003.

225 **"widespread view . . . that Bush was out of his depth":** Fred I. Greenstein, "The Leadership Style of George W. Bush," paper presented at the conference on "The Bush Presidency: An Early Assessment," Princeton University, Princeton, New Jersey, April 25-26, 2003.

225 **David Broder:** David S. Broder, "The Reticent President," *Washington Post,* April 22, 2001.

225 **Gallup survey:** Fred I. Greenstein, "The Leadership Style of George W. Bush," paper presented at the conference on "The Bush Presidency: An Early Assessment," Princeton University, Princeton, New Jersey, April 25-26, 2003.

225 **Frum planned to leave White House:** Cited in E. J. Dionne Jr., "Inevitably, the Politics of Terror; Fear Has Become Part of Washington's Power Struggle," *Washington Post,* May 25, 2003.

226 **Tenet and "bin Laden's fingerprints":** ABC News, September 14, 2002.

226 **December 4, 2001, description by Bush of his immediate reaction to September 11:** President George W. Bush, "President Meets with Displaced Workers at Town Hall Meeting: Remarks by the President in Town Hall Meeting," December 4, 2001.

226 **January 5, 2002, description by Bush of his immediate reaction to September 11:** President George W. Bush, "President Holds Town Hall Forum on Economy in California," Remarks by the President in Town Hall Meeting with Citizens of Ontario, January 5, 2002.

226 **Bush during September 11 speech to the nation:** President George W. Bush, "Statement by the President in His Address to the Nation," September 11, 2001.

227 **Bush told interviewer Card was the first person to tell him of September 11 crash:** Bill Sammon, "Suddenly, a Time to Lead: 'Difficult moment for America' Transforms the President," *Washington Times,* October 7, 2002.

227 **Fleischer reiterates that Card told Bush of crash:** Ari Fleischer, "Transcript of a Press Gaggle by Ari Fleischer," *Knoxville News Sentinel,* September 11, 2001, at web.knoxnews.com/web/kns/news/breaking/attack/texts/0911_0813pm.shtml.

227 **Woodward's account and Rove:** Sharon Churcher, "The Day the President Went Missing: The Remarkable Pictures That Show That Bush Was Spirited Away for 10 Hours on September 11," *Daily Mail,* September 8, 2002; ABC News, September 11, 2002, at http://www.cooperative research.org/timeline/2002/abcnews091102.html; and Dan Balz and Bob Woodward, "America's Chaotic Road to War: Bush's Global Strategy Began to Take Shape in First Frantic Hours After Attack," *Washington Post,* January 27, 2002.

227 **Bush stayed so as not to "upset" the children:** at http://stacks.msnbc.com/news/827074.asp and ABC News, September 11, 2002, at www.cooperativeresearch.org/timeline/2002/abcnews091102.html.

227 **Bush is alleged to have ordered flights grounded:** Robert Plunket, "The President in Sarasota," *Sarasota,* November 2001.

227 **FAA "begged" reporter to "maintain the fiction":** Joshua Green, "The Mineta Myth: How Bob Woodward Made the Secretary of Transportation a False Hero," *Slate,* April 1, 2002, at http://slate.msn.com/id/2063935.

227 **Ben Sliney ordered planes grounded:** Alan Levin, Marilyn Adams and Blake Morrison, "Part I: Terror Attacks Brought Drastic Decision: Clear the Skies," *USA Today,* August 12, 2002.

227 **Bush "trying to get out of harm's way":** "Interview of the President by Claus Kleber of Ard," May 21, 2002, at www.whitehouse.gov/news/releases/2002/05/20020521-10.html.

228 **Bush's flights on September 11:** Edwin Chen, "Bush Fled 'Harm's Way' with 9/11 Flights," *Los Angeles Times,* May 22, 2002 and at www.cnn.com/2001/US/09/11/chronology.attack/.

228 **Bush's second televised speech:** at www.whitehouse.gov/news/releases/2001/09/20010911-16.html.

228 **White House claimed threats against president:** Nicholas Lemann, "The Options: After the Morning of September 11th, the Presidency Changed, Too," *New Yorker,* October 1, 2001, 70.

228 **Fleischer stuck to story of threat:** at www.whitehouse.gov/news/releases/2001/09/20010915-5.html.

228 **White House operators "misunderstood":** Mike Allen, "White House Drops Claim of Threat to Bush," *Washington Post,* September 27, 2001.

229 **Carlson's Bush/Giuliani comparison:** Tucker Carlson, "Rudy Rules: Filling In for Bush, Giuliani Is Consoler-in-Chief," *New York,* September 24, 2001, at www.newyorkmetro.com/nymetro/news/sept11/features/5176.

229 **September 14 Bush address:** President George W. Bush, "President Bush Salutes Heroes in New York," Remarks by the President to Police, Firemen and Rescue Workers, September 14, 2001.

230 **90 percent approval rating:** Fred I. Greenstein, "The Leadership Style of George W. Bush," paper presented at the conference on "The Bush Presidency: An Early Assessment," Princeton University, Princeton, New Jersey, April 25-26, 2003.

230 **UN resolution condemning attacks:** *UN Security Council Resolution 1368 (2001),* adopted September 12, 2001.

230 **Michael Ignatieff:** Michael Ignatieff, "The Divided West," *Financial Times (London),* August 31, 2002.

230 **Wolfowitz and NATO:** Marc Champion, Charles Fleming, Ian Johnson, and Carla Anne Robbins, "How the Iraq Confrontation Divided the Western Alliance; France and Germany Strive to Check American Might," *Wall Street Journal,* March 27, 2003.

230 **Jacques Rupnik:** Eric Alterman, "USA Oui! Bush Non!" *The Nation,* February 10, 2003.

231 **"At some point, we may be the only ones left":** Bob Woodward and Dan Balz, "At Camp David, Advise and Dissent; Bush, Aides Grapple with War Plans," *Washington Post,* January 31, 2002.

231 **"my job isn't to nuance":** Stanley Hoffmann, "America Alone in the World: More Than Ever, America Needs Allies, but the Bush Administration Is Driving Them Away," *The American Prospect,* September 23, 2002, 20.

231 **"They hate our freedoms":** Dan Balz, "A Resolute and Focused Call to Arms," *Washington Post,* September 21, 2001.

231 **Bush told Rove "I'm here for a reason":** Bob Woodward, *Bush at War* (New York: Simon and Schuster, 2002), 205.

232 **Bush "really believes he was placed here . . . as part of a divine plan":** Michael Hirsh, "America's Mission," *Newsweek: Special Edition,* December 2002-February 2003, 10.

232 **bin Laden will be "sorely mistaken":** James Gerstenzang and Greg Miller, "Bush Warns of Long War," *Los Angeles Times,* September 16, 2001.

232 **"Wanted: Dead or Alive":** "Wanted: Dead or Alive; Bush Reasserts Demand to Afghans: Turn Over Bin Laden," ABCNews, September 17, 2001, at http://abcnews.go.com/sections/us/DailyNews/WTC_MAIN010917.html.

232 **Bush pronouncement without input from Cheney, Powell, or Rumsfeld:** George W. Bush, "Address to the Nation," September 11, 2001, at www.whitehouse.gov/news/releases/2001/09/20010911-16.html, and Bob Woodward, *Bush at War* (New York: Simon & Schuster, 2002), 30.

232 **Haqqani analysis:** Interview with Husain Haqqani, Carnegie Endowment for International Peace, Washington, D.C., March 6, 2002.

232 **Stanley Hoffmann:** Stanley Hoffmann, "America Alone in the World: More Than Ever, America Needs Allies, but the Bush Administration Is Driving Them Away," *The American Prospect,* September 23, 2002, 20.

233 **Paul Wolfowitz:** Paul Wolfowitz, "Department of Defense News Briefing," September 13, 2001, at www.defenselink.mil/news/Sep2001/t09132001_t0913dsd.html.

233 **Douglas Feith:** Nicholas Lemann, "After Iraq," *New Yorker,* February 17, 2003, 70.

233 **congressional authorization:** Authorization for Use of Military Force, 107th Congress, 1st sess., S.J. Res 23.

234 **Sir Michael Howard:** Sir Michael Howard, speaking to the Royal United Services Institute, republished as "Mistake to Declare This a 'War,'" *RUSI* 146, no. 6 (December 2001).

235 **"We're going to find him":** White House Notebook, "Naming Names, or Not," *Washington Post,* October 1, 2002.

235 **"mosquitoes with bombs":** Eric Alterman, "USA Oui! Bush Non!" *The Nation,* February 10, 2003.

235 **Walt and van Evera:** Nicholas Lemann, "The War on What?," *New Yorker,* September 16, 2002.

236 **Gallup poll:** Andrea Stone, "Kuwaitis Share Distrust Toward USA, Poll Indicates," *USA Today,* February 27, 2002; also see Miranda Green, "Islamic World Strongly Opposed to U.S. Foreign Policy, Survey Shows," *Financial Times (London),* February 27, 2002; and other polls available at www.gallup-international.com.

236 **Turkey and Pakistan polls:** Ibid. See also Carl Conetta, "The Pentagon's New Budget, New Strategy, and New War," *Commonwealth Institute Project on Defense Alternatives, Briefing Report #12,* June 17, 2002, at www.comw.org/pda/0206newwar.html; Carl Conetta, "Strange Victory: A Critical Appraisal of Operation Enduring Freedom and the Afghanistan War," *Commonwealth Institute Project on Defense Alternatives Research Monograph 6,* January 30, 2002; and Carl Conetta, "Operation Enduring Freedom: Why a Higher Rate of Civilian Bombing Casualties?" *Commonwealth Institute Project on Defense Alternatives Briefing Report 11,* January 18, 2002, at www.comw.org/pda.

236 **lowest level in twenty-two years:** Thomas L. Friedman, "Hummers Here, Hummers There," *New York Times,* May 25, 2003.

236 **Afghanistan:** Nicholas Lemann, "The War on What?," *New Yorker,* September 16, 2002, and Thomas Carothers, "Promoting Democracy and Fighting Terror," *Foreign Affairs,* January-February 2003.

236 **grievous defeat at Tora Bora:** Nicholas Confessore, "G.I. Woe," *Washington Monthly,* April 2003.

237 **bin Laden "present during battle for Tora Bora":** Barton Gellman and Thomas E. Ricks, "U.S. Concludes Bin Laden Escaped at Tora Bora Fight," *Washington Post,* April 17, 2002.

237 **United States chose to bomb only one of two escape routes:** Rod Nordland, Sami Yousafzai, and Babak Dehghanpisheh, "How Al Qaeda Slipped Away," *Newsweek,* August 14, 2002.

237 **sees Tora Bora as "a disaster . . . and never explained":** Nicholas Lemann, "The War on What?," *New Yorker,* September 16, 2002.

237 **U.S. intelligence was "supposed to have access to them":** Seymour Hersh, "The Getaway," *The New Yorker,* January 21, 2002.

237 **Rumsfeld demonstrated . . . U.S. government could not be trusted to account for its actions in wartime:** "Secretary Rumsfeld Interview with NBC *Meet The Press,*" United States Department of Defense, news transcript, December 2, 2001. For the airlift, see CNN, January 21, 2002, at www.cnn.com/transcripts/0201/21/ltm.10.html.

237 **Rumsfeld . . . claiming he did not know:** Dave Moniz, "Rumsfeld: No Evidence U.S. Let bin Laden Flee," *USA Today,* April 19, 2002.

237 **search for bin Laden had "lost at least half of its original strength":** Jane Mayer, "The Search for Osama," *The New Yorker,* August 8, 2003.

238 **"these guys were able to get away . . . because we let up":** Massimo Calabresi and Michael Duffy, "Letting Up on Osama," *Time,* August 11, 2003, 15.

238 **five hundred thousand new Afghan refugees and displaced persons:** Andrea Stone, "Kuwaitis Share Distrust Toward USA, Poll Indicates," *USA Today,* February 27, 2002; see also Miranda Green, "Islamic World Strongly Opposed to U.S. Foreign Policy, Survey Shows," *(London) Financial Times,* February 27, 2002; and other polls available at www.gallup-international.com. See also Carl Conetta, "The Pentagon's New Budget, New Strategy, and New War," *Commonwealth Institute Project on Defense Alternatives, Briefing Report #12,* June 17, 2002, at www.comw.org/pda/0206newwar.html; Carl Conetta, "Strange Victory: A Critical Appraisal of Operation Enduring Freedom and the Afghanistan War," *Commonwealth Institute Project on Defense Alternatives Research Monograph 6,* January 30, 2002; and Carl Conetta, "Operation Enduring Freedom: Why a Higher Rate of Civilian Bombing Casualties?" *Commonwealth Institute Project on Defense Alternatives Briefing Report 11,* January 18, 2002, at www.comw.org/pda.

238 **Bush demonstrated little patience for the hard work necessary to address . . . harsh consequences:** Barry Bearak, "Unreconstructed," *New York Times Magazine,* June 1, 2003.

238 **"a nation-building corps from America? Absolutely not":** George W. Bush, second presidential debate, October 11, 2000.

238 **Omar issued the tape from his hiding place in Afghanistan:** Syed Saleem Shahzad, "U.S. Shooting in the Dark in Afghanistan," *Asia Times,* June 28, 2003.

239 **bin Laden family spirited out of the country three days after September 11:** Patrick E. Tyler, "Fearing Harm, Bin Laden Kin Fled from U.S.," *New York Times,* September 30, 2001.

239 *Tampa Tribune* **report:** Kathy Steele, "Phantom Flight from Florida," *Tampa Tribune,* October 5, 2001.

240 **Saudis unwilling to freeze assets linked to bin Laden:** Jonathan Wells, Jack Meyers, and Maggie Mulvihill, "Ties to Saudi Elite May Be Hurting War on Terrorism," *Boston Herald,* December 10, 2001.

240 **"I'm living . . . in Saudi Arabia without any problem":** Katie Couric, John Hockenberry, and Bob Mckeown, "Sand Storm: Saudi Arabia does not allow US to gather intelligence there; various people discuss how terrorists find haven and recruits in Saudi Arabia," *Dateline NBC,* August 25, 2002.

240 **"I think [the Jews] were the protagonists of such attacks":** Alaa Shahine, "Saudi Interior Minister Says Jews Were Behind Sept. 11 Attacks," Associated Press, December 5, 2002, at www.signonsandiego.com/news/nation/terror/20021205-1451-attacks-saudi.html.

240 **Saudis . . . refuse to grant permission to U.S. agents to talk to any family members of the hijackers:** Katie Couric, John Hockenberry, and Bob McKeown, "Sand Storm: Saudi Arabia does not allow US to gather intelligence there; various people discuss how terrorists find haven and recruits in Saudi Arabia," *Dateline NBC,* August 25, 2002.

240 **left Saudi Arabia (and Pakistan) off the list:** John M. Broder, "U.S. Drops Armenian Men from List of Visitors Who Must Register," *New York Times,* December 19, 2002.

240 **CIA memo termed "incontrovertible evidence":** Dana Priest, "White House, CIA Kept Key Portions of Report Classified," *Washington Post,* July 25, 2003.

240 **Schumer complained of a "systematic strategy of . . . cover-up":** David Johnston, "Report of 9/11 Panel Cites Lapses by C.I.A. and F.B.I.," *New York Times,* July 25, 2003.

240 **the redacted papers . . . delineate "a coordinated network":** John B. Judis and Spencer Ackerman, "28 Pages," *TNR Online,* August 1, 2003.

241 **Saudis allocated more than $14.6 million to . . . Qorvis Communications:** Timothy Starks, "Saudi Arabia Spent $14.6 Million on P.R." *New York Sun,* December 30, 2002.

241 **Among major investors was Salem bin Laden:** Damien Cave, "The United States of Oil," *Salon.com,* November 19, 2001.

241 **Bush-bin Laden family connections span generations:** Oliver Burkeman and Julian Borger, "The Ex-Presidents' Club," *Guardian,* October 31, 2001.

241 **Among guests of honor was investor Shafig bin Laden:** Ed Vulliamy, "Dark Heart of the American Dream," *Observer,* June 16, 2002.

241 **"we settled on the one issue everyone could agree on":** Paul Wolfowitz, interview by Sam Tanenhaus, *Vanity Fair,* May 9, 2003.

242 **intelligence agencies thwarted by the Saudis:** Josh Meyer and Michael Slackman, "Security Push Preceded Attacks," *Los Angeles Times,* May 15, 2003.

243 **such an event was "almost a certainty":** David Rennie, "Attack on U.S. 'Almost Certain,'" *Daily Telegraph,* May 20, 2002.

243 **Rumsfeld added, "We do face additional terrorist threats":** Timothy Noah, "Crisis Over!" *Slate,* May 22, 2002.

243 **more suicide bombings were "inevitable":** Bill Miller and Christine Haughney, "Nation Left Jittery by Latest Series of Terror Warnings," *Washington Post,* May 22, 2002.

243 **"administration trying to fend off bruising bipartisan inquiry":** Romesh Ratnesar and Michael Weisskopf, "How the FBI Blew the Case," *Time,* June 3, 2002, 24.

243 **al Muhajir had no nuclear materials when arrested:** John Prados, "DEFCON Artists: How the Bush Administration Uses Terrorist Threats to Its Advantage," *The American Prospect Online,* June 12, 2002.

244 **Ashcroft warned of "a very serious threat":** Dan Balz, "Rhetorical Contradictions Flourish in War on Terrorism," *Washington Post,* October 3, 2001.

244 **entire department had only three experts on biological terrorism:** John Mintz, "At Homeland Security, Doubts Arise over Intelligence," *Washington Post,* July 21, 2003.

244 **"Senate more interested in special interests":** Jim VandeHei, "Daschle Angered by Bush Statement," *Washington Post,* September 26, 2002.

244 **Republicans were able to counter every political trend:** John C. Fortier and Norman J. Ornstein, "Congress and the Bush Presidency," paper presented at the conference on "The Bush Presidency: An Early Assessment," Woodrow Wilson School, Princeton University, April 25-26, 2003.

245 **"Laney's plane . . . a key piece of information":** Glenn W. Smith, "Homeland Security Department Used to Track Texas Democrats," *CommonDreams.org,* May 14, 2003, at www.commondreams.org/views03/0514-07.htm.

245 **political misuse of the government's police powers:** Molly Ivins, "Bucking the Texas Lockstep," *Washington Post,* May 15, 2003.

245 **Bush's "windfall of political capital":** Editorial, "A New Presidency: How Bush Should Spend His Windfall of Political Capital," *Wall Street Journal,* September 19, 2001.

245 **The two statements quoted were as follows:** President Bush, "*I have no ambition whatsoever to use [the War on Terror] as a political issue.* There is no daylight between the executive and the legislative branches," Associated Press, January 23, 2002; and Ari Fleischer, "*The President urges no one to politicize this [war] debate.* This is a very serious matter, and it needs to be handled seriously by everybody. The country will benefit from a healthy and civil discussion of this," September 27, 2002. Others included Senator Richard Shelby (R-AL) when asked if Republicans should use the war for political gain: "Absolutely not. And *as a Republican, I would deplore such tactics.* I think that what we've got to do in a bipartisan way, as Americans, win this war," *Crossfire,* CNN, March 4, 2002; and Vice President Dick Cheney said that making political hay of national security is "*thoroughly irresponsible and totally unworthy of national leaders in a time of war,*" *Washington Times,* May 17, 2002.

246 **"we will defeat them by expanding . . . world trade":** Staff, "Bush Links Terror Attacks to Trade Bill," *New York Times,* October 18, 2001.

246 **"The less dependent we are on foreign sources of crude oil":** Katharine Q. Seelye, "Bush Promotes Energy Bill as Security Issue," *New York Times,* October 12, 2001.

246 **on the need for agricultural subsidies:** George F. Will, "Steel and the National Security," *Washington Post,* February 14, 2002.

246 **George W. Bush on taxes and spending:** Timothy Roberts, "President Bush: Pressing for Tax Cuts to Strengthen America," *San Francisco Business Times,* October 17, 2001.

246 **why he required $170 million:** Mike Allen, "Bush Cites 9/11 on All Manner of Questions," *Washington Post,* September 11, 2003.

246 ***Doonesbury:*** Garry Trudeau, *Doonesbury,* June 1, 2003, at www.doonesbury.com/strip/dailydose/index.html?uc_full_date=20030601.

246 **Karl Rove told a Republican National Committee meeting:** Thomas B. Edsall, "GOP Touts War as Campaign Issue," *Washington Post,* January 19, 2002.

247 **sent out a letter to . . . potential donors:** Anne E. Kornblut, "Bush '04 Fund-Raising Cites War on Terrorism," *Boston Globe,* May 25, 2003.

247 **"the country remains more vulnerable than it should be today":** "Protecting the American Homeland," A Report of the Brookings Institution (Washington, D.C., 2003), at www.brookings.org/dybdocroot/fp/projects/homeland/budget.htm.

247 **"airport security . . . enhanced at best by cosmetic tweaks since Sept. 11":** Frank Rich, "How to Lose a War," *New York Times,* October 27, 2001.

248 **a mere 7 percent of what Abraham said would be needed just to get started:** Jonathan Chait, "Bush's Abysmal Failure on Homeland Security," *The New Republic,* March 10, 2003.

248 **"departure from the public unity that has characterized White House relations with congressional Republicans":** Dana Milbank, "House Republicans Sensitive to Criticism They Underfunded Homeland Security," *Washington Post,* March 8, 2003.

249 **"ill-prepared to handle a catastrophic attack on American soil":** John Mintz, "Study: 'First Responders' Underfunded," *Washington Post,* June 29, 2003.

249 **massive shortfalls in . . . skilled medical and scientific personnel:** David Johnston, "Report Calls U.S. Agencies Understaffed for Bioterror," *New York Times,* July 6, 2003.

249 **a November 2002 hiring freeze:** Stephen J. Schulhofer, "President on Security: Tough Talk, Soft Funding," *Miami Herald,* May 30, 2003.

249 **administration even tried to cut overseas nuclear security funding:** Eric Alterman, "Bush Goes AWOL," *The Nation,* May 5, 2003.

249 **"Bush plan for funding first responders amounts to double-entry bookkeeping":** Jonathan Chait, "The 9/10 President," quoted in *The New Republic,* March 10, 2003.

250 **cutting back on air marshals:** Sara Kehaulani Goo and Susan Schmidt, "Memo Warns of New Plots to Hijack Jets," *Washington Post,* July 30, 2003.

250 **Beers's anger at the Bush administration:** Laura Blumenfeld, "Former Aide Takes Aim at War on Terror," *Washington Post,* June 16, 2003.

251 **Screaming phone calls:** Jennifer 8. Lee, "Details Emerge of Post 9/11 Clash Between White House and E.P.A.," *New York Times,* October 10, 2003.

11. Invading Iraq

252 **President George W. Bush:** Quoted in Arianna Huffington, "We Don't Need No Stinkin' Proof," in *The Iraq War Reader: History, Documents, Opinions,* eds. Micah L. Sifry and Christopher Cerf (New York: Touchstone, 2003), 344.

252 **Major General Anthony Zinni:** Micah L. Sifry and Christopher Cerf, eds., *The Iraq War Reader: History, Documents, Opinions* (New York: Touchstone, 2003), 281.

253 **Asked how he would have prioritized U.S. commitments:** General Anthony Zinni, "A General Speaks on War with Iraq" (lecture, Middle East Institute, Washington, D.C., October 10, 2002), at www.cdi.org/terrorism/zinni-iraq-conditions.cfm.

254 **Zinni was informed:** Kathleen Kenna, "Americans Pay Price for Speaking Out," *Toronto Star,* August 9, 2003.

254 **possessed the willingness . . . to use these weapons against U.S. citizens:** See Malcolm Cooper, *The Birth of Independent Air Power* (London: Allen and Unwin, 1988).

255 **but might take the "extreme step" of assisting terrorists:** See President George W. Bush and Prime Minister Tony Blair, "President Bush, Prime Minister Blair Discuss Keeping the Peace; Remarks by the President and Prime Minister Tony Blair in Photo Opportunity," September 7, 2002, at www.whitehouse.gov/news/releases/2002/09/20020907-2.html; Joseph Curl, "Agency Disavows Report on Iraq Arms," *Washington Times,* September 27, 2002; Dana Milbank, "For Bush, Facts Are Malleable," *Washington Post,* October 22, 2002; and Dr. John Chipman, "Iraq's Weapons of Mass Destruction: A Net Assessment; An International Institute for Strategic Studies Dossier" (statement, Arundel House, London, September 9, 2002), at www.iiss.org/news-more.php?itemID=88. See also Eric Alterman, "Bush Lies, Media Swallows," *The Nation,* November 7, 2002, at www.thenation.com/doc.mhtml?i=20021125&s=alterman.

255 **a "serious threat to Iraq's neighbors":** See Brendan Nyhan, "Making Bush Tell the Truth," *Salon.com,* November 5, 2002, at www.salon.com.

255 **believed the claim was nonsense as well:** Dafna Linzer and John J. Lumpkin, "Experts Doubt U.S. Claim on Iraqi Drones," Associated Press, August 24, 2003.

255 **the Al Samoud-2 can actually travel less than two hundred miles:** Walter Pincus and Dana Milbank, "Bush Clings to Dubious Allegations About Iraq," *Washington Post,* March 18, 2003.

255 **designed to produce germ warfare agents:** President George W. Bush, "President Delivers State of the Union," January 28, 2003, at www.whitehouse.gov/news/releases/2003/01/20030128-19.html.

256 **no doubt that Saddam Hussein now has weapons of mass destruction:** Vice President Dick Cheney, "Vice President Speaks at VFW 103rd National Convention; Remarks by the Vice President to the Veterans of Foreign Wars 103rd National Convention," August 26, 2002, at www.whitehouse.gov/news/releases/2002/08/20020826.html.

256 **"We know they have weapons of mass destruction . . .":** Mitchell Landsberg, "Ample Evidence of Abuses, Little of Illegal Weapons," *Los Angeles Times,* June 15, 2003.

256 **"There is no doubt":** David Anthony Denny, "U.S. Central Command report," March 22, 2003, at http://usinfo.state.gov/topical/pol/terror/03032203.htm.

256 **"We know where they are":** Donald Rumsfeld interview, *This Week with George Stephanopolous,* ABC, March 30, 2003, at www.dod.gov/news/Mar2003/t03302003_ t0330sdabcsteph.html.

256 **"I'm absolutely sure":** Colin Powell, "Remarks after *Meet the Press,*" NBC, Washington D.C., May 4, 2003, at www.state.gov/secretary/rm/2003/20166.htm.

256 **"a kind of danger to us that we hadn't grasped before":** Robert Kagan and William Kristol, "What to Do About Iraq," *Weekly Standard,* January 21, 2002, republished in *The Iraq War Reader: History, Documents, Opinions,* eds. Micah L. Sifry and Christopher Cerf (New York: Touchstone, 2003), 244-45.

256 **none of the weapons cited was . . . ever found:** Mitchell Landsberg, "Ample Evidence of Abuses, Little of Illegal Weapons," *Los Angeles Times,* June 15, 2003.

256 **"We found them," the president claimed:** Jake Tapper, "Weapons of Mass Deception," *Salon.com,* June 6, 2003, at www.salon.com/news/feature/2003/06/06/wmd.

256 **"showed no positive hits at all":** Robert Scheer, "The Forgettable Truth—The War We're Winning Was Based on Lies," *Salon.com,* April 30, 2003, at www.salon.com/opinion/scheer/2003/04/30/WMD_truth/index.html.

256 **"They are exactly what the Iraqis said they were":** Peter Beaumont, Antony Barnett, and Gaby Hinsliff, "Iraqi Mobile Labs Nothing to Do with Germ Warfare, Report Finds," *The Observer,* June 15, 2003.

257 **this conclusion was rejected:** Douglas Jehl, "Iraqi Trailers Said to Make Hydrogen, Not Biological Arms," *New York Times,* August 9, 2003. See also Douglas Jehl, "Agency Disputes C.I.A. View on Trailers as Weapons Labs," *New York Times,* June 26, 2003.

257 **after extensive testing:** Douglas Jehl, "Iraqi Trailers Said to Make Hydrogen, Not Biological Arms," *New York Times,* August 9, 2003. See also Douglas Jehl, "Agency Disputes C.I.A. View on Trailers as Weapons Labs," *New York Times,* June 26, 2003.

257 **nuclear program to be in only the "very most rudimentary" state:** Dana Priest and Walter Pincus, "Search in Iraq Finds No Banned Weapons," *Washington Post,* October 3, 2003.

257 **"that is what the report said":** Dana Priest and Dana Milbank, "Iraq Sought Missile Parts, President Says," *Washington Post,* October 4, 2003.

257 **"they're simply not there":** Greg Miller, "Analysis of Iraqi Weapons 'Wrong,'" *New York Times,* May 31, 2003.

257 **"where an underground chemical weapons stash was supposed to be":** Barton Gellman, "In Search for Weapons, Army Team Finds Vacuum Cleaners," *Washington Post,* May 18, 2003.

257 **"But it was just a matter of emphasis":** John Cochran, "Reason for War? White House Officials Say Privately the Sept. 11 Attacks Changed Everything," ABC News, April 25, 2003.

257 **"For bureaucratic reasons":** Paul Wolfowitz, interview by Karen DeYoung, May 28, 2003, at www.defenselink.mil/transcripts/2003/tr20030528-depsecdef0222.html.

258 **"I'm not reading this. This is bullshit":** Jake Tapper, "Weapons of Mass Deception," *Salon.com,* June 6, 2003, at www.salon.com/news/feature/2003/06/06/wmd.

258 **lifted from a twelve-year-old doctoral dissertation:** Dan Plesch and Richard Norton-Taylor, "Straw, Powell Had Serious Doubts over Their Iraqi Weapons Claims; Secret Transcript Revealed," *The Guardian,* May 31, 2003.

260 **Nothing to support these claims was ever discovered:** Charles J. Hanley, "U.S. Justification for War: How It Stacks Up Now," *Seattle Times,* August 10, 2003.

261 **Gilbert Cranberg:** Gilbert Cranberg, ". . . Bring Back the Skeptical Press," *Washington Post,* June 29, 2003.

261 **"He has not developed any significant capability":** A videotape of Powell's remarks was

shown on MSNBC's *Countdown with Keith Olberman,* September 24, 2003, and a transcript can be found at www.msnbc.com/news/971717.asp.

261 **"We were reduced to dead reckoning":** James Risen, David E. Sanger, and Thom Shanker, "In Sketchy Data, Trying to Gauge Iraq Threat," *New York Times,* July 20, 2003.

262 **Many scientists contend:** Bob Drogin, "The Vanishing," *The New Republic,* July 21, 2003, 20.

262 **A detailed *Wall Street Journal* examination:** David S. Cloud, "Iraqi Scientists Recount Effort to Make Weapon Out of Ricin Program, One of the Threats Cited by the U.S., Was Dropped in '91, Baghdad Pharmacists Say," *Wall Street Journal,* July 18, 2003.

262 **instructed his intelligence service to do so:** Greg Miller and James Gersenzang, "Classified Iraq Data Released," *Los Angeles Times,* July 19, 2003.

262 **no reason to believe that substantial quantities remained:** Editorial, "The Legacy of Hans Blix," *New York Times,* June 30, 2003.

262 **"including VX, sarin, cyclosarin and mustard gas":** Robert Scheer, "Bad Iraq Data from Start to Finish," *The Nation,* June 11, 2003.

263 **"I think the burden":** Joe Conason, "Joe Conason's Journal: Pretzel Logic and Revised History," *Salon.com,* July 9, 2003, at www.salon.com/opinion/conason/2003/07/09/pretzel/index.html.

263 **Rumsfeld contended:** Timothy Noah, "Whopper of the Week: Donald Rumsfeld; Don Rumsfeld, meet Dick Cheney," *Slate.com,* May 23, 2003, at http://slate.msn.com/id/2083532.

263 **Cheney on *Meet the Press* in 2002:** Richard Cohen, "Never Mind the Weapons," *Washington Post,* May 7, 2003.

264 **"Mr. Hussein's dogged insistence":** Michael R. Gordon and Judith Miller, "Threats and Responses: The Iraqis; U.S. Says Hussein Intensifies Quest for A-Bomb Parts," *New York Times,* September 8, 2002.

264 **In fact no report and no evidence ever existed:** Gene Lyons, "A Crisis of Competence in the White House," *Arkansas Democrat-Gazette,* July 16, 2003.

264 **"The IAEA had found no evidence":** Walter Pincus, "Bush Faced Dwindling Data on Iraq Nuclear Bid," *Washington Post,* July 16, 2003.

264 **"They weren't our highest priority":** Barton Gellman, "Search in Iraq Fails to Find Nuclear Threat," *Washington Post,* October 26, 2003.

265 **Congress agreed to the president's request:** Seymour M. Hersh, "Selective Intelligence; Donald Rumsfeld Has His Own Special Sources. Are They Reliable?," *The New Yorker,* May 12, 2003, 44.

265 **"The most powerful argument that President Bush made":** Jake Tapper, "Weapons of Mass Deception," *Salon.com,* June 6, 2003, at www.salon.com/news/feature/2003/06/06/wmd.

265 **But when the IAEA requested backup information:** Michael Duffy and James Carney, "A Question of Trust; the CIA's Tenet Takes the Fall for a Flawed Claim in the State of the Union, But Has Bush's Credibility Taken an Even Greater Hit?," *Time,* July 21, 2003, 22.

265 **"The declaration fails to account for":** Walter Pincus, "CIA Did Not Share Doubt on Iraq Data; Bush Used Report of Uranium Bid," *Washington Post,* June 12, 2003.

265 **"He clearly has much to hide":** Seymour M. Hersh, "Selective Intelligence; Donald Rumsfeld Has His Own Special Sources. Are They Reliable?," *The New Yorker,* May 12, 2003, 44.

266 **an ABC/*Washington Post* poll:** John B. Judis and Spencer Ackerman, "The First Casualty," *The New Republic,* June 30, 2003, 14.

266 **"quite confident" that these views were passed:** Nicholas D. Kristof, "Missing in Action: Truth," *New York Times,* May 6, 2003, and Nicholas D. Kristof, "White House in Denial," *New York Times,* June 13, 2003.

266 **"Why don't they tell the truth?":** Dana Priest, "Uranium Claim Was Known for Months to be Weak," *Washington Post,* July 20, 2003.

266 **"Why don't we say the British say this?":** Joshua Micah Marshall, "A Rose Is a Rose Is a Rose," June 26, 2003, at www.talkingpointsmemo.com.

266 **Later, CIA sources claimed:** Walter Pincus, "CIA Asked Britain to Drop Iraq Claim; Advice on Alleged Uranium Buy Was Refused," *Washington Post,* July 11, 2003.

267 **"Lacking persuasive evidence":** Dana Milbank and Dana Priest, "Warning in Iraq Report Unread," *Washington Post,* July 19, 2003.

267 **did not want "a lot of footnotes":** Barton Gellman and Walter Pincus, "Depiction of Threat Outgrew Supporting Evidence," *Washington Post,* August 10, 2003.

267 **the inspectors were inside Iraq:** Dana Priest and Dana Milbank, "President Defends Allegation on Iraq," *Washington Post,* July 15, 2003.

267 **"this is just the president being the president":** Dana Milbank, *Reliable Sources,* CNN, July 20, 2003.

267 **the Niger story "did not rise to the level of certainty":** George Tenet, "In Tenet's Words: 'I Am Responsible' for Review," *New York Times,* July 12, 2003.

268 **"lacking persuasive evidence"**: Dana Milbank and Mike Allen, "Iraq Flap Shakes Rice's Image," *Washington Post,* July 27, 2003.

268 **What Dr. Rice ignores:** "16 Words," *The New Republic,* July 28, 2003, 8.

269 **"President Bush . . . did not entirely read"**: Dana Milbank and Dana Priest, "Warning in Iraq Report Unread," *Washington Post,* July 19, 2003.

269 **Robert Joseph:** James Risen and David E. Sanger, "New Details Emerge on Uranium Claim and Bush's Speech," *New York Times,* July 18, 2003.

269 **Bartlett dismissed this as "a conspiracy theory"**: Dana Milbank and Mike Allen, "Iraq Flap Shakes Rice's Image," *Washington Post,* July 27, 2003.

269 **memories were jarred, and memos discovered:** Michael Kranish, "Senator Says Bush Aide Pressured a Skeptical CIA on Iraq Data," *Boston Globe,* July 18, 2003.

269 **"And it is now clear to me that I failed in that responsibility"**: Maura Reynolds, "White House Admits CIA Warned It Before Speech," *Los Angeles Times,* July 23, 2003.

269 **Michael Gerson . . . found yet another warning dated October 5:** Dana Milbank and Walter Pincus, "Bush Aides Disclose Warnings from CIA," *Washington Post,* July 23, 2003.

269 **Scott McClellan:** Scott McClellan, "Press Briefing by Scott McClellan," July 17, 2003, at www.whitehouse.gov/news/releases/2003/07/20030717-5.html.

269 **Bush takes "personal responsibility"**: Mike Allen and Dana Milbank, "Bush Takes Responsibility for Iraq Claim," *Washington Post,* July 31, 2003.

269 **The question remains how Rumsfeld and Powell could continue:** Harold Meyerson, "Inconvenient Facts . . . ," *Washington Post,* July 17, 2003.

269 **Rumsfeld actually claimed to be unaware:** Timothy Noah, "Whopper of the Week: Donald Rumsfeld," *Slate,* July 10, 2003.

270 **Administration excuses also ignore:** Dana Priest and Dana Milbank, "President Defends Allegation on Iraq," *Washington Post,* July 15, 2003.

270 **"Who is it in the White House who was hell-bent"**: Timothy Noah, "Cheney Wraps His Glutes in the Flag," *Slate,* July 24, 2003.

270 **the secretary of state insisted on scrubbing:** Timothy Noah, "Is Libby the Phantom Bigfoot?," *Slate,* July 17, 2003.

270 **"They knew the Niger story was a flat-out lie"**: John B. Judis and Spencer Ackerman, "The First Casualty," *The New Republic,* June 30, 2003, 14.

270 **"compromised every operation"**: Andrew Buncombe, "Bush Officials Who Leaked Name of US Spy for Revenge Could Face Jail," *The Independent,* September 29, 2003.

270 **"that is not only a felony but directly can jeopardize lives"**: See Matthew Cooper, Massimo Calbresi, and John F. Dickerson, "A War on Wilson?," *Time Online,* July 17, 2003, at www.time.com/time/nation/article/0,8599,465270,00.html, and Greg Miller, "Critics See White House Double Standard on Leaks," *Los Angeles Times,* October 6, 2003.

271 **Vincent Cannistraro . . . charged:** Edward Alden, "Naming of Agent Aimed at Discrediting CIA," *Financial Times,* October 25, 2003.

271 **"We believe [Saddam] has, in fact, reconstituted nuclear weapons"**: John B. Judis and Spencer Ackerman, "The First Casualty," *The New Republic,* June 30, 2003, 14.

271 **IAEA official observed that its counterfeit character:** Seymour M. Hersh, "Selective Intelligence; Donald Rumsfeld Has His Own Special Sources. Are They Reliable?," *The New Yorker,* May 12, 2003, 44.

271 **The journalist feared she might lose her job:** Michael Isikoff and Evan Thomas, "Follow the Yellowcake Road," *Newsweek,* July 28, 2003, 22.

271 **what everyone now understands to be false information:** Walter Pincus, "Democratic Moves to Widen Intelligence Probe Defeated," *Washington Post,* July 26, 2003.

272 **"And that's just a lie"**: John B. Judis and Spencer Ackerman, "The First Casualty," *The New Republic,* June 30, 2003, 14.

272 **"The American people were manipulated"**: Jake Tapper, "Weapons of Mass Deception," *Salon.com,* June 6, 2003.

272 **"Wolfowitz treated the analysts' work with contempt"**: Walter Pincus and Dana Priest, "Some Iraq Analysts Felt Pressure from Cheney Visits," *Washington Post,* June 5, 2003.

272 **"pressed to tailor his analysis on Iraq"**: Douglas Jehl, "Powell Hails Man Who Cited Pressure on Iraq Data," *New York Times,* June 28, 2003.

272 **found himself the recipient of twenty thousand dollars:** Paul Sperry, "$20,000 Bonus to Official Who Agreed on Nuke Claim," *WorldNetDaily.com,* August 12, 2003.

273 **omitted the qualifications and countervailing evidence"**: John B. Judis and Spencer Ackerman, "The First Casualty," *The New Republic,* June 30, 2003, 14. See also Robert Dreyfuss, "More Missing Intelligence," *The Nation,* July 7, 2003, 4.

273 **"the Cabal"**: Seymour M. Hersh, "Selective Intelligence; Donald Rumsfeld Has His Own

Special Sources. Are They Reliable?," *The New Yorker,* May 12, 2003, 44. See also Robert Dreyfuss, "More Missing Intelligence," *The Nation,* July 7, 2003, 4.

274 **"without having been vetted":** House, Committee on Government Reform, "Members of Congress Call for Independent Commission on Iraq," 108th Congress, June 26, 2003, at www. house.gov/reform/min/pdfs_108/pdf_com/pdf_com_iraq_intelligence_commission_press.pdf.

274 **to bypass the experts in the Mossad:** Julian Borger, "The Spies Who Pushed for War," *The Guardian,* July 17, 2003.

274 **Republicans beat back an attempt:** Helen Dewar, "Senate Rebuffs Democrats' Moves to Challenge Bush on Iraq," *Washington Post,* July 17, 2003.

274 **"Well, it came from the White House":** Wesley Clark, interview by Tim Russert, *Meet the Press,* NBC, June 15, 2003.

274 **"Go massive. Sweep it all up":** Paul Krugman, "Pattern of Corruption," *New York Times,* July 15, 2003.

274 **"It was doable":** Bob Woodward and Dan Balz, "Combating Terrorism: 'It Starts Today,'" *Washington Post,* February 1, 2002.

275 **the letter warned:** Here is the letter in its entirety:

September 20, 2001

The Honorable George W. Bush
President of the United States
Washington, DC

Dear Mr. President,

We write to endorse your admirable commitment to "lead the world to victory" in the war against terrorism. We fully support your call for "a broad and sustained campaign" against the "terrorist organizations and those who harbor and support them." We agree with Secretary of State Powell that the United States must find and punish the perpetrators of the horrific attack of September 11, and we must, as he said, "go after terrorism wherever we find it in the world" and "get it by its branch and root." We agree with the Secretary of State that U.S. policy must aim not only at finding the people responsible for this incident, but must also target those "other groups out there that mean us no good" and "that have conducted attacks previously against U.S. personnel, U.S. interests and our allies."

In order to carry out this "first war of the 21st century" successfully, and in order, as you have said, to do future "generations a favor by coming together and whipping terrorism," we believe the following steps are necessary parts of a comprehensive strategy.

Osama bin Laden

We agree that a key goal, but by no means the only goal, of the current war on terrorism should be to capture or kill Osama bin Laden, and to destroy his network of associates. To this end, we support the necessary military action in Afghanistan and the provision of substantial financial and military assistance to the anti-Taliban forces in that country.

Iraq

We agree with Secretary of State Powell's recent statement that Saddam Hussein "is one of the leading terrorists on the face of the Earth. . . ." It may be that the Iraqi government provided assistance in some form to the recent attack on the United States. But even if evidence does not link Iraq directly to the attack, any strategy aiming at the eradication of terrorism and its sponsors must include a determined effort to remove Saddam Hussein from power in Iraq. Failure to undertake such an effort will constitute an early and perhaps decisive surrender in the war on international terrorism. The United States must therefore provide full military and financial support to the Iraqi opposition. American military force should be used to provide a "safe zone" in Iraq from which the opposition can operate. And American forces must be prepared to back up our commitment to the Iraqi opposition by all necessary means.

Hezbollah

Hezbollah is one of the leading terrorist organizations in the world. It is suspected of having been involved in the 1998 bombings of the American embassies in Africa, and implicated in the bombing of the U.S. Marine barracks in Beirut in 1983. Hezbollah clearly falls in the category cited by Secretary Powell of groups "that mean us no good" and "that have conducted attacks previously against U.S. personnel, U.S. interests and our allies." Therefore, any war against terrorism must target Hezbollah. We believe the administration should demand that Iran and Syria immediately cease all military, financial, and political support for Hezbollah and its operations. Should Iran and Syria refuse to comply, the administration should consider appropriate measures of retaliation against these known state sponsors of terrorism.

Israel and the Palestinian Authority

Israel has been and remains America's staunchest ally against international terrorism, especially in the Middle East. The United States should fully support our fellow democracy in its fight against terrorism. We should insist that the Palestinian Authority put a stop to terrorism emanating from territories under its control and imprison those planning terrorist attacks against Israel. Until the Palestinian Authority moves against terror, the United States should provide it no further assistance.

U.S. Defense Budget

A serious and victorious war on terrorism will require a large increase in defense spending. Fighting this war may well require the United States to engage a well-armed foe, and will also require that we remain capable of defending our interests elsewhere in the world. We urge that there be no hesitation in requesting whatever funds for defense are needed to allow us to win this war.

There is, of course, much more that will have to be done. Diplomatic efforts will be required to enlist other nations' aid in this war on terrorism. Economic and financial tools at our disposal will have to be used. There are other actions of a military nature that may well be needed. However, in our judgment the steps outlined above constitute the minimum necessary if this war is to be fought effectively and brought to a successful conclusion. Our purpose in writing is to assure you of our support as you do what must be done to lead the nation to victory in this fight.

Sincerely,

William Kristol

Richard V. Allen Gary Bauer Jeffrey Bell William J. Bennett Rudy Boshwitz Jeffrey Bergner Eliot Cohen Seth Cropsey Midge Decter Thomas Donnelly Nicholas Eberstadt Hillel Fradkin Aaron Friedberg Francis Fukuyama Frank Gaffney Jeffrey Gedmin Reuel Marc Gerecht Charles Hill Bruce P. Jackson Eli S. Jacobs Michael Joyce Donald Kagan Robert Kagan Jeanne Kirkpatrick Charles Krauthammer John Lehman Clifford May Martin Peretz Richard Perle Norman Podhoretz Stephen P. Rosen Randy Scheunemann Gary Schmitt William Schneider, Jr. Richard H. Shultz Henry Sokolski Stephen J. Solarz Vin Weber Leon Wieseltier Marshall Wittmann

275 **"I believe Iraq was involved":** Bob Woodward and Dan Balz, "Combating Terrorism: 'It Starts Today,'" *Washington Post*, February 1, 2002.

275 **"The coalition did not act in Iraq":** James Risen, David E. Sanger, and Thom Shanker, "In Sketchy Data, Trying to Gauge Iraq Threat," *New York Times*, July 20, 2003.

275 **the CIA claimed to have detected an Iraqi plot:** Seymour Hersh, "A Case Not Closed," *The New Yorker*, November 11, 1993.

275 **"focus on removing Saddam Hussein from power":** Richard Perle et al., "A Clean Break: A New Strategy for Securing the Realm," Institute for Advanced Strategic and Political Studies, Washington, D.C., and Jerusalem, at www.israeleconomy.org/strat1.htm.

275 **"to wean the south Lebanese [Shiites] away from Hezbollah":** Bryan Bender, "Democracy Might Be Impossible, U.S. Was Told," *Boston Globe*, August 14, 2003.

276 **unfettered by any restraints:** William Kristol and Robert Kagan, "Toward a Neo-Reaganite Foreign Policy," *Foreign Affairs*, July-August 1996. Quote is derived from Wesley Yang, unpublished essay, June 2003, provided by the author.

276 **Reagan's primary foreign policy achievement:** On May 2, 1982, Norman Podhoretz wrote of "The Neoconservative Anguish over Reagan's Foreign Policy" in the *New York Times Magazine*, arguing that Reagan has "in practice been following a strategy of helping the Soviet

Union stabilize its empire, rather than a strategy aimed at encouraging the breakup of that empire from within." According to Paul Nitze, during the early days of the START talks, "Pentagon civilian officials—particularly Richard Perle [then secretary of defense for international security policy] and Caspar Weinberger—were deliberately excluded from the discussion. Otherwise the howls and leaks from Weinberger and Perle and their supporters would have made the project impossible." For Podhoretz (among others), see John Ehrman's *The Rise of Neoconservatism: Intellectuals and Foreign Affairs, 1945-1994* (New Haven: Yale University Press, 1995) and for Nitze, Paul H. Nitze with Ann M. Smith and Steven L. Reardon, *From Hiroshima to Glastnost: At the Center of Decision* (New York: Grove Widenfeld, 1989).

276 **"American policy cannot continue to be crippled":** Steven R. Weisman, "Pre-emption: Idea with a Lineage Whose Time Has Come," *New York Times,* March 23, 2003.

276 **"transcends the issue of . . . Saddam Hussein":** "Rebuilding America's Defenses," Report of the Project for the New American Century, September, 2002, at www.newamericancentury.org/RebuildingAmericasDefenses.pdf.

276 **"When he ultimately asked Congress for the authority to go to war":** U.S. Congress, "Joint Resolution to Authorize the Use of United States Armed Forces Against Iraq," *New York Times,* October 11, 2002, at www.mtholyoke.edu/acad/intrel/bush/resolution.htm.

276 **"I can't make that claim":** George W. Bush, "President Bush Meets with Prime Minister Blair, Remarks by the President and British Prime Minister Tony Blair," White House press release, January 31, 2003.

276 **more explicitly in September 2003:** Dana Milbank, "Bush Disavows Hussein-Sept. 11 Link," *Washington Post,* September 18, 2003.

277 **Straw had seen no evidence:** Sebastian Rotella, "Allies Find No Links Between Iraq, Al Qaeda," *Los Angeles Times,* November 2, 2002.

277 **Former senator Max Cleland:** Shaun Waterman, "9/11 report: No Iraq link to al-Qaeda," United Press International, July 23, 2003, at www.upi.com/view.cfm?StoryID=20030723-064812-9491r.

277 **"[Saddam's] a bad Muslim," bin Laden replied:** Joshua Micah Marshall, Talking Points Memo, interview with Peter Bergen, August 21, 2003, at http://talkingpointsmemo.com/aug0303.html#0821031034pm.

278 **a direct contravention of the CIA's finding:** Walter Pincus, "Report Cast Doubt on Iraq-Al Qaeda Connection," *Washington Post,* June 22, 2003.

278 **"secretly, and without fingerprints,":** Matt Kelley, "Bush Overstated Iraq Links to al-Qaida, Former Intelligence Officials Say," Associated Press, July 17, 2003.

278 **"al Qaeda". . . was a constant feature of the president's speeches:** Joe Conason, "An Unproven Case, a Spurious War," *New York Observer,* March 25, 2003.

278 **Following a terrorist attack in Bali:** David Corn, "Bush's Biggest Whopper," *Salon.com,* July 24, 2003.

278 **"al Qaeda terrorists . . . are known to be in Iraq":** Mitchell Landsberg, "Ample Evidence of Abuses, Little of Illegal Weapons," *Los Angeles Times,* June 15, 2003.

278 **"It would take one vial":** President George W. Bush, "President Delivers State of the Union," January 28, 2003, at www.whitehouse.gov/news/releases/2003/01/20030128-19.html.

278 **"The battle of Iraq is one victory":** Quoted in Sam Schechner, "Today's Papers: Top Gun," *Slate,* May 2, 2003, at http://slate.msn.com/id/2082471.

278 **"the United States will not stand by":** "Citing 9/11, Bush defends Iraq war," *MSNBC,* July 14, 2003.

279 **"Why not document them?":** Arianna Huffington, "We Don't Need No Stinkin' Proof" in *The Iraq War Reader: History, Documents, Opinions,* eds. Micah L. Sifry and Christopher Cerf (New York: Touchstone, 2003).

279 **Even if Powell's charges were accurate:** John B. Judis and Spencer Ackerman, "The First Casualty," *The New Republic,* June 30, 2003, 14.

279 **"no strong evidence of connections to Baghdad":** Robert Scheer, "The Forgettable Truth: The War We're Winning Was Based on Lies," *Salon.com,* April 30, 2003, at www.salon.com/opinion/scheer/2003/04/30/WMD_truth/index.html.

279 **"Nothing has come to our notice":** Warren P. Strobel and Jonathan S. Landay, "Al-Qaeda Links to Saddam Doubted," *San Jose Mercury News,* June 27, 2003.

279 **"the administration was grossly distorting the intelligence":** Nicholas D. Kristof, "Save Our Spooks," *New York Times,* May 30, 2003.

279 **"dissident Iraqi activities overseas":** Joe Conason, "An Unproven Case, a Spurious War," *New York Observer,* March 24, 2003.

279 **meeting . . . said to have occurred in Prague:** The "single informant" is from James Risen, "Threats and Responses: The View from Prague; Prague Discounts an Iraqi Meeting," *New York Times,* October 1, 2002. Safire is quoted in Kate Taylor, "Did Mohamed Atta Meet an Iraqi Spy in

Prague?," at www.slate.com, September 3, 2003. Havel is quoted in David Rennie, "Havel Rebuts Report Linking Iraq to Sept 11," *The Telegraph*, October 22, 2002, at www.telegraph.co.uk/news/main.jhtml?xml=/news/2002/10/22/wirq22.xml. Cheney is quoted in Cynthia Tucker, "As Bush Milks Sept. 11, We Keep Drinking," *Atlanta Journal-Constitution*, September 10, 2003.

280 **When the high-level al Qaeda leader:** John B. Judis and Spencer Ackerman, "The First Casualty," *The New Republic*, June 30, 2003, 14.

280 **including one of the key planners:** Bill Keller, "The Boys Who Cried Wolfowitz," *New York Times*, June 14, 2003.

280 **any Iraq-al Qaeda ties denied:** Matt Kelley, "Bush Overstated Iraq Links to Al-Qaida, Former Intelligence Officials Say," Associated Press, July 12, 2003.

280 **no evidence:** Reuters, "Iraqi, Possibly Tied to 9/11, Is Captured," *New York Times*, July 9, 2003.

280 **"Saddam, if sufficiently desperate, might decide":** Greg Miller and James Gerstenzang, "Classified Iraq Data Released," *Los Angeles Times*, July 19, 2003.

280 **"Would be his last chance to exact vengeance":** Walter Pincus, "Oct. Report Said Defeated Hussein Would Be Threat," *Washington Post*, July 21, 2003.

280 **General Wesley Clark:** Micah L. Sifry and Christopher Cerf, *The Iraq War Reader: History, Documents, Opinions* (New York: Touchstone, 2003), 281.

280 **Daniel Benjamin:** Peter Slevin, "Striking Iraq Could Fuel Further Attacks on U.S.," *Washington Post*, March 16, 2003.

281 **"I can't use numbers":** Don Van Natta Jr. and Desmond Butler, "Anger on Iraq Seen as New Qaeda Recruiting Tool," *New York Times*, March 16, 2003.

281 **"a gift to Osama bin Laden":** Jessica Stern, "How America Created a Terrorist Haven," *New York Times*, August 20, 2003.

281 **"number-one security threat" in Iraq:** Bradley Graham, "General Cites Rising Peril of Terror in Iraq," *Washington Post*, August 22, 2003.

281 **"no substantive intelligence":** Robert Scheer, "White House's Cynical Iraq Ploy: 'Misspeak' First, 'Correct' It Later," *Los Angeles Times*, September 16, 2003.

281 **"We know he had a weapons of mass destruction program":** "Dateline NBC: Inside the White House at War," transcript, April 25, 2003.

281 **Wolfowitz warned of continuing threat:** Matthew Yglesias, "TV Guided How the Networks Did Bush's Bidding in Their Second-Anniversary Coverage of 9-11," *The American Prospect Online*, September 12, 2003.

281 **"a region from which the 9-11 threat emerged":** Terence Hunt, "Bush Says No Evidence That Saddam Hussein Involved in September 11 Attacks," Associated Press, September 17, 2003.

282 **"[I] should have been more precise":** Robert Scheer, "When Corrections Need Correcting," *Salon.com*, September 17, 2003.

282 **"there's no question":** Greg Miller, "No Proof Connects Iraq to 9/11, Bush Says," *Los Angeles Times*, September 18, 2003.

282 **February 2003 poll:** Ari Berman, "Polls Suggest Media Failure in Pre-War Coverage," *Editor and Publisher*, March 26, 2003.

283 **U.S. forces left canisters of radioactive material:** Judith Miller, "U.S. Inspectors Find No Forbidden Weapons at Iraqi Arms Plant," *New York Times*, April 16, 2003.

283 ***Washington Post* editorial:** Editorial, "Keep Looking," *Washington Post*, June 25, 2003.

283 **"Americans don't care":** Massimo Calabresi and Timothy J. Burger, "Who Lost the WMD?," *Time*, June 29, 2003, 32.

284 **"This isn't sticking":** David E. Sanger and Warren Hoge, "Bush Escapes Fury That Batters Blair," *New York Times*, June 26, 2003.

284 **2003 State of the Union:** George W. Bush, State of the Union Address, Washington, D.C., January 28, 2003.

284 **Donald Rumsfeld:** See Joost R. Hiltermann, "The Man Who Helped the Man Who Gassed His Own People," in *The Iraq War Reader: History, Documents, Opinions*, eds. Micah L. Sifry and Christopher Cerf (New York: Touchstone, 2003), 43.

284 **Dick Cheney:** John Le Carré, "The United States of America Has Gone Mad," in *The Iraq War Reader: History, Documents, Opinions*, eds. Micah L. Sifry and Christopher Cerf (New York: Touchstone, 2003), 437.

285 **The Congo:** Tom Masland, "Wars Without End," *Newsweek*, July 14, 2003.

285 **John Negroponte:** Maggie Farley and Maura Reynolds, "U.N. Measure on Iraqi Arms Nears Passage," *Los Angeles Times*, November 8, 2002.

285 **not a single nation's population:** Robert G. Kaiser, "The Briefing, Rumsfeld's E Ring Circus," *Washington Post*, March 22, 2003.

285 **so-called New Europe:** Fareed Zakaria, "The Arrogant Empire," *Newsweek*, March 24, 2003, 18.

286 **Jürgen Habermas:** Jürgen Habermas, "The Fall of the Monument," *The Hindu* (Madras, India), June 5, 2003.

286 **Secretary Powell:** Glenn Kessler and Mike Allen, "U.S. Missteps Led to Failed Diplomacy," *Washington Post,* March 16, 2003.

286 **Paul Wolfowitz:** H. D. S. Greenway, "Democracy, Neocon Style," *Boston Globe,* May 16, 2003.

286 **Representative Barney Frank:** Juliet Eilperin, "Frank Assails Wolfowitz for Remarks on Turkey," *Washington Post,* May 20, 2003.

286 **Security Council showdown:** Andrew Rawnsley, "Why We Don't Trust Bush," *The Observer,* January 15, 2003.

286 **yet another diplomat:** Glenn Kessler, "Forceful Tactics Catch Up with U.S.," *Washington Post,* February 16, 2003.

287 **Jacques Chirac:** Stanley Hoffmann, "America Goes Backward," *New York Review of Books,* June 12, 2003.

287 **Michael Walzer:** Michael Walzer, "What a Little War in Iraq Could Do," *New York Times,* March 7, 2003.

287 **Condoleezza Rice:** CBS News, *Face the Nation,* October 20, 2002.

287 **"still in a diplomatic phase":** ABC News, *This Week,* March 9, 2003.

287 **Richard Haas:** Daniel Eisenberg, "We're Taking Him Out," *Time,* May 13, 2003.

287 **"Bush has become the enemy":** Glenn Kessler and Mike Allen, "Bush Faces Increasingly Poor Image Overseas," *Washington Post,* February 24, 2003.

288 **President Bush:** Dana Milbank, "U.S. Faces Long Stay in Iraq, Bush Says," *Washington Post,* July 2, 2003.

288 **Lawrence B. Lindsey:** Elisabeth Bumiller, "White House Cuts Estimate of Cost of War With Iraq, *New York Times,* December 31, 2002.

288 **Eric K. Shineski:** Barbara Slavin and Dave Moniz, "How Peace in Iraq Became So Elusive," *USA Today,* July 22, 2003.

288 **Secretary Wolfowitz:** Peter Slevin and Dana Priest, "Wolfowitz Concedes Iraq Errors," *Washington Post,* July 24, 2003. See also www.defenselink.mil/transcripts/2003/tr20030727-depsecdef0462.html.

288 **Kosovo:** Fred Kaplan, "He Saw It Coming," Slate, August 5, 2003.

288 **James Dobbins:** James Dobbins, Rachel Swanger, John McGinn, Rollie Lal, and Andrew Rathmell, eds. *America's Role in Nation-Building* (La Jolla, CA: Rand Corporation, 2003). See also Fred Kaplan, "Blow-Back in Baghdad," Slate, July 8, 2003. See also Graydon Carter, "Editor's Letter," *Vanity Fair,* August 2003, 40, and Fred Kaplan, "He Saw It Coming," *Slate,* August 5, 2003.

288 **Wolfowitz asserted:** Michelle Goldberg, "From Heroes to Targets," *Salon.com,* July 18, 2003.

289 **Tommy Franks:** Esther Schrader, Edwin Chen, and John Daniszewski, "Gen. Franks Sees Troops Needed for Years in Iraq," *Los Angeles Times,* July 11, 2003.

289 **Paul Bremer:** Irwin M. Stelzer, "A Foreign Policy Worth Paying For," *Weekly Standard,* August 18, 2003.

289 **the *New York Times* discovered:** Jeff Gerth, "Report Offered Bleak Outlook About Iraq Oil," *New York Times,* October 5, 2003.

289 **Iraq is stuck with an enormous amount of foreign debt:** Donald Hepburn, "Nice War. Here's the Bill," *Washington Post,* September 3, 2003.

289 **Rumsfeld had already estimated the costs:** "Fantasy Budget," *Washington Post,* March 19, 2003.

290 **James Fallows:** James Fallows, "The Fifty-first State?," *Atlantic Monthly,* November 2002.

290 **Nordhaus:** William D. Nordhaus, "Iraq: The Economic Consequences of War," essay, Yale University, November 2002.

290 **Congressional Budget Office issued an estimate:** Richard A. Oppel Jr., "Congressional Unit Analyzes Military Costs in Iraq," *New York Times,* November 1, 2003.

290 **$87 billion price tag:** Richard W. Stevenson, "78% of Bush's Postwar Spending Plan Is for Military," *New York Times,* September 9, 2000. The $87 billion figure, as noted by the Center for American Progress, a liberal advocacy group, was roughly equivalent to two years of unemployment benefits, eighty-seven times what the federal government spends on after-school programs, and more than ten times the budget for the Environmental Protection Agency.

290 **Robert Dreyfuss:** Robert Dreyfuss, "More Missing Intelligence," *The Nation,* July 7, 2993, 4.

290 **Judith Yaphe:** Mark Fineman, Robin Wright, and Doyle McManus, "Washington's Battle Plan; Preparing for War, Stumbling to Peace," *Los Angeles Times,* July 18, 2003.

291 **U.S. Army War College study:** See Conrad C. Crane and W. Andrew Terrill, "Reconstructing Iraq: Insights, Challenges, and Missions for Military Forces in a Post-Conflict Scenario," Strategic Studies Institute, U.S. Army War College (Carlisle, PA), at www.carlisle.army.mil/ssi/pubs/2003/reconirq/reconirq.pdf.

291 **"resort to obstruction" and "so much tension":** Peter Slevin and Dana Priest, "Wolfowitz Concedes Iraq Errors," *Washington Post,* July 24, 2003.

291 **State Department's planning initiative:** Eric Shmitt and Joel Brinkley, "State Dept. Study Foresaw Trouble Now Plaguing Iraq," *New York Times,* October 19, 2003.

292 **"doubtful that the Iraqi population would welcome":** Jason Vest, "The War After the War," *Village Voice,* March 19-25, 2003.

292 **Chalabi was favored:** Karen DeYoung, "Role for Exile Leader Urged," *Washington Post,* April 4, 2003.

292 **Jonathan Landay:** Jonathan S. Landay and Warren P. Strobel, "No Real Planning for Post-war Iraq," Knight Ridder Newspapers, July 12, 2003.

293 **unreliable intelligence:** According to Seymour Hersh, "Chalabi's defector reports were now flowing from the Pentagon directly to the Vice-President's office, and then on to the President, with little prior evaluation by intelligence professionals. When INR analysts did get a look at the reports, they were troubled by what they found. 'They'd pick apart a report and find out that the source had been wrong before, or had no access to the information provided,' Greg Thielmann told me. 'There was considerable skepticism throughout the intelligence community about the reliability of Chalabi's sources, but the defector reports were coming all the time. Knock one down and another comes along. Meanwhile, the garbage was being shoved straight to the President.'" See "The Stovepipe," *The New Yorker,* October 27, 2003, 80-81.

293 **Bremer's description of the number as "really very low":** Laura King, "Baghdad's Death Toll Assessed," *Los Angeles Times,* May 18, 2003. See also Richard A. Oppel Jr., "U.S. Overseer Defends Occupation of Iraq," *New York Times,* August 13, 2003.

293 **congenital birth defects:** Military Toxic Projects, "Environmental Assessment of Depleted Uranium," at www.miltoxprj.org/assessment.htm.

293 **the chaos engendered by the U.S. invasion:** Peter Slevin, "Hussein Loyalists Blamed for Chaos," *Washington Post,* May 15, 2003.

293 **Pentagon also rebuffed efforts . . . :** Jonathan S. Landay and Warren P. Strobel, "No Real Planning for Postwar Iraq," Knight Ridder Newspapers, July 12, 2003.

294 **Henry T. Wright:** Shankar Vedantam, "Worst Looting May Be in Remote Parts of Iraq," *Washington Post,* June 12, 2003.

294 **Dr. Nawalaal Mutawalli:** "'One in 10' Iraqi treasures looted," BBC News, July 8, 2003, at http://news.bbc.co.uk/go/pr/fr/-/1/hi/entertainment/arts/3054974.stm.

294 **aversion to "nation-building":** Bush is quoted in the previous chapter during the presidential debates, claiming, "I think what we need to do is convince people who live in the lands they live in to build the nations. Maybe I'm missing something here. I mean, we're going to have kind of a nation-building corps from America? Absolutely not." Rumsfeld's views on the topic are also well known and consistent with Bush's. When asked about it in early 2002, he replied, "Another school of thought, which is where my brain is, is that why put all the time and money and effort in that? Why not put it into helping them develop a national army, so that they can look out for themselves over time?" Before she became Bush's national security advisor, Rice advised General Wesley Clark that, "she believed that American troops shouldn't be keeping the peace—they were the only ones who could kill people and conquer countries, and that's what they should be focused on doing." For Bush, see "Transcript of Candidate George W. Bush in the Second Presidential Debate," October 11, 2000, at www.c-span.org/campaign2000/transcript/debate_101100.asp. For Rumsfeld, see "Rumsfeld Stakeout at the Hart Senate Building," United States Department of Defense News Transcript, February 5, 2002. For Rice, see MSNBC.com, July 7, 2003, at www.msnbc.com/news/934709.asp.

294 **Basra:** Edmund L. Andrews, "Once Hailed, Soldiers in Iraq Now Feel Blame at Each Step," *New York Times,* June 29, 2003.

294 **gun-related killings in Baghdad:** Jeffrey Fleishman, "Baghdad's Packed Morgue Marks a City's Descent into Lawlessness," *Los Angeles Times,* September 16, 2003.

294 **Garner:** Barbara Slavin and Dave Moniz, "How Peace in Iraq Became So Elusive," *USA Today,* July 22, 2003.

294 **Resistance among Iraqis was increasing:** Bradley Graham, "Iraq Another Vietnam Quagmire? No and Yes," *Washington Post,* October 5, 2003.

294 **"acknowledging that it's not working":** David E. Sanger, "White House to Overhaul Iraq and Afghan Missions," *New York Times,* October 6, 2000.

295 **"The more successful we are on the ground":** "President Bush, Ambassador Bremer Discuss Progress in Iraq," October 27, 2003, at www.whitehouse.gov/news/releases/2003/10/20031027-1.html.

295 **McCain and "parallel to Vietnam":** Dana Milbank and Thomas E. Ricks, "Bush Says Attacks Are Reflection of U.S. Gains," *Washington Post,* October 28, 2003.

295 *Financial Times:* "Trapped in Vicious Circles in Iraq," *Financial Times,* July 2, 2003.

295 **a senior UN diplomat:** Fareed Zakaria, "Iraq Policy Is Broken. Fix It." *Newsweek,* July 14, 2003.

295 *Le Figaro:* Luc de Barochez, "The United Nations Refuses to Help George Bush in Iraq," *Le Figaro,* September 26, 2003.

296 **In Najaf:** Sam Schechner, "The Withdrawal Method," Slate, June 28, 2003. See also William Booth and Rajiv Chandrasekaran, "Occupation Forces Halt Elections Throughout Iraq," *Washington Post,* June 28, 2003; William Booth, "U.S. Soldier's Disappearance Is Still Shrouded in Mystery," *Washington Post,* June 28, 2003; and Edmund L. Andrews, "G.I. Dies, Others Are Wounded in New Ambushes in Iraq," *New York Times,* June 28, 2003.

296 **"marines who pull triggers":** Romesh Ratnesar with Simon Robinson, "Life Under Fire," *Time,* July 5, 2003.

296 **Laurence Pope:** Thomas E. Ricks, "Experts Question Depth of Victory," *Washington Post,* June 27, 2003.

296 **"guerrilla-type campaign":** Thom Shanker, "Yearlong Tours an Option for 'Guerrilla' War in Iraq," *New York Times,* July 17, 2003.

296 **Karen Kwiatkowski:** Karen Kwiakowski, "Career Officer Does Eye-Opening Stint Inside Pentagon," *(Akron, Ohio) Beacon Journal,* July 31, 2003.

297 **"misplaced bravado":** Editorial, "A Troubled Occupation in Iraq," *New York Times,* July 10, 2003.

297 **twenty U.S. soldiers:** Romesh Ratnesar with Simon Robinson, "Life Under Fire," *Time,* July 5, 2003.

297 **Mary Kewatt:** Dana Milbank, "Flap Over Iraq Charge Shows Bush Vulnerability," *Washington Post,* July 17, 2003.

297 **"At least six of us will lose our careers":** Robert Collier, "Pentagon Retaliates Against GIs Who Spoke Out on TV," *San Francisco Chronicle,* July 18, 2003.

297 **Drudge and ABC reporter:** Lloyd Grove, "The Reliable Source," *Washington Post,* July 18, 2003.

297 **Kristol on reconstruction:** Fred Kaplan, "Delusions of Empire," *Slate,* June 25, 2003.

297 **Carnegie study:** Andrew Moravcsik, "Striking a New Transatlantic Bargain," *Foreign Affairs* 82, no. 4 (July-August 2003): 85.

298 **World Bank:** John Cassidy, "Letter from Iraq: Beneath the Sand," *The New Yorker,* July 16 and 21, 2003, 73.

298 **CIA report:** Bryan Bender, "Democracy Might Be Impossible, US Was Told," *Boston Globe,* August 14, 2003.

298 **State Department study:** Greg Miller, "Democracy Domino Theory 'Not Credible,'" *Los Angeles Times,* March 14, 2003.

298 **Army War College Report:** Jason Vest, "After the War," *Village Voice,* March 19-25, 2003.

298 **Sunni Arabs . . . Shiites and Kurds:** Frank Smyth, "Saddam's Real Opponents," in *The Iraq War Reader: History, Documents, Opinions,* eds. Micah L. Sifry and Christopher Cerf (New York: Touchstone, 2003), 565.

299 **George Packer:** George Packer, "Dreaming of Democracy," *New York Times Magazine,* March 2, 2003.

299 **Kristol and principles of liberty and justice:** Fred Kaplan, "Delusions of Empire," *Slate,* June 25, 2003.

299 **"magical realism":** George Packer, "Dreaming of Democracy," *New York Times Magazine,* March 2, 2003.

299 **"bomb the shit out of you":** William F. Schulz, *Tainted Legacy: 9/11 and the Ruin of Human Rights* (New York: Thurnder's Mouth Press/Nation Books, 2003), 54.

299 **Jordan democracy advocates:** Fawaz Gerges, "Can Democracy Take Root in the Islamic World? Empty Promises of Freedom," *New York Times,* July 18, 2003.

300 **Ken Jowitt:** Ken Jowitt, "Rage, Hubris, and Regime Change," *Policy Review,* April 2003.

300 **Japan-Iraq analogy discounted by Dower and colleagues:** "As students of the Japanese occupation," they wrote, "we believe that the Bush administration's plans for war and occupation in Iraq are a historical mistake and strongly urge the United States to seek a peaceful solution to the present crisis." The list of historians signing the statement was as follows:

AWAYA Kentaro (Professor, St. Paul's University, Japan)
Hans H. BAERWALD (former Occupation official, Professor Emeritus, UCLA, U.S.)
Herbert P. BIX (Professor, Binghamton University, U.S.)
Bruce CUMINGS (Professor, University of Chicago, U.S.)
Ronald P. DORE (Associate Professor, London School of Economics, U.K.)

John W. DOWER (Professor, Massachusetts Institute of Technology, U.S.)
Jonathan DRESNER (Assistant Professor, University of Hawaii, U.S.)
Norma FIELD (Professor, University of Chicago, U.S.)
FURUKAWA Atsushi (Professor, Senshu University, Japan)
Andrew GORDON (Professor, Harvard University, U.S.)
Laura E. HEIN (Professor, Northwestern University, U.S.)
Glenn D. HOOK (Professor, University of Sheffield, U.K.)
HOSOYA Masahiro (Professor, Doshisha University, Japan)
KOSEKI Shoichi (Professor, Dokkyo University, Japan)
J. Victor KOSCHMANN (Professor, Cornell University, U.S.)
C. Douglas LUMMIS (Political scientist and writer, Okinawa, Japan)
Gavan MCCORMACK (Professor, Australian National University, Australia)
Richard M. MINEAR (Professor, University of Massachusetts, U.S.)
MIYAGI Etsujiro (Professor Emeritus, Ryukyu University, Japan)
Michael MOLASKY (Associate Professor, University of Minnesota, U.S.)
Joe B. MOORE (Professor, University of Victoria, Canada)
NAKAMURA Masanori (Professor Emeritus, Hitotsubashi University, Japan)
James B. PALAIS (Professor, University of Washington, U.S.)
Robert RICKETTS (Professor, Wako University, Japan)
Mark SELDEN (Professor, Binghamton University, U.S.)
SODEI Rinjiro (Professor Emeritus, Hosei University, Japan)
TAKEMAE Eiji (Professor Emeritus, Tokyo Keizai University, Japan)
TANAKA Toshiyuki (Professor, Hiroshima Peace Research Institute, Japan)
TOYOSHITA Narahiko (Professor, Kansei Gakuin University, Japan)
YUI Daizaburo (Professor, Tokyo University, Japan)

For the document itself, see http://japan.indymedia.org/feature/display_printable/45/index.php.

301 **"the guy who tried to kill my dad":** Transcript, "Showdown with Iraq: Bush Hits Colo., Ariz. Fund-Raisers," CNN Live Event/Special, September 27, 2002.

301 **"God told me to strike at al Qaeda":** Arnon Regular, " 'Road Map Is a Life Saver for Us,' PM Abbas Tells Hamas," *Ha'arretz*, at www.haaretz.com/hasen/pages/ShArt.jhtml?itemNo= 310788&contrassID=2subContrassID=1&sbSubContrassID=0&listSrc=Y.

301 **"tin-pot dictator":** Paul Krugman, "Waggy Dog Stories," *New York Times*, May 30, 2003.

301 **"we're taking him out":** Daniel Eisenberg, "We're Taking Him Out," *Time*, May 13, 2002, 36.

301 **John Brady Keisling:** "Former US Diplomat Says Rumsfeld Led Bush to War," *AFP* (Athens, Greece), August 17, 2003.

301 **Leo Strauss:** Gary J. Schmitt and Abram N. Shulsky, "Leo Strauss and the World of Intelligence (By Which We Do Not Mean *Nous*)" in *Leo Strauss, the Straussians and the American Regime*, eds. Kenneth L. Deutsch and John Murley (New York: Rowan and Littlefield, 1999), 407-21.

301 **Pippin . . . Holmes . . . Cropsey:** Seymour M. Hersh, "Selective Intelligence," *The New Yorker*, May 12, 2003, 44. See also *An Introduction to Political Philosophy*, ed. Hilail Gildin (Detroit: Wayne State University Press, 1990) and in *Leo Strauss, the Straussians and the American Regime*.

302 **codified as official U.S. government policy in September 2002:** National Security Strategy of the United States," at www.whitehouse.gov/nsc/nssall.html.

302 **Thomas Friedman:** Thomas L. Friedman, "Because We Could," *New York Times*, June 4, 2003.

303 **Olivier Roy:** Olivier Roy, "Europe Won't Be Fooled Again," *New York Times*, May 13, 2003.

303 **Douglas Feith:** Doyle McManus, "Pentagon Reform Is His Battle Cry," *Los Angeles Times*, August 17, 2003.

303 **Halliburton:** Neela Banerjee, "Bechtel Ends Move for Work in Iraq, Seeing a Done Deal," *New York Times*, August 8, 2003.

303 **320 million barrels:** Reuters, "Trade Deficit Remains High as Oil Imports Set a Record," *New York Times*, July 12, 2003.

303 **oil production is expected to fall:** Michel Renner, "Post-Saddam Iraq: Linchpin of a New Oil Order," in *The Iraq War Reader: History, Documents, Opinions*, eds. Micah L. Sifry and Christopher Cerf (New York: Touchstone, 2003), 581.

303 **Arab hatred for both the United States and Israel:** Those portions of the congressional September 11 report dealing with Saudi aid and encouragement to al Qaeda were redacted and remain classified, itself an indication of the influence they enjoy with the Bush administration and congressional Republicans. See Josh Meyer, "Report Is Wary of Saudi Actions. U.S. Officials Fear Riyadh May Have Given Hijackers Financial, Logistic Aid. Lawmakers Urge More Facts Be Made

Public," *Los Angeles Times,* July 25, 2003, at www.latimes.com/news/nationworld/nation/la-fg-saudi25jul25,1,253266.story?coll=la-home-headlines. The published portions of the report did acknowledge, however, "According to one U.S. government official, it was clear from about 1996 that the Saudi government would not cooperate with the United States on matters relating to Osama bin Laden."

Another U.S. official told investigators that "obtaining Saudi cooperation was unrealistic because Saudi assistance to the U.S. government on this matter is contrary to Saudi national interests."

And a third high-level U.S. government officer "cited greater Saudi cooperation when asked how the September 11 attacks might have been prevented," the congressional report said.

304 **"a huge recruiting device for al Qaeda":** Sam Tanenhaus, "Bush's Brain Trust," *Vanity Fair,* July 2003, 169.

304 **Francis Brooke:** John Cassidy, "Letter from Iraq: Beneath the Sand," *The New Yorker,* July 16 and 21, 2003, 73.

304 **oil reserves comparable to . . . Saudi Arabia:** Michael T. Klare, "Deciphering the Bush Administration's Motives," in *The Iraq War Reader: History, Documents, Opinions,* eds. Micah L. Sifry and Christopher Cerf (New York: Touchstone, 2003), 394-5.

304 **United States could order Iraqis to withdraw from OPEC:** Michael Ignatieff, "The Burden," *New York Times Magazine,* January 5, 2003.

304 **2000 PNAC report:** "Rebuilding America's Defenses," Report of the Project for the New American Century, September 2000, at www.newamericancentury.org/RebuildingAmericas Defenses.pdf.

304 **1992 DPG draft:** Salim Muwakki, "When Warriors Dissent," *In These Times,* August 11, 2003.

305 **ten-month deployment:** Anne E. Kornblut, "Bush Proclaims a Victory," *Boston Globe,* May 2, 2003.

305 **"They're the ones who put it up":** "Bush Steps Away from Victory Banner," *New York Times,* October 29, 2003.

305 **aides were happy to take full credit:** Editorial, "An Unfinished Mission," *Washington Post,* May 4, 2003.

305 **Wesley Clark:** "Clark Brings Political Message to Granite State," The Boston Channel, October 28, 2003, at www.thebostonchannel.com/news/2589225/detail.html.

306 **Bush managed to disappear from his reserve unit:** David Corn, "See Now They Tell Us," *The Nation,* May 19, 2003.

306 **more American servicemen would die in Iraq:** Richard A. Oppel, "G.I. Killed and 6 Are Wounded in Stepped-Up Attacks," *New York Times,* July 17, 2003.

306 **restricting soldiers' medical care:** Michael O'Hanlon, "Breaking the Army," *Washington Post,* July 3, 2003. See also "The Cost of Empire," *Newsweek,* July 17, 2003, 27.

306 **the 3rd Infantry Division:** Russ Bynum, "U.S. Troops to Get Longer Stay in Iraq," Associated Press, July 15, 2003.

306 **Stars and Stripes:** Bradley Graham and Dana Milbank, "Many Troops Dissatisfied, Iraq Poll Finds," *Washington Post,* October 16, 2003.

306 **administration's business-first ideology:** Paul Krugman, "Thanks for the M.R.E.'s," *New York Times,* August 12, 2003.

306 **If Donald Rumsfeld were here":** Michelle Goldberg, "From Heroes to Targets," *Salon.com,* July 18, 2003.

306 **General Zinni:** See Michael Elliott, "So, What Went Wrong?," *Time,* October 6, 2003, 33.

307 **George H. W. Bush:** George H. W. Bush and Brent Scowcroft, *A World Transformed* (New York: Knopf, 1998), 489-90.

12. The "Bungling Bully"

308 **"administration has proved to be incapable":** Jeffrey Sachs, "Comment and Analysis: A Distant World for Which Bush Cares Little," *Financial Times,* April 9, 2003.

308 **"Bungling Bully":** Editorial, "Bungling Bully," *Financial Times,* July 3, 2003.

309 **"perhaps the worst in American history":** Adam Gopnik, "Paris Journal: The Anti-Anti-Americans," *The New Yorker,* September 1, 2003, at www.newyorker.com/fact/content/?030901fa_fact1.

309 **"staggering" reconstruction costs:** Steven R. Weisman, with Felicity Barringer, "U.S. Abandons Idea of Bigger U.N. Role in Iraq Occupation," *New York Times,* August 14, 2003.

309 **He uttered these words:** Steven R. Weisman, with Felicity Barringer, "U.S. Will Ask U.N. for Move to Widen the Force in Iraq," *New York Times,* August 21, 2003, and Robin Wright and Maggie Farley, "U.S. to Seek International Efforts in Iraq," *Los Angeles Times,* August 21, 2003.

310 **"turn this bitter page":** Peter Beinart, "Sore Winner," *The New Republic,* May 12, 2003, at www.tnr.com/docprint.mhtml?i=20030512&s=trb051203.

310 **All of these fantastic stories . . . were vehemently denied by the French government":** Brian Knowlton, "France Says It Was Victim of Lies Fed by White House," *International Herald Tribune,* May 16, 2003, and Karen DeYoung, "U.S. Denies Campaign Against France" *Washington Post,* May 16, 2003.

310 **United States punished the Chileans:** Editorial, "The Price of Opposition," *Washington Post,* May 1, 2003.

311 **he stipulated Washington's expectation:** Luke Eric Peterson, "Trading Down," *The New Republic Online,* July 9, 2003.

311 **Bush decided to freeze military aid:** Kenneth Roth, "Open Letter to Colin Powell," June 30, 2003.

311 **hostility directed against America:** Alan Cowell, "A Worried World Shows Discord," *New York Times,* March 19, 2003.

311 **U.S. corporate brands began registering negative images with global consumers:** David Osborne, "Dire States," *The Independent,* July 17, 2003, at www.globalpolicy.org/globaliz/econ/2003/0717dire.htm.

312 **State of the Union:** "President Delivers State of the Union," January 29, 2002, at www.whitehouse.gov/news/releases/2002/01/20020129-11.html.

312 **Jörg Lau:** Author's interview.

312 **Frum and "axis of hatred":** David Frum, *The Right Man* (New York: Random House, 2002), 238-45.

313 **French warned other governments:** Douglas Frantz, "Iran Closes in on Ability to Build a Nuclear Bomb," *Los Angeles Times,* August 4, 2003.

313 **United Nations inspectors found enriched uranium:** Louis Charbonneau, "Iran Samples Show Enriched Uranium," Reuters, July 17, 2003.

313 **confirming their ability to complete the nuclear fuel cycle:** International Institute for Strategic Study, "Iran's Nuclear Ambitions," *Strategic Comments* 9, no. 2 (March 2003).

313 **hidden sites "spread all around":** Seymour M. Hersh, "The Iran Game—How Will Tehran's Nuclear Ambitions Affect Our Budding Partnership?" *New Yorker,* December 3, 2001.

313 **sufficient range to hit Jerusalem and Tel Aviv:** Nazila Fathi, "Iran Confirms Test of Missile That Is Able to Hit Israel," *New York Times,* July 8, 2003.

313 **his "friend" Putin's soul:** Thomas L. Friedman, "Soul Brother," *New York Times,* June 29, 2001.

313 **"a good fellow to spend quality time with":** David E. Sanger, "Russia Won't End Accord with Iran to Build Reactor," *New York Times,* September 27, 2003.

314 **Abbas Amanat:** Abbas Amanat, "A Risky Message to Iran," *New York Times,* February 10, 2002.

314 **Abramowitz and Laney; Cohen:** Eric Alterman, "Stop the Presses—State of Disunion," *The Nation,* February 10, 2003, at www.thenation.com/doc.mhtml?i=20030210&s =alterman.

314 **the president had become so emotional:** Quoted in Matthew Rothschild, "Bush's Messianic Military Mode," *The Progressive,* January 3, 2003.

315 **possesses "nuclear deterrence":** Anthony Faiola, "N. Korea Claims Nuclear Advance," *Washington Post,* October 3, 2003.

315 **"North Korea is much more of a threat":** Nicholas D. Kristof, "Grabbing the Nettle," *New York Times,* August 1, 2003.

315 **"That's how the president speaks":** Jake Tapper, "Did Bush Bungle Relations with North Korea?" *Salon.com,* March 15, 2001.

315 **General Wesley Clark:** NBC, *Meet the Press,* June 15, 2003.

316 **"We see a country that might export nuclear weapons":** Peter S. Goodman and Philip P. Pan, "N. Korea Threatens to Resume Missile Tests," *Washington Post,* January 12, 2003.

316 **North Korea has the fourth or fifth largest standing army on Earth:** Robert S. Norris et al., "NRDC Nuclear Notebook: North Korea's Nuclear Program, 2003," *Bulletin of the Atomic Scientists,* March-April 2003, 75.

316 **a transfer between North Korea and Iraq:** Dana Priest and Dana Milbank, "Iraq Sought Missile Parts, President Says," *Washington Post,* October 4, 2003.

316 **"North Korea shows once you get the weapons, you're immune":** Bill Keller, "The Thinkable," *New York Times Magazine,* May 4, 2003.

316 **"time is running out"**: Thomas E. Ricks and Glenn Kessler, "U.S., N. Korea Drifting Toward War, Perry Warns. Former Defense Secretary Says Standoff Increases Risk of Terrorists Obtaining Nuclear Device," *Washington Post*, July 15, 2003.

317 **"North Korea has the materials"**: Nicholas D. Kristof, "Grabbing the Nettle," *New York Times*, August 1, 2003.

317 **persuade several key Asian countries**: Michael R. Gordon, "U.S. Readies Plan to Raise Pressure on North Koreans," *New York Times*, December 29, 2002.

317 **stressed his independence from the United States**: Victor D. Cha and David C. Kang, "The Korea Crisis," *Foreign Policy*, June 2003.

317 **"It's a diplomatic issue, not a military issue"**: Romesh Ratnesar, "How Dangerous Is North Korea?," *Time*, January 5, 2003.

318 **"the 'lesson' of Korea seems to be"**: Michael Kinsley, "Morally Unserious," *Slate*, January 29, 2003.

318 **"You can't eat plutonium"**: Ivo H. Daalder and James M. Lindsay, "Nuclear Wal-Mart?," *The American Prospect* 14, no. 8 (September 1, 2003).

318 **Pakistan was eager to supply**: Seymour M. Hersh, "The Cold Test—What the Administration Knew About Pakistan and the North Korean Nuclear Program," *New Yorker*, January 27, 2003.

318 **"When we see starvation, we don't turn our back, we act"**: Editorial, "Talk Is Cheap," *The New Republic*, July 21, 2003.

318 **the least generous wealthy nation**: see www.foreignpolicy.com.

319 **USAID's budget**: Editorial, "Talk Is Cheap," *The New Republic*, July 21, 2003.

319 **no actual evidence**: Rachel L. Swarns, "U.S. Cuts Off Financing for AIDS Program, Provoking Furor," *New York Times*, August 27, 2003.

320 **the United States would "participate with the troops"**: Mike Allen, "Critics Assail Bush's Strategy of Restraint in Liberia," *Washington Post*, August 10, 2003.

320 **and Bush did next to nothing**: Editorial, "Liberia Denied," *Washington Post*, July 22, 2003.

320 **U.S. soldiers remained in the country a mere eleven days.**: Associated Press, "U.S. Marines Return to Ships off Liberia," August 25, 2003.

320 **various aids groups . . . have had their supplies . . . stolen**: Maggie Farley, Ann Simmons and Paul Richter, "Team in Liberia Sought Fast Aid," *Los Angeles Times*, August 17, 2003.

320 **"It baffles Liberians"**: Robin Wright, "Climate Worsens for Troops—The U.S. Squandered Its Opportunity to Send Peacekeepers to Liberia During a Cease-Fire, Analysts Say. Now It Faces a Combat Situation," *Los Angeles Times*, July 22, 2003.

321 **Douglas Farah described Taylor**: Douglas Farah, "The Tyrant We're Too Willing to Live With," *Washington Post*, August 3, 2003.

321 **Robertson considers Taylor a "fellow Baptist" and a "fine Christian"**: Ibid.

321 **African National Congress greeted Bush with a two-thousand-person protest march**: Dana Milbank and Emily Wax, "Critical of U.S. Policies, Africans Are Giving Bush Chilly Reception," *Washington Post*, July 10, 2003.

321 **"America has become a dirty word"**: Gitau Warigi, "Bush and Americanism in Africa," *The Nation*, July 6, 2003.

322 **"you can't go halfway"**: Dick Polman, "Neoconservatives," *Philadelphia Inquirer*, May 4, 2003.

322 **"just wage a total war"**: John Pilger, "John Pilger Reveals the American Plan," *The New Statesman*, December 16, 2002.

322 **"ours is the age of terrorism"**: Roy Gutman and John Barry, "Beyond Baghdad: Expanding the Target List," *Newsweek*, August 14, 2002.

322 **advocates within the administration for attacks**: Glenn Kessler, "N. Korea Arms Talks Appear Near—Pyongyang Seems to Accept U.S.'s Multilateral Format," *Washington Post*, August 1, 2003.

322 **"send a clear message to dictators like Kim Jong Il"**: Glenn Kessler, "N. Korea Seeks to Exclude U.S. Official from Talks," *Washington Post*, August 4, 2003.

322 **North Koreans term Bolton "human scum"**: Douglas Jehl, "New Warning Was Put Off on Weapons Syria Plans," *New York Times*, July 17, 2003.

323 **Syria's development of weapons**: Seymour M. Hersh, "The Syrian Bet," *New Yorker*, July 28, 2003.

323 **the offer was deliberately rejected**: Greg Jaffe, "Shift in Strategy Plays Down China, Calls Attention to Fighting Terror," *Wall Street Journal*, May 27, 2003.

323 **Rumsfeld envisions a force that will rotate**: Rumsfeld's number three, Undersecretary of Defense for Policy Douglas Feith, is quoted in the previous chapter, admitting that the decision to limit the number of troops sent in was "strategic and goes far beyond Iraq. This is part of his

[Rumsfeld's] thinking about defense transformation. It's an old way of thinking to say that the United States should not do anything without hundreds of thousands of troops. That makes our military less usable." See Barbara Slavin and Dave Moniz, "How Peace in Iraq Became So Elusive," *USA Today,* July 22, 2003.

323 **unwillingness of Donald Rumsfeld to commit sufficient troops:** Michael O'Hanlon, "Do the Math: We Need More Boots on the Ground," *Los Angeles Times,* August 12, 2003.

323 **destroy reenlistment incentives:** Irving Kristol, "Foreign Policy in an Age of Ideology," *The National Interest,* no. 1 (Fall 1985): 6-15.

324 **the United States could expect a period of conflict:** Theodore H. Draper, "Neoconservative History," *New York Review of Books* 32, nos. 21, 22 (January 16, 1986).

324 **Theodore Draper:** Josef Joffe, "Gulliver Unbound: Can America Rule the World?" Twentieth Annual John Bonython Lecture, presented at the Grand Ballroom, Sheraton on the Park in Sydney, Australia, August 5, 2003, at www.smh.com.au/cgibin/common/popupPrintArticle.pl?path=articles/2003/08/05/1060064182993.html.

324 **"hyper-puissance":** Eric Alterman, "USA Oui! Bush Non!" *The Nation,* February 10, 2003; Giovanni Borradori, *Philosophy in a Time of Terror: Dialogues with Jürgen Habermas and Jacques Derrida* (Chicago: University of Chicago Press, 2003), 28.

325 **"American inventions":** Jonathan Friedland, "Emperor George," *The Guardian,* April 2, 2003.

326 **"America is leaning on a rubber crutch":** Lawrence J. Korb, "The Pentagon's Eastern Obsession," *New York Times,* July 30, 2003.

326 **170 soldiers:** Andrew Higgins, "Chief Supporters for U.S. in Kabul: France, Germany, Afghan Team Shows America Needs More Allies for Peace Than to Make War," *Wall Street Journal,* June 17, 2003.

326 **The French even evacuated a hundred Americans from Liberia:** Josef Joffe, "Gulliver Unbound: Can America Rule the World?" Twentieth Annual John Bonython Lecture, presented at the Grand Ballroom, Sheraton on the Park in Sydney, Australia, August 5, 2003.

327 **"who would love to see the United States and Britain fail":** Niall Ferguson, "Hegemony or Empire?," *Foreign Affairs,* September-October 2003 at www.foreignaffairs.org/20030901fare viewessay82512/niall-ferguson/hegemony-or-empire.html.

327 **"We're not imperialistic. We never have been":** John B. Judis, "What Woodrow Wilson Can Teach Today's Imperialists. History Lesson," *The New Republic,* June 9, 2003.

328 **Americans "unambiguously to embrace [America's] imperial role":** Editorial, "America and Empire—Manifest Destiny Warmed Up?," *The Economist,* August 14, 2003.

328 **As the economist James Galbraith points out:** John B. Judis, "What Woodrow Wilson Can Teach Today's Imperialists. History Lesson," *The New Republic,* June 9, 2003.

328 **"Muslim clerics [have begun] demanding that Arab countries sell oil for euros, not dollars":** Jefferson Chase, "Europa, Europa—The Mixed-Up Debate over the New European Patriotism," *Boston Globe,* July 20, 2003.

329 **Tony Blair:** See Geoffrey van Orden, "Blair Goes French," *Wall Sreet Journal,* October 28, 2003.

329 **"could one day pose a real threat to U.S. dominance":** John B. Judis, "What Woodrow Wilson Can Teach Today's Imperialists. History Lesson," *The New Republic,* June 9, 2003.

329 **"Imperialism and democracy are at odds":** Editorial, "America and Empire—Manifest Destiny Warmed Up?," *The Economist,* August 14, 2003.

13. Conclusion

331 **Clinton administration:** Joan Didion, *Political Fictions* (New York: Alfred A. Knopf, 2001).

332 **Ashcroft likens civil libertarians to terrorist sympathizers:** Ronald Dworkin, "The Threat to Patriotism," *New York Review of Books,* February 28, 2002.

332 *New York Times* **editors:** Editorial, "Presidential Character," *New York Times,* September 9, 2003.

332 **"bipartisanship is another name for date rape":** John Aloysius Farrell, "Rancor Becomes Top D.C. Export; GOP Leads Charge in Ideological War," *Denver Post,* May 26, 2003.

332 **Rev. Franklin Graham:** "Franklin Graham Conducts Services at Pentagon," CNN, April 18, 2003, at www.cnn.com/2003/ALLPOLITICS/04/18/graham.pentagon/.

332 **net worth of America's four hundred richest:** Associated Press, "America's Richest People Get More; Microsoft's Bill Gates Remains at Top of the List," MSNBC, September 19, 2003, at www. msnbc.com/news/968977.asp?0dm=C2INB.

333 **$500 billion:** Ronald Brownstein, "Like Father, Like Son: The Economic Indicators Head South," *Los Angeles Times,* September 30, 2002, and Helen Dewar, "War Tab Jeopardizes Parties' Domestic Agendas; $87 Billion Request May Hurt Medicare, Other Priorities," *Washington Post,* September 29, 2003.

334 **Andrew Kohut:** Christopher Marquis, "World's View of U.S. Sours After Iraq War, Poll Finds," *New York Times,* June 4, 2003.

334 **"They're on their own":** Peter Slevin, "Reluctance to Share Control in Iraq Leaves U.S. on Its Own," *Washington Post,* September 28, 2003.

335 **"this is scripted":** Michael Crowley, "Bush Eats the Press," *New York Observer,* March 17, 2003.

335 **Lawrence McQuillam:** Mary Lynn F. Jones, "No News Is Good News," *The American Prospect,* May 2003, 40.

335 **"retribution if you don't play ball":** Dana Milbank and Jim VandeHei, "Bush's Strong Arm Can Club Allies Too; Lawmakers, Activists Say Tactics for Enforcing Loyalty Are Tough and Sometimes Vindictive," *Washington Post,* March 21, 2003.

336 **John Dean remarked:** James Harding, "Bush Rejects Independent Inquiry into Security Leak," *Financial Times,* September 30, 2003.

336 **attacked as "anti-Catholic":** Franklin Foer, "What It Takes," *The New Republic,* October 13 and 20, 2003, 23.

336 **Senator Richard Durbin:** Sarita Chourey, "Senator Fights Leak Allegation," *The Hill,* July 23, 2003, at www.hillnews.com/news/072303/leak.aspx.

336 **"stir up feelings":** Paul Krugman, "Let Them Hate as Long as They Fear," *New York Times,* March 7, 2003.

336 **"Everyone makes mistakes":** Quoted in Dana Milbank, "For Bush, Facts Are Malleable," *Washington Post,* October 22, 2002.

337 **there is no evidence:** Seth Porges, "Bus 9/11 Admission Gets Little Play; Story Doesn't Make Many Front Pages," *Editor and Publisher,* September 19, 2003, at www.editorandpublisher. com/editorandpublisher/headlines/article_display.jsp?vnu_content_id=1982860.

337 **"You can't distinguish between al Qaeda and Saddam":** Quoted in Arianna Huffington, "We Don't Need No Stinkin' Proof," in *The Iraq War Reader: History, Documents, Opinions,* eds. Micah L. Sifry and Christopher (New York: Touchstone, 2003), 344.

337 **Bush even justified the war:** President George W. Bush to Speaker of the House and the President Pro Tempore of the Senate, March 18, 2003, at http://usinfo.state.gov/topical/pol/terror/ 03031906.htm.

337 **Cheney described Iraq:** Dana Priest and Glenn Kessler, "Iraq, 9/11 Still Linked by Cheney," *Washington Post,* September 29, 2003.

337 **Sissela Bok:** Sissela Bok, *Lying: Moral Choice in Public and Private Life* (New York: Alfred A. Knopf, 1999).

338 **Richard Murphy:** Richard Murphy, "Letter to the Editor: My Tour of Duty in Iraq," *New York Times,* September 28, 2003.

338 **rather than read a complete newspaper story:** Editorial, "The Presidential Bubble," *New York Times,* September 25, 2003.

338 **"My faith frees me":** George W. Bush, *A Charge to Keep: My Journey to the White House* (New York: Morrow, 1999).

Index

★

Belgium, 328
Belloc, Hillaire, 328
Bender, Paul, 159
Benjamin, Daniel, 280
Benjamin Cardozo School of Law, 179
Bennett, William, 274
Berger, Sandy, 94, 216
Berman, Ari, 282
Bernstein, Jared, 42, 184
Bhutto, Benazir, 232
bidding procedures, 85
big business, 4, 147, 154, 202, 204, 331
Biggs, John, 79–80
bigotry, 125
Bilbo, Theodore, 134
Biloxi Sun Herald, 115
bin Laden, Osama, 90, 214, 215, 216, 217, 219,
    223, 225, 226, 230, 231, 232, 233, 234–35,
    237–38, 239, 240, 242, 250, 253, 274, 277,
    279, 280, 282, 304, 333
bin Laden, Salem, 241
bin Laden, Shafig, 241
bin Mahfouz, Khalid, 223
biological weapons, 244, 255, 256–57, 258–59,
    262, 277–78, 323
bipartisanship, 332
Black, William, 71*n*
Black Entertainment Television, 136
blackouts, 20, 21, 63, 69
Blair, Jayson, 335
Blair, Tony, 191–92, 205, 254, 264, 265, 276,
    283, 287, 326, 329
Blix, Hans, 258, 262
block grants, 50, 120, 167
Blount, Buford, 296–97
Blumefeld, Laura, 250
BND, 214
Bob Jones University, 126, 132
Boehlert, Eric, 223
Boehner, John, 141
Bok, Sissela, 337
Bolick, Clint, 156
Bollinger, Lee, 130
Bolton, John R., 194, 197, 302, 322–23
Bolton, Joshua, 46
Bond, Julian, 126, 162
Bonner, T. J., 183
Bookman, Jay, 197
Boot, Max, 328
border control, 91
Border Patrol, 183, 213
Boren, David, 226
Bork, Robert, 159, 163
Borosage, Robert, 181
Bosnia, 311, 326
Boston Globe, 71
Botswana, 203
botulinum toxin, 255
Bowling Alone (Putnam), 171
Boykin, William, 332
Boys and Girls Club, 49
Bradlee, Ben, 9
Brady Law, 175

Brandeis, Louis, 83
Brandwein, Ruth, 167
Bray, Thomas J., 13
breast cancer, 152
Bremer, Paul, 29, 289, 296, 309
Brennan Center for Justice, 135*n*
Bretton Woods accords, 325
Breyer, Stephen G., 98, 164
Britain, 294
British East India Company, 61
Broder, David, 51–52, 164, 225
Brokaw, Tom, 281
Bronson, Rachel, 290
Brooke, Francis, 304
Brookhiser, Richard, 190
Brookings Institution, 247, 250, 323, 336
Brooks, Renana, 8
Brookwood, 181–82
Brown, Sherrod, 109, 120
Brownstein, Ron, 57
Bruni, Frank, 3, 118
Bryan, William Jennings, 147
Bryant, Daniel J., 92
Buchanan, Bruce, 2–3, 128
Buffett, Warren, 54, 55–56, 209
Burdine, Calvin Jerold, 178
Bureau of Intelligence and Research (INR),
    257, 266–68
Burke, Thomas, 155
Bush, Barbara, 62
Bush, George H. W., 4, 10, 25, 30, 83, 119, 126,
    163, 168, 180, 188, 195, 196, 275, 286, 302,
    307, 324
Bush, George W., 1, 331–39
    academic record of, 128*n*
    anti–big government stance of, 90
    anti-spending ethic of, 49–51
    attempt to remake U.S. by, 10–11
    big business ties of, 5
    budget cuts of, 49–50
    business fraud and, 61–81
    in campaign of 2000, 1–2, 6
    casual attitude toward preparation of,
        188–89
    China standoff of, 198
    Christian Conservative support for, 5
    civil rights policies of, 125–37
    class warfare rhetoric of, 54–57
    crime policies of, 172–79
    dishonesty of, 6–7, 8–10, 335, 336–37
    dislike of reading of, 3
    early appraisals of, 3
    economic policy of, 6–7, 36–60
    education policy of, 138–47
    energy industry campaign contributions of,
        14, 18
    environmental policy of, 6, 12–35
    exaggeration of Iraqi threat by, 254–63
    executive power used by, 90–91
    family background of, 62
    feelings about world leaders of, 190–91
    gubernatorial fund-raising by, 114
    hard right agenda of, 2–3

resistance in postwar, 294
and September 11 attacks, 282
Shiites in, 298, 299
strain of occupation on military personnel in, 296–97
supposed Niger uranium purchases by, 264–71
troops deployed in, 306
UN sanctions on, 261
water shortages in postwar, 294
weapons of mass destruction of, 254–63
Iraq, war with, 3, 4, 6, 7–8, 40, 85, 252–307, 337–38
civilian deaths during, 293
costs of, 47, 288–97
as creating Arab democracy, 297–301
justifications for, 252–307
postwar contracts for, 65–66, 85
postwar force level in, 288–89
pre-war cost estimates for, 289–90
Iraqi Freedom, Operation, 90
Iraqi National Congress (INC), 273
Iraqi oil industry, 289
Iraq Survey Group, 264
Islamic charities, 217
Islamic fundamentalism, 324
Islamic schools, 90
Israel, 192, 231, 285, 287, 292, 302, 315, 324, 333*n*
Israeli-Palestinian conflict, 198
Italy, 311, 326, 333
Ivanic, Mladen, 311
Ivers, Kevin, 126*n*
Ivins, Molly, 132
Ivory Coast, 326

Jacobsen, Jay, 91
James A. Baker III Institute for Public Policy, 289
James Byrd Jr. Memorial Hate Crime Bill, 132
Japan, 298, 306, 317, 318
Japan, Imperial, 2
Japanese Americans, internment of, 82, 336
Jay Treaty, 163
Jefferson, Thomas, 11
Jeffress, Charles N., 180
"Jews for Jesus," 170
Joffe, Josef, 327
Johnson, Clay, 67
Joint Captured Enemy Material Exploitation Center, 264
Jordan, 299, 300
Joseph, Robert, 268–69
Jowitt, Ken, 300
Joyner, Tom, 136
judicial activism, 157, 158
judicial appointments, 133–34, 156–64, 245, 336
judicial ethics, 161
Judicial Watch, 74
Judis, John, 270, 273, 329
Jungle, The (Sinclair), 77

Justice Department, 31, 84, 159, 175
and corporate fraud, 76–77
Freedom of Information Act and, 87
immigration sweeps by, 98–100
lack of concern for terrorist threats by, 218
preventive detentions and, 101
racial profiling and, 98
TIPS program of, 97
tobacco lawsuits of, 122
University of Michigan case and, 127–29
and USA Patriot Act, 92, 93, 94, 95

Kadish, Ronald, 207
Kagan, Donald, 197
Kagan, Elena, 164
Kagan, Robert, 197, 198, 256, 275, 276, 302
Kamen, Al, 23
Kaminer, Wendy, 179
Kaplan, Fred, 209, 218
Kaplan, Lawrence F., 210
Karbala, Iraq, 283, 296
Kashmir, 210, 232, 233
Kass, Leon, 150
Kay, David, 257, 264, 316
Kean, Thomas, 223–24
Keenan, Nancy, 146
Keillor, Garrison, 39
Keisling, John Brady, 301
Keith, Damon J., 89
Kelliher, Joseph, 17–18
Kellog, Brown & Root, 65–66
Kennan, George, 235
Kennedy, Edward M., 109, 110, 141, 180, 336
Kennedy, John F., 5, 167, 333
Kennedy, Joseph, 79
Kennedy, Paul, 187
Kennedy, Robert F., Jr., 35
Kenya, 321
Kerry, John F., 22, 250
Kewatt, Mary, 297
Keynesianism, 39
Khalilzad, Zalmay, 194
Khobar Towers, 225
Kidd, Pamela, 181
Kim Dae Jung, 194, 315
Kim Jong Il, 314, 322
King, Alfred, 72
King, Larry, 126*n*
King, Martin Luther, Jr., 127, 128
Kinsley, Michael, 9, 128, 151, 318
Kirkpatrick, Jeane, 274
Kissinger, Henry, 89, 195, 222, 223
Klein, Joe, 2, 152
Klinefelter, Anne, 92
Knox, Alex, 141
Kohut, Andrew, 334
Korb, Lawrence, 225
Kosovo, 288, 289, 324–25, 326, 331
Krauthammer, Charles, 274–75
Kristof, Nicholas, 266
Kristol, Irving, 323–24
Kristol, William, 131, 197, 198, 256, 274, 275, 276, 297, 302, 312, 322

Wright, Henry T., 294
Wright, Robert, 218–19
Wright, Robin, 320
Wright Patterson Air Force Base, 278
Wyden, Ron, 85

Xerox, 181

Yaghi, Ali, 99
Yaghi, Shokriea, 99
Yale University, 62, 128n
Yang, Wesley, 275
Yaphe, Judith, 290
Yemen, 216
Yeoman, Barry, 123

Young, C. W. Bill, 248–49
Yousef, Ramzi, 214

Zakaria, Fareed, 199, 295
Zakheim, Dov, 194, 197
Zarqawi, Abu Mussab, 277, 279, 282
Zelikow, Philip, 223–24
Zerhouni, Elias, 150
Zhang Qiyue, 198
Zigler, Edward, 144
Zigler, James, 99
Zimbabwe, 285
Zinni, Anthony, 252, 253–54, 306–7
Zoellick, Robert, 204, 205, 311
Zubaydah, Abu, 243, 280